Bibliotheca
Valenciana

BIBLIOTHECA VALENCIANA
Translations and Commentary Copyright © José Leitão 2017.
All Rights Reserved Worldwide.
Images on pages 27-197 taken from *O Non Plus Ultra Do Lunario E Pronostico Perpetuo*, Lisbon: José Baptista Morando, 1857. Images on pages 303-503 taken from *Tratado De Los Animales Terrestres y Volatiles*, Benito Valencia: Benito Macè, 1672. Images on pages 577-587 taken from *Lunario Pronostico Perpetuo General y Particular*, Madrid: D. Julian Viana Razola, 1837. Images on pages 585-591 taken from *Libro y Tratado De Los Animales Terrestres y Volatiles*, Valencia: Iuan Chrysostomo Garriz, 1615. All images are in the public domain.
Printed in England.

ISBN 978-1-907881-81-7
10 9 8 7 6 5 4 3 2 1
A catalogue for this title is available from the British Library.

Except in the case of quotations embedded in critical articles or reviews, no part of this book may be reproduced or transmitted in any form or by any means, electronic or mechanical, including photocopying, recording, or by any information storage and retrieval system, without permission in writing from the publisher.

This book is not intended as a substitute for medical advice. The medical information contained in this book is of a historic nature and cannot substitute for the advice of a medical professional.

José Leitão has asserted his moral right to be identified as the author of this work.

First published in 2017 by Hadean Press
BM Box 6176
London
WC1N 3XX

Hadean Press is an imprint of Circle Six.
www.hadeanpress.com

MOST PRECIOUS

Bibliotheca Valenciana

Comprising of the books

THE NON PLUS ULTRA DO LUNARIO,
PHYSIOGNOMY AND VARIOUS SECRETS OF NATURE
& TREATISE OF THE ANIMALS

AUTHORED BY JERÓNIMO CORTEZ,
NOBLE SIR OF THE FAIR CITY OF VALENCIA

FOR THE BENEFIT AND PROSPERITY OF
ALL INDIVIDUALS, KINGDOMS AND REPUBLICS

TRANSLATED AND COMPILED FOR THE GRACE OF GOD BY

JOSÉ LEITÃO, CYPRIANISTA

Published by Hadean Press in the year of Our Lord of 2017

Contents

List of Tables in the Texts 9
Acknowledgments 11
Introduction 13
Consulted Bibliography 23

THE NON PLUS ULTRA DO LUNARIO
Prologue 29
Of the World and Its Division 31
Natural Prognostication of the Weather 125
Treatise of Rustic and Pastoral Astronomy 167
Treatise of some particular thing that the Majesty of God our Lord performed on the seventh day of the week 175
Another Treatise and particular things that the High Pontiffs ordered in favor of the Christian Religion, from Saint Peter to Gregory XIII 177
Memory of Universal Remedies 185

PHYSIOGNOMY AND VARIOUS SECRETS OF NATURE
First Treatise of the Natural Physiognomy of Man, According to the Method of Philosophy and Medicine 205
    Chapter I • By which one may know the temperament by the color of the face 205
    Chapter II • By which one will know which of the four humors dominates by the color of the body and thickness or thinness of it, and which conditions and properties this humor causes 205
    Chapter III • Of the signs of the four qualities 206
    Chapter IV • Of the signs of the complexion of the brain 206
    Chapter V • Of the signs of the complexion of the heart 207
    Chapter VI • Of the signs of the temperament of the liver 207
    Chapter VII • Of the signs of the temperament of the stomach 207
The Particular Physiognomy of Each Member and Part of the Body 209
    Chapter I • Of the hair 209
    Chapter II • Of the front 209
    Chapter III • Of the eyebrows 210
    Chapter IV • Of the eyes 210
    Chapter V • Of the nose 211
    Chapter VI • Of the mouth 212
    Chapter VII • Of the teeth 212
    Chapter VIII • Of the tongue 213
    Chapter IX • Of the voice 213
    Chapter X • Of laughter 213
    Chapter XI • Of the beard 213
    Chapter XII • Of the beard 214
    Chapter XIII • Of the physiognomy of the face 214
    Chapter XIV • Of the ears 214
    Chapter XV • Of the head 215
    Chapter XVI • Of the throat 215
    Chapter XVII • Of the back 215
    Chapter XVIII • Of the arms 216
    Chapter XIX • Of the hands 216
    Chapter XX • Of the chest 216

Chapter XXI • Of the belly *216*
Chapter XXII • Of the flesh of the body *217*
Chapter XXIII • Of the ribs *217*
Chapter XXIV • Of the muscles *217*
Chapter XXV • Of the buttocks *217*
Chapter XXVI • Of the knees *217*
Chapter XXVII • Of the legs *217*
Chapter XXVIII • Of the feet *218*
Chapter XXIX • Of the hunch *218*
Chapter XXX • Of stature *218*
Final Chapter • Of the correspondence of the spots and marks of the face with the various parts of the body *219*

Second Treatise of the Excellencies of Rosemary and its Quality *221*
Liqueur or Balm of Rosemary *224*
Medicinal Recipe *225*

Third Treatise of the Many and Great Properties of Aguardente *227*
The Virtues of the Sugary Aguardente *229*

Fourth Treatise of the Secrets of Nature and their Marvelous Effects *231*

Fifth and Final Treatise of the Elemental and Celestial Region *259*
First Part of this Treatise
Chapter I • Of the elemental region *259*
Chapter II • In which one says what is an element and why there aren't more than four *259*
Chapter III • Of the place and position of the elements and of some particular things about them *260*
Chapter IV • Of the nature and place of the earth *261*
Chapter V • In which is declared the shape and figure of the earth *261*
Chapter VI • Of the size and greatness of earth *262*
Chapter VII • Of the general division of the inhabitable earth *262*
Chapter VIII • Of the earthquakes and tremors the earth and the fire mouths which can be found on it *264*
Chapter IX • Of the nature and place of water *267*
Chapter X • Of the sea, rivers and fountains *268*
Chapter XI • Of the quality of air and the difference between air and wind and how this is caused *269*
Chapter XII • Of the divisions of the Region of air *270*
Chapter XIII • In which we deal in how the mists, dews, frosts, clouds, rain, snow and hails are made *270*
Chapter XIV • Dealing with thunder, rays and lightning and from what these are generated, how and where *271*
Chapter XV • Dealing with the Comets which are seen in the sky *273*
Chapter XVI • Dealing with the arch which is seen in the clouds and the flames that appear on the top of ship's masts *274*
Chapter XVII • In which it is proved the existence of elemental fire contrary to the opinion of many Philosophers *275*
Last Chapter • Which deals with the nature of fire and its activity *276*
Second Part of this Treatise
Chapter I • Of the first Heaven and the Moon which is found in it *277*
Chapter II • Of the second Heaven, in which one may find the Planet Mercury *278*
Chapter III • Of the third Heaven, in which one may find the Planet Venus *279*
Chapter IV • Of the fourth Heaven, in which one may find the Sun *279*

> Chapter V • Of the fifth Heaven, in which one may find the Planet Mars *280*
> Chapter VI • Of the sixth Heaven, in which one may find the Planet Jupiter *280*
> Chapter VII • Of the seventh Heaven, in which one may find the Planet Saturn *281*
> Chapter VIII • Of the eighth Heaven, in which is the multitude of the Stars *282*
> Chapter IX • Of the ninth, tenth and eleventh Heaven *282*

Dialogue of Doubts Referring to that Which was said in the Last Treatise of the Elemental and Celestial Region *285*
Treatise Brief and Very Curious *293*
Secrets which are added to this printing *296*
Other new secrets *299*

Treatise of the Animals of the Land and Sky
First Part of the Land Animals
> Chapter I • Of the Lion and its Excellences *311*
> Chapter II • Of the Donkey and its great Excellences *319*
> Chapter III • Of the Camel and its natural conditions *331*
> Chapter IV • Of the wolf and its perfidious conditions *334*
> Chapter V • Of the Lamb, Ram and Sheep *338*
> Chapter VI • Of the Goat and Buck *344*
> Chapter VII • Of the Dog and its great loyalty *348*
> Chapter VIII • Of the Fox and its great treasons *357*
> Chapter IX • Of the Pig and its advantages *360*
> Chapter X • Of the Deer and its properties *364*
> Chapter XI • Of the Cat and its cunnings *367*
> Chapter XII • Of the Ox and its advantages *371*
> Chapter XIII • Of the Ant and its great foresight and natural instincts *376*
> Chapter XIV • Of the Dragon *383*
> Chapter XV • Of the Elephant and its rare knowledge *387*
> Chapter XVI • Of the Horse and its arrogance *394*
> Chapter XVII • Of the Tiger or Panther *398*
> Chapter XVIII • Of the Beaver *402*
> Chapter XIX • Of the Unicorn *406*
> Chapter XX • Of the Mouse, and by its occasion we will say something of the Thief *410*
> Chapter XXI • Of the Frog *415*
> Chapter XXII • Of the Monkey or Simian *420*
> Chapter XXIII • Of the Lynx *423*
> Chapter XXIV • Of the Hare *427*
> Chapter XXV • Of the Rabbit *431*
> Chapter XXVI • Of the Crocodile *435*
> Chapter XXVII • Of the Chameleon *438*
> Chapter XXVIII • Of the Salamander *440*

Second Part of the Virtues and Properties of the Air Animals
> Chapter I • Of the Eagle *443*
> Chapter II • Of the Dove and its virtues *447*
> Chapter III • Of the bird called Halcyon *451*
> Chapter IV • Of the Mallards *452*
> Chapter V • Of the Geese or Goslings *453*
> Chapter VI • Of the bird called Bernace and of another called Carbates *454*

Chapter VII • Of all kinds of Birds which are placed in cages for the recreation of the ears and sight of man *455*
Chapter VIII • Of the birds of prey that are kept by many lords as entertainment and enjoyment in the hunt *458*
Chapter IX • Of the Rooster *463*
Chapter X • Of the Chicken *470*
Chapter XI • Of the Capon *472*
Chapter XII • Of the bird called Griffon or Grippes *473*
Chapter XIII • Of the Crane *474*
Chapter XIV • Of the Swallows *475*
Chapter XV • Of the Crow *477*
Chapter XVI • Of the bird called Woodpecker *478*
Chapter XVII • Of the Pelican *479*
Chapter XVIII • Of the Partridge *480*
Chapter XIX • Of the Turtledove *482*
Chapter XX • Of the Hoopoe *483*
Chapter XXI • Of the Peacock *484*
Chapter XXII • Of the Vulture *486*
Chapter XXIII • Of the Caladrius *488*
Chapter XXIV • Of the Phoenix *489*
Chapter XXV • Of the Stork *491*
Chapter XXVI • Of the Sparrow *492*
Chapter XXVII • Of the Owl *493*
Chapter XXVIII • Of the Cuckoo or Cubet *494*
Chapter XXIX • Of the Hooded Crow *495*
Chapter XXX • Of the bird called Swan *496*
Chapter XXXI • Of the Bees *497*

Appendix I • Tables and Calculations from the 1836 Barcelona edition of the Lunario *505*
Appendix II • Tables and Calculations from the 1837 Madrid edition of the Lunario *577*
Appendix III • Alternative illustrations to the Treatise of the Animals of the Land and Sky and Their Properties *585*
Index I • Authors mentioned in the texts *593*
Index II • Animals mentioned in the texts *601*
Index III • Ingredients mentioned in the texts *605*
Index IV • Illnesses mentioned in the texts *621*
Index V • Planets & Signs mentioned in the texts *625*

List of Tables in the Texts

The hours at which the Sun rises and sets throughout the whole of the year.	*36*
The hours in which the Sun rises and sets and the duration of the day.	*37-40*
Table of Correspondences.	*41*
Perpetual table of the Dominical letters.	*47*
Another way to find the Dominical letters.	*47*
To find the Golden number for any year.	*49*
Table of the fixed feasts.	*54*
To find the movable feasts by the Calendar until the end of the World.	*55*
The Movable Feasts.	*56-57*
The Calendars of the months, days and feasts of the whole year.	
January	*58*
February	*60*
March	*62*
April	*64*
May	*66*
June	*68*
July	*70*
August	*72*
September	*74*
October	*76*
November	*78*
December	*80*
The Planetary days and hours.	*83*
The hours of Moonlight in every day of the year.	*98*
To know perpetually at which hour of the day each high or low tide begins.	*99*
To know which sign the Moon is in.	*101*
The Signs the Moon is in each day.	*104*
Perpetual and general table for the prognostication of the years.	*107*
To know the true place of the Head of the Dragon.	*121*
Table of the location of the Head of the Dragon.	*123*
The beginning of the Canicular days in Cities and Several Places.	*126*
The Year in which the Golden number is 18.	*129*
The Year in which the Golden number is 19.	*130*
The Year in which the Golden number is 1.	*131*
The Year in which the Golden number is 2.	*132*
The Year in which the Golden number is 3.	*133*
The Year in which the Golden number is 4.	*134*
The Year in which the Golden number is 5.	*135*
The Year in which the Golden number is 6.	*136*
The Year in which the Golden number is 7.	*137*
The Year in which the Golden number is 8.	*138*
The Year in which the Golden number is 9.	*139*
The Year in which the Golden number is 10.	*140*
The Year in which the Golden number is 11.	*141*
The Year in which the Golden number is 12.	*142*
The Year in which the Golden number is 13.	*143*
The Year in which the Golden number is 14.	*144*
The Year in which the Golden number is 15.	*145*
The Year in which the Golden number is 16.	*146*

Translated by José Leitão

The Year in which the Golden number is 17.	*147*
Table of purges and bloodlettings.	*150*
The dominion of the Planets on the human body.	*151*
Astronomical judging of natural infirmities.	*151*
Table for the prognostication and successes of infirmities.	*153*
Perpetual table for the four Rows of the Dominical Letters.	*507*
Tables for the centennial leap years.	*508*
Table used for the Golden number for the centennial years.	*510*
Perpetual Table of the Golden number.	*511*
First Table of Equations.	*514-515*
Second Table of the Epacts for the common years.	*516*
To calculate the Movable Feasts from the year 1712 to 1741.	*518*
Perpetual Table of the Movable Feasts.	*519-520*
Table of the Times.	*521*
Table of the Movable Feasts.	*522*
To find the Letter of the Roman Martyrology.	*523*
The Calendar of the days and non-movable feasts.	
January	*524*
February	*525*
March	*526*
April	*527*
May	*528*
June	*529*
July	*530*
August	*531*
September	*532*
October	*533*
November	*534*
December	*535*
Effect of the Moon on the tides of the sea.	*537*
The years and days added to the first table of the conjunctions and fulls.	*542*
Tables of the conjunctions and fulls.	*543-573*
Conjunctions and fulls of the Sun and Moon for the various places in Spain.	*574*
Perpetual and General Table for the prognostication of the years.	*580*
Table of the perpetual fulls and conjunctions of the Moon.	*581-582*

Acknowledgments

As indispensable for the conclusion of this work, I would like to recognize the help provided by the Biblioteca Municipal Afonso Lopes Vieira of Leiria, for allowing me to consult the rare 1877 Porto edition of the *Lunario* from the Livraria de Afonso Lopes Vieira reserved collection. Being a son of the land, I know perfectly well that Leirienses, deep down in their core, are a mean and ill disposed bunch, consequently, I was more than pleasantly surprised by the eagerness and availability of the municipal library staff in aiding me in my research, particularly in the painstaking chore of digitalizing the 161 pages I requested.

While it may not seem like much, it was thanks to that that I was actually able to make sense of the contemporary edition of the *Lunario* by Lello Editores and much of the Bento Serrano mess. Your help saved me a few months of ungrateful work.

Introduction

Magic of the living lizard, dried in an oven

Take a live lizard, one with a blue back, place it in a new, very well-covered pan and put it in an oven to roast. As soon as it is well dried, grind it into a powder and place this in a sandalwood box.
The woman or man who wishes to captivate the heart of any other person, only needs to give them a pinch of this powder in some wine or coffee, and they will have this person at their command.
Jerónimo Cortez further says that this powder is also marvelous to pull out teeth with no pain whatsoever, simply by rubbing it on your gums.

in *The Book of St. Cyprian: The Sorcerer's Treasure*[1]

Worse than discovering that a reference is fake is discovering that it's too extensive…
There is a great deal of magic that doesn't seem to be regarded as such. This has probably something to do with the outdated Positivistic division of disciplines or maybe the belief that many practitioners have had through time that magic needs to be a separate activity from everyday life. All of this is fine and true, and on many occasions indeed a necessity, but this division becomes a difficult issue when you're talking about folk magic.

Even the name 'folk magic' is problematic and inductive to error, as this is largely a label given to certain cultural practices by outside observers and does not (or did not) actually exist among the practitioners of such processes. What is regarded as 'folk magic' is often a partial understanding of one of many expressions of a complex and intricate traditional world view of a people and, in its natural state, is not sterilely separated from other activities such as cooking, working a field, herding, singing and dancing or making babies.

Traditional life is a more or less skillful navigation through the cosmic web of power and potential, always in a state of emanation and becoming, and whose laws and rules are codified in culture. The human induced (non-spontaneous) growth of plants, cattle and other humans, the transformation of matter, the creation of art, beauty and life are all dependent on the individual skill of manipulating the cosmic potential[2] (Thelemites would rightly add 'according to Will'). Hence we can sing the old wordless *Aboio* to make our oxen more spirited and hardworking and the *Minha roda stá parada* when wheeling water out of a well… To toil – and human life is little more than toil – is to sing, and to sing is to seduce spirits and Gods, or, as we nowadays call it, do some magic. This means that if we ever expect to have any kind of understanding about the folk magic of any particular culture, as its worldview is not nicely packed into separate and standalone parts, we really have no other choice than to try to tackle that culture as a whole, which becomes even more of a challenge if we take into consideration that cultural expressions change over time.

So, when I first came across the name of Jerónimo Cortez 'Valenciano' while working on the Portuguese traditional grimoire *The Book of St. Cyprian*, and when the realization of what I was looking at started to sink in, I realized that this was not something I could just shrug off (in truth, just the fact that this name is mentioned in *The Book* should say something very significant in itself).

Like many others, I had been trained in the creed of the exclusive originality of magic – that there was something intrinsic in magic which was specific and unique to it – but reading the works by Cortez 'Valenciano' I found myself constantly having to grasp back at the memory that these were actually early modern treatises on Natural Philosophy and not folk magic grimoires.

---
1. Leitão, *The Book of St. Cyprian*, 195.
2. Just so we're clear, there is nothing natural about agriculture.

The fact was, simply, that there didn't seem to be much difference between the two: it was the same material, the same structure, the same preoccupations and the same pure fascination by a social class hungrily trying to leave its mark on the world.

This same hunger is the drive behind many folk grimoires, some of which are merely improper repackagings of material intended to produce an easy profit that got really out of hand and acquired a life of their own. In this there is a realization that we should take the opportunity to make, beyond the fantasies of secret pre-Christian pagan continuities: that unfortunately it is a fact that the old systems of ancient voiceless and wordless peoples have been largely lost to time, but what survived has found much of its life blood and a sustainable structure in the pages of this and other such vernacular treatises on astrology and 'medicine'. As also pointed out by Jim Baker,[3] when you're stepping into the world of folk practitioners (Cunning Men or whatever you call them in the place you're from), the lines always become blurry, and as we have it now, folk magic in Western Europe is largely and irremediably Christian, but this is far from a statement of despair. We need to gather our nerves and seek out where and how the vein of magic has by-passed reality, how it has taken to Christian and modern systems, how it has been redefined and itself redefined it, and this is what 'Valenciano' and these books collected here can help us with.

'Mestre de comptar'

Jerónimo Cortez (also alternatively spelled Jeronymo Cortès, Geronimo Cortes, Gerónimo Cortès or a few other variations)[4] seems to largely present himself as a mathematician, as stated in his first book, the *Arithmetica Practica*[5] (his only book not included in the current collection), but truthfully, of the man himself there isn't much to go on. The largest amount of information comes from the printing and trading permits requested by his widow and presented in the beginning of the 1615 edition of the *Libro e Tratado de los animals Terrestres y Volatiles* (presented in this book). From here we know that he was a Valencian, sometime in his life he lived in the city of Gandia, he married a woman named Angela Rull y de Cortez, had five children, died in 1611[6] and that's about it. But regarding his body of work on the other hand, we have quite a number of things that can be discussed.

There are basically four books attributed to this author: the already mentioned *Arithmetica Practica*, or, fully expanded, the *Arithmetica Practica muy util, y necessaria para todo genero de Tratantes, y Mercaderes, la qual contiene todo el Arte menor y principios del mayor, que son as raizes cubicas; y quadradas, con los usos, y provechos de ellas; las falsas posiciones al uso antiguo, y moderno declaradas. Contiene assi mesmo el modo, y arte de inventar, y reduzir unas monedas enotras, por reglas breves, con mucha variedad de perguntas, y respuestas, assi Arithmeticas, como Geometricas*, a book on arithmetic, mathematics and monetary conversions, which is actually an expansion of his earlier mathematical works, the *Tratado del cómputo por la mano, muy breve y necesário para los Ecclesiásticos* and the *Compendio de reglas breves com el arte de hallarlas e inventarlas; asi para las reducciones de monedas del Reyno de Valencia, Aragón, Barcelona y Castilla, como para las demás monedas de los otros Reynos;*[7] the *Lunario*, or the *El Non Plus Ultra*

---

3. Baker, *The Cunning Man's Handbook*, 316.
4. The reference to this author as *Valenciano* in, mainly, Portuguese editions of his works, and of which I am a victim, comes from the habit that almanacs and other similar books published in Portugal always have in their titles a clear reference to a city outside of Portugal. This was done for two reasons: first, the printing of such books was frowned upon in Portugal and assigning these to a foreign city was a common way of keeping the authorities from investigating the local printers; secondly, the attribution of such works to Spanish cities endowed them with an extra flare of authority, as, traditionally, Spain had been the origin of the most renowned Astrologers in Portugal, the first and foremost of which was the Jew Abraham Zacuto from Salamanca, author of the still much revered *Almanach Perpetuum*. Hence, Jerónimo Cortez in Portugal is sometimes simply referred to as *Valenciano*, the Valencian.
5. Salaverti i Fabiani, 'Una mostra de les necessitats cientifiques de la burgesia, l'Arithmetica Practica de Geronymo Cortés (Valencia, 1604)', 371-381.
6. Peris Felipo, 'Aportación a la divulgación zoológica valenciana del siglo XVII', 59-74.
7. Idem.

del Lunario y pronostico perpetuo geral, y particular para cada Reyno, y Provincia, a perpetual almanac, by far his most relevant and important work; the *Fisionomia y varios secretos de Naturaleza*, a book on physiognomy and natural secrets; and finally the *Tratado de Los Animales Terrestres, y Volantes, y sus Propriedades*, a bestiary.

Even if apparently completely different, what essentially binds these books together is that they occupy a very particular literary space in their time and, despite their disparate topics, all share a common purpose and functionality. First off, they are all (Catholic) moralistic books, transmitting in exemplary terms a full and complete view of the Universe as this was understood in their time, and they are meant to transmit knowledge to a wide, non-specialized and non-academic audience (not at all dissimilar from the *Bibliothèque Bleue* books). This last orientation arises primarily from the very moment in history when these books come into play: the boom of the Early Modern period, the rise of the merchant culture and increased literacy, which is put plainly into evidence by the *Arithmetica Practica*. This, even if still a mathematical treatise, is a book focused on practicality and application to commerce and trading, meant to answer the increasing interest in these topics by the newly educated lower classes of society.[8] Following this one, the *Lunario* is intended mostly for farmers, focusing on weather and event prediction, crop production and storage, while also containing instructions on proper health regiments for those who did not have access to a physician and other topics of popular interest (such as the occurrence of comets, an issue that had its own strand of devoted literature in 17th century Spain).[9] The final two, although not focused on commercial aspects, are mostly collections of classical, erudite and contemporary material, prepared with a concern for the dissemination of information of public interest (some originating from the discovery and novel study of America) to an 'extra academic scientific subculture' among the emergent middle class.[10] In this way, the focus of Cortez's literary production always stands on the feeding of information to new emergent social classes eager to expand themselves into previously inaccessible realms.

In the wider frame, this was essentially the common base behind the rise of vernacular literature in Iberia and Europe; a movement focused on the outside of the academies and on the commoners; books arranged and prepared for the consumption of a lower class.

One of the immediate results of this impulse, in this period in particular, was that a full Universal system of the Cosmos, the Catholic Clockwork Universe, the pinnacle of the full understanding of the Universe according to the old canonical authors, was finally revealed to the wide public, gradually framing and shaping all various practices (folk or otherwise) and the mysterious incongruities of the Church into a concise and practical whole. And, as also pointed out by Solomon,[11] the very fact that these books were published in the vernacular tongue presented them as belonging to this new reading class; that this new influx of information had been designed for a new audience and that it was meant to be claimed as such.

Of Magic and Imagination

Analyzing such novel vernacular books, we are then pressed with the question: what is indeed the difference between these vernacular medical/scientific treatises and a grimoire?

Some might go straight to an answer such as 'spirits', or the more direct 'one has magic', but these points are all purely circumstantial; they do not offer any elements for a definition in terms of the wider narratives that are repeated in every grimoire.

To say that yesterday's magic is tomorrow's science (or the other way around… it's really irrelevant) also does not touch on this point in any way, as it describes the evolution of ideas in purely dualistic terms which are largely fallacious. Also, the perception of what is magic or science

---

8. Salaverti i Fabiani, 'Una mostra de les necessitats cientifiques de la burgesia, l'Arithmetica Practica de Geronymo Cortés (Valencia, 1604)', 371-381.
9. Lanuza-Navarro, 'Astrological Literature in Seventeenth-Century Spain', 119-136.
10. Peris Felipo, 'Aportación a la divulgación zoológica valenciana del siglo XVII', 59-74.
11. Solomon, *Fictions of Well-Being*, 10.

is something which is entirely time dependent and not universally valid in any way (Positivism's dogma of a linear evolution of knowledge and technique, once again).

So, what is a grimoire (the real grimoires, the dirty disgusting ones, the workingman's grimoire) and what is a vernacular medical treatise, an almanac or a book of secrets? Put them side by side and these are parallel: they all claim their authority from old unverifiable sources (saying Chaldean, Dioscorides or that-guy-I-once-met really means the same to a man who doesn't own or has never read a single book); they all present a model of the functioning of the Universe and the tools and techniques to manipulate this; they all list a string of mundane pains and their solutions; they all claim to be sources of power arising from higher spheres; and finally, all of them are nasty. Basically, the same faith and frame of mind that would make a man pick up a grimoire and faithfully follow its apparently incongruent recipes would just as easily make a man pick up a medical treatise.

Even the inherent magical properties some of the more renowned grimoires claim to have as magical objects is not enough to make them stand out in this discussion, as, in the late medieval and early modern period, vernacular medical treatises themselves, when placed before the right audience, would come to attract this very same glamour. A particularly revealing example of this instance is mentioned by Solomon once again,[12] who describes the practice of a particular Valencian healer (a *metgessa*) which consisted of reflecting the text of a medical book onto her patients' bodies, so as in this way transmitting the healing virtue contained in the text (a handling which effectively made an otherwise scientific book into a magical object).

Such a process should not be seen as strange to magical practitioners, particularly the post-modern ones. Looking at it, the book first becomes an object of power and authority, a nexus for the patient's intent, will and expectations; arising from a physical stress (a possible illness or mundane obsession) the user (particularly if illiterate) is pushed to come up with a creative bridge between himself and what he sees as the release from his condition. As such, the use and manipulation of a medical treatise, be it the execution of its instructions or some other creative solution, and, finally, its consumption or application, functions like any standard textbook example of, say, a Chaos Magic sigil.

The magical thread can be further explored into one other very interesting and relevant aspect of this equation: the very act of reading. Our current concept of reading is *par excellence* one of the most private experiences of modern life, however this idea is born out of very particular circumstances of our time. We are mostly all literate, many of us have resources for the acquisition of books and books are inexpensive and readily available; all situations which are really an exception in the whole of human history. In the early modern period on the other hand, reading could at times become a collective or community activity,[13] giving rise to complex social networks of information trading. The most relevant aspect of this kind of distribution of information is that, as vernacular treatises started to make their way to the lower strand of society, it gave rise to the seeping of previously academic material into the traditional networks of transmission of folk and oral knowledge.

Speaking from experience, and underlying the relevance of the selection of works made for the current study, the Jerónimo Cortez books seem to have been the preferential ones for this kind of oral assimilation in Portugal.[14] Teófilo Braga explicitly mentions the *Lunario*, and particularly its engravings, as one of the main dispensers and framers of astrological/astronomical knowledge in rural Portugal,[15] this also being one of the greater precursors of the most famous Portuguese yearly almanacs: the *Borda d'Água* and the *Seringador*.

---

12. Idem, 12.
13. Idem, 10.
14. Similar occurrences are also common all around Europe with other books as, for example, we can find a few points in the 'Petit Albert' which are also contained in the Cortez books; although these are not likely to be directly connected but rather coming from similar (classical) sources. See for example Felix, T., *The Spellbook of Marie Laveau or The Petit Albert*, Hadean Press, 2012, 95 ('For Making Rotten Teeth Fall Out Painlessly').
15. Braga, 'Sobre as Estampas ou Gravuras nos Livros Populares Portuguezes', 497-512.

Title page illustrations of the Seringador (left) and the Borda-de-Agua (right) offered by Braga (no year given). The occurrence of elements from the cover of the Lunario (the compass and the globe, see below) in the illustration of the Borda-de-Agua is interesting to note.

Also, consulting Portuguese ethnographic records as late as the mid-20th century can also reveal procedures and 'folk magic' recipes coincident with those presented in the Cortez books, meaning that these were not only read but actually consumed by the very culture they entered.[16]

Ironically, these assimilated 'non-traditional' practices and recipes occasionally find themselves re-collected and re-organized back into pseudo-grimoires, presenting themselves now endowed with the glamour and authenticity of tradition. An illuminating example of this occurrence is the 1883 seven-part pseudo-grimoire *O Oraculo do Passado, do Presente e do Futuro* (Oracle of the Past, Present and Future) by Bento Serrano, a perfect example of how these books can become interchangeable with grimoires and other expressions of folk magic.

Taking our time with Bento Serrano, this name (which can be translated as Blessed of the Mountain) is found on numerous publications by the Porto based publisher *Livraria Portugueza*, frequently as a collector of poetry, folk riddles and stories,[17] although in the particular case of the *Oracle* he specifically refers to himself as an 'astrologer of the Estrela Mountain where he has resided for about thirty years, being his home a narrow cave which he uses as an office for his diligent astronomical writings'. Analyzing this lengthy book, and particularly its third part entitled 'The Oracle of Secrets', consisting of a list of 108 secrets, we can see that most of it is actually a repackaging of some of Cortez's collected secrets originally published in the *Fisionomia*,[18]

---

16. See for exemple Almeida A.G. (coord.), Guimarães, A.P. (coord.) and Magalhãe, M. (coord.), *Artes de Cura e Espanta-Males: Espólio de medicina popular recolhido por Michel Giacometti*, Lisbon: Gradiva, 2009.

17. See for exemple Serrano, B. (collr.), *A Praga Rogada nas Escadas da Forca*, Livraria Portugueza: Editora de Joaquim Maria da Costa, Porto, 1883.

18. One most notable exceptions is the first entry in this book, entitled "Secret 1 – taken from the book of St. Cyprian (the sorcerer) in order to make a man rise up in the air and float in the heights for 30 minutes without any harm coming to him", and it goes as follows:

Let a man lay down on the floor and place two other men standing by his feet and two others by his head. Once this is done say the following words, one after the other:

1st man – It smells like a dead body.
2nd man – Heavy as lead.
3rd man – Light as a feather.
4th man – Rise in the hour of God.

meaning that these are largely of an academic or classical origin instead of 'folk'. Still, Bento Serrano's appropriation of this material, coupled with the fact that he omits all references to any classical or early modern author mentioned by Cortez in the original, has meant that his book has been received, even by some modern researchers, as being of a purely folk origin,[19] this either out of credulity or the fact that trying to distinguish these from original folk practices, be it in terms of content or form, is nearly impossible. Apart from this, part two of Serrano's *Oracle* (*Oracle of the Halls*) also has many common points with the 1877 Porto edition of the *Lunario* and parts 5 and 7 (*Oracle of the Signs* and *Oracle of the Stars* respectively) also share much of their content with the descriptions of the Signs and Planetary influence present in this same book.

Throughout all of his work, it seems that Serrano had little problem in claiming Cortez's works as his own, although such is not without some poetry and sense, as these books and their contents had anyway already been previously claimed by large sections of the lower Portuguese classes as being genuine 'folk'. But still, some justice does need to be made for Serrano, as he does seem to have had some considerable individual knowledge of Astronomy, attested by his impressive record as an author of yearly almanacs, whose contents do not seem to originate in the *Lunario* (according to the catalog of the Portuguese National Library, his name features in 29 such books, the highest rate of all recorded authors of the genre, and all of these were published by the *Livraria Portugueza*).[20]

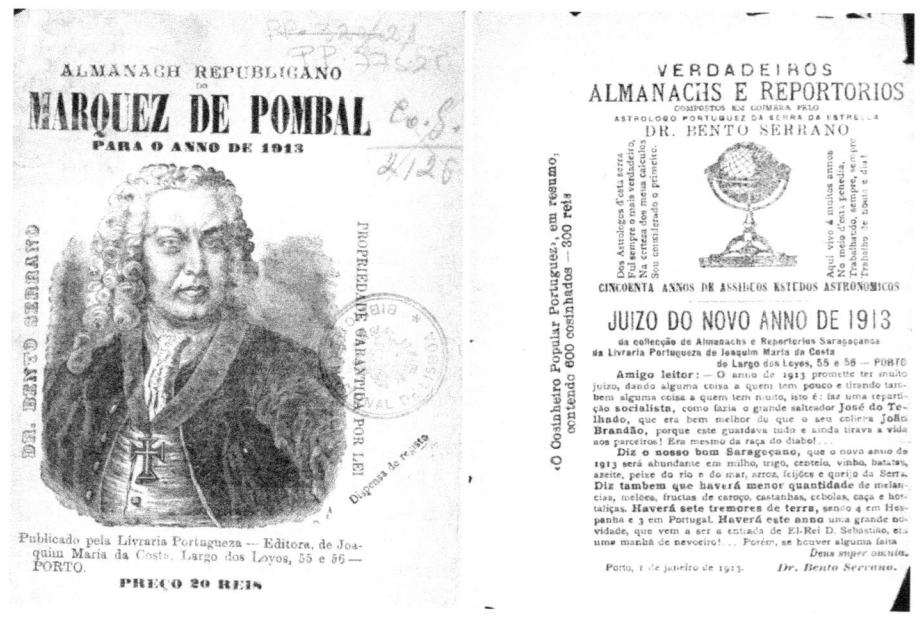

The Republican Almanac of the Marquis of Pombal for the year of 1913 published by the Livraria Portugueza and written by Dr. Bento Serrano (images from Biblioteca Nacional de Portugal, cota P.P. 7752 P.).[21]

After the above-mentioned words are said all should point their finger to him that he will start to rise through the air like a bird; after 30 minutes he will fall to the ground without any harm coming to him.
This secret was discovered by Lucifer, the prince of Hell.
19. Serrano, *O Oráculo dos Segredos*, 5.
20. Galvão, *Os Sucessores de Zacuto*, 197.
21. Serrano, *Almanach Republicano do Marquez de Pombal para o ano de 1913*, 1-2.

But returning to Cortez and the impressive revolution in the exchange of knowledge and information triggered by the rise of the various vernacular treaties in Iberia (and surely in other parts of the world), our question is still not answered. What exactly makes up the grimoire as a genre? Is that name given by its author or its readers? Is it the intention it is written or the intention it is read?

The arbitrary borders between Magic, Religion and Science, once so mighty and imposing, have fallen back into the nothingness they originally crawled out of, and if this is known why are we still trying to scratch lines on the water? Every time you do so you are abdicating a piece of your power and playing into The Man's game.

Many liberals will proclaim that borders are artificial and largely evil, but how many sleep better at night knowing there is a wall out there that effortlessly defines them in contrast to the 'other'? Many practitioners are no different in nesting behind the illusionary veil of magic which separates them from mainstream western society (and as a consequence automatically defines Christianity as a non-magical religion), maybe because doing away with it will force them to recognize that they are not in any way unique or special.

Abandon the borders and the plain purity of medical or astronomical texts and grimoires seems to simply be the following: I have a problem and this book has a solution. The nature of this solution, should it be natural or supernatural (if these are even distinguishable), is really of no concern or relevance to the debate.

On the current book

The current compilation cannot be called a 'complete works', as I did not include in it Cortez's first great book, the *Arithmetica Practica*, mostly because it's tremendously boring. Following on from *The Book of St. Cyprian*, my main interest here was to collect all of his works which might have had an influence on folk magic, practices and ideas, presenting among themselves a coherent, functional and usable worldview.

I do understand that this book is far from the excitement of *The Book*, and it will probably be of more use to academics than practitioners, but its source material is not in any way less relevant or less practical if we are ever hoping to have any kind of understanding of what folk culture is. This goal needs to be placed well beyond our strict perception of what magic is or what it should be.

Still, one might argue that this could have been achieved by the translation of any other set of vernacular treatises, but the truth is that, be it by chance or due to the whims of history, Jerónimo Cortez is special and unique. This name carries with it authority which is not easily found in the world. His books, particularly the *Lunario*, have been fundamental since their first original printing, and as soon these were translated into Portuguese in 1703 they rapidly became the most widely read books in the Brazilian Northeast for over two hundred years, shaping the religious sensitivity of the beautiful Sertanejo culture.[22] Many were the men on both sides of the Atlantic whose only book and sole treasure was the *Lunario*, who learned their first letters from its pages and who had a faith in it which could even challenge the Bible. It is then no surprise that this name would rightly feature in that other Bible of the people: *The Book of St. Cyprian*.

Even looking ahead in time, the relationship between St. Cyprian related literature and Cortez is everything but restricted to one single mention in the Portuguese version of *The Book of St. Cyprian*. The fingerprint of this author is visible throughout most folk-oriented practical literature, particularly in 19th century Portuguese low circulation publications. This is made plainly evident in such periodicals as Livraria Economica's *Almanach de S. Cyprian* (The Almanac of St. Cyprian), where numerous points taken directly from Cortez' *Lunario* and *Fisionomia* are presented under the title of 'Recipes of St. Cyprian'. Such also happens in another periodical entitled *Almanach da Tia Monica* (Almanac of Aunty Monica), which is heavy on repackaging material from the *Book of St. Cyprian* and including among this plenty of material from Cortez. Returning to the Bento Serrano bandwagon, this author, during this same time period, mostly though his *Verdadeiro Almanach das*

---

22. Vasconcelos de Almeida, *Saberes e Práticas de Cura no "Lunário Perpétuo" de Genónimo Cortés (1555 – 1615) e Sua Influencia no Nordeste Brasileiro*, 5.

Feiticeiras (True Almanac of the Sorceresses) and *Almanach Saragoçano das Feiticeiras* (Saragossan Almanac of the Sorceresses), insistently, and consistently, ties these two sources together.

Even crossing the Atlantic into Brazil offers us very similar observations, as a 1900 edition of the *Book of St. Cyprian* by Possidónio Tavares printed in Rio de Janeiro can equally be found which includes the already mentioned list of 108 secrets taken from Cortez's *Fisionomia*.

The future exploration of these publications and the variations and reconceptualizations they present of St. Cyprian practices and magic is surely demanded, but for now what this factually transmits is that by the end of the 19th century Cortez's books had been perfectly assimilated into Portuguese folk magic, St. Cyprian practices and its associated literature. This is an effective retroactive proclamation of the magical nature of these books.

They may not have been written as magic, but circumstances made them become magic by their reading.

Consequently, if we equally open our minds and our hearts to the greatest gift left to us by our ancestors, that of ingenuity, we can see that these writings are still today the same magical treasure trove they were read as in the 17th century and very explicitly became by the 20th century. They speak of the laws of the Universe and the methods of using these in immediate life; how you implement this information in your own practice and future reconceptualizations is, as it should be, up to your creative power.

The current collection is then comprised of the following translated books: *The Non Plus Ultra Do Lunario and Perpetual Prognostics, General and Particular for all Kingdoms and Provinces*, the *Physiognomy and Various Secrets of Nature* and the *Treatise of the Animals of the Land and Sky*.

Given the single purpose of usability and practicality of these books, over time there have been numerous editions and permutations of their content, particularly of the *Lunario* (counting 87 reprints worldwide,[23] the crown jewel of Cortez's work and considered one of the most successful books in Spanish history). This process is somewhat similar to what can be observed with, for example, *The Book of St. Cyprian* in later years. Like *The Book*, Cortez's works are seen as compilations of utility and their content is thus open for alterations and additions according to their location in time and space. Given this fact, we can find numerous editions of Cortez's books with the most disparate contents and consequently it did not seem entirely correct to me to restrict this compilation to the purely original editions.

As such the *Lunario* presented here was constructed having as a base the 1857 Lisbon edition, to which were added elements from the 1672 Valencia edition, the 1836 Barcelona edition, the 1837 Madrid edition and the 1877 Porto edition. It is important to note that those elements which seemed contradicting and incompatible with the base edition, or seemed to be entirely particular to the reprint in question and with little to do with the original thread of the *Lunario*, were not added (for example, the 1877 Porto edition lists a number of card games which do not seem relevant at all, although Bento Serrano seems to have liked them). Still, a few instances of contradicting tables and calculation have been added as Appendix I and II. Appendix I originates from the 1836 Barcelona edition, and is meant as an example of some of the alterations made to the *Lunario* which take into consideration the use of the Epact, which the original does not; Appendix II, originating from the 1837 Madrid edition, is added merely as an alternative using an altered Geocentric model.

The *Physiognomy and Various Secrets of Nature* (with a total of 67 counted reprints) was constructed having as a base the 1699 Lisbon edition, to which were added elements from the 1831 Paris edition. On the topic of folk magic and traditions, the *Physiognomy* becomes especially relevant due to the particular circumstances of 17th century Iberian medical literature. As already hinted at in the discussion of vernacular medical treatises, in Iberia there was in fact a constant overlap between university level conceptions of medicine and purely folk expressions of healing, with both these worlds being permeable to concepts from each other.[24] It should be noted that, as a traditionally Catholic region, the large majority of the early modern scientific and medical

---

23. Peris Felipo, 'Aportación a la divulgación zoológica valenciana del siglo XVII', 59-74.
24. Drumond Braga, 'Medicina popular versus medicina universitária en el Portugal de Juan V (1706-1750)', 209-233.

innovations, developed in mostly Protestant countries, were for a long time looked upon in Iberia with suspicion.[25] Consequently, the Iberian production of medical knowledge and literature in this time period ended up in a certain self-contained and self-referring loop, which gradually blurred the 'folk' and the 'literate' aspects of medicine. Of this particular 'hybrid' strand of medical treatises one of the most interesting examples, in my opinion, are the works of Francisco da Fonseca Henriques (whose influence can also be found in the *Book of St. Cyprian*),[26] but the *Physiognomy* is itself a perfect example of this situation and it should be read with this information in mind.

Finally, the third book of this collection, the *Treatise of the Animals of the Land and Sky* (counting only 4 reprintings), was constructed from the 1615 and 1672 Valencia editions, which were found to be completely similar in terms of written content, although containing different illustrations. As such, given the place this book in particular occupies in the tradition of zoological literature, the illustrations of the 1615 edition have been added in Appendix III.

At first glance, it is likely that the *Treatise* will be the least interesting of the three books for a magically oriented reader; however, I believe it offers a much needed reminder in terms of Medieval and Renaissance visual culture. Taking a small detour, being a bestiary, it fits into the long and rich literary trend initiated by the *Physiologus*, an anonymous treatise written either in Alexandria or Syria between the 2nd and 4th centuries[27] and having at its base the previous (pagan) zoology sources of Pliny, Aelianus, Aristotle and Plutarch.[28] But what effectively distinguished the *Physiologus* from these older sources was that it was composed with an inherent moral, didactic and doctrinal purpose, placing this preoccupation above any factual or scientific observation. This means that this was essentially a syncretic text mixing popular stories and early zoology, relating animals to the Christian conceptions of virtue or vice, either due to their factual or imagined behavior or supposed magical/natural abilities.[29]

Given its enormous popularity as a didactic text, the model of the *Physiologus* was repeated throughout the centuries, making up the literary tradition of the bestiaries,[30] all of which fit into the same moral intent and descriptions of the original text. These recurrent animal and moralistic descriptions being gradually assimilated into Christian rhetoric by writers such as St Isidore of Seville or Albertus Magnus[31] meant that, as editions followed each other, there was a gradual crystallization and stylization of visual and iconographical significance associated with particular animals. Thus, each animal described progressively became a concrete symbol of a certain vice or virtue, overlapping into other visual or plastic arts such as heraldry, architecture[32] and the later Emblem Books,[33] whose influence should not be underestimated by any conscious practitioner.

Focusing back on the *Treatise of the Animals*, even if following such a tradition, the same novelty and preoccupation that frames Cortez's other books is also quite visible in this one. As illustrated by the 1669 approval by Juan Bautista Ballester (see below), contrasting with other books of the genre, in this one 'are the most selected things compiled, so as they may be a field for the curiosity, learning and a document of vitality', meaning, a simplification and distillation of a vast literary tradition for a newly educated lower class, but, even if a good example of the bestiary genre, the *Treatise* is itself a very specific product of its time. An example of this is the fact that, as easily as Cortez quotes Pliny or Aelianus, he quotes contemporary and dissident authors and himself with equal authority, demonstrating a clear breaking down of a previously untouchable Cosmos and an increasing division between zoology-as-science and zoology-as-allegory (or between biology and emblem literature).

---

25. García Arranz, 'Livres d'amblèmes ou bestiaires modernes?', 269-286.
26. His *Medicina Lusitana e Soccorro Delphico a os Clamores da Natureza Humana* (1710) is a thrill ride.
27. García Arranz, 'Texto Clásico e Imagem Medieval', 27-40.
28. Idem, 'El Physiologus Como Fuente Gráfico-Textual de la Emblemática Animalística de la Edad Moderna', 73-114.
29. Idem, 'Texto Clásico e Imagem Medieval', 27-40.
30. Barbas, 'Monstros: O Rinoceronte e o Elefante, 103-122.
31. García Arranz, 'La Sabiduría Médica en los Animales Emblemáticos', 771-804.
32. Barbas, 'Monstros: O Rinoceronte e o Elefante, 103-122.
33. García Arranz, 'El Physiologus Como Fuente Gráfico-Textual de la Emblemática Animalística de la Edad Moderna', 73-114.

Finally, placing the *Treatise* next to the other two of Cortez's books collected here, one other thing does deserve to be underlined. As can be observed in the various stories put forward by Cortez in the *Treatise*, animals, as also presented by the bestiary tradition, were conceived as having a certain form of rationality,[34] almost on par with that of man but ultimately devoid of free will. This signified that their own behavior was 'exemplary' according to the moral laws of Nature and, consequently, God. Thus, the mystical contemplation of animal behaviors was a way of revealing the Divine designs of God and his laws,[35] making them perfect examples for the regulation of the conduct of humans (by both their virtues and vices, every animal had a purpose). This once again underlines the idea of the great Catholic Clockwork Cosmos, which reflected upon itself a perfect coherence of structure, organization and law. This means that in the *Treatise* one can find ample links back into humor theory and astronomy as covered in the *Lunario* and the *Physiognomy*, and these three books are essentially expositions of different angles of the same whole. Here everything has its place, purpose and function; the Universe is essentially complete and ultimately good, and it is up to man to find his place and path in an essentially divine and magical Universe.

At last, on a closing personal note, this book, as far as my Work is concerned, is probably nothing more than a footnote to *The Book of St. Cyprian*, and having composed it, and also looking at many of my future plans, I realize that the large majority of what I am still to write in this world will be nothing more than footnotes to *The Book of St. Cyprian*. This is the great danger of loving a book: every word, reference and side note can become a dangerous obsession, but at the end of the day the word 'devotion' needs to actually mean something.

And even if this book is larger than *The Book*, translating and putting it together didn't take one tenth of the toll on me as did *The Book*. If anything, and giving flesh to Cortez's promises of health and to my ancestor's beliefs in the inherent power of these books, this work was actually therapeutic and a form of rehabilitation after the physical and spiritual wreck translating *The Book* left me in.

True, this one is a big book, but contrarily to some others, it does not bite.

José Leitão

---

34. Idem, 'La Recepción de los Escritos Animalísticos de Plutarco en los Libros de Emblemas Europeos Durante Los Siglos XVI y XVII', 487-500.
35. Idem, 'Texto Clásico e Imagem Medieval', 27-40.

Consulted Bibliography

Almeida A.G. (coord.), Guimarães, A.P. (coord.) and Magalhãe, M. (coord.), *Artes de Cura e Espanta-Males: Espólio de medicina popular recolhido por Michel Giacometti*, Lisbon: Gradiva, 2009.

Anon., *Almanach da Tia Monica: Ensina a Fazer Toda a Qualidade de Bruxarias, Conforme Fazia S. Cypriano, e Outros Feiticeiros*, Lisbon: Livraria Popular de Francisco Franco 1886-1889, 1892-1895, 1905-1909.

Anon., *Almanach de S. Cypriano: O Feiticeiro*, Lisbon: Livraria Economica 1890, 1891, 1893, 1894.

Baker, J., *The Cunning Man's Handbook: The Practice of English Folk Magic 1550- 1900*, London: Avalonia, 2014.

Barbas, H., 'Monstros: O Rinoceronte e o Elefante: Da Ficção dos Bestiários à Realidade Testemunhal', in *Akten der V. Deutsch-Portugiesischen Arbeitsgespräche/Actas do V Encontro Luso-Alemão*, Köln-Lisboa: Zentrum Portugiesischsprachige Welt, 2000, 103-122.

Braga, T., 'Sobre as Estampas ou Gravuras nos Livros Populares Portuguezes', Portugália 1:3 (1901) 497-512.

Drumond Braga, I.M.R.M., 'Medicina popular versus medicina universitária en el Portugal de Juan V (1706-1750)', *Dynamis: Acta Hispanica ad Medicinae Scientiarumque Historiam Illustrandam* 22 (2002) 209-233.

Felix, T., *The Spellbook of Marie Laveau or The Petit Albert*, Hadean Press, 2012.

Galvão, R.M. (coord.), *Os Sucessores de Zacuto: o almanaque na Biblioteca Nacional do século XV ao XXI*, Lisbon: Biblioteca Nacional, 2002.

García Arranz, J.J., 'El Physiologus Como Fuente Gráfico-Textual de la Emblemática Animalística de la Edad Moderna', *Janus: Estudios sobre el Siglo de Oro*, 3 (2014) 73-114.

García Arranz, J.J., 'La Recepción de los Escritos Animalísticos de Plutarco en los Libros de Emblemas Europeos Durante Los Siglos XVI y XVII', in *Actas del IV Cimposion Español sobre Plutarco*, Madrid: Ediciones Clásicas, 1996, 487-500.

García Arranz, J.J., 'La Sabiduría Médica en los Animales Emblemáticos', in *Actas Del I Simposio Internacional de Emblemática*, Teruel: Instituto de Estudios Turolenses, 771-804.

García Arranz, J.J., 'Livres d'amblèmes ou bestiaires modernes?: Les traités animaliers d'Andrés Ferrer de Valdecebro et de Francisco Marcuello', in *Polyvalenz und Multifunktionalität der Emblematik/Multivalence and Multifunctionality of the Emblem:Akten des 5. Internationalen Kongresses der Society for Emblem Studies/Proceedings of the 5th International Conference of the Scociety for the EMblem Studies*, Frankfurt am Main: Peter Lang, 269-286.

García Arranz, J.J., 'Texto Clásico e Imagem Medieval: Una Aproximación a la Incidencia de la Literatura Antigua en el Bestiario Ilustrado', *Norba-Arte*, 17 (1997) 27-40.

Lanuza-Navarro, T., 'Astrological Literature in Seventeenth-Century Spain', *The Colorado Review of Hispanic Studies*, 7 (2009) 119-136.

Leitão, J., *The Book of St. Cyprian: The Sorcerer's Treasure*, Hadean Press, 2012.

Peris Felipo, F.J., 'Aportación a la divulgación zoológica valenciana del siglo XVII: El *Tratado de los animales terrestres y volátiles*', *Revista Historia Autónoma* 2 (2013) 59-74.

Salaverti i Fabiani, V.L., 'Una mostra de les necessitats cientifiques de la burgesia, l'Arithmetica Practica de Geronymo Cortés (Valencia, 1604)' in Garma Pons, S.(ed.), *El científico espanol ante su historia. La ciencia en Espana entre 1750-1850: I Congreso de la Sociedad Española de Historia de las Ciencias*, Madrid: Diputación Provincial de Madrid, 1980.

Serrano, B. (collr.), *A Praga Rogada nas Escadas da Forca*, Porto: Livraria Portugueza: Editora de Joaquim Maria da Costa, 1883.

Serrano, B. (Dr.), *Almanach Republicano do Marquez de Pombal para o ano de 1913*, Porto: Livraria Portugueza: Editora de Joaquim Maria da Costa, 1913.

Serrano, B., *O Oráculo do Passado, do Presente e do Futuro*, Porto: Livraria Portugueza: Editora de Joaquim Maria da Costa, 1883.

Serrano, B., *O Oráculo dos Segredos: Segredos úteis às pessoas para cura radical de muitas moléstias*, Sintra: Zéfiro Edições e Actividades Culturais, 2010.

Serrano, Bento (Dr.), *Almanach Saragossano das Feiticeiras*, Porto: Livraria Portugueza, 1895-1896, 1898, 19901, 1913, 1921.

Serrano, Bento (Dr.), *Verdadeiro Almanach das Feiticeiras*, Porto: Livraria Portugueza, 1887-1890.

Solomon, M., *Fictions of Well-Being: Sickly Readers and Vernacular Medical Writings in Late Medieval and Early Modern Spain*, Philadelphia: University of Pennsylvania Press, 2010.

Tavares, Possidónio, *O verdadeiro livro de São Cipriano*, Rio de Janeiro: H. Garnier 1900.

Vasconcelos de Almeida, A., *Saberes e Práticas de Cura no "Lunário Perpétuo" de Genónimo Cortés (1555 – 1615) e Sua Influencia no Nordeste Brasileiro*, Olinda: Editora Universitária da UFRPE, 2012.

Meu lunário tem antigas
Alquimias de almanaque.
Já enfrentou intempéries,
Roubos, incêndios e saques:
Dos homens, das traças, das garras das eras.
Carrega segredos, decifra quimeras,
Venceu todos os ataques

O meu lunário perpétuo
Sob o sol é luzidio.
Meu lunário foi forjado
Num fogo de desafio,
Que vibra, esquenta, atiça, aperreia,
Faísca, enlouquece, que pega na veia.
Pelos séculos a fio.

O meu lunário perpétuo
Guarda as vozes seculares
Do profeta de canudos
E do mártir dos palmares,
Sonhando com o reino do espírito santo
Na terra, no céu, em todo recanto.
Nos terreiros e altares.

O meu lunário perpétuo
É meu livro precioso,
Minha cartilha primeira,
Minha bíblia de trancoso.
João grilo, chico, malazartes, mateus,
Os órfãos da terra, os filhos de deus,
Heróis do maravilhoso.

Meu lunário é a memória
De um país que vai passando
Diante dos nossos olhos,
Rindo, mexendo, cantando.
Mestiço, latino, caboclo, nativo.
É velho, é criança, morreu e tá vivo...
Presente, mas até quando?

Meu lunário é conselheiro,
Meu folheto, é meu missal,
Atravessando os milênios,
Cada ponto cardeal.
De norte a sul, de pai para filho,
De lá para cá, meu livrinho andarilho,
Fabuloso romançal.

Antonio Nóbrega

THE NON PLUS ULTRA
DO LUNARIO

AND PERPETUAL PROGNOSTICS,
GENERAL AND PARTICULAR FOR ALL KINGDOMS AND PROVINCES

COMPOSED BY

JERÓNIMO CORTEZ, VALENCIANO

EMENDED ACCORDING TO THE PROOFINGS OF THE HOLY INQUISITION, AND TRANSLATED INTO ENGLISH BY

JOSÉ LEITÃO

And lastly it is added a curious invention of certain notes and rules so as one may be able to make prognostics and yearly discourses on the shortages or abundances of the year, and a memorial of universal remedies for various ailments.

Prologue

To the Discreet Reader

Saint Gregory the Nazarene says that good is not good unless it is used; for it is not enough to make a good thing if one does not proceed equally good. For this reason did Seneca say that by the ends does glory come, meaning that all effects caused by good are good; as all those by evil are evil; referring to the Gospel: *Arbor bona bonos fructus facit, & mala malos*. In this Lunario (dear Reader) have we seen such effects; for being this book so small we have yet seen the sublime and extraordinary vantages it has brought to all manner of people; as such, do not be surprised by the amount of printings made of it, for even more would be bought if more were to be printed, especially those of this new corrected edition.

And if the will of God is also his Law, and this Law is the precept that obliges us to love each other, then I, Christian as I am, and owing to the whole world (as says Saint Paul), let it fall upon my work, and may I print this book voluntarily once again, or, as Pindar says: would I be obliged to do anything else? And indeed to will is to do, and to do is to determine, and to determine is to labor, such as it is said: *obras son amores, que no buenas razones*; in such a use I then place it; and as this is the purpose to which all things are meant, according to Saint Augustine, may it make it worthy, and to it do I remit; may be judged and may one discover not only what is in its beginning, but also comprehend what is in its middle and find its ending pleasant; and as the final cause is the cause of all causes, mine has always been that of charity and wellbeing for all; and to sow nothing more than good deeds, as Cicero said, and to reap friends, as Terence, and also to make fools and amateurs out of Masters, as Titus Livy.

Vale.

Of the World

and

Its Division

By the world we mean the Universe, in which is contained the Heavens, Stars and Elements and all other created things. The Greeks called this universal machine *Cosmos*, and the Latin *Mundus*, which means ornament and adornment, due to the beauty and perfection it contains; this was created (according to the most respected Authors) in Autumn, around the month of September, being this conclusion based on the fact that the most remote of nations began the year in the month of September, as did the Egyptians, Persians, Greeks and all Orientals, and because our first Parents as soon as they were created ate of the forbidden fruit, and the natural and perfect time for ripe fruit is in the Autumnal Equinox. However it is most certain, and according to reason, that the world had its beginning in the Vernal Equinox, which is in the month of March as the Sun enters the first degree of Aries, which now happens on the 21st of the said month; and it was convenient that the world be created in this same period, for this time is more temperate and apt for the generation and augmentation of things than Autumn: the period in which things become diminished rather than increased, for being so close to Winter. One other more effective reason to prove that the world had its beginning in the Vernal Equinox is that Christ our Redeemer wished to die in Spring, and on a Friday, and he also wished to be put on the Cross at the sixth hour, at the time, day and hour our first parents broke the precepts of God. With this it is proven that the world had its beginning in the Vernal Equinox and not the Autumnal, for Christ did not wish to die in Autumn, but rather in Spring, on the fifteenth of the Moon of March, on a Friday, which was before April, with thirty three years of his life not yet completed.

The world is then divided into two parts: the Elemental and the Ethereal region. Of these we shall speak soon enough, and with the favor of God, with the brevity that the present Work requires.

Of Time

Time is the tarrying of the Equinoxial movement, or, as the Philosopher says, it is the measure of the movement of the first mobile, from which the measurement of the ages of the world as well as that of man and of all other larger or smaller parts of time are also born, as is also the alterations of things subjected to them. Time had its beginning (according to the writings of Saint John, Apocalypse, Chapter 10) at the creation of the world, which, according to the Hebrews, is said to have been created, at the time of the current printing, 5617 years ago.[36]

---

36. Translator's note: this refers to the year of 1857, date of printing of the Lisbon edition used as a base for this translation.

It took eight days from their formation for Adam and Eve, according to the most trustworthy opinions, to eat of the apple which God had forbidden; and since this day is time generally divided into three parts, according to the three Laws that God our Lord has given the world in different periods, these are: The time of the natural Law, which began in the time of our first Parents and lasted until the Law of the Scripture, which was in the time of Moses and which lasted 2512 years.

The second part had its beginning with the Law of the Scripture, written by Moses, which lasted until the Law of Grace, which was at the time of the true Messiah Christ our Redeemer, and lasted for 1488 years.

The third part began with the time of the Law of Grace given by Jesus Christ, true God and man, which has lasted since the death of the same Christ 1857 years ago.

Further down we shall divide Time in particular into Ages, Years, Months, Weeks, Days, Hours and Quarters. Even if it is possible to still divide it into larger or smaller parts, for the intelligence of this Repertoire, these are enough.

Of the Ages of Time

All the time past and still to come (according to the Sacred Scripture) is divided into six ages.

The first age had its beginning with Adam, and it lasted until the deluge; and according to Genesis, Chapter 5, lasted 1656 years.

The second age lasted from the deluge until Abraham, and it lasted 426 years.

The third age was from Abraham until the Law of Moses, and it lasted 430 years.

The fourth age lasted from the Law given by Moses until the beginning of the construction of the Temple of Solomon, and it lasted 480 years.

The fifth age lasted from the edification of the Temple until its destruction, and it lasted 476 years.

The sixth age lasted from the destruction of the Temple until the most joyous labor of the Virgin Mary and the happiest Birth of Christ our Redeemer, and it lasted 536 year.

With what was said above one can gather that from the beginning of the world until the Birth of Christ 4000 years were passed.

Of the ages of man

The ages of man (according to Galen) are five: Infancy, Adolescence, Youth, Virility and Senescence. This variety of ages arises from changes in some quality or another that, as time and years pass, loses a certain temperament and acquires another very different one.

The first age is called Infancy, or Childhood, and its quality is hot and humid, and lasts from birth until 14 years of age.

The second age, called Adolescence, or Boyhood, whose quality is hot and dry, and lasts from 14 to 25 years of age.

The third age is called Youth, which is very tempered in its beginning, and lasts from 25 to 40 years of age.

The fourth age is called Virility, and its quality is somewhat cold and dry, and lasts from 40 to 55 years of age.

The fifth age is called Senescence, or Old age and whose quality is of cold and excessive dryness, and it lasts from 56 until the end of one's life.

These five ages can be further reduced to four, which are: Childhood, Youth, Old age and Decrepitude, as can be seen below in a Table.

Of the Year

Year (*ano*) was derived from *ab innovatione*, for in each year are the grasses and plants renewed, and it is nothing more than an amount of time, or age, of twelve Solar months, which is the time taken by the Sun to pass, through its own movement, all the twelve Signs until it returns to the point where it was at the beginning of the year.

Julius Caesar established the year, which we use today, of 365 day and 6 imperfect hours: for their quantity is not precise, for we shall clearly see the belating of time and the anticipation of the Equinoxes. Such has been seen, as since the Council of Nicaea, which was 325 years after the coming of Christ to the World, until the year of 1700, the Equinox would have been anticipated by eleven days. Should this error not be corrected in the year of 1582, it would be so considerable that in many hundreds of years we would have Winter in June and Summer in December, as shall happen to those that do not accept the Gregorian Calendar. El Rey King Alfonso,[37] in that school of Astrologers and Philosophers he made, upon investigating the perfect quantity of the year determined it to be in fact 365 days, 5 hours, 49 minutes and 26 seconds, as one may see in his Tables.[38] And according to the opinion of El Rey King Alfonso (and received by every Astrologer) one cannot make up every 4 years a whole day, for one will be missing 42 minutes and 56 seconds. But keeping the simplicity of not counting the minutes, the Holy Mother Church uses the year as established by Julius Caesar, taking 6 hours for each year and dividing an entire day for four years; and for this reason the Holy Father Gregory XIII ordered that the calendar be updated in the year 1582, on the 5th of October, taking 10 days off of the mentioned month, and changing the Dominical letter G, that was then used, into a C, and for this cause does the order exist that from each 300 years we should remove one day.

Of the Month

Month is derived from *Metior, metiris*, which means to measure; it is one part of the twelve that measure the year. There are three types of months: the Regular months, the Solar months and the Lunar months. Regular months are the ones shown in the Calendars, and because the whole of the Roman Church makes use of them we call them Regular. The Solar month is the amount of time that the Sun takes in passing through one of the twelve Signs. Lunar months can be in three different forms: the month of Peragration, the month of Consequation and the month of Apparition. The month of Peragration is that amount of time the Moon takes in crossing all the 12 Signs, which is 27 days and 8 hours. The month of Consequation is that amount of time that the Moon takes, upon separating itself from the Sun by its own movement, to once again meet with the Sun, and this amount of time is 29 days and a half. The month of Apparition, or Medicinal month, according to the medics, is that amount of time that the Moon takes from when we see it in the New Moon after conjunction, until we see it again in this state after another conjunction.

The months are 12, and their names are: January and it has 31 days; February 28 and when it is a leap year it has 29; March 31; April 30; May 31; June 30; July 31; August 31; September 30; October 31; November 31; and December 31; which can be taken to memory with the following verses:

Thirty days has November
April, June and September
Of twenty eight there will be one
And all the rest thirty one.

Of the Week

The Week (*semana*) is an amount of time that contains seven days, and it originates in *Septem, & Mane*, which means seven mornings or seven lights; for in this period of time the Sun rises seven times.

---

37. Translator's note: Alfonso X of Castile, the Wise, a great patron of intellectuals and astronomers. If you ever touched upon the slightest corner of astronomy or astrology you owe him something.

38. Translator's note: the Alfonsine tables, created in Alfonso's Toledo School of Translator, comprising of Jewish and Muslim scholars.

The name of these days are the following: Sunday (*Domingo*), Monday (*Lunes*), Tuesday (*Martes*), Wednesday (*Miércoles*), Thursday (*Jueves*), Friday (*Viernes*) and Saturday (*Sábado*), which correspond to the 7 heavenly Planets. The Gentiles named Sunday the *dies Solis*, Monday, *dies Lunæ*, Tuesday, *dies Martis*, and so forth for all the others, for they thought, through Astrological knowledge, that the first hour on which the Sun rose on a Sunday was the hour of the Sun, and the first hour of Monday was the hour of the Moon and so forth. However, Our Holy Mother Church, by doing away with Gentility (in the time of Pope Sylvester) placed very different names on the days of the week, calling Sunday *dies Dominica*, or *prima feria*, to the second day *secunda feria*, to the third day *tertia feria*, and in this order with all the others, except Saturday, which is called *Sabbathum*,[39] which means relief and rest; for in that day did the Sacrosanct body of our Master and Redeemer Jesus Christ rest in the sepulcher.

Of the Day

Day is the same as saying light or clarity, for it is the illumination of our Hemisphere by the Sun that makes the day, which can be counted in three different ways; the Artificial, the Natural and the Astronomical. The Artificial Day, according to the Philosopher, is the amount of time from the Sunrise to the Sunset. It is called Artificial for in this time the Artifices work their trades and take care of their businesses. Natural Day is an amount of time of 24 hours, which is counted from the time of the Sunrise until the next time it rises and which may have several starting points, for the Chaldeans, Persians and Babylonians counted it from the Sunrise and the Hebrews from the Sunset. The Church, thinking on this more profoundly, starts the day at Midnight, for on that hour was her Bride-Groom and our Redeemer Jesus Christ born. The Astronomical is as the Astrologers take it, starting the day at Midday, lasting until the next Midday, counting the hours from 1 to 24, and in this way when they say 20 hours of the 5th of January, these are 8 of the morning of the 6th.

Of the Hour

An hour is one Part of those twenty four that the Natural day contains, or one of the twelve of the Artificial day, of which spoke Christ our Redeemer when he said to his Apostles: *Nonne duodecim sunt horae diei?* And Saint John, Chapter 11, mentions these artificial hours when he said: *Erat quasi horæ sexta quando crucifixus est Jesus*, which means that it was almost Midday when they crucified our Savior, being then understood the sixth hour of the 12 hours of the day. In such a way that to 6 in the morning the Hebrews called the Prime hour, and to the ninth the Third, and the twelfth hour the Sixth and to 3 in the afternoon the Ninth hour, as Saint Mathew mentions, Chapter 27: Now from the sixth hour there was darkness over all the land unto the ninth hour. This meaning: from Midday until three in afternoon. These names are still used by the Church in the praying of the Canonical Hours. The hour is divided into 60 minutes and the minute into 60 seconds.

Of the quarter of the hour

The Quarter is one of the four parts of an hour; it is the same as fifteen minutes, for four times fifteen make precisely 60 minutes, which is a whole hour.

---

39. Translator's note: Except for the Vatican, the renaming of the days of the week described here was only actually effective in Portugal, through the action of St Martin of Dume, archbishop of Braga, one of the oldest archdioceses in the world, where one may observe the Rite of Braga (as opposed to the Roman Rite). Currently the days of the working week are *Segunda-Feira, Terça-Feira, Quarta-Feira, Quinta-Feira* and *Sexta-Feira*.

Of the four periods of the year and their qualities

The year is divided into four periods of times: Spring, Summer, Autumn and Winter; and each of these parts (according to the Astronomers) contains three months.

Spring has its beginning on the 21st of March and its end at the 22nd of June, and its quality is hot and humid, and in this first part of the year is the sanguine humor predominant, and should Spring be too humid all fruits may come to rot while still on the tree branches and there will be an abundance of weeds, even if these are of little substance and use. If it is too hot, trees will produce flowers, fruits and leaves too early, and these will generate many pests, and roses will also blossom before their time and produce a weaker scent. If it is cold and dry it indicates a great deal of frost by the end of Spring which will destroy most fruit and make great damage on the production of grapes. If it is too dry there will be little wheat and less fruit, but these will be of a good quality. If it is cold fruit will generate later, but these will be good and in abundance.

Summer begins on the 22nd of July and ends on the 23rd of September, and its quality is hot and dry, and in this second part of the year the choleric humor is the predominant. If Summer is too humid its fruit will rot, and there will also be little wheat and barley and much disease. If it is too dry its fruits will be good and healthy, but their diseases will be quite acute. If it is too hot there will be an abundance of fruit with very little disease. If it is cold its fruits will come out of season and the year will be quite hard.

Autumn begins on the 23rd of September and ends on the 21st of December, and its quality is cold and dry; in this third part of the year the predominant humor is the melancholic. If Autumn is too humid grapes will rot and the wine will become clouded in Spring and while being transferred into bottles. If by the end of Autumn there is abundant rain then there will be little wheat and less barley in the following year; however should it be too dry there will be lack of any and all supplies and plenty of disease in the second part of the following year. If Autumn is too cold its fruits will have little taste, those such as pomegranates, olives, sugar cane and other such as these that are harvested in this time. If it is cold and temperamentally dry then it promises to be a good year of great health.

Winter starts on the 22nd of December and ends on the 20th of March; the quality of this quarter of the year is cold and humid, in which the phlegmatic humor is predominant. If Winter is hot and humid it will be baneful for plants and health. If it is too windy it will waste away all fruits and diminish all seeds.

Finally, should the natural qualities of the four times of the year be exchanged it is a sign of sterility and shortness of supplies and a diversity of sicknesses.

Of the Equinoxes and Solstices of the year

The Year has two Equinoxes and two Solstices, which are the two occasions when the days are equal to the nights, and the others are the occasions in which the day is the longest and shortest of the year.

The first Equinox is when the Sun begins to enter the Sign of Aries, which is on the 21st of March, and here the days are equal to the nights.

The other Equinox is when the Sun begins to enter the Sign of Libra, which is on the 23rd of September, and here once again are the days equal to the nights.

Of the Solstices, one is called Winter and the other Summer. The Winter Solstice is when the Sun begins to enter the Sign of Capricorn which is on the 22nd of December, and here are the shortest days of the whole year, registering: a day of nine hours and a quarter and a night of fourteen hours and three quarters.

The other Summer Solstice is when the Sun begins to enter the Sign of Cancer, which is on the 22nd of June, and here are the longest days of the year, registering: a day of 14 hours and three quarters and a night of nine hours and one quarter, as can be seen by the following Table.

The following table is understood as such: on the 23rd of January the Sun rises at 7 and one quarter, and is set at four and three quarters. And the day then has nine hours and two quarters and the night fourteen hours and two quarters. By taking this month as an example are the others understood.

This table is used so one may learn the hour at which the Sun rises and sets, how many hours has the day and night, throughout the whole of the year.

	Sun Rise		Sun Set		Day's Duration		Night's Duration	
	h.	q.	h.	q.	h.	q.	h.	q.
23rd of January	7	1	4	3	9	2	14	2
6th of February	7	0	5	0	10	0	14	0
18th of February	6	3	5	1	10	2	13	2
1st of March	6	2	5	2	11	0	13	0
11th of March	6	1	5	3	11	2	12	2
21st of March	6	0	6	0	12	0	12	0
2nd of April	5	3	6	1	12	2	11	2
12th of April	5	2	6	2	13	0	11	0
23rd of April	5	1	6	3	13	2	10	2
6th of May	5	0	7	0	14	0	10	0
20th of May	4	3	7	1	14	2	9	2
12th of June	4	2	7	2	15	0	9	0
26th of June	4	1	7	3	15	2	8	2
10th of August	5	0	7	0	14	0	10	0
22nd of August	5	1	6	3	13	2	10	2
2nd of September	5	2	6	2	13	0	11	0
13th of September	5	3	6	1	12	2	11	2
22nd of September	6	0	6	0	12	0	12	0
5th of October	6	1	5	3	11	2	12	2
15th of October	6	2	5	2	11	0	13	0
26th of October	6	3	5	1	10	2	13	2
7th of November	7	0	5	0	10	0	14	0
21st of November	7	1	4	3	9	2	14	2
22nd of December	7	2	4	2	9	0	15	0

One may also easily know the duration of the nights of the whole year by counting the time from when the Sun sets to when it rises the next day.

For example: Should I want to know the duration of the night of the 30th of January, I can see on the table below that the Sun sets when it's 17 hours and 55 minute; and as until Midnight there are 6 hours and 5 minutes, and from Midnight until the Sun rise of the 31st there are 7 hours and 44 minutes, I add the 5 hours and 5 minutes to the 7 hours and 44 minutes and I know that the night of the 31st of January has 13 hours and 49 minutes.

The following table shows, firstly, a column of days, common to all the months that each page contains; then, below each month it has the hours and minutes at which the Sun rises and at which it sets, and the hours and minutes that day has.

Note: One should know that every hour indicated is expressed in Universal time; which corresponds to the legal hour in the Winter time. In order to know that corresponding legal time in the Summer time one should add 60 minute to the values given.

Table of the hours in which the Sun rises and sets and the duration of the day

Day of the month	January			February			March		
	Sun rise	Sun set	Day	Sun rise	Sun set	Day	Sun rise	Sun set	Day
	h.m.	h.m.	h.m.	h.m.	h.m.	h.m.	h.m.	h.m.	h.m.
1	7:55	17:25	9:30	7:43	17:58	10:15	7:09	18:30	11:21
2	7:55	17:26	9:31	7:42	17:59	10:17	7:07	18:31	11:24
3	7:55	17:27	9:32	7:42	18:00	10:18	7:06	18:32	11:26
4	7:55	17:28	9:33	7:41	18:01	10:20	7:04	18:33	11:29
5	7:55	17:29	9:34	7:40	18:02	10:22	7:03	18:34	11:31
6	7:55	17:30	9:35	7:39	18:03	10:24	7:01	18:35	11:34
7	7:55	17:31	9:36	7:38	18:05	10:27	7:00	18:36	11:36
8	7:55	17:32	9:37	7:37	18:06	10:29	6:58	18:37	11:39
9	7:55	17:33	9:38	7:36	18:07	10:31	6:57	18:38	11:41
10	7:55	17:34	9:39	7:34	18:08	10:34	6:55	18:39	11:44
11	7:55	17:35	9:40	7:33	18:09	10:36	6:54	18:40	11:46
12	7:54	17:36	9:42	7:32	18:10	10:38	6:52	18:41	11:49
13	7:54	17:37	9:43	7:31	18:11	10:40	6:51	18:42	11:51
14	7:54	17:38	9:44	7:30	18:13	10:43	6:49	18:43	11:54
15	7:54	17:39	9:45	7:29	18:14	10:45	6:48	18:44	11:56
16	7:53	17:40	9:47	7:27	18:15	10:48	6:46	18:45	11:59
17	7:53	17:41	9:48	7:26	18:16	10:50	6:45	18:46	12:01
18	7:52	17:42	9:50	7:25	18:17	10:52	6:43	18:47	12:04
19	7:52	17:43	9:51	7:24	18:18	10:54	6:42	18:48	12:06
20	7:52	17:44	9:52	7:22	18:19	10:57	6:40	18:49	12:09
21	7:51	17:45	9:54	7:21	18:20	10:59	6:38	18:50	12:12
22	7:50	17:46	9:56	7:20	18:21	11:01	6:37	18:51	12:14
23	7:50	17:47	9:57	7:18	18:22	11:04	6:35	18:52	12:17
24	7:49	17:48	9:59	7:17	18:23	11:06	6:34	18:53	12:19
25	7:49	17:50	10:01	7:16	18:25	11:09	6:32	18:54	12:22
26	7:48	17:51	10:03	7:14	18:26	11:12	6:31	18:55	12:24
27	7:47	17:52	10:05	7:13	18:27	11:14	6:29	18:56	12:27
28	7:47	17:53	10:06	7:12	18:28	11:16	6:27	18:57	12:30
29	7:46	17:54	10:08	7:10	18:29	11:19	6:26	18:58	12:32
30	7:45	17:55	10:10				6:24	18:58	12:34
31	7:44	17:56	10:12				6:23	18:59	12:36

Continuation of the same table

Day of the month	April			May			June		
	Sun rise	Sun set	Day	Sun rise	Sun set	Day	Sun rise	Sun set	Day
	h.m.	h.m.	h.m.	h.m.	h.m.	h.m.	h.m.	h.m.	h.m.
1	6:21	19:00	12:39	5:39	19:29	13:50	5:14	19:56	14:42
2	6:20	19:01	12:41	5:38	19:30	13:52	5:13	19:56	14:43
3	6:18	19:02	12:44	5:37	19:31	13:54	5:13	19:57	14:44
4	6:17	19:03	12:46	5:36	19:32	13:56	5:13	19:58	14:45
5	6:15	19:04	12:49	5:34	19:33	13:59	5:13	19:58	14:45
6	6:14	19:05	12:51	5:33	19:34	14:01	5:12	19:59	14:47
7	6:12	19:06	12:54	5:32	19:35	14:03	5:12	19:59	14:47
8	6:11	19:07	12:56	5:31	19:36	14:05	5:12	20:00	14:48
9	6:09	19:08	12:59	5:30	19:37	14:07	5:12	20:01	14:49
10	6:08	19:09	13:01	5:29	19:38	14:09	5:12	20:01	14:49
11	6:06	19:10	13:04	5:28	19:39	14:11	5:11	20:02	14:51
12	6:05	19:11	13:06	5:27	19:39	14:12	5:11	20:02	14:51
13	6:03	19:12	13:09	5:26	19:40	14:14	5:11	20:02	14:51
14	6:02	19:13	13:11	5:25	19:41	14:16	5:11	20:03	14:52
15	6:00	19:14	13:14	5:25	19:42	14:17	5:11	20:03	14:52
16	5:59	19:15	13:16	5:24	19:43	14:19	5:11	20:04	14:53
17	5:57	19:16	13:19	5:23	19:44	14:21	5:12	20:04	14:52
18	5:56	19:17	13:21	5:22	19:45	14:23	5:12	20:04	14:52
19	5:55	19:18	13:23	5:21	19:46	14:25	5:12	20:04	14:52
20	5:53	19:19	13:26	5:21	19:46	14:25	5:12	20:05	14:53
21	5:52	19:20	13:28	5:20	19:47	14:27	5:12	20:05	14:53
22	5:51	19:20	13:29	5:19	19:48	14:29	5:12	20:05	14:53
23	5:49	19:21	13:32	5:18	19:49	14:31	5:13	20:05	14:52
24	5:48	19:22	13:34	5:18	19:50	14:32	5:13	20:05	14:52
25	5:47	19:23	13:36	5:17	19:51	14:34	5:13	20:05	14:52
26	5:45	19:24	13:39	5:17	19:51	14:34	5:14	20:05	14:51
27	5:44	19:25	13:41	5:16	19:52	14:36	5:14	20:06	14:52
28	5:43	19:26	13:43	5:16	19:53	14:37	5:14	20:06	14:52
29	5:41	19:27	13:46	5:15	19:54	14:39	5:15	20:05	14:50
30	5:40	19:28	13:48	5:15	19:54	14:39	5:15	20:05	14:50
31				5:14	19:55	14:41			

Continuation of the same table

Day of the month	July			August			September		
	Sun rise	Sun set	Day	Sun rise	Sun set	Day	Sun rise	Sun set	Day
	h.m	h.m	h.m	h.m	h.m	h.m	h.m	h.m	h.m
1	5:16	20:05	14:49	5:38	19:47	14:09	6:06	19:07	13:01
2	5:16	20:05	14:49	5:39	19:46	14:07	6:07	19:05	12:58
3	5:17	20:05	14:48	5:40	19:45	14:05	6:08	19:04	12:56
4	5:17	20:05	14:48	5:41	19:44	14:03	6:09	19:02	12:53
5	5:18	20:05	14:47	5:42	19:43	14:01	6:10	19:00	12:50
6	5:18	20:04	14:46	5:43	19:42	13:59	6:10	18:59	12:49
7	5:19	20:04	14:45	5:44	19:41	13:57	6:11	18:57	12:46
8	5:20	20:04	14:44	5:45	19:40	13:55	6:12	18:56	12:44
9	5:20	20:03	14:43	5:45	19:38	13:53	6:13	18:54	12:41
10	5:21	20:03	14:42	5:46	19:37	13:51	6:14	18:53	12:39
11	5:22	20:03	14:41	5:47	19:36	13:49	6:15	18:51	12:36
12	5:22	20:02	14:40	5:48	19:35	13:47	6:16	18:49	12:33
13	5:23	20:02	14:39	5:49	19:33	13:44	6:17	18:48	12:31
14	5:24	20:01	14:37	5:50	19:32	13:42	6:17	18:46	12:29
15	5:24	20:01	14:37	5:51	19:31	13:40	6:18	18:45	12:27
16	5:25	20:00	14:35	5:52	19:30	13:38	6:19	18:43	12:24
17	5:26	20:00	14:34	5:53	19:28	13:35	6:20	18:41	12:21
18	5:27	19:59	14:32	5:53	19:27	13:34	6:21	18:40	12:19
19	5:27	19:58	14:31	5:54	19:25	13:31	6:22	18:38	12:16
20	5:28	19:58	14:30	5:55	19:24	13:29	6:23	18:37	12:14
21	5:29	19:57	14:28	5:56	19:23	13:27	6:24	18:35	12:11
22	5:30	19:56	14:26	5:57	19:21	13:24	6:25	18:33	12:08
23	5:31	19:55	14:24	5:58	19:20	13:22	6:25	18:32	12:07
24	5:31	19:55	14:24	5:59	19:18	13:19	6:26	18:30	12:04
25	5:32	19:54	14:22	6:00	19:17	13:17	6:27	18:29	12:02
26	5:33	19:53	14:20	6:01	19:16	13:15	6:28	18:27	11:59
27	5:34	19:52	14:18	6:02	19:14	13:12	6:29	18:25	11:56
28	5:35	19:51	14:16	6:02	19:13	13:11	6:30	18:24	11:54
29	5:36	19:50	14:14	6:03	19:11	13:08	6:31	18:22	11:51
30	5:37	19:49	14:12	6:04	19:10	13:06	6:32	18:21	11:49
31	5:37	19:48	14:11	6:05	19:08	13:03			

Continuation of the same table

Day of the month	October			November			December		
	Sun rise	Sun set	Day	Sun rise	Sun set	Day	Sun rise	Sun set	Day
	h.m	h.m	h.m	h.m	h.m	h.m	h.m	h.m	h.m
1	6:33	18:19	11:46	7:04	17:36	10:32	7:36	17:16	9:40
2	6:34	18:18	11:44	7:05	17:35	10:30	7:37	17:15	9:39
3	6:35	18:16	11:41	7:06	17:34	10:28	7:38	17:15	9:37
4	6:36	18:15	11:39	7:07	17:33	10:26	7:39	17:15	9:36
5	6:36	18:13	11:34	7:08	17:32	10:24	7:40	17:15	9:35
6	6:37	18:11	11:34	7:09	17:31	10:22	7:41	17:15	9:34
7	6:38	18:10	11:32	7:10	17:30	10:20	7:42	17:15	9:33
8	6:39	18:08	11:29	7:11	17:29	10:18	7:42	17:15	9:33
9	6:40	18:07	11:27	7:13	17:28	10:15	7:43	17:15	9:32
10	6:41	18:05	11:24	7:14	17:27	10:13	7:44	17:15	9:31
11	6:42	18:04	11:22	7:15	17:26	10:11	7:45	17:15	9:30
12	6:43	18:02	11:19	7:16	17:26	10:10	7:46	17:16	9:30
13	6:44	18:01	11:17	7:17	17:25	10:08	7:46	17:16	9:30
14	6:45	18:00	11:15	7:18	17:24	10:06	7:47	17:16	9:29
15	6:46	17:58	11:13	7:19	17:23	10:04	7:48	17:16	9:28
16	6:47	17:57	11:10	7:20	17:22	10:02	7:48	17:17	9:29
17	6:48	17:55	11:07	7:21	17:22	10:01	7:49	17:17	9:28
18	6:49	17:54	11:05	7:22	17:21	9:59	7:50	17:17	9:27
19	6:50	17:53	11:03	7:24	17:20	9:56	7:50	17:18	9:28
20	6:51	17:51	11:00	7:25	17:20	9:55	7:51	17:18	9:27
21	6:52	17:50	10:58	7:26	17:19	9:53	7:51	17:19	9:28
22	6:53	17:49	10:56	7:27	17:19	9:52	7:52	17:19	9:27
23	6:54	17:47	10:53	7:28	17:18	9:50	7:52	17:20	9:28
24	6:55	17:46	10:51	7:29	17:18	9:49	7:53	17:20	9:28
25	6:56	17:45	10:49	7:30	17:17	9:47	7:53	17:21	9:28
26	6:57	17:43	10:46	7:31	17:17	9:46	7:53	17:22	9:29
27	6:58	17:42	10:44	7:32	17:17	9:44	7:54	17:22	9:28
28	7:00	17:41	10:41	7:33	17:16	9:43	7:54	17:23	9:29
29	7:01	17:40	10:39	7:34	17:16	9:42	7:54	17:24	9:30
30	7:02	17:39	10:37	7:35	17:16	9:41	7:55	17:24	9:29
31	7:03	17:37	10:34				7:55	17:25	9:30

Of the Elemental Region and the Elements

The Elemental region is everything that is created between the Lunar Sphere and the center of the earth, all of which is composed of 4 simple parts to which we call the Elements and these are the following: Earth, Water, Air and Fire. These are called simple bodies for they are not composed by any other bodies, as all the remaining bodies are composed from them.

The Earth naturally, as a dense body, is in the middle and center of the Universe, whose quality is cold and dry and has a roundness, according to the best opinions, of 6480 leagues: one could walk the whole of the earth by walking 10 leagues everyday in one year, nine months and 13 days. Its diameter, which is the distance from this part of the earth until the other under it, is 2061 leagues and a little over half. By which we can extract that to the center, or hell, there are 1030 leagues and 3 quarters.

Right above the Earth we have Water, whose quality is cold and humid, and according to the opinion of the Philosophers, is 10 times greater than the Earth in rarity,[40] not quantity.

After the Earth and Water follows Air, whose quality is hot and humid, and is 10 times greater than Water in rarity. We will not discuss the winds at this point, for we shall do so in a more appropriate time, so as to make it clearer to the Navigators.

The fourth Element is Fire, which is above the region of Air, whose quality is hot and dry, and is ten times rarer and simpler than Air.

By the following Table will one know the qualities of the four elements, the four parts of the world, the four winds, the four parts of the year, the four humors, the four ages of man and the nature of the twelve Signs.

The Qualities	Hot and humid	Hot and dry	Cold and humid	Cold and dry
The 4 Elements	Air	Fire	Water	Earth
The 4 parts of the World	Midday	Occident	Orient	Septentrion
The 4 Winds	South Meridional	West/Ponente	East/Levante	North/Tramontana
The 4 parts of the Year	Spring	Summer	Winter	Autumn
The 4 humors	Sanguine	Choleric	Phlegmatic	Melancholic
The 4 ages	Infancy	Youth	Old age	Decrepitude
The qualities of the 12 Signs	Gemini Libra Aquarius	Aries Leo Sagittarius	Cancer Scorpio Pisces	Taurus Virgo Capricorn

---

40. Translator's note: lack of density.

Of the number and nature of the winds

Wind (according to the Philosophers) is an exhalation, like a breath, hot and dry, that is produced in the entrails of the earth and, after exiting it, by virtue and strength of the rays of the Sun, moves around it with the strength and vehemence as we many times see and experience. The efficient cause of the Winds, as was said, is the Sun, repulsing and attracting to itself exhalations, which being evaporations, and wanting to rise to greater heights, are expelled by the coldness which is in the middle region of the Air; and, seeing as they are expelled in different directions, so are the winds differently moved through the roundness of the earth; and according to the lands and regions they traverse are they so named and receive different qualities and cause different effects. In olden times the Philosophers merely used 12 different Winds, and of these, four they referred to as the Cardinal Winds, for they are born and blow through the four parts of the World and the other eight they called the Collateral.[41] The first of the Cardinals is named South and Meridional for it blows from the region of the Midday, and others call it Riverwind; it is hot, humid and powerful, it generates clouds, except in Africa, where it causes serenity; it is also pestilential, as Saint Isidore says. The Collateral of this Wind, to the direction of the Sunset is called Libonotus and South-southwest; it is slightly hot and excessively humid; it is a harmful and sickening wind.

---

41. Translator's note: this layout of the winds/direction is quite distinct from the usual compass roses or wind roses, of either 4, 8, 16 or 32 winds/directions. The one being described here is actually the Classical wind compass of ancient Greece and Rome, although it is quite difficult to know which one Cortez is actually following.

The other Collateral, which is to the Orient, is called Penicias[42] and South-southeast, and it is hot and humid, gathers clouds, is healthier and frequently causes rain.

The second Cardinal Wind is called Tramontana and North, which is opposed to the Meridional; it is cold and dry, causes cold, stops showers, tightens the bodies, purifies the humors, drives away corrupt airs and pestilence and causes serenity, this also has two Collateral Winds.

The Collateral Wind that is to the Occident, called Circius and Northwest, and sometimes North-northwest, is temperately cold and excessively dry: it usually causes hail and snow, and in the province of Narbonne (according to Pliny) it blows so furiously that it can rip the tiles off of roofs.

The other Collateral wind, which is to the Orient, is called Aquilo and Northeast, and it is of a cold and dry nature, harmful to flowers and ripe fruit, it freezes and is abrasive to vines; it appear to sap the strength and virtue of trees, reduces the clouds, causes thunder and is quite strong. When this wind is blowing Pliny advices that no sowing should take place and no seed should be cast to the ground.

The third Cardinal Wind is called Levante and East: it is cold and humid and it generates clouds; this wind frequently makes it rain in Valencia, it is greatly helpful for the growth of herbs and flowers, and it conserves health. It has two Collaterals, one to the Midday, called Eurus and East-northeast and another for Tramontana, or North, called Grecale or East-southeast, which are benign according to their main quality.

The fourth Cardinal comes from the Occident and is called Ponente and West: its nature is cold and dry in Valencia; when the wind blows it softens this cold, melts snow, causes infirmities and expectoration and sometimes thunder and rain. One of its Collaterals is Corus and West-northwest: it is moderately humid and excessively cold, it is a harmful and pestilent wind. In the Orient it is said that it causes showers and in India serenity.

The other Collateral is Asirico[43] and West-southwest: it is temperately cold and excessively humid, rainy and tempestuous; it frequently causes storms, thunder and lightning.

Warning so as to keep one's supplies

Cellars and other places where one keeps wine should be placed in such a way as to receive sunlight and the Northern winds, for the wine will be kept fresh and dry, and will be better preserved, this according to Pliny, Book 4; and one should never keep sour wine in a cellar for it will contaminate the rest of it.

Barns should have windows opened to the North, for in this way the wheat will conserve itself for longer than it would with light and wind from any other direction.

Also, all fruit which is picked for storage should be in a place that receives light from the North, for this wind is cold and dry, and is natural for conservation of wines, wheat and fruit, such as pomegranates, grapes, nuts, almonds, pears, *camoesas*[44] and others such as these, as shall be said below. These fruits should be picked, so as to better conserve themselves, in the waning Moon, after midday, or during the most intense period of the Sun.

Sleeping quarters should receive light from the Orient, for this is good for the conservation of health, as well as to keep one's quarters clean and sane.

In this same fashion should libraries and offices receive light from the Oriental part, so as to keep them clear of moths and mildew.

Olive oil requires light from the Midday, or to be kept in a warm place during Winter and in a cool place during Summer; so as it may receive these conditions, it is good if it is kept in an underground, as is the custom in many places.

---

42. Translator's note: the name of this wind is frequently given as Euronotus, previously described by Aristotle, together with the Libonotus, as a non-wind. The name given by Cortez is a reference to Phoenicia, as this wind was considered to only exist in this region.

43. Translator's note: This wind is more frequently referred to as Africus. The name given by Cortez is a clear reference to Assyria.

44. Translator's note: a particular kind of apple.

Of the Ethereal or Celestial Region

Up to this point we have dealt with the Elemental Region with the greatest possible brevity, it is convenient now that we say something about the Celestial Region, to which Aristotle (Book 1 *de Caelo*, Chapter 8) calls the fifth essence, this with equal brevity, and whose nature is very different from that of the four Elements. This Ethereal or Celestial Region contains eleven Heavens, according to the most common opinion and also by that of the Astronomers. The first, in natural order, and eleventh relatively to us, as the Theologians say, is the Empirium Heaven, home and resting place of the Faithful, which is not subjected to any movement, as the other Heavens are.

Immediately after the Emperium is the tenth Heaven, or the tenth sphere, found by El-Rei King Alfonso, and accepted as the first mobile, for because of its movement are all the inferior Heavens dragged in a complete circle of twenty four hours around the Earth.

The ninth Heaven or Sphere found, and considered by Ptolemy as the first mobile, is the Heaven called Crystalline, where some men of knowledge believe that the waters mentioned in Genesis are kept. And Bede[45] says in Book 1 *de Natura rer.*, Chapter 4, that they were kept there after the flooding of the world in the great deluge.

In the natural order, after the Crystalline Heaven, we have the eighth Heaven, or Firmament, in which are all the fixed Stars except the seven planets, or, by another name, the Errant Stars, which are in the seven orbs or inferior heavens. These are called Planets, or wandering Stars, for they never are equally separated from each other, as all others in the Firmament or eighth Heaven. Of these Stars, or Planets, we shall speak in particular below.

Rule so as to know at night the hour by the North

North is a Star considered to be in the eighth Heaven, which is very close to the point around which all Orbs move. This Star, or North, is towards the Tramontana, which will be recognized by turning one's face to the East, and the brightest star that is found before the left shoulder is that which is called North, by which sailors and navigators guide themselves at night. With this star and with one other, which is in the tail of the Bosina,[46] the most resplendent one called the Horological, will the hour of the night be known in any period of the year.

Once the North is found, turn your face towards it in such a way as your right arm is facing the East and your left the West. Thus positioned imagine a Cross in the North, with one arm reaching above your head, the other at your feet and the other two arms of the Cross reaching to the West and East. Now imagine a circle around the North, which contains the four arms of the cross. One should note that the Horological, which describes the limit of the circle, goes on a full circle around the North in the space of 24 hours, in such a way as from one of the arms to the other it takes 6 hours; and in this way will the quarter part of the cross be divided into six parts, each representing one hour.

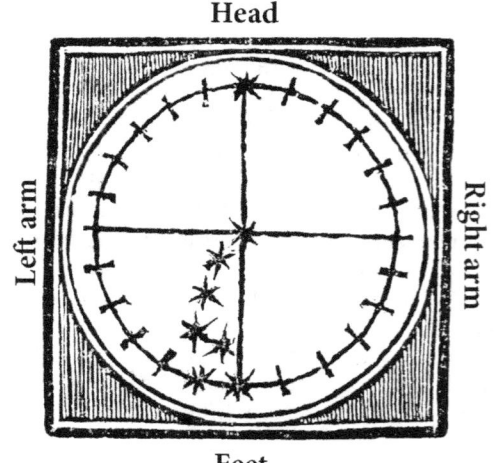

---

45 Translator's note: St Bede.
46 Translator's note: Ursa Minor.

The above being understood, one should consider the time of the year, for in the first of the month of May, the Horological Star marks midnight in the arm of the cross which comes before one's head; at the first of August it marks midnight in the left arm of the cross; in the first of November the mentioned start marks midnight in the arm of the Cross which falls before the feet; and on the first of February one will find midnight in the right arm.

Further down we shall note that these points of midnight will, every fifteen days, change in one hour, in such a way as on the first of May one will find the midnight of the Horological Star in the arm of the Cross which befalls the head, in fifteen days after this, which will be on the sixteenth of May, the said Star will mark one hour further towards the left arm of the cross, and in another fifteen days it will mark midnight in the second hour of those six which are between the two arms. Knowing the four points where the Horological Star marks midnight, consider the first of May and that the said star is removed from the midnight point towards the right by three sections (representing 3 hours). One can then say that it is 9 at night, for these are the three parts of the six that it takes from one arm to the other until it reaches midnight. And if three more hours pass from the arm at the front of the head to the right arm, one can say that it is three in the morning. And with this discourse and consideration will one know the hours during the night, on any period of the year, without missing a single point. Yet this practice is tiring and somewhat difficult to use with certainty, for it depends on astronomical observation

Rule so as to know, by one's hand and the Sun, the hour of the day

Since we have given the rule so as one may know the hours by night without needing a bell clock, it will also be good if we provide another rule so as one may know the hour of day by one's hand; so as everyone will at all times have a clock with them. Those who wish to know the time by their hand should turn their backs straight to the Sun and to be sure of this stick a rod on the ground and position the shadow it casts between your feet. Thus positioned, place a straw or small stick, as long as your index finger, on your hand over your life line (which is the one around your thumb) and having your left arm in a straight line to your left foot, with the hand of this arm not be raised or lowered beyond the arm, turn this hand so as the thumb no longer casts a shadow on its palm. Note that at the Sunrise of anytime of the year, the straw on your hand will cast a shadow on the index finger. Now let us suppose that the Sun rises at five in the morning, this shadow will be cast on the extremity of the index, and if it instead is cast on the extremity of the middle finger, this will mean it is six, and if it is cast on the next finger it will be seven, and if it is cast on the edge of the little finger it is eight; if it is cast lower than this it will be nine, if it is cast on the middle phalange of this finger it will be ten, on the lower phalange it will be eleven and if the shadow goes into the palm of the hand in front of the straw it will be twelve.

Now, to know the time after midday, one should note that the shadow will once again rise through the same places as it came down in the morning: as such, by having the shadow cast on the lower phalange of the little finger, it will be one, coming up to the second it will be two, to the third it will be three, and on the tip of this finger it will be four, on the other finger it will be five, on the middle finger six and on the index seven. We further warn that, should the Sun come out at six in the morning, one should perform these calculations by the phalanges closest to the extremities of the fingers, going also down the little finger to the point we have indicated in the previous example, and coming up through the same phalanges will the hours of the afternoon be revealed. If the Sun rises at seven in the morning, one will do this calculation by the middle phalanges of the finger, always starting by the index. And because experience will further instruct you on this procedure, I will not go any further; for the example of the five in the morning Sunrise will be enough to understand the hours one should take in the months of May, June, July and August; for six those of March, April, September and October; for seven those of November, December, January and February.

Of the Dominical letters

The Dominical letters are the first seven letters of the alphabet: A, B, C, D E, F, G.

Each one of these letters corresponds to a year and these mark the day of the week that year begins with, and consequently, every Sunday of that year.

The following table shows the days of the week and their corresponding Dominical letter:

A – Sunday
B – Saturday
C – Friday
D – Thursday
E – Wednesday
F – Tuesday
G – Monday

The leap years have however two letters: the first marks the Sundays until the day of Saint Mathias at the 24th of February, and the other the Sundays for the rest of the year.

The following table starts with the houses which contain the letters BA corresponding to the year of 1600, and it ends where we have the letter C and 1627; for every twenty eight years we return to the houses of the BA, by this being the time the Sun takes to perform its revolution.

The unit years (from 1 to 99) are counted from the houses of the BA to the right, going up in this same order; the hundreds (from 100 to 199) are counted by going up perpendicularly through the column of the leap years (the one with two letters in each house), but this solely for the first four houses, meaning 1600, 1604, 1608 and 1612. One should be warned that in the counting of the hundreds in this way, going up the four houses of the column, only those which fall in the house of the BA will have two letters, and all others which may fall in any other houses will not be leap years, this by reason of the three days which need to be suppressed each 400 years so as to compensate for the small excess of the day added in the leap years.

It is for this reason that, by the leap years being those you can perfectly divide by 4, one excludes those years of 1700, 1800, 1900, 2100, 2200, 2300, 2500, 2600, 2700, 2900, 3000, 31000 and in this way with the first 3 of each century.

One should also be warned that the years of 1900, 2100, 2200 and 2300 and all those centennials that are not leap years will only be given the second letter in retrograde of the two which would be given should they be leap years.

Example: The year of 1900 would have the Dominical letters of GC should it not be one of the centennials in which the leap is suppressed; and for this reason the Dominical letter of that year will be G, which is the second by the retrograde order (by counting from the right to the left), and in 1901 it would be F, in 1902 E, in 1903 D, in 1904 CB, in 1905 A, etc. And as the year 2000 is a centennial leap year, and there is no suppression of the Dominical letter, for this reason it will follow the order of the letters until the year of 2100, which would be CB should it be a leap year; but as this is one of the centennials in which this is suppressed, it will merely be C, which is the second letter, and 2101 will have B, 2102 A, 2103 G, 2104 FE, etc.

One should also be warned that in the centennials that are not leap years the month of February only has 28 days, and Saint Mathias is on the 24th like in a regular year.

All other years thus counted which may fall in the second house (1604), third (1608) and fourth (1612), will only have as a Dominical letter the second of the two, as ways said above.

Counting the unit years, as was mentioned before, those which fall in the houses of the first column will be leap years and will have two letters.

First example: Wanting to know the Dominical letter corresponding to the year of 1877, which is not a leap year, I will note that the letters FE, which are in the house of 1608, equally correspond to the year 1800, which is to the left; starting to count the 77 units beyond 1800 from the house immediately to its right, meaning 1 for 1609, 2 for 1610, 3 for 1611, 4 for 1612, 19 for 1627, 20 for

1600 and so forth you will find 77 in the house of 1601, in which there is the letter G, which is the Dominical letter of the said year.

Second example: wanting to know the Dominical letter for the year of 1880, which will be a leap year, I will start to count 80 units from the same house in the same order as the previous example, ending in the house 1604, whose letters are DC, which are the Dominical letters for the mentioned year.

Third example: What will be the Dominical letter for the year of 1900? As 1900 is in front of 1612, it corresponds to the letters AG; by being 1900 one of the centennials that every 400 years is not a leap year, as was mentioned, it will solely have the second of those letters, which will be G.

Fourth example: What will be the Dominical letter for the year 2400? As the centennial years, out of brevity, can be counted on the first four lower houses of the leap column, by going up I will count 2000 in the one of 1600; 2100 in the one of 1604; 2200 in the one of 1612; and returning to the first, 2400, whose Dominical letters will be BA for that year, in such a way as the centennials which may fall in the houses of 1604, 1608 and 1612 will not be leap years.

Perpetual table of the Dominical letters

			GF 1624	E 1625	D 1626	C 1627
			ED 1620	C 1621	B 1622	A 1623
Years			CB 1616	A 1617	G 1618	F 1619
	1900	....	AG 1612	F 1613	E 1614	D 1615
3000	1800	....	FE 1608	D 1609	C 1610	B 1611
	1700	....	DC 1604	B 1605	A 1606	G 1607
2000		....	BA 1600	G 1601	F 1602	E 1603

One may also find the Dominical letter in the following way:

Divide the year by 4, in order to take out the leap years and in order to know if this is one of these; add the result of this division to the year; should this be before the Gregorian reform (in 1582) add 5 more to this; should it be between 1582 and 1699 subtract 5; if it is between 1700 and 1799, subtract 6; if it is between 1800 and 1899, subtract 7; and so forth; then divide the total by seven, and the remaining of this division will be the number of the sought Dominical letter (should this not be a leap year) according to the following table.

1	2	3	4	5	6	7
G	F	E	D	C	B	A

Should it be a leap year the remaining of this division will give you the second letter, and as such it will be the one immediately to its right.

Perpetual wheel of the Dominical letters

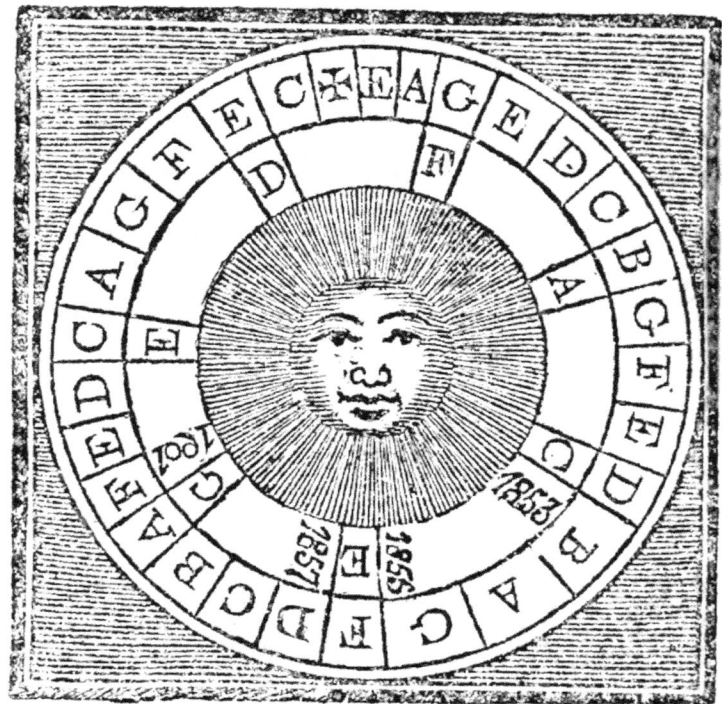

By the above wheel will one also find the Dominical letter or letters which will serve in each year perpetually until the year of 1900, starting from the letter G which is the first on the right side of the Cross, and is written above the year of 1855. This letter G served the year of 1855 as Dominical, and in the following year the Dominical letters will be FE; F from the first day of the year until the day of Saint Mathias, and the E, which is written below, for the rest of the year of 1856, and in the year of 1857 the Dominical letter will be D. And let us also warn that the number of years written in the wheel makes it perpetual, and their declaration will be found in the table of yearly prognostication.

Of the Golden number

Four hundred and thirty years before the coming of Our Lord Jesus Christ, a Greek man called Meton discovered the exact revolution of the Moon in 19 Solar years, or 235 lunations, there being one single day of difference in the space of 312 years. This discovery was so important that the Greeks called this the Golden number, which is also called the Lunar Cycle, for after 19 years the conjunctions of the Moon are repeated in the same civil years.

In the following table one may find the Golden number for any year; but for that one should first observe the first column to the left, which contains the years of the age of Christ, or the vulgar years, from 1800 to 3600, counting in every 100 years, and to each hundred you will have the corresponding Golden number in front of it, which is the second column to the right.

When we wish to know the Golden number of any of the mentioned hundreds followed by any unit, one should count the number in front of it in the third column, moving to the right and down as many numbers as units one may want to add to the preceding hundred.

So as this may be understood let us look at the following example: Should I want to know the Golden number for the year of 1879 I will see that the year of 1800 has the Golden number of 15 in the second column, and as such I will count 1 in the third column, which contains the number 16, and on to the right I will count 2, which contain 17, and 3 on the one that has 18, 4 on the one with 19 and so forth from left to right until I complete 79 units, and the same should be done with any other number of this or any other century.

When one wishes to know the Golden number of a year beyond 3600, the last of this table, one should just place 3700 in the place of 1800, 3800 in the place of 1900 and so forth going up the hundreds.

Years	Golden number				
1800..	15	16	17	18	19
1900..	1	2	3	4	5
2000..	6	7	8	9	10
2100..	11	12	13	14	15
2200..	16	17	18	19	1
2300..	2	3	4	5	6
2400..	7	8	9	10	11
2500..	12	13	14	15	16
2600..	17	18	19	1	2
2700..	3	4	5	6	7
2800..	8	9	10	11	12
2900..	13	14	15	16	17
3000..	18	19	1	2	3
3100..	4	5	6	7	8
3200..	9	10	11	12	13
3300..	14	15	16	17	18
3400..	19	1	2	3	4
3500..	5	6	7	8	9
3600..	10	11	12	13	14

One may also find the Golden number of any year by adding to this one unit and dividing it by 19, being that what remains from this division will be the Golden number of the sought years, and when one does not have anything remaining the Golden number will be 19.

Example: I wish to know the Golden number of the year of 1994. I add one unit and I have:

1995 |19
0095 105
  00

The remaining is 00 or a Golden number of 19.

Perpetual wheel of the Golden number

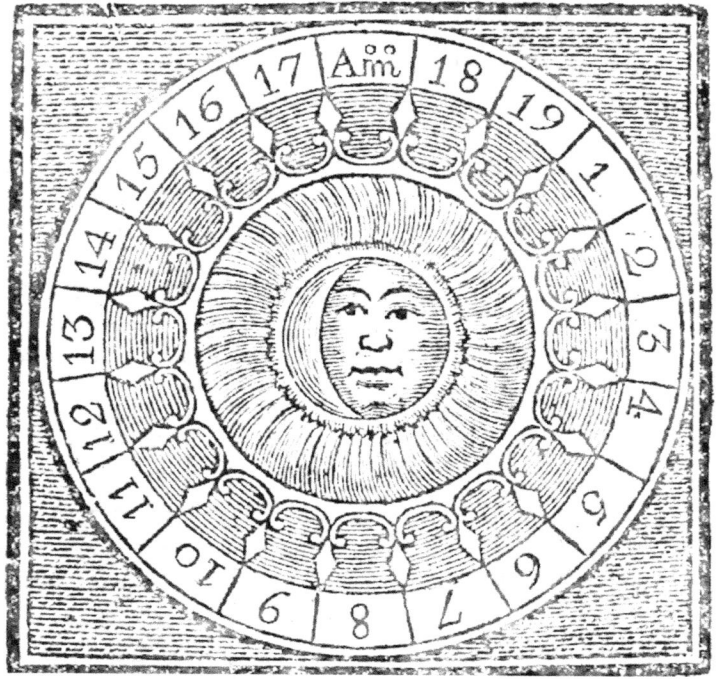

By the above wheel will one also find the Golden number for each year, knowing that once we reach nineteen one should start counting once again from one. And to better understand this wheel I shall demonstrate with a few examples.

In the year of 1862 the Golden number will be 1, and in the second house of the wheel, starting our counting from the house where the 1 is, in the following year of 1863 the Golden number will be 2, and in the year of 1864 it will be 3, and in the year of 1865 it will be 4, and so forth for the remaining years, increasing one unit with each year; and upon reaching 19 one shall count 1 as the Golden number, which will be the year of 1881.

Of the Solar or Dominical Cycle

The Solar or Dominical cycle is the time of 28 years in which the Sun does its revolution, after which the same Dominical letters take place in the same days of the week.

It is called Solar cycle not because it has to do with the course of the Sun, but rather for having to do with Sunday, which the Romans called *dies solis*; and these named the days of the week by the seven Planets.

One may find the number of the solar cycle by adding 9 to the year and dividing this by 28; the remainder of this division will be the number of the solar cycle, and should there be no remaining number, than this will be 28.

Difference between the Civil and Sinodal year

The Civil year has { lunar 354 days
solar 365 days

The Sinodal year has { lunar 354 days, 8 hours, 48 minutes and 10 seconds
solar 365 days, 5 hours, 48 minutes and 45 seconds

It is this excess of 5 hours, 48 minutes and 45 seconds which constitutes the day that every four years is added to the leap years; and because this day also exceeds that quantity, three years out of 400 are not leap years, as was said when mentioning the Dominical letters.

Of the Advent, and when it begins

The Advent is an amount of time of almost a month, and it is always counted from the Sunday closest to the feast of Saint Andrew,[47] and it ends on the eve of the Birth of Jesus Christ our Lord. During this time the Holy Mother Church gives graces to God for that greatest grace he gave to humankind by wanting to come to the world made man. Should Saint Andrew fall on a Monday, Tuesday or Wednesday, the Advent begins on the previous Sunday. If Saint Andrew is on a Thursday, Friday or Saturday, the Advent begin the following Sunday. And should Saint Andrew be on a Sunday, then the Advent begins that very day. For good use of memory one should keep the following verse: From before or from behind the Sunday, the one closest to Saint Andrew, the Advent thou shall count.[48]

Of the Nuptial Blessings

Nuptial Blessings are those blessings that brides and grooms receive when they hear the nuptial Mass; and as in such Blessings there is always such joy and banquets and carnal copulation, for these reasons the Holy Mother Church in certain times prohibits them and in others allows them. The Holy Council of Trent in Session 24, chapter 10, ordered that there should not be Nuptial Blessings from the first Sunday of the Advent until the Epiphany,[49] and from the first day of Lent until the Octave of Resurrection of Easter, *inclusivé*.

Of the four Ember Days

The Ember Days are certain fasting, which the Church celebrates in the four parts of the year, established by Saint Callixtus Pope. The reason why the Church celebrates these fasting in the four parts of the year is (as Saint John of Damascus says) to settle the movements of the four humors in the body during the four seasons of the year, and this by reason of the celestial movements. As such one fasts the first Ember days on the Wednesday, Friday and Saturday of the second week of Lent, which is in Spring, so as to repress in us the blood, that in this time is usually the dominating humor, which inclines one to the vices of the flesh and vainglory.

The second Ember Days are fasted in Summer in the week before the Holy Trinity,[50] so as to repress the cholera, which is dominant in this time, and moves men towards rage, hate and deceit.

The third Ember Days are fasted in Autumn, on the Wednesday, Friday and Saturday after the Holy Cross,[51] so as to diminish and thin in us the melancholy, that in such time usually predominates and move us to sadness and avarice.

---

47. Translator's note: Andrew the Apostle, on the 30th of November;
48. Translator's note: The original Spanish reads «Por delante, ó por detrás, de la Dominica, que es mas cercana a San Andrés, el Adviento contarás»;
49. Translator's note: The original indicates the Day of Kings, the day in which the three wise men (Reyes Magos/Mage Kings) worshiped the new born Jesus, on the 6th of January;
50. Translator's note: Trinity Sunday, the first Sunday after Pentecost.
51. Translator's note: Feast of the Holy Cross, 14th of September.

The last Ember days are fasted in Winter, on the Wednesday, Friday and Saturday after the Saint Lucia,[52] so as phlegm does not increase in us, for in this time it usually predominates and causes sloth and bodily and spiritual weakness.

Of the Septuagesima

The Septuagesima means 70 days, which one starts counting on the Sunday we call the Septuagesima Sunday. In this Sunday one no longer sing the Alleluia in mass, and instead one sing the office which begins with: *Cercáronme los gemidos de la muerte, los dolores del infierno me rodearon, en mi tribulación clamé*; and this lasts until the Quasimodo Sunday.

This celebration is the memory of the 70 years that the children of Israel were held captive in Babylonia. In this time of captivity our own exile is represented; and in the same way that they, after 70 years, had the joy of being set free and had been given permission by Cyrus, king of Persia, to return to their country; likewise we, in the sixth age were liberated by the Redeemer of the human Lineage. The Septuagesima has, with the Sundays that follow it, great mysteries, as any curious may see in Saint Gregory, on the Homily on the Gospel: *Ductus est*.

Of the Easter of Resurrection

No other Movable Feast has made the Church so preoccupied with the time on which one should celebrate it then this one of the Easter of Resurrection; for having established this one are all the others established. From this point did the astronomical solar years arise.

Easter is a Hebrew word: for this is what they called their Passover, which the people of Israel celebrate in memory of being set free by God from Pharaoh's captivity. The time of the celebration was given to Moses by God by telling him that this should always be done on the 14 days of Moon of Nisan, first month of the Lunar year, which always began in the next Moon after the Summer Equinox; and any time this mandate was not met did God send them great punishments. This holy and solemn day of Easter, contains in it much more, for this is the day in which the Holy Mother Church celebrates the Resurrection of our Redeemer Jesus Christ, and teaches us the mystery of the sacrifice of the Lamb, which was Christ on the Cross for the redemption of human kind; and also for the redemption of the sons of Israel, when the Angel killed all the first born children of Egypt, except those marked with the blood of the Lamb upon their door.

Of the Litanies

Litany is a Greek word with means rogation; this is done twice in a year; this first on the day of Saint Mark, and these are called the greater; these were established by Saint Gregory, Pope, over a great plague which ran through Rome called Inguinal, because of certain swellings it caused on men, from which they died of a sudden death or of other times by sneezing and yawning, from which one has the custom of saying "God bless you", after a sneeze. The second one was established by Saint Mamertus, bishop of the French Vienne after experiencing great earthquakes which destroyed many houses in Vienne, and the horrible noises and groans made by wolves and other fearful beast that came down into the city and ate many people; in order to appease the Divine Majesty he ordered that the whole world pray the Rogations on the Monday, Tuesday and Wednesday before Ascension. And these Litanies are called the minor.

Of Ascension and Pentecost

Forty days after the resurrection of the Son of God, the Church celebrates the marvelous Ascension into the Heavens. The Easter of Pentecost, or the coming of the Holy Spirit over the Apostles, also represents the many things which the people of Israel experienced during the three feasts which last 7 days, which were Passover, when they sacrificed the Lamb; the feast of the

---

52. Translator's note: 13th of December.

celebration of when they received the Law on Mount Sinai; and the festivity they call Scenopegia, which means of the Tabernacles; in such a way as 50 days after Easter the Israelites celebrate the time when they received the Law and so does the Church celebrate the solemnity of the Holy Spirit, 50 days after the resurrection; and as the people of Israel, 50 days after the sacrifice of the Passover Lamb in Ramatha, came to Mount Sinai to receive the Law; these same days were given to the Apostles by the Holy Spirit in the height of the Cenacle, which was on the mount of Zion, as it seems in Exodus.

The feast of the Holy Trinity

This feast didn't use to have a fixed day in the ancient Church, not even a special day dedicated to it; for in every festive day is this generally honored, but as from this resulted the rising of so many heresies and such great errors against the essential unity and distinction of the Divine Persons, the Holy fathers ordered that some sort of special memory of the Holiest Trinity be made, in addition to that which was already made in every festive days with the verse *Gloria Patri*; so as in this way all Christians would agree that the Father, the Son and the Holy Spirit were three distinct Persons and one single true God.

Of the Corpus Christi

Pope Urban IV in the year of 1263, so as the entire Christian nation would celebrate with a proper office the institution that our Lord Jesus Christ, Son of the glorious sacrament, ordered that the solemnity and memory of the Holy Eucharist should be celebrated on the Thursday after the octave of Pentecost. He granted great graces to all Faithful who were present in these festivities, and that the canonical hours of the night and day be said in the Churches. This Holy Pope Urban was followed by Pope Clement, Martin and Eugene, who granted and conceded innumerable indulgences to the Faithful Christians over this so solemn feast of the Corpus, that, as all other Movable Feasts, has countless mysteries; for through the Holy Sacrament do we reach Glory.

Of the fixed feasts

The knowledge of the days of the week on which the fixed feasts will take place, or any other event, is not only curious but of great utility, and we need only use the following table by which one will rapidly know on which day this or that Saint will fall, should this be not movable; this as well as any other event, given that it is known on which day of the month it has happened or will happen.

One should always be warned that in the leap years there are always two Dominical letters, and we should only use the first of these from the start of the year until Saint Mathias and the second from this day until the end of the year.

First example: On which day did the feast of Saint Anthony occur in 1877?

Firstly I should know the Dominical letter of that year; and knowing that it is G, and that this Saint's feast day is on the 13th of June, I shall count this number of 13 in the row of the month of June starting on the E, returning to the beginning of the row each time I arrive at its end and after 13 I will arrive at the letter C, and seeing as I have four houses before G, or four days before Sunday, I will know that the feast of Saint Anthony was on a Wednesday that year.

Second example: On which day of the week was the Lisbon earthquake of the 1st of November of 1755?

By learning the Dominical letter of that year I will see that this was the letter E, and by going to the row of the month of November of the table of the fixed feasts I will count 1 on the letter D, and as there is one letter left before E, or one day until Sunday, I will know that the earthquake was on a Saturday.

Third example: I wish to know the day of the week of the acclamation of King John IV, on the 1st of December of 1640.

By knowing that this was a leap year, and that its second letter is a G, which rules it from the day of Saint Mathias until the end of the year, I will count 1 (the day of the month when this event happened) in the first house of the month of December; and as I have one day until Sunday, I will know that the acclamation of King John IV was on a Saturday.

Fourth example: On which day of the week was the 1st of February of 1880?

By knowing that 1880 was a leap year and it had the letters DC, I will use the first of these letters; and not the second, for the 1st of February is before the day of Saint Mathias, which falls on the 25th of that month; and by going to the row of February I will count 1 on the house of the D; and as there is nothing more to count to reach that letter I will know that the 1st of February of the mentioned year was on a Sunday.

Table of the fixed feasts

January	A	B	C	D	E	F	G
February	D	E	F	G	A	B	C
March	D	E	F	G	A	B	C
April	G	A	B	C	D	E	F
May	B	C	D	E	F	G	A
June	E	F	G	A	B	C	D
July	G	A	B	C	D	E	F
August	C	D	E	F	G	A	B
September	F	G	A	B	C	D	E
October	A	B	C	D	E	F	G
November	D	E	F	G	A	B	C
December	F	G	A	B	C	D	E

The particular and brief prognostication for each Kingdom and Province of the Universe

Even if in the past I have concluded something about particular prognostications for each Kingdom and Province, as may be seen in those works on Agriculture, I however wish to offer much more in the current one. And as such, he who wishes to know anything in particular which may come to happen naturally in his Kingdom on each year, may he note and be warned, as so discreetly said the much learned master Astrologer Leopold of Austria, in which month of the year are the first thunders heard; and taking note of this month, may he go to the Calendar of the months and Saints and on the right side page, on the bottom, he shall find four or six notable and natural things which shall happen that year in that Kingdom where the first, not the second, thunder was heard, starting from the month of January.

Of the full Moons, perpetual and general conjunctions of the Moon by the Calendar of the months

So as to know perpetually, both inside as outside of Spain, the proper day of the conjunction and fullness of the Moon by the Calendar of the months, one should check the Golden number of the year in question, should he wish to know about the full or new Moon. By knowing the Golden number (which can be found in the current Lunario in a perpetual wheel) he shall seek it on the left and right margins of each month, and in front of the day in which the said Golden number is placed this will be the conjunction and full Moon; we further warn that on the left side are the conjunctions, or new Moons, and on the left side the full Moons. For example, in the year of 1862, in the month of January it will be a new Moon on the twenty-eighth, and full Moon on the fourteenth of February; for in this year the Golden number will be 1, the same 1 which, in the month of January, is on the left side in front of the twenty eight and on the right side in front of the fourteen, and so forth with all the other months.

Method of finding the movable feasts by the Calendar until the end of the World

The movable feasts are eight: Septuagesima, Ash Wednesday, Easter, Rogations or Litanies, Ascension, Pentecost, Trinity Sunday and the Corpus Christi, with the feast of S Vincent Ferrer, in the Kingdom of Valencia also following the order of the movable feasts. These are called movable feasts for they do not have a fixed place in the calendar, as do all the remaining feasts, by which reason they are called fixed.

In order to know on which day and which month these feasts will take place, all one needs to know is the Golden number and the Dominical letter of the year one wishes to enquire. Knowing the Golden number of that year look in the Calendar from the seventh of March until the fourth of April, and upon finding it count fifteen more days, *inclusivé*, and on the first Dominical letter of that year that you find, after these fifteen days, that will be Easter. And should the fifteenth day coincide with the Dominical letter of that year, one should not count it, but rather the next one. Once Easter is found one may find the remaining feasts by knowing how distant they are from Easter; which may be learned in the following Table, but remembering that the Septuagesima and Ash Wednesday are always before Easter.

From Easter to the Septuagesima	64 days
From Easter to Ash Wednesday	47 days
From Easter to Saint Vicente Ferrer	9 days
From Easter to the Rogations	37 days
From Easter to Ascension	40 days
From Easter to Pentecost	50 days
From Easter to Trinity Sunday	57 days
From Easter to Corpus Christi	61 days

Further note that all these days are counted inclusively, meaning, counting the day of Easter until the following feast, as can be understood by this example: I wish to know on which day and month the Septuagesima will fall in 1862. Let us find Easter by the above rule and we shall find the twentieth of April; now count back from the day of Easter 64 days, and where you find the number four, that will be the Sunday of Septuagesima, which is on the sixteenth of February, and with this rule one may find all other movable feasts.

For greater clarity we offer the following table where one may find the dates of the movable feasts solely by their Dominical Letter and Golden number.

Table of the Movable Feasts

Dominical Letter	Golden Number	Ash Wednesday	Easter
A	14	8th of February	26th of March
G	15	28th of February	15th of April
F	16	13th of February	31st of March
E D	17	4th of March	19th of April
C	18	24th of February	11th of April
B	19	9th of February	27th of March
A	1	1st of March	16th of April
G F	2	21st of February	7th of April
E	3	5th of February	23rd of March
D	4	25th of February	12th of April
C	5	17th of February	4th of April
B A	6	8th of March	23rd of April
G	7	21st of February	8th of April
F	8	13th of February	31st of March
E	9	5th of March	20th of April
D C	10	25th of February	11th of April
B	11	9th of February	27th of March
A	12	1st of March	16th of April
G	13	21st of February	8th of April
F E	14	6th of February	23rd of March
D	15	25th of February	12th of April
C	16	17th of February	4th of April
B	17	9th of March	24th of April
A G	18	22nd of February	8th of April
F	19	13th of February	31st of March
E	1	5th of March	20th of April
D	2	18th of February	5th of April

Ascension	Pentecost	Corpus Christi	Advent
4th of May	14th of May	25th of May	3rd of December
24th of May	3rd of June	14th of June	2nd of December
9th of May	19th of May	30th of May	1st of December
28th of May	7th of June	18th of June	29th of November
20th of May	30th of May	10th of June	28th of November
5th of May	15th of May	26th of May	27th of November
25th of May	4th of June	15th of June	3rd of December
16th of May	26th of May	6th of June	1st of December
1st of May	11th of May	22nd of May	30th of November
21st of May	31st of May	11th of June	29th of November
13th of May	23rd of May	3rd of June	28th of November
1st of June	11th of June	22nd of June	3rd of December
17th of May	27th of May	7th of June	2nd of December
9th of May	19th of May	30th of May	1st of December
29th of May	8th of June	19th of June	30th of November
20th of May	30th of May	10th of June	28th of November
5th of May	15th of May	26th of May	27th of November
25th of May	4th of June	15th of June	3rd of December
17th of May	27th of May	7th of June	2nd of December
1st of May	11th of May	22nd of May	30th of November
21st of May	31st of May	11th of June	29th of November
13th of May	23rd of May	3rd of June	28th of November
2nd of June	12th of June	23rd of June	27th of November
17th of May	27th of May	7th of June	2nd of December
9th of May	19th of May	30th of May	1st of December
29th of May	8th of June	19th of June	30th of November
14th of May	24th of May	4th of June	29th of November

Here we give the Calendar of the months, days and feasts of the whole year; noting that the feasts which have a ✠ are fixed. In this calendar one will find the new and full Moons of each month by the above instructions. As also the work of Agriculture of each month, as well as the crescent and waning Moons.

Golden number			JANUARY, 31 days		Golden number
	A	1	✠ Circumcision of the Lord	a	13
17	b	2	St. Isidore Bishop and Martyr	b	
	c	3	St. Anterus Pope	c	2
6	d	4	St. Eugenia and her companions	d	10
	e	5	St. Simeon Stylites	e	
3.14	f	6	✠ Day of Kings	f	
	g	7	St. Theodorus Monk	g	7
11	A	8	St. Lawrence Giustiniani	h	15
19	b	9	∗ St. Julian Martyr	i	18
	c	10	St. Paul 1st hermit	K	4
	d	11	St. Hyginus Pope and Martyr	l	
16.8	e	12	St. Satyrus Martyr	m	12
	f	13	St. Hilary Bishop	n	
	g	14	∗ Martyr of Sinai and Raithu	o	1
5	A	15	∗ St. Maurus	p	
13	b	16	Martyrs of Morocco	q	9
	c	17	St. Anthony the Abbot	r	17
10.2	d	18	Cathedra Petri	s	6
	e	19	St. Dionysius Carmelite	s	
	f	20	∗ St. Sebastian Martyr	t	
	g	21	*Fast.* St.Agnes Virg. Mart. *Sun in Aquarius*	v	14
7	A	22	✠ St. Vincent Martyr	u	3
15	b	23	St. Ildephonsus Bishop	x	11
18	c	24	Our Lady of Peace	y	
4	d	25	St. Paul's Conversion	z	19
	e	26	St. Polycarp Bishop and Martyr	2	8
12	f	27	St. John Chrysostom	5	
1	g	28	St. Agnes and St. Cyril	a	16
	A	29	St. Francis de Sales	b	5
9	b	30	St. Martina Virgin and Martyr	c	
	c	31	St. Peter Nolasco	d	13

Conjunctions of the Moon, or perpetual and general new Moons

Perpetual and general full Moons

Works for January, according to Pliny

In the crescent Moon of January, Farmers should graft those trees that have an early flower, like almonds, peaches, plums and other similar trees. They should sow orange, lime and cider seeds in warms lands. Also plant roses, grapevines and perform layerings.

In the waning it is convenient to cut building wood from those trees that lose their leaves, as also stakes for vines, pruning should only be done on those that are in warm lands, trim trees, clear the old wheat, fertilize the grapevines and farmlands, plant garlic and onions. Pliny says, Book 18, that everything that needs to be harvested for storage, cut, pruned or trimmed, should be done in the waning Moon.

If in this month the first thunders are heard, it signifies fertility of fruits and sterility of the woods and fields, abundance of water, sickly winds, alterations in population, death of men and cattle, this in the Kingdom where they are heard.

Golden number			FEBRUARY, 28 days		Golden number
17	d	1	*Fast*. St. Brigit Virgin	e	
	e	2	✠ Purification of Our Lady	f	2
6	f	3	✶ St. Blaise Bishop	g	10
	g	4	St. Andrew Corsini Carmelite	h	
14.3	A	5	St. Agatha Virgin and Martyr	i	18
11	b	6	St. Dorothea Virgin and Martyr	K	7
	c	7	St. Romuald Abbot	l	15
19	d	8	St. John of Matta	m	
	e	9	✶ St. Apollonia Virgin and Martyr	n	4
8	f	10	St. Scholastica Virgin	o	
16	g	11	St. Euphrosyne Virgin 3rd Order of Carmel	P	12
	A	12	St. Eulalia Virgin and Martyr	q	
	b	13	St. Gregory Pope	l	1
13.5	c	14	St. Valentine Martyr	f	9
	d	15	Transfer of the body of St. Anthony	s	
2	e	16	St. Juliana Virgin	t	17
0	f	17	St. Faustinus with 44 companions Martyrs	v	6
	g	18	St. Theotonius	u	
18	A	19	St. Susana Virgin and Martyr. *Sun in Pisces*	x	3
	b	20	St. Eleutherius Bishop	y	14
7	c	21	St. Hilarius Pope	z	11
15	d	22	Cathedra Petri	2	
	e	23	*Fast*. St. Gerald Archbishop of Braga	5	9
4	f	24	St. Matthias Apostle	a	
12	g	25	St. Aventanus Carmelite	b	8
	A	26	St. Felix with 24 companions Martyrs	c	16
1	b	27	St. Alex Martyr with 3 companions	d	
9	c	28	St. Romanus Abbot	e	5.14

In a leap year this month has 29 days

Works for February, according to Palladius[53]

In the crescent Moon of February it is custom to plant hemp and linen, and it is also proper to plant some vegetables, melons, cucumbers, mustard, early pumpkins, grafting pear and apple trees as well as other similar plants. Plant laurel, ivy, myrtle, transplant orange and lemon trees, poplars and cypresses, plant grapevines and perform layerings, grafting them in temperate lands.

In the waning Moon of February reeds and osier are cut to make baskets and other works, although Palladius says that these are better cut in the waning of January. One may prune the vineyards, dig them, add stakes, prepare hedges, prune late blooming trees and check the bee hives when there is good weather. Finally, this whole month is dangerous for illnesses of the feet.

If in this month the first thunder is heard, this indicates the death of rich and powerful men, sicknesses of the head, ear pain, frost and little fruit, according to Leopold.

---

53. Translator's note: probably Rutilius Taurus Aemilianus Palladius, a Roman writer from the fourth or fifth century, mostly known for his book of Agriculture *Opus agriculturae*.

Golden number			MARCH, 31 days		Golden number
	d	1	St. Rudesind Bishop	f	
17	e	2	St. Simplicius Pope	g	2
	f	3	Beginning of the novena of St. Xavier	h	
6	g	4	St. Adrian Martyr	i	10
	A	5	St. Eusebius Bishop	K	
14.3	b	6	St. Victor and Victorinus Martyrs	l	18
	c	7	✶ St. Thomas Aquinas	m	7
11	d	8	St. John of God	n	
19	e	9	St. Frances of Rome Virgin	o	15
	f	10	St. Alexander Pope	p	
	g	11	St. Candidus with 20 companions Martyrs	q	4
	A	12	✶ St. Gregory Pope	r	
8.16	b	13	St. Euphrasia Carmelite	s	1.13
	c	14	Transfer of the body of St. Bonaventure	s	
	d	15	St. Longinus Martyr	t	9
13	e	16	St. Cyriacus Martyr	v	17
2	f	17	St. Patrick Bishop	u	
	g	18	St. Gabriel Archangel	x	6
10	A	19	St. Joseph husband of Our Lady	y	
18	b	20	St. Joachim father of Our Lady	z	14
	c	21	St. Benedict. *Sun in Aries*	2	3
7	d	22	St. Helena Queen	5	11
	e	23	St. Felix Martyr	a	
15	f	24	*Fast*. St. Mark Martyr	b	19
	g	25	✠ Annunciation of Our Lady	c	
4	A	26	St. Theodore and 4 Martyrs	d	
12	b	27	St. Rupert Bishop	e	8
1	c	28	St. Alexander Martyr	f	16
	d	29	St. Berthold Carmelite	g	5
9	e	30	St. Angela of Foligno Franciscan	H	
13	f	31	St. Isabel Queen of Bohemia	i	13

Conjunctions of the Moon, or perpetual and general new Moons

Perpetual and general full Moons

Works for March, according to Palladius

In the crescent Moon of March it is good to plant melons, cucumbers, thistles and pumpkins; and on hot lands sow corn, linen, grain, amaranth, lettuce, and all sour pips, and in temperate lands plant fig trees.

In the waning of March one should hoe the land and wheat, plow the fields so as they don't grow too many weeds, trim the fig trees, mulberries and all other late blooming trees. The pruning of the grapevines should not exceed the waning of this month, for they already start to sprout. During this time it is also good to change the wine recipients and store it in cellars or attics. Finally, this month generates bad humors and head diseases are dangerous.

If in this month the first thunder is heard, this means that there will be great winds, and abundance of grass, bread, dissension, amazements and death, according to Leopold, in this Kingdom where they are heard.

Golden number			APRIL, 30 days		Golden number
	g	1	Conversion of St. Mark Martyr	K	2
6	A	2	St. Francis of Paola	l	
	b	3	St. Theodosia Virgin	m	10
14	c	4	St. Adrian Martyr	n	18
3	d	5	St. Vincent Ferrer	o	
11	e	6	St. Gerald Carmelite	p	7
	f	7	St. Euphemia Virgin	q	15
19	g	8	St. Apollonia Martyr	r	
	A	9	Transfer of the body of St. Monica	s	
	b	10	St. Macarius	s	4
8	c	11	St. Leo Pope	t	12
16	d	12	St. Julius Pope	v	1
5	e	13	St. Hermengild Martyr	u	9
	f	14	St. Maximus Martyr	x	
13.2	g	15	St. Helena Virgin	y	17
	A	16	St. Encratia	z	6
10	b	17	St. Anicetus Pope and Martyr	2	
	c	18	St. Eleutherius Bishop	5	14
18	d	19	St. Hermogenes Martyr	a	
	e	20	St. Marcellinus. *Sun in Taurus*	b	3
7	f	21	St. Anselm Archbishop of Canterbury	c	
15	g	22	St. Senorina	d	11
	A	23	✶ St. George defender of Portugal	e	19
	b	24	St. Aber Bishop	f	
4.12	c	25	✶ St. Mark Evangelist	g	8
	d	26	St. Peter of Rates	h	
1	e	27	St. Anastasius Pope	i	5.16
9	f	28	St. Vitalis Martyr	K	
	g	29	St. Peter Dominican	l	13
17	A	30	St. Catherine of Siene Dominican	m	

Conjunctions of the Moon, or perpetual and general new Moons

Perpetual and general full Moons

Works for April, according to Avicenna

In the crescent Moon of April it is good to sow or plant any kind of vegetable, such as melons, cucumbers, pumpkins, leek and capers. It should be noted that most vegetables can be planted during most of the year: from January until August, or even in very rainy seasons. In this month, in the crescent Moon, planting cuttings of mulberry trees will be more successful than in other months. It is good to graft the poplars, apricot and peach trees.

In the waning of April it is good to start watering the wheat if the region is very hot and dry. This month is a very good time to clean the beehives from parasites and spiders that take refuge in them. Finally, it is healthy for one to purge himself during this month, and any sickness of the throat is dangerous.

If in this month the first thunder is heard it means that it will be a prosperous year, abundant in wine, cattle and wheat in dry places and mountains; however, it also indicates danger at sea (according to Leopold) in the Kingdoms where they are heard.

Golden number			MAY, 31 days		Golden number
6	b	1	St. Philip and St. James Apostles	n	2
14	c	2	St. Athanasius Bishop	o	10
	d	3	Feast of the Cross	p	
3	e	4	St. Monica Widow	q	18
	f	5	St. Pius 5th Rule of the Dominicans Pope	r	7
11	g	6	St. Ioannis ante Portam Latinam	s	
19	A	7	St. Stanislaus Bishop and Martyr	s	15
	b	8	Apparition of St. Michael Archangel	t	
	c	9	St. Gregory Nazarene	v	
8	d	10	St. Anthony Archbishop of Forence	u	4
16	e	11	St. Maxima Martyr	x	1.12
5	f	12	Blessed Joanna Virgin	y	
	g	13	✱ Our Lady of the Martyrs	Z	9
13	A	14	St. Boniface Bishop	2	17
2	b	15	St. Mancio Portuguese Martyr	5	
	c	16	St. Simon Stock Carmelite	a	6
10	d	17	St. Possidonius	b	14
	e	18	St. Felician Bishop	c	
18	f	19	St. Ivo Franciscan	d	
7	g	20	St. Bernardine Confessor	e	3
	A	21	St. Timothy Martyr. *Sun in Gemini*	f	11
15	b	22	St. Romanus Abbot	g	19
	c	23	St. Michael Bishop	h	
	d	24	Transfer of the body of St. Dominic	i	8
4	e	25	St. Mary Magdalene de Pazzi	K	16
12.1	f	26	St. Philip Neri	l	
9	g	27	St. John Pope and Martyr	m	5
	A	28	St. Germain Bishop	n	
17	b	29	St. Maximus Bishop	o	13
	c	30	St. Felix Pope and Martyr	p	2
14.6	d	31	St. Petronilla Virgin	q	

Conjunctions of the Moon, or perpetual and general new Moons

Perpetual and general full Moons

Works for May, according to Palladius

The crescent Moon of May is a good time to clean the saffron, take the honey from the hives and put the goats together with their males. It is also a good time to plant any sour pits, and should they be new, these will take better than the old ones. One can plant any kind of vegetable and graft peach, apricot, almond, cider and orange trees.

The waning of May is an admirable time to take tiles and other clay thing to the furnaces, for if they are made and heated in this period they will be quite singular. It is good to plow the fields that will be planted in Autumn, if it is a cold land, one may also castrate the calves, pigs and lambs. Finally, any harm or damage done to the arms is dangerous in this month, and even more if healed with iron.

If in this month the first thunders are heard (the first of the year) it signifies an abundance of water and lack of birds; but great quantity of bread and vegetables in the Kingdom where these are heard.

Golden number			JUNE, 30 days		Golden number
	e	1	St. Nicodemus Martyr	r	10
3	f	2	St. Marcellus Pope and Martyr	s	18
	g	3	St. Francis Bishop and Martyr	s	
	A	4	St. Alexander Bishop	t	7
11	b	5	St. Marcian Martyr	v	
19	c	6	St. Claudianus Martyr	u	15
	d	7	St. Lucian Martyr	x	
8	e	8	St. Severinus Bishop	y	4
	f	9	St. Melania 3rd Order of Carmel	z	1
16	g	10	St. Onuphrius Hermit	2	9.12
5	A	11	✶ St. Barnabas Apostle	5	
	b	12	*Fast.* St. Basil Martyr	a	17
13	c	13	✠ St. Anthony	b	
	d	14	St. Marcellus Bishop	c	5
2	e	15	St. Vitus and Modestus Martyrs	d	
10	f	16	St. Aurelian Bishop	e	14
18	g	17	St. Thude advocate of cough	f	
	A	18	St. Mark Martyr	g	3
7	b	19	St. Gervase and Protase	h	11
15	c	20	St. Silverius Pope and Martyr	l	
	d	21	St. Aloysius Gonzaga	K	19
4	e	22	St. Paulinus. *Sun in Cancer*	l	8
12	f	23	*Fast.* ✶ John of Sahagún Martyr	m	
	g	24	✠ Birth of St. John the Baptist	n	16
1	A	25	St. Amandio Bishop	o	
9	b	26	St. John and Paul Martyrs	p	5
17	c	27	St. Ladislaus King of Hungary	q	
	d	28	*Fast.* St. Leo Pope	r	13
6	e	29	✠ St. Paul and St. Peter Apostles	s	2
14	f	30	✶ St. Martial	s	10

Conjunctions of the Moon, or perpetual and general new Moons

Perpetual and general full Moons

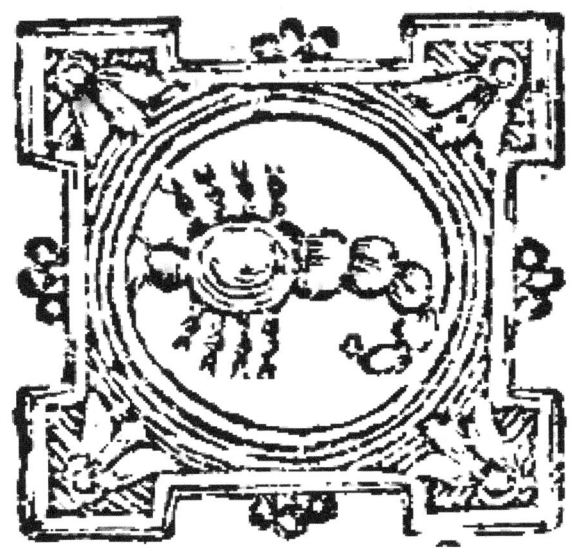

Works for June according to Palladius

In the crescent Moon of June one may graft any tree with thick bark, such as laurels, cider orange, fig, olive, almond and other similar trees, and in cold lands it is also good to sow corn, harvest the garlic, plant borage, cabbage and other vegetables that do not come early.

In the waning of June it is good to harvest favas, grains and other dry vegetables. Palladius says that in the waning Moon one should not water the fig trees, for it will cause the figs to be ripe early and also become better and more delicious. Wool, which should be sheared now, will be better at this time than at any other, for it is sweatier. Finally, during this month illnesses of the bosom, stomach and liver are dangerous.

If in this month the first thunder is heard, it signifies abundance of bread and fish; however, there will be a shortage of fruit, restlessness among the peoples and river floods, according to Leopold, in the Kingdoms in which these are heard.

Golden number			JULY, 31 days		Golden number
	g	1	St. Quentin Martyr	t	18
3	A	2	Visitation of Our Lady	v	
	b	3	St. Gregory Martyr	u	7
11	c	4	St. Laurianus Mart. Isabel Q. of Portugal	x	
19	d	5	St. Anselm Martyr	y	15
	e	6	St. Dominica Virgin and Martyr	z	
8	f	7	St. Victorinus and 10 Martyrs	2	4
	g	8	St. Procopius Abbot	5	
16	A	9	St. Cyril Bishop and Martyr	a	1.12
5	b	10	The seven Martyr Brothers	b	
	c	11	Transfer of the body of St. Benedict	c	9
13	d	12	St. Proculos and St. Hilarion	d	
2	e	13	St. Anacletus Pope and Martyr	e	17
10	f	14	St. Bonaventure Doctor	f	6
	g	15	St. Henry Emperor	g	14
18	A	16	Our Lady of Mount Carmel	h	
	b	17	St. Alexis Confessor	i	3
7	c	18	St. Marina Virgin and Martyr	k	
15	d	19	St. Justa and Rufina	l	11
	e	20	St. Margaret Virgin and Martyr	m	19
4	f	21	St. Victor Martyr	n	
	g	22	St. Mary Magdelene	o	8
12	A	23	St. Apollinaris. *Sun in Leo*	p	16
1	b	24	*Fast.* St. Christopher	q	
	c	25	St. James Apostle	r	5
6	d	26	St. Anne Mother of Our Lady	s	
17	e	27	St. Pantaleon Martyr	s	13.2
6	f	28	St. Innocent Pope	t	
	g	29	St. Martha Virgin and St. Beatrix	v	10
14	A	30	St. Rufinus Martyr	u	
3	b	31	St. Ignatius Loyola	x	18

Conjunctions of the Moon, or perpetual and general new Moons

Perpetual and general full Moons

Works for July, according to Palladius

In the crescent Moon of July it is customary to plant turnips, carrots, onions and mustard. It is also good to cover the grapevine trunks so as they do not become burnt by the Sun and cut the weeds from the lands, which will not grow back in this time as they do in others.

In the waning it is greatly advantageous to reap the wheat, so as it will better preserve itself, and the same is true for almonds. Finally, anxiousness and diseases of the heart are dangerous in this month, as well as purges, blood lettings, baths and sleeping during the midday.

If in this month the first thunders are heard, this indicates great troubles in the Kingdom, commotions among the people, lack of bread and abundance of fruit, according to Leopold, in the Kingdom where they are heard.

Golden number			AUGUST, 31 days		Golden number
	c	1	Cathedra Petri	y	
	d	2	Our Lady of the Angels of Porziuncola	z	7
11	e	3	Invention of St. Stephen	2	
	f	4	St. Dominic Confessor	5	15
19	g	5	✶ Our Lady of the Snows	a	4
8	A	6	Transfiguration of the Lord	b	
16	b	7	St. Catejan and St. Albert	c	12
	c	8	St. Cyriac Bishop	b	
5	d	9	*Fast*. St. Romanus	e	9.1
2.13	e	10	St. Lawrence Martyr	f	17
	f	11	St. Susanna Martyr	g	
	g	12	St. Clare Virgin	h	
10	A	13	St. Hippolytus Martyr	i	6
	b	14	*Fast*. St. Eusebius	k	14
18	c	15	✠ Assumption of Our Lady	l	
7	d	16	✶ St. Roch Confessor	m	3
	e	17	St. Mammes Martyr	n	11
15	f	18	St. Helena	o	19
	g	19	St. Luiz Beltran Bishop	p	
4	A	20	✶ St. Bernard Abbott	q	
	b	21	✶ St. Anastasius Martyr	r	8
12	c	22	St. Timothy	s	16
1	d	23	*Fast*. St. Lupus Martyr	s	
9	e	24	St. Bartholomew Apostle. *Sun in Virgo*	t	5
17	f	25	St. Louis King of France	v	2
	g	26	St. Victor Martyr	u	13
6	A	27	St. Rufus Confessor	x	
	b	28	✶ St. Augustine Doctor of the Church	y	10
14	c	29	Beheading of St. John the Baptist	z	18
3	d	30	St. Rose Dominican	2	
	e	31	St. Raymond Nonnatus	5	7

Conjunctions of the Moon, or perpetual and general new Moons

Perpetual and general full Moons

Works for August, according to Palladius

In the crescent and waning Moon of August it is good to fertilize the fields in which wheat will be planted and also to dig out the onions for storage, and after rain one should sow the lupines, radishes, turnips and late cabbages.

It is during this time that it is custom to dry figs, peaches and plums and plant favas and collards. Finally, in this month the company of women and midday naps are most dangerous, and baths aren't good; purges and blood lettings shouldn't be done unless under great necessity.

If during this month the first thunders are heard it signifies great mortality of fish in the ocean and in four legged animals, quietness and peace in the Republics and much sickness in the Kingdom where they are heard, according to Leopold.

Golden number			SEPTEMBER, 30 days		Golden number
11	f	1	St. Giles Abbot	a	
	g	2	St. Brocard Carmelite	b	15
19	A	3	St. Euphemia Virgin and Martyr	c	
8	b	4	St. Rosalia Franciscan	d	4
	c	5	St. Victorinus Bishop Martyr	e	12
16	d	6	St. Eugene Bishop	f	
5	e	7	*Fast.* St. John Martyr	g	9.1
	f	8	Nativity of Our Lady	h	
13	g	9	St. Gregory Martyr	i	17
2	A	10	St. Nicholas of Tolentino	k	
	b	11	St. Theodora Carmelite	l	6
10	c	12	St. Valerian Martyr	m	
18	d	13	St. Philip Martyr	n	14
	e	14	✶ Feast of the Cross	o	3
7	f	15	Transfer of the body of St. Vincent	p	11
15	g	16	St. Cornelius Pope and Martyr	q	
	A	17	Stigmata of St. Francis	r	19
4	b	18	St. Thomas of Villanova	s	
	c	19	St. Januarius Martyr	s	8
12	d	20	*Fast.* St. Eustachius Martyr	t	
1	e	21	St. Matthew Apostle	v	16
9	f	22	St. Maurice Martyr	u	5
	g	23	St. Linus Pope and Martyr. *Sun in Libra*	x	
17	A	24	St. Gerard Carmelite	y	2.13
6	b	25	St. Firmian Bishop	z	
	c	26	St. Cyprian and St. Justina	2	10
14	d	27	St. Cosmas and St. Damian	5	
	e	28	St. Wenceslaus Duke	a	18
3	f	29	St. Michael Archangel	b	
	g	30	St. Jerome Doctor of the Church	c	7

Conjunctions of the Moon, or perpetual and general new Moons

Perpetual and general full Moons

Works for September, according to Palladius

In the crescent Moon of September it is good to sow rye, barley, favas, lupines and mimosas in hot lands, for in cold ones it is better if these were sown beforehand.

In the crescent it is very good to plant linen that is not watered.

The waning of this month is the natural time for the grape harvest, but this should not be done when the Sun is at its peak. It is good to plow, dig and fertilize the lands for vegetables, or to sow three month seeds, which are corn and millet. Finally, during the whole of this month blood lettings are good, and any illness of the kidneys and buttocks is dangerous.

If in this month the first thunders are heard they indicate that the beginning of the year will be dry, but the end will be humid. Also there should be an abundance of bread, but this will be expensive and there will be the threat of the death of popular people (according to Leopold) in the Kingdoms in which these are heard.

Golden number			OCTOBER, 31 days		Golden number
11	A	1	✶ The Martyrs of Lisbon	d	15
19	b	2	The Angels of our Guard	e	
	c	3	St. Claudianus Martyr	f	4
8	d	4	St. Francis Confessor	g	
16	e	5	St. Placid Martyr	h	1.12
	f	6	St. Bruno founder of the Carthusians	i	
5	g	7	St. Mark Pope	k	
	A	8	St. Demetrius Martyr	l	9
13	b	9	St. Dionysius	m	17
2	c	10	St. Francis Borgia	n	
	d	11	St. Placidia Virgin	o	5
18	e	12	St. Cyprian Bishop	p	14
10	f	13	St. Chelidonia Virgin	q	
	g	14	St. Eduard King of Bohemia	r	3
7	A	15	St. Teresa of Avila	s	11
15	b	16	St. Martin	s	
	c	17	St. Lucina of Rome Virgin	t	19
4	d	18	✶ St. Luke Evangelist	v	
12	e	19	St. Peter of Alvantara	u	8
1	f	20	St. Irene Virgin and Martyr	x	16
	g	21	The eleven thousand Virgins	y	
9	A	22	St. Mark Bishop	z	5
17	b	23	St. Severinus Bishop	2	
6	c	24	St. Furtunatus. *Sun in Scorpio*	5	2.13
	d	25	✶ St. Crispin and Crispinian	a	
	e	26	St. Evaristus Pope and Martyr	b	18
1	f	27	*Fast*. St. Sabina	c	11
	g	28	St. Jude and St. Simon Apostles	d	
3	A	29	St. Felician Martyr	e	
	b	30	St. Serapion Bishop and Carmelite	f	7.15
11	c	31	*Fast*. St. Quentin Martyr	g	

Conjunctions of the Moon, or perpetual and general new Moons

Perpetual and general full Moons

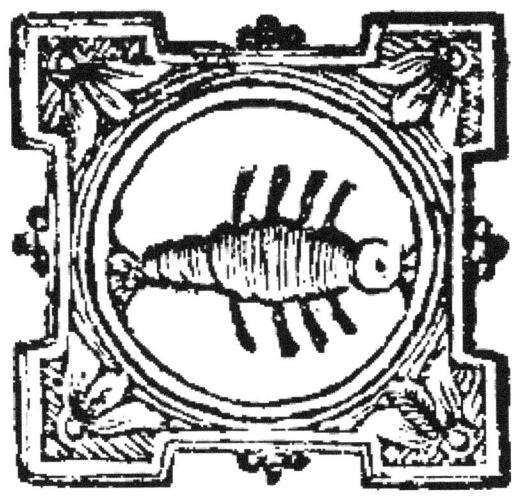

Works for October, according to Avicenna

In this month one should make the olive oil meant for food, and one may also pick the grapes from dry and belated places; it is a very good occasion to sow every kind of grain that are meant to make bread, such as wheat, rye, barley and others like these. One may also plant favas and lupines. It is advisable to pick the acorns, chestnuts, hazelnuts, nuts, pomegranates, quince pears and all late fruit. One may plant cherry trees, wild cherry, and pear and apple trees. Finally, every wound made in this month is hard to heal, and worse still are those diseases in hidden areas.

If during this month the first thunders are heard it indicates wind storms, shortness of bread and fruit, a small grape harvest and the death of fish and cattle in the Kingdoms where these are heard, according to Leopold.

Golden number			NOVEMBER, 30 days		Golden number
19	d	1	✠ Feast of all Saints	h	
8	e	2	Celebration of the dead	i	
	f	3	St. Germanus Martyr	K	4.12
16	g	4	St. Charles Borromeo Cardinal	l	
5	A	5	St. Zachary	m	
	b	6	St. Leonard Confessor	n	9
13	c	7	St. Florentius Bishop	o	
2	d	8	Santi Quattro Coronati	p	17
	e	9	The Saint of the Order of St. Dominic	r	6
10	f	10	The dead of the Order of St. Dominic	r	
18	g	11	St. Martin Bishop	s	14
	A	12	St. Martin Pope	s	
7	b	13	Feast of all Saint of St. Benedict	s	
15	c	14	Feast of all Saint of Carmel	v	3.11
	d	15	Celebration of the dead	u	19
	e	16	St. Eucherius Bishop	x	
4	f	17	St. Gregory Thaumaturgus	y	8
12	g	18	St. Romanus Martyr	z	
1	A	19	St. Elizabeth Queen of Hungary	2	16
9	b	20	St. Felix of Valois	5	
	c	21	✶ Presentation of Our Lady	a	5
17	d	22	St. Cecilia Virgin Martyr	b	2.13
	e	23	St. Clement Pope. *Sun in Sagittarius*	c	
6	f	24	✶ St. Chrysogonus Martyr	d	
14	g	25	St. Catherine Virgin and Martyr Dom.	e	10
	A	26	St. Peter Alexander Bishop and Martyr	f	18
	b	27	St. Facundus and St. Primitivus Martyrs	g	
3	c	28	St. Gregory Pope	h	7
11	d	29	*Fast.* St. Saturninus	i	
9	e	30	St. Andrew Apostle	K	15

Conjunctions of the Moon, or perpetual and general new Moons

Perpetual and general full Moons

Works for November, according to Avicenna

In this month it is a custom to plow the fields and lands that produce useless weeds, so as these may die and not grow again; also one should clear the trees of dry branches and fertilize them. The same is also true of the grapevines, which can very well be planted on dry and hot lands. It is also a good time for layering and planting garlic.

The waning of this month and the next is a very good time for brines and to cut wood for construction. Finally, this month is good for baths and blood lettings to cure any illness; it is however a bad month for illnesses of the legs, even more in this land, which is more humid than most others.[54]

If in this month the first thunders are heard it signifies the lack of sheep, abundance of wheat, contentment and joy among men, good weather, good rain and the fruit will fall from their tress before the right time (according to Leopold) in the Kingdom they are heard.

---

54. Translator's note: I assume he's talking about Valencia.

Golden number			DECEMBER, 31 days		Golden number
	f	1	St. Eligius	l	
8	g	2	St. Bibiana Virgin	m	4
16	A	3	✶ St. Francis Xavier	n	12
	b	4	✶ St. Barbara Virgin and Martyr	o	1
5	c	5	St. Gerald Archbishop of Braga	p	
	d	6	✶ St. Nicholas Bishop	q	9
13	e	7	St. Ambrose Doctor of the Church	r	17
1	f	8	✠ Our Lady of Conception	s	
10	g	9	St. Leocadia Virgin and Martyr	s	6
	A	10	St. Eulalia Virgin	t	14
13	b	11	St. Damasus Portuguese Pope	v	
	c	12	St. Justin Martyr	u	3
7	d	13	St. Lucia Virgin and Martyr	x	11
15	e	14	St. John of the Cross	y	
	f	15	St. Eusebius Bishop	z	19
	g	16	St. Valentine and his companions	2	
4	A	17	St. Francis of Siena	5	3
12	b	18	✶ Our Lady of Expectation	a	
1	c	19	St. Clement Bishop Carmelite	b	16
9	d	20	*Fast.* St. Dominic Abbot	c	5
17	e	21	St. Thomas Apostle	d	
	f	22	St. Honoratus. *Sun in Capricorn*	e	2.13
	g	23	St. Victoria Virgin and Martyr	f	10
6	A	24	*Fast.* St. Gregory Martyr ✶ until the Kings	g	
14	b	25	✠ Birth of Christ our Lord	h	18
3	c	26	1st Octave St. Stephen	i	7
	d	27	2nd Octave St. John the Evangelist	k	15
11	e	28	3rd Octave Holy Innocents	l	
	f	29	St. Thomas Archbishop of Canterbury	m	4
19	g	30	St. Sabinus Bishop and Martyr	n	
8	A	31	St. Sylvester Pope	o	

Left margin: Conjunctions of the Moon, or perpetual and general new Moons

Right margin: Perpetual and general full Moons

Works for December, according to Palladius

In truth there is little work to be done in this month, however, any kind of vegetable can be planted so as to be harvested in Spring. The wood that is cut in the waning of this month is very durable. The curious farmer will never lack work in this month, as says Palladius, such as gathering hay, spreading fertilizer where it is necessary, press esparto, make ropes, prepare vats, clean pots and wine cellars; he may also fix ditches and gates.

Many more things could be said regarding Agriculture in each of the months, however, the brevity of this work, and the smallness of this volume does not permit more than this. Diseases of the knees are dangerous.

If in this month the first thunders are heard, this denotes prosperous health and a good year, peace and agreement among peoples, according to Leopold, in the Kingdom in which they are heard.

Here we shall give the principle of natural and general prognostication of the weathers and times by the first day of the year, by addressing the seven days of the week (ut scribit Leopold of Austria), whose names represent the Planets of Heaven, which are: Saturn, Jupiter, Mars, Sun, Venus, Mercury and Moon; and the qualities and effects these cause on those who are born under their domain; the Physiognomy they give to each one and the conditions, trades and arts unto which one may dedicate himself.

Before we enter into the prognostication of the years I wish to describe a Proverb which runs through the schools, among Astrologers and Christians, for it is most appropriate for what we will deal with, and which says: *Astra movent hominess, sed Deus Astra movet*. Which means that the Stars move, incite and incline men to several effects, causing the same to every other created thing in this world, living and sensitive, and infusing in them their own qualities, both good and bad. However this Proverb further says that God moves the Stars, providing them with his infinite power and eternal wisdom, that innate and communicating virtue to infuse men and all other things with their properties and nature, by which each one follows their natural tendency. From this we have another ancient Aristotelian Proverb, which says: *Quod à natura inest, simper inest*. Which means: that which each one has by nature only with difficulty will he separate from himself, rather, he will easily conserve it. Such is the truth, we experience this every day in ourselves and in others. However, it is also certain that a man with discretion and prudence can dominate any bad intention which may reside in his nature; thus, with great reason was it said: *Sapiens dominabitur Astris*. Which means: The Wise man will be the lord of the Stars, changing the luck and harshness of nature into something mild and soft, and the bad tendency into a good and delectable one. As God, may he be forever blessed and praised, gave man that strength of free will, I say that neither all the Stars in the Heavens, nor the demons of Hell, nor all the other created things, are enough to force a man to do anything he does not wish to do, even less will they be able to constrain him if he is aided by the grace of his Creator. I then say that the Stars may incline men, but not constrain or force them; and it is this inclination that we wish to talk about in all these discourses on the natural prognostication of the Planets, while submitting myself on every point to the correction and obedience of the Holy Mother Roman Catholic Church.

As each Planet corresponds to one day of the week, its influence starts at the moment of the Sun rise, and one counts the hours from 1 to 24, which is the hour before the Sun rise of the next day; and as each Planet rules one hour one after the other, it so happens that the one which rules the 1st hour also rules the 8th, the 15th and 22nd, and in the same way the one which rules the 2nd hour of that day also rules the 9th, the 16th and the 23rd, and the one which rules the 3rd also rules the 10th, the 17th, and the 24th, and thus forth for all others.

Example: Which Planets will influence the hours of the 9th of February?

By knowing the Dominical letter of the year, and that that day was on a Monday, which is the day of the Moon, one may see in the table of the Sun rise at which time this happened, and as such we will know that this was at 7, which is the 1st hour of the Moon and which will last until 8; the second will last until 9 and in this way the 24th will be between 6 and 7 of the next day. Given this, in the 1st, 8th, 15th and 22nd hour, the Moon will rule; in the 2nd, 9th, 16th and 23rd, Saturn will rule; in the 3rd, 10th, 17th and 24th, Jupiter will rule; in the 4th, 11th, and 18th, Mars will rule; in the 5th, 12th and 19th, the Sun will rule; in the 6th, 13th and 20th, Venus will rule; in the 7th, 14th and 21st, Mercury will rule; and in this way all days and hours of the week will be filled, as can be seen by the following tables:

Sunday – Sun	Monday – Moon
1st hour of the Sun rise belongs to the Sun	1st hour of the Sun rise belongs to the Moon
2nd hour of the Sun rise belongs to Venus	2nd hour of the Sun rise belongs to Saturn
3rd hour of the Sun rise belongs to Mercury	3rd hour of the Sun rise belongs to Jupiter
4th hour of the Sun rise belongs to the Moon	4th hour of the Sun rise belongs to Mars
5th hour of the Sun rise belongs to Saturn	5th hour of the Sun rise belongs to the Sun
6th hour of the Sun rise belongs to Jupiter	6th hour of the Sun rise belongs to Venus
7th hour of the Sun rise belongs to Mars	7th hour of the Sun rise belongs to Mercury
8th hour of the Sun rise belongs to the Sun	8th hour of the Sun rise belongs to the Moon
And in this order the Planets will infuse their influence until the 24th hour	And in this order the Planets will infuse their influence until the 24th hour
Tuesday – Mars	**Wednesday – Mercury**
1st hour of the Sun rise belongs to Mars	1st hour of the Sun rise belongs to Mercury
2nd hour of the Sun rise belongs to the Sun	2nd hour of the Sun rise belongs to the Moon
3rd hour of the Sun rise belongs to Venus	3rd hour of the Sun rise belongs to Saturn
4th hour of the Sun rise belongs to Mercury	4th hour of the Sun rise belongs to Jupiter
5th hour of the Sun rise belongs to the Moon	5th hour of the Sun rise belongs to Mars
6th hour of the Sun rise belongs to Saturn	6th hour of the Sun rise belongs to the Sun
7th hour of the Sun rise belongs to Jupiter	7th hour of the Sun rise belongs to Venus
8th hour of the Sun rise belongs to Mars	8th hour of the Sun rise belongs to Mercury
And in this order the Planets will infuse their influence until the 24th hour	And in this order the Planets will infuse their influence until the 24th hour
Thursday – Jupiter	**Friday – Venus**
1st hour of the Sun rise belongs to Jupiter	1st hour of the Sun rise belongs to Venus
2nd hour of the Sun rise belongs to Mars	2nd hour of the Sun rise belongs to Mercury
3rd hour of the Sun rise belongs to the Sun	3rd hour of the Sun rise belongs to the Moon
4th hour of the Sun rise belongs to Venus	4th hour of the Sun rise belongs to Saturn
5th hour of the Sun rise belongs to Mercury	5th hour of the Sun rise belongs to Jupiter
6th hour of the Sun rise belongs to the Moon	6th hour of the Sun rise belongs to Mars
7th hour of the Sun rise belongs to Saturn	7th hour of the Sun rise belongs to the Sun
8th hour of the Sun rise belongs to Jupiter	8th hour of the Sun rise belongs to Venus
And in this order the Planets will infuse their influence until the 24th hour	And in this order the Planets will infuse their influence until the 24th hour
Saturday – Saturn	
1st hour of the Sun rise belongs to Saturn	
2nd hour of the Sun rise belongs to Jupiter	
3rd hour of the Sun rise belongs to Mars	
4th hour of the Sun rise belongs to the Sun	
5th hour of the Sun rise belongs to Venus	
6th hour of the Sun rise belongs to Mercury	
7th hour of the Sun rise belongs to the Moon	
8th hour of the Sun rise belongs to Saturn	
And in this order the Planets will infuse their influence until the 24th hour	

Of the quality and natural prognostication and effects of the Planet Saturn

This planet has its seat in the seventh Heaven and in the natural order is the first of the Planets, which is cold and dry, melancholic, earthy, masculine and diurnal; it is an enemy of the human nature. It causes great labors, famines, afflictions, sterility in its year and shortness of supplies. It brings weeping and sighing, imprisonment, destruction, pilgrimages, death. It represents restlessness, disquiet, tardiness, miseries and suspiciousness. On those of its nature, this Planet usually causes boredom, sadness, melancholy, anxiety, sorrow, wonder, anguish, loneliness and isolation. It has dominion over the old, invalid and loners, over those of greed, usurers, sad and melancholic; over vile men, miserable and suspicious; over gluttons, sorcerers, magicians and necromancers, and over those who open graves, roam among the dead and do humble and lowly activities.

Prognostications of the Planet Saturn

The day of this Planet is Saturday, its hour is the first of the Sunrise and the eighth after it. If the year begins on a Saturday it will be dry and sterile of supplies, the Winter will be long and cold with little water. In Spring it will be windy. In Summer humid. Autumn will be dry and fresh. It indicates shortness of wheat, wine, olive oil, honey will be almost nonexistent. Linen will be rare and expensive. There will be an abundance of fruit but little fish. This Planet shows that in this year there will be a great deal of weddings, that some houses will become ruined and collapse. Tertian and Quartan[55] fevers in any and all regions of the world, due to the intemperance caused in bodies. Many old men will find the end of their days in this year, for being a time too contrary to them. It denotes mortality in small cattle, more even in sheep and silk worms; *sed Deus super omnia*.

---

55. Translator's note: a type of periodical fever that is a common symptom of Malaria.

The Physiognomy given by Saturn

Those who are born under the dominion of this Planet are of a cold and dry nature. They usually have a large and ugly face, medium sized eyes, inclined towards the ground, one bigger than the other; the nose is big and thick, the lips also thick, joined eyebrows, the face will tend to be dark, their hair black, hard and course, some teeth bigger than the others and ill proportioned, extremely hairy chest filled with nerves and dry muscles, the subtle veins will be very visible, the legs long and crooked, the same for the hands. And if Saturn was at the West, this makes men pasty, of small stature, with little beard, clear and straight hair.

The conditions infused by Saturn

The Saturnine, are imaginative, shy and deep of thought, friends of Agriculture. They are inconstant, sad, melancholic, filled with deceit, perfidious and, according to the Philosopher, very lustful due to the vanity that is generated in their complexions. They love solitude, they are disturbed by great tumults, festivities and joys; they are angered over little things, and they greatly fear boredom; however, all these bad influences and inclinations will be overcome by the wise and prudent man with discernment and free will.

To which things the Planet Saturn inclines

The Saturnine are inclined to the letters and all things related to study, especially to philosophy and other areas of knowledge; for these are greatly given to study and are friends of the secrets of nature and even of the mechanical and liberal arts. To many of these does this Planet incline to be farmers, tanners and stone masons; to others it inclines to being shoe cobblers and glove makers; to others it inclines to the trade of burying the dead, house masters, hermits and hunters; these are also very apt for working in the quicksilver, lead and tin mines, as well as other metals, and these are usually very venturous in discovering mines and treasures, and finding old and ancient things; finally these are also greatly apt for religious and cloistered life; for they are great enemies of conversation and any form of commerce.

This Planet (according to Alfraganus[56]) is larger than the earth 95 times; its metal is lead, its light has an ash color and its dominion is earth, from which it is separated by 28 million 80 thousand and 650 leagues; its body has 659 thousand and 560 leagues.

---

56. Translator's note: Abū al-'Abbās Aḥmad ibn Muḥammad ibn Kathīr al-Farghānī, a Muslim astrologer from the IXth century, involved in the calculation of the diameter of the Earth and whose work became extremely influent in Europe in the XIIth century.

Of the quality and natural prognostication and effects of the Planet Jupiter

This Planet has its seat in the sixth heaven. It is hot, humid, airy, sanguine, masculine, diurnal and greatly beneficial to the human nature by its natural temperament; and as such, by its influence is the air clarified and healthy winds run and the rains are of great benefit for the land. It is through its influence that Summer softens its heat and Winter its cold. It diminishes infirmities and drives away pestilence by purifying the air. It is common for this Planet to cause friendship among men, agreement, quiet, peace, tranquility and benevolence, especially in the Jovial.

It has dominions over wise, honest and self-conscious men; over the liberals, just and merciful; over the loyal, well inclined, magnificent and virtuous; over just and merciful Judges, helpers of the poor and givers of charity; over those inclined towards women, joyful and loving; over the well disposed, prudent and handsome; over the cautious and fearful of God.

Prognostications of the Planet Jupiter

This Planet's day is Thursday, its hour the first and the eighth. In a year that begins on the day of Thursday the Winter will be temperate, Spring windy, Summer pleasant and Autumn rainy. There will be an abundance of wheat and supplies. There will be a great shortage of wine, of all other fruit there will be abundance, little honey, and there will be no shortage of bacon or fresh fish. By the benevolent influences of this Planet will great peaces and accordance be made, this given the free will of man, as was said.

The Physiognomy given by Jupiter

Those who are born under the dominion of this Planet are of a good stature, well disposed and temperate, somewhat blond, brown harsh beards, sanguine sight and neither very strong nor acute, the eyes will be black and handsome, the forehead large and fleshy, big and well composed teeth, the hair blond and not thick; they will eventually go bald and finally their veins are well exposed.

The conditions infused by Jupiter

The Jovial are peaceful men, modest, friendly, without falsehood or deceit; they are tempered in eating and drinking; virtuous, faithful, given to knowledge; they are not vindictive, however they will become enraged by just cause; they follow their promises with loyalty; they take care of things with great discretion, usually giving good and sound advice, they understand things with great ease and without great effort, for their cunning is clear; they are very apt for generation, they live healthy and are finally well conditioned.

To which things the Planet Jupiter inclines

The Jovial are inclined to things of the Church, religion and devotion; for they are peaceful, virtuous and modest people, and to many this Planet inclines to become judges and notaries and to others to become *mayordomos*,[57] councilmen, priests tending to the poor, for these are apt for any kind of piety and for any kind of literate positions and dignities.

This Planet (according to Alfraganus) is larger than the earth 95 times; its metal is tin. It has dominion over the air and is 17 million 280 thousand and 200 leagues away from the earth; its body has 615 thousand and 600 leagues.

---

57. Translator's note: A semi-archaic Spanish title indicating a high level caretaker, usually given to someone of noble descent.

Of the quality and natural prognostication and effects of the Planet Mars

This Planet is in the Fifth Heaven; it is hot, dry, choleric, igneous, masculine and nocturnal, enemy of the human kind by its terrible nature. This Planet is the cause of the resolution of the winds, the cold, storms, frost, hail, darkness and, in its time, great heat waves, distempered and ill complexioned winds, causers of infirmities; it is of such a contrary and perverse nature and quality that it moves the tempers of mortals to conflict, struggles, divisions, war, partiality, disputes, bloodshed and enmity. It also commonly causes robbery, arson, death, injury, affronts and sudden rage in armies.

It has dominions over men of war, over the choleric, criminal, inconstant and liars; over gluttons, shameless and belligerent; over fighters, swordsman, reckless and furious men; over thieves, roadside robbers, and malicious, deceiving, plotters and envious men; over the perfidy, inconstant, mad, frenetic, irate and bloodthirsty.

Prognostications of the Planet Mars

This Planet's day is Tuesday, its hour is the first and the eighth. In the year which begins on this day the Winter will be very cold, rainy, dark and with plenty of snow. Spring will be humid, Summer hot, Autumn dry. There will be many misfortunes at sea, storms and shipwrecks. There will be lack of wheat as well as in all other small grains. Honey and olive oil will be average; vegetables will be abundant, there will be little wine, and the fruits will be average. There will be great mortality in small cattle due to the overabundance of blood and a great heat will reign. This Planet denotes infirmity and death in the feminine gender, some sudden deaths of some illustrious persons, and great *vitam cum morte commutabunt*. And finally there will be issues and contentions among tyrants.

Physiognomy given by Mars

Those who are born under the dominions of this Planet have a large face, ugly and with a few red spots, they have few other signs, little hair, red or ginger, an acute and frightful stare, long neck, bright and bitter eyes, big and open noses, white teeth, separated from each other and unevenly proportioned, little beard and a slightly bent body. And if Mars was at the West, it denotes that they will have a thick neck, subtle legs, a stride of great long steps, thick feet, small ankles and a large head.

The conditions infused by Mars

Those of Martian nature are usually choleric, filled with rage, lacking in reason and words, seekers of struggle and fights, enemies of peace and quietness, great friends of their similar, gambling and women; they are usually deceitful and liars, without any mercy; they are inclined to steal; however the wise and prudent is lord of the Stars and all his inclinations.

To which things the Planet Mars inclines

The Martial, and those subjected to the Planet Mars, are inclined for all things to do with fire and weapons; and as such they tend to be artillery men, blacksmiths and locksmiths; others will be gunsmiths, pot and bell makers and glass blowers, others will be inclined to be surgeons or butchers; to others of this nature it inclines to be gamblers and swordfighters.

This Planet (according to Alfraganus) is larger than the earth one and a half times and one eight part more. It has dominion over fire and its metals are iron and copper and it is distant from the earth in 2 million 379 thousand leagues; its body has 10 thousand and 539 leagues.

Of the quality and natural prognostication and effects of the Sun

This Star is placed in the middle of the seven Planets, which is in the fourth Heaven, as King and Lord of them all, and from which they receive light. It is hot, temperately dry, diurnal and masculine, by which all fruit becomes ripe, all herbs and plants reach their perfection. It is so grand the influence of this Star, and God our Lord gave it such generating virtue that the Philosopher came to say that *Sol & homo generant hominem*. Which means that the Sun and man begat man. Of this Star does Hali[58] say that, from its influence, are all things on earth born and are all vegetative and animal creatures generated; this Star inspires, moves and incites men to important positions, government, liberties, honor and dignities, causing authority, ambition and gravity, and many times cruelty, depending on the Planet that may join it.

It has dominion over Kings, and great Lords; over serious and magnanimous men, over grand and magnificent advice and finally over all of those that are advisors to Kings and great Lords.

Prognostications of the Sun

The day of this Star is Sunday, its hour is the first and the eighth. In the year that begins on a Sunday, the Winter will be somewhat harsh, Spring tempered, Summer excessively hot, Autumn windy. There will be an abundance of supplies: of wheat, barley, and as well as all other grains. Of wine, olive oil and honey there will be a good harvest, and in such a year there will not be any shortness of fruit. And finally there will be a lot of cattle, both large and small. This Star signifies that there will be fighting and issues between gentlemen and noblemen; that many things will be spoken of Princes and Great men. And finally that there will be some divergences, even if everything will end in peace and understanding, and many young men and boys will die. *Sed Deus super omnia*.

---

58. Translator's note: A common latinisation of the Arabic "Ali". This can either refer to Ali ibn Ridwan (Abu'l Hasan Ali ibn Ridwan Al-Misri) or Hali Abenragel (Abû l-Hasan 'Alî ibn Abî l-Rijâl), but it is most likely the latter, as this was one of the authors translated in Alfonso the Wise's Toledo school.

Physiognomy given by the Sun

Those born under the dominion of the Sun are white and with plenty of flesh; they have a round face, medium sized mouth, and somewhat thick lips; the forehead is round, the eyebrows thin, the teeth white and well shaped, the nose straight and well proportioned, the neck and chest round, the body straight and well built. They are usually strong and with a good humor.

Conditions infused by the Sun

The Solar are grave, honest and frank men, of great advice; they wish to be honored; they are of a loyal temper, well spoken and generous; they are usually constant and magnificent.

To which things the Sun inclines

Those who are dominated by the Sun are inclined to seek positions of rulership and dignity; as such they are apt to be governors, regents and prelates; to be captains, pilots and field masters; to be shepherds of men and cattle; finally, they are apt and convenient for any art or trade dealing with silk, gold and silver

This Star (according to Alfraganus) is larger than the earth 166 times. It has dominion over fire and its metal is gold; it is distant from the earth in 1 million 213 thousand 333 leagues; it body has 1 million 75 thousand 680 leagues.

Of the quality and natural prognostication and effects of Venus

This Planet has its seat in the third Heaven. It is cold, temperately humid, aqueous, feminine, nocturnal and somewhat phlegmatic, a friend of the human nature. This Star is the brightest of the night after the Moon, and is the one usually called Morning Star; it shows itself occasionally during the day after the Sun has risen, especially in Winter.

It has dominion over women, young boys, Musicians, the well spoken, the joyful, the good fortunate, the just and prudent; over the thankful and merciful; and finally over all those who make a point to present themselves with hygiene and cleanliness.

Prognostications of the Planet Venus

This Planet's day is Friday; its hour is the first and eighth. The year that begins on this day will not be lacking in water. Winter will be heavy and very cold. Spring windy. Summer humid and pleasant. Autumn will have its dry and windy parts and others with plenty of water. There will be plenty of supplies even if expensive. The grape harvest will be plentiful and good. There will be an abundance of olive oil and honey. It also denotes illnesses of the eyes and many young boys will die from pox and many grave and esteemed men will go through difficult labors. There will be plenty of processions and dissensions in many parts of the world. Small cattle will have a great mortality. And finally there will be a few earthquakes felt in several areas.

Physiognomy given by Venus

Those who are born under the dominion of this Planet have a round fleshy face, blushed and somewhat red; joyful, black and restless eyes; black handsome eyebrows somewhat joined; straight hair, even if some will have it curly, they usually carry some mark on their face, a crooked nose, a thicker lower lip, medium sized mouth, handsome neck, narrow chest, small stature, very little flesh and robust legs. If Venus was at the East at the hour of birth, this will make the person thick, white and of good stature. If it was at the West she will be small of body and bald.

The conditions infused by Venus

The Venereal are of a hot, humid and phlegmatic complexion, they are usually eloquent, prudent, joyful and fortunate, thankful, friendly, just and merciful, of sweet words, lovers of music and pastimes, dancing, games, leisure, inclined towards women, composed and ornate. Finally they take pleasure in being well groomed and with sweet smelling clothes; very rarely will they have an inclination towards the letters.

To which things the Planet Venus inclines

Those of the nature of Venus are inclined for joyful trades and arts, showy, elegant and pleasant; such as the arts of singing and playing instruments. Others are inclined to be poets, organists, music masters; other may become embroiderers, gilders, painters; weavers, needle masters and wax workers; some might become actors or comedians.

This Planet (according to Alfraganus) is smaller than the earth 270 times; its metal is copper and it has dominion over the shameful part of both man and woman and is distant from the earth 32 thousand and 650 leagues; its body has 175 leagues.

Of the quality and natural prognostication and effects of Mercury

This Planet has its seat in the second Heaven and it is masculine, diurnal and of an indifferent nature, for it assumes the nature of the Planet with which it is joined; this in such a way that if it is joined by a good Planet its quality and nature will be good; and if it is joined with a bad Planet its complexion will be bad as will be its influences; in this way do we see it with experience, that there are men of this same nature, that while joined with good men turn good and while with the bad also become as them.

This Planet has dominion over poets, scribes, men of letters, painters and mathematicians, over inventors, jewelers and embroiderers and finally over all dealers and merchants.

Prognostications of the Planet Mercury

The day of this Planet is Wednesday, its hour is the first and the eighth. In the year that begins on this day Winter will be harsh but not very cold. Spring will be humid and not too good. Summer will be exceedingly hot. Autumn temperate. Of wheat and other grains there will be a good harvest. The grape harvest will be good. Olive oil will be abundant, but there will still be famine in some areas. Further on, it will indicate death in some principality, and further miscarriages and many new things will happen this year.

Physiognomy given by Mercury

Those who are born under the dominion of this Planet have a medium height, a broad and risen forehead, a somewhat long face. A long and sharp nose; small and pretty eyes, not completely black; broad and long eyebrows; black and shallow beard; thin lips; straight hair that curls at the tips; unevenly placed teeth and long fingers.

The conditions infused by Mercury

The Mercurial are usually cunning, skillful, diligent and wise; they are inventors and industrious. They are good for any art. They are friends of traveling to strange lands and are great negotiators.

To which things the Planet Mercury inclines

The Mercurial are inclined to be notaries, scribes, imaginaries and painters; others are inclined to be arithmeticians, mathematicians, dealers and merchants; others to be sculptors, printers, stonecutters, great negotiators and matchmakers.

This Star of Mercury is much smaller than the Moon, and the Moon is much smaller than the earth, as we shall see. Its metal is quicksilver and it is distant from the earth 125 thousand and 125 leagues; its body has a thousand miles, which are 200 Italian leagues.

Of the quality and natural prognostication and effects of the Moon

    This Planet has its seat in the first Heaven, and is the closest to us. It is cold, humid, aqueous, nocturnal and feminine, to which is attributed humidity and the production of all vegetative things, by the great humidity this Planet infuses. Some have taken up the contemplation of the properties of the Moon, and they have grown more than a little tired at trying to understand its effects, however, this is as wanting to dry out the ocean, for its changes are so various and so admirable its secrets that it is not possible to know them all, but, as is our motive here, I shall mention a few of its general effects. Firstly one should notice that the effects of the crescent Moon are very different from the waning; and as such, every prudent person always takes note of the crescent and waning of the Moon regarding many and diverse things related to agriculture and bodily health. Pliny says in Book 13, Chapter 32, that all things that are cut and sheared, so as to preserve them for a long time, should be cut and sheared on the full or waning Moon, for wood that is cut on the crescent is immediately taken by the beetles, this if it is from a deciduous tree. Animals that are castrated in the crescent are in danger of dying, and fruit which is picked and plants which are watered in the crescent become damaged much faster than in the waning (so says Palladius). One should note one other effect of the Moon, which is, so as to generate males, one should join the males and females on the crescent. The same for chickens when one wishes for more male chicks than female; should the desire be the opposite one should do this during the waning.

Another marvelous effect of the turning or conjunction of the Moon

    Jacob of Palermo,[59] Italian, says that whoever wishes to know the point of conjunction of the Moon should take a silver jug and fill it with a small amount of sea water and olive tree ash,

---

59. Translator's note: uncertain reference.

that, on the moment of conjunction, the ash will dissolve and the water will turn murky. This same author also provides the cause for this effect, saying that as the Moon has direct dominion over silver, olive trees and sea water, by the time of its conjunction these elements demonstrate the nature they receive from this Planet. This Planet has dominion over sailors, over those who roam rivers, lakes or any body of water; over the phlegmatic and the lazy and those who sleep too much.

Prognostications of the Moon

The day of this Planet is Monday, its hour is the first and the eighth. A year that begins on this day will not have shortness of water. Winter will be temperate. Spring cool. Summer moderate. Autumn very humid. There will be little wheat but plenty of all other grains. Wine and olive oil will be average. Animals will have infirmities and these shall be so abundant as to cause great admiration; among the mighty there shall be schisms and betrayals; women will suffer from *mal de madre*.[60] And finally there will be little silk and less honey, for many bees and silk worms will die.

Physiognomy given by the Moon

Those born under the dominion of the Moon are very white and phlegmatic men; they have a full, round and placid face; their eyes are average and somnolent, one being larger than the other, they have some signs or spots on their face, united eyebrows, a rhomb nose and a small mouth.

Conditions infused by the Moon

Those of the nature of the Moon are inconstant, vagabonds, sleepy and have many small illnesses; they are inclined to sail, roam the water and lakes and are lazy and slow in making up their mind.

To which things the Moon inclines

Those of the nature of the Moon are inclined to various things and also to vary in all of these; among them some become fishermen and navigators; others are inclined to be merchants, tavern owners, innkeepers and other similar trades.

This Planet (according to Alfraganus) is 39 times smaller than the earth. Its metal is silver; it has dominion over brackish water, peaches and olive trees, and it is 9 thousand and 847 leagues away from the earth; its body has 166 leagues.

By the signs and Physiognomy that each Planet gives to each one, will the knowledge of such things arise from the natural condition which they infuse and cause; this because it is certain that should you have the conditions of Mars then you are Martian; of Jupiter Jovial of Mercury Mercurial, etc.

Rule so as to know if the Moon is new or old

Every time that the horns or tips of the Moon are turned towards the side of the Sunrise it is a new Moon; if they are turned to the side of the setting Sun it is an old Moon, or waning; and to aid in one's memory this verse is most useful, and it goes: «*Luna cresciente, puntas a Oriente, Luna menguante, puntas adelante.*»[61]

---

60. Translator's note: "Mother's ill", a common name used since medieval times for hysteria. *Madre* in this context is a euphemism for vagina.
61. Translator's note: Crescent Moon, tips to the Orient; waning Moon, tips to the front.

Table so as one may know the hours of Moonlight in every day of the year

AGES OF THE MOON

Crescent	Waning	Hours of Moonlight	
Days	Days	Hours	Quarters
1	29	0	4
2	28	1	3
3	27	2	2
4	26	3	1
5	25	4	0
6	24	4	4
7	23	5	3
8	22	6	2
9	21	7	1
10	20	8	0
11	19	8	4
12	18	9	3
13	17	10	2
14	16	11	1
15	15	12	0

One should be further warned that if it is a crescent Moon, the Moonlight is counted after the Sunset; if it is waning the Moonlight is before the Sunrise.

Marvelous effect of the Moon on the fluxes and refluxes of the sea

Among the various and many effects that the Moon usually causes, one of them, and quite strange, is the flux and reflux of the sea, which rises and lowers twice in a period of little over twenty four hours by the movement of the Moon, and usually detains itself six hours and a fifth part in each rise and low. These fluxes and refluxes usually happen on every Ocean coast and on a few of the Mediterranean, and sometimes are these rising and lowering, such as on the coast of Panama, that the beach is extended by a length of two leagues, sometimes more sometimes less.

As it is convenient and necessary for sailors to know the hour of the day when the tides start, so as they may enter with their ships in the harbors and docks without danger, it is not less important for a Medic to know this marvelous secret; for, as Pliny writes, and Petrus Aponensis[62] confirms, every animal that dies a natural death never does so on the rising tide, but rather on the lowering tide; this is a most worthy thing of being noted and it has been proven by Medics.

For one to know perpetually at which hour of the day each high or low tide begins, one should first know which day of the Moon it is on the day we wish to know the tide. To know the days of the Moon one may do so with the following Table, on the first column at the left, and after that to the right, one will find the hour at which every high and low of the sea begins on that day. And one should know that the following Table is made up of five columns; the first column of this Table starts with what is understood as the day of the new Moon, which is not a complete day, for it is assumed to begin at midday and ends at the midday of the following day. The first day of the

---

62. Translator's note: Also known as Pietro d'Abano a XIIIth and XIVth century Italian philosopher and astrologer.

Moon is understood as beginning at the midday of that day noted at the edge with the number 1, and it ends in the midday of the number 2; for it is supposed that the first day does not begin but after twenty four hours and four fifths. The letter A at the side of the hours indicates afternoon, and the M indicates morning. On the fifth column one will find the small letters m.d., which signifies midday and m.n., midnight.

Days of the Moon	1st high tide			1st low tide			2nd high tide			2nd low tide		
	H.	f.		H.	f.		H.	f.		H.	f.	
0	3	0	M	9	0	M	3	2	A	9	3	A
1	3	4	M	10	0	M	4	1	A	10	2	A
2	4	3	M	10	4	M	5	0	A	11	1	A
3	5	2	M	11	3	M	5	4	A	12	0	m.n.
4	6	1	M	12	2	A	6	3	A	12	4	M
5	7	0	M	1	1	A	7	2	A	1	3	M
6	7	4	M	2	0	A	8	1	A	2	2	M
7	8	3	M	2	4	A	9	0	A	3	1	M
8	9	2	M	3	3	A	9	4	A	4	0	M
9	10	1	M	4	2	A	10	3	A	4	4	M
10	11	0	M	5	1	A	11	2	A	5	3	M
11	11	4	M	6	0	A	12	1	M	6	2	M
12	12	3	A	6	4	A	1	0	M	7	1	M
13	1	2	A	7	3	A	1	4	M	8	0	M
14	2	1	A	8	2	A	2	3	M	8	4	M
15	3	0	A	9	1	A	3	2	M	9	3	M
16	3	4	A	10	0	A	4	1	M	10	2	M
17	4	3	A	10	4	A	5	0	M	11	1	M
18	5	2	A	11	3	A	5	4	M	12	0	m.d.
19	6	1	A	12	2	M	6	3	M	12	4	A
20	7	0	A	1	1	M	7	2	M	1	3	A
21	7	4	A	2	0	M	8	1	M	2	2	A
22	8	3	A	2	4	M	9	0	M	3	1	A
23	9	2	A	3	3	M	9	4	M	4	0	A
24	10	1	A	4	2	M	10	3	M	4	4	A
25	11	0	A	5	1	M	11	2	M	5	3	A
26	11	4	A	6	0	M	12	1	A	6	2	A
27	12	3	M	6	4	M	1	0	A	7	1	A
28	1	2	M	7	3	M	1	4	A	8	0	A
29	2	1	M	8	2	M	2	3	A	8	4	A
30	3	0	M	9	1	M	3	2	A	9	3	A

And so as this Table be made easy and understandable we propose an example: be it that we wish to know the tides at the 9th of the Moon (which is the amount of days since the last conjunction until the day we wish to inquire), we check the number 9 in the first column on the left and immediately corresponding to it, on the right in the second column, which has two divisions as all others, one will find in the first division 10 hours and in the second one fifth of an hour, which are 12 minutes, and the letter M at the right, which signifies that those times are in the morning, and this will be the time of the first high tide.

This first low tide will be found in the third column at 4 hours and 2/5 of the afternoon of this same day of the 9th of the Moon.

The second high tide will be found in the fourth column at 10 hours and 3/5 of the same afternoon of this day of the 9th of the Moon.

The second low tide will be found in the fifth column at 4 hours and 4/5 of the morning of the next day of this 9th of the Moon

If one wishes to know the low tide before the first high tide of the 9th of the Moon, remove from the 10 hours and 1/5 of Morning, on which is the first high tide, 6 hours and 1/5, arriving at 4 hours in the Morning, which is a low tide; should one wish to know the high tide before this low tide, remove from the 4 hours 6 hours and 1/5 more and one will have 9 hours and 4/5, which was the high tide of the afternoon of the same day.

Second example

Should one wish to know the tides on the 24th of the Moon, following the same line as above, one will find the first high tide at 10 hours and 1/5 in the afternoon. The first low tide is at 4 and 2/5 in the morning of the next day, as the 24th of the Moon began on the midday of that day. The second high tide is at 10 hours and 3/5 of the same morning. The second low tide is at 4 hours and 4/5 in the afternoon of the next day following the 24th of the Moon.

But should you want to know the high tide before the high tide of the second column remove from the 10 hours and 1/5 6 hour and 1/5, arriving at 4 hours of the afternoon, and reducing further 6 hours and 1/5 one will arrive at 9 and 4/5 in the morning of the 23rd of the Moon, which is the previous high tide.

So as to know which Sign the Moon is in

To know the Sign in which the Moon is in each day, one should go to the Calendar of the months and check on the day we wish to know the corresponding letter on the right side of the A B C, and once the letter is known one should also know the Golden Number of that year (which is also in this Lunario) and once this is known, seek in the following Table the Golden number and once this is found go down these letters on the right side until you find the letter in the Calendar. Once this is found check in front of it on the left side the corresponding Sign, for it is in this Sign that the Moon is in that day.

Golden Number	I	II	III	IV	V	VI	VII	VIII	IX	X	XI	XII	XIII	XIV	XV	XVI	XVII	XVIII	XIX
Aries	g	x	n	d	v	K	a	l	h	z	p	e	u	l	b	s	i	a	t
Aries	h	y	o	e	u	l	b	s	i	2	q	f	x	m	c	t	K	5	u
Aries	i	z	p	f	x	m	c	t	K	5	r	g	y	n	d	v	l	a	u
Taurus	K	2	q	g	y	n	d	x	l	a	s	h	z	o	e	u	m	b	x
Taurus	l	5	r	h	z	o	e	u	m	b	s	i	2	p	f	x	n	c	y
Taurus	m	a	s	i	2	p	f	x	n	c	t	K	2	q	g	y	o	d	z
Gemini	n	b	s	K	5	q	g	y	o	d	v	l	a	r	h	z	p	e	2
Gemini	o	c	t	l	a	r	h	z	p	e	u	m	b	s	i	2	q	f	5
Cancer	p	d	v	m	b	s	i	2	q	f	x	n	c	s	K	5	r	g	a
Cancer	q	e	u	n	c	s	K	5	r	g	y	o	d	t	l	a	s	h	b
Leo	r	f	x	o	d	t	l	a	s	h	z	p	e	v	m	b	s	i	c
Leo	s	g	y	p	e	v	m	b	s	i	2	q	f	u	n	c	t	K	d
Leo	s	h	z	q	f	u	n	c	t	K	5	r	g	x	o	d	v	l	e
Virgo	t	i	2	r	g	x	o	d	v	l	a	s	h	y	p	e	u	m	f
Virgo	v	K	5	s	h	y	p	e	u	m	b	s	i	z	q	f	x	n	g
Libra	u	l	a	s	i	z	q	f	x	n	c	t	K	2	r	g	y	o	h
Libra	x	m	b	t	K	2	r	g	y	o	d	v	l	5	s	h	2	p	i
Scorp.	y	n	c	v	l	5	s	h	z	p	e	u	m	a	s	i	2	q	K
Scorp.	z	o	d	u	m	a	s	i	2	q	f	x	n	b	t	K	5	r	l
Sagitt.	2	p	e	x	n	b	t	K	5	r	g	y	o	c	v	l	a	s	m
Sagitt.	5	q	f	y	o	c	x	l	a	s	h	z	p	d	u	m	b	s	n
Capri.	a	r	g	a	p	d	u	m	b	s	i	2	q	e	x	n	c	t	o
Capri.	b	s	h	2	q	e	x	n	c	t	K	5	r	f	y	o	d	v	p
Aquar.	c	s	i	5	r	f	y	o	d	v	l	a	s	g	z	p	e	u	q
Aquar.	d	t	K	a	s	g	z	p	e	u	m	b	s	h	2	q	f	x	r
Pisces	e	v	l	b	s	h	2	q	f	x	n	c	t	i	5	r	g	y	s
Pisces	f	u	m	c	t	i	5	r	g	y	o	d	v	K	a	s	h	z	s
Pisces	g	x	n	d	v	K	a	s	h	z	p	e	u	l	b	s	i	2	t

Rule so as to know how many hours of Moonlight will each night have

Count how many days there are from the new Moon to the day you wish to know and multiply them by three, dividing this number by four you will have that amount of hours of that night. And the same you can do with the days from the old Moon, and the value after the division by four, after the multiplication, are the hours which will take the Moon to come up on that night. And if after the division you have an excess of one, this will mean a quarter of an hour, if it is two it is two quarters and three is three quarters. And note that each night the Moon is halted in our Hemisphere, if it is a new Moon, three quarters of an hour, and if it is an old Moon, it will be delayed in its rise another three quarters each night.

New invention and very curious and true Table so as to know in which Sign the Moon is in each day

To also know in which Sign the Moon is in each day, one should see how many Moon days there are in that month, and the day one wishes to know, and this number you can then search in the left side of the following Table, and in front of that number, in the column corresponding to the month of the day one wishes to know, one shall find the Sign in which the Moon is in that day; and so as this may be facilitated we shall give an example: be it that I want to know, on the 12th of September of the year of 1663 in which Sign the Moon was in, and by the above rule I find it was in Aquarius, for the conjunction of the Moon was on the 1st of that month, and from the 1st to the 12th are 11 Moon days (not counting the first one of the conjunction) and this number 11 is found in front of the Sign of Aquarius, which is in the column which corresponds to the month of September, and so I say that on the 12th of September the Moon was in the Sign of Aquarius. And for those who wish to know in which Sign was the Moon on the very day of conjunction, one does not need more than to see in which Sign the Sun was on that day (this by the Calendar) for the Moon is in that same Sign on that day; and note that below you shall find the Table of the Signs which are good or bad for bloodlettings and purges.

Table of the Signs the Moon is in each day

Days of the Moon	Signs of January	Signs of February	Signs of March	Signs of April	Signs of May	Signs of June
1	Aquarius	Pisces	Aries	Taurus	Gemini	Cancer
2	Aquarius	Pisces	Aries	Taurus	Gemini	Cancer
3	Pisces	Aries	Taurus	Gemini	Cancer	Leo
4	Pisces	Aries	Taurus	Gemini	Cancer	Leo
5	Pisces	Aries	Taurus	Gemini	Cancer	Leo
6	Aries	Taurus	Gemini	Cancer	Leo	Virgo
7	Aries	Taurus	Gemini	Cancer	Leo	Virgo
8	Taurus	Gemini	Cancer	Leo	Virgo	Libra
9	Taurus	Gemini	Cancer	Leo	Virgo	Libra
10	Taurus	Gemini	Cancer	Leo	Virgo	Libra
11	Gemini	Cancer	Leo	Virgo	Libra	Scorpio
12	Gemini	Cancer	Leo	Virgo	Libra	Scorpio
13	Cancer	Leo	Leo	Virgo	Scorpio	Sagittarius
14	Cancer	Leo	Virgo	Libra	Scorpio	Sagittarius
15	Cancer	Leo	Virgo	Libra	Scorpio	Sagittarius
16	Leo	Virgo	Virgo	Libra	Sagittarius	Capricorn
17	Leo	Virgo	Libra	Scorpio	Sagittarius	Capricorn
18	Virgo	Libra	Libra	Scorpio	Capricorn	Aquarius
19	Virgo	Libra	Scorpio	Sagittarius	Capricorn	Aquarius
20	Virgo	Libra	Scorpio	Sagittarius	Capricorn	Aquarius
21	Libra	Scorpio	Sagittarius	Sagittarius	Aquarius	Pisces
22	Libra	Scorpio	Sagittarius	Capricorn	Aquarius	Pisces
23	Scorpio	Sagittarius	Capricorn	Capricorn	Pisces	Aries
24	Scorpio	Sagittarius	Capricorn	Aquarius	Pisces	Aries
25	Scorpio	Sagittarius	Capricorn	Aquarius	Pisces	Aries
26	Sagittarius	Capricorn	Aquarius	Aquarius	Aries	Taurus
27	Sagittarius	Capricorn	Aquarius	Pisces	Aries	Taurus
28	Capricorn	Aquarius	Pisces	Pisces	Taurus	Gemini
29	Capricorn	Aquarius	Pisces	Aries	Taurus	Gemini
30	Capricorn	Aquarius	Pisces	Aries	Taurus	Gemini

Table of the Signs the Moon is in each day

Days of the Moon	Signs of July	Signs of August	Signs of September	Signs of October	Signs of November	Signs of December
1	Leo	Virgo	Libra	Scorpio	Sagittarius	Capricorn
2	Leo	Virgo	Libra	Scorpio	Sagittarius	Capricorn
3	Virgo	Libra	Scorpio	Sagittarius	Capricorn	Aquarius
4	Virgo	Libra	Scorpio	Sagittarius	Capricorn	Aquarius
5	Virgo	Libra	Scorpio	Sagittarius	Capricorn	Aquarius
6	Libra	Scorpio	Sagittarius	Capricorn	Aquarius	Pisces
7	Libra	Scorpio	Sagittarius	Capricorn	Aquarius	Pisces
8	Scorpio	Sagittarius	Capricorn	Aquarius	Pisces	Aries
9	Scorpio	Sagittarius	Capricorn	Aquarius	Pisces	Aries
10	Scorpio	Sagittarius	Capricorn	Aquarius	Pisces	Aries
11	Sagittarius	Capricorn	Aquarius	Pisces	Aries	Taurus
12	Sagittarius	Capricorn	Aquarius	Pisces	Aries	Taurus
13	Capricorn	Aquarius	Pisces	Aries	Taurus	Gemini
14	Capricorn	Aquarius	Pisces	Aries	Taurus	Gemini
15	Capricorn	Aquarius	Aries	Aries	Taurus	Gemini
16	Aquarius	Pisces	Aries	Taurus	Gemini	Cancer
17	Aquarius	Pisces	Taurus	Taurus	Gemini	Cancer
18	Pisces	Aries	Taurus	Gemini	Cancer	Leo
19	Pisces	Aries	Taurus	Gemini	Cancer	Leo
20	Pisces	Aries	Gemini	Gemini	Cancer	Leo
21	Aries	Taurus	Gemini	Cancer	Leo	Virgo
22	Aries	Taurus	Cancer	Cancer	Leo	Virgo
23	Taurus	Gemini	Cancer	Leo	Virgo	Libra
24	Taurus	Gemini	Cancer	Leo	Virgo	Libra
25	Taurus	Gemini	Leo	Leo	Virgo	Libra
26	Gemini	Cancer	Leo	Virgo	Libra	Scorpio
27	Gemini	Cancer	Leo	Virgo	Libra	Scorpio
28	Cancer	Leo	Virgo	Libra	Scorpio	Sagittarius
29	Cancer	Leo	Virgo	Libra	Scorpio	Sagittarius
30	Cancer	Leo	Virgo	Libra	Scorpio	Sagittarius

Rule so as to know from memory in which Sign and in what degree is the Moon in each day

To know in which Sign and in what degree is the Moon in each day, one should precisely note and take care of three things. The first is that on the day of the turning, or conjunction (which is the same thing), the Sun and the Moon are in the same Sign. The second is that the Sun is the whole month in the same Sign and the Moon is never more than two and a half days, more or less, in each Sign. The third is to know on which day of each month the Sun enters each Sign, which can be found in the Calendar of the months and Saints, and also where we deal with these same Signs. Once these three things are known, and the day on which the conjunction of the Moon, or new Moon, was, count the day from this same conjunction day until the day you wish to know the Sign and degree of the Moon, double this number and add one; the amount of fives you can make out of this number is the movement that the Moon has taken from the Sign in which it had its conjunction or turning. And, if besides the fives you have any amount left, each one will be worth six degrees towards the next Sign. And because practice makes theory easier, we shall give an example: be it that I wish to know what Sign and degree is the Moon in on the 20th of October of the year of 1663; according to the above, I will know that the Moon was on that day at six degrees of Gemini, for the conjunction of the Moon was on the 1st of October, being the Sun in Libra, from the 1st of October to the 20th are 20 days, whose double is 40 and plus one is 41, a number in which there are 8 fives, which represent eight Signs, and one further point, which is worth 6 degrees on the ninth Sign. Then, counting from Libra, *exclusivé*, we arrive at Gemini; for since the Sun was in Libra during the conjunction so was the Moon, and so as one may know the order of the Signs we give it here: Aries, Taurus, Gemini, Cancer, Leo, Virgo, Libra, Scorpio, Sagittarius, Capricorn, Aquarius, Pisces.

Another rule even more necessary than the previous one so as to know in which
Sign the Moon is in on each day

Multiply by four the days of the Moon, and as many tens as you can make from this number those will be the number of Signs the Moon will be separated from the Sign of its last conjunction; and if beyond the tens that you get you have any amount left, each will be worth one degree towards the next Sign; and so as this may be better understood we propose an example: given that we want to know in which Sign the Moon was in on the 15th of May of the year of 1638, by this rule I find that it was in the 8th degree of Gemini, for the past conjunction was on the 13th of May, and the Sun was in the Sign of Taurus; from the 13th of May until the 15th, *exclusivé*, are two days, which multiplied by four make the number 8, from which we cannot make any tens to represent any Sign, and as there are no tens we have eight degrees of Gemini, in which the Moon was in on the 15th of May. And do note that this rule is of great accuracy and truth.

Marvelous effects of the Moon by the Signs regarding supplies

If the January Moon enters in the crescent in the Sign of Aquarius, this indicates that the year will be abundant of bread and all other supplies. And if it enters in the waning it indicates illness, sadness and labors, with river floods and storms at sea.

If the February Moon enters in the crescent in the Sign of Pisces, it will be the cause of low prices and great commodity. And if it enters in the waning it indicates abundant rain.

If the March Moon enters in the crescent in the Sign of Aries, and if it is to the Septentrional side, it signifies restlessness. However, if it enters in the waning, it denotes a good and prosperous year.

If the April Moon enters in the crescent in the Sign of Taurus, it indicates that there will be great joy and contentment; however, if it enters in the waning it indicates the opposite.

If the May Moon enters the Sign of Gemini in the crescent, it indicates revolutions and changes in that region for those who are of that Sign. And if it enters in the waning it signifies a great deal of rain.

If the June Moon enters the Sing of Cancer in the crescent, it indicates revolts, confusion and changes in the Empire of Africa, and if it enters in the waning it indicates an abundance of rain.

If the July Moon enters the Sign of Leo in the crescent, it indicates good profit for farmers on their harvest. And if it enters in the waning it signifies labors, danger and infirmities.

If the August Moon enters in the crescent in the Sign of Virgo, this announces great revolutions of winds, earthquakes and storms. And if it enters in the waning it indicates a good year and prosperous in terms of health and supplies.

If the September Moon enters the Sign of Libra in the crescent, it indicates an abundance of every kind of grain. However, if it enters in the waning it indicates storms and revolts.

If the October Moon enters the Sign of Scorpio, which dominates the Kingdom of Valencia, in the crescent, it denotes envy and disputes among learned men. However, if it enters in the waning it denotes a good and prosperous year and abundance in the same Kingdom.

If the November Moon enters the Sign of Sagittarius in the crescent there will be no shortage of rain and olive oil. But if it enters in the waning it denotes hunger and also plague.

If the December Moon enters the Sign of Capricorn in the crescent it denotes great misfortunes and storms at sea. However if it enters in the waning it indicates a lot of joy for the farmers.

Note and be warned curious Reader, that all these significances and effects will be mostly felt in those Kingdoms and Provinces which are dominated by each one of the twelve Signs. And he who wishes to know all the general and particular lands that are subjected to each one of the 12 Signs, know that this is indicated below in the declaration of the Signs themselves.

Below is the declaration of the following perpetual and general Table for the prognostication of the years

In this Table there are five columns. In the first at the left you have the Dominical letters of each year. In the second you have the years, starting from 1855, and this column may last until the end of the World, knowing that once these years are done one may go back to its beginning and start over. In the third column one will find the day on which each year will begin. In the fourth one will find the Planets that represent each first day of the year. In the fifth one will find information regarding supplies for each year. And so as this Table may be understood better I shall propose two examples: be the first in the year of 1855, which is written at the top of the column, in front of which is the Dominical letter G, and that year begins on a Monday, whose Planet is the Moon, and in front of this there is the indication of an Average of supplies. And those who wish to have a greater knowledge of the prognostication and successes of the year should read what is written regarding the Planet of the Moon, where this is expressed in detail; and as such, in this order one will know the prognostication of the coming years. Second example is for the year of 1883, which is not written in the following Table, but corresponds to the year of 1855, and so forth for every other year. On this point a curious may doubt or contend that this Table cannot be perpetual, seeing as in 100 years the Dominical letters will change, and once again in 100 years, and further still in another 100 years, and so every 400 years they will change and switch three times: once every hundred years during 300 (as is expressly mandated by the Gregorian Calendar), this being due to the leap years. This was thus arranged so as time may be kept and the Equinoxes, particularly the Summer one, do not move because of Easter. Immediately a curious will say: If this is so, how is it that in certain times and years the Dominical letters change? The Table cannot be perpetual; for once the Dominical letter changes so will the first day of the year change and as a consequence also the effects of the Planets. To this doubt and objection I answer that at the left edge of the mentioned Table there are three numbers; which are the first years in which the Dominical letters are changed; and one should note and take care that in the place of these three numbers one should note, in their proper order, all other coming years in which the letters are changed. And this will happen, during every 400 years, three times; and as such, the year in which the letters are changed is the first number in the Table; the year in which the letters change a second time is noted by the second number; and as such, the third time the letters are changed is noted by the third number, and in this order, until the end of the World, will this last with the observation of the Gregorian Calendar, which will last forever; and as such will this Table be perpetual.

Year in which the Dominical letter changes	Dominical letter		Year of Christ	First day of the year	The seven Planets	Of the supplies
	G		1855	Monday	Moon	Average
	F	E	1856	Tuesday	Mars	Shortage
	D		1857	Thursday	Jupiter	Abundance
	C		1858	Friday	Venus	Abundance
	B		1859	Saturday	Saturn	Shortage
	A		1860	Sunday	Sun	Abundance
1901	F		1861	Tuesday	Mars	Shortage
	E		1862	Wednesday	Mercury	Average
	D		1863	Thursday	Jupiter	Abundance
	C	B	1864	Friday	Venus	Abundance
	A		1865	Sunday	Sun	Abundance
2001	G		1866	Monday	Moon	Average
	F		1867	Tuesday	Mars	Shortage
	E	D	1868	Wednesday	Mercury	Average
	C		1869	Friday	Venus	Abundance
2101	B		1870	Saturday	Saturn	Shortage
	A		1871	Sunday	Sun	Shortage
	G	F	1872	Monday	Moon	Abundance
	E		1873	Wednesday	Mercury	Average
	D		1874	Thursday	Jupiter	Average
	C		1875	Friday	Venus	Abundance
	B	A	1876	Saturday	Saturn	Abundance
	G		1877	Monday	Moon	Shortage
	F		1878	Tuesday	Mars	Average
	E		1879	Wednesday	Mercury	Shortage
	D	C	1880	Thursday	Jupiter	Abundance
	B		1881	Saturday	Saturn	Shortage
	A		1882	Sunday	Sun	Abundance

Declaration of the 12 Signs, their qualities and effects

In the ninth Sphere, which is called the crystalline Heaven, the Astronomers consider a circle which has the name of Zodiac, three hundred and sixty degrees long and twelve wide, which they divided into 12 equal parts which are the 12 Signs, and each of these parts, or Signs, has thirty degrees. Their names are the following: Aries, Taurus, Gemini, Cancer, Leo, Virgo, Libra, Scorpio, Sagittarius, Capricorn, Aquarius and Pisces. These names were given to them by the effects they caused (and still cause) when the Sun entered each of them, which, by another name, are referred to as the Planetary Houses; for, being the Planets in their corresponding Sign or House, they will have greater strength and more vigor than outside of it, and each Sign is 273 million 870 thousand and 47 leagues long, and is 22 million, 318 thousand and 258 leagues wide.

And should any curious wish to know which Sign is the House of which Planet, I shall say this with brevity. The Sign of Leo is the House of the Sun; Cancer of the Moon; Capricorn and Aquarius are the Houses of Saturn; Pisces and Sagittarius of Jupiter; Aries and Scorpio of Mars; Libra and Taurus of Venus; Gemini and Virgo of Mercury (of these Houses or Signs we shall say a few secrets and natural effects they have on those who are sick while the Moon is on these Signs or Houses). Following my intent, I shall say that, entering the Sun on each of these Signs, they cause many and various effects, as we shall see in their corresponding declaration.

Of the quality and effects of the Sign of Aquarius, which begins on the 21st of January, for this is when the Sun enters this Sign

This Sign is depicted by a man with a vase in his hands, casting out water, which denotes plenty of water and the falling of rain. This Sign is of a hot and humid nature, it imprints heat and distempered and harmful dryness, for it corrupts the air, and as such damages every living thing and plant. The Sun commonly enters this Sign on the 21st of January, and from the time it does so until it leaves the days grows in one hour. This Sign is airy and masculine, diurnal and fixed, for while the Sun is in it the Winter is fixed; this Sign is the diurnal and pleasure House of Saturn, and nocturnal and diurnal determent of the Sun.

It has dominion over the Provinces of Aragon, Bohemia, Saxony, Ethiopia, Dalmatia, Arabia, Sogdiana, Azavia, Piedmont and India. Over the cities of Constancia, Jerusalem, Urbino, Pavia, Monferrato. And in Hispania over Zamora, Medina, Palencia and Seville. In Portugal over Bragança, Guarda and Castelo Branco.

A man who is born under the rising of this Sign will be of average height, cautious, secretive, of healthy entrails, venturous in all he undertakes; it is indicated that he will receive some blow from iron, and is in danger from water; he will have an inclination to travel to foreign lands, where he will fare better than in his own motherland. It is denoted that, should he return, he will return rich and prosperous; and he should take care from being taken by passion, for it will affect him in excess. *Incerto quodam anno erit in dubio vita sua.* It is also denoted that he will have a great illness before his thirties, and should he cure it, he is promised, according to his nature and complexion, to reach 68 years of life.

If it is a female, it denotes that she will be very moderate, a friend of her own opinions, and she is in danger of losing everything she may come to gain with her industry and work; it is also indicated some form of danger from water, and that from her middle age on this will improve; before she turns 38 she should have two illnesses. The first when she is 24 and the second when she is 35 and promises, according to her nature and temperament, to reach 82 years of life.

Of the quality and effects of the Sign of Pisces, which begins on the 19th of February, for this is when the Sun enters this Sign

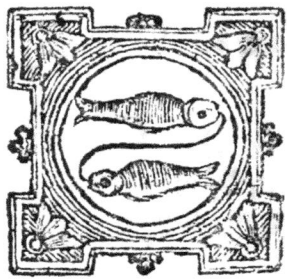

This Sign is represented by two fish and it signifies that, as the fish are humid and always in water, so is the weather humid and abundant in water when the Sun enters this Sign. It is a feminine Sign, nocturnal, aquatic and common to Winter and Spring. It is of a cold and humid nature, from which it infuses and imprints coldness, distempered and harmful humidity to lake and fountain waters, causing corruption in them by making them brackish. The Sun enters this Sign commonly on the 19th of February, and from the time the Sun enters it until it leaves the day grows by an hour and a half; this Sign is the nocturnal and diurnal House of Jupiter, exaltation of Venus, fall and nocturnal determent of Mercury and his sadness.

It has dominion over the Provinces of Persia, Ireland, Normandy, Portugal, Lydia, Sicily, Pamphylia, the Garamantes, Masamones and Prussia. The cities of Cologne, Venice, Regensburg and Alexandria. In Hispania over Orense, Santiago and parts of Seville. In Portugal over Braga, Fafe, Guimarães and Amarante.

The male who is born under the rising of this Sign will be a friend of visiting many lands, have a great delight in roaming the sea, joy for food, by which he may develop an illness if his Planet does not aid in his complexion. It denotes that he will be a man of few words, and will be inclined to abandon his motherland, that he will have a grave illness when he is 15, another when he is 30 and a third one when he is 38; but it is promised, according to his nature that he will live until 65.

A woman will suffer from the eyes, she will be very honest and merciful, and suffer from the *mal de madre*. And finally she should keep herself from fire, for it is denoted great danger from this, and an infirmity when she is 12, another when she is 20 and 21 and another when she is 30. She is promised, according to her nature, 59 year of life.

Of the quality and effects of the Sign of Aries, which begins on the 21st of March

This Sign is represented by a ram; it is of a fiery nature, hot and dry, by which it imprints heat and temperate dryness. It is diurnal, mobile and masculine. It is a House of Mars and exaltation of the Sun, fall of Saturn and determent of Venus. The Sun enters this Sign at the 21st of March; this day constitutes and begins the first Equinox, which means that the day is the same as the night; from the time the Sun enters this Sign until it leaves, the day grows by an hour and a half. It has dominion over the Provinces of England, France, Germany and Poland minor. The cities of Florence, Naples, Padua, Venice, Kracow, Sumala and Pergamon. In Hispania over Zaragoza, Tortosa, Plasencia and Valladolid. In Portugal over Coimbra, Leiria, Santarém, Tomar and Mafra.

A male who is born under the rising of this Sign will be crafty, prudent and of a noble temper, he will also be a friend of talking; he will fall in love with ease, but this will pass briefly. It denotes that he will many times talk to himself, and he will never be too rich nor too poor and he will easily keep his friends and will have to live with *mortuorum causa*.

It is denoted some remarkable sign in his body, and damage dealt by some four legged animal and a blow from iron and he will pass through some misfortunes and labors. Finally, it is also shown that he will have a dangerous infirmity before he is 22, and should he survive it he should reach, according to his nature, 75 years, and that those mentioned 22 *forsan ducet uxorem*.

If it is a female she will be wrathful and very clever in her action; of good mind and resourceful; this Sign denotes that if she marries she will become a widow, and that she will have a dangerous infirmity in her head or knees, from when she is 7 until 12, and promises, according to her nature, to live for 46 years. Both the male and female will experience great poverty, but they will recover everything due to their own industry and work.

Of the nature and effects of the Sign of Taurus, which begins on the 20th of April

This Sign is represented by a Bull, and it is of an earthy, cold and dry nature, but temperate however; by this reason, by entering the Sun in it are many sensitive things generated and all vegetation increases and grows. This Sign is nocturnal and feminine; the Sun enters it commonly on the 20th of April and from this time until it leaves, the day increases by one hour; this Sign is the House and delight of Venus, exaltation of the Moon, determent and sadness of Mars. It has dominion over the Provinces of Persia, Mehdya, Sweden, Asia Minor, Ireland, Egypt, Armenia and Cyprus. In cities over Capua, Salerno, Bologna, Sena, Verona, Ancona, Trier, Parma, Mantua, Palermo. In Hispania over Girona, Osma, Toro, Badajoz, Astorga and Jaén. In Portugal over Elvas, Portalegre, Estremoz and Vila Viçosa.

The male who is born under the rising of this Sign is denoted to be cheeky, pretentious and haughty of hearth; he will be inclined to leave his motherland and go to strange lands, where he will fare better; and should he marry, he will acquire position and status through his wife. It is denoted that he will be bit by a dog; if he is a businessman he will be venturous in buying and selling. Finally it is shown that he will be under danger from water, more than once if he is not careful and *infortunia mulierum causa*; he will have some illness at 12 and another when he is 30 and a third one when he is 40, and should he survive it he should live, according to his nature, until 64 years of age.

A female denotes that she will be careful and determined, and she will have the inclination to go to strange lands; she will be fertile and will have many children and *Plures indicat enim habere maritos*; finally it is denoted that she will suffer a fall from a high place and an infirmity when she is 16 and another when she is 33. This Sign promises her, according to her nature, 66 year of life.

Of the nature and effects of the Sign of Gemini, which begins on the 21st of May

    This Sign is represented by two young boys embracing, it denotes softness in the weather caused by the entering of the Sun in this Sign, which is of an airy, hot and humid nature, and as such infuses and generates a very temperate weather for all plants, trees and things of vigor. It is the diurnal House of Mercury and determent and sadness of Jupiter. This Sign is masculine and diurnal, and is common to Spring and Winter, infusing heat and temperate dryness. The Sun enters this Sign commonly on the 21st of May and until it leaves the day increases by half an hour.

    It has dominion over the Provinces of Hyrcania, Cyrenaica, Marmarica, part of Egypt, Armenia and Margiana. The cities of Trento, Sète, Vita, Pau, Nuremberg, Brussels, Lyon and Magnesia. And in Hispania over Sigüenza, Murviedo, Cordoba and Talavera. In Portugal over Covilhã, Vila Real and Abrantes; and in the Azores the islands of Terceira, S. Jorge, Faial and Pico.

    The male born under the rising of this Sign will be of good disposition and a liberal; it denotes that his nature will incline him live outside of his motherland, and that he will tread many paths, he will be a person of great credit and will own much; it shows that he will be diligent in his affairs and that he will be in danger from water; he should keep himself from rabid dogs, for it is prognosticated that he will be wounded by one; and finally it is denoted that he will suffer from 4 infirmities by the time he is 30 years old, and that from that age on he will live healthily, and it is promised, according to his nature, that he will live for 68 years.

    If it is a female it is denoted that she will be very constant, esteemed, taken into high regard and inclined for holy matrimony. Ill accomplished things will weigh heavily on her and she may suffer from some ailments; but this Sign promises, according to her nature, 62 years of life.

Of the quality and effects of the Sign of Cancer, which begins on the 22nd of June

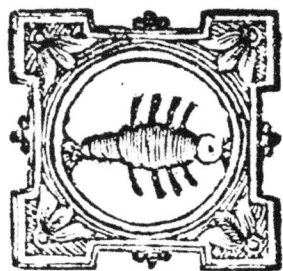

This Sign is represented by a fish called Crab, whose nature is watery, cold and humid, feminine, nocturnal and movable; for entering the Sun in it is the quality of the weather changed, infusing humidity and temperate coldness, apt and convenient for nutriment. The Sun enters this Sign on the 22nd of June and until it leaves the day is reduced in half an hour; this Sign is the diurnal and nocturnal House of the Moon, exaltation of Jupiter, determent of Saturn and fall of Mars.

It has dominion over the Provinces of Numidia, Holland, Norway, Zeeland, Bithynia, Burgundy, Scotland, Rhodes, Lydia, Ethiopia, Africa, Colchis and Phrygia. The cities of Constantinople, Milan, Pisa, Luca, Venice, Tunis, Geneva. And in Hispania over Compostela, Lisbon, Granada and Barcelona. In Portugal over Viana, Porto, Braga, Aveiro and Penafiel.

The male who is born under the rising of this Sign will be of an average stature, secretive, humble and joyful. It denotes that he will go through some labors over agreements and that he will defend the causes of others, as he is inclined to be a court Claimant; as such he will acquire many claims, and it is denoted that he will spend a lot of money. It is shown that he is in danger from water, fire and iron, and that he will be arrogant and of great reputation; it is also denoted that he will suffer from small infirmities and it is promised that he will live, according to his nature, until 73 years of age.

If it is a female it is denoted that she will be diligent, careful and given to grief, which will be short lived and she will be very grateful. It is shown that she will go through some restlessness over her children and family. She will have many children and is in danger of falling from a high place and that she will find some hidden things, but these will be of little worth. It is denoted that she will live healthily, and it is promised, according to her nature, to reach the age of 70 years.

Of the quality and effects of the Sign of Leo, which begins on the 23rd of July

This Sign is of a fiery nature, hot and dry in excess; it is masculine, diurnal and fixed, for while the Sun is in this Sign heat is constant and firm; during its time vigorous things are destroyed and dried. The Sun enters this Sign commonly at the 23rd of July and until it leaves the day is diminished by one hour; this Sign is the diurnal and nocturnal House of the Sun, sadness of Saturn and his determent. It has dominion over the Provinces of Sicily, in part, and other parts of Apulia, Bohemia, the coast of the Red Sea, Chaldea, Italy, Greece, Turkey, Pontus, the Alps and Macedonia. In cities over Rome, Ravenna, Cremona, Osma, Cretón, Damascus, Prague. And in Hispania over Murcia and Leon. In Portugal over Barcelos, Ponte de Lima, Póvoa do Varzim and Famalicão.

The male who is born under the rising of this Sign will be of a good disposition and of a pleasant presence, haughty and with great temper; it is denoted that he will be daring, arrogant, eloquent and that, should he apply himself to the letters, he will be very wise and learned; he will reach great dignities or positions, and he will see a great deal of lands; and should he marry he will have enough to live by, for his wife will have an inheritance. Finally it is denoted that there will be some danger of a blow by iron, that he will be in peril at sea and he will be venturous in business and in some time *inveniet pecuniam absconditam*.

A female will be beautiful, terrible and strong. It is denoted that she will suffer from stomach pain, she will be a great lover of honor and will come to own a farm. Finally she will be charitable to the poor and is in danger of suffering from blood flow.

The male is denoted to suffer from 6 infirmities throughout the course of his life, and when he is 40 one of these will be extremely dangerous, but should he survive it this Sign promises him 71 year of life.

The female will have infirmities of excessive blood throughout her life, and she will live, according to her nature, for 71 years.

Of the quality and effects of the Sign of Virgo, which begins on the 24th of August

    This Sign is of an earthy nature, cold and dry; it is represented as a damsel, indicating the sterility of the earth by the infertility of the damsel when the Sun enters this Sign. It is feminine, nocturnal, melancholic and common to Autumn and Summer; the Sun enters this Sign commonly on the 24th of August, and from this time until it leaves the day is diminished by an hour and a half. This Sign is the House, pleasure and exaltation of Mercury, the fall of Venus and nocturnal determent of Jupiter.

    It has dominion over the Provinces of Greece, part of Persia, Babylonia, Assyria, Mesopotamia, Sicily, Rhodes and the island of Candia. In cities over Pavia, Paris, Ferrara, Toulouse, Poreča and Corinth. In Hispania over Lleida, Toledo, Avila and Algeciras. In Portugal over Lisbon, Setúbal, Portimão; in the Azores the island of S. Miguel and the island of Madeira.

    The male born under the rise of this Sign will be honored, chaste and of a noble condition. It is denoted that he will be a self-conscious and variable man and that he will have wealth; but he will also fall into great poverty over not knowing how to rule or manage himself.

    A woman will be self-conscious, diligent and very devout. It is denoted that she will fall from a high place and will for some time live with an infirmity. Finally it is shown that both the man and the woman who are born in this Sign will have a great pleasure in living cleanly and chastely, and they will go through great labors.

    The man, it is shown, will have some infirmities until he is 30, promising the Sign that he will live, according to his nature, until he is 84 years old.

    The woman denotes a serious infirmity from her 30 years until she is 36, and it is promised, according to her nature, that she will live for 77 years.

Of the nature and effects of the Sign of Libra, which begins on the 23rd of September

This Sign is represented as two equal scales, signifying the equality of night and day when the Sun enters this Sign; and here is constituted and begins the second Equinox. It is a masculine Sign, diurnal and mobile, for entering the Sun in it the Summer wanes and Autumn begins. It is of a hot and humid and airy nature, and it imprints heat and crass humidity, for it is the reason for the condensation and thickening of the air in such a way that it is extremely harmful to all living things, and in such a way does it condense the air with vapors that are dense (when the Sun enters this Sign), cold and thick, that it causes great and contagious diseases. The Sun enters this Sign commonly on the 23rd of September, and until it leaves the day is diminished by one hour and a half; this Sign is the diurnal House of Venus, fall of the Sun, exaltation of Saturn and diurnal determent of Mars.

It has dominion over the Provinces of Austria, Crespelia, Bactria, Regio, Tucia and Syria. In the cities it has dominion over Palencia, Lodi, Parma, Ghent, Vienna, Augusta. In Hispania over Burgos, Almería and Salamanca. In Portugal over Almeida, Mirandela, Chaves; in the Azores the islands of Corvo, Flores and Graciosa.

The male who is born under the rise of this Sign will be honorable and venturous in that which he may embark on, and caring in the dealings with his friends. It denotes that he will be inclined to go to strange lands, where he will fare better than in his Motherland, and he will be a man of good understanding. Finally he will have enough for his sustenance, and will go through some drawbacks and labors.

If it is a female she will be joyful and very affable and will have some burns on her feet and will have a few infirmities. It denotes that she will be inclined to pilgrimages and to walk the World.

The male denotes some infirmity at the age of 6, another at the age of 18, and another at the age of 35, should he survive them, this Sign shows, according to his nature, that he will live for 77 years, and the woman for 66.

Of the quality and effects of the Sign of Scorpio, which begins on the 24th of October

    This Sign is represented by an animal called Scorpion, whose effects correspond to its name, which are to bite and sting; and as such, when the Sun enters this Sign it starts to sting and bring in the cold with storms, thunder and lightning.

    It is cold and humid, feminine, nocturnal and fixed, for in this time it is fixed in Autumn with its intemperance and bad influences. The Sun enters this Sign on the 24th of October and from this time until it leaves, the day is diminished in one hour; this Sign is the nocturnal House and joy of Mars, fall of the Moon, determent and sadness of Venus.

    It has dominion over the Provinces of Scotland, Syria, Mauritania, Gaetuli, Cappadocia, and Judea. In cities over Messina, Padua, Aquileia, Crema and Bugia. And in Hispania over Valencia, Xátiva, Segovia, Tudela, Braga, Málaga and Burgos. In Portugal over Évora, Beja, Faro, Tavira and Lagos.

    The male who is born under the rise of this Sign denotes that he will have bad habits, he will be deceitful, lustful and stubborn; unclear in his business and inclined to theft; and that he will be grave, affable and of good words, even if false, *sed sapiens dominubitur Astris*. It is denoted that he will suffer from pain in his genitals and stomach, he will be in danger from iron and finally he will be inclined to travel through different lands; and he will be so subtle and cunning in his sayings and deeds that no one will understand him and he will not be very wealthy nor very poor. It is also shown that he will have some infirmities, even if small; and that this Sign promises, according to its nature, 61 years of life.

    If it is a female, she will be friendly, strong and terrible, to which is denoted *habere cicatrices, maximum periculum vitea*, and she will live with infirmities. And this Sign promises, according to its nature, 72 years of life.

Of the quality and effects of the Sign of Sagittarius, which begins on the 23rd of November

This Sign is represented by a Centaur who is shooting arrows, which represents the effects caused by the Sun during the time it is joined with this Sign, which is to shoot rain, frost, thunder and lightning. It is of a fiery nature, hot and dry; it is masculine, diurnal and common to Autumn and Winter. The Sun enters this Sign commonly at the 23rd of November and from this time until it leaves the day is reduced by one hour. This Sign is the diurnal House of Jupiter and its pleasure, it is the diurnal determent of Mercury.

It has dominion over the Provinces of Hispania, Arabia Felix, Slavonia, Dalmatia, Etruria and part of Liguria. In the cities over Malta, Avignon, Jerusalem, Asti, Milan. And in Hispania over Jaén, Calahorra and Medinaceli.

The male who is born under the rising of this Sign will be self-conscious, affable, honest and venturous; he will be inclined to sail, which will cause him to own land, and he will suffer some damage from a four legged animal, and will have some infirmities. The first when he is 7 years old, the other when he is 18 and another when he is 28; he will live, according to his nature, for 67 years.

If it is a female it is denoted that she will be imaginative, fearful and self-conscious, and she will acquire wealth and will be a good administrator. Finally, in the same way as the man, the woman will be inconstant, fickle, even if merciful and of a good consciousness. It is denoted an infirmity when she is 4 years old, another at 22 and another at 30; she is promised, according to her nature, 57 years of life.

Of the nature and effects of the Sign of Capricorn, which begins on the 22nd of December

This Sign is represented by a goat, an animal which climbs trees and the greatest inclines it can find. As such the Sun, when it enters this Sign, is rising for us, for the days will begin to increase. It is of an earthly nature, cold and dry, and it is feminine, nocturnal and movable; for it leaves Autumn and enters Winter. The Sun enters this Sign commonly on the 22nd of December, and from the time it enters until it leaves the day increases by half an hour; this Sign is the nocturnal House of Saturn, exaltation of Mars, fall of Jupiter and determent of the Moon.

It has dominion over the provinces of Macedonia, Barbary, Portugal, Romandiola, Albania, Moscovy, Gedrosia, Thrace, Caria, India and part of Slavonia. In cities over Verona, Forli, Savoy, Turin, Faenza and Constantinople. And in Hispania over Tortosa, Soria and Carmona.

The male who is born under the rise of this Sign will be wrathful, vain and a liar. It is denoted that he will many times be talking to himself; he will be somewhat melancholic, spirited and inclined to war, *& guadebit bonis alienis*. And finally *habebit curam de animalibus quadrupedibus* and he will go through some tribulations *mulieris causa*.

He will live with infirmities, but it is promised, according to his nature, 77 years of life.

If it is a female, she will be of a perverse nature, and she may be lost if she does not take hold of her levity. It is denoted that she will be bitten by an animal of four legs and that she is in danger of falling from a high place; she will suffer some infirmities, but small however; and this Sign promises, according to her nature, 69 years of life.

Astronomical rule so as to know the Sign of the hour on which a person is born

To know each one's Sign it is no longer a necessity to make any Astrological calculations, one merely needs to know three things. The first is to know in which Sign was the Sun on the day one was born. The second, at which hour did the Sun rise on that day. The third, which one should know with great certainty, is the hour when one was born. Once these three things are known, you can count from the hour the Sun came out until the one in which the person was born, *exclusivé*, and for every two hours count a Sign, and start counting from the Sign the Sun was on that day, which is the natural one for each person. The above explanation can be understood and facilitated with 2 examples: the first is of a person who was born in Valencia on the 4th of the month of August at one in the afternoon in the year of 1587, even if the year does not need to be known. I say that the Sign of this person is Scorpio, for in Valencia at August 4th the Sun rises at 5 in the morning (as can be seen in the present Lunario in a Table above), and until one in the afternoon eight hours pass, which represent four Signs; for, counting from the Sign on which the Sun was on at that time, which was Leo, until the fourth Sign, *inclusivé*, I find Scorpio; and this is the Sign that dominates this person. In the second example a person was born in Italy on the 10th of October at eleven thirty in the afternoon; and according to the rule, I say that her Sign is Gemini, for the Sun on the 10th of October is in the Sign of Libra (as can be seen in the Calendar of this Repertoire) and the Sun on this day always rises at five thirty, which is an hour earlier than in Valencia; from five thirty in the morning to eleven thirty in the evening there are eighteen hours, which represent nine Signs, and the ninth Sign counting from Libra, in which was the Sun in that day, is Gemini, and this we say is the proper Sign of this person born in Italy. We should also warn that if, beyond the even number of hours one has an extra hour, one should count the next Sign; if the extra does not amount to a full hour then it should not be counted, for it does not interfere with this rule. If any curious asks me of what those Signs which the *Lunarios* and Repertoires talk about are worth, when they say that one who is born under the rising of this Sign is of such and such character, I respond that those characters are common and general to all who are born within that whole month of 30 days. And even if they cause many and great effects on those born on those days, this however is not the same as the Sign of the particular hour of birth, and as such one may judge much better and truly with the Sign of our present rule than by the other. But, the curious may still doubt by saying: For which reason do I take every two hours to be a Sign? To which I respond that the Sign in which I am giving the rule is the one on the Horizon at the time of birth, and that each Sign takes two hours to rise, and this is the cause why we take one Sign every two hours after the Sunrise, and should one be born in the morning before the Sun rises, one should make these calculations from the Sunrise of the previous day. The curious may also ask: how does one know the hour at which the Sun rises on each day in Italy and in other parts of Hispania and outside of it? To which I respond that after the Table of the full and the conjunctions of the Moon, there is a Table with many Towns and Cities, both in Hispania and outside of it, by which one may know the hour in which the Sun rises in all of them; with the further warning that in the Cities in which there is the indication of adding some time found there, one should subtract from the hour in which the Sun rises in Valencia; and in the cities in which it is said to remove the time shown there, one should add to the hour that in Valencia the Sun rises. One should note this rule.

Of the Eclipses of the Sun and the Moon

For the perfection of this perpetual Lunario it seemed to me proper to address something regarding Eclipses, with the brevity that this work requires.

I say that the Eclipse of the Sun isn't any other thing but the body of the Moon placing itself between us and the Sun, in such a way that it blocks our light and the rays of the Sun; and this happens in the conjunction of the Moon, however, we must advert that for a Solar eclipse two things must happens. The first is that the Sun and the Moon be in conjunction. The second is that both Planets are found on one of the two points which the Astronomers call *Caput & Cauda*

Draconis. And as such not every conjunction of the Sun and the Moon generate an Eclipse of the Sun, unless the Sun and the Moon are in one of the said two points, and according to this, by being farther and closer of the *Caput* or *Cauda Draconis*, will the eclipse of the Sun be smaller or greater.

The Eclipse of the Moon is not anything else than its deprivation of light caused by the shadow of the earth, which reaches the orb of the Moon and beyond. In such a way that, entering the body of the Moon into the shadow of the earth, it is deprived of its light (and this is the Eclipse) for this means that the Moon is diametrically opposed to the Sun, from which it receives light and clarity. And for an Eclipse of the Moon to happen two things have to occur. The first is that the Sun and the Moon are opposed. The second is that one of the Luminaries are in one of the above mentioned points of *Caput* or *Cauda Draconis* and the other of the Luminaries in the other point. And if any curious wishes to know what thing is the *Caput* or *Cauda Draconis*, I say that the Astronomers consider a 12 degree strip in the Sky to which they call the Zodiac, through which the Sun travels by its own movement; this path, through where the Sun moves, is called Ecliptic; and let us further say that the Moon, by its own movement, is never parted from the width of the strip of the Zodiac; however, it sometimes travels through the Ecliptic part, the path of the Sun, and other times by another part. For when the Moon passes from the North part to the South, or the Midday, it crosses the Ecliptic, or, saying it in a better way, crosses the path of the Sun, and this point, on which it crosses is called *Cauda Draconis*. And when the Moon crosses from the South part to the North part once again, or crosses the said Ecliptic, to that point they call *Caput Draconis*. The Lunar Orb moves three degrees and a little more on each day; and since we are talking of eclipses I offer here the practice to know in which sign this is to be found perpetually.

Explanation of the following table of the true place of the Head of the Dragon[63]

This table is divided into three columns: the first contains the number of the years, from 1 to 93, for these are the amount of years that the Head of the Dragon takes to complete its full revolution, and after 93 years it returns to the beginning with the difference of 1 degree and 15 minutes; in the second column one has the years from 1712 until 1804, and during these years one does not need to add anything to the table; in the third column one has the Signs, and these signs are numbered in the following way: Aries 0, Taurus 1, Gemini 2, Cancer 3, etc. This is marked on the top of the table as S, the degrees are marked as D and the minutes with M.

Should you want to know in which Sign and degree was the head of the Dragon in March of the year of 1712, one does not need to do anything else but search for this year in the table, and by its side we find 9 in the Sign, 22 degrees and one minute; the 9, taking Aries to be 0, corresponds to Capricorn, on which the Head of the Dragon can be found on the first day of March, at 22 degrees and one minute; and this is the same for every other year.

This is the calculation for the first day of March, but should you want to know the degrees of the 14th of March, you must go to the Days, always taking one less day than the one intended, which is 13, and the head of the Dragon will be in the Sign 11, 29 degrees and 19 minutes, which, summed up with the Sign 9, 22 degree and 1 minute, as can be seen in this small table, adds up to Sign 9, 21 degree and 20 minutes, and so I may say that this was the position of the head of the Dragon on the 14th of March; and in this way one may achieve this calculation for all days, keeping in mind the tables of months and days.

S	D	M
9	22	1
11	29	19
9	21	20

---

63. Translator's note: I only found the Table in question in the Barcelona 1836 and 1848 editions, being an exact copy in both of them. Still, even a superficial analysis reveals that this table is incomplete, starting in 1720 instead of the mentioned 1712. No attempt was made on my part to correct this error or any others that it may contain, and I present it here as it is presented in the originals.

Another example for the years

I wish to know on the first of March of 1820 in which Sign the Head of the Dragon is in. I find this year of 1820 by taking 1712, which is the year I start the counting of the first column of 93, and by counting forward I find the number 108, and to this I add one, as a general rule, which results in 109. To these I subtract the 93 and I obtain 16, which in the Table corresponds to the year of 1727, which is the one which corresponds to the year of 1820, and I see that here we have the Sign 0, 1 degree and 42 minutes, to which I still have to add one degree and 15, with which I obtain 0 Sign, 2 degrees and 57 minutes. And so I say that the Head of the Dragon on the 1st of March of the year of 1820 was in 2 degrees and 57 minutes of the Sign of Aries.

Table of the location of the Head of the Dragon

Table	Years	S	D	M	Table	Years	S	D	M
9	1720	4	27	16	35	1746	11	24	22
10	1721	3	27	52	36	1747	11	1	1
11	1722	3	8	32	37	1748	10	40	40
12	1723	2	19	13	38	1749	9	18	18
13	1724	1	29	55	39	1750	9	7	7
14	1725	1	9	31	40	1751	4	17	40
15	1726	0	21	12	41	1752	7	28	20
16	1727	0	1	42	42	1753	7	28	20
17	1728	11	12	13	43	1754	7	8	59
18	1729	10	13	10	44	1755	6	19	38
19	1730	10	3	50	45	1756	6	0	18
20	1731	9	14	31	46	1757	5	10	59
21	1732	8	25	11	47	1758	4	21	35
22	1733	8	5	47	48	1759	4	2	16
23	1734	7	16	26	49	1760	3	12	56
24	1735	6	27	7	50	1761	2	4	13
25	1736	6	7	47	51	1762	1	14	53
26	1737	5	18	27	52	1763	0	25	34
27	1738	4	29	6	53	1764	0	6	14
28	1739	4	9	27	54	1765	11	16	52
29	1740	3	20	27	55	1766	10	27	31
30	1741	3	1	5	56	1767	10	8	11
31	1742	2	11	45	57	1768	10	10	52
32	1743	1	22	25	58	1769	9	29	30
33	1744	1	5	1	59	1770	8	10	19
34	1745	0	13	36	60	1771	8	20	51

Table	Years	S	G	L	Day	Months	S	G	L
61	1772	7	1	31		March	11	28	22
62	1773	6	12	7		April	11	26	46
63	1774	5	22	48		May	11	25	6
64	1775	5	3	48		June	11	23	31
65	1776	4	15	9	Day	July	11	21	54
66	1777	3	24	46		August	11	20	15
67	1778	3	5	26		September	11	18	40
68	1779	2	16	6		October	11	17	1
69	1780	1	26	46		November	11	15	16
70	1781	1	7	24		December	11	13	48
71	1782	0	18	3		January		Day	
72	1783	11	28	45	1	February			
73	1784	11	9	25	2	S D M	16	S D M	
74	1785	10	20	2	3	11 29 27	17	11 29 9	
75	1786	10	0	42	4	11 29 45	18	11 29 6	
76	1787	9	11	22	5	11 29 50	19	11 29 2	
77	1788	8	22	3	6	11 29 47	20	11 29 0	
78	1789	8	24	0	7	11 29 44	21	11 28 56	
79	1790	7	13	20	8	11 29 41	22	11 28 53	
80	1791	6	24	0	9	11 29 38	23	11 28 50	
81	1792	6	4	41	10	11 29 34	24	11 28 57	
82	1793	5	16	17	11	11 29 31	25	11 28 44	
83	1794	4	25	58	12	11 29 28	26	11 28 40	
84	1795	4	6	48	13	11 29 25	27	11 28 43	
85	1796	3	17	17	14	11 29 22	28	11 28 37	
86	1797	2	27	53	15	11 29 10	29	11 28 24	

Of how one may know the effects that an Eclipse usually causes

By the Sign, or House, in which any of the eclipse Luminaries is to be found, may anyone know (without being an Astronomer) the effects that a certain Eclipse causes. In such a way that if an Eclipse Luminary is found in one of the twelve Signs, or houses of the Planet Mars, we say, with Ptolemy, Book 2 Chapter 7, that the effects of that Eclipse will be Martial, which can be read in the chapter of the Planet Mars above. And if the eclipse Luminary is found in any of the other Signs, or Houses of the other Planets, one should seek the effects on the Chapter of the Planets, whose Sign, or House, is the Eclipse Luminary on. We advert that the 12 Signs are called Planetary Houses, as is said and declared in this Lunario in the chapter on the Signs.

Of the time on which the effects of the Eclipses begin

Once the hour of the Eclipse is known, and the hours that artificial day will have, one may know the time on which its effects start. And so as this may be better understood, let us suppose that the Sun will be eclipsed two hours after it has risen above the Horizon, and that the day had twelve hours; I say that the effect of such an Eclipse will start in two months, which are the sixth part of the year, for those two hours are the sixth part of the day of twelve hours, which we suppose are the hours of the artificial day. And if the day had ten hours, the effects would be felt two months and twelve days after, for those two hours are the fifth part of ten hours which we said this day had; thus the fifth part of the year is the said two months and twelve days. And if the day had fourteen hours, the effects would take a seventh part of the year to manifest, which is one month and twenty days; for those two hours are the seventh part of the fourteen hours we said the day had; and with this order and proportion will other Eclipses be understood in the other larger or smaller days of the year; and the same that was said about the Eclipse of the Sun can be said of the Eclipse of the Moon.

Of the time that the effects of the Eclipses last

If the eclipse Luminary lasts one hour in its Eclipse, and if it is a Solar one, its effects will last one year. And if it is a Moon eclipse, its effects will last merely one month. And if the Solar Eclipse lasts two hours, its effects will last two years, and the Moon two months; and thus proportionately for all other Eclipses.

On how one may know in which part of the World the effects of an Eclipse will be executed

By knowing in which Sign is the eclipse Luminary, one will know in which part of the world the effects of an Eclipse will be executed. For in the lands, provinces and cities that are subjected to a given Sign will the effects be executed. The lands, provinces and cities that are subjected to the twelve Signs are found before the calendar of those Signs, where one may see which lands or provinces they dominate in general and in particular. One will easily know in which Sign the Luminary is by the Tables of the particular conjunctions. We advert that the Solar Eclipse always happens on the conjunction of the Moon and the Moon Eclipse on the full Moon; and in front of every full Moon or conjunction one may find the corresponding Sign.

Natural Prognostication of the Weather

taken by the Comets of Aristotle, Pliny, Ptolemy

Of the Comets, their nature and general effects

Comets aren't anything else than (according to the Philosophers) great amounts of hot and dry exhalations attracted by the earth from up high by virtue and natural force of the Sun and the remaining Stars; and taking these exhalations to the supreme region of the air, where, for being so close to the sphere of fire, by the natural ventilation of the air, inflame themselves and according to their density these may last for a greater or smaller amount of time without falling apart. These Comets and signals (according to the affirmation of all Philosophers and also by experience) are always, or for the most part, omens of misfortune, such as wars, dependences, famines, shortages and plagues, as well as the death of Princes and great Lords.

One should note that by the shape and dispositions of the Comets, and the colors that they display, one may know their influences, effects and qualities. The same may be applied to the Eclipses regarding color.

If the Comet or Eclipse has a slightly black color, tending to the green, it is of the nature of Saturn and it denotes death, pestilence, great cold, ice, snow and darkness of the air, storms, earthquakes and deluges with hunger and lack of supplies.

If the Comet has a white color, slightly towards saffron, it is of the nature of Jupiter, and it denotes the death of a King or powerful man. The shape of this Comet is large and round, resembling a human face.

If the Comet has a bright red color and a long tail, it is of the nature of Mars. And if it appears in the Oriental region with its head low and its tail high, it denotes for the Occidental region great hungers, wars, earthquakes, shortage of water and the destruction of Cities and Kingdoms.

If the Comet appears to be very white and horrible in its aspect, and close to the Sun, it will be of its nature; it denotes changes in States, meager harvest of fruit, death of Kings and rich and powerful men.

If the Comet appears with a golden color it will be of the nature of Venus, and if its aspect is similar to the Moon, with a great mane, leaving behind it some rays, it denotes damage to powerful men and new cults, namely to the regions where the tail is pointing to.

If it appears with several colors, or of a bluish color, with a small body and long tail, it is of the nature of Mercury; it denotes the death of a Prince, riots, famines, wars, poverty, great lightning and thunder.

If it appears with a bright silvery color and is so resplendent that it exceeds the clarity of the other Stars, it is of the nature of the Moon, and it signifies abundance in supplies, especially if Jupiter is in the sign of Cancer or Pisces. And one should note that if the Comet appears in the Oriental region, its effects will be felt very shortly in the lands that are subjected to the Sign in which it appears. And if the Comet appears in the Occidental part, its effects will be greatly delayed.

Of the Canicular days,[64] when they begin and end

I understand that many wish to know the cause of the Canicular days and when they begin and end, and as such I will declare these three things with brevity. In the eighth Sphere there are two Constellations which are of the nature of Mars, and they are called *Canis Minor* and *Canis Major*. *Canis Minor*, it is said, according to Ptolemy, consists of two stars, which are of the nature of Mercury and Mars. Some learned men affirm that this *Canis Minor* is the cause of the Canicular days (as says Pliny, Book 18, Chapter 28, and El-Rei King Alfonso in the *Tabulis Astronomicis*, whose opinion we wish to follow, for it seems to me to be more according to reason and experience) which normally rises with the Sun on the Orient of Valencia around the time this Planet enters the first degree of the Sign of Leo, which is at the 24th of July. And thus the Canicular days begin in the Kingdom of Valencia at the 24th of July and end on the 2nd of September. The common opinion among Astrologers and experienced Medics is that the Caniculars last for 40 days, which is the time the Sun detains itself from its rise with the Canicular until it passes through the whole figure of the Sign of Leo. This duration of time, and Canicular days, are strong and dangerous, and during this time Hippocrates says, and also advised Medics, that one should not offer any medicine to any sick person. During this time, Pliny says in his *Natural History*, Book 2, that wine changes and goes sour; and that the dogs become sick with rabies due to the heat and dryness that the Sun, Sign and the Canicular imprint on this period; and as such I advise and plead that during the Canicular one has the care, more than in any other time, to provide water for the dogs, so as they may temperate their natural heat, which is excessive during this time; and this should be done so as to prevent the great damage and injury they may cause with rabies, and may God free us from it. Amen.

Table of the beginning of the Caniculars in Cities and Several Places

Cities and Towns of Hispania and India	The days and months	Cities and Towns of Hispania and India	The days and months
Valencia	24th of July	Villena	23rd of July
Majorca	24th of July	Alicante	23rd of July
Origuela	22nd of July	Seville	23rd of July
Minorca	24th of July	Lisbon	24th of July
Cordoba	23rd of July	Calatrava	24th of July
Cartagena	23rd of July	Alcántara	24th of July
Murcia	22nd of July	Barcelona	25th of July
Granada	22nd of July	Toledo	25th of July
Malaga	22nd of July	Madrid	25th of July
Úbeda	23rd of July	Cuenca	25th of July
Goa	10th of July	Ceylon	5th of July
Onot	9th of July	Malacca	26th of July
Barcelona	9th of July	China	15th of July
Mangalore	8th of July	Chaul	13th of July
Kannur	8th of July	Diu	14th of July
Kochi	7th of July	Mombasa	26th of July
Kollam	6th of July	Mozambique	16th of July

---

64. Translator's note: Dog days.

Prediction from one year to the next by the day in which the Canicular begins

Diophanes[65] writes that if on the day the Canicular start the Moon is in the Sign of Aries, it denotes that the next year there will be a great amount of water and little wheat, with an abundance of olive oil and a great mortality of cattle.

If it is in the Sign of Taurus, there will be no shortage of labors, miseries and rain and frost, with little production of bread.

If it is in the Sign of Gemini, there will be plenty of bread and wine, with abundance of fruit; however there will be great illnesses.

If it is in the Sign of Cancer, there will be lack of water and greater lack of wheat.

If it is in the Sign of Leo, wheat, wine and olive oil will be abundant; there will be a good price in other fruits; there will be an earthquake, flooding and storms at sea.

If it is in the Sign of Virgo it denotes a fertile year, given that there shall be plenty of movement in pregnant women, plenty of water and cattle will not be worth much.

If it is in the Sign of Libra there will be very little olive oil, a great deal of wine and little wheat; there will be plenty of almonds, nuts, pine nuts as well as hazels and chestnuts.

If it is in the Sign of Scorpio there will be mortality of bees and other critters, there will be terrible airs and little silk.

If it is in the Sign of Sagittarius there will be no shortage of water, wheat and birds; there will be little cattle however.

If it is in the Sign of Capricorn there will be an abundance of water, but many grasshoppers and danger of some contagion.

If it is in Aquarius there will be a lack of wheat and water, however there will be plenty of locusts and some contagious danger.

If it is in the Sign of Pisces, it denotes rain, plenty of wheat and wine, even if there will be a lack of birds but no lack of infirmities. And this should be thought from one year to the next, as is the will of God our Lord.

How one will understand the Perpetual Lunario that follows and, by this same Lunario, how one will understand the previous prognostications

The Perpetual Lunario that is to follow is ruled by the Golden number and by knowing what the Golden number is in the year one is in; we shall find this same number on the top of the columns of the Lunario below, from which we will find the new, full, crescent and waning quarters of the Moon, days, hours and degrees of the Signs and time; we advert that the first column of each page has the months of the year, the second column the names of the aspects assigned to the new Moon, the crescent quarter, the full Moon and the waning quarter. The third column is of the days of the month in which we have a new, quarter and full Moon. The fourth column is the limited hours of these aspects. The fifth column is the degrees of the said aspect. The sixth column is the Sign of which these degrees belong to, on which we have that aspect. The seventh gives the significance of the weather indicated by that quarter. And after we have found the new Moon we wish to know of, and also knowing the day and hour, we shall see the degrees and corresponding Sign. This Sign and degrees we will read in the previous prognostication, and in it we will find the weather which comes next. And this same diligence we will perform in the crescent quarter, full and waning quarter of each Moon. The Reader should note that, not rarely, there will be a square with five rules for the four crescent, full, waning and new Moon; as many times happens that a month may have two new Moons or two full Moons, which then require five numbers. And thus, one should also note that the Golden number cannot go above nineteen, and arriving at eighteen it turns once again to one and thus does this living wheel run perpetually. By this reason, supposing that in this Lunario there is no mention of any years from 1651 to 1669, one should once again begin in the years nominated to 1670 and thus forth until reaching the end of the Lunario, and once again returning to the beginning and running the living wheel perpetually,

---

65. Translator's note: Diophanes of Nicaea, a first century agricultural writer.

keeping all prognostications in the same order that in the previous Chapter we have mentioned. And even if in some months the full Moon might arrive first than the new Moons, this should not be seen as a mistake, but rather, this is a necessity; for when the Moon is new, from the 17th of a month forward, it is not possible to have a full Moon in that same month, for between the new and the full there is a fifteen day interval, or at least fourteen and a half; for this reason the Moon, which is new on the above mentioned time, will be full in the beginning of the next month. And thus one should also be warned that this Lunario makes mention of 1651 in its beginning, this is for the reason that in that year there is a Golden number of one, and as in 1614 there is a Golden number of nineteen we govern ourselves by the last number of the Lunario. And if we wish to know the Moons of the year of 1613, we govern ourselves by these pages, going backwards in the order of the Golden number, and we can learn the Moons of any other past year, by keeping the same rule as going into the future.

We further advert that the prognostications that are to follow regarding the times of the new, full, crescent and waning Moons should not be understood as if they are the precise hour and minute of the conjunction, opposition or quarter that will trigger that weather; but rather that most of the quarter to follow will have the weather according to the prognostication.

Year in which the Golden number is 18							
Month	*Aspect*	*Day*	*Hour*	*Degree*	*Signs*	*Weather*
January	Full	6	6	17	Cancer	Abundance of water
	Wan.Quar.	13	12	23	Libra	Revolted weather
	New	20	8	2	Aquarius	Clouded Sun
	Cres.Quar.	28	11	8	Taurus	Thunder or winds
February	Full	4	18	17	Leo	Good weather
	Wan.Quar.	11	3	22	Scorpio	Humid weather
	New	19	2	1	Aries	Water or clouds
	Cres.Quar.	27	5	8	Cancer	Heavy weather
March	Full	6	5	15	Virgo	Cold and wet
	Wan.Quar.	13	20	21	Sagittarius	Variable weather
	New	20	19	7	Aries	Variable weather
	Cres.Quar.	2	21	7	Cancer	Variable weather
April	Full	4	13	14	Libra	Variable weather
	Wan.Quar.	11	10	20	Capricorn	Bad weather
	New	19	12	29	Taurus	Water, cold and windy
	Cres.Quar.	27	8	5	Leo	Intense Sun
May	Full	2	11	14	Scorpio	Wind or thunder
	Wan.Quar.	11	1	20	Aquarius	Harsh weather
	New	19	4	29	Taurus	Water, cold and windy
	Cres.Quar.	26	17	5	Virgo	Cloudy weather
June	Full	2	6	12	Sagittarius	Calmness
	Wan.Quar.	9	17	19	Pisces	Good weather
	New	17	17	27	Gemini	Gloomy weather
	Cres.Quar.	24	20	3	Libra	Good weather
July	Full	1	15	10	Capricorn	Cool weather
	Wan.Quar.	9	10	17	Aries	Calmness
	New	16	4	25	Cancer	Cool weather
	Cres.Quar.	24	1	1	Scorpio	Cool weather
	Full	31	3	8	Aquarius	Little water
August	Wan.Quar.	8	3	16	Taurus	Harsh weather
	New	15	14	23	Leo	Calmness
	Cres.Quar.	22	6	29	Scorpio	Harsh weather
	Full	29	16	7	Pisces	Cool weather
September	Wan.Quar.	6	20	14	Gemini	Good weather
	New	13	23	21	Virgo	Harsh weather
	Cres.Quar.	20	14	27	Sagittarius	Change in weather
	Full	28	8	5	Aries	Good weather
October	Wan.Quar.	6	13	13	Cancer	Some water
	New	13	8	19	Libra	Changing weather
	Cres.Quar.	20	1	27	Capricorn	Windy weather
	Full	28	2	5	Taurus	Cool weather
November	Wan.Quar.	5	2	13	Leo	Quite weather
	New	11	17	19	Sagittarius	Water and wind
	Cres.Quar.	18	16	26	Aquarius	Calmness
	Full	26	20	6	Gemini	Snow and humid
December	Wan.Quar.	4	13	12	Virgo	Humidity
	New	18	3	20	Sagittarius	Good weather
	Cres.Quar.	11	11	26	Pisces	Water with wind
	Full	26	14	6	Cancer	Abundance of water

Year in which the Golden number is 19					
Month	Aspect	Day	Hour	Degree	Signs	Weather
January	Wan.Quar.	2	22	12	Libra	Revolted weather
	New	9	5	25	Capricorn	Wind or thunder
	Cres.Quar.	17	7	27	Aries	Revolted weather
	Full	25	5	6	Leo	Good weather
February	Wan.Quar.	1	5	12	Scorpio	Humid weather
	New	8	5	21	Aquarius	Clouded Sun
	Cres.Quar.	16	4	17	Taurus	Thunder or wind
	Full	23	19	6	Virgo	Cold and wet
March	Wan.Quar.	2	12	11	Sagittarius	Variable weather
	New	9	20	20	Pisces	Water of mist
	Cres.Quar.	17	1	27	Gemini	Loaded weather
	Full	24	5	5	Libra	Variable weather
	Wan.Quar.	31	2	11	Capricorn	Changing weather
April	New	8	13	20	Aries	Variable weather
	Cres.Quar.	16	17	26	Cancer	Variable weather
	Full	23	14	3	Scorpio	Wind or Thunder
	Wan.Quar.	30	6	6	Aquarius	Intense Sun
May	New	8	5	18	Taurus	Water, cold and wind
	Cres.Quar.	16	6	25	Leo	Intense Sun
	Full	22	22	2	Sagittarius	Calmness
	Wan.Quar.	29	18	8	Pisces	Good weather
June	New	6	21	16	Gemini	Gloomy weather
	Cres.Quar.	14	16	23	Virgo	Clouded weather
	Full	21	5	30	Sagittarius	Calmness
	Wan.Quar.	28	8	6	Aries	Calmness
July	New	6	11	14	Cancer	Cool weather
	Cres.Quar.	13	23	21	Libra	Good weather
	Full	20	13	28	Capricorn	Cold weather
	Wan.Quar.	28	1	5	Taurus	Harsh weather
August	New	5	1	13	Leo	Calmness
	Cres.Quar.	12	4	19	Scorpio	Cold weather
	Full	19	23	26	Aquarius	Water or clouds
	Wan.Quar.	26	14	3	Gemini	Good weather
September	New	3	12	11	Virgo	Harsh weather
	Cres.Quar.	10	9	17	Sagittarius	Change in weather
	Full	17	11	25	Pisces	Harsh weather
	Wan.Quar.	25	12	2	Cancer	Some water
October	New	2	23	19	Libra	Changing weather
	Cres.Quar.	10	2	17	Capricorn	Variable weather
	Full	17	22	24	Aries	Good weather
	Wan.Quar.	25	7	2	Leo	Quiet weather
November	New	1	20	9	Scorpio	Water with wind
	Cres.Quar.	8	1	16	Aquarius	Calmness
	Full	15	20	24	Taurus	Cold weather
	Wan.Quar.	23	1	2	Virgo	Humid
	New	30	19	9	Sagittarius	Good weather
December	Cres.Quar.	7	13	15	Pisces	Water with wind
	Full	15	15	25	Gemini	Snow and humid
	Wan.Quar.	23	14	1	Libra	Revolted weather
	New	30	6	9	Capricorn	Wind or thunder

Year in which the Golden number is 1					
Month	Aspect	Day	Hour	Degree	Signs	Weather
January	Cres.Quar. Full Wan.Quar. New	6 14 22 18	5 12 1 23	15 24 2 8	Aries Cancer Scorpio Aquarius	Revolted weather Abundance of water Humid weather Sun behind clouds
February	Cres.Quar. Full Wan.Quar. New	5 13 20 27	1 1 10 15	16 18 1 17	Taurus Leo Sagittarius Pisces	Thunder or wind Good weather Variable weather Water or clouds
March	Cres.Quar. Full Wan.Quar. New	6 13 21 28	20 18 18 6	16 18 1 6	Gemini Virgo Capricorn Aries	Good weather Humid Changing weather Variable weather
April	Cres.Quar. Full Wan.Quar. New	5 12 19 26	6 7 23 23	5 17 29 6	Cancer Libra Capricorn Taurus	Variable weather Variable weather Windy weather Water, cold and wind
May	Cres.Quar. Full Wan.Quar. New	5 11 19 26	10 15 6 14	14 16 27 5	Leo Scorpio Aquarius Gemini	Intense Sun Wind or thunder Harsh weather Calmness
June	Cres.Quar. Full Wan.Quar. New	2 9 17 25	1 23 14 5	13 19 26 4	Virgo Sagittarius Pisces Cancer	Harsh weather Calmness Good weather Cool weather
July	Cres.Quar. Full Wan.Quar. New	3 9 17 24	15 8 2 17	11 15 24 2	Libra Capricorn Aries Leo	Good weather Cool weather Calmness Calmness
August	Cres.Quar. Full Wan.Quar. New Cres.Quar.	2 8 15 23 29	23 23 16 6 6	9 17 23 1 7	Scorpio Aquarius Taurus Virgo Sagittarius	Cool weather Little water Harsh weather Harsh weather Changing weather
September	Full Wan.Quar. New Cres.Quar.	6 13 20 28	5 12 16 1	12 21 30 5	Pisces Gemini Virgo Capricorn	Cool weather Good weather Changing weather Variable weather
October	Full Wan.Quar. New Cres.Quar.	5 13 19 28	20 4 9 17	13 20 9 5	Aries Cancer Libra Aquarius	Good weather Some water Changing weather Calmness
November	Full Wan.Quar. New Cres.Quar.	4 12 19 27	14 1 12 4	15 20 27 4	Taurus Leo Scorpio Pisces	Cool weather Quiet weather Water with wind Water with wind
December	Full Wan.Quar. New Cres.Quar.	4 12 19 26	9 19 23 24	12 20 25 4	Gemini Virgo Sagittarius Aries	Snow and humid Humidity Good weather Revolted weather

Year in which the Golden number is 2						
Month	*Aspect*	*Day*	*Hour*	*Degree*	*Signs*	*Weather*
January	Full	3	9	14	Cancer	*Abundance of water*
	Wan.Quar.	11	12	20	Libra	*Revolted weather*
	New	18	8	28	Capricorn	*Wind or thunder*
	Cres.Quar.	25	2	4	Taurus	*Revolted weather*
February	Full	2	4	1	Leo	*Good weather*
	Wan.Quar.	10	3	21	Scorpio	*Humid weather*
	New	16	18	28	Aquarius	*Sun behind clouds*
	Cres.Quar.	23	18	4	Gemini	*Loaded with change*
March	Full	2	23	14	Virgo	*Cold and wet*
	Wan.Quar.	10	13	20	Sagittarius	*Variable weather*
	New	17	4	28	Pisces	*Water or mist*
	Cres.Quar.	24	13	4	Cancer	*Variable weather*
April	Full	1	15	13	Libra	*Variable weather*
	Wan.Quar.	8	21	19	Capricorn	*Changing weather*
	New	15	15	27	Aries	*Heavy weather*
	Cres.Quar.	23	7	3	Leo	*Intense Sun*
May	Full	1	4	12	Scorpio	*Wind or thunder*
	Wan.Quar.	8	2	17	Aquarius	*Harsh weather*
	New	15	2	25	Taurus	*Water with wind*
	Cres.Quar.	23	1	2	Sagittarius	*Cloudy weather*
	Full	30	14	9	Virgo	*Calmness*
June	Wan.Quar.	6	7	5	Pisces	*Good weather*
	New	15	15	23	Gemini	*Gloomy weather*
	Cres.Quar.	23	18	1	Libra	*Revolted weather*
	Full	30	27	8	Capricorn	*Cool weather*
July	Wan.Quar.	5	13	13	Aries	*Calmness*
	New	13	15	15	Cancer	*Cool weather*
	Cres.Quar.	20	8	28	Libra	*Good weather*
	Full	27	6	5	Aquarius	*Little water*
August	Wan.Quar.	4	22	12	Taurus	*Harsh weather*
	New	11	20	20	Leo	*Calmness*
	Cres.Quar.	19	21	27	Scorpio	*Humidity*
	Full	25	14	3	Pisces	*Cool weather*
September	Wan.Quar.	2	10	10	Gemini	*Good weather*
	New	10	19	19	Virgo	*Harsh weather*
	Cres.Quar.	17	8	25	Sagittarius	*Change in weather*
	Full	24	22	3	Pisces	*Good weather*
	Wan.Quar.	30	2	0	Cancer	*Some water*
October	New	10	5	8	Libra	*Changing weather*
	Cres.Quar.	17	16	25	Capricorn	*Windy weather*
	Full	24	8	2	Taurus	*Cool weather*
	Wan.Quar.	31	20	9	Leo	*Quiet weather*
November	New	8	10	17	Scorpio	*Water with wind*
	Cres.Quar.	15	23	24	Aquarius	*Cloudy weather*
	Full	22	20	2	Gemini	*Snow and humid*
	Wan.Quar.	30	17	9	Virgo	*Humidity*
December	New	8	10	17	Sagittarius	*Good weather*
	Cres.Quar.	15	7	23	Pisces	*Water with wind*
	Full	22	11	3	Cancer	*Abundance of water*
	Wan.Quar.	29	13	9	Libra	*Revolted weather*

Year in which the Golden number is 3					
Month	Aspect	Day	Hour	Degree	Signs	Weather
January	New	6	23	18	Capricorn	Wind of thunder
	Cres.Quar.	13	7	24	Aries	Revolted weather
	Full	22	4	3	Leo	Good weather
	Wan.Quar.	29	19	14	Scorpio	Humid weather
February	New	5	10	19	Aquarius	Sun behind clouds
	Cres.Quar.	2	1	23	Taurus	Thunder or wind
	Full	19	23	3	Virgo	Cool weather
	Wan.Quar.	28	1	9	Sagittarius	Variable weather
March	New	6	20	17	Pisces	Water or mist
	Cres.Quar.	13	15	23	Gemini	Loaded weather
	Full	21	17	2	Libra	Variable weather
	Wan.Quar.	30	14	16	Capricorn	Changing weather
April	New	5	5	22	Aries	Variable weather
	Cres.Quar.	13	12	1	Cancer	Variable weather
	Full	20	20	5	Scorpio	Wind or thunder
	Wan.Quar.	28	28	7	Pisces	Harsh weather
May	New	4	4	14	Taurus	Water, cold and wind
	Cres.Quar.	11	11	21	Leo	Intense Sun
	Full	20	20	29	Scorpio	Wind or thunder
	Wan.Quar.	28	27	9	Pisces	Good weather
June	New	2	2	15	Gemini	Gloomy weather
	Cres.Quar.	10	10	20	Virgo	Cloudy weather
	Full	18	18	27	Sagittarius	Calmness
	Wan.Quar.	25	13	3	Aries	Calmness
July	New	2	10	10	Cancer	Cool weather
	Cres.Quar.	10	6	18	Libra	Good weather
	Full	17	22	26	Aquarius	Cool weather
	Wan.Quar.	24	14	1	Taurus	Harsh weather
	New	31	2	9	Leo	Calmness
August	Cres.Quar.	9	1	10	Scorpio	Cold weather
	Full	16	6	23	Aquarius	Little water
	Wan.Quar.	22	21	29	Taurus	Harsh weather
	New	30	13	8	Virgo	Harsh weather
September	Cres.Quar.	7	17	15	Sagittarius	Changing in weather
	Full	14	15	22	Pisces	Harsh weather
	Wan.Quar.	21	7	28	Gemini	Good weather
	New	29	5	6	Libra	Changing weather
October	Cres.Quar.	5	7	14	Capricorn	Variable weather
	Full	13	23	21	Aries	Good weather
	Wan.Quar.	21	20	27	Cancer	Some water
	New	29	23	6	Scorpio	Water with wind
November	Cres.Quar.	5	18	13	Aquarius	Calmness
	Full	12	9	20	Taurus	Cool weather
	Wan.Quar.	20	13	27	Virgo	Humidity
	New	28	17	7	Sagittarius	Good weather
December	Cres.Quar.	5	4	13	Pisces	Water with wind
	Full	12	20	22	Gemini	Snow and humid
	Wan.Quar.	19	9	27	Virgo	Cold with change
	New	26	9	6	Capricorn	Wind or thunder

Year in which the Golden number is 4					
Month	Aspect	Day	Hour	Degree	Signs	Weather
January	Cres.Quar.	3	11	13	Aries	Revolted weather
	Full	10	12	21	Cancer	Abundance of water
	Wan.Quar.	18	6	28	Libra	Revolted weather
	New	25	3	7	Aquarius	Sun behind clouds
February	Cres.Quar.	1	19	12	Taurus	Thunder or wind
	Full	9	17	21	Leo	Good weather
	Wan.Quar.	17	2	28	Sagittarius	Humid weather
	New	24	3	6	Pisces	Water or mist
March	Cres.Quar.	3	3	12	Gemini	Loaded with change
	Full	11	1	21	Virgo	Cool with change
	Wan.Quar.	18	11	28	Sagittarius	Variable weather
	New	26	22	6	Aries	Variable weather
April	Cres.Quar.	2	13	1	Cancer	Variable weather
	Full	10	3	21	Libra	Variable weather
	Wan.Quar.	17	13	27	Capricorn	Changing weather
	New	25	7	4	Taurus	Water, cold and wind
May	Cres.Quar.	2	1	10	Leo	Intense Sun
	Full	10	7	19	Scorpio	Wind or thunder
	Wan.Quar.	17	1	25	Aquarius	Harsh weather
	New	25	16	3	Gemini	Gloomy weather
	Cres.Quar.	31	15	8	Virgo	Cloudy weather
June	Full	8	5	17	Sagittarius	Calmness
	Wan.Quar.	15	7	24	Pisces	Good weather
	New	22	3	1	Cancer	Cool weather
	Cres.Quar.	29	7	8	Libra	Good weather
July	Full	7	14	15	Capricorn	Cool weather
	Wan.Quar.	14	3	21	Aries	Calmness
	New	21	9	29	Cancer	Cold and changeable
	Cres.Quar.	28	23	5	Scorpio	Cool weather
August	Full	5	23	12	Aquarius	Little water
	Wan.Quar.	12	17	19	Taurus	Harsh water
	New	20	6	28	Leo	Calmness
	Cres.Quar.	27	17	4	Scorpio	Change in weather
September	Full	4	6	22	Pisces	Cool weather
	Wan.Quar.	11	22	18	Gemini	Good weather
	New	18	22	26	Virgo	Harsh weather
	Cres.Quar.	26	11	3	Capricorn	Variable weather
October	Full	3	5	10	Aries	Good weather
	Wan.Quar.	10	6	16	Cancer	Some water
	New	18	6	25	Libra	Cold with change
	Cres.Quar.	26	11	3	Aquarius	Calmness
November	Full	3	14	10	Taurus	Cool weather
	Wan.Quar.	9	18	16	Leo	Quiet weather
	New	17	9	25	Scorpio	Water with wind
	Cres.Quar.	24	18	2	Pisces	Water with wind
December	Full	2	2	9	Gemini	Snow and humid
	Wan.Quar.	9	9	16	Virgo	Humidity
	New	17	12	25	Sagittarius	Good weather
	Cres.Quar.	24	7	2	Aries	Revolted weather
	Full	31	12	10	Cancer	Abundance of water

Year in which the Golden number is 5					
Month	Aspect	Day	Hour	Degree	Signs	Weather
January	Wan.Quar.	7	3	16	Libra	Revolted weather
	New	15	17	26	Capricorn	Wind or thunder
	Cres.Quar.	22	16	2	Aries	Thunder or wind
	Full	29	11	10	Leo	Cold with change
February	Wan.Quar.	5	23	16	Scorpio	Humid weather
	New	14	5	26	Aquarius	Sun behind clouds
	Cres.Quar.	21	10	2	Gemini	Loaded with change
	Full	28	11	10	Virgo	Cold with change
March	Wan.Quar.	7	19	17	Sagittarius	Variable weather
	New	14	15	25	Pisces	Water or mist
	Cres.Quar.	22	6	1	Cancer	Variable weather
	Full	29	4	9	Libra	Variable weather
April	Wan.Quar.	6	14	16	Capricorn	Changing weather
	New	13	13	24	Aries	Variable weather
	Cres.Quar.	20	13	26	Cancer	Variable weather
	Full	27	20	8	Scorpio	Wind or thunder
May	Wan.Quar.	5	7	15	Aquarius	Harsh weather
	New	12	7	22	Taurus	Water, cold and wind
	Cres.Quar.	19	22	28	Leo	Intense Sun
	Full	27	14	7	Sagittarius	Calmness
June	Wan.Quar.	4	10	13	Pisces	Good weather
	New	11	14	20	Gemini	Gloomy weather
	Cres.Quar.	18	9	29	Virgo	Cloudy weather
	Full	26	1	8	Capricorn	Cool weather
July	Wan.Quar.	4	7	11	Aries	Calmness
	New	10	23	28	Cancer	Cool weather
	Cres.Quar.	17	22	24	Libra	Good weather
	Full	25	25	3	Aquarius	Little water
August	Wan.Quar.	2	15	10	Taurus	Harsh weather
	New	9	5	16	Leo	Calmness
	Cres.Quar.	16	14	23	Scorpio	Cool weather
	Full	24	13	1	Pisces	Good weather
	Wan.Quar.	31	21	8	Gemini	Cool weather
September	New	7	15	21	Virgo	Harsh weather
	Cres.Quar.	15	8	18	Sagittarius	Change in weather
	Full	22	7	26	Pisces	Cool weather
	Wan.Quar.	30	2	3	Cancer	Some water
October	New	7	3	14	Libra	Changing weather
	Cres.Quar.	15	3	21	Capricorn	Revolted weather
	Full	22	16	29	Aries	Good weather
	Wan.Quar.	29	8	5	Leo	Quite weather
November	New	5	18	13	Scorpio	Water with wind
	Cres.Quar.	12	21	21	Aquarius	Calmness
	Full	21	3	28	Taurus	Cool water
	Wan.Quar.	28	6	5	Virgo	Humidity
December	New	5	5	14	Sagittarius	Good weather
	Cres.Quar.	12	16	21	Pisces	Water with wind
	Full	20	13	28	Gemini	Cold and humid
	Wan.Quar.	27	6	5	Libra	Revolted weather

Year in which the Golden number is 6					
Month	Aspect	Day	Hour	Degree	Signs	Weather
January	New	4	7	13	Capricorn	Wind or thunder
	Cres.Quar.	12	7	21	Aries	Revolted weather
	Full	18	22	28	Cancer	Abundance of water
	Wan.Quar.	26	22	5	Scorpio	Humid weather
February	New	3	2	4	Aquarius	Sun behind clouds
	Cres.Quar.	10	19	21	Taurus	Thunder or wind
	Full	17	10	28	Leo	Good weather
	Wan.Quar.	24	16	5	Sagittarius	Variable weather
March	New	4	5	15	Pisces	Water or snow
	Cres.Quar.	12	4	21	Gemini	Loaded with change
	Full	18	6	28	Virgo	Cool with change
	Wan.Quar.	25	11	5	Capricorn	Variable weather
April	New	2	10	15	Aries	Variable weather
	Cres.Quar.	9	10	20	Cancer	Variable weather
	Full	16	22	28	Libra	Variable weather
	Wan.Quar.	24	6	4	Aquarius	Harsh weather
May	New	1	22	2	Taurus	Water, cold and wind
	Cres.Quar.	8	16	18	Leo	Intense Sun
	Full	16	22	25	Sagittarius	Wind or thunder
	Wan.Quar.	24	1	3	Pisces	Good weather
	New	31	7	10	Gemini	Gloomy weather
June	Cres.Quar.	7	2	16	Virgo	Cloudy weather
	Full	14	2	3	Sagittarius	Calmness
	Wan.Quar.	22	1	1	Aries	Calmness
	New	28	15	8	Cancer	Cool weather
July	Cres.Quar.	6	5	14	Libra	Good weather
	Full	14	18	32	Capricorn	Cool weather
	Wan.Quar.	22	4	30	Aries	Calmness
	New	28	22	6	Leo	Calmness
August	Cres.Quar.	4	10	22	Scorpio	Cold weather
	Full	12	8	12	Aquarius	Little water
	Wan.Quar.	20	15	28	Taurus	Harsh weather
	New	27	7	4	Virgo	Harsh weather
September	Cres.Quar.	3	6	11	Sagittarius	Change in weather
	Full	11	20	19	Pisces	Cold weather
	Wan.Quar.	18	23	26	Gemini	Good weather
	New	25	10	3	Libra	Changing weather
October	Cres.Quar.	3	23	10	Capricorn	Variable weather
	Full	11	8	18	Aries	Good weather
	Wan.Quar.	18	6	25	Cancer	Some water
	New	24	11	3	Scorpio	Water with wind
November	Cres.Quar.	1	19	10	Aquarius	Calmness
	Full	9	19	18	Taurus	Cold weather
	Wan.Quar.	16	13	24	Virgo	Quite weather
	New	24	5	3	Sagittarius	Good weather
December	Cres.Quar.	1	15	10	Pisces	Water with wind
	Full	9	6	28	Gemini	Snow and humid
	Wan.Quar.	16	20	24	Virgo	Humid
	New	24	1	3	Capricorn	Wind or thunder
	Cres.Quar.	31	21	10	Libra	Revolted weather

Year in which the Golden number is 7							
Month	Aspect	Day	Hour	Degree	Signs	Weather
January	Full	7	10	18	Cancer	Abundance of water
	Wan.Quar.	15	6	14	Libra	Revolted weather
	New	22	20	4	Aquarius	Wind or thunder
	Cres.Quar.	29	23	10	Taurus	Thunder or wind
February	Full	6	5	1	Leo	Good weather
	Wan.Quar.	13	19	20	Scorpio	Humid weather
	New	21	13	28	Pisces	Water or snow
	Cres.Quar.	28	20	4	Gemini	Loaded with change
March	Full	7	14	10	Virgo	Cold with change
	Wan.Quar.	15	10	23	Sagittarius	Variable weather
	New	22	3	3	Aries	Variable weather
	Cres.Quar.	20	6	0	Cancer	Variable weather
April	Full	6	2	18	Libra	Variable weather
	Wan.Quar.	13	3	23	Capricorn	Average weather
	New	21	5	3	Gemini	Gloomy weather
	Cres.Quar.	28	12	8	Leo	Intense Sun
May	Full	5	1	12	Sagittarius	Variable weather
	Wan.Quar.	13	11	21	Aquarius	Harsh weather
	New	19	5	1	Gemini	Gloomy weather
	Cres.Quar.	28	10	7	Virgo	Cloudy weather
June	Full	4	7	24	Sagittarius	Calmness
	Wan.Quar.	11	14	20	Pisces	Good weather
	New	19	18	28	Gemini	Gloomy weather
	Cres.Quar.	25	23	4	Libra	Revolted weather
July	Full	3	14	1	Capricorn	Cool weather
	Wan.Quar.	11	7	19	Aries	Calmness
	New	18	11	25	Cancer	Cold and changeable
	Cres.Quar.	25	5	2	Scorpio	Cool weather
August	Full	2	2	10	Aquarius	Little water
	Wan.Quar.	9	23	17	Taurus	Harsh weather
	New	16	2	25	Leo	Calmness
	Cres.Quar.	24	5	1	Sagittarius	Change in weather
	Full	31	9	8	Pisces	Harsh weather
September	Wan.Quar.	8	12	16	Gemini	Good weather
	New	15	17	22	Libra	Cold and changeable
	Cres.Quar.	22	1	29	Sagittarius	Change in weather
	Full	30	17	5	Aries	Good weather
October	Wan.Quar.	8	0	15	Cancer	Some water
	New	15	7	22	Libra	Changing weather
	Cres.Quar.	22	17	28	Capricorn	Windy weather
	Full	30	0	7	Taurus	Water, cold and windy
November	Wan.Quar.	6	8	4	Leo	Quiet weather
	New	13	20	21	Scorpio	Water with wind
	Cres.Quar.	20	11	28	Aquarius	Calmness
	Full	28	1	7	Gemini	Snow and humid
December	Wan.Quar.	5	7	14	Virgo	Humidity
	New	13	8	22	Pisces	Good weather
	Cres.Quar.	20	8	28	Sagittarius	Water with wind
	Full	28	1	7	Cancer	Abundance of water

| Year in which the Golden number is 8 ||||||
Month	Aspect	Day	Hour	Degree	Signs	Weather
January	Wan.Quar.	4	1	14	Libra	*Revolted weather*
	New	12	19	22	Capricorn	*Wind or thunders*
	Cres.Quar.	19	5	19	Aries	*Revolted weather*
	Full	26	18	7	Leo	*Good weather*
February	Wan.Quar.	3	9	13	Scorpio	*Humid weather*
	New	10	14	22	Aquarius	*Sun behind clouds*
	Cres.Quar.	18	1	29	Taurus	*Thunder or wind*
	Full	25	4	7	Virgo	*Cold with changes*
March	Wan.Quar.	3	9	12	Sagittarius	*Variable weather*
	New	12	8	22	Pisces	*Water or clouds*
	Cres.Quar.	20	17	29	Gemini	*Charged with change*
	Full	27	14	6	Libra	*Variable weather*
April	Wan.Quar.	3	7	12	Capricorn	*Changing weather*
	New	1	1	21	Aries	*Variable weather*
	Cres.Quar.	18	6	28	Cancer	*Variable weather*
	Full	25	8	5	Scorpio	*Wind or thunder*
May	Wan.Quar.	2	19	10	Aquarius	*Harsh weather*
	New	10	21	10	Taurus	*Water, cold and wind*
	Cres.Quar.	17	14	26	Leo	*Intense Sun*
	Full	24	11	4	Sagittarius	*Calmness*
	Wan.Quar.	31	12	9	Pisces	*Good weather*
June	New	8	23	17	Gemini	*Gloomy weather*
	Cres.Quar.	15	22	24	Virgo	*Cloudy weather*
	Full	22	23	1	Aries	*Cool weather*
	Wan.Quar.	30	15	8	Capricorn	*Calmness*
July	New	7	7	16	Cancer	*Cool weather*
	Cres.Quar.	15	2	22	Libra	*Changing weather*
	Full	22	7	1	Aquarius	*Little water*
	Wan.Quar.	29	2	9	Taurus	*Harsh weather*
August	New	6	14	14	Leo	*Calmness*
	Cres.Quar.	13	6	20	Scorpio	*Cool weather*
	Full	21	3	28	Aquarius	*Little water*
	Wan.Quar.	28	16	5	Gemini	*Good weather*
September	New	4	12	12	Virgo	*Harsh weather*
	Cres.Quar.	11	13	18	Sagittarius	*Change in weather*
	Full	19	19	26	Pisces	*Cool weather*
	Wan.Quar.	27	8	4	Cancer	*Some water*
October	New	4	7	11	Libra	*Changing water*
	Cres.Quar.	11	23	17	Capricorn	*Windy weather*
	Full	19	13	26	Aries	*Good weather*
	Wan.Quar.	26	23	3	Leo	*Quiet weather*
November	New	2	7	10	Scorpio	*Water with wind*
	Cres.Quar.	10	12	15	Aquarius	*Calmness*
	Full	17	6	26	Taurus	*Cool weather*
	Wan.Quar.	25	2	3	Virgo	*Humidity*
December	New	2	6	11	Sagittarius	*Good weather*
	Cres.Quar.	9	5	17	Pisces	*Water with wind*
	Full	17	20	26	Gemini	*Snow and humid*
	Wan.Quar.	24	22	3	Libra	*Revolted weather*
	New	31	21	10	Capricorn	*Wind or thunder*

Year in which the Golden number is 9					
Month	Aspect	Day	Hour	Degree	Signs	Weather
January	Cres.Quar.	7	17	17	Aries	Revolted weather
	Full	15	10	26	Cancer	Abundance of water
	Wan.Quar.	23	6	3	Scorpio	Humid weather
	New	31	14	10	Aquarius	Sun behind clouds
February	Cres.Quar.	6	22	17	Taurus	Thunder or wind
	Full	14	21	18	Leo	Good weather
	Wan.Quar.	21	13	3	Sagittarius	Variable weather
	New	28	8	11	Pisces	Water or clouds
March	Cres.Quar.	7	18	18	Gemini	Charged with change
	Full	15	6	26	Virgo	Cool with change
	Wan.Quar.	22	20	3	Cancer	Changing weather
	New	30	2	10	Aries	Variable weather
April	Cres.Quar.	7	12	17	Leo	Variable weather
	Full	13	4	25	Scorpio	Variable weather
	Wan.Quar.	20	5	1	Capricorn	Harsh weather
	New	28	8	9	Taurus	Water, cold and wind
May	Cres.Quar.	7	3	16	Leo	Intense Sun
	Full	13	13	23	Scorpio	Wind or thunder
	Wan.Quar.	20	17	28	Aquarius	Harsh weather
	New	28	8	9	Gemini	Gloomy weather
June	Cres.Quar.	2	6	14	Virgo	Cloudy weather
	Full	10	7	22	Sagittarius	Calmness
	Wan.Quar.	18	4	27	Pisces	Good weather
	New	26	9	5	Cancer	Cool weather
July	Cres.Quar.	5	13	13	Libra	Good weather
	Full	11	18	19	Capricorn	Cool weather
	Wan.Quar.	18	19	25	Aries	Calmness
	New	26	6	4	Leo	Calmness
August	Cres.Quar.	3	5	10	Scorpio	Cold weather
	Full	9	6	26	Aquarius	Little water
	Wan.Quar.	17	12	24	Taurus	Harsh weather
	New	24	15	2	Virgo	Harsh weather
September	Cres.Quar.	1	10	8	Sagittarius	Change in weather
	Full	7	20	15	Pisces	Cold weather
	Wan.Quar.	15	7	23	Gemini	Good weather
	New	22	23	30	Virgo	Harsh weather
	Cres.Quar.	30	16	7	Capricorn	Variable weather
October	Full	8	13	15	Aries	Good weather
	Wan.Quar.	16	0	22	Leo	Some water
	New	23	8	30	Scorpio	Changing weather
	Cres.Quar.	30	23	6	Pisces	Calmness
November	Full	6	7	15	Aries	Cold weather
	Wan.Quar.	14	11	21	Leo	Quiet weather
	New	20	18	29	Scorpio	Water with wind
	Cres.Quar.	28	11	7	Pisces	Water with wind
December	Full	6	2	15	Gemini	Snow and humid
	Wan.Quar.	14	11	22	Virgo	Humidity
	New	21	6	30	Sagittarius	Good weather
	Cres.Quar.	28	1	6	Aries	Revolted weather

Year in which the Golden number is 10					
Month	Aspect	Day	Hour	Degree	Signs	Weather
January	Full	4	19	15	Cancer	Abundance of water
	Wan.Quar.	12	0	22	Libra	Revolted weather
	New	18	20	30	Capricorn	Wind or thunder
	Cres.Quar.	26	18	6	Taurus	Thunder or wind
February	Full	3	10	16	Leo	Good weather
	Wan.Quar.	11	10	22	Scorpio	Humid weather
	New	17	11	30	Capricorn	Wind or thunder
	Cres.Quar.	25	12	6	Gemini	Loaded with change
March	Full	4	22	13	Virgo	Cold with change
	Wan.Quar.	11	18	21	Sagittarius	Variable weather
	New	19	3	29	Pisces	Water or mist
	Cres.Quar.	26	10	6	Cancer	Variable weather
April	Full	3	8	14	Libra	Variable weather
	Wan.Quar.	10	0	20	Capricorn	Changing weather
	New	17	19	28	Aries	Variable weather
	Cres.Quar.	23	5	5	Leo	Intense Sun
May	Full	2	15	14	Scorpio	Wind or thunder
	Wan.Quar.	9	6	19	Aquarius	Harsh weather
	New	17	10	27	Taurus	Water, cold and wind
	Cres.Quar.	24	21	4	Virgo	Harsh weather
June	Full	1	22	11	Sagittarius	Calmness
	Wan.Quar.	8	14	17	Pisces	Good weather
	New	16	1	25	Gemini	Gloomy weather
	Cres.Quar.	23	11	2	Libra	Good weather
	Full	30	6	8	Capricorn	Cool weather
July	Wan.Quar.	7	23	15	Aries	Calmness
	New	15	14	23	Cancer	Cool weather
	Cres.Quar.	22	22	30	Libra	Good weather
	Full	29	14	7	Aquarius	Little water and heat
August	Wan.Quar.	5	12	13	Taurus	Harsh weather
	New	13	15	21	Leo	Calmness
	Cres.Quar.	21	7	29	Scorpio	Cool weather
	Full	28	1	5	Pisces	Cool weather
September	Wan.Quar.	4	20	12	Gemini	Good weather
	New	11	14	20	Virgo	Harsh weather
	Cres.Quar.	19	14	27	Sagittarius	Change in weather
	Full	26	15	4	Aries	Good weather
October	Wan.Quar.	3	22	11	Cancer	Some water
	New	10	10	19	Libra	Changing weather
	Cres.Quar.	18	20	26	Capricorn	Windy weather
	Full	26	7	3	Taurus	Cool weather
November	Wan.Quar.	2	19	11	Leo	Quite weather
	New	10	1	19	Scorpio	Water with wind
	Cres.Quar.	17	3	25	Aquarius	Calmness
	Full	25	2	4	Gemini	Snow and humid
December	Wan.Quar.	2	14	10	Virgo	Humidity
	New	9	21	19	Sagittarius	Good weather
	Cres.Quar.	17	12	24	Pisces	Water with wind
	Full	24	21	4	Cancer	Abundance of water

\	Year in which the Golden number is 11					
Month	*Aspect*	*Day*	*Hour*	*Degree*	*Signs*	*Weather*
January	Wan.Quar.	1	8	11	Libra	*Revolted weather*
	New	8	8	19	Capricorn	*Wind and thunder*
	Cres.Quar.	15	17	25	Aries	*Revolted weather*
	Full	23	16	4	Leo	*Good weather*
February	Wan.Quar.	31	11	11	Scorpio	*Humid weather*
	New	6	19	19	Aquarius	*Sun behind clouds*
	Cres.Quar.	14	14	14	Taurus	*Thunder or wind*
	Full	22	8	4	Virgo	*Cold with change*
March	Wan.Quar.	1	13	11	Sagittarius	*Variable weather*
	New	8	8	18	Pisces	*Water or mist*
	Cres.Quar.	14	7	24	Gemini	*Loaded with change*
	Full	22	22	3	Libra	*Variable weather*
	Wan.Quar.	29	22	10	Capricorn	*Changing weather*
April	New	6	21	17	Aries	*Variable weather*
	Cres.Quar.	14	1	24	Cancer	*Variable weather*
	Full	22	8	2	Scorpio	*Wind or thunder*
	Wan.Quar.	30	4	9	Aquarius	*Harsh weather*
May	New	6	21	16	Taurus	*Water, cold and wind*
	Cres.Quar.	13	1	22	Leo	*Intense Sun*
	Full	21	16	1	Sagittarius	*Calmness*
	Wan.Quar.	29	9	8	Pisces	*Good weather*
June	New	5	2	15	Gemini	*Gloomy weather*
	Cres.Quar.	12	13	21	Virgo	*Cloudy weather*
	Full	19	23	29	Sagittarius	*Calmness*
	Wan.Quar.	26	24	5	Aries	*Calmness*
July	New	4	17	12	Cancer	*Cool weather*
	Cres.Quar.	12	5	20	Libra	*Good weather*
	Full	19	6	27	Aquarius	*Cool weather*
	Wan.Quar.	25	21	3	Taurus	*Harsh weather*
August	New	3	6	11	Leo	*Calmness*
	Cres.Quar.	10	18	18	Scorpio	*Cool weather*
	Full	17	13	25	Aquarius	*Little water and heat*
	Wan.Quar.	24	7	1	Gemini	*Good weather*
September	New	1	8	9	Virgo	*Harsh weather*
	Cres.Quar.	8	6	16	Sagittarius	*Change in weather*
	Full	15	23	23	Pisces	*Cool weather*
	Wan.Quar.	22	21	30	Gemini	*Good weather*
October	New	1	11	8	Libra	*Changing weather*
	Cres.Quar.	8	17	15	Capricorn	*Windy weather*
	Full	15	11	22	Aries	*Revolted weather*
	Wan.Quar.	22	14	29	Cancer	*Some water*
	New	30	17	7	Scorpio	*Water with wind*
November	Cres.Quar.	7	1	15	Aquarius	*Calmness*
	Full	14	18	22	Taurus	*Cool weather*
	Wan.Quar.	22	10	30	Leo	*Quiet weather*
	New	29	13	8	Sagittarius	*Good weather*
December	Cres.Quar.	6	7	14	Pisces	*Water with wind*
	Full	13	21	22	Gemini	*Snow and humidity*
	Wan.Quar.	21	7	29	Virgo	*Humidity*
	New	29	1	8	Capricorn	*Wind or thunder*

| Year in which the Golden number is 12 ||||||||
Month	Aspect	Day	Hour	Degree	Signs	Weather
January	Cres.Quar. Full Wan.Quar. New	4 12 20 27	15 16 3 10	14 23 30 8	Aries Cancer Libra Aquarius	Variable weather Abundance of weather Revolted weather Sun behind clouds
February	Cres.Quar. Full Wan.Quar. New	3 11 18 25	10 11 22 20	14 23 30 8	Taurus Leo Scorpio Pisces	Thunder or wind Good weather Humid weather Water or mist
March	Cres.Quar. Full Wan.Quar. New	5 13 20 27	12 1 12 7	14 23 30 7	Gemini Virgo Sagittarius Aries	Loaded weather Cool with change Variable weather Variable weather
April	Cres.Quar. Full Wan.Quar. New	3 11 18 25	2 20 23 18	13 23 29 6	Cancer Libra Capricorn Taurus	Variable weather Variable weather Changing weather Water, cold and wind
May	Cres.Quar. Full Wan.Quar. New	3 11 18 25	17 7 7 6	14 21 29 6	Leo Scorpio Aquarius Gemini	Intense Sun Wind or thunder Harsh weather Gloomy weather
June	Cres.Quar. Full Wan.Quar. New	1 9 16 23	10 16 12 20	10 19 25 2	Virgo Pisces Sagittarius Cancer	Cloudy weather Calmness Good weather Cool weather
July	Cres.Quar. Full Wan.Quar. New Cres.Quar.	1 9 16 23 30	3 1 17 10 20	9 17 23 1 7	Libra Capricorn Aries Leo Scorpio	Good weather Cool weather Calmness Calmness Harsh weather
August	Full Wan.Quar. New Cres.Quar.	7 14 22 29	7 5 1 13	14 22 30 6	Aquarius Taurus Leo Sagittarius	Little water Harsh weather Harsh weather Changing weather
September	Full Wan.Quar. New Cres.Quar.	5 13 20 28	14 7 17 4	13 20 28 5	Pisces Gemini Virgo Capricorn	Cool weather Good weather Harsh weather Variable weather
October	Full Wan.Quar. New Cres.Quar.	4 11 18 26	13 17 0 7	13 19 26 4	Aries Cancer Libra Aquarius	Good weather Some water Changing weather Calmness
November	Full Wan.Quar. New Cres.Quar.	3 11 18 23	3 8 14 4	11 18 27 4	Taurus Leo Scorpio Pisces	Cool weather Quiet weather Water with wind Water with wind
December	Full Wan.Quar. New Cres.Quar.	2 9 17 24	9 19 23 13	10 18 27 3	Gemini Virgo Sagittarius Aries	Snow and humid Humidity Good weather Revolted weather

	Year in which the Golden number is 13					
Month	Aspect	Day	Hour	Degree	Signs	Weather
January	Full	1	17	10	Cancer	Abundance of water
	Wan.Quar.	8	23	18	Libra	Revolted weather
	New	16	21	27	Capricorn	Wind or thunder
	Cres.Quar.	23	21	3	Taurus	Thunder or wind
	Full	31	11	13	Leo	Good weather
February	Wan.Quar.	7	20	18	Scorpio	Humid weather
	New	14	12	17	Aquarius	Sun behind clouds
	Cres.Quar.	22	1	3	Gemini	Cold with change
	Full	1	13	10	Virgo	Cold with change
March	Wan.Quar.	9	16	19	Sagittarius	Variable weather
	New	16	22	17	Pisces	Water or mist
	Cres.Quar.	23	12	2	Gemini	Loaded with change
	Full	1	5	10	Libra	Variable weather
April	Wan.Quar.	8	9	18	Capricorn	Changing weather
	New	15	6	25	Aries	Variable weather
	Cres.Quar.	22	1	1	Leo	Intense Sun
	Full	29	15	10	Scorpio	Wind or thunder
May	Wan.Quar.	7	7	17	Aquarius	Harsh weather
	New	14	14	23	Taurus	Water, cold and wind
	Cres.Quar.	21	11	30	Leo	Intense Sun
	Full	29	14	8	Sagittarius	Calmness
June	Wan.Quar.	6	8	15	Taurus	Good weather
	New	13	1	22	Gemini	Gloomy weather
	Cres.Quar.	20	1	28	Scorpio	Cool weather
	Full	28	4	6	Capricorn	Revolted weather
July	Wan.Quar.	5	10	13	Aries	Calmness
	New	12	6	19	Cancer	Cool weather
	Cres.Quar.	19	18	26	Libra	Good weather
	Full	27	21	4	Aquarius	Little water and heat
August	Wan.Quar.	3	19	11	Taurus	Harsh weather
	New	10	16	17	Leo	Calmness
	Cres.Quar.	18	11	25	Scorpio	Cool weather
	Full	26	5	3	Pisces	Cool weather
September	Wan.Quar.	2	1	9	Gemini	Good weather
	New	9	4	16	Virgo	Harsh weather
	Cres.Quar.	17	5	24	Sagittarius	Change in weather
	Full	24	15	1	Aries	Good weather
October	Wan.Quar.	1	9	8	Cancer	Some water
	New	8	19	15	Libra	Changing weather
	Cres.Quar.	16	23	23	Capricorn	Revolted weather
	Full	24	1	30	Aries	Good weather
	Wan.Quar.	31	16	6	Scorpio	Humidity
November	New	7	12	14	Scorpio	Water with wind
	Cres.Quar.	15	15	22	Taurus	Calmness
	Full	21	11	29	Aquarius	Snow and humidity
	Wan.Quar.	28	5	6	Pisces	Good weather
December	New	7	7	15	Sagittarius	Good weather
	Cres.Quar.	15	5	23	Pisces	Water with wind
	Full	22	21	29	Gemini	Snow and humid
	Wan.Quar.	29	21	6	Libra	Revolted weather

Year in which the Golden number is 14					
Month	*Aspect*	*Day*	*Hour*	*Degree*	*Signs*	*Weather*
January	New	6	2	15	Capricorn	*Wind or thunder*
	Cres.Quar.	13	16	22	Aries	*Revolted weather*
	Full	20	7	30	Cancer	*Abundance of water*
	Wan.Quar.	27	16	7	Scorpio	*Humid weather*
February	New	4	19	15	Aquarius	*Sun behind clouds*
	Cres.Quar.	12	1	23	Taurus	*Thunder or wind*
	Full	19	19	1	Virgo	*Cold with change*
	Wan.Quar.	26	13	7	Sagittarius	*Variable weather*
March	New	5	14	16	Pisces	*Water or mist*
	Cres.Quar.	12	7	22	Gemini	*Loaded with change*
	Full	20	0	30	Virgo	*Cool with change*
	Wan.Quar.	27	9	7	Capricorn	*Changing weather*
April	New	3	22	14	Aries	*Variable weather*
	Cres.Quar.	10	14	20	Cancer	*Variable weather*
	Full	18	1	28	Libra	*Variable weather*
	Wan.Quar.	26	3	6	Aquarius	*Harsh weather*
May	New	3	7	13	Taurus	*Water, cold and wind*
	Cres.Quar.	10	21	19	Leo	*Intense Sun*
	Full	18	16	26	Scorpio	*Wind or thunder*
	Wan.Quar.	25	18	4	Pisces	*Good weather*
June	New	1	15	11	Gemini	*Gloomy weather*
	Cres.Quar.	8	7	17	Virgo	*Cloudy weather*
	Full	15	13	26	Sagittarius	*Calmness*
	Wan.Quar.	22	8	4	Aries	*Good weather*
	New	30	23	9	Cancer	*Cool weather*
July	Cres.Quar.	7	18	16	Libra	*Good weather*
	Full	15	21	23	Aquarius	*Cold weather*
	Wan.Quar.	23	15	1	Taurus	*Harsh weather*
	New	31	5	8	Leo	*Calmness*
August	Cres.Quar.	6	9	15	Scorpio	*Cold weather*
	Full	14	22	22	Aquarius	*Little water*
	Wan.Quar.	21	22	29	Taurus	*Harsh weather*
	New	29	19	6	Virgo	*Harsh weather*
September	Cres.Quar.	5	12	13	Sagittarius	*Change in weather*
	Full	13	2	21	Pisces	*Harsh weather*
	Wan.Quar.	20	1	27	Gemini	*Good weather*
	New	27	11	5	Libra	*Changing weather*
October	Cres.Quar.	4	21	12	Capricorn	*Variable weather*
	Full	12	17	19	Aries	*Good weather*
	Wan.Quar.	19	10	26	Cancer	*Some water*
	New	27	5	4	Scorpio	*Water with wind*
November	Cres.Quar.	3	16	11	Aquarius	*Calmness*
	Full	11	2	16	Taurus	*Cool weather*
	Wan.Quar.	18	17	26	Leo	*Quite weather*
	New	25	7	5	Sagittarius	*Good weather*
December	Cres.Quar.	3	11	11	Pisces	*Water with wind*
	Full	10	13	19	Gemini	*Snow and humid*
	Wan.Quar.	18	3	26	Virgo	*Humidity*
	New	25	15	4	Capricorn	*Wind or thunder*

Year in which the Golden number is 15					
Month	Aspect	Day	Hour	Degree	Signs	Weather
January	Cres.Quar.	2	4	12	Aries	*Revolted weather*
	Full	8	23	20	Cancer	*Snow and humidity*
	Wan.Quar.	15	17	26	Libra	*Revolted weather*
	New	23	21	4	Aquarius	*Sun behind clouds*
	Cres.Quar.	31	18	12	Taurus	*Thunder or wind*
February	Full	7	2	13	Leo	*Good weather*
	Wan.Quar.	14	11	25	Scorpio	*Humid weather*
	New	22	13	4	Pisces	*Water or mist*
	Cres.Quar.	2	4	12	Gemini	*Harsh weather*
March	Full	9	3	19	Virgo	*Cool with change*
	Wan.Quar.	16	5	25	Sagittarius	*Variable weather*
	New	24	15	4	Aries	*Variable weather*
	Cres.Quar.	31	12	11	Cancer	*Variable weather*
April	Full	7	18	19	Libra	*Variable weather*
	Wan.Quar.	15	1	25	Capricorn	*Changing weather*
	New	22	1	3	Taurus	*Water, cold and wind*
	Cres.Quar.	30	17	9	Leo	*Intense sun*
May	Full	7	9	18	Scorpio	*Harsh weather*
	Wan.Quar.	14	18	24	Aquarius	*Wind or thunder*
	New	22	9	1	Gemini	*Gloomy weather*
	Cres.Quar.	29	22	7	Virgo	*Harsh weather*
June	Full	6	1	16	Sagittarius	*Calmness*
	Wan.Quar.	13	11	22	Pisces	*Good weather*
	New	20	15	29	Gemini	*Gloomy weather*
	Cres.Quar.	28	5	5	Cancer	*Variable weather*
July	Full	7	18	16	Capricorn	*Cool weather*
	Wan.Quar.	15	21	21	Aries	*Calmness*
	New	23	15	1	Cancer	*Cool weather*
	Cres.Quar.	31	5	8	Scorpio	*Cool weather*
August	Full	6	9	15	Aquarius	*Little water*
	Wan.Quar.	14	22	22	Taurus	*Harsh weather*
	New	21	22	29	Leo	*Calmness*
	Cres.Quar.	29	19	6	Sagittarius	*Changing in weather*
September	Full	5	12	13	Pisces	*Cool weather*
	Wan.Quar.	13	2	21	Gemini	*Good weather*
	New	20	1	27	Virgo	*Harsh weather*
	Cres.Quar.	27	11	5	Capricorn	*Variable weather*
October	Full	4	21	12	Aries	*Good weather*
	Wan.Quar.	11	17	19	Cancer	*Some water*
	New	17	10	26	Libra	*Changing weather*
	Cres.Quar.	24	5	4	Capricorn	*Variable weather*
	Full	30	18	28	Taurus	*Cool weather*
November	Wan.Quar.	5	16	11	Leo	*Quiet weather*
	New	11	2	16	Scorpio	*Water with wind*
	Cres.Quar.	18	17	26	Aries	*Revolted weather*
	Full	25	7	5	Gemini	*Snow and humidity*
December	Wan.Quar.	3	11	11	Virgo	*Humidity*
	New	10	13	19	Sagittarius	*Good weather*
	Cres.Quar.	18	3	26	Aries	*Revolted weather*
	Full	25	15	4	Cancer	*Abundance of water*

| Year in which the Golden number is 16 ||||||
Month	Aspect	Day	Hour	Degree	Signs	Weather
January	Wan.Quar.	5	6	15	Libra	Revolted weather
	New	12	20	21	Capricorn	Wind or thunder
	Cres.Quar.	20	1	1	Taurus	Thunder or wind
	Full	28	1	9	Leo	Good weather
February	Wan.Quar.	3	17	15	Scorpio	Humid weather
	New	11	15	23	Aquarius	Sun behind clouds
	Cres.Quar.	18	17	30	Taurus	Thunder or wind
	Full	26	11	8	Virgo	Cold with change
March	Wan.Quar.	5	6	14	Sagittarius	Variable weather
	New	13	9	22	Pisces	Water or mist
	Cres.Quar.	20	6	1	Cancer	Variable weather
	Full	27	23	8	Libra	Variable weather
April	Wan.Quar.	4	22	4	Capricorn	Changing weather
	New	12	21	22	Aries	Variable weather
	Cres.Quar.	19	16	9	Cancer	Variable weather
	Full	26	11	6	Scorpio	Wind or thunder
May	Wan.Quar.	3	5	13	Aquarius	Harsh weather
	New	11	7	21	Taurus	Water, cold and wind
	Cres.Quar.	18	1	27	Leo	Intense Sun
	Full	25	16	4	Sagittarius	Calmness
June	Wan.Quar.	2	9	11	Pisces	Good weather
	New	10	4	19	Gemini	Gloomy weather
	Cres.Quar.	17	3	26	Virgo	Cloudy weather
	Full	24	15	23	Capricorn	Cool weather
July	Wan.Quar.	2	2	10	Aries	Calmness
	New	9	14	27	Cancer	Cool weather
	Cres.Quar.	16	6	23	Libra	Good weather
	Full	23	15	1	Aquarius	Little water and heat
	Wan.Quar.	31	18	8	Taurus	Harsh weather
August	New	7	22	15	Leo	Calmness
	Cres.Quar.	14	12	21	Scorpio	Cool weather
	Full	22	6	29	Aquarius	Good weather
	Wan.Quar.	30	9	7	Gemini	Good weather
September	New	6	6	13	Virgo	Harsh weather
	Cres.Quar.	13	22	21	Sagittarius	Change in weather
	Full	21	12	29	Pisces	Cool weather
	Wan.Quar.	29	23	7	Cancer	Some water
October	New	5	15	12	Libra	Changing weather
	Cres.Quar.	12	12	19	Capricorn	Windy weather
	Full	20	16	27	Aries	Good weather
	Wan.Quar.	28	9	5	Leo	Quiet weather
November	New	4	2	12	Scorpio	Water with wind
	Cres.Quar.	11	5	19	Aquarius	Calmness
	Full	19	18	27	Taurus	Cool weather
	Wan.Quar.	26	12	4	Virgo	Humidity
December	New	3	18	12	Sagittarius	Good weather
	Cres.Quar.	11	1	19	Pisces	Water with wind
	Full	19	1	27	Gemini	Snow and humidity
	Wan.Quar.	26	2	4	Libra	Cloudy weather

Year in which the Golden number is 17						
Month	*Aspect*	*Day*	*Hour*	*Degree*	*Signs*	*Weather*
January	New	6	2	15	Capricorn	*Wind or thunder*
	Cres.Quar.	13	16	22	Aries	*Revolted weather*
	Full	20	7	30	Cancer	*Abundance of water*
	Wan.Quar.	27	16	7	Scorpio	*Humid weather*
February	New	4	19	15	Aquarius	*Sun behind clouds*
	Cres.Quar.	11	1	23	Taurus	*Thunder or wind*
	Full	17	19	1	Leo	*Good weather*
	Wan.Quar.	24	13	7	Sagittarius	*Variable weather*
March	New	1	15	11	Pisces	*Water or mist*
	Cres.Quar.	8	7	17	Gemini	*Loaded with change*
	Full	16	13	26	Virgo	*Cold with change*
	Wan.Quar.	24	8	4	Capricorn	*Changing weather*
	New	30	23	9	Aries	*Variable weather*
April	Cres.Quar.	5	22	14	Cancer	*Variable weather*
	Full	12	14	20	Libra	*Variable weather*
	Wan.Quar.	18	1	28	Aquarius	*Harsh weather*
	New	26	3	6	Taurus	*Water, cold and wind*
May	Cres.Quar.	3	7	13	Leo	*Intense Sun*
	Full	10	21	19	Scorpio	*Wind or thunder*
	Wan.Quar.	18	16	26	Pisces	*Good weather*
	New	25	18	4	Gemini	*Gloomy weather*
June	Cres.Quar.	5	14	16	Virgo	*Cloudy weather*
	Full	12	7	22	Sagittarius	*Calmness*
	Wan.Quar.	20	0	30	Pisces	*Good weather*
	New	27	9	7	Cancer	*Cool weather*
July	Cres.Quar.	4	21	13	Libra	*Good weather*
	Full	13	8	20	Capricorn	*Cool weather*
	Wan.Quar.	22	20	18	Aries	*Calmness*
	New	27	14	5	Leo	*Calmness*
August	Cres.Quar.	3	5	11	Scorpio	*Cool weather*
	Full	10	23	19	Aquarius	*Little water*
	Wan.Quar.	19	2	26	Taurus	*Harsh weather*
	New	25	22	2	Virgo	*Harsh weather*
September	Cres.Quar.	1	15	9	Sagittarius	*Change in weather*
	Full	9	15	18	Pisces	*Cool weather*
	Wan.Quar.	17	15	25	Gemini	*Good weather*
	New	24	17	2	Libra	*Changing weather*
October	Cres.Quar.	1	5	8	Capricorn	*Windy weather*
	Full	9	8	16	Aries	*Good weather*
	Wan.Quar.	17	9	24	Cancer	*Some water*
	New	23	16	1	Scorpio	*Water with wind*
	Cres.Quar.	30	22	7	Aquarius	*Calmness*
November	Full	8	1	17	Taurus	*Cool weather*
	Wan.Quar.	15	10	22	Leo	*Quiet weather*
	New	22	3	1	Sagittarius	*Good weather*
	Cres.Quar.	29	18	8	Pisces	*Water with wind*
December	Full	7	16	16	Gemini	*Snow and humidity*
	Wan.Quar.	14	17	23	Virgo	*Humidity*
	New	21	16	1	Capricorn	*Wind or thunder*
	Cres.Quar.	29	15	8	Aries	*Revolted weather*

To prognosticate, in sum, the weather for the whole year

Knowing that for the knowledge of the weather it is necessary to raise a figure of the revolutions of the year, of the real entry of the Sun in Aries, and seeing as not everyone can be a Mathematician, we shall give satisfaction by the following rules so as all may have knowledge of the weather through them.

One should note that those of experience arrived at this knowledge of the year by the twelve days between Saint Lucia and Christmas, taking each day for one month; and for every quarter day a quarter of a month; and thus at the day of Saint Lucia at midnight until six in the morning one will count the first eight days of January; from six in the morning until midday one will take the weather from the eighth until the fifteenth of the said month; and from midday until six in the afternoon one shall take the weather from the fifteenth until the twenty third of January; and from six in the afternoon until midnight of the next night one shall take the weather from the twenty third until the end of January, and the same way for the following day with the month of February and the third for March, and so forth for each one until all months are done, meaning the twenty second of December.

In a similar way can one also acquire knowledge of the weather throughout the year by the four main winds, by their courses from the day of Saint John the Baptist until Saint Peter's day and by the one which blows the most during these days, which should be known: on the twenty fourth of July, which is Saint John's day, until the twenty ninth, which is Saint Peter's day, this wind will then be the one which will blow the most during the year. And the main winds are these: North, South, East, West. And let us remind that the East wind comes from the rising Sun and the West from the setting Sun.

Thus, blowing in these days the North wind, which is cold and dry, so will be the year.

And if in the mentioned days the strongest wind is the South, which is humid and cold, so will equally be the year.

And if in the mentioned days the West wind blows the strongest, which is hot and humid, so does it denote the year.

But do note that what we say regarding the North and South should be regarded in reverse to those who live South of the Equinoxial line, for those North denotes water and South dryness.

Following are some greatly advantageous and necessary Astrological advertences for bloodlettings

Four things (according to Avicenna) should be observed in a bloodletting; these are: the time, the age or custom, the strength and character of the subject. Furthermore, the same Avicenna says that one should note two particular hours for bloodlettings: the hour of election and the hour of necessity. The hour of election, which is the convenient one for the bloodletting, shall be a hot hour, which is one after the rise of the Sun and after digestion has been finished, and after the expelling of any over-fluids. For these elected hours to be good it is necessary to follow the warnings of the learned and wise Astrologers. The other hour for bloodlettings, that of necessity, is when an infirmity is urgent and demands a bloodletting, such as an acute fever, a suffocation, a frenzy, an apoplexy and others of the sort, which do not admit Astronomical prorogations or considerations; for these infirmities, within instants, end a man's life. Taking into consideration the hour of election, and the supposed rules of the expert Medics, regarding age and time, we say as Ptolemy in *Centiloquium, verb.* 20, that it is a dangerous and fearful thing to do a bloodletting while the Moon is in the predominant Sign of the part of the body where one will do the bloodletting. And this point is of such importance that it would be pure ignorance not to observe it.

Of the harmful and advantageous times to do a purge

There is a rule greatly observed by the expert Medics that prohibits medical laxatives in the excessive heat of Summer and in the greatest cold of Winter. This same thing Hippocrates seems to confirm in the 5th Aphorism, in the 4th particular where he says that *Sub Cane, & anie Canem molesta sunt pharmaca, & medicamentorum usus diffifilis*. Which means: on the Canicular days, and on the days of great cold, one should not take a purge.

The best time of the year to have a purge, for those who do not have great necessity, is Spring. A purge is very dangerous, and even more a bloodletting, as was said above, when the Moon is in conjunction and opposed to the Sun, and this still holds true one day before and one day after this moment.

One should not take a purge while the Moon is in a ruminating Sign, such as Aries, Taurus and Capricorn; this because they cannot retain anything in their stomach, rather vomiting as experience shows; should one wish to purge through vomiting these will be good times. While Leo is in ascendant is a good time for vomiting.

Anytime the Moon is in the Aqueous Signs a purge will be very beneficial. However one should be warned that if the purge is in the form of a drink, it is convenient that the Moon is in Scorpio. And if it is in the form of a solid or electuary, the Moon should be in the Sign of Cancer. And if it is in as a pill the Moon should be in Pisces; and in this way the effects will always be very good and healthy. A purge made while Jupiter is in its house and in Ascendant will not have any effect; rather, very grave consequences are inferred into the health of the sick, for being this Planet in these conditions in the hour of the purge, it will turn it into the quality of the disease.

During great weather changes Hippocrates says, in the book *Aere, Aquis, & Locis*, that one should not offer medicine, nor cauterizations, nor make incisions in one's members; these same rules should be kept for the two Solstices and Equinoxes. And these Astrological considerations are of such importance to Medicine that, according to the same Hippocrates, in the book *Epidemiæ*, there wasn't a single Medic who was not an Astrologer, for in the quoted book he says it in this way: *Hujusmodi Medicus est qui Astrologiam ignorant, nemo &c.*

Table of the purges and bloodlettings,
so as to know when they are good or bad

SIGN	DOMINION	PURGE	BLOOD LETTING
Aries	Head	Bad	Good
Aries	Head	Bad	Good
Aries	Head	Bad	Good
Taurus	Neck	Bad	Bad
Taurus	Neck	Bad	Bad
Gemini	Arms	Indifferent	Bad
Gemini	Arms	Indifferent	Bad
Cancer	Chest	Good	Indifferent
Cancer	Chest	Good	Indifferent
Leo	Heart	Bad	Bad
Leo	Heart	Bad	Bad
Leo	Heart	Bad	Bad
Virgo	Belly	Bad	Bad
Virgo	Belly	Bad	Bad
Libra	Buttocks	Indifferent	Good
Libra	Buttocks	Indifferent	Good
Scorpio	Genitals	Good	Indifferent
Scorpio	Genitals	Good	Indifferent
Scorpio	Genitals	Good	Indifferent
Sagittarius	Thighs	Indifferent	Good
Sagittarius	Thighs	Indifferent	Good
Capricorn	Knees	Bad	Bad
Capricorn	Knees	Bad	Bad
Aquarius	Shins	Indifferent	Good
Aquarius	Shins	Indifferent	Good
Pisces	Feet	Good	Indifferent
Pisces	Feet	Good	Indifferent
Pisces	Feet	Good	Indifferent

Dominion of the Planets on the human body

Saturn	Arms
Mars	Bile
Venus	Kidneys
Moon	Head
Jupiter	Liver
Sun	Heart
Mercury	Lungs

Strange Astronomical judging of natural infirmities

D	1	If any person falls ill, and knows with certain the day on which this infirmity started, and desires to know its success, count the days that have passed since the beginning of the Caniculars in his kingdom until the day the illness began, counting them *inclusivè*, and from this number of days subtract the number 36, as many times as possible, and the remaining number should be searched in this page and the letter that is found in front of this number will declare the success of the infirmity, noting that D denotes death, L life and A denotes an arduous and long infirmity.	19	A
L	2		20	D
A	3		21	D
L	4		22	
A	5		23	L
D	6		24	D
D	7		25	D
A	8		26	L
L	9		27	L
D	10		28	M
L	11		29	A
L	12		30	D
D	13		31	A
L	14		32	D
A	15		33	L
L	16		34	L
L	17		35	L
D	18		36	L

And if the number that is in front does not have a letter this indicates doubt regarding life or death. The curious reader should note this rule.

Another judging of infirmity

Guido of Arezzo[66] writes that if one wishes to pass judgment on an infirmity, if it shall be deadly or curable, one should take the urine of the sick and mix it with the milk of a woman who is raising a boy, and if both these things mix, the milk and the urine, then this is a sign of life; if these, however, do not mix, then the prognosis is death.

---

66. Translator's note: Guido of Arezzo the younger, a professor at Parma and amanuensis and editor of Robert Frugart's surgical books. Not to be confused with Guido of Arezzo the music theorist.

Another judging of infirmity

Bernardo Granullachs[67] writes in his *Chronographia* that in order to know if one will live or die from a sickness, one should take a drop of blood from this person, as soon as the bloodletting is performed, and drop it in a vase of very clear water, and if the blood falls to the bottom without dissolving this is a sign of life and the sick will not die from that illness; however, if it dissolves and becomes suspended on the surface, without any part of it arriving at the bottom, then it denotes a life threatening danger.

Following is an admirable and strange judgment of infirmities by the ages of the Moon from Nicolas Florentinus,[68] a most expert Medic

One cannot deny that the Stars and celestial bodies cause many and various effects in humans, and the Star or Planet that causes the greatest ones is the Moon, both by its proximity to us as by the shifting of its phases. Nicolas Florentinus says that in order to judge the success of an infirmity one should know two things. The first is the day on which the said infirmity began, or when the first indisposition started, and the second the day of the last conjunction. Knowing both these things one will take note of the days since the last conjunction until the day that the infirmity started, *inclusivé*. Once this number is known one will look for it in the following Table, and in front of the number one will find the success of the infirmity. One should note and be warned that, while the Moon does influence many things, God our Lord may order something very different, as is his power. And so as this rule may be made clear, we propose an example: a person was made sick on the 6th of February of 1829, I check the days from the last conjunction of the Moon, which was on the 29th of the month of January until the 6th of February and I find that there are 9 days counted inclusively as indicated; now I find in the following Table this same number 9, and in front of it I see that it indicates a serious illness, however, not deadly; as such, by this example all the rest will be understood.

---

67. Translator's note: a difficult reference to place, but this seems to have been a XVIth century astrologer from Barcelona reported to have written his own Lunario.

68. Translator's note: Also known as Nicolas Salernitanus, a XIIIth century medic or surgeon of French origins but exiled in Italy.

Table for the prognostication and successes of infirmities

1. Should one get sick on the very day of the conjunction of the Moon, he should be fearful until the fourteenth, twenty first and twenty eighth day of his sickness, however he will recover after this time.
2. This denotes danger until the fourteenth day; afterwards there will be improvements.
3. It denotes little work and soon he will recover.
4. There will be a great danger until the thirty first day of illness, after which, should he survive, he will heal.
5. It is shown a laborious infirmity, but not deadly.
6. It denotes that, should he not recover immediately there will be a laborious infirmity; but at the fifth of next month's Moon he will recover his health.
7. He will soon recover.
8. If in twelve or fourteen days he is not better there will be danger.
9. This is a serious illness, but he will not perish.
10. It denotes a danger of death before the fifteenth day.
11. It denotes that he will soon heal or die.
12. It denotes that if in fifteen days he does not heal he will die.
13. He will have a laborious infirmity up to the eighteenth day, after which, should he survive, he will heal.
14. It shows that he will be sick until the fifteenth day, after which he will recover.
15. If in fifteen days he is not well he will be in danger, or, as another Author mentions, he will fall to the utmost extreme.
16. He will suffer until the twenty eighth day, if he survives then he will heal.
17. It denotes health if he survives eighteen days.
18. If he does not heal quickly then the infirmity will be long and life threatening.
19. It denotes than he shall have his health back soon, if he is well cared for.
20. It denotes danger of death on the ninth or seventh day, from which, should he survive, he will heal.
21. If in six day he does not die, after next month's Moon he will recover his health.
22. In ten or twelve days he will recover his health.
23. Even if with some trauma, he will be fine next month.
24. If in twenty two days he is not well, in next month's Moon he will be in danger of death.
25. If in six days he doesn't die, he will recover (even if with great labor).
26. Serious and dangerous infirmity.
27. It denotes that from this infirmity he will fall into another.
28. There will be danger of death before the twenty first day.
29. Little by little he will recover.
30. Arduous infirmity; however, with care and diligence he will soon recover.

Of the election of baths

It is not less important, in its proper time and place, to have a good decision on taking a bath as it is for a purge or bloodletting; but one should notice that a bath can be taken for two reasons, for cleanness and for health. If it is for cleanness it is quite enough that the Moon is in the Sign of Libra or Pisces, and the person in question will be extremely clean. If the bath is taken for health reasons one should consider the sickness and if it requires humidity or dryness. If it requires humidity, such as a blockage, shrinkage of the nerves or others similar to these, it is convenient to wait until the Moon is in Cancer, Scorpio or Pisces, for these are aqueous Signs and its nature is humid. If the sickness, however, requires dryness, such as paralysis, it is convenient that the Moon is on an igneous Signs, such as Aries, Leo and Sagittarius, whose nature is dry, and as such the bath will have a great benefit.

By this figure one shall see over which members and entrails the seven Planets and twelve Signs have dominion over

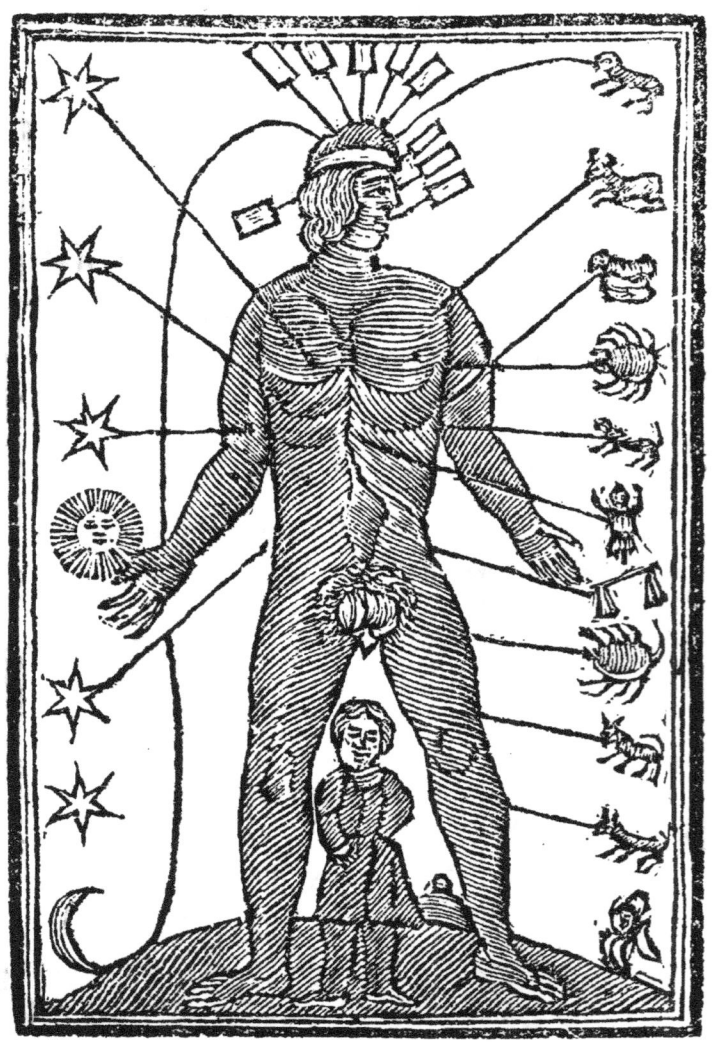

Of the benefit of bloodlettings on various part of the body as well as suction cups

In the middle of the forehead there is a vein, whose bloodletting serves for the relief of headaches, no matter how old they are, and this is even truer if such a pain is on the backside of the head; it is also useful to treat hemicranias, discharges from the eyes and infirmities of the face, such as morphea, recent leprosy and frenzy. And on each corner of the eyes there is a vein which is used to clarify the sign, and for all infirmities of the eyes.

On the inside of the upper lip one shall find two veins, which are used against all eye rheum.

Under the tongue, deep down, there is a vein whose bleeding is used to remove eye pain, swellings of the face, jaw ache, nose stench and itches.

The bleeding of the cephalic vein is good for eye and ear pain.

There are three veins under each knee, whose blood extraction is good for kidney swellings.

The saphenous vein, which is under the curves of one's legs, is used to remove ear pain.

In the middle of the smallest finger of the foot and hand there is a vein which is used for Ophthalmology, hot swellings and knee pain.

On the tip of the nose there is a vein used to stop the flow of tears. On each side of the face, under the jaw, there is a vein that, if bled, is of great value for the sight.

Two other veins on the front of the tongue are good for tonsillitis and swellings.

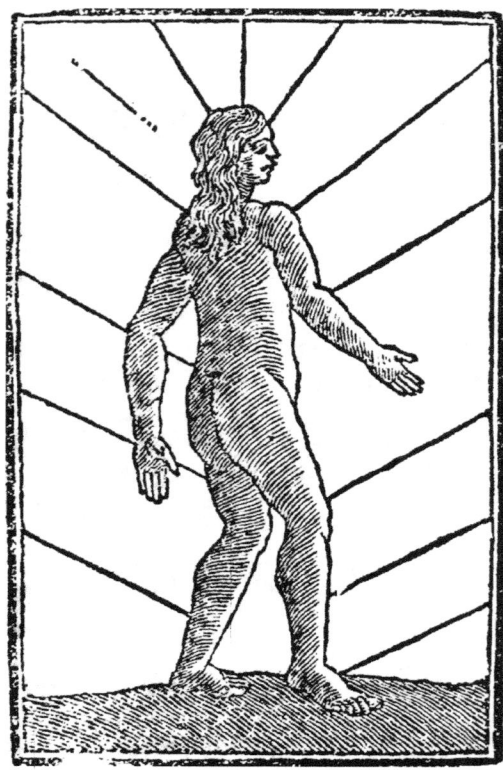

The middle, or common vein of the arm, is used to remove pain from the head, heart, lungs and from the whole body.

The basilic and the hepatic vein, which is the one belonging to the liver, is used to cure headaches and remove the flow of blood from the nose.

In the middle of the head there is a vein whose bleeding is used to remove migraines, no matter how old the pain may be.

Two veins found inside the foreskin are used for heart pain.

Bloodletting of the vein found between the thumb and the index finger is used to avoid head and eye pain.

The vein which is between the ring and little finger is used for crises of the spleen, and intense heating.

Above the shins there are two veins which are called the sciatic and their bleeding is used to remove arthritic pain, or sciatica and excessive blood flow.

Behind the ears one will find two veins that, if bled, are used for the same as the sciatic veins and even more for eye sight.

Some Astrological considerations for bloodlettings

Since we have declared the harmful times for bloodlettings, it will be appropriate to offer which times will be good and convenient to make good use of these.

For the choleric it is very useful to do a bloodletting when the Moon is in an aqueous Sign, such as Cancer, Pisces and Scorpio, this in the last fifteen degrees.

To the phlegmatic it will be of great use to do a bloodletting when the Moon is in hot Signs (with the exception of Leo), such as Aries and Sagittarius.

To the melancholic it is convenient to do a bloodletting when the Moon is in an airy Sign (except Gemini), such as Libra and Aquarius.

Finally, the sanguine may do a bloodletting in any Sign in which the Moon may be at, keeping with the rules of Medicine and Astrological warnings explained up to this point.

Suction cups may be used on any Sign on which the Moon may be at, except Taurus. The cause of this is because this Sign passes through certain starts which are of the nature of Mars.

Of suction cups

A suction cup placed in the middle of the head removes swellings in the face, foulness from the nose and itching in the eyes.

A suction cup on the buttocks is good for swellings of the thighs.

A suction cup placed on the back is good for chest pain.

Suction cups placed under the bellybutton remove stomach pain and colic.

Suction cups placed on the thighs are used to remove hotness in this same area.

Suction cups placed under the legs are used to cure fistulas and wounds in the thighs and to avoid all phlegmatic humor.

A suction cup in the middle of the neck is used to remove swellings of the eyebrows, and to clear one's sight.

A suction cup under the buttocks is used to cure a heavy body.

Finally a suction cup placed under the thigh is used to avoid certain infirmities such as hemorrhoids, menstruation, blood flows, and itches on one's spine.

Healthy advice, worthy of being taken by any Christian heart

Any time the celestial bodies determine that a theft or a runaway slave shall not found, and any infirmity shall be dangerous, prolonged or deadly, it is most wise to resort to God and his Saints; for it is most certain that these can hold back the celestial influences and make it so as lost and stolen things are found, as has been done so many times by the Blessed Saint Antony of Lisbon, of the Order of Saint Francis, to those who, with confidence, ask him through the following verses, which the church prays in honor of this same Saint. These go as follows:

> *Si quæris miracula,*
> *Mors, error, calamitas,*
> *Dæmon, lepra, fugiunt,*
> *Ægris surgunt sani.*
> *Cedunt mare, vincula,*
> *Membra, resque perditas,*
> *Petunt, & accipiunt*
> *Juvenes, & cani.*
> *Vers. Pereunt pericula,*
> *Cessat & necessitas,*
> *Narrent hi, qui sentient,*
> *Dicant Paduani.*
> *Gloria Patri &c. Cedunt &c.*

And in truth I say, for the glory of God Our Lord and praise of the glorious Saint, that not a few times has it happened to me to find lost or stolen things by means of these verses. And believe those who hear me that even if what you seek is delayed, do not lose faith nor cease to say these verses many times, for you will certainly not be denied, if such is what is convenient. I say convenient, for even if it is true that we know of what we are asking for, it is an even a greater truth that God our Lord knows much better what is convenient for us; and thus He sometimes concedes to what we ask for by intercession of the Saints, and other times he does not, as one time happened to a great lady from the City of Valencia who, being greatly molested and tormented by a cancer, performed a novena to the Blessed Saint Louis Bertrand of the Order of Saint Dominic, pleading to him with great devotion for health. And upon finishing the novena she was healthy and free of such issue. After some days of being healthy this said lady heard from a certain Preacher of that City that many times labors, disgraces and infirmities were the reason for many Christians to be rewarded with Heaven. And having heard this the good lady decided to make another novena to the Blessed Saint Louis Bertrand, praying to him that, should that infirmity he had removed from her be her reason to be awarded Heaven, that he should please give it back to her. And once the petition was finished did her previous cancer return; and shortly after she died, and piously is it believed that she is enjoying the company of God in Heaven. These two miracles are authenticated by D. Miguel Espinosa, Bishop of Morocco and Canon of Valencia.

Returning to our verses to the Paduan, you may use it not only to find lost and future things, but also freedom from many and great labors and miseries, for it has a very effective virtue: such as driving the devil away, preventing errors and calamities, freeing one from death, leprosy and other evils, by which a sick person may return to good health and the needy find their remedy. To these verses does the ocean, the wind and storms obey; and further still those who are weak and paralyzed will be set free and healthy through the devotion of these verses. And do note something strange, which is that the Holy Mother Church permits that anyone petition God for a miracle through these verses, as the first three words go: *Si quæris miracula*. All of this I said for those who suffer from theft and other similar labors, so as they do not raise any Astronomical figures, for no advantage will be gained from these, quite the contrary, they are the cause of great infamy, suspicion and heartbreak, as the same Astronomers will tell you and experience has shown, and of this truth I have been a witness.

Greatly useful and necessary health regiment to conserve and extend one's life, taken from the Medicine of Avicenna

A lot do we owe (dear reader) to the learned Medics and experts, for with their industry and knowledge (through God) do they free us from many labors and infirmities, returning our lost health to us; however, I think we owe them more for having left us the rules by which we may not only conserve our health, but also extend our lives. And as many times the body grows sick over the lack of health of the soul, it will be good to firstly provide an Ecclesiastic rule and regiment, so as each one of us may, with the favor of God, conserve the health of their souls, which is the grace and principal means to conserve the health of the body.

Charissime, time Deum,
Et fuge a non timentibus eum.

This first verse tells us the method and rule that one should follow in order to conserve the health of the soul, which is the fear of God and to keep away from those who do not fear him; for, as the Ecclesiastes says, Proverb 15: *Quit timet Deum faciet bona;*[69] which means: He who fears God will do good things, which are the conservative medicines for the soul and prevention of many miseries, labors and infirmities of the body. This verse further says that to preserve the holy fear of God, it is convenient that we stay away and flee from those who do not fear him, for, as the Proverb says: *Cum sancto sanctus eris & cum perverso pervertiris*; and thus, by losing fear is respect lost, and from losing respect is the total ruin of the spiritual and bodily health born.

---

69. Translator's note: this reference seems to be wrong, the only similar lines in Ecclesiastes seem to be in 5:6 (tu vero Deum time), 7:19 (quia qui timet Deum, nihil negligit), 8:12 (ego cognovi quod erit bonum timentibus Deum) and 12:13 (Deum time, et mandata eius observa).

Si Medico carebis hæc tria tenebis,
Mentem lætem, requiem & moderatam diætam

These verses say that if by any chance we find ourselves in a place where there are no Medics or medicine, we should find and use three things, and as such we will have no need for Medics or medicine. The first thing is to be in a joyful mood, for the Wise says in Proverb 17 n.22: *Ætatem animus gaudens floridam facit*; which means: the joyful mood makes the age blossom, conserving itself boastful, robust and strong. To the contrary the Wise says in the same place: *Animus tristis dessiccat ossa*. Which means: the gloomy mood not only destroys the flesh, but also consumes the bones and ends life. The second thing that we must seek to conserve the health of the body and that of the soul, which is quietness and calmness of spirit, is to keep away from us all excessive bodily care, for it troubles and disturbs one's mood, and drives away sleep and rest, as Avicenna says *doct*. 3 Chapter 1: *Nimiæ curæ diminuunt dies*. Which means: excessive care diminishes and make one's life shorter. The third thing we must above all else conserve is the temperateness of eating and drinking, which is the cause of great good, both bodily and spiritual; and its contrary carries with it an infinite number of evils, such as infirmities of the body and restlessness of the soul, of which we shall mention below.

Lumina mane, & manus gelida lavet aqua:
Si esse vis sanus, ablue sæpe manus.

The first verse says that it is very healthy to wash one's hands, eyes and face with very cold water, first thing in the morning, for Avicenna says that besides the contentment and advantage the senses receive, the brain is comforted and one's sight becomes humid, strong and much clearer. The second verse says that performing the above plenty of times conserves one's health.

Mane quisque modicum pergat.
Modicum sua membra extendat.

These verses say that, in order to conserve one's health, it is convenient to, once one is out of bed, to walk around in a small space and stretch one's members, for according to the writings of Avicenna, with this moderate morning movement are the over fluids of the first and second digestion *ad evacuandas fæces, & urinam*, and with these movements are the vital spirits attracted to the members and outer parts of the body, and these are thus made robust and fortified, and the spirits of the brain made thinner.

Crines pecte, dentesque juvabis,
Et ita cerebrum, membraque evacuabis.

These verses declare how important it is for one's health to comb one's head in the morning and clean one's teeth, for, from the first does one acquire three advantages, and from the second are three harms averted. The advantages from combing the head are the following: The first is that the head is made cleaner and relived of heavy humors. The second is that the pores are dilated and opened, and thus are the vapor from the brain evacuated. The third, and greatest advantage, according to Avicenna, *tract*. 3 Chapter 1, is that one's sight is clarified and freed from thick and salty humors, and this rule is of particular advantage for those of old age. The harms that are avoided by cleaning one's teeth are these: the first is for the reason of limes and filth that attaches itself to the gums, which not only corrode and blacken the teeth but also corrupt the breath, causing great bother and disgust to the person in question and all those around her. The second harm, according to Avicenna, is that this breath infects the stomach and corrupts the nutrients. The third harm is that, corrupting the nutrients, corrupted vapors rise to the brain, harming and disturbing it.

Nigridem dentum, atque fœtorem,
Tot malum tollit, atque dolorem

These verses say that the root of oregano boiled with wine whitens and strengths the teeth, and, as Avicenna says, Chapter 3, not only removes pain from the gums and teeth, but also conserves a good fragrance if one washes the mouth with this wine two or three times a day.

Nobilis est ruta, quia lumina reddit acuta,
Auxilioque rutæ vir quippe videbit acute.

Theses verses praise rue, and with good reason, for by rubbing one's eyes with it is one's sight made sharper. Avicenna writes that, dripping the juice of rue into one's eyes, sharpens and strengthens the sight. Another Author writes that washing one's eyes with white wine, boiled with rue, conserves the sight and makes it much more penetrating, and such is excellent.

Omnis mensa male ponitur, absque sale.
Vas condimenti debet proponi denti.

The first verse says: a table is not properly set without salt. And the second verse says that the first thing that should be put in front of a man who is about to eat is salt, and so claims Sadoleto[70] with this verse: *Sal primo debet poni, primoque reponi*; which is the same as stated above, for any meat taken to the fire without salt is extremely dull and lacking in taste; and for that is the following verse said: *Sapit esca male, quæ datur absque sale*. Meaning that meat without salt, not only has no taste, but is further unpleasant. By eating salt moderately along with any food are many advantages taken and some ills avoided. Firstly, it helps with digestion, it tightens the muscles, cures nausea, moves the appetite and generates good pleasure while eating. Salt avoids corruption of the humors, *aperta penetrationem veneni per poros*. Too much salt, or excessively salty meals waste away one's sight, for they dry the humidity of the eyes by which they are conserved. It causes great itching all over the body and generates mange, for the excessive salt creates a stinging, abrasive and penetrating humor from where (according to the Almansor,[71] Chapter 3) mange, leprosy and other ills arise from.

Post piscis nuces, post carnes caseum manduces:
Caseus est sanus, si dat avara manus.

The first verse says that health will be greatly conserved if after eating some fish one eats some kind of nut; and, according to Avicenna, this should be nutmeg, which not only reduces the phlegm, which fish usually generates, but (according to the same author) comforts the stomach and sight. Furthermore, the verse says that after eating meat it is convenient for one's health to eat some cheese, for it settles the food and makes for good digestion &c. *Faciet descendere cibum ad fundum stomachi ubi magis viget digestio*. This is due to the fact that cheese causes food to drop to the lowest part of the stomach, where digestion occurs with the greatest efficiency. The second

---

70. Translator's note: uncertain reference, the only relevant Sadoleto I know of is Jacopo Sadoleto, an Italian cardinal of the XVth and XVI century. However, a very similar line does also feature in Thomas Cogan's (1546 – 1607) *Haven of Health*:

Sal primo poni debet, primoque reponi,
Omnis mensa male ponitur absque sale.

This same line also appears in the book *Elementa Sanitatis, Ex Libris Medicis*, but its author seems to be obscure.

71. Translator's note: see following footnote.

verse says that cheese is good but only if eaten in small amounts, and Rhazes'[72] Almansor says that old cheese is good for the phlegmatic and fresh for the choleric, for one does not feel the salt in fresh cheese as much as in the old.

Panis sit fermentatus,
Bene coctus, & oculatus;
Quem si sumpseris calidum;
Ægrum te puta, & pallidum.

These two verses declare the condition for good bread: the first is that it is well leavened, for it is of a light digestion. The second is that it is well baked, for in any other way it will be greatly harmful, heavy and of bad digestion. The third is that it is soft on the inside, have many vacancies and as such have no viscosity. The second verse says that bread should not be eaten hot, and thus wrote Avicenna by saying: *Panis non comedatur calidus, qui non est apud naturam receptabilis.* This being for the reason that hot bread is not well received in nature, for it causes thirst and blockage, and because those who eat it as such continuously have a pale face.

Natura vino conservatur,
Si vero moderate sumatur.

These verses say that with wine is nature preserved, however, this should be moderately and temperately, as Avicenna writes, Chapter 4: *Scias quod salus conservatur & virtus augmentatur vino convinienti, ac moderato.* This means that health is preserved and natural virtue increased with a good wine, drunk in moderation. But should it be drunk vulgarly without temperance Pliny says it is greatly harmful to one's health and prejudicial to one's virtue; for it causes many and great infirmities, such as: gout, paralysis, leprosy, mange and hotness. Too much wine damages the head, disturbs the senses, reduces memory, clouds one's reasoning and numbs the tongue. Philo,[73] Medic, says that wine drunk without temperance increases one's rage, occupies the brain, weakens the nerves, and diminishes strength. Finally, too much wine burns the blood, corrupts the humors, corrodes the entrails and shortens one's life; it also sows discord, uncovers secrets, discredits a person and affronts their generation. Plato left the following written as a law (3 *legum*), that soldiers should not drink wine, at least not in excess, for besides weakening their strength and numbing their cunning, it causes drowsiness, which is not desired in a war, much less in the Christian republics. Being the great Orator Demosthenes asked on how he could talk so eloquently, he answered by saying that he had spent more on olive oil for study than on wine to drink. Of the glorious father Saint Dominic it is written that he abstained from wine for ten years so as to better penetrate the divine and human letters. Also it is said of the wise Solomon and Daniel that they abstained from wine so as to be further enlightened by the wisdom of God, unto whom we should pray for grace, so as we may drink of Him and that his divine Majesty may be served and our health increased.

Post prandium nihil, aut parum dormire,
Post cænam vero mille passus ire.

The first verse prohibits sleep after eating, unless it is a small amount, for, should it be in excess, this causes great damage, such as indigestions of the stomach, headaches, severe blockage of the veins, and, according to Avicenna, from this does fever, catarrh, debilitated appetite and an extraordinary tiredness and laziness of the members occurs. Hippocrates says, Proverb 2, that

---

72. Translator's note: Muhammad ibn Zakariyā Rāzī, a Persian polymath from the IXth century. The Almansor, or *Liber ad Almansorem*, the Latin translation of his *Kitab al-Mansouri fi al-Tibb* was extremely popular among European medics in later years, being merely one of his many works.

73. Translator's note: Likely Philo of Tarsus, the inventor of a famous electuary mentioned by Galen, contemporary of Emperor Augustus.

when sleep is natural, habitual and received with temperance it is healthy, but when it is in excess it is harmful. The second verse says that for the preservation of health it is convenient to have a small walk after supper, or perform some kind of mild exercise, because going to bed directly after supper generates many inconveniences, such as those declared in the following verses:

Ex magna cœna stomacho sit máxime pœna.
Ut sis nocte levis, sit tibi cœ brevis.

The first verse says that from having too much food for supper there is a great penalty and harm to the stomach, and even more if one goes to bed immediately after eating; for it prevents sleep, causes restlessness, aggravates the mind, causes great boredom and the eruption of scabs on the face. In order to free ourselves from such inconveniences, the second verse says that supper should be light and moderated, and we should follow the advice of the following verses:

Post cœnam mille passus,
Omnibus assuetam jubet servare diætam
Hippocrates sic esse, nisi sit mutare necesse.

These verses say that Hippocrates orders in his Aphorisms that, in order to conserve health, one should keep a constant diet. And we should say that by diet we do not only mean the eating and the drinking in general and the hours one has reserved for these, but also all bodily exercises that one is accustomed to. Hippocrates then says of both things that *non debet fieri subita, vel repentina matatio*. Which mean that if one is accustomed to work and physical exercise, and all of the sudden is struck by idleness, this will be the occasion for him to lose his health. And the same he says of those who eat and drink moderately and offer themselves to excessive and extraordinary consumptions. And as such we see many that for having abandoned their usual foods immediately fall ill; and those accustomed to exercise, upon abandoning it immediately notice this in their health, for *consuetude est altera natura*. This means that custom turns to nature and one should not change this unless it is out of necessity, as the following verse says.

Sibona vina cupis, hæctria servabis in cunctis:
Fortia, formosa, fragrantia veluti rosa

These verses say that in order for wine to be good it must have three properties, which are: be strong, have a good color and even better scent. Strong wine, drunk temperately is greatly advantageous and healthy for the body, for it feeds and nourishes. Good colored wine, besides causing great contentment to the sight, is appetizing and generally better. Wine with fragrance and a good scent is greatly comforting, generates good blood and invigorates the subtle spirits.

Caro caprina, leporina, atque bovina,
Melancholica est ægrotisque maligna.

These verses means that goat (male), hare and ox are not good to preserve one's health; this because (as Rhazes' Almansor says, Chapter *de anima*) such meats generate thick humors, and make the blood turn melancholic. Isaac[74] writes (*in diætis universalibus*) that ox and billy goat meat is hard, heavy and of a bad digestion, and that these generate melancholic and heavy humors. Finally all meat coming from an animal with sharp fur is not good for the preservation of health, and the worst of the above mentioned meats (according to Avicenna) is that of billy goat, and the best (according to Galen) is pork back fat; however, for those who are ill, neither one or the other is of any worth, but rather these are quite malignant and harmful.

---

74. Translator's note: Isaac Israeli ben Solomon, a IXth and X[th] century Jewish physician, the book mentioned (*Diætæ Universales*) is the Latin translation of the first twelve chapters of his book *Kitab al-Adwiyah al-Mufradah wa'l-Aghdhiyah*.

Et caro porcina sine vino peior caprina
Cum his tribus vina non erunt nociva.

These verses mean that one should not drink water after having eaten bacon, for this meat is worse than that of goat and of those other animals mentioned above; but, if taken with moderate wine, it will not be harmful, but rather healthy

Inter prandendum sit sæpe, parumque bibendum,
Ac si sumpseris ova, sint libi blanda, & nova.

The first verse warns us that while eating we should drink little and in small amounts, for according to Arnaldus de Villa Nova:[75] *Talis potus juvat transitum cibi, & præparat stomachum ad suscipiendum cibum sequentem.* This is, that drinking in these small amounts, not only aids the transit of the consumed food, but also prepares the stomach to receive other dishes. The second verse says that should we eat eggs we should seek that these are soft and fresh, for these are better and of a better nutrient than the hard ones; they are of easier and lighter digestion, generate good and subtle blood and without overflow. These eggs, says Avicenna, are very good for the weak, old and the recovering.

Singula post ova pocula sume nova.

This verse says (taking into consideration the above mentioned rule) that over each egg one should drink a sip of good wine; for, according to the author of these verses, who is Arnaldus de Villa Nova, it settles the stomach and greatly helps the penetration of nutrients into the members.

Balnea, Venus, emissioque sanguinis,
Ista nocent oculis, sed vigilare magis.

These verses mean that excessive baths, the venereal act and bloodlettings are damaging to the sight; however, much worse for the sight is to make a nightly vigil. For, according to Avicenna, baths, wine and the venereal act warm and dry to the highest degree the humid and cold nature of the eyes; and in this way is the eye sight weakened and diminished; and too much bloodlettings also debilitates it. However the second verse says that too many vigils is much more damaging on the sight, for it dries the humidity of the eyes, which is of no small damage; especially the vigils one makes while studying, writing or while looking attentively at any small thing. One should note the great damages made by the venereal act, that the constant evacuation of semen causes aging and the whitening of one's hair earlier in life.

Esuriet, sitiet, vigilet, qui rheuma tenet,
Hoc bene tu serva, si vis depeller rheuma.

These verses say that eating little, drinking even less and too many vigils dry and expel the rheum from the eyes and head, because with hunger is the humidity of the stomach dissipated and with thirst the same happens to that of the brain. And finally, too many vigils prevent the rising of vapors to one's head, and thus says the second verse, together with the first, that all rheum is consumed and finished.

---

75. Translator's note: a XIIIth century alchemist, astrologer, physician and translator from Aragon, master of Ramon Llull and, according to legend, of Saint Elizabeth of Portugal.

Fœniculum, verbena, rosa, celidónia, ruta,
Ex istis fit aqua quæ lumina reddit acuta.

These verses mean (according to the Almansor) that from these five simple things is a substance and liquid made which is most wonderful for the eyes, with which is one's sign comforted, sharpened and clarified. These are fennel, verbena, rose, tetterwort and rue, which are must praised and approved by any learned Medics.

Est modicum granu, magnumque virtute sinapis,
Quod caput expurgat, & lacrymare facit.

These verses say that mustard grains are small in size, however they are great in virtue and quality; according to Avicenna, they are hot and dry to the fourth degree, of which Palladius says they should be harvested during the waning Moon; for they are better at this time than in the crescent, and can preserve their virtue for a longer period of time. It would be enough of praise to this little seed to have this little grain of mustard compared to Christ our Redeemer the Holy living and pure Faith. However, for all of our benefit, we will say some of the properties and virtues of this grain, according to Pliny, Book 29, Chapter 8, Dioscorides, Book 2, Chapter 140 and Avicenna, Book 2, Chapter 84. Firstly it purges the head, and with its mordacity induces sneezing and tears and distills rheum through the nose. It thins all thick and viscous humors, and is thus healthier for the phlegmatic; and to all others it unclogs the liver and the spleen. It prevents infirmities, mainly those that originate in the phlegmatic humors. It is good against paralysis of the tongue and other members. The smoke from this seed drives away lizards and all other venomous[76] animals, and this smoke, received from below, makes women have their rules,[77] cleanses the *madre*,[78] removes all urinary impediments and is also valid for the quartan fever, cures ringworm, face rash, mange, clarifies the voice, helps with digestion, removes pain and coldness from the chest and finally dissolves all sand and stones from the bladder.

Dicitur salvia, quasi salvatrix,
Est naturæ humanæ conciliatrix.

So many are the virtues and properties of sage, and it is so favorable to the human nature, that with great reason is it called with the above names, and of it these other verses say the following: *Cur moriatur homo cui salvia crescit in horto?* Which says: So much is the virtue and excellence of sage that he who uses it will never be ill. But to this we may answer with another verse, which goes: *Contra vim mortis non est medicamentum in hortis.* Which means: there is no herb or medicine which is of any worth or remedy against death. Of the properties of this plant, however, we have written extensively in our book *Physiognomy*.

Mentitur mentha se sit depellere denta.
Ventris lumbrico stomachi, vermesque nocivos.

These verses say that mint has the virtue of killing and casting out roundworms from the belly, should its juice be taken first thing in the morning before breakfast, or, should it be dried, drunk, as a powder with white wine, or simply just eaten. This herb is good against rabid dog bites; if made into a paste, and mixed with salt, olive oil and vinegar, it removes the venom[79] from

---

76. Translator's note: the original word is *peçonha* (ponzoñosos in the Spanish editions) which is a quite more complex concept than simple venom. *Peçonha* has a certain connotation of evil, as this is a noxious property of "evil" and poisonous animals.
77. Translator's note: menstruation.
78. Translator's note: vagina.
79. Translator's note: *Peçonha*.

scorpion bites. Crescentiis[80] says, Book 6, Chapter 64, that the juice from this herb, taken with honey is an antidote for poison, both taken as a liquid and a solid; from this herb it is said that scorpions and other poisonous animals flee. Avicenna says in his *Canon*, Book 2, the Chapter on Mint, that by putting this herb in milk it will not go sour.

Ut minus ægrotes, non inter fercula potes.

This verse means that in order to live healthily we should not drink between lunch and supper, at least not before three or four hours have passed, should the thirst not be great to the point of necessity; for, drinking before digestion is finished wastes away the stomach, creates over fluids, generates bad humors, aggravates the body and removes the appetite. Those who wish to live without bothers, and heal from many infirmities, may drink very little and always with thirst. And above all, eat little and more will you live: *intelligenti pauca*.

Marvelous effects of the Moon, by the signs and the first thunder of the year

If the first thunder of the year is heard when the Moon is in the Sign of Aries, this denotes an abundance of grass and pasture for cattle, also anxieties in those of Martial and Saturnine nature, causing some to make rash decisions due to the choleric humor which governs them; in others it will cause desperation, due to the overflowing of melancholy they have. But the wise and prudent will dominate all of this with his free will.

If the first thunder of the year is heard when the Moon is in Taurus, this denotes great fertility in the mountains and a better harvest in the highlands than in the vales; and there will be an abundance of small cattle and even greater amount of wine.

If the first thunder of the year is heard while the Moon is in the Sign of Gemini this denotes rain, frost, abundance of bread and vegetables, and a shortage of all kinds of poultry, but not of birds of prey however.

If the first thunder of the year is heard while the Moon is in the Sign of Cancer, it denotes hunger, revolutions in those places dominated by this Sign and there will be a lot of grasshoppers, causing great damage to wheat and all fruits in any lowlands, and there will also be an abundance of water.

If the first thunder of the year is heard while the Moon is in the Sign of Leo, this denotes riots in some Kingdoms, that supplies will be sufficient and that some Principal or magnate will die.

If the first thunder of the year is heard while the Moon is in Virgo, this denotes that there will be great threats from enemies, spies and deaths among large animals.

If while the Moon is in Libra the first thunder of the year is heard, this denotes that the year will start dry and end extremely humid and supplies will be expensive.

If the first thunder of the year is heard when the Moon is in the Sign of Scorpio there will be a bad grape harvest, great mortality of fish and small cattle, abortions among women and there will be no shortage of terrible winds.

If while the Moon is in Sagittarius the first thunder of the year is heard it denotes that there will be moderation in rain and this will be rewarding, even if there won't be that much fruit and there will be many arguments and issues among housekeepers.

If while the Moon is in Capricorn the first thunder of the year is heard, it denotes dependence among men and sadness and plague in some of the lands subjected to this Sign.

If, while the Moon is in Aquarius the first thunders of the year are heard, it denotes an abundance of water and great agitation, amazement and alterations among the people, with terrible and unhealthy winds.

If while the Moon is in Pisces the first thunder of the year is heard there will be a great drought and, when its time comes, great cold and freezing, plenty of wine, little fruits and plenty of disease, not deadly however.

---

80. Translator's note: Petrus de Crescentiis, or Pietro de' Crescenzi, a XIIIth and XIVth century Bolognese jurist, writer of the *Ruralia Commode*, a book on agriculture.

One should further be warned that all these prognostications will mostly happen in those lands which are subjected to the Sign in which the first thunder is heard.

Important warnings for farmers

So as all that one may sow produces a good harvest, a farmer should always sow during a new Moon and this either in Taurus, Cancer, Virgo, Libra or Capricorn, and in this way will he see a great and strange difference in what he sows and what he harvests.

Very curious and useful secret for farmers

In order to know, from one year to the next, what grains or seed will be most abundant, an Andalusian Astronomer writes, and is further mentioned by the most learned Zamorano in his *Chronology*,[81] in Letter 80, that if one sows, on a piece of good and humid land, four of five castes of all seeds, such as: wheat, barley, corn, favas and chickpeas, one month before the Caniculars, and in case of necessity waters the said seed, those which fare the best and grow with the greatest strength on the day of the beginning of the Canicular, which on the 24th of July in Lisbon and 21st in Madrid, of this one plant there will be the greatest abundance in the following year; and those plants which seems to be weak and dying on that same day, of those there will be very few in the next year.

---

81. Translator's note: this refers to Rodrigo Zamorano, a Sevillian cosmographer, pilot and mathematician, and the book mentioned is the "Cronologia y reportorio de la razon de los tempos" from 1594.

Treatise
OF RUSTIC AND PASTORAL ASTRONOMY

IMPORTANT FOR FARMERS, SHEPHERDS AND NAVIGATORS

The signs of earthquakes by several methods

When any Comet appears displaying a black, red or green color, this denotes earthquakes.

When the ocean swells and alters itself without there being any wind there will be an earthquake or a great storm.

When birds seem to flee in panic, they denote an earthquake.

When the water in the wells becomes murky and one feels a bad odor without any exterior cause for it, then this denotes an earthquake, and very soon.

When one sees that all farm animals are frightened, this denotes an earthquake.

When earthquakes happen during the night, they are always close to the morning, and during the day they are close to the midday, for during those times the air is usually quite still.

In Summer and Autumn there are more earthquakes than in any other time, and they are also more frequent in those places close to the sea and in the mountains.

The signs of plague by various methods

When the Southern wind blows and it doesn't rain, and as quickly as it is cold it is also hot, and one has intermittent rain, then this is a sign of pestilence and grave infirmities.

When in Summer it is extremely dry, in Spring very cold and humid, in Autumn hot and one has also a dry Winter, this denotes plague and other illnesses due to the switching of the nature of the weather.

After any earthquake or any great famine, one should always fear pestilence.

When on the same day the air alters itself a great deal of times, and the following day it presents itself clear and very cold, immediately followed by extreme heat, then this denotes pestilence.

When reptiles are seen multiplying in abundance, flies are greatly increased and nocturnal birds are seen coming out during the day frightened, this denotes pestilence.

When the Southern wind blows too many times in Spring, it denotes acute fevers and belly ache, especially in women or in those who have a humid complexion.

When it rains and the Southern wind blows during Spring and Autumn, it denotes illness in Winter.

The signs of shortage by various methods

When Comets with very long tails appear, these denote shortages and lack of fruit.

When the weather is switched, meaning that when it is supposed to be cold it is instead hot, this denotes a great shortage.

When during any Eclipse one sees a black, green or red sign, this denotes a shortage.

When in Winter there is a lot of rain it is a sign of shortage.

When in the beginning of Summer there is a lot of rain and frost, it denotes shortage.

Signs of storms by the Sun

When, before the Sun rises, many clouds are gathering around it, this denotes a storm.

When the Sun appears to be large and yellow at dawn, even on a clear day, it denotes that on this same day there will be a storm with thunder and lightning.

When the Sun rises green or blue, it denotes a rainy storm.

When the Sun appears as if it is concave, it denotes a storm with rain.

When the Sun is seen to have many circles of various sizes, it denotes a storm with rain and wind.

When the Sun sets very bright with a few black or green spots, it denotes a storm with water and wind.

If, while the Sun is setting, it is raining, then this may indicate a windy storm for the following day.

Signs of serenity by the Sun

When the Sun rises clear and temperate, without any clouds around it, it denotes that that day will be serene and clear, with some dryness.

If, while rising, the Sun has any circle, and if this slowly fades away, it equally denotes serenity and a clear day.

If when the Sun is setting there are no clouds, it denotes serenity for that night and the following day.

Signs of wind by the Sun

If, when the Sun is rising, it shows any kind of concavity, it denotes humid winds.

When the Sun appears yellow in the morning, with some clouds under it, it denotes Septentrional winds.

If the Sun appears red in the morning it signifies dry winds.

When the Sun, while rising, spreads out the clouds, some to the South and some to the North, it denotes humid winds with water.

When the Sun rises and sets with a green or blue color, surrounded by think clouds, it denotes hard and humid winds.

When, while rising, the Sun is seen to be bigger than usual, there will be strong winds by the third day.

When the Sun has many circles around it, it denotes storms and wind, and if it has a single one of many colors it denotes the same.

When the Sun sets looking very fiery it denotes winds from the East, more or less strong, and dry.

Signs of serenity by the Moon

If the Moon has sharp and resplendent tips during the three days before or after the conjunction, opposition or quarter, it denotes serenity for that whole quarter.

If the quarter or full Moon has the part facing the Septentrion thinner and brighter, it denotes serenity.

If the Moon, at the fourth day, has its tips thin and is extremely resplendent, it denotes serenity for that whole Moon.

If the Moon, at the time of its rise, is clear and without any clouds around it, it denotes serenity.

If at the time of its rise the Moon shines its light all around itself, it signifies serenity.

If the Moon has some circles around it, and if these are white, yellow or red, it denotes serenity.

Signs of wind by the Moon

When the Moon is very red, three days before or after its conjunction, or has a circle of this same color, this denotes extremely strong wind.

When the Moon, being new, has very thin, rosy and resplendent tips, which also seem to move, this denotes terrible wind.

When the Moon, before the fourth day, does not show sharp tips, but rather these appear blunt, it denotes continuous winds for practically that whole Moon, and these shall come from the West.

When, on the fourth day, the Moon reveals its tips to be broad, and if these appear to move, it denotes strong and wet winds.

When, on the fourth day, the Moon has a red circle there will be wind.

When the Moon shows itself red, no matter the time of year, there will be wind.

When the Moon rises from the Horizon, or sets, and is seen to be red and not very resplendent, this denotes extremely strong winds at the third day.

When the Moon has any black or green circle with several gaps, this denotes strong winds.

When the Moon is full and has any circle, and inside this circle there is a cloud, then this denotes terrible winds.

Signs of rain by the Moon

When the Moon, before its conjunction, or after being full for three days shows its tips to be thick and dark, that signifies that it will rain at the quarter Moon.

When the Moon appears, after its turning,[82] to be dark and green, it denotes that there will be rain soon.

When the Moon shows its Austral tip to be thick and dark, it will rain before the full Moon.

When the Moon is not visible before the fourth day, and there are Western Winds, then this denotes great rains.

When the Moon has its turn[83] on a Tuesday it usually rains; if by any chance it rains on the first Tuesday after its turn, the rain will last for a quarter Moon.

Signs of storms by the Moon

When the Moon, before its conjunction and opposition, for three days, and three days more after, shows its tips to be thick rather than sharp, and these also seem to move, this denotes a storm at sea for an extended period of time.

When the Moon appears to sparkle in the water, and over the rows of a boat, it denotes a storm.

When the Moon has many dark and intermittent circles it denotes bad weather with water and wind.

When the Moon is very bright at the sixteenth day of its age, it denotes that there will be a storm soon, both on land and sea.

When the Moon appears very reddish and has a purple circle, it signifies that there will be a storm with hail and lightning.

---

82. Translator's note: uncertain translation.
83. Translator's note: uncertain translation.

Signs of cold by the Sun, Moon and birds

When the Sun appears in Winter to be extremely resplendent or red, it denotes cold for the following day.

When the Sun rises or sets and has a lead color circle, it signifies cold for the following day.

When the Moon is green or has the color of lead during its quarters, or is on any of the earthly Signs, it denotes great cold for that quarter.

When many small birds of different species gather to seek food in any village, it denotes great mists.

When scroll and paper, during humid weather are suddenly dry, it denotes a change in weather with great cold.

Signs of serenity by the Stars

When the Stars are still and resplendent, it denotes serenity.

When one sees exhalations that look like Stars traveling from one part to the other, this denotes serenity with the winds.

When the fixed Stars and Planets have some circle around them, and this is white, yellow or red, it denotes serenity and if they have any other circle, and it is red, there will be serenity with the winds.

Signs of wind by the Stars

When the Stars at night seem to be extremely resplendent, and moving, there will be hard wind on the following day.

When the Stars, or in a more correct way, the bright exhalations, travel from one part to the other, these denote winds in the region they are traveling to.

When the Stars appear to be bigger than usual, this denotes winds by the third day.

When in the four parts of the World the Stars or Comets move from one part to the other, they denote terrible winds with thunder and lighting.

When certain Stars are seen to move and quickly hide, these denote stormy winds.

When in some Stars one sees red or yellow circles, this denotes wind.

When the Stars called The Seven Sisters manifest themselves more resplendent than usual it denotes wind in that region.

Signs of cold by the Stars

When in Winter the Stars are extremely resplendent, or seem to move, they denote cold with great winds.

When one sees a great density of Stars in the Heavens, it is a sign of great cold and shift in the weather.

Signs of wind by the clouds

If, during a clear and serene sky, some cloud appears on the horizon, it denotes winds, and these are to begin from that same region.

When the clouds move towards diverse regions and are very thin, this signifies winds.

When some thick clouds are surrounding high places, it denotes winds.

When clouds appear in the Orient as fleeces of wool, it denotes extremely wild winds from the Austral.

When, at Sunset and afterwards, extremely red clouds appear at dusk, these denote winds. And if the clouds extend towards the South there will also be water.

When the Arch of the Sky appears in the morning, it denotes wind in the afternoon of the same day.

When the Arch of the Sky appears while the weather is serene, it signifies wind.

When the Arch of the Sky appears yellow or red around any Star, it denotes wind.

Signs of serenity by the Arch of the Sky

When the Arch of the Sky appears during stormy and cloudy weather, it denotes serenity.

When at the Sunrise and Sunset the Arch of the Sky appears, it denotes serenity.

When the Arch of the Sky appears in the afternoon it always denotes serenity, and if it appears in the morning it denotes wind in the afternoon.

When one sees, on the horizon, lightning without thunder, with few clouds, it denotes serenity.

Signs of serenity by the birds and fish

When the hawks are still and peaceful by the creeks it denotes serenity.

When the swans, when going across the water, cross each other and do not dive, this denotes serenity.

When the cranes are flying high and keeping quiet without any squawking, this is a sign of serenity.

When the pigeons are constantly flying from one place to the other, and singing, this denotes serenity.

When the goshawks are playing with each other up in the sky, this denotes serenity.

When the mosquitoes gather in great numbers and produce great buzzing after Sunset, this denotes serenity.

When the crows open their mouth while looking at the Sun, this denotes serenity.

When the river or ocean fish are seen jumping out of the water, this denotes serenity.

Signs of wind by the birds and fish

When the swallows are flying close to the ground or water, with their wings touching the surface, this denotes extremely strong winds.

When the sheldrakes stretch their feathers with their beaks, this denotes winds.

When the dolphins jump through the air and come very close to land, this denotes winds.

When the cormorants are constantly cleaning their wings and feather, while many others are making a great noise, this denotes winds.

Signs of rain by the birds and land animals

When the sheldrakes are swimming and produce louder noises than usual, this means that it will rain.

When flies gather greatly in the Sun, this means that it will rain.

When the pigeons come back later than usual to their pigeon house, this denotes rain.

When the crows make sharper noises than usual, and carry straws in their beaks, this denotes that it will rain shortly.

When the owls sing during the Sunset, this denotes rain.

When the frogs are singing and the moles digging the earth, making great mounds of it, this means it will rain shortly.

When the oxen, after it has rained, are grazing extremely fast, it denotes that there is still more rain to come.

Signs of storms by the birds and fish

When squid is seen jumping outside of the water, this denotes a storm.

When the dolphins are jumping over the water, and coming very close to land, this denotes a storm.

When water birds are getting away from the sea on to land, this denotes a storm soon to come.

When the sheldrakes and goslings make more noise than usual, this denotes a storm.

When cranes are very calm and relaxed by the sea shore, this denotes a storm.

When the seagulls are seen leaving the sea and going to the rivers, this denotes a storm with water and wind.

When the swallows fly over the water, and almost touch the surface with their wings, it signifies storms of water and wind.

When the hawks flap their wings a lot, and are constantly flying over the creeks, this denotes a storm.

Signs of storms by the land animals

When ants are extremely busy, and they move away from the place they were before, then they denote with great certainty that there is a storm coming soon.

When the wounded and those with gout complain a lot, it denotes that soon there will a storm and it will be cold.

When the cows are seen smelling the earth and then raising their heads to the sky, then they denote a storm.

When sheep are hitting each other and then raising their heads to the Heavens, then they denote a storm.

Signs of serenity by senseless causes

When, during the first light of the day it is colder than usual, then this is a sign of serenity.

When the tips of the mountains are extremely bright, then this denotes serenity.

When, at dawn, one sees a great mist, it denotes serenity for two days.

When, before the Sunrise, one sees many vapors and fog over bodies of water or fields, it is a sign of serenity.

When after some rain one sees on the sail of a ship some shapes, this denotes serenity.

Signs of wind by senseless causes

When the bells become louder than usual it is a sign of humid winds.

When the fire sparks more than usual, it denotes winds.

When the embers on the fire attach themselves to the pots sitting on it, it denotes wind.

When the mountains and sea emit a great rumble, it denotes stormy winds and storms at sea.

Signs of rain by senseless causes

When water taken from wells is warmer than usual it denotes humidity.

When the bells sound harder than usual, without there being wind, they denote that it will rain soon.

When door locks are hard to open and salted meat is humid, it denotes humidity.

When salt gets humid it is a sign of change in weather from dry to humid.

When the soot on the chimney starts falling by itself and in great amounts, it denotes that it will rain soon.

When any smell is felt stronger than usual it denotes humidity and rain.

Signs of storms by senseless causes

When the foam of the sea is spread through various parts of the surface of the water, this denotes storms.
When the sea is greatly agitated while the weather is serene, it is a sign of a strong storm.
When leather feels thicker than usual it denotes a windy storm.
When the first light of the day is yellow, it denotes a storm.

Signs of wind by lightning

When there is lightning to the West or North, it denotes a change in weather accompanied by winds.
When in Summer there is abundant thunder, it denotes wind from the region where they are heard.
When in the morning one hears thunder, there will be wind in the afternoon.

Signs of storms by the clouds and lighting

When it seems that clouds are at the same height as the mountains, it denotes storms.
When many clouds surround the Sun, without covering it completely, it denotes storms.
When lightning is seen in all four parts of the world, it denotes a storm with rain and wind.

Signs of rain by the clouds and the Arch of the Sky

When wind is blowing and in that region there are thick and dark clouds it is certain that it will rain shortly.
When at the West or Midday, one sees some clouds resembling tufts of wool it denotes that it will rain at the third day.
When at Sunset one sees a very white cloud, stretching towards the West, and in the middle of it there is another very dark cloud, it denotes that it will rain shortly and there will be wind.
When the Arch of the Sky appears before midday, it denotes rain in the afternoon and wind.
When the Arch of the Sky appears in the afternoon it denotes soft rain.
When one sees two Arches of the Sky it denotes rain.

Annotations

Signs of cold in humid weather signify serenity.
Signs of heat in cold weather denote rain.
Signs of cold and rain together denote snow.
Signs of cold and dryness denote frost.
Signs of wind in any weather are always strong, but more so in Summer and Autumn.

Signs of the fertility, sterility or infirmities of the year by the rustic method

The fourth day of January, should it be clear and serene, denotes great fertility; if it is windy it denotes sterility.
The seventh day of January, if it is clear and serene denotes infirmity in young boys; and if at night there are great winds, it signifies sterility and hunger.
The eighth day, if it is serene, will make fruit come later, but there will be a great abundance of these; and if at night there is wind it promises infirmities, particularly in scholarly men.
The ninth day, if it is serene and with winds at night, promises fertility in vegetables and fruits.
The tenth day, if it is serene and clear, denotes a sterile year.

The eleventh day, if it is windy in the morning, there will be a great abundance of fish and war, and if it is windy at night there will be a plague.

The twelfth day, if it is serene, denotes a multiplication in sheep; and if it is windy signifies plague.

The thirteenth day, if it is serene promises great storms, and if at night there is any wind many sheep and goats will die.

The fourteenth day, if there is an extraordinarily bright Sun, and if it is windy at night, it indicates a plague and a lot of infirmities.

The fifteenth day, if it is serene and with wind at night, signifies war.

The first day of February, if it is clear and serene, promises a great deal of wine.

The fourth day of February, if it is clear denotes fertility; windy signifies war; cloudy or foggy denotes plague.

Treatise

of some particular thing that the Majesty of God our Lord performed on the seventh day of the week

Of Sunday, the first day of the World

The World had its beginning on a Sunday, as is written in Genesis. *In principio creavit Deus cælum, & terram,* and it was created 5856 years ago.

On a Sunday shall all the labors and miseries of this life also be ended; for according to Guillaume Durand[84] in the *Rationale* such is the day the World will end.

On a Sunday was the Blessed Virgin Mary, Mother of Jesus Christ, God and true man, born.

On a Sunday was the desired Messiah Jesus Christ born for our blessing.

On a Sunday, first day of the year, month and week, Christ began shedding his blood, the day on which he received that sweetest name of Jesus.

On a Sunday, ninth of March, did Christ perform that solemn banquet to more than five thousand people with five loaves of bread and two fish, as is written in Saint John, Chapter 6.

On a Sunday, the one they call Palm Sunday, did the most sweet and humblest Lamb Jesus Christ enter Jerusalem, triumphing over his enemies who had him condemned to death.

On a Sunday, fifth of April, did the Redeemer of life resurrect from among the dead.

On a Sunday did finally the Church receive that mercy and singular benefit which was the coming of the Holy Spirit over the Apostolic College.

Of Monday, the second day of the World

On Monday did God create the Firmament from among the waters, and separated the superior from the inferior, naming the Firmament Heaven.

Of Tuesday, the third day of the World

On Tuesday our God and Lord created the earth, which he ordered to produce herbs, trees and plants which produced fruits and seeds, according to the nature they received from his Divine hand.

Of Wednesday, the fourth day of the World

On Wednesday the One God in Three persons created the Sun, the Moon and the Stars, so as they may bring us joy and light our day and night. On a Wednesday, twenty fifth of March, Christ, for our good, was condemned to death in the tribunal of the Jews, whose sentence was confirmed by Pilates in his tribunal on Friday the third of April.

---

84. Translator's note: Guillaume Durand (1230-1296), a French canonists, liturgical writer and bishop of Mende, the book mentioned is the *Rationale divinorum officiorum,* a liturgical treatise.

Of Thursday, the fifth day of the World

On Thursday the Majesty of God our Lord created the fish of the waters and the birds of the air, giving them the virtue of growth and multiplication with his holy blessing, words and commandments.

On this day, on the fourteenth of the Moon of March, which was on a second of April, Christ our Redeemer ate the Easter Lamb with his disciples, on which day he institutionalized the Holy Sacrament of the Altar.

Of Friday, the sixth day of the world

On Friday God almighty created all the animals of the earth, distinct in species, for the service of man.

On this day the Majesty of God created our first father and mother in his image and likeliness, making them able to achieve Heaven and lords of the earth.

On a Friday, twenty fifth of March (4003 years after the creation of the World) did the Son of God incarnate in the humble loins of the Virgin Mary; on which day was the Moon in conjunction with the Sun and not without mystery, for the true Sun of Justice was being joined *per carnis assumptionem* with the beautiful Moon Mary.

On a Friday was the Precursor Baptist born, which was on the twenty fourth of June.

On a Friday, the sixth of January, was the Redeemer of life baptized by Saint John the Baptist, at 29 years and 12 days of age of the same Christ.

On a Friday, on the first of the Moon and first day of the Hebrew month, which is called Nisan, which was on a twentieth of March, Christ resurrected Lazarus, after being dead for four days.

On a Friday, in the fifteenth of the Moon of March, which was on a third of April, did the Redeemer of the human kind die on a cross, having thirty three years not yet completed.

Of Saturday, seventh day of the World

On Saturday, the last day of the week, and seventh of the creation of the world, the Majesty of God our Lord rested, ceasing from the creation of new substance.

On a Saturday, eighth of December, was the Virgin our Lady conceived without original sin.

On a Saturday, sixth of January, did Christ operate that first miracle, which was to convert water into wine in Canaan of Galilee, having thirty one years of age.

On a Saturday did the Virgin our Lady die, at the age of 60 years, minus 23 days, according to Nicephorus Callistus,[85] who says that the Virgin Mother of God lived for further eleven years after the death of her Son Jesus Christ, God and true Man.

Curious astronomical warning of the seven days of the week

Those who are born on a Sunday, according to the Astronomical courses, are usually handsome, proud and secure.

Those who are born on a Monday are inconstant, lazy and sleepy.

Those who are born on a Tuesday are usually inclined towards religion.

Those who are born on a Wednesday are usually industrious, resourceful and inclined to travel the world.

Those who are born on a Thursday are usually modest, peaceful and quiet.

Those who are born on a Friday usually have a terrible condition, and usually live for a long time.

Those who are born on a Saturday are strong and important.

---

85. Translator's note: Nikephoros Kallistos Xanthopoulos, a great Greek ecclesiastic historian.

Another Treatise

and particular things that the High Pontiffs ordered in favor of the Christian Religion, from Saint Peter to Gregory XIII

Saint Peter was the first Pontiff who led the Church after Jesus Christ our Redeemer, by whose hand and power he was elected the universal Sheepherder of all the faithful. He reigned in the Church for 36 years 5 months and 12 days. He celebrated the first Council with the Apostles in Jerusalem, in which the Law of Moses and Idolatry were forbidden.

Linus, from Tuscany, ordered women to enter the Temples with their head covered.

Cletus, Roman, was the first to put into the Apostolic letters *Salutem, et Benedictionem Apostolicam*.

Clement, Roman, ordered that Notaries be spread throughout all lands so as to write the lives and deeds of the Saintly Martyrs.

Anacletus,[86] Athenian and Martyr, ordered that a priest be ordained by a bishop, and that in the consecration of a Bishop three others should be present.

Evaristus, Greek, considered it to be incest any marriage not consecrated by a Priest.

Alexander I, Roman, ordered that a Priest not say more than one Mass per day, and he also added to the Canon of the Mass the following: *Qui pridie quiam patereur*, and that water be mixed with wine so as to consecrate it and that holy water be present at the entrance of every door and private home, so as to keep demons away and relief worrying consciousnesses.

Sixtus, Roman, ordered that in Mass *Sanctus* be said three times, and that no one should deal in sacred things unless he had been Ordained.

Telesphorus, Greek, reinstated the holy fasting of Lent, that Saint Peter had established, and also that every Priest say three Masses on the day of our Lord's Nativity, and that the *Gloria in excelsis* be sung in solemn Masses

Hyginus, Greek, ordered that at Baptism and Confirmation there should be Godparents.

The Pope Pius, Italian, ordered that the celebration of the Resurrection be made on a Sunday

Anicetus, Syrian, ordered that all Clergy members wore a crown and not carry long beards.

Soter, from Campania, restored the holy custom of Priests blessing weddings, and that otherwise none would be considered married.

Zephyrinus,[87] Roman, ordered that Christians communed in Easter for the Resurrection.

Callixtus, Roman, ordered fasting on the four Ember days, and that Ordinations be given on these days, for before this time these were given only once in the month of December.

Urban I, Roman, ordered that chalices and patens be made of silver and not glass, as before, and that no one should be made a Bishop without being a Priest first.

---

86. Translator's note: to the best of my knowledge, in the official Catholic succession of Pontiffs this Pope Anacletus does not in fact exist, rather, there seems to be a confusion in dates and identification around Pope Cletus/Anacletus.

87. Translator's note: Cortez skips Popes Eleuterus and Victor.

Fabian,[88] Roman, ordered that on Holy Thursday the Oil and Confirmation be consecrated, and he established the Prothonotary.

Stephen,[89] Roman, established the Priestly vestments and the altar cloth.

Dionysius,[90] Monk, organized the Parishes and Dioceses by Curates and Prelates.

Felix, Roman, ordered that the Temples be consecrated, and that Mass should not be celebrated in an unholy place.

Eutychian, Tuscan, ordered that Martyrs be buried with the Chasuble and that the fruits of the Altar be blessed.

Caius, Dalmatian, established that no heretic should have the right to accuse a Christian.

Marcellus,[91] Roman, ordered that Councils not be celebrated without the authorization of the Pontiff, in whose time the College of Cardinals was institutionalized. In the time of Pope Eusebius the *Lignum Crucis* was found on a third of May.

Miltiades, African, ordered the end of fasts on Sunday, both in Lent and not, which was later removed.

Sylvester I, Roman, ordered that the Bishops should consecrate the Confirmation and the Baptism.

Mark, Roman, ordered that after the Gospel one should sing the Creed on all solemn days, as was determined at the Council of Nicaea.

Julius I, Roman, ordered that Priests should not be cited to a secular Judge, but rather an Ecclesiastic one.

Damasus,[92] Portuguese, ordered that at the end of the Psalms the *Gloria Patri* should be sung, and that in the beginning of the Mass the Confession should be said.

Siricius, Roman, ordered that the bigamous not be admitted into the Priesthood.

Anastasius, Roman, ordered that everyone should be standing during the recitation of the Gospel.

Innocent I ordered that in Mass, and on solemn days, peace be given unto the people.

Zosimus, Greek, ordered that the Paschal candle be blessed on the Holy Saturday.

Boniface, Roman, ordered that no one perform a Mass before they were thirty.

Celestine, Campanian, ordered that the Psalms be sung in Antiphon before Mass.

Felix,[93] Roman, ordered that the Churches be consecrated by a Bishop.

Felix IV,[94] Roman, ordered that the Extreme Unction be given to the sick at the appropriate time.

Boniface II ordered that the people be separated from the Priesthood during the celebration of Liturgy.

Vigilius,[95] Roman, ordered that the Virgin MARY be called the Mother of God.

Pelagius I, Roman, ordered that the Priests pray the seven Canonical hours each day.

Gregory,[96] Roman, ordered the singing of the Psalms and the giving of the ash in Lent, to which he further added four more days and established the Antiphons, the Kyries, the Hallelujahs and the Offertory: *o Deus in adjutorium* at the beginning of the Canonical Hours. He added the Canon of Mass, and that after the Consecration there should be a prayer of *Pater noster*. He ordered the greater Litanies, the Stations of Rome, Music schools, the worshiping of the Cross on Holy Friday and may other things, and was the first to name himself *Servus servorum Dei*.

Sabinian, Tuscan, divided the Canonical Hours into Prime, Terce, Sext, None and Compline, Matins and Lauds.

---

88. Translator's note: Cortez skips Popes Pontian and Anterus.
89. Translator's note: Cortez skips Popes Cornelius and Lucius.
90. Translator's note: Cortez skips Pope Sixtus II.
91. Translator's note: Cortez skips Pope Marcellinus.
92. Translator's note: Cortez skips Pope Liberius.
93. Translator's note: Cortez skips Popes Sixtus II, Leo, Hilarius and Simplicius.
94. Translator's note: Cortez skips Popes Gelasius, Anastasius II, Symmachus, Hormisdas and John.
95. Translator's note: Cortez skips Popes John II, Agapetus and Silverius.
96. Translator's note: Cortez skips Popes John III, Benedict and Pelagius II.

Adeodatus,[97] Roman, ordered that the children of Godparents could not marry the children of their *Compadres*.

Boniface, Neapolitan, ordered the establishments of the Feast of All Saint, and mandated that those who received homily in Churches could not be removed from them.

Vitalian,[98] Campanian, establish the Church Chant and Organ, and composed the Ecclesiastical rules.

Pope Leo II[99] ordered that Baptism be performed on any day.

Sergius I,[100] Syrian, ordered that the *Agnus Dei* be sung three times after raising of the Host to God.

Stephen IV,[101] ordered that no secular person rise to the Pontifical dignity, unless he came from an Ecclesiastical degree.

Sergius II,[102] Roman, also called by the name *Os porci*, which means "pig's mouth", being this the origin of the custom of Pontiffs changing their names.

John VIII[103] declared murderers to be irregular.

Adrain III,[104] Roman, ordered that for the creation of a new Pontiff it was not necessary to wait for the consent of the Emperor.

John XVI,[105] Roman, established the celebration and feast of the Souls in Purgatory in the whole Church.

Nicholas II,[106] Savoyard, organized the election of the Pontiff by the Cardinals.

In the time of Adrian IV[107] an extremely bright Cross appeared on the Moon.

Gregory IX[108] ordered that the Hail Mary be prayed, the bells be rung and the *Salve Regina* be sung every night at Church; and these bells were invented by the Bishop of Nolla, Campania, and it is from this fact that Durand says these have the name of *Campanæ*, and this was over six hundred years ago. And before these were invented the Christians were called into Church by trumpets, which were played from the top of their Temples.

Innocent IV,[109] Genovese, ordered that the Cardinals wear red caps, so as to represent that they are ready to shed their blood for the Church.

Urban IV,[110] French, established the festivity of *Corpus Christi*.

Boniface VIII[111] ordered the first year of Jubilee, which should repeated every hundred years.

---

97. Translator's note: Cortez skips Popes Boniface III and Boniface IV.
98. Translator's note: Cortez skips Popes Honorius, Severinus, John IV, Theodore, Martin, Eugene
99. Adeodatus II, Donus and Agatho.
100. Translator's note: Cortez skips Popes Benedict II, John IV and Conon.
101. Translator's note: Cortez skips Popes John VI, John VII, Sisinnius, Constantine, Gregory II, Gregory III, Zachary, Stephen II, Paul, Stephen III, Adrian and Leo III.
102. Translator's note: Cortez skips Popes Paschal, Eugene II, Valentine and Gregory IV.
103. Translator's note: Cortez skips Popes Leo IV, Benedict III, Nicholas and Adrian II.
104. Translator's note: Cortez skips Pope Marinus.
105. Translator's note: John XVI is usually taken to be an Antipope, with the next John being numbered in sequence as John XVII. I don't know if this is what is intended or just a genuine error, as there are a few others such cases in this list. Nonetheless, Cortez skips Popes Stephen V, Formosus, Boniface VI, Stephen VI, Romanus, Theodore II, John IX, Benedict IV, Leo V, Sergius III, Anastasius III, Lando, John X, Leo VI, Stephen VII, John XI, Leo VII, Stephen VIII, Marinus II, Agapetus II, John XII, Benedict V, Leo VIII, John XIII, Benedict VI, Benedict, VII, John XIV, John XV, Gregory V, Sylvester II.
106. Translator's note: Cortez skips Popes Gregory V, Sylvester II, John XVII, John XVIII, Sergius IV, Benedict VIII, John XIX, Benedict IX, Damasus II, Leo IX, Victor II and Stephen IX.
107. Translator's note: Cortez skips Popes Alexander II, Gregory VII, Victor III, Urban II, Paschal II, Gelasius II, Callixtus II, Honorius II, Innocent II, Celestine II, Lucius II, Eugene III and Anastasius IV.
108. Translator's note: Cortez skips Popes Alexander III, Lucius III, Urban III, Gregory VIII, Clement III, Celestine III, Innocent III and Honorius III.
109. Translator's note: Cortez skips Pope Celestine IV.
110. Translator's note: Cortez skips Pope Alexander IV.
111. Translator's note: Cortez skips Popes Clement IV, Gregory X, Innocent V, Adrian V, John XXI, Nicholas III, Martin IV, Honorius IV, Nicholas IV and Celestine V.

Clement VI[112] reduced the mentioned Jubilee year to every fifty.

Sixtus IV,[113] Savonesi, ordered that the above mentioned Jubilee be awarded every twenty five years, and this Pontiff confirmed the Feast of the Conception of the Virgin and approved the Office of that day.

In the time of Innocent VIII the title of Holy Cross was founded in Rome, and in this same time were the Indies discovered and found.

Leo X,[114] Fiorentini, conceded the remission of all sins of those who took upon the Crusade and gave alms for the war on the Turks, and in that year the sect of Martin Luther had its beginning, which was in the year of 1513.

In the time of Pope Clement VII,[115] Fiorentini, began the Order of the Society of Jesus by the Holy Priest Ignatius of Loyola, Spanish from Gipuzkoa, in the year of 1539.

Pius V,[116] Alexandrian, was the one who made the famous league with Spain, Venice and the Papal States of Italy against the Turks, by which league, with the favor of the Virgin MARY, did John of Austria achieve that famous victory in the naval battle against the Turks near the golf of Lepanto, on October seven, day of our Lady of Remedy in the year of 1571, which was a Sunday, Feast of the Rosary.

Gregory XIII, Bolognese, emended the time, fault and error of the Roman Calendar in the year of 1581, on the fifth of October, by taking 10 days from the said month, with the sound advice of great doctors, and no more days could be taken because of the celebration of Easter.

Those who say, without any foundation, that there was a Pope called John (Joan) who was a woman, they should know that such is fiction, fable and a lie invented by the Heretics with their hate towards the Holy Apostolic See, for there isn't any recorded history that says that such a thing ever existed, neither is such a thing recorded in the Catalog of Pontiffs.

The Litanies ordered by Pope Gregory I, added by Saint Ambrose, Bishop of Milan and Doctor of the Church, and who had them prayed over the whole of his Bishopric are the following: Free us Lord, from the logic of Augustine; for being a Gentile and Arian, had such great logical power that it was feared that he would pervert many with his arguments. Later Augustine converted through Saint Ambrose, who baptized him himself, and both of them composed that Chant so celebrated and esteemed by the Church, *Te Deum Laudamuns*, with Saint Ambrose saying one verse and Saint Augustine saying the other.

Treatise and virtue of the Agnus Dei

It will not be less important or curious than the above for the good Christian reader to know who was the first Pope to establish the *Agnus Dei*, and how this is worked, by whom, who does its blessing and consecration work and what are its virtues.

Of Pope Leo III, Roman, who rose to the Pontifical dignity in the year of 796, we know for certain that he was the first to establish the *Agnus Dei*, for he sent one of his *Agnus Dei* to Emperor Charlemagne (who he had recently crowned) writing to him in the following way:

Thou should know, Great Charles, that from the Balm and clear wax and Holy Sacramental Oil are the Agnus Dei made, of which I now give thee one, and I offer it as a grand gift, as born from the fountains and sanctified by the secret mysteries of Sacrifice.

In our own time the *Agnus Dei* are solely made of clear white wax and nothing else, as is described in the Roman Rite, Book 1, last Chapter: One should know that the Pope does not bless

---

112. Translator's note: Cortez skips Popes Benedict XI, Clement V, John XXII and Benedict XII.
113. Translator's note: Cortez skips Popes Innocent VI, Urban V, Gregory XI, Urban VI, Boniface IX, Innocent VII, Gregory XII, Martin V, Eugene IV, Nicholas V, Callixtus III, Pius II and Paul II.
114. Translator's note: Cortez skips Popes Alexander VI, Pius III and Julius II.
115. Translator's note: Cortez skips Pope Adrian VI.
116. Translator's note: Cortez skips Popes Paul III, Julius III, Marcellus II, Paul IV and Pius IV.

the *Agnus Dei* each year, as some think, but solely in the first year in which he is made Pontiff, and from that day on every seven years and no more.

Once these forms are made, greater or small, of white and very clear wax, the Pope's Sacristan and his Chaplain and Clerics take them and imprint on them the Lamb, express figure of Jesus Christ the sinless Lamb. After this is done they take them to the Pope's Chapel where, in his Pontifical dressings, he blesses an amount of water with many prayers and orisons; he then takes some of the balm and casts it into the holy water in the form of a Cross, saying: Lord, see it as fitting to consecrate and bless this water with this ointment and by our blessing: In the name of the Father, the Son and the Holy Spirit. And similarly he takes the Oil and casts it over the water as a Cross, saying the same words. He then takes the *Agnus Dei*, tightly wrapped in a white towel, and he places them on the said holy and consecrated water and baptizes them, and from there do the other Prelates remove them with silver sieving spoons and place them in a proper place to dry. And once again the Pontiff says over the *Agnus* many prayers and orisons, pleading to the Lord that all the Faithful who, with purity and devotion, carry these, may be given all that is good and may they be free from evil.

Virtues of the Agnus Dei

Firstly the *Agnus Dei* has the virtue of freeing those who carry it with devotion and confidence from all enemies, both visible as invisible.

It has also the virtue of keeping us and freeing us from many dangers, both spiritual and material, as the Holy Father asks in his prayers and orisons when he blesses the *Agnus Dei*, and by means of the said *Agnus* are many gifts, privileges and graces achieved, and even more, the remission of venial sins.

It also has the very effective virtue to raise and free a person from mortal sin, should she carry it with great devotion.

He who carries it will also be protected from storms, torments, lighting and thunder.

He will also be preserved from the plague, *gota coral*[117] and sudden death, as the High Pontiff asks God in one of the orisons he prays when he is consecrating it.

It also frees one from fire, ghosts, visions and frights, and also from the snares of the devil.

It also has the great virtue to free women who are in labor from all danger, giving them strength and confidence in that great distress.

One should also note a great excellence and virtue of the *Agnus Dei*, which is that if a woman is in labor, and is in danger of not being able to give birth, she should be given three small pieces of this to drink in some water and, with faith, she will give birth without injury or danger, and it is a wonderful thing that all mothers who take this will have given birth before the third pain arrives; and this should be given as soon as it becomes obvious that there is any danger. And have the devotion of saying:

Agus Dei, meserere mei.
Qui passus es pro nobis, miserer nobis.

Questions and answers between the Reader and the Author of this work over some difficulties on the Astronomical names

Reader: Speaking of the Planets and Signs, you mention their quality and the effects they cause, however, you do not declare the difference between these by which we may know which are of the Planets or the Signs or if the Planet is greater that the Signs, for I see that you described the Planets as much greater than the Signs; and why do you describe the Planets with human features, some different from the others; and the Signs as animals and other different aspects, and if they are in the Heavens why do you paint them with earthly aspects?

---

117. Translator's note: a typical name given to an undefined number of neurological symptoms, some of which are characteristic of epilepsy.

Author: Much material do you cover and a great field did you discover dearest Reader, and to respond to you a whole book would be necessary; however, I will answer to all of that and I shall explain myself with the greatest possible brevity: and responding to the first doubt may all the others be understood. The difference between the Planet and the Sign is that the Planet is a single Star and is found alone and single in one of the seven Spheres or inferior Heavens, and the Sign is not a Star, but rather a part of the Heaven, one of those twelve by which the Astronomers divide the Zodiac, considering them to be in the ninth sphere, which is after the eighth or Starry Heaven; and for that reason will you understand how greater is the Sign relative to the Planet, the great difference of that which is up in Heaven from that which is painted in the Lunarios and Almanacs, for the Planets are Stars and the Sign is a piece of Heaven where the infinity of the Stars are represented.

About that which you ask, of how to know of the Planet or the Sign, I answer: The Sign is an easy thing to know, if we remember that the Sun, on each month, enters one of the twelve Signs, and during a whole month is the Sun in this Sign, as is declared in the Signs themselves and in the Calendar of the months and Saints, and as such, regarding the knowledge of the Signs, there is no difficulty. The Planets you may not so easily know, unless you use some Ephemerides, which is a book on Astrology where one may see drawings of the Sky, being possible to know thus in which part of this each of the seven Planets may be found. It is also true that at night, if one is able to find the trajectory of the Sun, one may find some of the Planets, and recognize them by their colors; for the Star of Mars is always red and bright; the Star of Saturn is gray, close to the color of lead; and should you want to know the colors of the other Planets you may find them in the treatise of the Comets. Finally I respond on why the Astronomers represent the Planets with human aspects of different conditions, and the Signs as animals and other senseless figures that they surely do not require; I then say that the reason why they represent the Planets with such figures is because of the effects they cause and infuse in men. And thus you will see that they represent the Sun as a King and great Lord for two reasons: the first is because those born under his dominion are made to be magnanimous, royal, liberal and of a noble temper and given to rule, reign and govern. The second reason why he is painted as a King is because he is in the middle of the seven Planets, giving them all light and clarity. The Planet Mars is represented with a fierce aspects of an armed man, for he causes those who are born under his dominion to be cruel, warriors, enemies of peace and quietness, and seekers of fighting (as is said in the proper place of this Planet as well as of all others, and as such I will not deter myself). Regarding the different figures of the Signs, one should notice that some are represented with human figures over the various effects they cause and others by other figures over some kind of resemblance between this and what they represent. Like the Sign of Libra, which is represented as two equal plate balanced, denoting the equality of time caused by the Sun when entering this Sign of Libra, as the days become the same as the nights, and there is temperance between hot and cold, representing an equality between the heat of the passing Summer and the incomparable cold of Winter.

Reader: Greatly did knowing these finer things relieve me more than anything else in the Lunario, for even if seemingly not important, in truth, I ignored them.

Author: Do not think that I declare this to every man, for I know that there are many still who can actually teach me, and so I do not speak to these, but rather to those who do not know; by which reason, should you have any other doubt, please ask it, for I know that many do not ask of these small things and because of this they ignore them.

Reader: My consciousness tells me you are right, and so I say that I rather ask than ignore, so will you tell me why do you call the Signs the houses of the Planets?

Author: If you remember, when speaking of the Signs I pointed this out, but I shall repeat it for you have asked me. Know that every time that the Planets are found in their own Signs they have greater strength and dominion than if they are found in Signs which are strange to them, and for this reason we say that a certain Sign is the house of a certain Planet; as can be seen by the Sun when it enters the Sign of Leo, which is his house, where he shows to a much greater extent his virtue, strength and heat than in any other Sign.

Reader: You are right, in no other place does a man hold greater dominion than in his own house; however, you further say that some Signs are diurnal houses and others nocturnal houses.

Author: Know that the Signs whose nature is hot are called diurnal, and those that are cold are called nocturnal, just like the day has greater virtue by its heat than the night by its cold.

Reader: I am satisfied with this declaration; however, why do you call the Sign of Leo the diurnal and nocturnal house of the Sun?

Author: I shall tell you this. Know that the Sign of Leo, as he is hot, is called a diurnal house; however, comparing the heat of this Sign with the heat of the Sun, he is called a nocturnal house of the same Sun, because the heat of the Sun is so much greater than the heat of the Sign of Leo.

Reader: I am satisfied; however why it is said that some Signs are masculine and others feminine, and which are which?

Author: In good Philosophy the igneous and airy Elements are active and the aqueous and earthly Elements passive, and by consequence is the active called masculine and the passive feminine; and thus the Astronomers call the Signs of watery and earthly nature feminine. The masculine ones are: Aries, Gemini, Leo, Libra, Sagittarius and Aquarius. The feminine are: Taurus, Cancer, Virgo, Scorpio, Capricorn and Pisces.

Reader: I may say that your responses give me great contentment and I will further ask more, and so I plead to you that you tell me why do the Astronomers say that a Sign is the joy of some Planet and that another is the determent of another Planet.

Author: You know that a Sign in which a Planet shows greater virtue and strength, causing greater influence, is called its joy; and that Sign in which the strength of the Planet is reduced is called the determent of that Planet, and so we say that Leo is the joy of the Sun; for once the Sun enters in it, it manifests to a greater extent its heat, virtue and strength than when it enters in Aquarius, which is called the determent of the Sun, for when entering the said Sign of Aquarius, the Sun diminishes its strength and heat.

Reader: I have one question or doubt left, which is that you tell me which are the causes of why some Signs are said to be the exaltation of a certain Planet and other Signs the diminishing of another Planet.

Author: Know that when any Planet enters any Sign, in which the said Planet begins to manifest its virtue and influence, that Sign is called the exaltation of that Planet, as it happens when the Sun enters the Sign of Aries, which is on the eleventh of March, in which Sign the Sun starts to manifest to us its virtue and influence, and by this reason is it called the exaltation of the Sun. And this is the opposite with the Sign of Libra, which is the determent of the Sun, for upon entering this Sign on the twenty third of September, it begins to diminish its influence and heat, and in this way one may understand this for the other Signs and Planets.

Reader: I give you graces. But tell me in particular over which things does each Planet infuse and have dominion over, so as, knowing which Planet will be Lord of the year, we shall know of what things there will be abundance.

Author: I say it with joy, and I shall start with the Moon.

Things that are subjected to the Moon

It has dominion over all things humid and in particular donkeys, oxen, fish, white birds and sea birds. Over pumpkins, cucumbers, quince pears and melons, lettuce, purslane and chicory. In illnesses it has dominion over epilepsy, paralysis, shrinkage of the members and *gota coral*. In man over the head, belly, chest, stomach and the left side of the body. In color over white and saffron. Its greatest dominion is in the West.

Things that are subjected to Mercury

Mercury has dominion over quicksilver, over lead and coins and precious stones. In animals over goats, deer and all those that are quick and light; in birds over those that can talk. Over silk worms and bees; in trees over walnut, orange, lemon and pomegranate trees, lemon balm, linen, ginger and sugar cane. In colors, over vermilion and gray mixes; in infirmities over those of the spirit, thought, disquiets, doubts, vomit, common fever, tuberculosis, epilepsy and melancholy, and all of those arising from any unknown dryness. In the members it has dominion over the brain, tongue, mouth, nose, nerves, memory, fantasy, hands and legs. In the mechanical and liberal arts, over writing, music, singing, painting, sculpture and carving. This Planet has greater dominion over the Septentrional.

Things that are subjected to Venus

Venus has dominion over women, musicians and young people. In metals and mines, over copper, quicksilver, sal ammoniac and orpiment. Over saffron, roses, carnations, dates, musk, amber, pearls and balms; over servals, does, serpents, ants and spiders. In birds, over doves and hoopoes. In trees, apples trees and all of those that emit a singular smell. In colors, white tending towards green. In the human members over the kidneys, the shameful parts, buttocks, liver, bellybutton, vulva, nose and sperm. In infirmities, over fistulas, swellings of the liver and stomach coldness. Its greatest strength and dominion is to the Midday.

Things that are subjected to the Sun

The Sun has dominion over all that lives, both sensitive and insensitive, natural and corporeal, and in particular over gold and rubies, hyacinth and other stones; over saffron, peony, myrrh, incense and fig. Over fig, pomegranate and mulberries trees; over laurel, aquilaria, rosemary and hot and dry species. Over lions, crocodiles, rams, bulls, horses and dragons; over the heart and stomach of man; over the brain, nerves and the right eye. In infirmities over those that are hot and dry, cancer of the mouth and illnesses of the eyes. Finally it has its greatest strength in the East.

Things that are subjected to Mars

Mars has dominion over copper, iron, glass and places of ordinary fire in particular. In the animals over dogs, wolves, foxes and leopards. Over basilisks, goshawks, scorpions, vultures and birds of prey; over pepper, mustard, cumin, fennel, rue, scammony, cicuta, horseradish, onion, leek and red wine; in the human body over the liver, bile, veins and genital members. In infirmities over hot, acute and sanguine fevers, mange and itches, leprosy, and tertian, holy fire and migraines. In colors, over bright red. The strength of this Planet is in the West.

Things that are subjected to Jupiter

This Planet has particular dominion over tin and in stones over crystal, sapphire, chalcedony an coral; over sage, mint and marjoram; over wheat, rice, barley, grains and sugar; over nuts, almonds and pine nuts; over eagles, chickens and peacocks and all animals with cloven hooves; over amber, musk and camphor; in tastes over the sweet; in color over green and citrine. In the human body over the liver, ribs, blood, sperm and cartilages. In infirmities over stupor, apoplexy and schizophrenia; over those arising from corrupt blood and those that kill during sleep. The greatest strength of this Planet is in the Septentrional region.

Things that are subjected to Saturn

This Planet has dominion over lead, black and heavy stones and magnets. In animals over elephants, camels, pigs, moles and black cats. In birds over ostriches, owls, bats and nocturnal birds. In trees over *zambujeiro*,[118] oaks and cork oaks; over lentils, lupines, grass pea and acorns; styrax, cerussite, olive oil, chestnuts, cucumbers, onions and gourds. In the human body over the spleen and bladder. In colors over black and ash. Finally in infirmities it has dominion over all those preceding the melancholic humor. And this Planet dominates Ethiopia.

---

118. Translator's note: a type of olive tree endemic to the Madeira and Canary islands. *Olea europaea*.

Memory of Universal Remedies

for ordinary infirmities, made by Carlos Estevão and João Lihaut, Medics of the city of Paris.[119]

For continuous fever

It is of prime importance for continuous fever to place fresh egg whites well mixed with chimney rust, some salt and strong vinegar over the wrists of the patient, all tied together in a linen cloth. It is also good to take a sea squill, remove its inside and quickly tie it tightly to the patient's right wrist. Many also cure this by macerating chards or garden sorrel into a drink that once taken at the height of the fever breaks it. Others make dressings of this same substance and apply it to the wrists. Others take the seed of a herb called plantain and place it in water over night, giving this same water to the patient with some sugar.

For the common quartan fever

For the common quartan fever (and this is also good for anything else) take small or common sage, hyssop, *losna*,[120] parsley, mint, artemisia and clover; macerate this with coarse chimney rust and extremely strong untempered vinegar, making this into small dressings which are applied to the wrists. For this same problem it is also good to take the inside of two hot white loaves of bread, right off the oven, place these in vinegar and distill them in an alembic, and two hours before the fever returns one should give two ounces of this water to the patient.

For the tertian fever

Root of broadleaf plantain macerated with an equal amount of water and wine. Also possible is the juice of this same herb and giving it to the patient some time before the tertian. The juice of purslane and chayote does the same. For this same illness, the most effective remedy, according to some Medics, is to take in the morning, before one eats anything, two ounces of pomegranate juice, and immediately anoint the wrists and soles of the feet with popal balm with two drachma[121] of spider webs, and repeat this until the fever passes.

For headache arising from heat

Headache caused by heat is cured by placing cloths soaked with rose water or plantain, lichwort, lettuce and purslane juice together with vinegar over the forehead of the patient; or also, soak a cloth with two egg whites beaten together with rose water and place that on the forehead of the patient, making sure it covers the whole forehead. You may also cure this by washing the

---

119. Translator's note: Of all the various version of the *Lunario* I consulted, this section was only present in the 1857 Lisbon edition. Partly as a consequence of this, I was unable to confirm these two references.
120. Translator's note: this may either refer to absinthium/wormwood or southernwood.
121. Translator's note: a variable unit of volume, usually slightly above 3.5 ml.

head with tepid water in which vine leaves, sage, white lotus and roses have been boiled, and the remaining water should be used to wash the legs and feet.

For frenzies

For frenzies caused by a patient's continuous fever it is good to place over his head the liver or kidney of a ram, immediately after it is killed, or a large chicken or pigeon, killed and opened in half, over the back.

For excessive sleep

For those who sleep too much, it is good to give them burnt partridge feathers or old shoe soles or donkey nails or human hair to smell.

To cause sleep

For those who cannot sleep they should take the seed of the sleepy plant,[122] henbane, lettuce and the juice of the black nightshade[123] or the milk of a woman who is raising a baby girl, or ground-ivy leaves macerated with the white of one egg, and place this in a dressing on the forehead and this person will sleep.

For excessive redness of the face

To remove excess redness from the face it is good to wash it with water in which barley or oat straw has been boiled, adding some orange juice.

For weak sight

To cure a weak sight you can take fennel, common verbena, tetterwort, rue, euphrasia and roses, in equal amounts, and distill everything in an alembic; when you wish to use this medicine, put three or four drops in the eye right in the morning and afternoon, and this is a good remedy. It is also good to boil fennel, rue and euphrasia and receive that vapor in the face.

For sore eyes

You can remove eye pain with a boiling of *macela*,[124] lilies, and fennel grains in a mix of water and wine; to use this medicine you should fold a linen cloth into four parts and place it wet with this infusion over the eyes. A woman's milk, beaten with an egg white and placed over the eyes is also good.

For blood in the eyes

You will remove blood from the eyes by beating an egg white with rose or plantain water, soaking a cloth in it and placing it over the eyes.

For cataracts

Cataracts, or misty eyes, are removed by taking one or more fresh eggs of the day, boiling them in ash until they are hard and then cutting them into quarters so as their yolks can be removed. Then fill the eggs with rock sugar, or the whitest sugar you can find, place everything in

---

122. Translator's note: *Mimosa pudica*.
123. Translator's note: the original name of this herb literally translates as "*Moura* herb"
124. Translator's note: *Achyrocline satureioides*.

a clean cloth and squeeze it until a liquid or liqueur comes out; use this on occasions, by letting a drop fall in the eye of the patient and he will be cured.

Also good for this ailment is a liquid made from white vitriol, rock sugar, rose water, whites from hard eggs, all strained thought a cloth as described above, and take this in the morning and afternoon. Other also have successes with *tutia*[125] water, which is prepared by taking a bowl of *tutia*, half an ounce of *almecega*[126] and have everything melted in rose water and wine, a bowl of each, and place everything in a bottle of wine, putting it under the Sun for three days; you should hide this bottle every time the Sun is cloudy.

For ear pain

You can cure ear pain by taking rose oil, a little vinegar and putting it into the ailing ear, and place over this some *macela* and lily juice.

For a buzzing in the ear

For a buzzing in the ear it is good to put into it rue, spikenard or sour almond oil, or *aguardente*.[127]

For deafness

Drop into the ear onion or old man's beard juice mixed with honey or juice from the peel of the horseradish mixed with rose oil.

To stop a nose bleed

For those who have a nose bleed, they should have their extremities tied as tightly as possible and have a dressing of wild nettles placed over the nose, also he should hold in his hand roots and leaves of agrimony, or extremely cold water in his mouth, which should be slowly changed. Also very good are sage leaves and that central vein that the quince pears and other such fruits have placed inside his nose, and around the neck; more importantly placing cooling herbs over the jugular vein, such as lichwort, plantain, lettuce and others.

For teeth and gum pain

Make a boiling of henbane root with vinegar, rose water, and put a portion of this in the mouth every once and a while. The same can be done with a garlic bulb lightly roasted on ashes and macerated, placed over the teeth or ailing gums, as hot as possible; we further warn that firstly a small portion of this same paste should be placed on the ear of the side of the face where the pain is.

To comfort loose teeth

Take *alambre*,[128] rose water and make a boiling with this, or take the root of quinquefolium and *alambre* and apply it to comfort the teeth.

---

125. Translator's note: An impure form of zinc oxide frequently found on the walls of ore furnaces.
126. Translator's note: plants of the *Protium* genus.
127. Translator's note: a strong distilled grape spirit.
128. Translator's note: uncertain translation, but possibly a distilled juice from the black poplar.

To remove bad breath

Take anise, carob pods, *almecega* and root of the blue lily, boil everything with wine and use it to wash the mouth of the patient, this will remove the odor.

For tonsillitis

A good remedy is to take a whole swallow's nest, make a dressing from this with *macela* oil and sweet almonds and apply it to the throat.

For sharp back and flank pain

Take three ounces of blessed thistle, one spoon of white wine and six egg yolks from very fresh eggs, this mix you will give to the patient, tepid, as fast as he can consume it, and it is a great remedy. It is also good to make ash or dust of the virile member of an ox, and give that ash to the patient mixed with a drachma of white wine, only if the pain isn't too severe; and should it be severe, with blessed thistle or barley water it is a remarkable remedy. If taken for three days it will completely remove the pain.

The way to prepare the said ash is to cut the nerve or member of the ox into very small pieces, and place them in a small and new pan, over a hot fire with plenty of very hot ashes and embers around it. One should check on this occasionally until everything is turned into dust, which will take no less than a whole day.

To stop hiccups

It is good to hold one's breath, do stretches, get tired and go thirsty. It is also good to cast some cold water on the patient's face, or scare him with something that surprises him.

For vomiting

A slice of toasted bread dipped in mint juice and pulverized with *almecegas* and placed warm over the stomach, and by changing it every three hours the vomiting will stop. It is also good to take two bunches of mint and one of roses and boil them in wine, then to these boiled herbs you should add powdered *almecegas*, and all of this should be made into a dressing and placed over the stomach of the patient; if the vomit comes with great heat it will be good to boil some mint and roses with vinegar and dip the toast in rose oil, and place this as a dressing on the pit of the stomach and it will remove all sorts of vomit.

For stomach pain

Take a shallow bowl of ash sprinkled with wine and wrapped in a cloth and place it over the pain. It is also good to take coarse bread crumbs, heated in the oven and macerated with *macela* oil and placed over the pain, wrapped in a linen cloth.

For the liver

The best thing one can do to temper this heat is to frequently drink water of lettuce, sorrel and purslane, first thing in the morning, and this is extremely refreshing.

To remove the yellowing hue from the face

Take the bark of a hawthorn, harvested in the morning, and a batch of wet parsley. Macerate this with white wine and strain this through a clean cloth and drink it for two or three days in the morning and afternoon, and all the yellowness will disappear and a good color will return. It should be said that even if this remedy is extremely effective it should not be given to a pregnant woman, however, instead of this you may place on her wrists and the on soles of her feet macerated bark of holm oak, leaves of greater celandine and wild *macela* with wine, and this made into a dressing; otherwise, take some worms, wash them in white wine and dry them, then take a small spoon of this powder with white wine.

For hydropsy

Make a beverage of macerated broom grass seeds and white wine, or make a beverage with the juice of the root of the blue lily and *asato*,[129] also with white wine. It is also a proven remedy to take a few laudanum capsules and roast them in the oven, grind and sieve them and take them in an egg or some white wine, during nine mornings.

For hardness of the spleen

It is good to drink wine on which a deer tongue, asparagus and mandrake have been boiled; it is also important to take, first thing in the morning, a broth of half boiled crambes.

For colic

An important remedy for colic is to drink *macela* water, or the boiling of hemp seeds, or wine which had a campanula root in it for ten or twelve hours; but should you not want a remedy which is taken orally, then skin a lamb and place the skin, as it is, over the pain; a dressing of wolf dung is also very good against colic.

For diarrhea

For those cases that this arises from the humors, drink milk in which a steel, hot iron or gold bar is immersed, or eat roasted rice; otherwise, take a drachma of *almecega* with an egg white, and place a dressing of boiled untempered wheat flower and red wine over the bellybutton.

To stop bleedings

You will stop a bleeding if you drink three or four ounces of garden nettles or plantain, which will help greatly, also you may use broth from well boiled cabbages or pomegranate juice or a salad of plantain and sorrel.

So as to not spit out blood

For those who are spitting blood, they should drink water or boiling of *solda*,[130] plantain or snake grass or knotgrass, or alternatively swallow a mouthful of *almecega*.

For a bad heart

Drink two or three ounces of borage water or lemon balm water, or take two pig's hearts, three deer antlers, two nutmegs, carnations and sweet basil seeds, three drachma of each, flowers from every month,[131] borages, plantain, rosemary, a bunch of each, and make an infusion with

---

129. Translator's note: uncertain reference, but likely asarabacca, *Asarum europaeum*.
130. Translator's note: *Polypodium vacciniifolium*.
131. Translator's note: uncertain translation.

malvasia[132] or hippocras wine and let it rest overnight, then distill it in an alembic and use that, which is extremely helpful.

To produce milk

You will make milk come to a wet nurse by using fresh fennel juice or powered cow fat, and she will have plenty of milk

To diminish milk

Take the root of the greater celandine, which, boiled and kneaded with strong vinegar and placed over the breasts will dry the milk. Also a dressing of boiled fava beans or rue, sage, mint, *losna* and fennel, and incorporated with *macela* oil is very good.

For roundworms

You will kill roundworms by making the patient drink mint, purslane or rue juice, and also placing a dressing over the bellybutton with *losna*, asphodel and ox bile.

For kidney stone

It is good to drink broom grass, poaceae or silverweed water, in which the powder of burnt egg shells has been added, or loquat seed, and you will find a great remedy for kidney stone; and should you want an external one, place over the kidneys a dressing of lichwort, cypress roots and campanula leaves boiled in wine; however, what is more effective is to take a bath in which watercress, mallows, althaea, vines, broom grass flowers and *macela* were boiled, and while in the bath have a small bag of bran over the shoulders, and this if the stone is in the kidneys.

For bladder stone

If the stone is in the bladder then it will be good to take sour lime juice with white wine, or pear pits, placing them in white wine; and once they are dry grind them into a powder together with broom grass seeds, chayote, asparagus, saxifrage, melon, cucumber and pumpkins, and use this with white wine. It is also good to make a remedy from walnut shells and cherry tree gum, and take this with white wine.

For urinating in bed

For those who urinate in their beds, without having the ability to retain it, there is nothing better than eating a roasted goat liver, or drink with some wine a hare's brain or pig's bladder.

For painful urination

Use the boiling of four cold seeds, and after you urinate, place your member in milk serum; sometimes the drinking of goat milk cures the burning sensation.

To stop a woman's menstrual flow

If the woman drinks plantain juice with powdered cuttlefish bone, or powdered bones from sheep's feet, or from sea shells, or coral, or deer antlers, or burnt walnut shells, or ten or twelve grains of red peonies, she will stop the menstrual flow. From the outside it is also good to make

---

132. Translator's note: a caste of grapes.

a dressing with chimney rust mixed with egg whites and annual mercury[133] juice or brassica maritima[134] and place this above the arm and below the belly. For this ailment what is also widely used is cherry tree gum in an infusion of plantain juice placed over the location of the flow with a small syringe, or at least placing over the breasts leaves from the greater celandine.

For the white purge

It is good to drink plantain juice or purslane water; or the powder of a sponge burned in a pan, and externally by making holm oak or fig tree ashes and boiling in these some pomegranate peels, holm oak acorns, betony leaves and roots, a little of *alambre* and salt, and make a fumigation of this, or a bath, should that be more pleasant.

To cause a purge

If you wish for a woman to have her rules[135] give her each morning two ounces of artemisia water, or the boiling of poaceae, loquat pits and celery roots, cinnamon, saffron, round turnip roots and over all of this as much myrrh as fava beans. It is also very good to have a bath in water where one has boiled artemisia, mallows, altheae, lilies, *macela* and other similar herbs; and while in the bath she should rub her thighs and buttocks, while holding a small bag filled with artemisia, greater celandine, chervil, celery, betony, loquat pits and other similar things underneath.[136]

For separations of the Madre[137]

For separations of the Madre in women one should rub their arms and legs and tie them tightly, and place suction cups on the thighs and rub her stomach up until the bellybutton, also make fumigations of foul smelling things, such as partridge feathers, soles of old shoes, while applying sweet and smoothing scented things to the venereal parts, such as marjoram, thyme, catnip,[138] pennyroyal, amber, artemisia, musk and brassica maritima which must have grown to a considerable height; it is also convenient to make her drink *losna* water onto which fifteen rose or peony seeds have been dropped with wine; and if the woman is pregnant there is no better remedy than that which may be applied by her husband, for being all of the above dangerous for her.

For an out of place Madre

For a drooping or out of place *Madre*, the arms of the patient should be raised and tightly tied, place suction cups on her breasts and make perfumes of sweet smelling things and foul smelling things underneath; it is convenient to make her drink powder from deer antlers, and dried laurel leaves with strong white wine. It is also good to make a dressing of macerated garlic cloves and place this over the belly, so as the *Madre* will return to her place.

For inflammation of the Madre

For an inflammation of the *Madre* it is good to put over it plantain, black nightshade or knotgrass juice; or apply a dressing of barley flour, pomegranate peels and plantain, black nightshade or knotgrass juice, and the inflammation will be gone.

---

133. Translator's note: *Mercurialis annua*.
134. Translator's note: *Brassica maritima Tardent*, a synonym for *Brassica oleracea L.*
135. Translator's note: menstruation.
136. Translator's note: this particular instruction might actually mean that the bag has to be held inside the vagina.
137. Translator's note: uncertain translation, but I think what is being discussed is a widening of the vagina, meaning that these recipes and meant to tighten it once again.
138. Translator's note: uncertain translation.

Inflammation of the virile member

The same is also good for inflammations of the virile member, adding some dry roses.

For early birth

A woman who usually gives birth before time should eat ox nerve powder, prepared in the same way as we have described for the ailment of *pleuritude*,[139] and she should always carry a diamond on her finger, for this stone has great virtues in retaining creatures in the womb.

It is also said that the skin a snake sheds, dried and made into a powder and given with the inner soft part of the bread is very efficient in preventing abortion.

For childbirth difficulties. A water prepared for childbirth, the Madre, stomach and retention of breath and urine.

For the woman who is in labor and is unable to give birth, she should be given a boiling of artemisia, rue, betony and *macela* or parsley juice with vinegar, or white wine or hippocras wine in which cinnamon, date pits, cypress roots or *macela* flowers were immersed; and when the pain becomes sharper, give her some hippocras wine or a spoon of water prepared in the following way: place three ounces of cinnamon in a jar of *aguardente* and after three days strain this through a very clean cloth and add one ounce of fine sugar, and a third of the amount of the *aguardente* in rose water; conserve it like this in a glass jar for whenever it is necessary; this is very good remedy for any indisposition of the *Madre*, weakness of the stomach, retention of breath and urine and many other infirmities.

For sciatic pain

Apply over the pain a dressing made from wet bread crumbs boiled in cow or sheep milk, mixed with two egg whites and a little saffron; in another way, prepare a dressing of mallow roots, altheae, viola and mallow leaves, *macela* and melilot water, all of this boiled in water or a broth of tripe; after macerated and incorporated with two egg whites, linseed flour, pig's lard and *macela* oil; or even better and easier is to take cow manure, fava bean flour, wheat bran, cumin seeds and water with honey; all of this mixed into a dough, and equally made into a dressing and then placed over the pain or inflammation and then add some sulfur, naval tar, which in Latin is called *zopissa*, and mix everything well; it is also good to squeeze over this some elderwort and vine juice, boiling it in rue and worm oil, and made unto an unguent with some wax and rubbed over the location.

Windy[140] inflammation

You will resolve the windy inflammation by taking salt, drying it very well in a frying pan over a fire and then placing this between two cloths and put over the inflammation.

For very red inflammations

You will remove red inflammations by making a dressing of viola flowers and leaves, henbane flowers, black nightshade leaves, *macela* flowers, lilies and after all of this is boiled it should be applied on the region in question. It is also good to take knotgrass juice and mix it with some red wine and barley water and make a dressing of all of this and place it over the inflammation.

---

139. Translator's note: uncertain translation and the reference to the previous preparation seems to elude me, unless its referring to the ox penis used *For sharp back and flank pain*.

140. Translator's note: uncertain translation.

To soften an abscess

You will soften an abscess by placing over it a dressing of leaves and root of mallows, altheae and white bread crumbs, all boiled together, and then mixing in one egg white and some saffron; if the abscess is very cold then you may add to this boiling some roots of elecampane, elderwort, lilies, old man's beard and *macela* flowers.

For tumors

A tumor will become softer by taking wheat flour, egg whites, honey, and pig's lard; boil everything together in hot water and make a dressing.

For every kind of gout

Make a dressing of red cabbage, elderwort, fava bean flour, *macela* flowers and roses, all made into a well mixed powder, and placed over the pain. It is also good to take some roots and leaves of scabious, comfrey, wild sage and boil everything in wine; then macerate everything very well, add lily oil, *aguardente*, nerves from an ox's or cow's foot and mix everything and make a dressing with it.

For mange

You will cure mange by taking two parts of Venice turpentine[141] (you should wash this with cold water, four or five times, if it is rose water so much the better), then, with fresh butter, one egg white and the juice from one sour orange, make an unguent; then anoint the area and pass it through the hot air arising from a fire. It is also good to take some liquid storax and another part of pig's lard, everything mixed, and with this anoint your hands and with them the afflicted areas, for three or four nights.

For bug bites

If any person is bitten by any critter, it is convenient that they drink the juice of ash leaves with some white wine; these same leaves macerated as a dressing should also be put over the bite.

To remove any creature which has entered the body

When any critter or snake enters the body of any person when she is asleep, the best remedy is to breathe in, through a funnel, the smoke from burning old shoe soles, and the creature will exit from below.

For scrofula

Take some chicken fat, two ounces of wormwood oil and one ounce of hot wax, mixed and allowed to coagulate; this unguent you should place on some threads and place this over the wound for five or six days; after this, leave the wound be until it creates a crust and after this leave it until it becomes white and dry by itself; and as it starts to shed away, be sure to remove any dead skin so as no mark is left, and take some baby fat and anoint the wound gradually to close the flesh properly.

---

141. Translator's note: not the same as regular turpentine.

Oil of great virtue for cancer, scrofula once they are open and for every kind of foul, cancerous and fistulous wounds

Take a *canada*[142] of saltless olive oil, two *oitavas*[143] of male incense[144] powder, and one *oitava* of myrrh powder; and put all of this to boil while stirring it continuously; afterwards add ten ounces of turpentine to all of this in a pot, and boil until everything is well incorporated, and once you remove it from the fire cover it very well and leave it like this until it cools down and put it in a very well covered glass bottle.

You can place this oil on threads of small cloths, always in a very small quantity.

One other remedy for the great ill of scrofula

Grind some gun powder very well in a mortar and pestle and weigh amounts of this of roughly the same as three wheat grains, and take this same amount of *solimão*,[145] in such a way as on each sore there is the weight of six grains of these things, and also three of *trovisco*[146] seeds; and if the sore is very large, put more of each of these things on it, in the amount you see most proper, and do this the following way:

Take some soft sheep leather and put in it, on the inside, some turpentine, and over it place those powders, so as they may cover the sore; and leave it like this for three or four days, and once these are past remove the leather and the sore will be gone, and after it is gone do the following:

Take some chicken fat, the necessary amount, the oil linseed segregates when it is boiled, oil from the critters which are called chicken's bread,[147] and on equal parts of all of this drop some white wax until you make an unguent which can be put on some threads and on any scrofula; after these are removed be careful with what you eat for many days.

Another remedy for cloudy eye or cataracts, which is very proven

Take a bread made with rough flour, while this is still half baked in the oven but still hot, fill it with new or virgin white honey, as it is called, and place it in a clean alembic; once distilled the water which is thus extracted may be put in very small amounts in the eye in question, it is given that it will sting the patient, but he must endure it; before this water is used the patient should purge himself in the following way:

This syrup, taken every three days, consists of two ounces of eyebright water and two ounces of rose syrup and afterwards perform the purge in this way:

Six drachma of *diacratano*[148] incorporated in wine, and also take some honey and afterwards you may use the above mentioned water.

For severe eye pain or eyes which are extremely red and inflamed

Take a small portion of plantain and another of barley into a cloth; all of this well mixed you then boil in a *quartilho*[149] of white wine and a *canada* of water until this volume is reduced to half; with this water you will then wash the eyes; also, if you put into this water, during the boiling, a small portion of greater celandine, and before anything make two bloodletting from the salvatella

---

142. Translator's note: an old variable unit of measurement usually ranging from 1.5 to 2 liters. In Lisbon it usually stood for 1.4 liters.
143. Translator's note: an old unit of measure of 3.5856 g.
144. Translator's note: this refers to incense which is segregated naturally from the plant, and not extracted by any artificial technique.
145. Translator's note: a common name for corrosive sublimate, or mercuric chloride.
146. Translator's note: A common name given to a number of plants, most likely the *Daphne lauerola*, *Daphne gnidium* and *Thymelaea villosa*.
147. Translator's note: the larva of the *Diloboderus abderus*.
148. Translator's note: uncertain translation, but possibly diacatolicon, a purger.
149. Translator's note: an old unit of measure consisting of 0.35 liter, one quarter of a "canada".

vein, and taking five ounces of blood from each arm, taking care to take less should the person be weak, but in any case the patient should be bled at least once from each arm; and once this is done take the following syrup:

Two ounces of syrup of *quinque radicibus*;[150] for the purges this should be three *oitavas* of *mechoação*[151] and another three of this syrup, and two spoons of honey.

When one feels great stinging in the eyes and these also display great inflammation, take a herb called *acolodina*,[152] which should be boiled with dill and vine leaves, and all this should be very well boiled and with the water from this wash the eyes.

Another remedy for liver sores, new and old, and for all kinds of fistulas, mange, itches which appear on the face, for red harsh pimples on any part of the body. With this remedy many marvelous effects have been obtained

Take an *arratel*[153] of old bacon and clean it very well from any salt, without washing it, and make some holes in it along the side which has skin and place some wicks[154] in these, so as these go through the whole piece of bacon, then make some cuts in it, that should not go completely through, and put an ounce of finely ground sulfur in these. After all of this is done place the bacon in a roasting spit and light the wicks while having a bowl under the bacon. All which drips into the pan you will allow to coagulate and then you will change this into another heated pan and having the unguent melted, or at least hot, dip a feather in it and anoint the afflicted area once a day, being that during the night is the best time.

A most excellent water for sores of the liver

Two *quartilhos* of plantain water and one of rose water, one and a half ounces of flower of sulfur and boil everything in a glazed bowl for about half an hour; put this in a glass vase and soak some cloth in it and place this over the sores or skin rash, while not putting your hand directly in the water, so you should use a straining spoon to do this.

Another water for the same itches and swellings and for spongy flesh and to remove any signs of wounds

Take two *quartilhos* of plantain water and one of rose water and two ounces of potash alum and boil this until the alum is melted; take this from the fire and place it in a glass vase and soak some small fine cloths in this liquid and place these over the said ailments.

Another water to heal corrupt and foul smelling sores and resolve and dry swellings

Take a *canada* of sea water, two ounces of potash alum and boil this until the alum is melted and place this immediately in a glazed vase and wash the affliction with it and place cloths soaked with this water over the sore.

These three different waters described here are of a marvelous virtue and have shown their good effects very clearly.

---

150. Translator's note: a remedy made from roots of butcher's broom, wild celery, fennel, parsley and asparagus. A diuretic and expectorant.
151. Translator's note: *Convolvulus mechoacana*.
152. Translator's note: uncertain translation.
153. Translator's note: an old unit of measure, in 1499 settled as 0,459 kg.
154. Translator's note: uncertain translation.

Another remedy for the spleen

Take fennel, tamarisk, parsley, asparagus and celery roots, clean them from any dirt and macerate everything very well with a stone and put them in a pan with a *canada* of old saltless olive oil and half a *canada* of very strong white vinegar and a *quartilho* of sour orange juice and boil everything until all the vinegar and orange juice disappear, add a small *luberno*,[155] very well ground, sieved and mixed and put a *quarta*[156] of wax so as it will coagulate; mix this well and after it is coagulated anoint the spleen with it in the mornings and nights, in such a way as it doesn't reach the liver, and place over it a blue linen cloth soaked in chicory water and heat it with your hands or over the hot air from a fire and tighten a towel over the belly, and continue this for one to two weeks.

For jaundice, a very well proven remedy

Take some agrimony and extract its juice, take one spoon of this and drop it inside an egg from which you should have removed the white, and place it over the fire, and while this is warm give this to drink to the patient in the morning and afternoon for nine days, and before these days are over (God be wiling) he will have recovered his health.

For those who cannot retain anything in their stomach

Quince pears, very well cleaned, both inside and out, boiled in extremely strong vinegar and mashed in a stone cup and mixed with some well ground mustard; once this is well incorporated and still hot, place it in a linen cloth; spread over this some carnation dust and place it over the stomach and in two days he will be fortified.

For stomach pain by a cold cause

Two ounces of sweet almond oil, one ounce of *losna* oil, a portion of wax, very little (just the amount necessary for it to coagulate), a little incense and little of dry coriander powder; you should put the powder in as it coagulates, so as it does not sink, and before it is hard pass a linen cloth by this unguent, making it waxy; this cloth, placed over the stomach, makes a healthy work.

For hemorrhoids which are on the outside

Take pig's manure, put this on a fire and fumigate the sores with the smoke arising from it.

A very well proven powder for wounds

Take a flint stone and put it over some very hot embers. When the stone is blazing hot throw it into some very strong vinegar and those dust particles which are left in the bottom of the vinegar put them to dry and after that you may use them on any wound.

Another remedy to close sores

Dry quince pears, picked in the month of May, with their flowers, and after they are well dried make them into a powder which you will offer as a drink with wine or water, three or four times, and soon they will heal.

---

155. Translator's note: uncertain translation.
156. Translator's note: an old unit of measure, 3,45 liters.

A secret of great marvel for the bad airs

The root of a herb called *brinzo*[157] (which may be found near Santarem in a mountain neighboring Almoste, mainly in a farm they call "of the poplar", on the way to Santarem) very well macerated, adding a small quantity of mustard, which should be less than a third of the root, and once again macerated and very well incorporated. Immediately placed in a glazed bowl with boiling saltless olive oil and the fumes rising from this mix should be used to fumigate the ailing region; and after this fumigation have some powder of this same herb placed on a brazier and perfume with this that which was previously fumigated, keeping everything hot; and this is most proven, while keeping the area warm. The root of the said herb, carried by the neck in contact with the skin, is greatly affirmed for the preservation from bad airs.

For stone pain[158]

Take a handful of black grains[159] very well washed, and place them for one day and one night in two *canadas* of water, in a new pan, where it should then be boiled until you have only one *canada* left; then drop half a dozen of well washed parsley roots in it and after you are left with the single *canada,* strain that boiling through a clean cloth into a glazed pan, and each morning take a mug of this liquid, warm, where you should drop a shard of sugar every time you heat it up. As I have said, put a shard of white sugar every time you heat this syrup up and take it in the morning before you have anything else to eat, and from this syrup the patient should take fifteen portions, and he shouldn't eat any fish or harmful food.

LAUS DEO,
VIRGINIQUE MATRIS SINE LABE CONCETÆ

---

157. Translator's note: uncertain translation.
158. Translator's note: although I have no such confirmation, this is probably kidney stone.
159. Translator's note: this likely to be either a vegetable or mineral substance I'm not familiar with.

PHYSIOGNOMY

AND

VARIOUS

SECRETS OF NATURE

CONTAINING FIVE TREATISES ON
DIFFERENT SUBJECTS, ALL REVISED &
IMPROVED IN THIS LAST PRINTING

TO WHICH ARE ADDED MANY NOTABLE THINGS OF
GREAT UTILITY

COMPOSED BY JERÓNIMO CORTEZ,
NATURAL OF THE CITY OF VALENCIA.

NOW TRANSLATED INTO ENGLISH BY JOSÉ LEITÃO

IN 2017

THESE ARE THE AUTHORS FROM WHOM ALL THAT IS CONTAINED IN THIS WORK WAS EXTRACTED

Regarding Physiognomy these are the authors: Taisnerius,[160] Escoto[161] and Pedro de Ribas.[162]

Regarding Rosemary and *aguardente* these were: Arnaldus,[163] Pliny, Herrera,[164] Master Zapata,[165] surgeon, and Galen in the section of the simple; and many others such as: Dioscorides,[166] Theophrastus,[167] Serapion[168] and Crescentiis.

Regarding the secrets of nature these are: Mizaldus,[169] Pliny, Cardano,[170] Florentinus,[171] Albertus[172] and Licenciado Aranda[173] and the Italian Porta.

Regarding the position and place of the elements and the notable things caused and generated by these, as the treatise of the celestial region, these are Pliny, Alfraganus and Aristotle, prince of the Philosophers, as well as other infinite and grave Authors, who, for being so many, I will not mention.

---

160. Translator's note: Johannes Taisnerius, or John/Jean Taisnier, a XVIth Belgium writer who, among the great varieties of topics he wrote about, composed works of Palmistry and physiognomy.

161. Translator's note: likely to be Johannes Scotus Eriugena, an Irish philosopher and theologian of the IXth century.

162. Translator's note: Hard reference to place, but probably a Saragossan priest occasionally referred to as Petrus de Ribas.

163. Translator's note: Arnaldus de Villa Nova.

164. Translator's note: Gabriel Alonso de Herrera (1470 – 1539) a Spanish author mostly known over his book *Obra de Agricultura*, which was in constant use since its original printing until the beginning of the XXth century.

165. Translator's note: uncertain reference.

166. Translator's note: Pedanius Dioscorides, writer of the influential *De Materia Medica*.

167. Translator's note: Most likely the Greek philosopher, who also wrote on biology and botany in particular. Another alternative would be Paracelsus, but his works were highly persecuted in Spain.

168. Translator's note: Likely Serapion of Alexandria.

169. Translator's note: Antonio Mizauld, Antoine Mizauld or Antoninus Mizaldus, a XVIth century French physician and astronomer.

170. Translator's note: Gerolamo Cardano, a greatly influential XVIth century Italian mathematician and astrologer.

171. Translator's note: Nicolas Florentinus.

172. Translator's note: Albertus Magnus.

173. Translator's note: uncertain reference.

WARNING

In this printing there are included many curious, useful and advantageous secrets for the common good, and some games for laughter and fun, taken from other famous Authors and very well received.

TO THE READER

In all works of nature, prudent reader, it has shown itself so astute, prudent and provident that the Philosopher came to say: *Quod nihil naeturæ fit frustra*; and this means that nature never worked anything at random and without cause; but rather, that in all its aspects it attended to some good purpose and utility. Among the works in which it showed itself most ingenious, astute and or of a great art, was in the natural physiognomy of man, in that part which is animal, pointing its finger to what are good or bad compositions and natural inclinations of each one and further still the goodness or malice of the soul, as many times the body follows one's good or bad temperament. In such a way as the good or bad inclination is known by the disposition of the members and features of the face; for nature, at the time of generation of man or animal, disposes all the parts and members of the human body according to the qualities of the four humors, in the measure in which these are lacking or exuberant. And as such, those who are of a cold temperament will naturally be shy and of little strength, and those of a hot temperament are usually cheeky, animate and of great effort; for from coldness is fear and pusillanimity born and from heat comes boldness, cheekiness and strength, for heat is of a more active nature than coldness. And the description of those who are of a cold or hot temperament is found right at the beginning of the third Chapter.

What I ask of you, dear Reader, is that you accept this curiosity with benevolence, for I offer it in the same way; as also I offer the labor of consulting the great authors for the virtues of rosemary, the properties of *aguardente* and various secret of nature; declaring the place and position of the four elements and the heavenly bodies, and the effects of some over the others. Submitting myself in everything to the censorship and obedience of the Holy Mother Roman Catholic Church.

VALE.

LICENSES

BY THE HOLY OFFICE

The Book entitled Physiognomy and Various Secrets of Nature composed by Jeronimo Cortez, which this petition mentions, except on that which is crossed out, may be printed, and after it is printed it should be returned for further examination and selling license, without which it cannot be sold.
Lisbon 29th of July of 1687

Jeronymo Soares   Bishop Friar Manoel Pereyra   Bento de Beja Noronha
Pedro de Ataida de Castro   Friar Vicente de Santo Thomás

This book may be printed, having the licenses of the Holy Office and Ordinary and after it is printed it should return in order to be re-confirmed and taxed, and without this it may not be sold.
Lisbon 15th of August of 1687

Mello P. Marchão   Azevedo Rebeyro

This book is taxed in one hundred and fifty *reis* on paper.
Lisbon 19th of September of 1699.

Pereyra Oliveyra

FIRST TREATISE

OF THE NATURAL PHYSIOGNOMY OF MAN, ACCORDING TO THE METHOD OF PHILOSOPHY AND MEDICINE

PHYSIOGNOMY isn't anything else beside the ingenious and artful science of nature, by which one may know the good or bad temperament, the virtue or the vice of man, by that part in him which is animal.

CHAPTER I

By which one may know the temperament by the color of the face

A whitish color on the face, like plaster or tin, denotes a cold temperament,
A rosy and embery color, mixed with white and with a lot of freckles, denotes a hot temperament.
A whitish face, with a large white spot and many red spots, denoted a temperate temperament.
A good or swarthy color signifies good temperament.
A purple color on the face or nails denoted a terrible nature.

CHAPTER II

By which one will know which of the four humors dominates by the color of the body and thickness or thinness of it, and which conditions and properties this humor causes

He who is thin of flesh and has a light skin, rosy in the proper places, denotes a dominion of cholera. And thus the choleric are naturally furious, irate and friends of fighting. They are usually tall of stature, with little flesh and pale, their hair is rough and red and they are more inclined for the bad than for the good and they usually dream of things to do with fighting and fire, and they are given to fighting with each other.

Those that have a lot of flesh, white skin and somewhat rosy, denote a dominance of blood. The sanguine are naturally fair and handsome with straight hair; they are cheeky, even if shameful and friends of music and the sciences, benign, liberal and merciful; they usually dream of joyful things and pleasures that they enjoy: such as finding treasures, being present at banquets, soirées and balls.

A body which is of a swarthy color and is full of flesh denotes a dominion of blood with a mixture of melancholy. And thus the melancholic are of a sad condition, fearful and with a swarthy color, greedy and not given to sleep and not very good eaters; they have their veins well hidden and clear eyebrows. These usually dream of sad things which may cause grief, such as the feeling of falling from a high place or as if they're running from a bull, or they feel themselves in some bind or notable danger.

A body which is not very thick, between pale and swarthy denotes a dominion of phlegm and some melancholy; and do note that the phlegmatic are naturally sleepy, rough of cunning and with thick hair; they are usually fearful, greedy and have a weak waist (I mean the venereal waist). Their dreams are largely of humid things, such as seeing themselves in rivers, lakes or somewhere fresh.

A body, which is normally hot to the touch, is of a hot temperament. One which feels cold is of a cold temperament. One which is found rough is of a dry temperament. And one which is soft is of a humid temperament.

A body which sweats easily and in good amount denotes that it is of a good and temperate complexion; if, on the contrary, with a lot of exercise it does not sweat a lot, it is of a cold and dry temperament.

A body which is light and well developed denotes a good and temperate complexion.

A body which seems to move with a great load on it, and feels heavy, denotes that it is full of humors.

Chapter III

Of the signs of the four qualities

Those who are of a warm nature naturally grow a great deal and very fast, and they rarely become fat, and should they do, they will become increasingly thinner and elegant, making their veins more visible; these have a very thick breath and a firm, strong and full voice; they are good eaters, better digesters, have an abundance of hair and they are usually spirited and confident.

Those of a cold complexion are slow growers and have their veins exposed; they have a short breath and a thin voice; they do not have a great desire for the venereal act, they eat little and are bad digesters; they have a pale or rosy color, long and straight hair, are fearful and not given to work, although they are usually very cunning.

Those of a humid complexion have soft flesh, with hidden spots, they are light and of little strength; they are fearful and also become frightened over little; they do not sleep well and their eyes cry on many occasions; they have little and thin hair and have the ability to learn any art.

Those of a dry complexion are rough to the touch, dry, and strong and patient workers with their joints very exposed; they eat averagely and have a very hard and harsh hair.

Those who have the four qualities in their proper proportions are temperate and can boast good health; they eat and drink well and gladly and they are very joyful and content, sleep well and with a good breath; they feel light and don't sweat too much, sneeze occasionally and usually have a rosy face; they are hot to the touch, their five senses work perfectly; the distempered bodies are in every operation different from the tempered ones.

Chapter IV

Of the signs of the complexion of the brain

Those who have a brain of a hot complexion have an abundance of hard hair, they see very far and they are straight in their reasons and sense; they are vigilant in their business and their thoughts are high and they always aspire to great things and finally they always have their eyes and nose dry, unless they have a cold.

Those who have a brain of a humid complexion have soft flesh, they are usually lascivious and sanguine, they have an abundance of hair and overfluidity from their noses and frequent headaches, having the constant risk of having a sanguine illness and not living for very long; they become easily frightened and are very merciful.

Those who have a brain of a cold complexion are slow of cunning, rough of understanding and hard of capacity, somewhat lazy; they do not grow much hair and they make many vigils, they are firm in their purposes, cunning, skillful and subtle.

Those who have a brain of a dry complexion see very far and their hair turns gray very early, becoming bald shortly after; they have very dry eyes and nose and they have a lot of headaches and these have a wild and rude cunning.

Chapter V

Of the signs of the complexion of the heart

Those who have a heart of a hot temperament have a rapid pulse and a very hairy chest, they are very daring in their actions, harsh with words, avaricious in giving and hot to the touch; they are presumptuous, stubborn, irate and lustful and they always have a great appetite.

Those who have a heart with a cold complexion have a slow pulse, bare chests, are cold to the touch and not very given to food; they have a tight breath, thin and weak voice, they are tardy in their works, rough in their condition, bad eaters and they don't drink very often, they are frightened by little and they are not venereal.

Those who have a heart of a humid temperament are hairy, and this grows on them a great deal and very quickly, except on their chest; their bodies are soft to the touch, somewhat thick and not very white; by the most part they are fearful, shy, not very discreet and not good for work.

Those who have a heart of dry complexion have a hard pulse and they are thin of flesh, having very exposed veins and short and rough hair.

Chapter VI

Of the signs of the temperament of the liver

Those who have a liver of a hot complexion have a rosy face, large veins, are usually strong and their urine is very bright. These are greatly harmed by eating hot food by nature, which immediately gives them an inflammation, for these have an abundance of choleric humor and hair throughout their bodies and lower regions.

Those who have a liver of a cold complexion have thin veins, are weak and have an abundance of phlegm, by which reason they are frequently spitting and blowing their noses, ordinarily they have practically white urine, are filled with gases and they don't have much hair in their lower regions.

Those who have a liver of a humid temperament have murky blood, a very thick body and their belly easily gets swollen; many times they display a pale face.

Those who have a liver of a dry complexion have little blood, are thin of body, bad digesters and their faces are somewhat rosy.

Chapter VII

Of the signs of the temperament of the stomach

Those who have a stomach of a hot complexion are good digesters and have a great appetite, for they constantly wish to eat and drink and they suffer from occasional head and eye aches. These are quick to be enraged but this will quickly pass.

Those who have a stomach of a cold temperament don't digest well what they eat and they have a weak appetite and they are rarely hungry or thirsty; they will enjoy good health in their head and eyes.

Those who have a stomach of a humid complexion drink very little, have an abundance of spit and overfluidity in their noses, they suffer from vomit and revolutions in their stomachs and headaches.

Those who have a stomach of a dry complexion have harsh tongues and throats and are constantly thirsty.

HERE BEGINS
THE PARTICULAR PHYSIOGNOMY
OF EACH MEMBER AND PART OF THE BODY

Chapter I
Of the hair

Those who have the hair on their head soft, thin and very straight, are naturally shy, peaceful of heart, of weak strength, gentle, humble and convenient for everything.

Thick, short and spiny hair signifies strength, daring and deceitfulness, but these have a favorable fortune.

Rough hair denotes harshness of temper and simplicity in a man, and in a woman shamelessness and daring.

Those that have it villous in the front and temples are naturally simple, vain and venereal, and not very discreet, *et cito credentes*. I say naturally for a man can make himself contrary to the signs given to him by nature with his industry.

Those who have very harsh hair are very gullible, and slow in their work; they have a weak memory, much greed and short initiative.

Those who have red hair are naturally greedy, have a bad mouth and are deceitful; however, he who is wise will dominate all.

Those with hair almost red are convenient for anything with virtue and kindness; they are frequently secretive, loyal and diligent, even if unfortunate, they are peaceful, quiet and of good customs.

Those with hair almost white denote a good condition, these are skillful, self-conscious and of good temper; but these are however weak of heart, fearful and of adverse fortune.

Those who in their youth are grayish are usually variable, daring, vain and very inclined to the venereal act.

Chapter II
Of the forehead

Those who have a very risen forehead are liberal towards their friends and family, they are usually tractable, joyful, virtuous and of a good understanding.

Those who have a flat forehead, without any wrinkles, usually denote vanity, simplicity, *et cito credentes*, and some seek noise without any cause.

Those who have the extremes of their forehead small are naturally simple, covetous and courteous, even if they become enraged easily, and these are gullible.

Those who have a round forehead in the extreme of the temples, and this without any hair, have a good temper, clear understanding, much boldness, great heart and daring; and finally, these are covetous of beautiful things and honor.

Those who have a wrinkly forehead, and concave in the middle, are shameless, petulant and they have a great heart, even if simple and of variable fortune.

Those who have a large forehead reach very little of Solomon, and they give evidence of madness.

Those who have a forehead in the proper proportions are of great understanding and good capacity.

Chapter III

Of the eyebrows

Very arched eyebrows, which rise a great deal in the middle, signify greed, spirit and vainglory, daring and skill.

Those who have lowering eyebrows, when they speak or are looking anywhere, are signaled to be malicious, cheaters, traitors, greedy and lazy, even if secretive and silent.

Those who have light eyebrows, with little hair, are naturally simple, vain and of little work, very peaceful in their company.

Those who have joined eyebrows and cropped from below, and these are also rough, are signed to be shameless, lazy, suspicious, greedy and stubborn.

Those who have wide eyebrows are arrogant and shameless.

Those who have short eyebrows, almost white or red, are skilled and convenient for many things, even if these are fearful and not very given to work and very convertible *ad bonum et ad malum*.

Those who have their eyebrows very close together are cunning, covetous and very secretive, even if in some things they are cruel, greedy and of little venture.

Those who have a great deal of hair in their eyebrows are abundant in thoughts and malice, and they have a good voice.

Chapter IV

Of the eyes

Those who have large, thick and very open eyes, are naturally lazy, daring, secretive, envious and in some things shameful; they have a weak memory, small intellect, great fury and great covet.

Those who have very deep and almost hidden eyes, naturally see very well and with great depth; however these are usually suspicious, malicious, treacherous, fearful, of great wrath and worse customs; they have great memory, lie frequently, are daring, greedy, cruel and are inclined to cheat, mock and deceive, and of these the prudent one should keep away.

Those who have very bulging eyes have a short sight and cunning; they are simple, indiscreet and inconstant, even if shameful, liberals and of good breeding.

Those who have very low eyebrows have a sharp sight; they are naturally malicious and lazy, even if secretive and well spoken.

Those who have very small and round eyes are usually weak of complexion and genius, they are simple, shameful and easy in their belief; but these are liberal, even if harsh and contrary to fortune.

Those who have viscous eyes are naturally cunning, deceitful, envious, indiscreet and greedy; they are usually liars, angry and malicious. Even if I do know a few viscous persons who in their dealings and customs are very good, virtuous and true, this because through discretion and prudence they have corrected what the stars have communicated to them by nature.

Those who have the pupils of the eyes painted or golden, and are vague in their stare, that is, they are constantly looking over here and over there, are of a great spirit, even if venereal, and these are inclined to beautiful things, to lying, vanity and shedding blood.

Those who have eyes which wink a lot are inconstant, presumptuous, false, treacherous and hard in believing.

Those who have the pupils of their eyes black are shy and not very discreet.

Those who have moving eyes, constantly moving from one part to the other, demonstrate a great wrath, malice and little fidelity in things, and these are great seekers of noise and inclined to steal.

Those who have very fixed eyes and do not blink are marked for great malice.

Those who have reddish or crying and sanguine eyes are naturally angry, greedy and full of disdain; they are usually cruel, civil, shameless and liars; they are vain, disloyal and deceitful, even if these are easily moved to compassion and mercy.

Those who have round eyes, like those of an ox, are simple and malicious; they have little memory and are slow in their understanding and hard in their capacity.

Those who have eyes which are average in their proportions, tending to the black, are somewhat peaceful, gentle, loyal and true; they have a good temper, great intellect and are of good breeding.

Chapter V

Of the nose

Those who have a somewhat long and thin nose are daring, angry, vain, careful and easy to convert from one opinion to another.

Those who have a long and hooked nose, with its tip pointing down, are cunning, secretive, serviceable, loyal and decided.

Those who have a blunt nose are naturally boisterous, inconstant and weak of heart.

Those who have a crooked nose in the middle, and the tip pointing upwards, are variable and of variable fortune.

Those who have the sides of the nose thick are simple in good and cunning in evil, these are usually secretive and fortunate.

Those who have a nose that is thin in its tip and thick in the rest of it, are quick to anger and quarrel over nothing; they are usually disdainful, cunning, malicious and have a great memory.

Those who have a nose that is very round in its extremities, and with small nostrils, are greedy, even if faithful and liberal, *et cito credentes*.

Those who have a very long nose and a thin tip are decided, daring and liberal; they are usually secretive and amicable.

Those who have a crooked nose turning upwards and this is somewhat long and thick in the tip, are naturally daring, greedy, bold, angry and very covetous; they are usually cheats, have a bad mouth, are offensive and liars.

Those who have their nose very risen in the middle are inconstant, *cito credentes*, mendacious, aggravating, even if of a good temper and strong nourishment.

Those who have a very red nose, and this is naturally colored, are covetous, cruel, of rough temper and hard capacity.

Those who have the tip of their nose flat on the top are peaceful, gentle, loyal, secretive, laborious and of a good intellect.

Those who have the tip of their nose somewhat hairy and the meat of the nostrils somewhat thick and thin to the tip are variable, inconstant and of good condition.

Those who have wide and thick nostrils are of a hard temper, simple, envious and somewhat vainglorious.

Those who have their nostrils very closed and covered are indiscreet, greedy and friends of war, and these are harsh of fortune.

Those who have their nostrils narrow and thin are cunning, loyal and modest.

Those who have their nostrils wide and thick are treacherous, false and of harsh temper and are greedy and lustful.

Chapter VI

Of the mouth

Those who have a large and wide mouth are naturally shameless, cheeky, talkative, gossipers, gluttonous, greedy and friends of war.

Those who have a small mouth are peaceful, modest, loyal, secretive, fearful, temperate and shameful.

Those that continuously have a bad odor in the mouth are signaling a spent liver, and these are usually vain, indiscreet, *cito credentes*, and with a great intellect.

Those who always have a good odor coming from their mouth indicate that they are sane in their insides; these usually are discreet in their speaking, prudent in their giving, prudent in their silence, and cunning in their negotiating.

Those who have thick and preeminent lips indicate that they do not have much foresight; they are very simple and light in their believing.

Those who have their lips somewhat thin and not turning outwards are discreet, cunning, secretive, angry and of great genius.

Those that have well colored lips, and more to the thin than thick, are usually of a good condition, even if variable, but these are more inclined to good than evil.

Those who have one lip thicker than the other are more simple than discreet, of variable fortune, slow intellect and rough temper.

Chapter VII

Of the teeth

Those who have very small and weak teeth, and in their positioning are clear and short are naturally shy, secretive, gentle, faithful and variable, even if of a short life.

Those who have uneven teeth and these are badly placed in the gums, some crooked and others straight, are very ingenious, daring, cunning, even if envious and somewhat disdainful.

Those who have crooked and thick teeth are usually dissolute, simple and of little capacity. Those that have tough and well closed teeth are usually very self confident and spirited, but these are friends of carrying news, and these are friends of high things, and they usually live for a very long time.

Well closed and strong teeth denote a long life; these are discreet, constant, strong and good eaters.

Chapter VIII

Of the tongue

Those who have a tongue given to talking are variable in their dealings and indiscreet in their negotiating.

Those who have a slow tongue are wrathful, vain, inconstant and terrible, but these are possible to placate.

Those who have a fat and harsh tongue are cunning, wise and well raised; even if malicious, cruel and treacherous.

Those who have a thin tongue are naïve, cunning and fearful, *et cito credentes*.

Chapter IX

Of the voice

Those who have a low and full voice are naturally daring, strong and very greedy, gluttonous and fast with their hands.

Those who have a weak and thin voice have little breath and good understanding, even if these are shy and weak of heart.

Those who have a clear and fast voice are usually discreet, true and ingenious, and somewhat vainglorious.

Those who have a firm voice in their singing are cautious, warned, ingenious and strong.

Those who have a trembling voice are suspicious, shy, lazy weak and ingenious.

Those who have a very high tone voice are strong, daring, injurious and faithful to their opinion.

Those who have a very resonant voice are shy, indiscreet, vain and inconstant.

Those who have a soft, constant and pleasing voice are peaceful, secretive, shy and greedy.

Chapter X

Of laughter

Those who laugh easily and give out great shouts are signaled to have a large spleen and these are naturally simple, vain, foolish, inconstant and not very secretive.

Those who laugh only a little and late are discreet, cunning, secretive, loyal and inconstant, and these have a clear genius.

Those who are very difficultly moved to laughter are intelligent, patient and very cunning; these are usually ingenious, greedy, bookish and diligent in their things.

Those who laugh easily, and while laughing cough or yawn, and those who twist their necks or lips, are false, arrogant and treacherous; they are wrathful, *et cito credentes*, and variable.

Chapter XI

Of the beard

Those who have a thick beard are naturally peaceful, secretive and variable; these are usually loyal and of a harsh genius.

Those who have a sharp beard and somewhat fleshy, have a good temper, a great heart and high thoughts.

Those who have their beard separated in the middle are peaceful, secretive and serviceable.

Those who have a sharp beard and of little flesh are daring, angry and friends of war.

Those who have a curly beard turning outward, with an opening or break in the middle of the jaw are treacherous, lousy, deceitful, greedy, daring and inclined to stealing.

Chapter XII

Of the beard[174]

Those who have a well composed, thick and regular beard have a good nature and an appeasable condition; and the contrary is true of those with a badly composed beard.

The woman who has many hairs on her chin, near the beard, is of a strong nature and terrible condition, and she is extremely hot and for this reason she is extremely lustful and of a manly condition.

The woman who is entirely free of hair is mostly of good complexion, shy, shameful, gentle, peaceful and obedient.

Chapter XIII

Of the physiognomy of the face

Those who have a very meaty and wide face are naturally shy, joyful, liberal, secretive, even if of a weak memory; they are importunate, presumptuous and have a bad mouth.

Those who have a thin face are given to work and fatigue, but these are constant, they are also angry, merciful and of good understanding.

Those who have a small and round face are simple, weak, shy and of little memory.

Those who have a face which is too long and thin are cheeky with their tongue, simple in their work, quarrelsome and greedy.

Those who have a very flat face, neither thick nor risen, are of a good condition, affable, amiable, serviceable, loyal and of adverse fortune.

Those who have an average face in the proper proportion are men of truth, ingenious, easy, cunning and of good memory.

Those who have a yellowish face do not have a perfect health, neither do they have a good condition, for these are malicious, deceitful, greedy, treacherous and liars, and they are usually also money grabbing, envious, vain and presumptuous.

Those who have a well colored face are of a good complexion and have a good understanding, but these are variable.

Chapter XIV

Of the ears

Those who have big, fat and ill proportioned ears are naturally simple and very lazy, of thick nourishment, bad memory and even worse quality.

Those who have very small and thin ears are of good temper, clear intellect and much prudence; they usually are secretive, peaceful, cunning, honest, clean and shameful.

Those who have somewhat long or wide ears are daring, gluttonous, shameless, indiscreet, vain and of little work.

---

174. Translator's note: this is not an error, this repetition is present in the original.

Chapter XV

Of the head

Those who have a big and round head are naturally discreet, cunning, secretive and these are usually loyal, ingenious, imaginative, hard workers and constant.

Those who have an elongated head, with a big and misshapen face are very simple, malicious, vain, envious and friends of bringing news.

Those who move their heads too much are indiscreet, inconstant, deceitful, vain, simple, prodigious and unreasonable.

Those who have a thick head and a wide face are suspicious, cunning and spirited, secretive, daring and not very shameful.

Those who have a fat head and not very proportionate, with a thick and short neck, are discreet, cunning, secretive, ingenious, faithful, tractable and true.

Those who have a small head and a thin throat and tongue are weak of heart, indiscreet, cunning and stubborn; these are however, teachable even if of a harsh fortune.

Chapter XVI

Of the throat

Those who have a white throat are naturally shy, liars and dissolute.

Those who have a thin throat are shy, of weak heart and variable, *et cito credentes*.

Those who have a long neck and long feet are fearful, pusillanimous, variable, envious and not secretive at all.

Those who have a short neck are cunning, greedy and secretive; these are constant, angry and discreet; these are usually also ingenious and lovers of peace and quiet.

Chapter XVII

Of the back

Those who have a somewhat small and thin back are naturally shy, peaceful and of little labor.

Those who have a wide and sturdy back are strong and of great labor and suffering; they are usually angry, loyal and friends of peace and quiet.

Those who have a curved back and bent to the inside are cunning, secretive, deceitful and ingenious.

Those who have a flat back and without any hair are modest, peaceful, greedy and variable. Those who have one side of their back larger than the other are slow of mind, daring, greedy, false and treacherous.

Those who have very risen backs are inconstant, daring, have a bad mouth, are simple and shameless.

Those who have a hairy, thin and very elevated back or spine are naturally shameless, malicious, bestial and of bad understanding, weak and of little work.

Those who have a fat back are vain, strong, slow and of great deceit.

All who have thin and elongated backs are amazed with little, and they have a bad mouth, and these believe in everything with ease.

Chapter XVIII

Of the arms

Those who have their arms so long that when these are straight can reach their knees with their hands are naturally liberal, greedy, daring, solicitous, simple and of lowly thoughts, even if serene in their command.

Those who have arms that are shorter than their stature requires are ingrate, greedy, daring, friends of weapons and quarreling.

Those who have their arms tough with nerves and flesh are presumptuous, haughty, covetous of great and delectable things and not very discreet and friends of praise.

Those who have very hairy arms are malicious, suspicious, lustful and of weak memory.

Those who have their arms without hair are of great anger, little memory and much cunning and deceit.

Chapter XIX

Of the hands

Those who have long, soft and thin hands are of good understanding, weak memory and much loyalty; they are usually peaceful, serviceable, discreet and of good handling.

Those who have thick and short hands are simple, vain and slow of understanding; these are usually very given to work and anger.

Those that have hairy hands, with curved hairs and fingers are lustful, vain and liars.

Those who have fingers curved upwards are liberal, serviceable, cunning and of great anger; these are also secretive and of a good genius.

Those who have hands that are shorter than of their fingers are greedy, covetous, thoughtful and of much labor and these are usually cunning and of firm purposes.

Chapter XX

Of the chest

Those who have wide and thick chests are naturally strong, daring, greedy, tyrant, cunning and covetous.

Those who have narrow chests in the middle are usually of a high genius, sudden intellect, good advice and true; they are usually wise, ingenious and of much wrath.

Those who have a very hairy chest are cunning, liberal, serviceable, of great lust and spirit, but these are however inconstant.

Those who have a flat, thin and hairless chest are shy, secretive and have a good life; they are usually also pacific, ingenious, but these are heavy with conversation.

Chapter XXI

Of the belly

Those who have a large belly are natural drinkers, more than eaters; these are slow and disdainful; however they are loyal and have a great heart.

Those who have a small and extended belly are of much work and constant; they are usually well spoken, tractable; even if variable and of contrary fortune.

Chapter XXII

Of the flesh of the body

Those who have soft and bland flesh are naturally shy and weak of heart; even if these are of good understanding, short memory and variable fortune.
Those who have harsh and hard flesh are strong, daring, vain, greedy and of variable fortune.
Those who have fat and white flesh are forgetful, shameful, shy and careful in their dealings.

Chapter XXIII

Of the ribs

Those who have stout ribs, full of meat, are naturally strong, furious and half mad; and this comes from having too much heat, which causes such fury that it clouds their judgment, and these are also simple.
Those who have very thin and small ribs, with little flesh, are weak of heart, cunning and of little labor.

Chapter XXIV

Of the muscles

Those who have very thick muscles with harsh hair are naturally lustful and not very chaste.
Those who have flat muscles with few hairs, and these are thin and straight and are usually quite chaste.

Chapter XXV

Of the buttocks

Those who have meaty and pulpy buttocks are naturally strong, daring, greedy and proud or arrogant.

Chapter XXVI

Of the knees

Those who have fat knees are naturally shy, vain and of little labor, even if very liberal.
Those who have thin knees are strong, daring, secretive and great walkers.

Chapter XXVII

Of the legs

Those who have sturdy legs, or thick with flesh and bones, and these are hairy, are naturally secure, slow, strong and of average cunning.

Those who have thin legs, and not very hairy, are shy, weak, faithful, serviceable and of good understanding.

Those who have their legs completely devoid of hair are chaste, weak of heart and these are amazed with very little.

Those who have very hairy legs are marked to be as such in their secret parts, and consequently these are vain, simple and inconstant.

Chapter XXVIII

Of the feet

Those who have feet thick with flesh, long and rough, are naturally simple, strong and good and these have a slow intellect.

Those who have slow, subtle, thin and bland feet are shy, weak, wise and of little labor; even if these are of good understanding and great genius.

Chapter XXIX

Of the hunch

Those who have a hunch on their backs are most wise and ingenious; but these are false, malicious and of bad memory.

Those who have a hunch in the front are the double of the previous one, but these are more simple than wise.

Chapter XXX

Of stature

Those who have a tall and straight stature, more to the thin than fat, are usually cheeky, cruel and greedy, of great wrath and presumptuous; but these are faithful and constant.

Those who have a tall and somewhat crass stature are usually strong, stubborn and ingrate; even if these are prudent and have foresight.

Those with a short and crass stature are signed to be suspicious and of much wrath, but these do not have much foresight and they are somewhat envious. Those who have a short stature, thin and very straight are naturally wise, ingenious, secretive, tiresome and of good temper; even if somewhat vainglorious.

The curious reader should know and be adverted that that which he may have read in the current treatise of physiognomy of one part or member of the body, as these are so many, and each one of them having its own particular judgment, that the effects of one member may contradict that of another. He should thus search and research that what one part of the body says of it does not contradict another part of the said body; and in this way he may be able to understand and judge with prudence the good and the bad which was transmitted by nature.

And he should be further adverted that nature does not force nor determines those who have free will to follow this or that; for the wise and prudent is a master of all his actions and he can, with his industry, avoid that which is bad and follow that which is good, and as such here we give the signs that each part of the body indicates. And do not think this to be useless, and all should give grace to God; for the more rebellious one has his nature, the more merit will he gain before his Creator if with prudence he rules and dominates himself.

Natural and true rule

Any person who may have a color or position of their eyes similar to that of some animal, this will extend to his complexion and consequently to his customs, unless he, with his discretion and free will, changes himself.

Final Chapter

Of the correspondence of the spots and marks of the face with the various parts of the body

It is natural that every spot or mark on one's body will have a correspondence in some other part of the body.

The marks which are found on the forehead correspond to the area from the neck until the chest; proportionately, the right side of the forehead to the right side of the neck or chest; and these are naturally good for the management of land.

The spots or marks which are found on the eyes correspond to the nipples; and these are naturally ill inclined.

Those which are found on the nose correspond to the cleavage of the chest; and these are naturally inclined to roam the world.

Those which are found on the jaw correspond to the buttocks, and each side corresponds to its own side: meaning the right side of the jaw to the right buttock and the left side to the left buttock; and of these Taisnerius says that they should not be trusted.

Those which are found on the lips or mouth correspond to the genitals; and of these it is said that they will marry at their own will.

Those which are found on the beard correspond to the shoulders; and of these it is said that they will become rich.

Those that are found on the sides of the beard correspond to the arms, each arm to its own side, as was said according to the method of prudence; and of these it is said that they will have wealth and a bad stomach.

Those which are found on the ears correspond to the thighs; and of these it is said that they will be prosperous.

Those which are found behind the ears correspond to the shoulder blades; and of these it is said the same as the ones before.

Those which are found on the neck correspond to the back, and if these are on the bottom of the neck they correspond to the white of the eyes; and of these it is said that they should be careful over some blow to the head.

Those which are found on the hands correspond to the feet, each hand to its foot and each finger to each toe; and of these it is said that they will have many children and both men and women will travel thought distant lands.

One should note that a sign or spot which is found on the face, should it be small, its correspondence on the body will be great.

SECOND
TREATISE
OF THE EXCELLENCIES OF
ROSEMARY AND ITS QUALITY

Rosemary is of a hot and dry nature, it is aromatic, sweet smelling and in this way comforts all parts and members, both interior and exterior, of the body; it invigorates and fortifies the senses, dries all humidities and coldness, obstructions and contagious ills.

Finally, rosemary does not admit to melancholy, sadness, tremors or faintness of heart, and its roots, branches, bark, leaves and flowers have almost infinite virtues, which, those we have collected and taken from the great authors, we will faithfully name for the glory of God our Lord and enjoyment of Man.

The small and most tender seeds of rosemary, eaten every morning with bread and salt, fortify the head and the brain and conserve a clear, robust, sharp and strong sight.

The flowers and leaves of rosemary, made into a powder and carried in contact with the body, drive away the enemies of the same body, which are the fleas, lice and bedbugs.

These same powders carried in contact with the body, on the left side, prevent melancholy and bring much joy to the heart.

Rosemary leaves, well macerated or chewed and placed over a fresh wound, will cure and close it marvelously.

The flower of rosemary, eaten on an empty stomach with honey from this same plant and a slice of warm bread, greatly conserves the health and prevents the generation of buboes, rotten blood and gout, and rather to the contrary, should anyone have one of these ills it will cure it.

Rosemary drives away every poisonous animal, and its smoke is useful against every plague and contagious ill.

Burnt branches or trunk of rosemary, made into a powder, can be used to whiten the teeth and fortify them and also prevent the generation of worms in them and also coldness.

Alonso de Herrera writes and mentions in his *Agricultura* that in a house in which it is custom to burn rosemary no filthy spirits will be able to inhabit.

A woman who usually eats rosemary flowers with rye bread will not suffer from *mal de madre*; for eating this will repress the bad humors and dry her humidity and it will cure any and all interior disarrangement of any person that thus uses it.

The flowers and leaves of rosemary, placed inside a chest among clothes will conserve them from moths and will transmit to them a very pleasant smell.

Those who usually wash their bodies with water in which rosemary was boiled will acquire a good healthy color and they will conserve their good health and youthful disposition.

Houses, that due to being dark and damp aren't usually healthy, by fumigating them with rosemary are these conserved healthy and dry.

Should anyone have catarrh, by receiving smoke from the bark of rosemary through the nose, will the whole head be purged and be made healthy.

Should anyone fall ill due to coldness or a bad air, while sweating they should take a bath of rosemary and they will soon recover.

Macerated rosemary leaves, made into a dressing and placed over the *quebraduras*[175] of a young boy will make an excellent cure, for it will close the wound and fortify it in nine days.

Also note a marvelous secret well experimented for any *quebradura* which is that macerated green carobs placed over these will cure and close them in less than eight days.

Rosemary flowers, mixed with boiled and beaten honey, made into a conserve and taken in the morning and afternoon, will drive away any ill and preserve from every affliction proceeding from phlegm, viscosities and coldness.

Green rosemary flowers, or dried and made into a conserve with sugar and taken in the morning with a glass of white wine, prevents fainting of the heart, widens the breath, comforts the digestion and removes gases and stomach pain, and finally it prevent the urge to vomit.

Rosemary leaves, boiled with white wine and applied very hot as a paste over the genitals, will make one urinate abundantly should one have a blockage.

If a woman receives from below a breath of boiled rosemary, it will cleanse her *madre*, comfort it and repair it for conception.

Rosemary leaves, boiled in white wine and placed as a paste, as hot as it can be endured over hemorrhoids, will tighten, dry and remove all pain from them, by doing this three times a day, for three days.

Those who have joint pain due to some cold humor, by washing this area occasionally with very hot water where rosemary was boiled, will cure any pain from any region on which this is done.

If from the wine used to boil rosemary one makes *aguardente* and with this wash any region afflicted by mange or cancer many times, this will heal.

Those who drink this same liqueur before going to bed will be preserved from any hidden diseases. And in the same way acquire a good memory.

If one washes a child with water from the boiling of rosemary, he will be raised very clean and free from itching and mange.

In a time of plague it is extremely healthy and advantageous to burn a great deal of rosemary inside houses and on the streets, for this thins the airs and drives away the plague.

Rosemary honey, so say it the learned, is the best of all, both for the making of electuaries, medicine, as also sweets and conserves.

Virgin rosemary honey should be boiled to remove eye mists, clear the sight and to purify the faces of women.

Bees that make rosemary honey do not fall ill as often as those that make it from other flowers.

Rosemary juice, dripped inside the ears, removes pain arising from coldness, heals wounds, dries putrefaction and kills any worm generated in them.

Rosemary juice taken through the nose removes foul smells, dries the catarrh, cures the cold and any other wound and any evil which is usually generated in this area.

Rosemary leaves, chewed and brought inside the mouth on an empty stomach, remove the bad breath arising from worn out teeth and they cause joy and a sweet smell.

Chewed rosemary, brought under the tongue for some time on an empty stomach, usually clears it up and removes phlegm, when it swells up because of this phlegmatic humor.

This same virtue is said to be much more efficient to make one speak fluently, and its other virtues are numberless and some may be found in the *Agricultura* of Alonso de Herrera, Book 3, Chapter on sage.

Rosemary boiled in vinegar is used to fortify the teeth which are shaking, it tighten the gums and removes the pain if one washes the mouth with this hot vinegar.

Burnt rosemary leaves and bark are used to purge the rheum from the teeth and fortify them, by rubbing them with this ash.

Note an admirable and peregrine secret most proven and experimented of rosemary water placed under the Sun and used to cure the eyes which may have spots, cataracts or be clouded.

---

175. Translator's note: a possible translation for this can be breakings, as in a broken or fractured bone.

Take a large bunch of green and fresh rosemary and place it inside a new glass jar, with their tops to the bottom and in such a way as they do not touch the bottom. Cover the vase with a folded linen cloth and over this cloth place some yeast, so as it covers the whole mouth of the vase, and over this place another folded cloth and tie it very well so as no breath may escape and place this vase under the Sun during serene weather for three or four days and you will distill a very important water for the eyes, as was said. Do note that after you have distilled this water one should place it in a small bowl which should be placed under the Sun in serene weather once again for a few days; and this water will turn from white to yellow and be made thick, and one should also grind some rock sugar into it and one should put three drops of this water in each eye in the morning, again at midday and another time before going to sleep; and with the favor of God you will heal.

Whoever washed their mouth every morning with the boiling of rosemary water, will preserve this from ever corrupting, remove all swelling and heal all wounds in the mouth and gums; and should he have any inflammation it will soon disappear.

The woman who doesn't have much milk to raise her child should eat rosemary leaves and flowers, and these will cause an abundance of good and healthy milk, for it purifies the blood and comforts the digestive virtue.

Rosemary juice, mixed with sugar and taken every morning and every night before going to sleep is good against anxiety and afflictions of the chest; it does away with blockages and congealed blood in the stomach, helps digestion, reduces thirst and incites the appetite.

Rosemary juice with sugar, taken in the same way as before, resolves any gases and mitigates every stomach and belly pain.

Rosemary sticks and twigs, made into a powder are marvelous to tighten the posterior way and it comforts the intestines which may be coming out of that region. By using this powder three times it will be fortified.

Rosemary flowers and leaves powdered, taken with good wine and white honey, mitigates spleen and liver pain and it consumes the melancholic humor, which offends the spleen and purifies the blood which is generated in the liver.

Fresh rosemary flowers, boiled in good white wine and taken a few sips in the morning, unclogs the melancholy, opens the entrails, widens the heart, settles the stomach, comforts the digestion, removes gases and prevent vomiting.

Very good red wine, boiled with rosemary root or flowers and drunk, removes colic and gout pain, represses dysentery or belly fluxes, even if these are very old.

Rosemary powder drunk with white wine removes any viscous and thick humors and any obstruction from the veins or belly, and it also breaks bladder stones, throwing them out and comforting that area.

Whoever suffers from urinary flow due to debility or weakness of that region, by drinking the powder of rosemary leaves or root with white wine, will repress the flow and fortify that part and if this remedy is maintained he will be fully healed.

Rosemary leaves and roots, boiled in vinegar, are used to remove pain from the legs and from tired feet, be this due to walking or due to some bad humor, this by washing these regions with this vinegar.

Those who might have lost their appetite should take two or three soup spoons of rosemary boiled in wine in the morning and the will to eat and sleep will once again awaken in him, his stomach and all parts of the body will be comforted.

Dioscorides and Arnaldus say that boiled rosemary has the same effect as theriac against poison. They further say that wherever there is any rosemary no poisonous animals or spider will be able to exist.

By washing the face with a linen cloth and some rosemary water this will be made beautiful, fresh and lustrous; and if this is made with wine boiled with rosemary, instead of water, it will be much better; as not only does it cause these effects but, if you use it every day, the face will never become wrinkled or old, but it will rather be conserved fresh, beautiful and every spot will be removed.

Whoever washes and rubs their head with water of boiled rosemary, mixed with some vinegar, will do away with any dander and any humor which may be condensed there and it will fortify the hair and clear the memory.

Rosemary flowers placed in wine which is about to go bad will conserve it and sustain it for many years, giving it a smooth smell and taste.

Rosemary charcoal is much better for painters to draw with than any other.

Finally, to rosemary baths do the mentioned authors call the bath of life, for it removes pain, both from the joints as from any other part of the body, removes tiredness, prevents suffocation of the heart while sleeping, or when in dreams one becomes frightened and it seems as there is some kind of weight over the chest; it give strength and vigor in old age, conserves youth and it renews and fortifies the members and enlivens the senses; whoever uses rosemary evaporation, every fifteen days, until he is made to sweat, will be preserved from every illness and he will be renovated as an eagle.

LIQUEUR OR BALM OF ROSEMARY

which has the same virtues as Arabian balm

Arnaldus de Villa Nova writes in the above mentioned work and in the *Fysico Mater,*[176] Question 10, Chapter 1, and the most wise Herrera in his *Agricultura*, Book 3, Chapter 34, as well as other very learned authors, that from rosemary flower an admirable liqueur is made which has the same properties and virtues as the Arabian balm. These author then say that one should take rosemary flowers, very well developed, and clean them thoroughly, and these should be placed inside a very thick bowl, as much as can fit in it. This should be very well covered with a linen cloth and a scroll, so as no breath may escape from inside, and after this it should be buried in warm manure for a month, after which all the flowers will be found to have become a liquid, and once this is taken and strained into another bowl, with the flowers needing to be very well squeezed, bury it in a small mound of sand under a serene Sun as before, and it should be covered by sand for a month and this rosemary balm will be made ready, and casting one drop of this in water it can be seen to reach all the way to the bottom, as is said of the Arabian balm.

The virtues of the liqueur or rosemary balm

This liqueur or rosemary balm has the virtue and property of healing any wound, be it new or old.

It also has the property to bind the flesh around wounds, making it so as not mark, or a greatly reduced one, be left, as is said of the Arabian balm.

By casting two drops of this liqueur into the eyes it cures any mists and cataracts in them, and it comforts and clears the sight marvelously.

By anointing weakened members and shrunken nerves with this balm they are unshrunken and fortified.

This liqueur reduces hand and head tremors, should these not be due to extremely old age and it comforts the heart admirably by anointing it on the left side of the body.

One should note and be warned that should the face be anointed with this liqueur once a day it will be preserved fresh, as that of a boy, without growing wrinkles, and should these already be on one's face they will soon disappear.

This liqueur removes any pain arising from coldness from the joints and also from any other part of the body, even if not due to coldness.

Finally it is useful for those suffering from colic and for all women suffering from *mal de madre*, this by anointing that region which is in pain with the said liqueur; and for infinite other afflictions is this liqueur or rosemary balm useful.

---

176. Translator's note: uncertain reference.

MEDICINAL RECIPE

of the must and rosemary wine, which contains many and admirable virtues

The most learned doctor Arnaldus de Villa Nova wrote a rare and most useful secret of the must and rosemary, whose virtues and properties are worthy to be known by all. The mentioned Arnaldus says that one should take the flowers and the most tender leaves of rosemary and cast them into a the vase of must (which is wine as soon as you squeeze it out of the grapes) and leave them there until this must finishes boiling and afterwards it is ready for use. And Arnaldus confirms that this secret was communicated to him in the city of Babylon by a Moor who was a great Philosopher, Medic and Astronomer. This same recipe is mentioned by Josefo Cirurgico[177] in the books of Medical secrets. And these two authors say that, should there not be any must available, then one should take some excellent red wine which should have a good and smooth smell and one should cast the rosemary flowers into this and let it boil until it is reduced to one third of the original volume. And let one be warned that in one *almude*[178] of wine or must one can cast three *arrateis*[179] of flowers and tender leaves of rosemary.

The virtues and properties of the must with rosemary

Any person who occasionally drinks some sips of this wine in the morning and afternoon will conserve their health and renew their boyish disposition.

Drinking this wine removes all pain from the stomach arising from cold or cholera, or from abundance of blood and phlegm.

This wine is used to heal and remove side pain arising from cold or from the congealing of a stone.

This wine has the virtue of, if drunk first thing in the morning or after dinner, purging the stomach, retaining vomit and curing colic.

Those who have lost their appetite and their will to eat, by drinking this wine will recover their will.

The smell or fragrance of this wine comforts the brain, gives pleasure to the senses and joy to the heart.

Many and great effect does this wine cause if drunk every morning and afternoon, for it fortifies all the members of the body, comforts one's substance, conserves the youthful disposition and delays old age.

Those who usually wash their faces every morning with this wine and a cloth, after having washed themselves with cold water, should know that this conserves their face fresh and beautiful, appeasing and without marks or wrinkles.

By washing one's mouth with this wine are the teeth admirably conserved and the gums fortified, wounds are healed and every day one will have a good smelling breath.

Fistulas and wounds are cured by this wine by frequently washing them and placing a clean linen cloth, wet with this wine over it.

Those who feel exceedingly weak and debilitated because of some illness should be given a few slices of bread that has been made wet with this wine, and this will give great renewal to their members and great joy to their heart, and they will regain their strength and vigor much quicker.

If one mixes this wine with rain water and gives it to drink to those with phthisis they are greatly healed; and this says Master Zapata, which he himself has proven and experimented many times. And further still it has the virtue of healing continuous, tertian and quartan fevers.

This wine is very appropriate to retain fluxes from the belly by drinking it.

---

177. Translator's note: uncertain reference.
178. Translator's note: an old variable unit of measure originating in the Arabic *al-mudd*, the most official one being 16,8 l.
179. Translator's note: an old variable unit of measure, from 1499 it was established as 0.4590 kg.

This wine has virtue against poison, be it drunk or eaten. And further does the above mentioned author say that fine theriac cannot be made without this marvelous rosemary wine.

This wine is even further used mixed with theriac and drunk, for it removes tremors from the hands and head and it also detains the passions of women that arise from the *madre*, which it also marvelously prepares for conception.

Those suffering from gout should drink this wine frequently and they also should wash their afflicted area with it, and they will heal perfectly.

Those suffering from stones or sand in the bladder should drink this wine on an empty stomach and not only does it melt away the sand but also causes a clear urination and it also prevents more stones from being generated.

This same wine is used to break away any blockage; it causes a good proportionate sleep, increases the memory and drives away sadness from the heart.

Finally, drinking this wine on an empty stomach and before going to bed after a light dinner, will unclog the liver, provoke appetite and brings joy to the entrails, comfort the brain, sharpen the senses, dilate the breath, incite urination, give vigor and strength to all members of the body, admirably aiding the convalescent and is notable for comforting old men, augmenting their natural heat.

The reader should be warned that if he looks closely to the virtues here mentioned about rosemary, that he will count more than two hundred of them.

THIRD TREATISE

OF THE MANY AND GREAT PROPERTIES OF AGUARDENTE

Before we mention the properties of *aguardente* it will be good for us to check the ingredients used in its making so as it may have all the virtues and effects that will be mentioned below. In two *almudes* of the best red wine one should cast the following ingredients: half an ounce of white ginger; two *oitavas* of cloves; two *oitavas* of milium solis;[180] half an ounce of nutmeg; half an ounce of dried orange peel from the month of May; half an ounce of rosemary flowers; half an ounce of sage leaves; and all these materials should be ground and cast into that same wine and after six hour of infusion one can have the *aguardente* made and use it whenever there is a necessity for it and whose properties are the following:

Firstly, should you want to preserve the hair on your head and a black beard, you should wet that region with this water with a wet cloth each day, and it will be preserved black; and you should be warned that it will grow much more than usual.

Do note this secret, which should you have nits or lice, all of these will die and not return when they are made wet with this water.

Should anyone have a rash on their head, by shaving their hair and wetting their head with a cloth with this water, three or four times a day, they will soon be healed.

By drinking this water you will cure catarrh and also remove any pain one may have in the body, and, should you wet that aching region with this water, so much faster will it be removed.

Should anyone have an acquired deformation on their fingers by washing them with this water many times he will heal.

Should anyone have any redness on their face, by washing it with this water three or four times a day, it will be healed.

Should anyone be weak, by washing themselves occasionally with this water will they be made well.

Those who have lost their hearing over some cold should cast two or three drops of this water, warm, inside their ear and they will once again hear well, and, should there be any illness or pain inside these due to some loud noise, this will also be resolved by covering the ear with some cotton.

This water is also used to remove mists and cataracts from the eye and it is also good for any abnormal ear growths.

This water marvelously cures tooth pain by placing over the ailing tooth a little cloth with this water, warm, and the mouth should be closed during the time the cloth is still warm and once this dissipates you should replace it until the pain disappears, which should be very soon.

---

180. Translator's note: a medicinal plant featured in some medieval sources, I am uncertain if it is the *Lithospermum officinale* or some plant of the Milium genus. The 1831 Paris edition has Grains of Paradise instead, *Aframomum melegueta*.

Those who might have cancer, wounds or inflammations in the mouth, by washing it many times with this water it will heal.

This water, if drunk, has the property to remove stupor and reverse the shortening of the nerves, it is useful and greatly helpful to paralytics.

This water mixed with theriac has a great virtue to heal the bites of venomous animals and it also prevents any harm made from the drinking of poison.

Drinking this water is of great advantage to those that have *gota coral*. And in those who have this, by drinking this water three times this ailment will never return to them.

Drinking this *aguardente* is very advantageous to those who have a bad heart, and also to those who are taken over by an ill in which they lose their senses and fall to the ground. And note that by drinking this water three times this evil will not take them.

If you wash with this water the harness wounds on any beast of burden it will heal, no matter how old the wound is and one should not fear that any corruption will grow on this wound.

This water has so much virtue that it kills roundworms and any creature living inside the belly, and this is from the first time it is drunk. Should it be a boy half a glass is enough, should it be an older person a whole glass.

This drink cures kidney pain and colic; and the use of this water prevents these two terrible pains and even worse ones which are usually generated hidden from sight.

If with this *aguardente* one mixes a third part of rose water and with this mixture one washes the face it will be preserved fresh, beautiful and pleasing to the eye.

This water removes any foul smell from the mouth or arising from the stomach or from any other part, by washing the foul smelling region or drinking this water.

This water has the virtue to remove apoplexy from the tongue by washing it regularly, and it will be released from excessive phlegm.

This water is extremely useful for a disease called *Suber*,[181] which is a lethargy which makes a person sleepy and weak in all members and with very great difficulty does she awake, and by putting this water in their nose and washing their face with it will she lose all sleep.

Those who drink this water will not suffer from migraines or headache, nor from head distillations which is something which torments many.

Drinking this water removes all melancholy and all blockages from the nose and it tempers the black colic.

By washing wounds with this water will pain and malice be removed from them, and also the numbing feeling some of these have.

By washing wounds with this water is all pain, malice and stupor removed.

If any piece of meat is placed inside this water for twenty four hours it will be preserved from all corruption.

Those who have tertian and quartan fevers should drink this water at the time of the illness and they will heal.

Drinking this water increases the natural heat of the body and it reduces the overfluidities of the body.

Those who have urination pain will do well in drinking this water and if they can't retain their urine by weakness of that region, by drinking this same water will that part be fortified and they will urinate at the convenient times.

Those who have stones in the urinary tract or any other fleshy blockage, should use this water in a syringe and they will break this stone and remove the excess flesh and they will once again urinate correctly.

Drinking this water cures any illness of the intestine as well as stomach pain caused by coldness.

Drinking this water prevent the ill of *mal de madre* and it makes its purge correctly.

Those suffering from gout should wash the ailing part with this water or even drink it and it will heal.

---

181. Translator's note: uncertain translation.

Those who have lack of hair due to an abundance of phlegm, by washing that region with this water and drinking it will it once again grow.

Drinking this water has the virtue of purifying the blood, fortifying the nerves and clearing the sight.

If this water is cast into some wine which is turning sour it will return to its original state and casting it in good wine will preserve it.

Those having cough or a very old fluidity, by drinking this water will they be made better.

A woman, carrying a dead child in her womb, not being able to cast it out, by drinking this water will be able to do so, for it causes great effort and resoluteness to bear those distresses.

This water represses the flow of blood from the nose or from any other part, this by washing the region where blood is coming out.

Note a rare and marvelous secret to staunch and repress blood from the nose which is proven:

Take green bark from a fig tree and macerate it very well, and immediately place this over the nose and also offer this to smell and the blood will stop and be repressed.

Should anyone be bitten by a rabid dog, by washing the bite with this water, continuously, and also drinking from it, they will not become ill.

Those who get pierced by some thorn should wash the region with this water a great deal of times, and the thorn will be cast out.

Should anyone have red markings on their face, by washing it with this water for nine days will this be removed.

Whoever has any kind of swelling in the jaw, or in any part of the body due to a cold humor, by placing over the inflammation a linen cloth with this water, being that as soon as it dries it should once again be made wet, the humor will soon be dispelled.

Should you cast inside this water any betony leaves and then drink it, it will make the sight sharper and should they have a swollen spleen, in such a way as it makes moving hard, it will be cured; and it will also purify the blood in their liver.

Those who have eye inflammations, constantly crying and a debited sight can use this water to wash them, and once they are dry it will fortify their sight and clear their tears of all sanguine humor.

FOLLOWING ARE THE VIRTUES OF THE

SUGARY AGUARDENTE

taken from Master Zapata, Surgeon of the King of France

One can barely put into words the great advantage and great smoothness of the sugary *aguardente*, for as Master Zapata writes, it is so great its virtue and so excellent its liqueur that just its taste and experience can offer judgment of its valor and admirable efficiency. This author says that this *aguardente* is made from very good red wine, pure, smooth and of an excellent scent, this before mixing the other ingredients which will be pointed out. Take then three ounces of sugar water and another three ounces of *aguardente* and half an ounce of rose water; and by mixing these three waters they will make up a most remarkable compound which one may use whenever it seems right, without any fear of doing harm, but it will rather cause so much good and pleasure that one will never do without it.

Method of making the sugary water

Master Zapata says that one should cast an *arratel* of fine sugar into a bowl and over this as much rain or cistern water as is necessary to cover the sugar and half a finger more above the sugar level, then mix or shake this bowl until the sugar is melted; this is the sugar water which is to be mixed with the *aguardente*. And note a secret of sugar and *aguardente* which is that if you cast sugar into pure *aguardente*, without mixing it in any other water, that it will never melt the sugar, nor will it be converted into this *aguardente*.

This sugary *aguardente* is greatly praised by Master Zapata, and with good reason, for beyond its taste and smoothness, it has many great virtues and utilities as I have many times experienced.

Firstly, drinking this sugary water unclogs the liver in a most notable way, it takes away any kidney illness, it helps in doing away with the hardness and swelling of the spleen, expels any gases from the body and heal any debility and weakness of the stomach, head and from any other members.

This water may be used by pregnant women, for it will not do any harm to them, but rather it will cause them a great good and strength for labor.

Those who are recovering from some disease and wish to quickly have their strength back, regain the will to eat and joy of working, should drink this water on an empty stomach and some other time during the day and they will recover all which was said.

If old men drink this water it will conserve and sustain them for a long time with good strength and vigor, without any hand or head shaking; for it not only increases their natural heat but it also offers them nutrients.

Finally this water can be given to those who have a fever and are suffering from great thirst, this if in three ounces of sugar water one does not cast more than one ounce of *aguardente* and one drachma of rose water; and this will cause two healthy effects: one will be the mitigation of their great thirst, and the other the diminishing of their fever to the point of removing it.

FOURTH
TREATISE
OF THE SECRETS OF NATURE AND THEIR
MARVELOUS EFFECTS

SECRETS OF THE VIRTUES AND PROPERTIES OF THE FINEST AND MOST PRECIOUS STONES

Secrets and virtues of the magnet stone which is commonly called lodestone

The magnet stone has the virtue to attract to itself iron, steel, sand, olive oil and many other things. The first one to notice its virtues was Aristotle.

Iron, once touched by a magnet stone will attract to itself more iron, should you approach this stone with several iron rings, some will attach themselves to each other in such a way as to suspend themselves attached to the magnet stone.

Those who are inclined to gamble and other apparent lightlessness have invented and still invent, with the virtue of this magnet stone, a thousand and one curiosities and sleights of hand that to those who don't know any better may think them to be enchantments.

By means of the virtue of this stone may one know the time of day, which is what is used in those clocks coming from Flanders and Italy, whose truth and experience we see and touch every day with our hands.

By the virtue of this magnet stone is navigation made possible, for with this stone may one cause the navigation needle to always point to the North, and no matter to which direction the ship is turned towards, this needle is always fixed towards the North, and the cause for this is the magnet stone which was used to touch this needle.

This has the virtue of closing wounds and removing pain, of separating white sand from the black and should it be anointed with garlic is loses all its virtue, valor and strength.

Secrets and virtues of jacinth

Jacinth has many colors, but the green and bright purple ones are the best, and from these a powder can be made, which if taken through the mouth is most cordial and useful against typhus fever and it defends whoever carries it from lighting and storms.

By bringing jacinth in contact with the body it comforts the heart and brightens one's cunning.

Whoever carries jacinth with them is defended against poison and corrupt airs.

Jacinth has the virtue of cooling down madness, preventing melancholy and the manifestations of ghosts and visions.

Half a league from Toledo, near a monastery, there is a fountain near the Tagus where one may find jacinth, for there are so many of these in that place that water is simply running over them.

Secrets and virtues of diamond

Diamond is understood to be superior to all other precious stones, this due to its great hardness and by the many and admirable virtues it possesses. And for a diamond to be very fine it should be clear, tend towards the blue and be pure and bright as a Sun beam.

Those who carry a fine diamond with them will be preserved from heavy and harmful dreams, representations of visions and ghosts and mainly from fears and tremors.

Whoever carries a diamond with them cannot become a target of the eye (which is to be infected by an evil intent) nor will he suffer from the danger of poison, as the poet Dionysus writes in these verses.

Hic fulget lymphata adamas, qui pectora sanat.
Et prohibet miseris oculta dogma veneni

Diamond is useful and of great utility to pregnant women, both to preserve them and also to comfort them during labor.

If a diamond is rubbed against any other stone or metal it will leave a clear trace.

Diamond is the opposite and enemy of the magnet stone, for in its presence and proximity the magnet stone loses its virtue and attraction strength.

Should anyone rub two fine diamonds together these will become attached and strongly united.

King Phillip the Third had a diamond which was valued at one hundred and seventy thousand *cruzados*.

The greatest diamond that exists is the size of a great hazelnut.

Diamonds cannot be carved by any other thing than another diamond, for it is so hard in its nature that no iron will imprint on it, and yet, it is made softer with the blood of a kid goat.

Secrets and virtues of Emerald

An emerald which is fine has very pleasant color to the sight and brings greater joy and recreation than all meadows and most delicious pastures of all fields.

If the emerald is fine, so says Saint Albertus Magnus, it has such virtue that it does not consent that there be any commerce between men and women without cracking, should it be carried in contact with one's body.

Emerald has an admirable virtue and property in that it mitigates the stimuli of the flesh and it infuses chastity to whomever carries it with them.

Emerald generates good memory and is useful against venom and storms.

Licenciado Aranda writes in the book he so learnedly filled with concepts and sentences, that in Geneva there is an emerald which is the size of a plate; which is highly venerated as a relic; for according to tradition Christ our Lord ate from it on the Last Supper and it is called *Paropside Domini*.

Secrets and virtues of Sapphire

Sapphire and Ruby have almost the same virtues and properties, their only difference is that Ruby is much more red, embery and bright; and the sapphire is of a celestial and very transparent color.

Sapphire is widely praised for many medicines and antidotes against all poison.

Sapphire has the virtue of staunching nose bleeds and the fleshy growths that are usually generated in the eyes.

Sapphire is a marvelous aid to fortify and clear one's sight, by passing this same stone over the eyes many times.

Those who have very high fever, by placing this stone under their tongue it will slow and mitigate the heat and burn of the said fevers.

This stone is very useful against poison and it defends the whole body from corrupted airs.

Secrets and virtues of the Bezoar stone

This stone has admirable virtues for it is effective against all poison and venom, should it be drunk as a powder.

Whoever carries it with them will be free from melancholy and melancholic illnesses.

This stone represses fevers, cures tertian and quartan, preserves from leprosy, mange and itch, no matter how old, it is good against pox, measles and impetigo, strengthens the weak and debilitated by increasing their will to eat, should they take it as a powder.

This stone facilitates childbirth, clears the kidneys and bladder from sand, expels any worms, eels, vipers, snakes and any venomous animal bite.

If powder from this stone is put on any wounds made from a poison arrow it will remove its poison; by casting this powder on any open scrofula or cancer, it will operate a marvelous effect.

Secrets and virtues of the Carbuncle[182]

This stone can shine even in the greatest darkness without there being any other light present and this virtue it receives from the Sun.

This stone is used against all venom, and should this be in any vase, it immediately discovers it just by being placed near this stone.

Luis Bartholomeo[183] says that while in the Indies he saw in the possession of the king of Peru some carbuncle that could shine in such a remarkable way in the greatest darkness that it seemed like they had transparent bodies, so penetrating was the light of those carbuncles.

Secrets and virtues of the Eagle stone

This is called an Eagle stone for (according to Albertus Magnus) eagles usually carry this stone to their nests. The color of this stone is like that of chestnut peel and inside this stone there is a second one, which can be heard if this is shaken; and it is also called by the name of pregnant stone.

This stone operates any childbirth in women, by tying it to the leg, under the groin.

Powder from this stone, if drunk, is useful for all venom and blockages.

The small stone which is inside the Eagle stone, made into a powder and drunk with water, cures any stabbing pain in less than 24 hours. The tertian and quartan can be cured if these powders are taken before the beginning of the cold weather. It removes the *mal de madre*, and drinking this powder with wine kills roundworms.

Secrets and virtues of the Acates or Agate, Jasper and Ivory

This Agate stone has a rare virtue which is that should it be cast into water it will light up and burn, and should it be cast into olive oil it will be extinguished. If made into a powder and given to drink to a woman who is not a damsel it will cause her to immediately urinate, and should she be a damsel it will not have any effect.

Jasper stone

Green jasper stone is the best, and by tying it to the inside of a woman's thigh it abbreviates labor.

---

182. Translator's note: Almandine.
183. Translator's note: uncertain reference.

Whoever brings jasper stone with them, while entering the sea, will not get sea sick or have any blood flow, and by bringing it over the stomach it gives a great effort, strength and it also represses vomit.

Ivory is the tooth of an elephant, which, if carried with a person comforts the heart, conserves the liver and staunches white purges from women.

Secrets and virtues of the Pantaura, Turquoise, Agate and Amethyst stone

Pantaura stone has the virtues of all stones, as writes Apollonius of Tyana, and as the magnet stone attracts iron, so does the Pantaura attract every other precious stone; whoever carries it with them will not be touched by any venom and will be free from all that which all other stones free a man from.

Turquoise stone

Turquoise is used against falling and it drives away tremors.

Agate greatly conserves the sight and gives good speech to all those who carry it and it is useful against poison.

Amethyst stone

This stone has the virtue to prevent the ill effects of intemperately drunk wine, this by carrying it.

Secrets and virtues of the swallow stone

The experimenter says, and also the above mentioned Albertus, that in the head of the swallow there are two very small stones, one white and one red, whose virtues are the following:

It is said that whoever carries with them the white swallow stone will never be bothered by thirst and their mouth will always be fresh.

It is said that if someone has a blood flow and puts this stone around the neck that the blood will immediately stop.

It is also said that it has the virtue to aid women during childbirth, just as the Eagle stone.

They further say that casting the same white stone into a vase of water and leaving it there for nine nights will cause that when this water is drunk it will remove gout and fever, should this person have these.

It is also said that whoever carries the red swallow stone is freed from many diseases.

Secrets and virtues of the skin snakes shed

Burnt snake skin, placed over any wound will make it well and should there be any thorns or spikes in the flesh, it will attract it until it comes out.

And let all be warned that whoever carries the dust of this skin with them will be preserved from leprosy and any poison. And know that the said powder has great virtues and many properties; but the skin should be burnt when the Sun is in Aries, which is from the 21st of March until the 20th of April.

Secrets and virtue of the Nicolaus, Asteroid and Heliotrope stone

The Nicolaus stone saddens and causes melancholy to whoever carries it with them.

The asteroid stone, cast into wine or vinegar, moves without any one touching it.

The heliotrope stone lengthens the life of anyone who carries it with them; and it also constantly communicates many other properties which are of the nature of the Sun.

In Scotland a certain quality of spongious stones are produced, and by straining sea water through them it becomes fresh and drinkable.

Secrets and virtues of some fountains

The properties of fountains are so many and their effects so admirable that if these were not reported by such celebrated men no one would believe them and I wouldn't dare mention them; but as such grave authors have mentioned them I will also write them here and I will cite the names and the places where these are mentioned.

In the Cyrenaica province Pomponius Mela[184] said that there is a fountain of such property that at midnight its water boils to the highest degree and at midday it is once again cold and peaceful.

In the Canary islands, there are two fountains that, if drunk from, one will cause perpetual laughter and the other perpetual sadness.

In India, and in Ethiopia, said Pliny, there is a fountain whose waters are used as olive oil for lamps and these are also good for food, as actual olive oil; the same is said by Theophrastus.

Solinus[185] and Theophrastus said that there are two fountains of such virtues that should a woman drink from one of them she will be made sterile and should she drink from the other she will be ready to conceive. The same is said by Saint Isidore in Book 14 of his *Etymologiae*.

In Beotia there are two fountains and drinking from one will cause loss of memory and drinking from the other will cause its augmentation.

In Guinea there is a fountain which is called of Jacob that every three months its waters change color, namely gray, red, green and white.

In Judea, Pliny writes, Book 32, there is a fountain that every Saturday becomes completely dry.

In the castle of Emmaus there is a fountain whose water will cure any infirmity, both of men and irrational animals; where according to tradition Christ our Lord washed his hands when his disciples invited him to eat, in this same castle of Emmaus.

Near the Garamantes, which are a people of Africa, Pliny writes in the above mentioned place that there are two fountains of such different nature that one is so cold that it cannot be drunk and the other so hot that one cannot place a hand under its flow without burning himself.

Aristotle writes that there is a fountain whose waters are of such nature that should one play a flute or any other instrument in its proximity it will boil and become so agitated as to go over its boundaries, and should the music stop it will once again become calm.

Baptista Fulgoso[186] writes that in England there is a fountain that should any wood be placed inside it, it will turn to stone within a year.

In France, this same author says, that there is an extremely cold fountain that sometimes spits out flames from the same place from where its water comes out.

Leonicus[187] mentions, Book 3, Chapter 83, that in a certain island of Cyclops there is another fountain whose water can never the mixed with wine.

Pomponius Mela writes and claims that in Macedonia there is a fountain that should you place a torch in it, it will be extinguished, and should you put in one which is extinguished it will come out lit. And from this did Juan de Mena[188] claim that there is a fountain in the world which can give and steal fire. And just so you do not think this to be a fable and my own invention, one should know that Saint Isidore makes mention of this fountain in Book 1 of the *Etymologiae*. And Saint Augustine mentions this same fountain in Book 1 of *De Civitate Dei*, as does Pliny in his natural history.

---

184. Translator's note: An early Roman geographer.
185. Translator's note: Gaius Julius Solinus, a third century writer of books of worldly curiosities and wonders.
186. Translator's note: Uncertain reference, but probably a Spanish chronicler.
187. Translator's note: Nicholas Leonicus Thomaeus.
188. Translator's note: A XVth century Spanish poet.

The same Leonicus, in the above mentioned place, mentions a fountain in Lycia which flows blood.

Celio[189] says that in a certain part of France there is a fountain that emits such a concerted noise and so loud and pleasant, that it cures all sadness and melancholy of all who hear it.

On the island of Cuba there is a fountain which flows such thick water that it is used as tar for ships.

Nicholas Leonicus mentions a fountain which is on the island of Naxos which, on a certain day of the year, a certain water flows which tastes like wine.

Marco Polo writes in the book of his Navigations that in the province of Zarçania[190] there is a lake which gathers the water of several fountains of the surrounding hills and in which there isn't a single fish, except between Lent and Easter, and after that they once again disappear.

In Gorgona there is another river which does not have any fish except in Lent, and once this is over they once again disappear.

In Serra da Estrela there are two extremely large lakes, which the bottom of one was never found; and both of these become altered when there is a storm at sea; nothing living grows in them and occasionally pieces of ships are found there, while the sea is more than 20 leagues away.

In one of the Canary islands there is a tree that distills so much water through its leaves that it sustains all it inhabitants and also all irrational animals, and this island is called La Gomera.

Father José de Acosta[191] refers in the history of the Indies, Book 3, Chapter 29, that in Bolivia[192] there is a fountain whose water, as soon as it immerges, turn to a very white salt and this is very good for food.

Father Acosta further says that in Peru, where you have the lead mines, there is a hot water fountain that as soon as water flows out it turns to stone, from which all the local building are constructed, in Huancavelica, which is close to this mountain.

Saint Isidore, Book 15 of *Etymologiae*, mentions many extremely cold fountains in Sardinia and others which are extremely hot, all very close to each other.

Near the town of Estremoz, in Portugal, there is such a copious fountain that one may call it a river, and as Winter approaches it gradually dries until it completely ceases its flow, and as soon as Summer begins it immediately starts pouring again and it moves many mills. By virtue of this same water it also happens that these mills become covered with stone, and the same happens to any bread or board, in such a way that should anyone throw a loaf inside this water, it will be covered by stone.

In Andalucía, in a mount called Maxna there is a fountain near the Villa de D. Luis de la Cueva, which is so cold that, should you cast a cow's leg inside, in six hours it will be frozen, and no man has ever been able to keep his hand inside this water for over the time it takes to pray a Hail Mary.

Paul of Venice,[193] Book 1, Chapter 13, says that in a mount in Armenia, where Noah's Ark landed, there is a fountain which expels a liqueur, similar to olive oil, but which is not good for eating, but it is still very good for burning and making unguents.

Aristotle, prince of philosophers, in *De mirabilibus auscultationibus*, mentions a certain fountain in Sicily which seems more miraculous than natural, near which should anyone make an oath, and write this on a tablet and cast it into the water, if his oath is true the tablet will float, otherwise it will sink and the person who wrote it will burst into flames and be reduced to ash.

Pomponius Mela, in *De situ orbis*, Chapter 8, writes of a strange marvel of a certain fountain which they call Sun, in the province of Cyrenaica, and this is such that by placing one's hand in front of the stone from which the water flows, this will grow and rise so as to flow around the hand, and should one remove the hand it will return to normal and lower itself as before. This author writes of another effect and marvel of this fountain, which is that as the Sun rises and goes

---

189. Translator's note: uncertain reference.
190. Translator's note: uncertain reference.
191. Translator's note a XVIth century Spanish naturalist of South America.
192. Translator's note: uncertain translation.
193. Translator's note: a XIVth and XVth century priest, a philosopher and theologian.

up through the sky, so does this fountain become gradually cooler, and from the midday on it heats up again until midnight, and from then until the morning it starts to cool down once again as the Sun rises; and by this cause is this fountain called the Sun.

Lucio Siculo,[194] Book 3, says that in Villanueva del Obispo there is a very abundant fountain, but as soon as the Sun enter in the Sign of Libra, which is at the 23rd of September, it completely dries and not a single drop of water falls from it until the Sun enters the Sign of Aries, which is at the 21st of March, when it once again begins to flow.

Near Tentugal, Coimbra, there is another fountain which they call Fervença, which boils anything which is thrown inside it, be it whole trees or live animals.

Solinus and Saint Isidore, Book 3, *Etymologiae*, claim that there is a fountain in Sardinia which can cure every infirmity of the eyes. And these authors further add that if any thief washes his eyes with this water he will become blind, should he be guilty of theft, but should he be innocent his eyes will become lighter than they were before.

In the province of Entre Douro e Minho, near a hermitage of Saint James, there is a small river that on the eve of the day of that Saint becomes filled with leeches and people who go on a pilgrimage with some illness, on entering this water are rushed by these leeches which suck their blood and heal them.

Saint Albertus Magnus writes of a fountain in Germany which is so cold that anything cast inside it turns to stone.

Aristotle, in the above mentioned book, says that in the Promontory[195] there is a fountain which flows blood, and this casts such a foul odor that it is impossible to sail past that part of the sea, where this bloodied water enters the ocean.

Aristotle also claims that in this same place, near the Cyclops, there is a very clear fountain, but it has such a bad quality that anyone drinking from it immediately dies.

Nicholas Leonicus, Book 3, Chapter 83, writes of a lake which generates an innumerable amount of fish and he says that when the day is calm and still, over the waters appears an abundance of olive oil, which is very good for eating, light and medicinal and that all the neighboring villages collect a great amount of olive oil on those days.

Father José de Acosta writes in his history of the Indies, Book 1, Chapter 19, that in the natural baths of the Incas there are two fountains of such an opposite nature, that from one flows boiling water and from the other extremely cold water, which is like snow; and because these fountains are so close to each other it causes great amazement.

He further says that in Peru there are many fountains which can cure the *Morbo Gallico*[196] should one wash in them, and the cause of this is because these waters pass by lands with a great abundance of sarsaparilla, which has particular virtues to heal similar diseases.

And those wanting to know more properties of water, and greater marvels of the fountains should read Nicholas Leonicus, Book 1 Chapter, 32, Saint Augustine, Book 21 of *De Civitate Dei*, Chapter 5, Vitruvius, Book 8, Chapter 4 and many others who wrote of this, such as Pliny, Pomponius, Lucio Siculo and Saint Albertus Magnus, among others.

Secret in order to turn sea water into drinkable water

Aristotle says that in order to make sea water into drinkable water one should make a vase of wax, and make sure it is very well closed. Place this vase in sea water, in such a way as it is completely covered by water and all the water that enters this vase through the pores in the wax will be drinkable. The same will happen if you use a new clay vase, as long as it has its mouth closed.

---

194. Translator's note: Lucio Marineo Sículo, a Sicilian historian who lived most of his life in Castile.
195. Translator's note: uncertain translation.
196. Translator's note: The French disease, Syphilis.

Natural secrets to conserve chastity and repress the stimuli of the flesh

Macencio[197] writes that the juice of a herb called *sagunta*[198] if drunk on an empty stomach will repress the impulses of the flesh and its leaves, placed over the genitals have the virtue of placating the incentives of lust.

Avicenna writes that rue, if eaten, mitigates the ardor of the flesh in a man, but in a women it does the opposite, as it activates them in excess.

Master João[199] says that verbena has a great virtue and efficiency in repressing lust, for if placed on the lower back it greatly placates the excitements of the flesh. The same author further says that verbena juice, if drunk, causes impotence in whoever drinks it for a period of seven days. Dioscorides writes that the fruits produced by the cedar tree, macerated, or the juice from its leaves, if placed on the genitals will remove the desire for venereal acts. Michael Scot with great foundation says that cold and sour things are very well accommodated with chastity and conserve it; on the contrary sweet, hot and scented things destroy and spoil everything. However, if we are to talk spiritually and catholically, what defends chastity the most is fasting, discipline and frequent prayer and great devotion.

Very sure and experimented secrets so as to preserve beds free of bedbugs, rooms free of fleas, houses free of flies, mosquitoes and mice

Take a glue made from leftover leather melted in boiling water, and let it be very clear and thin and mix it with olive oil; and while it is still hot rub the boards around the bed with it in such a way as the floor around the bed is covered with this boiling and you will obtain two very good effects. The first of these is that the bed will appear as it is made of chestnut tree wood. And the second one is that no bedbugs will grow in it, as I have myself experimented.

Against fleas

Place a pan of water over the fire and cast in it two *vintães of solimão*[200] and let it boil very well; after that spray the quarters with this and afterwards sweep it very well and be sure that all fleas in there will die, disappear and never return again. But this needs to be made twice a week.

Against flies

Take some honey and flour and mix this with a little bit of clear water and cast in this some arsenic or *resalgar*[201] and place this mixture in small plates where flies may reach it and you shall see how many will begin to fall, for they will start dying. The same effect may be accomplished by ground gold pepper melted in water and placed in a few vases spread through the house; but do take care that no dog or chicken reaches these, for they will die.

Against mosquitoes

Burn some wild cumin in the room where the mosquitoes are in and these will immediately fall dead and flee; also, should you wash your face with water infused with wild cumin, mosquitoes

---

197. Translator's note: uncertain reference.
198. Translator's note: uncertain translation.
199. Translator's note: most likely João Faras, also referred to as João Emenesau, a Spanish physician and astronomer of the XVth century.
200. Translator's note: uncertain translations. *Vintém* can both mean a unit of weight (112,05 grams) or a type of coin, and *solimão* can mean mercuric chloride or Solomon (as in the Biblical king). So, this either reads 224.1 g of mercuric chloride or two Solomon coins, which would be two coins with pentagrams imprinted on them, frequently used in Iberia as talismans and for divination purposes. Logic would dictate that it would be the first option, but I really can't rule out the second one.
201. Translator's note: arsenic oxide.

will not come anywhere near the face. In other places and books one may find many other secrets about this, very notable and hard to believe and so I cite the authors which mention these.

Against mice

Manage to catch a live mouse, either a big or medium in size, and make two things to it: either skin its head and place in the opening a little bit of ground salt and release it; for with the burning and rage he feels he will drive away all other mice; or make another thing, should it seem easier: tie to its neck the rattle of a snake with a very clear sound, and it will make all others run away, and thus you will be free from the great enemies of all housekeepers, saving a lot in expenses and harm. Another even better secret is even easier. Take some new plaster and sieve it, mixing it with ground cheese and place this in various places of the house and it will be very entertaining to see the mice eating this delicacy and become bloated throughout the house, and should there be any water for them to drink it will kill them even faster, for as soon as the plaster touches the water or anything humid it immediately turns to a mass and this is a secret with no danger.

Curious and advantageous secret so as to preserve your shoes new and with luster, should these be of leather

When your shoes, sandals or boots start to lose their luster and color, buy one *dinero*[202] of tanner ink (the one which they use to treat and darken the skin), wet a wool cloth with this, rub the shoes and let them dry. After they are dry rub them with another cloth, this one dry or wet with orange juice, which is better, and you will see that they will recover their previous dark luster; so much so that they will seem as if new, and this experiment I have made not few but many times; for those of us with a low income and high expenses should save on one thing so as we may spend on another.

Secret to make olive oil in a lamp last longer

Take a small broom shrub, the one with small leaves (for there are two types of them) and burn it; bleach this ash and boil it, so that it will turn into a salt, which, if put into a lamp will make olive oil last one third longer than its normal time. Pink potassium alum and common salt, like the one used for food, have this same property, but they are not as good as the broom shrub salt.

Secret to increase lamp oil

Take a *canada* of olive oil and place it over the fire and immediately put four ounces of Greek tar into a *vintem* of pink potassium alum, grind everything and mix it very well until this is all homogeneous, and immediately after you may used this in a lamp. This may be produced in greater or smaller amounts by following these proportions.

Secret to multiply good and strong vinegar at little cost

During the time of the grape harvest, take some bagasse from the bottom of the grape vise after these have been squeezed, and in this mix one hundred pots of water, four *arrateis* of green samphire, two of elderberry flowers and a vase of the best and strongest vinegar and leave this for twenty or thirty days, after which you should squeeze everything and obtain a very strong and aromatic vinegar. And by keeping these proportions one may make more or less of this.

---

202. Translator's note: Either a Spanish unit of measure I am not familiar with, or a specific denomination of early-modern Spanish currency (this word currently means 'money').

Secret to multiply wax

Take one *arroba*[203] of lard from a male goat and one dozen Mallard eggs, only the yolks, half boiled, well beaten, and cast these into the lard with another *arroba* of wax. Everything is put over a fire and mixed until it is melted and well mixed and it will be converted into yellow wax from which one may do anything one wishes.

Secret to know if wine has water in it or not

Creponte[204] says that in order to know if wine has any water in it; one should cast in it a few shavings of wild pear. If this floats in the wine then it is pure, but should it sink one will know that water has been added to this wine. Another warning: take a flat oat straw, wax it with lard and put it into the vase of wine. Should this have any water in it there will be very tiny drops of water attached to the straw when you take it out. Another way: fill a new pan with wine and leave it there for two days, after this time all the water in it will be gone. Another: take a small stone of lime and drop some wine on it, if this has any water the stone will immediately melt, otherwise it will become even harder. Another: cast some of the wine into a pan of very hot olive oil, should this have any water it will make a great mess and agitation, should it be pure nothing will happen.

Secret in order not to get drunk

Philonius says that in order not to get drunk, some time before, one should eat roasted sheep lungs. Or, before drinking wine, eat some collard greens with vinegar, and in this way wine will not harm you, given that you do not drink in exaggeration. However the best remedy to not get drunk is what I have used in the sixty three years in which I have not drunk any wine, and I find such satisfaction in water that to me there is no greater delicacy on the most splendid of tables; and I wish that what is usually said would be practiced, which is that wine should be sold in pharmacies and used as medicine. Should anyone recognize the discredit that the vice of over drinking causes and wishes to free themselves from getting drunk, do note what Pliny writes, which is to place two thick living eels inside a vase of wine and after these are drowned give this wine to him who usually drinks too much and he will be completely fed up with wine, for this causes a rare bother and aversion. For this same effect powdered bastard balm, drunk, is also used.

Secret to remove water from wine

Cato[205] and Pliny write that in order to remove water from wine one should make a vase of vine wood and pour the wine in this, and should it have water, all the wine in it will be strained leaving only the water, and should it be pure the vase will be left empty.

Secret of a bowl that, being filled with water and uncovered,
can be put upside down that it will not spill

Place a bowl or bottle filled with water or wine inside a small cube or bucket, made of wood or copper, which is better, and cast over the bottle or bowl and under it a quantity of snow, and over this some fine salt. Little by little turn the bottle until all the snow has melted, and after this strain this water and once again cast more snow with salt over it, and leave it be until it is melted without moving the bottle, and the same should be done a third time and all the water or wine

---

203. Translator's note: An old unit of measure, coming from the Arabic *ar-rub*, usually equivalent to 14,688 kg.
204. Translator's note: uncertain reference.
205. Translator's note: possibly Marcus Porcius Cato, or Cato the Elder, a Roman statesman of the IInd century.

in the bottle will become frozen. And this can be done in the height of Summer and it will seem like an impossible thing. By putting this bottle upside down be certain that not a drop will fall, as has the Duke of Gandia Dom Francisco de Borja experimented, who sent a bowl of frozen water in Summer to the Patriarch Dom João de Ribeyra Archbishop of Valencia, who in return for such a curious secret sent him back another bottle of frozen wine, which was an ever greater marvel.

Secret to turn a red rose, or carnation, white

Fumigate the carnation or rose with sulfur and immediately they will turn from red to white and in this way you may have a fully white garden, as I have myself made once to great admiration of the garden owner.

Curious and entertaining secret

Gather a little bit of mercury in a tube, and while this is very well covered place inside this a piece of hot bread, and one will see the mercury heat up so much that the bread will start to leap throughout the table. The same can be seen should you fill a hazelnut with mercury and cast it in hot water, for as the mercury heats up the hazelnut will start jumping.

Another secret of the bottle or bowl

Should you want to make water go up into an empty bowl or bottle, heat this recipient well and place it upside down with its mouth under water and you shall see it rise through the bottle while it is hot; and so as this may be kept so continuously burn some paper under the bottom of the bottle and it won't stop until it is completely full, and this is proven.

Another secret of the bowl

Should you want a bowl filled with wine that, while being hung in the air and broken, will not spill any wine, take a nicely clean calf bladder and place this inside the bowl, and this bladder should be of the same size of the bowl when it is filled with air, and tie the opening of the bladder to the bottom of the bowl and then fill it with wine. Hang this in the air and when it is struck with a stick in such a way as to break it, the wine will be kept in the bladder and it will not spill. This is proven.

Another secret of the bowl

Should you want to place a bowl of water on top of your head, and not touching it with your hands, still be able to drink this, take a long wheat straw which should reach from your mouth to the bowl. Place one end of this in the bowl and the other in your mouth and you will be able to drink without losing a single drop; and so as the tip of the straw may be kept inside the bowl, tie a small stone to it; and in this same way you may have this bowl of water in your hand, having your arm extended and still be able to drink from it.

Another secret of the bowl

Should you want to read or write during the night and have a light as clear as the Sun, take water from a cistern and distill it in a glass alembic instead of the common ones, if possible, and when this is distilled put this water into a thin clear glass bowl and when you wish to read or write place a candle behind this bowl and it will create such a resplendently clear light that it will allow you to see as clearly as the midday Sun, and this has been proven many times. The same also happens with water which was not distilled in an alembic, but this light will not be as clear. And do note that this light does not offend one's sight.

Secret of the egg

A fresh egg placed in a bowl of fresh water will sink to the bottom; and if the water is salty it will float. This secret has been experimented by curious women marinating olives, that in order to see if the water has enough salt they place a fresh egg into this, and if it floats they understand that there is enough salt, and should it sink they add more salt, and in this way they know if this water has enough salt to marinate olives.

This same experiment is used by those who make bleach, so as to know if this is strong enough; should it be strong the egg will sustain itself in the water, and if it is weak it will sink to the bottom; and the stronger the bleach the more manifested is the floating of the egg over the water. This is proven.

Secret of the egg so as to place it whole inside a bottle

Take an egg and place it to soak for two or three days in strong vinegar and the shell will become so soft that you may slip this inside a bottle, no matter how narrow it has its mouth; and when the egg is inside the bottle put some cold water into this, and the egg will return to its previous condition; and in order to take it out, remove this water and place some vinegar in and you will be able to take it out. This is proven.

Secret of the egg and the leech

Should you want to have an egg that rolls around the house by itself, take an empty egg, strong enough that the shell is kept in one piece while the inside has been blown out through a hole, place a leech inside it and cover the hole with wax. Take a bowl of water and agitate it near the egg; as the leech by natural instinct recognizes and feels the sound of the water, it will follow that noise in the direction of the bowl and the egg will begin to move; and those who do not know of this secret will be very confused and this is proven; and do note that the leech should be from a bog, those which are very dark and thick.

Rare secret of the egg and line

Tie a line around an egg and place it to cook in the middle of some embers, and let this be covered with living fire, and it will be seen that the egg will be cooked and the line will not burn or break, and this is proven.

Incredible secret for those who have not seen or tested it

Should you want to fry fish or eggs on paper instead of a pan, take a piece of paper and make this into the shape of a four corner hat and cast some olive oil on it and place this over a candle or lamp. The olive oil will start to boil and you may fry your fish or eggs, and this is proven

Secret of the two painted faces on a wall that light and put out candles

Paint two large faces on a wall, and in the middle of their mouths make two little holes; in one of these place some ground and very well dried saltpeter and in the other powdered sulfur; should you approach a lit candle to the mouth, near the hole with the saltpeter, it will be extinguished, and if immediately afterwards you approach the wick to the hole with the sulfur it will once again light; but note that the wick must touch the saltpeter and the sulfur.

Secret to make a large chicken, while still alive, appear dead and roasted on a table and another secret to make it jump and run

Take some celery juice and mix it with refined *aguardente* and drop inside this mixture two pieces of bread and feed this to the chicken on an empty stomach; shortly after the chicken will fall to the ground numb and in that same instant remove all of its feathers and anoint it with white honey mixed with strong saffron, in such a way as the chicken will look very dark and place this on a plate in such a way as it looks roasted. When you wish to make it come to life and jump away, wet its beak with some strong vinegar, in such a way as this will fill its throat and it will suddenly rise and run away from the table, and this has been proven.

Secret and rare marvel

Saint Basil and Saint Ambrose write about a bird, which they call halcyon, which makes its nest in the sand near the sea in Winter and which in seven days generates and hatches its eggs and in another seven days has its young flying. These Saintly Doctors say that in these fourteen days that this bird takes to raise its young never does the sea alter itself, but will instead remain very serene and quiet. This marvel and prodigy is well observed by sailors, and they call these days the halcyonic days and they are very certain that during these fourteen days there will not be any torments at sea.

Secret of the dog heart

Baptista Aranda[206] writes in his book of concepts that whoever carries with them a dog's heart does not have to fear any other dogs, for they shall run from him. This same author says that ants will flee from the heart of a bird called hoopoe.

Secret of the dog's eye

Battista della Porta[207] writes in his book of secrets that whoever carries an eye from a black dog will never be barked at by other dogs; this because the said eyes emit a scent that all dogs can feel due to their strong sense of smell, and they will not dare bark or bother you.

Important secret for one's memory

Should you want to augment your memory take some bear fat, white wax and melt these two things together, being that the fat should be twice as much as the wax. Then take a herb called valerian and another called euphrasia, either dried or fresh, and grind these very well and mix them with the melted fat and wax, and once again put this over the fire until it becomes thick, always mixing it with a stick. With this unguent anoint the forehead and the back of your head occasionally, and your memory will increase in a notable way, and this is proven.

Secret for a married couple with no children

In a married couple with no children, in order to know in which one the natural defect lies, one should take the urine of both of them, husband and wife, in two vases and cast into each of them some wheat bran; the vase in which critters will start to grow indicates the one with the natural defect and this person will not be able to procreate or conceive.

---

206. Translator's note: uncertain reference, but the same as Licenciado Aranda.
207. Translator's note: Giovanni Battista della Porta, a XVIIth century Italian polymath and occultist, writer of the book *Magia Naturalis*.

Secret to have a clear and good voice

Take some elderberry flowers and dry them under the Sun, then grind them and cast this powder into some wine and drink this on an empty stomach and it will cause a good and clear voice.

Celery and verbena juice also make the voice very clear, but one should be warned that verbena juice makes the genitals cold. Both these effects are proven.

Secret of Artemisia

An author writes that a herb called Artemisia infuses joy and good spirits in those who carry it next to their heart. The powder from this herb, drunk with some white wine, immediately cures the tiredness of a journey. And it has another rare virtue, which is that a traveler who carries it with him will feel much less tired than otherwise. This herb receives these virtues from a Star that the Astrologers call Algol. This herb has another virtue which is to conserve wine for many years by casting these powders into the liquid, but one should dry the herb in the hotness of an oven. It has another virtue of driving flies away from any house, should it be boiled with goat's milk and with this boiling one washes the walls and doors of the house, and all flies will immediately leave and never return.

Secret for those who have blood flows[208]

Eat a dozen roasted hazelnuts before going to bed and it will staunch, this has been proven.

Secret to make parsley grow in twenty four hours

Take virgin lime, iron powder and some dirt made up of Dove manure, all this well ground and mixed. Plant in this mixture the parsley and water it with young pigeon blood and *aguardente*, and after twenty four hours it will have grown.

Secrets and virtues of sage

In the Salenternian school there are many writings on the virtues of sage, among which one may count that those who have the custom to eat its leaves in a salad or in a pan will very rarely fall ill; and this also greatly helps with digestion, removes any evil and pain from the chest and stomach, arising from coldness, strengthens every member and debilitated nerves, comforts and brings joy to the heart, breaks away thick humors from the bladder and facilitates urination. This herb distilled in an alembic is also good against paralysis and *gota coral*. Its conserve is most helpful to preserve health, removing any ill from the heart, it also has a great virtue to loosen the tongue which is slow, this by placing a leaf of this herb under the tongue in the morning.

Secret to make flames come out from an unlit vase

An author writes that one should take a duck's egg and empty it through a small hole, and it should be well dried. Fill this with quicklime and fine sulfur, both very well ground and in equal proportions, and cover this hole with white wax. Put this egg into a vase filled with water and it will spit flames. This is proven.

Secret so as not to be able to cook meat in a pan placed over the fire during the whole day

Take a thick lead paste and place it on the bottom of the pan, and the meat will not cook even if kept there for the whole day, this has been proven.

---

208. Translator's note: In some editions this same recipe is given to prevent involuntary urine flow.

Secret for headaches or migraines

Take some vitriol powder and apply it to the nostrils, and be sure that this is not too much and you will see that it immediately make you sneeze and purge your nose, and it will end the pain which causes these great ills.

Proven secret against jaw pain

Take two vine leaves and the same amount from elderberry and some pepper grains and place all of this in a boiling of very red and old wine with a little bit of salt. After it is well boiled take it from the fire and gargle this hot wine, three or four times and the pain will soon disappear.

Secret to cast burlap on the fire and have this not burn

Douse the burlap in *aguardente* and cast it into a fire and you will see that it will be engulfed in flames but not burn. But you should be warned to remove it from the fire before the *aguardente* is entirely consumed, because after that it will really burn.

Secret and joke to make people sneeze terribly from below

Take some chestnut peels and ant eggs, all mixed and ground into a powder and cast this into something which you should offer as a drink and you will see marvels. This is proven.

Secret to make all who are in the house sneeze from below and above

Take three or four hot peppers and place these on some embers, covered with ash, in such a way as the embers are not touching the peppers, but there should be an abundance of embers over them. As the peppers become hotter they will start emitting a subtle and thin smoke which is not felt until it causes the above mentioned effect, and the house should be well closed, and this has been proven.

Secret in order to make one's face look like a dead man at night

Take one *vintem* of sulfur and a hand full of salt, grind these together and place them in a bowl over a fire. When this is almost burnt drop into this bowl two *vintens* of *aguardente* (should it be strong so much the better) and all the ingredients will start burning with the *aguardente*, and this light will make the faces of all those present look like as they were dead, fainted and disfigured in such a way as they will appear more dead than alive, and this is proven. And be warned that there shouldn't be any other light in the house.

Proven secret so as to make that not a single hair should grow

Shave all the hair you may wish with a razor and anoint that region with Arabic Gum melted in fumitory juice or bat's blood, which is even better, and no hair will grow. The same effect will be done by cat manure melted in vinegar.

Secret so as one's beard and hair always be conserved black

Have a thin lead comb made, and use this to comb your beard and hair and they shall always conserve themselves black.

Secret to conserve one's beard and hair blond

Take chestnut tree leaves, pomegranate peels and distill these in a glass alembic and use this water to carefully wash the hair and beard for fifteen days and these will conserve themselves blond.

Secret so as the beard and hair turn from white to black

Take leaves from a black fig tree, dry them and turn them into powder, mixing them with *macela* oil. Anoint the beard and hair many times with this mix and they will turn black.

Secret so as one's nails and hair grow slowly

Cut the hair and nails during the waning Moon while this is in the Signs of Cancer, Pisces or Libra, and they will grow very little

Secret so as one's nails and hair grow faster

Cut the nails and hair on the crescent Moon while this is in the Signs of Taurus, Virgo or Libra, and you shall see that they will grow faster.

Secret and important warning for great advantage of farmers

In order to have good sowing row and even better harvest farmers should observe that when they sow the Moon should be in the Sign of Taurus, Cancer, Virgo, Libra or Capricorn, and they will find a great and rare difference in the fields and harvest.

Secret and curious and advantageous warning for students

All fathers who have their sons studying the letters should note this warning; and this is that when you start sending them to school, so as they may learn to read, write, count, study mathematics or any other discipline, seek with those who know these things if the Moon is in an amicable aspect with the Planet Mercury; for they will learn what they study with less labor and more perfection. And if the Moon and Mercury, on this occasion, are in the sign of Gemini or Virgo, so much the better for the student.

Secret to make fire without a flint stone or a lighter

Take a dry laurel stick and another from a mulberry tree or vine, which is even better, and by rubbing these together energetically they will grow so hot that you will be able to make a fire with a little gun powder or wick. This secret was used by spies in the time of Caesar so as not to be seen or heard by their enemies.

Another rare secret in order to light a fire with water

Take an *arratel* of fresh quicklime and very well refined saltpeter, *tutia* stone, sulfur, one ounce of each; all of this ground in a mortar and pestle and sieved should be put in a new linen cloth and tied shut. Place this inside a new clay pan, very well closed and covered with clay; place this inside a lime furnace and after it cools down you may break the pan and you will find this mix made into a stone. When you make this stone wet it will start burning.

Secret to light a fire with the Sun's rays

Take a piece of crystal or glass, crystalline and concave and put it under the Sun's rays and place at the point where the rays join a piece of wool cloth or a wick, and this will immediately light itself. Another: take a mirror and anoint one side of it with sulfur oil and place the other side under the Sun's rays. Place a wick under the ray which comes out of this and it will immediately burn.

Secret to cool wine with a hot thing

Take a piece of crystal and place this in some embers or ashes that are not ablaze. When this crystal is very hot place it in some wine that it will become cool. This is proven.

Secret to make strong vinegar

Take a bottle of wine and put this to boil inside a pan with water, and as soon as it is boiled cast inside it some heated pieces of new tiles and soon it will turn into very strong vinegar.

Very proven secret to turn a clouded wine into a clear one

Alonso Herrera writes in his *Agricultura* that into wine which is clouded and losing its color, as many times happens, one should mix two egg whites to three *almudes* of wine, and the whites should be very well beaten with clean sand or salt, which is even better, and then cast inside the wine and thoroughly mixed. In four days the wine will be clear and with a good color.

Most excellent secret to conserve wine

Take some dry orange peels, from oranges picked in the month of May, and grind them into a powder and cast them into the vase of wine and it will not go sour. Do note and be adverted of another virtue and property of these same powders, which is that should the wine start to go sour, by casting these powders in it, not only does it stop this process but it will also make it very temperate and it will return to its original state. For thirty *almudes* of wine one should use six ounces of orange powders to conserve and season it.

Rare secret so as sour wine returns to its first and good state

For that wine which has become completely sour Herrera also says in his *Agricultura* that one should roast an *oitava* of walnuts in the oven, and while these are still very hot, cast them into the wine vase, covering this immediately with a cork of barkless willow, in such a way as there will not be any evaporation. This secret will cause great admiration should it be true, for it will make death turn into life and this seems impossible, especially after its heat and spirit force has been lost, that which the medics call quintessence. But this is so easy to experiment and at so little cost, that whoever is curious may make this test and certify it.

Important secret so as not to get sea sick or throw up

When someone wants to embark he should place a small conger over the heart, in contact with the skin and he should remain seated on the ship and he doesn't need to fear seasickness or vomiting, this has been proven.

Very curious and natural secret for farmers

In order to know from one year to the next which grain or seed will have the greatest abundance, an Andalucían Astronomer says (according to the most wise Zamorano in his

Cronologia) that one should sow in a tract of good humid land four or five grains of each seed, such as wheat, barley, corn, rye, fava beans and chickpeas, one month before the Canicular days, and should it be necessary water these seeds; the ones which will fare the best on the first day of the Caniculars, which is on the 24th of July, will be the ones with the most abundance in the next year. And those seeds which are seen to be the most debilitated and weak, of those there should be a shortage in the next year.

Secret so as fruit is grown without pits

When the trees are in bloom make a hole in the branch of the tree, in such a way as it goes from one side to the other of the branch, and you will see that the fruits from that branch will be born without pits. So says Giovanni Battista della Porta.

Secret to make a wick that is never spent

Take that kind of alum which dissolves into threads and gather a number of these, enough to make a wick and twist them together, placing it in a lamp. And this will never grow smaller. Perez de Moya.[209]

Secret so as to make everything which is inside a pan jump out

Fill a hazelnut with mercury and cover the hole very well with a little stick and cast this same hazelnut into a lidless pan. When this starts to boil everything inside that pan will jump out, given that these are small things.

Secret to make coal which will last for a month and a year

Take some vine coal, grind this into powder and knead it with very strong refined *aguardente* and cover this with vine ash and it will conserve itself for over a month. And should you have some excess coal, and you make the above diligence, and after this has been lit, cover it with juniper ash and it will be lit for a whole year, so say it Bartholomew of England[210] and Vincencio[211] in the gloss of the Psalm *ad Dominum cum tribulare*.

Secret so as to see in the night without any fire light

Take a great deal of fireflies, which are a kind of worm that shines in the night, and keep them for a period of fifteen days; after this place them in a glass alembic and distill them in a soft fire and they will produce a water that if placed in a small clear glass dome will give out such illumination that you may read and write in this light.

Secret to write letters that cannot be seen except over a fire

Take some powdered sal ammoniac, dissolve this in water and write with this liquid, and this will not be visible unless it is placed near a flame or candle light. The same effect is done by lime juice.

---

209. Translator's note: this name is simply dropped here without any kind of reference to why, but it is likely that this secret was taken from this author. Anyway, this refers to Juan Pérez de Moya, a XVIth century Spanish mathematician and mythographer.

210. Translator's note: Bartholomeus Anglicus, a XIIIth century Franciscan author, writer of the book *De proprietatibus rerum*.

211. Translator's note: uncertain reference.

Secret to write letters that cannot be read unless in water

Take a pink alum stone and grind this into powder and melt it in water; anything written with this liquid cannot be read unless the paper is placed in water, and this is proven.

Secret to remove olive oil stains from paper or scroll

Take the bones from a lamb's foot, have them burn in an oven, grind them into powder and sieve them; by placing these powders over an olive oil stain, and applying some good weight on them for three days, the olive oil will be gone.

Secret to remove an ink blot from paper or scroll

Place over the ink blot the juice from a white onion and shortly after subtly rub the blot with a wool cloth and it will be removed, this if the ink hasn't passed to the other side of the paper or scroll.

Secret of the lard and vinegar

Should one want to sculpt some figure or letters into any stone, one should heat some lard and with this write or paint whatever it is one wishes onto a stone, and by placing this into a vase where it will be covered in vinegar it will corrode and dig into the stone everything which is not covered with lard, and thus will the letters be sculpted in the stone.

Secret and subtlety of hand

Should you want to cut an apple in two or four pieces, leaving the peel untouched, take a thin sewing needle with a white silk thread and insert this between the peel and the flesh of it (starting near the stalk or the other end), and anywhere the needle comes out once again insert it in the same hole until you go around the whole apple and return to the first point. Now pull the two silk threads and the apple will be cut in two as if by a knife, and the peel will be left in one piece. Should you want this to be cut in four parts once again repeat this as was said but in a different direction.

Secret of the three pieces of paper

Take three small pieces of paper of equal width and different lengths and put all three together in such a way as these will be equal on one end and roll them up. Now unroll them again and you will see that the piece in the middle will have passed to the top, and that the one at the top will have passed to the middle; this is a thing worthy of being noted, that this effect is not only due to them being rolled up but also unrolled. And one should be warned that sometimes this will happen and other times not, and this is due to the position of the pieces of paper and the way in which you arrange them.

Natural secret in order to know if a woman is pregnant with a boy or a girl

Note which foot a pregnant women uses to take the first step out of the house, or the first one she uses to go up some stars, for if she first lifts her right foot it is certain that she is carrying a girl and if she lift the left then she is carrying a boy. The cause of this, according to good philosophy, is that a boy is generated on the right side, and his weight is more to that side than to the left, and thus one will raise the left foot more easily to help with the carrying of this weight, and by this reason we can say that it is a boy; and a girl is generated on the left side, and its weight is then more to that side than the right, and so it is natural that this foot is the first to be lifted.

Principle secret to dry the milk from a woman's breast

Note this secret to dry a woman's breasts of milk, no matter how full and hard she has them. Take some elderberry leaves and place them, flattened and clean over the breasts and these will immediately start to decrease and dry, and this has been proven plenty of times. Another very important secret for the same effect is that one should take a herb called annual mercury and place this on a small plate over a fire with a little bit of rose oil, and when this is hot place it over the breasts, covering them with some cloth, and after three days one will not feel any milk or any sort of pain; and this has also been proven and experienced many times, but do not ignore this first method, which is easy and certain.

Secret for hemorrhoids

For those who are molested by hemorrhoids, they should take a herb which is called cinquefoil and which is born near streams and field ditches, and you should carry it in contact with your chest, in such a way as it does not fall, and you will find that as this herb dries so will the hemorrhoids dry and heal. But these will however dry much better with ox penis[212] powder.

Secret in order to know beforehand if there will be an abundance of wine

Mizaldus writes that if the hoopoes sing before the grape vines are in blossom it is most certain that there will an abundance of wine that year.

Secret in order to make very strong vinegar

Cast into the vinegar vase some pieces of barley bread and it will be made very strong, according to Mizaldus. The same will happen if you cast some bile or lamprey oil in it, or half a dozen of date pits, or more, according to the quantity of vinegar.

Secret to make wine into vinegar

Battista della Porta says that you should take some salt and pepper, and grind everything, adding a little bit of very sour yeast, and all of this mixed should be cast into the wine, and it will turn to vinegar. Vinegar can be made faster than this if you cast into it a new tile heated into an ember, five or six times, and this is proven.

Secret so as calves will follow a man

Aristotle says, *libro de animalibus*, that should anyone put some small pieces of yellow wax on the horn of a calf, it will follow whoever does this.

Secret to make beasts return to their owners' houses

Saint Albertus Magnus writes that one should anoint the forehead of the beast with red squill juice and one should not fear for they will not get lost or stolen.

Secret so as to make a beast unable to eat

Before they eat rub their tongue with lard, and these will not be able to eat anything unless their tongues are very well cleaned with salt and vinegar.

---

212. Translator's note: In some editions this ingredient is substituted for *yerba del buey*, *Cissus trifoliata*.

Secret so as any horse or any other cattle cannot pass through a street

Saint Albertus Magus writes that one should make a tiny rope out of the intestine of a wolf and place this across the street, covered with sand or dust, and you shall see that no horse or cattle will pass through this, even if they are severely beaten; and it is said that Saint Thomas Aquinas, disciple of Saint Albertus Magnus tried this experiment.

Secret for the rest of traveling beasts

Pliny writes that one should take the larger teeth of a wolf and that these should be tied to the neck of the horse, and it will not be harmed or get tired along their travels.

Secret so as a donkey will not heehaw and a horse not neigh

Simonete[213] writes that one should tie a somewhat large and heavy stone to the donkey's tail and it will not heehaw while it is there; and should you tie a rock with some holes to the head of a horse it will not neigh.

Secret so as a ram will lose its natural inclination to charge

Constantino[214] writes that one should make a hole in both of the ram's horns, close to the ears, and it will lose its tendency to bump its head.

Secret of the pregnant sheep

Dimidio[215] writes that in order to know the color of the lamb which a sheep is carrying in its womb, one should look at the tongue of this same sheep, and if it is black then so will be the color of the lamb, and should it be white then the lamb will be white, and should she have a spotted tongue then so will be the lamb.

Secret so as a wolf will not make pray of any sheep

Anatolius[216] writes that one should tie a red squill around the head of the sheep leader, and no wolf will harm any sheep from that flock

Secret so as no kid goats will run away

Florentinus and Zoroastes[217] write that if you cut the beard off a goat it will not run away.

Secrets and properties of the wolf

The Natural Philosophers write that the wolf has a natural property which is that if it discovers and sees a man before that man sees it, his voice will turn so hoarse that he will not be able to shout in order to make the wolf run away.

---

213. Translator's note: uncertain reference.
214. Translator's note: uncertain reference.
215. Translator's note: uncertain reference.
216. Translator's note: uncertain reference, but it's most likely to be Vindonius Anatolius, a IVth century Greek writer of a book on agriculture.
217. Translator's note: uncertain reference.

Secret so as wolves will not be able to reach any cattle herd

Rhazes writes in the Almansor that if one hangs a wolf's tail in the pen or cattle corral, other wolves will not get to it.

Secret to make ants flee

Agrippa says that you should put a hoopoe heart in the place where ants are, and they will quickly flee from that place.

Another secret, writes Diafanes,[218] is that if you take a few ants and burn them, casting them afterwards in the ant hill, they will very quickly run from that location.

Secret so as frogs will not croak

Mizaldus writes that to stop the most harmful croaking of frogs, one should put over the water or lake where they sing some small bowls with one or two small candles, and you will be free from this bother.

Secret to catch lots of eels

Cast into the lake or still water the herb called sumac, or just its juice, and many eels will rush to this place in such a way as these may be caught with bare hands.

Secret to catch fish with one's hands

Take some fish feed and a ground salted cheese and mix all of this with wheat flour until it turns into a hard paste. Then make some tiny pellets with this and cast them where you see that there are fish and these will immediately come to this scent, and as they eat they will start coming to the surface sick, and one may catch them with one's own hands.

Another secret to catch fish in abundance

Mathias Bion[219] writes that in order to catch plenty of fish it is convenient to fish on the 6th day of the Moon and on the 29th, given that the day is not cloudy or windy.

Secret to catch birds with your hands

Saint Albertus Magnus writes that one may take any grain and mix it with wine dregs and juice from a herb called cicuta, which is very well known in pharmacies, and place this somewhere where birds may reach it and they will begin to fall drunk with no way of waking up, and one may pick them up with their own hands.

Another secret to catch birds

Alexios[220] writes that one should take the bile of an old ox and mix it with white henbane juice and let this boil for a while with some corn or any other grain. Then cast this wherever one may finds birds or pigeons and all those that eat will fall to the ground, in such a way as you can just pick them up with your hands.

---

218. Translator's note: uncertain reference.
219. Translator's note: uncertain reference.
220. Translator's note: uncertain reference.

Secret so as to know the gender of the eggs a chicken is roosting

Aristotle says, and Avicenna confirms, that if roosting chickens have with them very round and small eggs these will be female; and if these are long and sharp at the end, they are all males.

Secret to conserve and increase pigeons

Dimidio writes that if one feeds cumin seeds to pigeons and anoints them with some sweet smelling unguent, when they leave the pigeon house they will bring with them other outside pigeons, and these will join them in your house. And do note that the cumin seeds are to conserve and the unguent to attract. This same author mentions another secret, which is that if you wish for your pigeons and those of other people to not delay or stop while entering your pigeon house, that you should fumigate this with incense and sage.

Secret so as to remove stains from dresses and also from scrolls and leather

Take some wild chard and boil its roots in some water, and with this water wash the stains that they will disappear.

Secret to polish and clean gold and silver from embroideries or tissues

Take a small mirror and calcinate this until its powders are impalpable, and after this take a sponge or some other cloth with these same powders and rub the material with it; afterwards remove this powder with a small brush and it will be as new.

For gold pieces take some curcuma root made into a powder and proceed as explained above, taking a sponge with these powders.

Secret in order to polish and clean silver without this being consumed

Take some burnt straw and mix this ash with water until it has the consistency of honey. Rub your plates or other pieces with this and dry them well.

Secret to remove oil stains from paper

Take some live lime as a fine powder and place these powders between the sheets and it will remove the oil. The same can be done with burnt sheep bones.

Secret to know if a woman is a virgin or not

Alexios writes that one should melt a little bit of sal ammoniac with well water, and you give this drink to a woman and if it immediately gives her a great urge to urinate, then she is not a virgin.

Another secret to know is a person is a virgin or not

Measure the neck or throat with a folded line and take the two ends of this line and tie them. Then try to pass with the person's head through this circle and if you can do this then this person is not a virgin. And if it does not fit through the circle then it is a sign that she is still a virgin.

The cause of this is that when a person loses her virginity her neck becomes thicker, and thus may one know when someone has lost the most priceless treasure of chastity, as soon as their voice becomes deeper due to their neck dilation.

Very curious secret in case a person falls into the sea so as she does not sink to the bottom, even if she does not know how to swim

Take a leather strap, as thick as three fingers made from tanned leather, long enough to go around the body, either over or under the shirt. Then take another strap, as thick as four fingers, made of the same leather, and sew the two straps very tightly with a strong string; then grease everything very well with lard, and you should be warned that one end of the straps should be left unsewn, through which you will blow into to fill it with air, and when this is filled you should sew this end of the straps very strongly, just as before. Tie this around you whenever going into the sea and you needn't fear any kind of danger from water or from drowning, even if you do not know how to swim and even if you weigh twenty *arrobas*; and with this strap it is very easy to learn how to swim.

Secret to cut glass

Take a piece of steel and shape one end of it to a very sharp tip, and place this in the fire until it is very hot and incandescent, then touch the glass very lightly with it, while casting some cold water drops in the path you mark with the steel and you will cut the glass. And if you use this to cut a cup you may use it to drink, and this has been proven.

Secret to melt glass

Take the blood of a kid goat and the juice from a herb which in Latin is called senecio, and in common tongue groundsel, and place the glass to boil with these two ingredients and it will become as soft as wax.

Very curious secret so as fire does not burn

Saint Albertus Magnus writes that one should take ruby of arsenic and alum stone in equal part, and all of this very well ground and mixed with knotgrass juice, and anoint your hands with this mixture and you may take any fire on them that they will not burn; and in the same way one may wash his hands with boiling olive oil or water that if you have your hands anointed with this compound you will not be burn.

Another secret so as fire does not boil, burn or do any harm

Saint Albertus Magnus writes that one should take some ictiocola, which is known in the pharmacies, and mix it with pure vinegar, wetting a cloth with this mixture and with this anoint your hands and face. And you can drop boiling water or olive oil on them that they will not burn.

Another secret so as fire does not burn

Pallopio[221] writes that one should take altheae powder, mix it with egg whites and anoint one's hands or feet or any other part of the body with this mixture, and this will never be burned.

Secret of a certain fire that the more water you add to it the more it lights up

Saint Albertus Magnus writes that if one takes living sulfur, which is the natural one without any fire, barrel sludge and a gum which can be found in pharmacies and is called *lançarote*,[222]

---

221. Translator's note: uncertain reference, although it might refer to either Palladius or the anatomist Gabriele Falloppio.
222. Translator's note: uncertain translation.

picola,²²³ boiled salt, petroleum, common olive oil and all of this mixed and placed to boil for a while, if you cast this onto a cloth and light it, if you try to put it out with water it will light itself even more; and this may only be put out with vinegar.

Curious secret for laughter and practical joke

Saint Albertus Magnus writes that if one takes the blood of a turtle and wets a piece of cotton cloth with this and makes a lamp wick. When one lights this lamp, and it is lit for a while, you will hear what you have never heard. And note that this Author did not specify if this should be a male or female turtle.

Secret to have a lamp burning under water

Saint Albertus Magnus writes that one should take some wax, sulfur and vinegar in equal parts, and place this to boil until the vinegar is all gone; and after this mixture is congealed use it to make a candle, this will be able to burn under water.

Secret so as a person will not be able to sleep in bed

Saint Albertus Magnus writes that one should put over the bed a swallow's eye, and he says that whoever lies on that bed will not be able to sleep while that eye is there, but I have not made an experiment of this.

Secret so as a ring will jump without anyone touching it

Take a copper or silver ring, and in the space meant for a precious stone, place some drops of mercury and cover this with a silver sheet so as it may not escape. After this cast the ring inside a pan with boiling water, in such a way that the mercury will begin to heat up and the ring will start jumping, to the admiration of those who do not know of this secret. Instead of a ring one may use a silver or copper hazelnut, or even just a natural hazelnut, very well covered with foil, tar or plaster.

Secret so as women, especially the pregnant ones, cannot eat that which is placed in front of them

Florentinus writes that one should put a little bit of *alfavaca*,²²⁴ still attached to the root, under their plate without them knowing it, and he says that they will be unable to eat anything that is on that plate.

Secret so as a pan will not boil, no matter how much fire it has

Mizaldus writes that one should put over the pan, in the place of the lid, a turtle shell, and he says that any water or olive oil in it will never boil.

Secret so as wasps won't sting, even if one is walking among them

Mizaldus writes that one should take some marshmallow and anoint one's hands and face with the juice from this plant mixed with olive oil and they will not harm you.
And if you carry this same herb with you, should it be fresh and still have its root, bees will not sting. And in the case that a bee or wasp does sting you, then, this same author says that you should anoint that region with common olive oil and it will not swell. This is proven.

---

223. Translator's note: uncertain translation.
224. Translator's note: plants of the *Ocimum* genus.

Secret so as to have a bowl placed on top of some embers and have it not break

A certain Author says that for one to place a bowl of water or any other liqueur over some embers and have it not break he should put a green twig inside it. But I have proven that even without placing a stick inside this it will boil but not break.

Secret to break a bowl easily just by blowing on it

You should eat one or two garlic cloves and then blow on a glass bowl and it will break, which will never happen if you haven't eaten the said garlic; and it is not enough to chew them, but also to swallow them, and one should keep the breath on the glass from some time, so as to make it hot.

Secret so as no one will be able to put out a candle until it is completely spent

Take some red and yellow wax and knead it with a little of virgin sulfur, as well as some mineral salt and camphor, and make a candle out of this. And you should also be warned that the wick should also be made wet with the same sulfur and camphor, very well ground; and all of this incorporated you may light the candle and no matter how much you want to put it out by blowing on it or even with water it will not be extinguished until it burns down, and this is said by Gaudencio.[225]

Secret so as you may read letters at night in the dark and not in any other way

Take some crystal powder and some made from the tails of those worms that glow in the night, which are called fireflies, and mix these with some egg whites and write with this on a very white paper. Once this dries these letters will not be able to be read except at night and in the dark.

Secret to remove a tooth, or all of them, and the patient will not feel a thing, and this is proven

Take a living lizard and place it in a very well covered new pan, so as it may not escape, and place it to dry in an oven; and when it is well roasted make a powder of it and rub this powder on the gums of the jaw, or tooth, which is in pain, be it rotten or not; and this will soften the flesh in such a way that with one's hand, one may remove all the teeth with very little effort.

Marvelous secret to increase memory and conserve health

Experience writes that one should take half a *tostão*[226] of olive oil, pumpkin root, *mirabolanos*,[227] any kind of scammony, laurel berries and dry roses, half a drachma of each, saffron, one scrupulum, of myrrh one and a half scrupulum, and all of this very well ground and mixed. Make some pills from this mix of such a size as they can be eaten with lettuce juice and, every three days, in the morning, take five of these, not eating anything else until midday. And you should be warned to eat good substances for these will make you evacuate, cleaning your whole body of bad humors; and you will get three advantages from this: that you will increase your memory, have a good retention and conserve your heath, for it cleans the body from bad humors.

---

225. Translator's note: uncertain reference.
226. Translator's note: this probably refers to a unit of measure of wither volume or weight which I am not familiar with.
227. Translator's note: fruits from the *Prunus mirabolanus* I believe.

*Admirable secret to repress the runs and make them fully stop,
no matter how continuous they may be*

In order to make the runs stop one should note this very smooth and wonderful recipe which has been experimented by many, me among them; and in truth I claim its efficiency, in such a way that it should be written in golden letters. The recipe is that one should boil four ounces of roses for fifteen minutes and afterwards strain this water and cast in half an ounce of horehound[228] syrup, one ounce of rose syrup, another of quince syrup, and all of these can be found in the pharmacy. Mix all of this and take it hot every hour, as long as two or three hours have passed since you last ate, and you will see a very rare effect; and this shall be done for three days, three times a day and I claim that even taking it a single time will cure you. And should you want to comfort your stomach you should anoint the belly with *almecega* oil.

Secret to cure hiccups quickly

Two secrets to cure hiccups; one is particular to those who do not know of it and the other is general for anyone. The first is to give a sudden scare or surprise the person with some good or bad news, and in the same instant he will no longer have the hiccups. Another better and safe secret is that they should take, or someone else should make this person take, a mouthful of water and gargle for the amount of time they can hold their breath, and once this is done they will be free from hiccups, and both of these secrets are proven.

Natural secret which seems more like a miracle than nature

In a handbook I have found this secret, which I did not have the chance to verify. The secret is that in Summer time, when the swallows are raising their young, one should observe when one of these has already laid all of their eggs; and with all vigilance they should take them, in such a way as this is not seen by their parents and place them in a pan of boiling water, and these should be boiled in a short time, having lost their original color; in this same instant remove these eggs and return them to the nest where they were before, and as the swallows will not have any knowledge of what has happened they will continue to roost them, and upon seeing that they do not develop in the normal time, thinking that this is due to their own fault, they will immediately seek a herb, which they know due to their natural instinct, and place it over the eggs. This herb has the virtue and efficiency to regenerate the eggs, and in a few days they will return to their original condition and these will generate baby swallows. This is surely a thing worthy of being noted, should it be true. And this author says that this herb has many virtues and he left them printed. And I do not doubt that it has them and that they will be surely great.

END OF THE SECRETS OF NATURE

---

228. Translator's note: *Marrubium vulgare*.

FIFTH AND FINAL
TREATISE

OF THE ELEMENTAL AND CELESTIAL REGION, IN WHICH ONE DESCRIBES THE NATURE OF THE FOUR ELEMENTS AND HEAVENLY BODIES AND THE MANY AND VARIOUS EFFECTS WHICH THEY CAUSE.

THIS MATTER IS DIVIDED IN TWO PARTS, THE FIRST CONTAINING FOUR TREATISES REGARDING THE FOUR ELEMENTS

First part of this Treatise

CHAPTER I

Of the elemental region

By elemental region we comprehend everything which is contained from the orb of the Moon to the center of the Earth. And it is called elemental for it is composed of the four elements or simple bodies, which are fire, air, water and earth, which, as instruments and universal principles of all mixed and composed bodies, the Divine Majesty gave them those first four qualities, so contrary among themselves as heat, cold, dryness and humidity as the work of corruption and conservation of all elemental things. One should note that of these so diverse four qualities each element has two: one as agent, by which it works, and another as patient, from which it suffers; thus fire has heat, by which it works and resists, and dryness from which it suffers; and air resists and works with humidity and it suffers from heat; coldness is the work of water and humidity its suffering; and earth works with dryness and suffers from coldness. From this diversity of qualities a continuous war and a perpetual conflict between the four elements is in place, as each will naturally try to conserve its species and remain in the being which God gave them without stepping out one single point from the natural disposition that is made between them. In the same way as in a chapel of many voices a very perfect and pleasant consonance is formed, so too is nature, as the most skilled chapel master of all these diversities and opposing natures of the elements, which make a perfect conformity, with a rare and admirable correspondence among itself, making a diverse union and natural connection with these four elements, together with their qualities, composing the sphere and elemental region in a certain, rightful and wonderful proportion.

CHAPTER II

In which one says what is an element and why there aren't more than four

An Element is a simple body without any mixture from another body, and it is in such a way simple that its parts do not have any diversity, nor are they composed of anything else, contrarily to the elemental bodies. The elements are not, nor can they ever be, more than four, as is proven by Aristotle by citing that the four qualities (which are heat, cold, humidity and dryness) can be combined in six ways, and from these combinations two are incompatible and cannot be naturally put together by being completely opposing qualities; and these are heat and cold, dryness and humidity. From what was said the compatible combinations which may be mixed are the following.

Elemental combinations:

Heat and Dryness
Heat and Humidity
Cold and Dryness
Cold and Humidity

And so the compatible combinations and mixtures cannot be more than four and these are naturally found in the Elements. Thus it is proven and concluded that there cannot be more than four Elements

Some might say that the Elements are divided between the mixed and composed, such as the atoms, which may be discovered by the Sun's rays when these enter through a hole in any dark region, and these can also be found in a example of greatly flawed reason, which is that if one burns a green branch, from its extremities one can see some evacuation of humidity, which is similar to the Element of water, and also smoke, which represents fire, and also humid vapors which are of the nature of air. And finally these consider ash to be of the nature of earth, and from this they gather and mean to prove that the elements are made into very small particles in all things, in the same way as we have mentioned of the atoms of the Sun. This has been proven false and against all natural reason and good Philosophy (in one word) for the Elements are not formally mixed and composed, but only virtually according to their own properties.

Chapter III

Of the place and position of the elements and of some particular things about them

The proper and natural location and position of the Elements is one on top of the other, surrounding each other. And the cause of this is because all of them have an intrinsic principle of motion, by which each of them goes straight to its proper location. Thus, earth is the densest and heaviest of them, and naturally it occupies the lowest and infinitesimal place of the Universe and the farthest away from Heaven, as will be explained in particular below.

Water, as it is less dense, has the second place, which is above the earth, and by being flexible it runs through the surface, entrails and the depths of the earth. The air, being lighter, has the third place, surrounding all of the water and earth. Finally fire, being purest and lighter than all the others, has its location in the fourth and highest place of the Universe. These locations and position of the four Elements was ordered thus so as fire, with its great heat, would repress the humidity of the air, and the hot quality of the air would mitigate the cold nature of the water, and the humidity of the water temperate the overwhelming dryness of the earth, and in this way this last one could fructify and provide us, according to its time, with our necessities. One should be further adverted that the elements, by being in their proper locations, to not have any weight, and outside of it they do; as can be seen by putting a man under water, and even if carrying eighty loads of water, these will not weigh on him, but should these be taken out of their element then no man will be able to carry them; the same can be noted with air, for one can see that a bag filled with air has the same weight as one which is empty, and the cause of this is because this is in its proper and natural location, and taking this same bag filled with air and placing it under water will reveal its weight, strength and resistance as soon as it leaves its natural location, and this is true of all the other elements.

TREATISE

Of the first element

Chapter IV

Of the nature and place of the earth

Earth is naturally cold and dry, and, as is shown by experience, is dense and very heavy, and by this cause it has its natural seat in the middle of the Universe, as the place equally distant from Heaven by all sides. Some imagine and believe, and still many do profess, that the earth is miraculously sustained in the air, this without considering the many inconveniences which are to follow and which are against all good reason and natural philosophy. For if the earth was miraculously sustained in the air, should this miracle ever cease it would fall to some part, given its immense weight. Falling to a lower region we have seen that it is impossible, and so it would rather go up than go down, and this is against the nature of anything heavy. For it would fall to some side, which must be false, for one would have to conclude that the earth would be the highest points and the Heaven that surrounds it the lowest point. That the Heaven surrounds the earth cannot be denied, for the Sun, the Moon and the Stars say and manifest it every day by rotating around it, and in order to fall into Heaven this would need to be lower than the earth is. And from this we may come to another greater inconvenience, which is that the men and the animals which roam on that other side of the earth would have to be walking with their head down and their feet up, which is impossible, and thus it is proven that the earth is at the bottom and Heaven above, both on its top as on the opposite side of it. And if this is true, as is clearly proven, then one sees that there is no need for miracles to sustain the earth floating in the air, for it cannot naturally rise to any part of Heaven, nor to one side nor to the other; and a true miracle would be that it should move either way the length of half a finger, for this would truly be against its nature. But we will always say that all creation is a continuous miracle of God the Almighty.

Among the many and great foolishnesses that Muhammad wrote in his *al-Quran*, one of them was that the earth was sustained over the horns of an ox, which was on top of a fish, and when this fish moves then one has earthquakes. Surely the Moors his henchmen can brag that Muhammad was so wise and such a great philosopher that he understood and said such a great vanity and foolishness, for, should ever that ox scratch its tail with its horns, he would cast us and the whole world through infinity. It seems to me that it is good to write this bad note on Muhammad, so as his loyal followers may see how much of a barbarian and senseless and infamous and ill born he was, who caused such perdition of the bodies of those who have followed him in the past, present and will do so in the future.

Chapter V

In which is declared the shape and figure of the earth

The earth, together with the water, makes a whole spherical and round body; and even if there are ups and lows, mountains and vales, these are not enough to prevent the roundness of the earth, for when one compares this with the whole of its body, one sees that they are smaller than grains of sand. And as a round ball might have a few bumps, this isn't a reason to say that it is any less of a ball, and the same we say of the earth. The truth of the earth and water making a round body cannot be better seen in no other part than in the ocean, for as soon as a ship enters high sea one immediately loses sight of land and shortly after of all tall buildings and after that one also loses sight of the mountains, and the cause of this is nothing else than the fact that the earth and water have a round figure. The proof of this truth can also be seen in the fact that a sailor on top of a mast can see more land than one on the deck of the ship; being true that the higher one goes, the farther away from the earth he is, the fact that he can see more land cannot have any other cause than the roundness of these two Elements, the water and the earth. What has been said can be further proved more wisely and sensibly with a tangible and visible example, and this is the following: when the Sun rises it gives its light firstly to the Orientals and only after, little by little, does it become manifested to the Occidentals, and the cause of this is that the earth and the water are round, for should it be any other way, should the earth be flat (as Empedocles said) when the Sun rises in the Orient, all would see it, and this is not as experience proves it. This same thing is proven by Aristotle very wisely, in Book 2 of *De Cælo*, by saying that all shadows follow the form of the body, which causes them, and from this one may infer that the earth is round; for when the Moon appears to be eclipsed due to the shadow of the earth, this same shadow covering the body of the Moon is round; and from this one may say that the earth is round and not flat.

Chapter VI

Of the size and greatness of earth

It is so great the machine and body of the earth that only its roundness has six thousand four hundred and eighty leagues; and from its center to the surface, where it is said hell lies, one has one thousand and thirty leagues, more or less; from where one may gather that from one part to its opposite one has two thousand and one and a half leagues. And even if all of this is true (as we will prove), comparing the whole earth and water with the eighth and starry Heaven, it is much smaller than a grain of sand; for according to Alfraganus, the said Heaven is three hundred and seventy and six thousand times larger than the whole earth. And one should not marvel, for the same author says that the said starry Heaven has a circumference, by its concave side, of two hundred and thirty five million and two hundred and ninety three thousand leagues, as we will mention below.

The above mentioned measurements are known due to the divisions that the Astronomers have made of the Sky, by dividing it into three hundred and sixty degrees, or equal parts, corresponding to equal parts of the earth, which are however different from the ones in the Sky, for these are much larger than the ones down here. Thus each degree of the Sky corresponds to a part of the earth, which has been proven to have eighteen leagues by the use of the Astrolabe, as has the Astronomer Munhoz[229] from Valencia experimented many times, and whose opinion I wish to follow for being an exceedingly celebrated man. In this way, dividing the earth into three hundred and sixty equal parts, as was said, each part would have eighteen leagues, and the whole of the earth will have the above mentioned six thousand four hundred and eighty leagues.

Chapter VII

Of the general division of the inhabitable earth

The ancient Cosmographers divided the earth, which to them seemed inhabitable, into three principal parts, which are Asia, Africa and Europe; however, by the mercy of God another part, much greater and fertile than the other mentioned three parts, has been discovered, which is the new world of the West and East Indies, and whose discovery happened in the year of one thousand and four hundred and ninety two, by Don Christopher Columbus.

---

229. Translator's note: uncertain reference.

Europe is the smallest of the four parts, in which most of Christianity lives. It is a very temperate land and convenient for the inhabitation of the human kind, for in it abound all sorts of supplies, and it grows temperate men of great understanding and greater will and effort than any other generated in the four parts of the earth. Europe is counted, according to Ptolemy, in thirty four Provinces, which are: France, Hispania, Germania Greater and Lesser, Franconia, Sweden, Thuringia, Italy, Moravia and Pannonia Superior and Inferior, in which one has Austria, Hungary and Poland, Greater and Lesser. Following are great Thrace, Palodia, Lorraine, Pomerania, Russia, Vandalia, Obarnaria, Illyria, Liburnia, Dalmatia or Sclavonia, Greece and Samartia. After these one further has Crete, Negroponto, with many islands near it, such as Corsica, Sardinia, Majorca and similar others.

Following is the second part of Africa

Africa, according to Josephus,[230] Book 1, Antiquities, took its name from a grandson of Abraham called Affer, who passed through that region with his army and settled there, having given it his own name. This second part of the world, according to Pomponius Mela and Ptolemy, Book 1, Chapter 4, has twelve very large and most distinguished Provinces. The first towards the Setting Sun and in front of Gibraltar is Mauritania, where it is said is located one of the columns of Hercules and the mount of Abyla. After this is the much dilated Numidia, where is located, by our miseries and sins, the stepfather and bottomless pit of the Christians, Algiers, Morocco, Bugia, Tunis, Acmula and Carthage. After Numidia comes Massilia, Massomones, Asbiras and the land of the Carthaginians. Further in the direction of Egypt are Murmaridas, an indomitable peoples of Gentiles, Negretos, Phatusios and the Garamantes; and to the side of the Midday are the Ethiopia, Meroë and the Kingdom of Prester John, which is said to be from the Indies. This also contains many great islands as are the Canaries, Cape Verde, Madagascar and São Tomé. This land generates great and ferocious beasts, such as the Elephants, Dragons, Tigers, Lions and Basilisks and it is very abundant and fertile in supplies and Serpents.

Of Asia, third part of the world

Asia is much larger than Africa or Europe; it is a fertile and temperate land, which is divided into Asia Major and Minor (according to Ptolemy in his *Cosmographia*), and it contains thirty three Provinces and is situated (according to Saint Anselm) between the Indus and the Tigris river. Its Provinces are Persia, Assyria and Media, Mesopotamia and Chaldea, Babylon and the great Arabian Desert. It then follows with the whole land of Palestine, Phoenicia, Syria, Egypt, where was founded the famous city of Thebes, whose walls had one hundred gates, and to the Septentrion one has Sarmatia and the celebrated lands of the Amazons. To the Midday are the regions of Colchis, Iberia and Albania and to the West one has Scythia which reaches the Hyperborean mounts until the Hyrcanian sea with the infinite neighboring peoples of the Caucasus Mountains. To the Oriental part are Hyrcania, Armenia, Cappadocia, Bithynia, which is close to the foul Arabs, where one has Turkey. Asia Minor is situated between Cappadocia and Egypt. To the Meridional part are the Provinces of Phrygia, Galatia, Lydia, Mysia, Troas, Caria, Pontus, Lycia, Sicily and Pamphylia. In this part of Asia, Pliny writes, as well as other great authors, that there are a great different kinds of men, for there are those who are very wild, some who are born with two heads, other with a single foot, and which is so large that they take shelter under its shade, and others which are born with a single eye in the middle of their forehead. Finally there is a certain generation of men who are so small which, given this reason, are called Pigmies, and who are in war with the grackles, and these live for such little time that they do not grow over ten years old.

---

230. Translator's note: Titus Flavius Josephus, a first century Roman-Jewish scholar, writer of the *Antiquities of the Jews*.

Of the fourth part of the inhabitable earth

The Indies, the new world, called America, or fourth part of the inhabitable earth, is greater and richer in metals, especially in gold and silver, than the above mentioned other three parts, and its discovery had its start, by the kindness and clemency of the Creator, in the year of 1492. The man who gave principle to so admirable convenience, felicity and richness was the good fortunate and more than happy Don Christopher Columbus, by discovering to the side of the Setting Sun the great America, which is surrounded by most of its part by sea, as an island. The first to start to conquer and win the lands of the Indies and plant the Holy and pure Faith of Jesus Christ was Hernán Cortés, who left from Cuba in the year of 1518 with eleven ships and only five hundred Spaniards and arrived at the great Province and Kingdoms of Mexico, subjecting it with its great infinity of Indians to the rule and obedience of Emperor Charles, this in three and a half years. With the passing of time the discovery of the new world had increased, up until the Antarctic region by the Spaniards, who have shed plenty of blood, their own and that of others, in the rebellious and strong Conquest of Arauco, in the unbreakable Province of Chile, being the result of this most harsh campaign the well born and most fortunate Valdivia. And with these new examples of human diligence and Spanish covet, by cruising these seas, more and more Provinces were discovered, so great and so dilated as the Province of Paria, as Venezuela and Santa Marta, from Cartagena until the Cape of God, where one finds the Río de la Plata and Peru. Farther on there are the Provinces of Yucatan and Honduras, with the new Hispania, which is greater than the whole of France, Italy and our Hispania and Germany, for this is more than four hundred leagues in length. To the Midday of these Provinces one will find the ones of Guatemala and Nicaragua and to the West the Provinces of the Nueva Galicia and between the Septentrion and the East there are the great Florida and the land of Cod, with the greatly dilated Province of Lavrador. Finally one has so many islands and Provinces discovered in the new world that these would be endless and it would be a great bore to mention all of them. What I can say is that, excluding the lands in the two Arctic and Antarctic poles, all of it is discovered and crisscrossed by the tireless and most joyful investigators from Portugal and Spain.

Chapter VIII

Of the earthquakes and tremors of the earth and the fire mouths which can be found on it

Before we say anything of the earthquakes it is convenient that we offer a declaration of the three Regions that the most learned say make up the same earth. In the first region grow the fruits, trees and plants, that sustain man and the land animals. In this same region are the fountains born, the rivers flow, the mountains are raised and the mouths of fire appear, or as the common call them, the mouth of Hell; and according to good philosophy, this region is not deeper than six or seven *estados de homem*[231] under the earth. In the second region of the earth are the vapors and exhalations, made hot by the strength and virtue of the rays of the Sun, by the influence of the Stars and Planets; here are all metals generated, such as gold, silver, copper, iron, tin, brass, lead and mercury; here are also created the minerals, which can be ground, such as sulfur, alum, coppers and soda ash, etc.

The third region is not known to produce anything, for it is taken as certain that the virtue, strength and heat of the Sun's rays cannot reach there, and thus this third and last Region is the purest and simplest earth of the above two Regions. The tremors and earthquakes are caused in the second region, and they proceed from the many hot exhalations which are generated in the intimate concavities of the earth, which, as they are multiplied by the virtue and strength of the rays of the Sun, Planets and Stars, unable to find a place to rise, shake the earth with a strange violence so as they may escape, causing great tremors and great earthquakes in the same earth.

---

231. Translator's note: an old unit of measure I'm not familiar with.

These cause, and have caused, great damage in the world, bringing down mountains, ruining houses, destroying peoples and Cities, similar to gunpowder which, placed inside mines and caves can bring down buildings and break rock and cast away walls and fortresses; and these same things are caused by the lit exhalations of the earth's entrails, when these cannot find a way up to escape.

Of this truth we have plenty of testimonies and examples in our Europe, especially those of the City of Ferrara in Italy, which in our own days has been destroyed by a great earthquake which happened in that location. The new world suffers much more from these great labors than the other regions of the earth; the cause of this is due to its proximity to the sea and water, for rivers, lakes, bogs and the sea meld the crevices and openings which the earth usually has, and in this way the exhalations of the earth do not have an escape route. And these have caused a strange and horrible earthquake in the year of 1586 in the Indies, which according to Father José de Acosta, was felt in a hundred leagues in length and fifty of width and destroyed a City called of the King.[232] These same exhalations which are generated in the second region of the earth cause the mouths of fire, which may be found in several regions of the world, for when these encounter any mineral or sulfurous earth, these become lit and upon finding some kind of escape, that incandescent matter starts exiting through there, and occasionally these can be immensely big flames, other times these are horrifying and amazing fogs. These mouths of fire will last as long as there is combustible matter to consume; and some of these have been known to last five hundred years, others three hundred years and others fifty, depending on the matter or wood (if one can call it that) that they have to conserve this fire. The stones which are called pumice are born from the fire of these mouths which are near the sea. These become cold and spongious and they are very strong and apt for scrubbing, scraping, cleaning and soften harsh and hard things. The mountains (a few learned men write) are caused by the upward intention of the mentioned exhalations when these cannot find a concavity in the region where they are generated. Others claim that the mountains were discovered in the time of the Deluge, over the fact that the water would have eroded the earth in many and diverse parts of the world. I for one say that the reason for mountains wasn't one or the other, but rather that when the immense Majesty of the Creator formed the earth, it created the mountains for its beauty and service of men, who take so much utility and use from them, and they still do, both their neighbors as those living far from them. Moses writes in Genesis, Chapter 7, that in the time of the general Deluge, all the high and low mountains were covered by water. And he further says that the water was higher than the highest mountain by fifteen cubits, and that Noah's Ark stopped over the mountains of Armenia, from where one may gather that before the Deluge mountains already existed, and these were not discovered in the time of the Deluge as some wish to claim.

---

232. Translator's note: Lima, Peru.

TREATISE

OF THE SECOND ELEMENT

CHAPTER IX

Of the nature and place of water

Water (as was mentioned in the first treatise) is naturally cold and humid, and is heavier than air and not as much as the earth, and by this cause it has its proper place in the roundness and surface of the earth, as was written in Genesis, Chapter 1. From where one may gather clearly that the whole surface of the earth was surrounded by water, for it was necessary that God ordered it to recede and retire to a certain part so as the earth could appear and fructify and produce herbs, trees and plants for the sustenance of man and the maintenance of all animals, both flying and terrestrial. And knowing that the Eternal and Ruling God ordered that the water recede to one part, this does not mean that this is of a repugnant nature (as some might think), but as the creator arranged all things most appropriately, his Divine Providence ordered that in the roundness of the earth there would be many and great concavities where water, as fluid and heavy, could gather itself and where it would inhabit without receiving force or violence. The lowest place of the whole surface of the earth is the place of the sea; and for this reason all the water of the rivers and fountains, by being fluid, naturally run towards the sea, as the lowest place and their natural location; for as the earth is round so is the water, and it does not rest until it reaches its center and natural seat. It is also true that it was necessary that the supreme Artifice of all creatures place a term on the waters; *Ne transirent fines sous*; for by being water so naturally fluid and so easy to move and change from one part to the other, it would be possible for it to once again cover the earth and embrace the whole of it, as it was in the beginning of creation and once again in the time of the general Deluge. And this may once again happen, not only due to the terrible winds and torments which happen at sea, but also due to the great tumescence and rise through which the Moon may cause nefarious dilations of the waters and the deep seas, which would be impossible (by speaking naturally) to face and repress should the Majesty of God our Lord not have placed that mighty and eternal hold on them so as they would not once again pass the limits of the deeps and rivers. Water is a very efficient element and mightier than the others, for it surrounds the earth, taking hold of it, and it rises through the air with the virtue of the Sun, causing clouds, rain, dew, snow, hail and mists. Finally, with its natural strength it beats and puts out fire, which is such a strong, voracious and consuming element. Water is extremely important and principal mean and remedy of our corporeal and spiritual life, for God Our Lord ordered that not only it be used for our refreshments and conservation from natural heat, but he also wanted our regeneration and Baptism to be made through water, of which Moses writes in Genesis, Chapter 7, that it was also the means by which the world was cleansed and purified from the great sins which in the time of the Deluge were covering the earth, rising higher than the highest mountain by fifteen cubits and not leaving a single living thing in the whole universe except those which, by commandment of God, entered the Ark made by Noah. Finally, the earth without water becomes sterile, useless and without any production, in such a way as its whole would turn to dust and crack down to the abysses, and with the convenience of being watered it is conserved fresh, pleasant and apt for the production of all which is necessary for human life, of the multitude and infinity of fish, which are continuously created in it, and all for the service of man.

Chapter X

Of the sea, rivers and fountains

Sea means bitterness, and it is called this because it is so salty, however, speaking morally, it is called bitter over the great labors, heartbreaks and bitterness that men receive at every step of traveling through it; but all of this is beaten by the covet of the mortals, together with their natural inclination for sailing, due to all that the waters have to offer. The cause of being the sea salted, almost all of the philosophers say, Aristotle, Book 3, Chapter 3, is due to the virtue and strength of the Sun's rays, for by elevating the most subtle particles of water, the thicker and earthly ones remain behind, due to being heavier; but I say that such bitterness does not proceed from these sayings, but rather from the principle of supreme Providence, which created those waters salty and bitter so they could be more apt to conserve the infinity of fish which are created in it, and so as these waters do not admit inside themselves corruptions or any sort of rottenness, for they are thus very pleasant and healthy for fish, and even for sailing are these much better than the fresh ones, due to being thicker and helping in the flowing of ships, which can be proven by placing a fresh egg in fresh water, in which it immediately sinks, and placing it in salt water makes it float. The ocean is the end and beginning of the waters, for from it are the rivers and fountains born, and to it do these once again end up as is written in Ecclesiastes, Chapter 1, by saying that the rivers return to their beginning to once again flow. And even if it is true that every day and hour thousands and thousands of rivers enter the sea, this does not overflow nor does it grow any more than if they didn't; the reason for this is because the sea is the natural place and receptacle of all water and it also has its drains, the places from where all this received water disappears and enters other places. Rivers proceed and are caused from the congregation and joining of many fountains; and should this joining be of many or few fountains, so are the rivers greater or smaller. Fountains are caused as thus: as the water travels through the veins and concavities of the earth, every time these find a closed passage, not being able to turn back due to the great quantity of water which follows it, and not being able to also sink into the depths due to the thickness and density of the earth, it rises up out of necessity, and from this a fountain is born. However, a curious might ask me why the rivers and fountains aren't salted or bitter like the sea water, if it is true that it has its principle in the sea, as is written in the mentioned place of Ecclesiastes. To this I respond that as the winds receive the qualities of the regions through where they pass, losing the one which they had in the beginning of their movement and acquiring a very different one due to these accidents (as the Philosophers say) so it happens with the waters of the rivers and fountains, by passing different lands, little by little they lose that harshness and bitterness which they bring from the sea, acquiring a different softness and sweetness. It is also true that if fresh water passes through a salty or sulfury land, these will become salty and bitter as our experience shows of many wells and fountains in various regions of the world.

TREATISE

OF THE THIRD ELEMENT OF AIR

Chapter XI

Of the quality of air and the difference between air and wind and how this is caused

Wanting to prove that air exists, as some think that it doesn't over the fact that they don't see it, would be to want to prove that what we breath is such a clear and manifest thing; for even if we do not see it or perceive it with our sight over the fact that this element does not have a color, with our sense of touch do we perceive it, as well as with a thousand other ways do we certify and are convinced that it exists. And it is most convenient that the air does not have a color for many reasons, but mainly over that fact that it would block our singular sight of the Heaven and Stars and the circular motions of the Orbs with their Planets. The nature of air is hot and humid, given that it is much more humid than hot; and if sometimes we feel it cold this is but an accident, as the Philosophers say, and it is not natural, for the rising from the earth and water of so many exhalation of the same nature of water and cold earth, cools down the air, and by this reason do we feel it cool and even cold. Wind differs from air in that it is not an element, as the air, but it is as smoke and exhalations of an element; and it also differs from air, which is hot and humid, by being hot and dry, as can be seen by the fact that it dries much more than air. Wind isn't anything else than some hot and dry exhalation that the Sun extracts from the Earth with the virtue and strength of its rays (given that Seneca intends that wind is air moved and violently expelled). However the truth is that wind is generated from the said hot and dry exhalations, which, wanting to rise with their natural lightness and subtlety, are expelled by the coldness of the middle Region of air, which is its contrary; and not being able to rise any more, nor go down from where they came, for being too light, they breach from the part or parts around them, through the sides of the middle Region; and according to the aspects of the Planets and Stars, are thus moved and expelled around the earth through different lands and angles, from where the winds receive natures different from their own, and so do they cause diverse and various effects down here. If by any chance the said winds are expelled from the Meridional region, these are of a hot and humid nature, and they aren't very healthy, for the hot and humid produces the corruption of the humors. These winds usually cause many clouds, many lightnings and much rain. If the winds are expelled from the Septentrional region they receive a cold and dry quality; and even if these are very harmful to fruit, they are very good for the bodily health and rarely do these cause rain. If the said exhalation or winds are expelled from the Levante, these will have a cold and humid nature, even if very smooth, pure and subtle, and these conserve health and generate many clouds and cause augmentation to plants. Finally if these are expelled from the Occidental region, they will augment their own nature, for it is hot and dry, and these tend to temper the cold, cause catarrh, infirmities and sometimes rain and thunder; the same do I say of the collateral winds that each of these four winds has near them. Aristotle is right in saying that the winds are motioned air; but he however does not forget to mention that the origin of these are the hot and dry exhalation, which, by slowly congregating, are converted into wind.

Chapter XII

Of the divisions of the Region of air

The Philosophers divide the air into three parts or Regions, and these are the high, low and middle, whose qualities are very different from one another (even if these are so by mere accident). The highest Region of air is hot and dry, by accident, for it is close to the element and sphere of fire. In this Region are the Comets generated, as we will see below. The lowest Region of air is of the same nature of air, even if these qualities are received accidentally, and so it is hot over the reverberation of the Sun's rays and humid from the neighboring waters which are humid. In this Region are the mists, dews and frosts generated; and even if it is true that the lowest region is hot, when compared to the high Region it is most cold.

The middle Region of air is of a very cold nature; for it does not have any participation from the fire above and the reverberation of the Sun's rays on the earth cannot reach it. And as this cold of the middle region is fortified over being surrounded by the heat of the two high and low Regions, surrounding it by all sides, not giving it any room to extend and dilate, and because of this it is condensed, tightened and fortified, as can be understood in ourselves, as in Winter we have greater heat and strength in the stomach to digest what we eat than we do in Summer; for as the natural heat is surrounded and tightened by the external cold, it is more united and fortified. The same happens in the middle Region, and thus in Summer it is more compressed and tightened and as a consequence it is colder, over the great reverberation of the Sun's rays, which in Summer is greater than in Winter. From this one may understand the cause of the water in wells and fountains being colder in Summer and warmer in Winter; this is because in Winter the earth becomes very cold and as in Summer and Spring, when the Sun's rays fall more directly over the earth we inhabit, these are the cause for the cold to recede down to the veins of water, refreshing them and turning them from hot to cold. And on the contrary, when the Spring and Summer are gone, and the earth is made cold by Winter, this makes the great heat of the earth recede to the lower regions and heat up these same cold waters with the retraction of the heat, which the Sun left in the earth during the time of Summer. The cause of the coldness of Winter is the separation of the Sun (not from the earth, as this distance is constant) from our Zenith, or in a simpler way, from our head, for when the Sun is traveling in a more frontal position, over our heads, its rays fall more directly on the earth we inhabit, and in this way they cause a great reverberation and much heat, and on the contrary, when the Sun is not on our top, but rather somewhat separated from this, its rays do not fall so directly on our climate and Region, but these fall more to the sideways; and thus they do not cause so much reverberation on the earth and consequently this does not cause so much heat, and from this does Winter arise with its cold. And a more or less colder Winter is caused by the Sun separating itself more or less; and to this is added the various aspects which are formed among the Planets, Sun and Stars, and also from the differences of the winds which blow, and which are subjected to the mentioned aspects.

Chapter XIII

In which we deal in how the mists, dews, frosts, clouds, rain, snow and hails are made

The Sun and the Stars, with the strength of their rays, take and attract from the water and earth two different bodies and subtle smokes; one the Philosophers call vapors and the other exhalation. From the vapors, for being humid and cold in their nature, are the above mentioned natural things generated, which are the mists, dews, frosts, etc. Of which the first three are generated in the first Region of air, the other four in the second Region. Mist is made and caused by very subtle vapors, taken and lifted from the earth by a weak native heat, and as this cannot resist the cool air of the first Regions with which it first enters into contact, slowly these gather together and condense close to the earth as a kind of smoke, and this is mist. These mists do not usually happen during the day, but rather at night and in the morning, for as the Sun rises in the Orient, as they are so subtle they are immediately consumed and dissipated. Dew is caused and generated by the same vapors as mist, however, as these are very few and thin and more humid, these do not have enough heat to rise into the middle Region of air, so these stay in the first Region, not far from the earth, and as night falls with its coolness, these are condensed and made thicker and are converted into water and dew, which they call "of the morning". These dews are usually generated in temperate weathers, as Spring and Autumn, and not in Summer and even less in Winter, for excess heat consumes them and the excess cold condenses them into frost, and from what was said one will understand how frost is made.

Here are declared the things which are generated in the second Region

Clouds are caused by some very humid and hot vapors which rise from the earth, and being that the heat of these vapors is enough to allow them to rise to the middle Region of air, there they condense and are made thick with the strength of that cold air which naturally tightens them; these condensed and tightened vapors are the clouds, and once these are formed they are moved by the air and ventilated from one region to the other, until the strength of the Sun's rays, once the heat which caused them to rise is dissipated, starts to melt them from the bottom up, causing thus rain in the same way as it happens in an alembic, that with the heat and strength of fire is risen and raised as a vapor from the herbs or humid things placed inside, and as soon as they touch the cold metal cover are converted into water, and they once again go down through their open tap.

To rain frogs seems like a ridiculous and fabulous thing, as this was an impossible thing, but it is not. Not only does philosophy teach this but experience as well, for many people have seen them fall and I, in my early years, saw countless of them fall in the market and plaza of the See of Candia, and almost everyone in that town was greatly amazed; and I say almost for there were those men who were learned and wise and knew that raining frogs, which come from the middle region of air, is a possible and natural thing, and thus they were not only not surprised, but they didn't even make much of it, and this to all others was a wonder and a monstrosity. Snow is also made from the vapors when these rise thick and in quantity, be it in the first Region or the second, where they condense as snow, and if the Northeastern wind is blowing with its natural heat, it will melt, little by little the mentioned vapors or clouds and as these fall and surge through the frigid airs, so are they condensed and frozen, falling as very white flakes (for it is a property of cold to make things white) and this is snow. It is customary for snow to fall in very high and cold places, such as on mountains and very rarely in low and hot lands, planes and vales, this because even if the heat arising from the low lands is little it is enough to melt the snow as this is falling in its direction, converting it to very thin and subtle water, and thus it happens that as it rains in the vales, it snows in the mountains.

Hail isn't anything else than frozen rain drops. That as the water falls from the melted fogs, and it is spread into drops, and as air on these occasions is very cold, it tightens them in such a way as to convert them into hail.

Chapter XIV

Dealing with thunder, rays and lightning and from what these are generated, how and where

Thunder, rays and lightning are caused and generated by the exhalation, which the Sun and the Stars raise from the earth, and these, due to being hot and dry, naturally rise rapidly to the third Region of air, for being of this same nature (for as Aristotle says: *Omnes simile simile quærit*; and this mean that everything seeks its similar), however, as they encounter the second cold

Region, with some thick fogs formed by humid vapors, being unable to rise further, they are gathered inside the clouds, and thus united and tightened are made stronger, and become livelier with the heat they have, helping to this effect the coldness of the cloud and the Region, causing an even greater tightening and gathering of the exhalation, and in this way they light up and burst through the weakest part of the cloud. From this great rupture, which has such strength and violence, is thunder born, just as it happens when placing an extremely hot iron into very cold water, which produces a great blast. The same happens with chestnuts and acorns when placed whole inside a fire, bursting with a great blast for having their heat very tightened; and the same does experience show us with gunpowder in artillery pieces and muskets. These lit exhalations are then what we call lightning, causing such great light and splendor that they can disturb a man's sight, and these same lit exhalations, shot with such velocity from among the clouds is what we call rays, whose strength and subtlety is such that it breaks anything in its path. And in this way, should any ray hit a man, it will burn his eyes without causing any damage to his clothes, and if it hits a sword it breaks and melts it without harming the hilt. The same happens if it should hit any pouch, as it will destroy the money inside and not the pouch itself. And even if it is true that the thunder, lightning and ray are caused at the same exact time, one does not hear the thunder as soon as the lightning is seen; the cause of this is that sight is more optimal and quick to see than hearing to hear; and in this same way when someone hits something with a mace, and we are standing at a distance, we see the hit and only after that do we hear it, and yet the blow and the noise were done at the same time. Sometimes it happens that a stone falls at the same time as the ray, as Aristotle proves in Book 4, *Meteorologica*, saying the following: just as in the entrails of the earth are generated stones and metals by the mixture of humid vapors with the hot exhalations, in the same way are stones created by this same reason in the mentioned second Region of air, and by this reason does lightning sometimes carry a stone, even if more often it is just fire and no stone. Lightning, Pliny says, never pierces the earth more than five feet, by which reason he advises, should we want to take cover from lightning, that we should go into an underground place, or carry some laurel with us, or a seal fur pelt; but even if this is thus, I would advise one to carry with them an *Agnus Dei*, which has virtue not only against lightning, but against every kind of storm and against many other visible and invisible dangers, this because they are made by the Holy Pontiff which has power for this and much more. And thus it is appropriate to write here the virtues of the *Agnus Dei*; and the way in which the Holy Pontiff blesses them. And one should be warned that the Pope does not bless the *Agnus Dei* in each year, but only in the first year in which he is made Pontiff, and from that day on only every seven years.

Once these forms are made, greater or small, of white and very clear wax, the Pope's Sacristan and his Chaplain and Clerics take them and imprint on them the Lamb, express figure of Jesus Christ the sinless Lamb. After this is done they take them to the Pope's Chapel where, in his Pontifical dressings, he blesses an amount of water with many prayers and orisons; he then takes some balm and casts it onto the holy water in the form of a Cross, saying: Lord, see it as fitting to consecrate and bless this water with this ointment and by our blessing: In the name of the Father, the Son and the Holy Spirit. And similarly he takes the Oil and casts it over the water as a Cross, saying the same words. He then takes the *Agnus Dei*, tightly wrapped in a white towel, and he places them on the said holy and consecrated water and baptizes them, and from there do the other Prelates remove them with silver sieving spoons and place them in a proper place to dry. And once again the Pontiff says over the *Agnus* many prayers and orisons, pleading to the Lord that all the Faithful who, with purity and devotion, carry these may be given all that is good and may they be free from evil.

Virtues of the Agnus Dei

Firstly the *Agnus Dei* has the virtue of freeing those who carry it with devotion and confidence from all enemies, both visible and invisible.

It has also the virtue of keeping us and freeing us from many dangers, both spiritual and material, as the Holy Father asks in his prayers and orisons when the blesses the *Agnus Dei*, and by means of the said *Agnus* are many gifts, privileges and graces achieved, and even more, the remission of venial sins.

It also has the very effective virtue to raise and free a person from mortal sin, should she carry it with great devotion.

He who carries it will also be protected from storms, torments, lightning and thunder.

He will also be preserved from the plague, epilepsy and sudden death, as the High Pontiff asks God in one of the orisons he prays when he is consecrating it.

It also frees one from fire, ghosts, visions and frights, and also from the snares of the devil.

It also has the great virtue to free women who are in labor from all danger, giving them strength and confidence in that great distress.

One should also note a great excellence and virtue of the *Agnus Dei*, which is that if a woman is in labor, and is in danger of not being able to give birth, she should be given three small pieces of this to drink in some water and, with faith, she will give birth without any danger, as I have seen many times. And she should have the devotion of saying:

Agus Dei, meserere mei.
Qui passus es pro nobis, miserer nobis.

Chapter XV

Dealing with the Comets which are seen in the sky

A Comet isn't anything else besides an aggregate of inflamed exhalations, some of which are generated in the first Region of air and some of which are caused in the third. When these exhalations are few and thin they have no strength or heat to pass through the middle Region of air, staying in the first, where they are moved and ventilated from one part to the other by the air, still, with the heat and dryness they possess they will inflame, but due to their subtlety and little matter they soon burn out and disappear. These Comets are the stars that the vulgar say roam around at night. And even if they do seem to move, these Comets do no such thing, but rather that exhalation is inflamed from one end to the other, and a flame can be seen traveling along its length; this is the same as lighting fire to a line of gunpowder on the floor, should we be standing away it seems that the light is moving, thus these Comets, while their fire lasts, which is their consumption, seem as Stars that run from one part to the other.

Comets are generated in the third and highest Region of the air, and these are made from a thicker exhalation than this first one; and as they have enough heat to resist the coldness of the middle Region, they pass on to the third, which is extremely hot by being near the element of fire. These exhalations, arriving at this Region, are inflamed and light up, both due to the continuous movement of the air around the Universe, as also due to their heat being also increased because that region is very hot. These Comets thus inflamed usually last many days and months, depending on the matter of which they are formed and which is being consumed; these sometimes move from the Levante to the Ponente, following the motion of the air, which carries them along the Heavens, and other times they do not keep with this regular movement, for we have seen them a few times traveling from the Ponente to the Levante, and from the Septentrion to the Midday. From these movements of the Comets, so diverse and contrary to the natural movement of the Heavens, one can prove the lack of opinion of a few Philosophers and Astronomers, who claim the Comets are caused and generated in the ethereal region, being a condensation of celestial matter. Should this be so, the Comets would necessarily follow the movements of Heaven, however (as was said) they many times do not. Consequently the said Comets are not formed of Heavenly matter.

These Comets, which are generated in the supreme Region of air, according to Pliny and Ptolemy, always, or at least in most times, denote great evils and harm. The cause of this is because the said Comets are generated from hot and very dry exhalations, an evident sign that the earth from which they are rising is very inflamed and dry. And as the said exhalations stretch out along the air, they spread their terrible nature, and they infect, corrupt and dry, and anywhere they pass they alter the humors of the human body, causing infirmities, wraths, sicknesses, ill will, inciting also war and discord, which are the causes of many changes in Kingdoms and states. Those wishing to know the effects that each kind of Comet usually causes, according to the Sign in which they appear and Planet, should consult our Perpetual Lunario of the times, where this is expressed perfectly.

Chapter XVI

Dealing with the arch which is seen in the clouds and the flames that appear on the top of ship's masts

The Arch which sometimes is seen is caused by two clouds of different colors, one which is very resplendent and which is placed in front of another which is very dark and obscured, both in such a disposition and melting away in water and dew. Being then both clouds in this position, as the Sun's rays hit the darker one on its lower side, these are multiplied, and that clarity is reflected in the clearer cloud, causing an arch of different colors, for if we could see this effect where it happens we would not see anything, neither arch nor colors, or the vapors and exhalations, which are positioned between our sight and those reverberations of the rays with the clouds, causing the colors and arch. More often these arches appear during the afternoon or in the morning, because the Sun always causes this arch on the contrary side of that in which it is traveling; from where one may gather that in the morning the arches appear at the Occident and in the afternoon in the Orient; and when these appear in the North it will necessarily be midday, or very close to this.

Sometimes it happens that something as a small fire appears on the top of a ship's masts, and also, in armies, on the soldier's pikes and on top of their heads. The cause of these little fires is no other than viscous and very dry exhalations which are lifted from the earth, and upon touching the cold air of the first Region, due to the humidity and coldness of the night, they tighten and condense close to the earth, and being ventilated and moved from one part to the other, they are inflamed and appear as small blue fires.

These fires usually appear where one has a gathering of people, as in armies and ships, for these exhalations mix with the hot vapors arising from soldiers and sea fairing folk; and when a storm gathers they are condensed even more, and as they inflame themselves the air carries them from one part to the other and they find the tops of ships, where they attach themselves and burn until the vapor or subtle smoke from which they were generated is consumed; and occasionally these will move from one part to the other, before they are consumed, and this is due to the hard winds which on such occasions are common. To these fires many sailors, ignoring their cause, call Saint Elmo, and the common call "holy body", and these are great advocates for them, helping them overcome many dangers and storms at sea. These same fires appear, as mentioned, on top of the heads of soldiers, attaching themselves many times to their pikes. At this point one may doubt and ask the reason why these lit exhalations do not cause any burning or any kind of harm to the heads and spears where they sit. To this one may respond that this happens due to this matter being so prepared and this fire being so subtle that it only consumes the matter on which it was generated. This same thing also happens with good and fine gunpowder, which if placed on someone's hand and lit only burns itself and does not offend the hand. The same also happens with *aguardente,* in such a way as one may wash their hand with it, or some cloth or even hair, and this will burn without these things being offended. And thus, as the matter on which these fires are generated and lit is so subtle and prepared, that light does not have the strength and fire to bun any other matter different from that on which it is generated.

TREATISE

OF THE FOURTH ELEMENT OF FIRE

Chapter XVII

In which it is proved the existence of elemental fire contrary to the opinion of many Philosophers

Elemental fire has its proper and natural seat over the third Region of air, by being ten times as rare as this same air, as is agreed by every school of good philosophy. Many Philosophers deny not only the existence of elemental fire over the said Region of air, but even that this exists outside of it (as Titelmanus[233] refers in his Philosophy), for they say that should it be so, then we would necessarily be able to see it, given that fire is naturally bright and incandescent; and thus they conclude that if we do not see it then it must not exist. Others have said that, should elemental fire exist, that it would be necessary for it to have matter on which to burn, for being this its natural activity of consumption, as is experienced in every moment in which material fire is burning, and once this is all consumed it naturally disappears. Saying that there is combustible matter up there, so that the said fire might conserve itself, is not admitted among Philosophers, for, should there in fact be such matter up there, it would inflame, light and condense (as some say) and from this there would be a great deal of inconveniences, as that which would prevent our sight of the Heavens, Stars and Planets and their movements, and one would not enjoy the influences of the Sun, Moon and Heavenly bodies, and from this one may gather and infer that there is no elemental fire. Others, such as Cardano, Book *De subtilitate rerum*, say that elemental fire might be mixed and introduced together with air, but this would completely consume the humidity of the same air, as it happens with material fire. To the first question one responds that elemental fire cannot have nor receive light, nor can it be visible as the material one, for it cannot burn bright, nor light itself; this due to it being so pure, simple and rare; for by being air ten times thicker than fire one already cannot see it, and this cannot even receive any color in itself, much less can elemental fire, being ten times rarer than air. And thus the reason of not seeing it is not valid, for we also do not see air, and we cannot say that it does not exist, for we sometimes feel it hot, others cold and other times temperate; and on elemental fire no sense can touch, this due to the simplicity and rarity it has. However, it is certain that the elements are four, as Aristotle proves in the *Meteorologica* and, all concede to this, and that these are earth, water, air and fire. And as it was said that earth is the heaviest, it is in the lowest point of the universe; and water, for being ten times rarer than earth is above this; and for the same reason fire, being ten times rarer and subtler than air will be on top of this same air, as it in fact is. To the second reason one may respond that the elements, while being in their natural and proper seats, do not have necessity of any strange matter to conserve themselves, as I have proven in the first treatise on this matter in the third chapter, but these, if taken from their natural place, have the necessity of matter to sustain themselves, as can be seen by a lit candle whose flame appears to rise to it natural sphere, and thus we can see that as soon as the matter which sustained it is consumed, it disappears and it loses that bright heat which it has by matter, on which it was sustained.

---

233. Translator's note: Likely Franciscus Titelmanus, a XVIth century Belgian author, writer of the *Compendium Naturalis Philosophiae*.

Last Chapter

Which deals with the nature of fire and its activity

The element of fire is naturally hot and dry, exceeding with its heat the heat of air, and with its dryness the dryness of earth; given that fire is hot in its nature, in no way does it generate anything in itself, as some might think, but it rather scorches everything which is applied to it, and of this truth we have plenty of experience.

There is no shortage of those who say that in fire is generated, raised and sustained an animal which they call Salamander, and they say this happens in glass furnaces, and to prove this they claim that in air is the Chameleon sustained, and in water is where fish are generated and sustained, and from the earth is the toad and mole sustained, as well as many other creatures, and in the same way this happens with the Salamander, which is created in fire and sustained there. I however have this as a fable and that we should believe that which experience demonstrates. By fire being naturally so active, some Philosophers intend that elemental fire burns in its sphere; and if we do not see it burning or lighting up it is because there is no combustible matter there, others however follow a different path, saying that even if there should be any combustible matter it would not inflame or burn, due to the great rarity of elemental fire, and neither does elemental fire have the necessity of this for its sustenance (as was proven above and declared in its proper place) as we see with air, that by being much more humid than water it does not make things wet, and this is due to its great rarity and division of its parts that they sooner make things which are wet dry, and the cause of this is the ventilation of the said air. For if air is thus, that it does not make anything wet wherever it passes, due to its great rarity, much less does elemental fire burn in its sphere, as this is even rarer than air. And one should be warned that no man can be considered learned in Philosophy if he considers elemental fire hot in the same way as a hot furnace would be should they remove its fire, leaving only the wood inside; for it would only be left hot, not burning, and this because there wouldn't be any artificial fire inside; in this same way, even if elemental fire had any combustible matter, it would not light itself; and this should be enough for one to understand that elemental fire does not burn as does the artificial one.

SECOND PART OF THIS

TREATISE

OF THE ETHEREAL OR CELESTIAL REGION

CHAPTER I

Of the first Heaven and the Moon which is found in it

Having mentioned the elemental Region with the most possible brevity, it is convenient that we now say something about the orbs and Stars or Planets which are found in these with the same brevity, for volume and time does not allow us to extend ourselves as this matter requires.

The Heavens, which are subjected to a continuous motion (according to modern Astronomers) are ten; and with the Emperium Heaven they are eleven, which is not subjected to any motion for it is a place of rest and breath, where the blessed rest and wait.

I say with Cardano, an expert astrologer, that the first Heaven, which is the closest to us, is separated from the earth, by its concave part, six thousand, two hundred and forty seven leagues; and in this there is but one body, which is the Moon, and whose body has a grandeur of one hundred and seventy six leagues; and thus, should it be in the eighth Heaven, given the distance, it would be so small that we would not be able to see it.

This Orb or Heaven, in which the Moon resides, has a circumference of seven hundred, fifty six thousand and eleven hundred and sixty eight leagues, and its body has a thickness of one hundred and eighteen thousand and seventy eight leagues.

The Moon travels from the Levante to the Ponente, in one hour, thirty thousand five hundred and thirty two leagues. The Moon has a cold and dry nature, even if accidentally it is somewhat warm due to the light it receives from the Sun.

The ancient Astronomers came to understand, by their Astronomy, that the seven days of the week are subjected to the natural movement of the seven Planets, from which these took their names by which many nations call these same days; thus to Monday they called the day of the Moon, to Tuesday that of Mars, Wednesday the day of Mercury, Thursday the day of Jupiter, Friday the day of Venus, Saturday the day of Saturn and to Sunday the day of the Sun, as those dominate these days of the week; further still, the Astronomers think that in each hour of each day of the week one of these Planets reigns and that they still do. From what was said one can gather that the day of the Moon is Monday, and that its hour is the first hour of the Morning when the Sun rises and the eighth after it has risen; and so highly was this Planetary hour taken by the ancient Astronomers that these would not give a single step, or do anything of any importance without first observing which Planet was reigning in each hour in which they wanted to do anything. And one should note that by the Planet which dominated the hour of the birth of each man they could tell the temper, inclination and condition of each one, and depending on each person's inclination and faculty, he was thus proposed and raised by his parents to that same faculty, art or letter, to which his natural inclination would aid him a great deal. And God our Lord always wished that, and I say this one, twice and a hundred thousand times, that God wished that in the various republics there were always learned people who knew how to extract the natural inclination of each one and who could know the art or faculty that these could perform and accommodate to; and in this way everyone would be skilled and artful and greatly intelligent in all they might undertake. But unfortunately, he who is good for the letters is made into an officer, merchant or sailor; and he who is not good for them is made to study, and there are many in this condition and they live most miserably; and by our disgrace no one takes note of their elected faculty or art, in which their natural inclination would aid and favor them, and in this way they would live joyously and well rested. And so each one may know, without being an astronomer, to which art, letters or faculty they can apply themselves, so as they may follow their intent easily and live happily, they should note and be adverted of the signs and Physiognomy which each Planet imprints on those who are born under their dominion, by which one may know and collect what is the Planet that dominates him and to which faculty or art he is better fitted and convenient, so as with will and affection he may apply himself and be made into a good artifice.

Signs and Physiognomy of the Moon

Those who are born under the dominion of the Moon are pale and somewhat blond; the face is round, pale and handsome, medium sized eyes, not completely black and not very strong; the eyebrows are united, they have some freckles or spots on their face.

Those who are born under the dominion of the Moon are inclined to sailing, fishing and roaming the waters and lakes; these are not good for the letters or any merchant trade, for they have a weak memory and are inconstant and very given to sleep, which is not something which is good for letters or trading.

Chapter II

Of the second Heaven, in which one may find the Planet Mercury

The second Heaven is distant from the concave part of the earth by one hundred and twenty five thousand and twenty five leagues, whose circumference has one million, nine hundred and fifty eight thousand, eight hundred and eight leagues, and its body has a thickness of three hundred and twenty five thousand, eight hundred and eighty leagues. In this second Heaven only one Star is to be found, and its name is Mercury, and its body has a roundness of one fifth of an Italian league, which is a thousand paces. This Star travels from the Levante to the Ponente eighty one thousand, six hundred and twenty leagues in one hour.

This Star, or Planet, is of an indifferent nature, and it has such a property as to convert itself into the nature of the Planet with which it is joined; in such a way as the Mercurial, when among the good, become good, and perverse with the bad.

Those who are born under the dominion of this Planet are apt and convenient to be painters, singers, sketchers, men of letters, merchants and writers. These will understand and learn Arithmetic, Mathematic, Philosophy, Astrology and any mechanical art with great ease; mainly those of goldsmith, painter, sculptor, for these have an inventive and subtle cunning, and these are great friends of poetry and things of secret or cunning.

Signs and Physiognomy of Mercury

The Mercurial are of an average height, have little flesh and a broad forehead, projected outward, long and sharp nose; small and handsome eyes; a not completely black beard, short and light; the lips are thin as is the hair, and this is straight; the teeth are not well formed and are crooked. Finally these are of good customs, even if easy to convert *ad bonum, et ad malum*.

Chapter III

Of the third Heaven, in which one may find the Planet Venus

The third Heaven is separated from the concave part of the earth by three hundred and twenty five thousand, six hundred and fifty leagues, and whose roundness has three million, one hundred and ten thousand leagues, and its body has a thickness of one million, eight hundred and fifty eight thousand and three hundred and fifty leagues. In this third Heaven there is a single Star which is the Planet Venus, which is called the Morning Star.

The body of this star has a roundness of a little more than one hundred and seventy five leagues. This Star travels from the Levante to the Ponente five hundred and forty six thousand, two hundred and fifty leagues in one hour.

This Planet, or Star of Venus, is of a hot and humid nature.

Those of the nature of Venus are better for the palace and the service of great lords than they are for the letters; and these will learn any mechanical art in which one requires gentleness quite well, and above all music.

Signs and Physiognomy of Venus

Those of the nature of Venus have a full and round face, somewhat evident and black, joyful and restless eyes, black eyebrows, united and handsome, straight hair, curved nose, average mouth with a slightly thicker lower lip, handsome neck and a tight chest. And if Venus was at the Orient when they were born, they will have a pleasing stature, light and well grown. And if it was in the Occident they will have a small stature, and be bald with some sign on their face. These are hot, humid and phlegmatic; they are usually eloquent, prudent, and well fortunate; they are also friends of parties, pastimes, ornaments, curious dresses, sweet smelling things, music, dancing and very rarely are they given to the letters.

Chapter IV

Of the fourth Heaven, in which one may find the Sun

The fourth Heaven is separated from the concave part of the earth by two million, three hundred and seventy nine thousand leagues, which has a circumference of fourteen million, two hundred and eighty thousand leagues and its body has a thickness of one million, one hundred and ninety five thousand leagues.

In this fourth Heaven there is only one body, and this is the Sun, which is in the middle of the seven Planets, as their king and lord, communicating to these its light and splendor.

This Planet, or Heavenly body of the Sun, is larger than the whole earth one hundred and sixty six times and its body has a roundness of one million, sixty five thousand and six hundred and eighty leagues. The Sun travels from the Levante to the Ponente five hundred and ninety five thousand leagues in one hour.

The nature of this Planet is hot and temperately dry, by whose actions are improved and perfected all the fruits of the earth, and by it do all the plants and herbs of the fields grow and reach perfection. And God our Lord gave it such virtue and excellence that the Philosopher came to say that the *Sol & homo generat hominem*; and this means that the Sun and man generate men.

All those which are born under the dominion of the Sun are good rulers, regents and governors; these are fitted for important positions and for the exercise of public office. These are good for the invention of new things and arts.

Signs and Physiognomies of the Sun

The solar are of a hot and temperately dry completion, they are fair and with plenty of flesh; they have a light face, average mouth, not very thick lips, round forehead, thin eyebrows, clear and handsome eyes, straight and well proportioned nose, round neck and chest, straight and well formed body.

These are grave, honest and tall men of great advice; these have a royal spirit and desire to be honored; they are generous, well spoken and constant; finally they aspire to position and rule, honors and dignities.

Chapter V

Of the fifth Heaven, in which one may find the Planet Mars

The fifth Heaven is separate from the concave part of the earth by two million, three hundred and seventy nine thousand leagues, and it has a roundness of one hundred and three million, eight hundred and fifty five thousand and two hundred leagues, and it body has a thickness of fourteen million, nine hundred and twenty nine thousand and two hundred leagues.

In this fifty Heaven there is the Star of the Planet Mars, whose body has a roundness of ten thousand, five hundred and thirty leagues. This Planet travels four million, three hundred and twenty seven thousand and three hundred leagues in one hour.

The Martial are apt and good for anything relating to fire, as weapons artificers, artillery men, sword makers, locksmiths and blacksmiths; they are also apt for butchers and surgeons, as well as for other similar trades and ministries.

Signs and Physiognomy of Mars

Those who are born under the dominion of this Planet have a large and ugly face with some red spots and freckles; subtle and amazed sight, long necks, lit and reddish eyes, large or very open noses, wide, white and ill proportionate teeth; very little beard and a somewhat bent body. And in the case that Mars was in the Occident at the time of birth, this will cause a thin neck, delicate legs with a long stride, very raised chest and feet, small heels and large head.

These are choleric to the extreme and filled with wrath, ready with their hands and late with their reason and words, seekers of noise and brawls, enemies of peace and quiet, they are deceitful, liars, and friends of discord; they are daring, restless, cruel and without mercy; they are inconstant, persistent, inclined to thefts; but the wise and prudent will be the lord of the stars and all his evil tendencies by keeping with the commandments.

Chapter VI

Of the sixth Heaven, in which one may find the Planet Jupiter

The sixth Heaven is separated from the concave part of the earth by seventeen million, three hundred and eight thousand and three hundred leagues and it has a circumference of one hundred and sixty eight million, five hundred and forty four thousand and five hundred leagues, and its body has a thickness of ten million, seven hundred and eighty one thousand, five hundred and fifty leagues.

In this Heaven there is a single Star which is called the Planet Jupiter, whose body is larger than the whole earth by ninety four times, and this Star has a roundness of six hundred and fifteen thousand and six hundred leagues. This Planet travels from the Levante to the Ponente seven million, twenty two thousand, six hundred and eighty seven leagues and a half in one hour.

This Planet has a hot and humid nature, very favorable to the earth, men and irrational animals.

Those who are born under the dominion of this Planet are apt for the study of any letter and faculty, for they usually have a clear cunning and subtle understanding; they are good for Religion, judges, lawyers, republic positions and also to regency and government; finally they are good for any mechanical art, except those which are of the Planet Mars; they are given to marriage and procreation, and they are prudent in governing their house and family.

Sign and Physiognomy of Jupiter

The Jovial are of a very good stature, well disposed, temperate, fair and somewhat blushed, brown and harsh beard; these have a sanguine sight and are neither very strong nor very week; the eyes are black and handsome; the forehead large and fleshy; the teeth well proportioned and nicely closed; slightly whitish hair and not very abundant, in such a way as they will be bald, and they have thick and well exposed veins.

These men are peaceful, modest, amicable without any deceit; they are virtuous, faithful, given to knowledge and they are not vengeful, they keep their promises, treat their things with discretion and finally these can give good advice.

This Planet has its strength in the Septentrion and it dominates the provinces of its Signs, Pisces and Sagittarius, and its metal is tin.

Chapter VII

Of the seventh Heaven, in which one may find the Planet Saturn

The seventh Heaven is separated from the earth, on the concave part, by twenty eight million, eighty nine thousand, five hundred and fifty leagues and it has a circumference of two hundred and thirty five million, one hundred and ninety three thousand leagues and its body has a thickness of eleven million, one hundred and twenty four thousand and seven hundred and fifty leagues.

In this seventh Heaven there is a Star which is called the Planet Saturn, whose body is larger than the whole earth by 90 times, and thus this Star has a roundness of five hundred and eighty nine thousand, six hundred and eighty leagues. The Planet travels from the Levante to the Ponente nine million, eight hundred and three thousand, six hundred and eighty leagues. This Star is of a cold, dry and melancholic nature, and it is contrary to the human nature.

Those who are born under the dominion of this Planet are good for any kind of letters and arts, both liberal and mechanical, for they are usually as melancholic as their Planet Saturn; and thus they are greatly given to study, imaginative and lovers of the sciences and of understanding fundamentally all that which they learn and study, this in such a way as they tend to forget all other pleasures and delights, loving loneliness in exchange for reaching that which they study and the majority of the ancient philosophers are of the nature of Saturn; finally these will be good farmers, stonemasons, hermits, shoe cobblers, curators and grave diggers; and those who walk among the dead.

Signs and Physiognomy of Saturn

The Saturnine usually have a big and dry face; average eyes inclined towards the earth, with one bigger than the other; fleshy noses, thick lips, joined eyebrows, dark face, black, hard and course hair; uneven teeth, hairy chests, long legs and not very straight; they are full of nerves, dry and with very thin and well exposed veins. And should Saturn be on the Occidental side, this will cause those who are born to have a small stature, pasty skin, little beard and whitish and straight hair; they are deep of thought, they love in excess and are bored to the extreme.

It has dominion on the first climate and the lands of Ethiopia and the provinces of its two Signs, Aquarius and Capricorn, it has its strength in the Orient and its metal is lead.

Chapter VIII

Of the eighth Heaven, in which is the multitude of the Stars

The eighth Heaven is separated from the concave part of the earth by forty million, five thousand and five hundred leagues, and it has a circumference of one hundred and seventy three million, eight hundred and seventy nine thousand and forty seven leagues and two thirds, and its body has a thickness of twenty one million, seven hundred and eighty five thousand and eight hundred and thirty eight leagues and one third.

In this eighth Heaven or firmament are all Stars fixed, which discover themselves and become visible at night, except those seven we have named, which are in their own orbs or Heavens. The whole of this starry Sky travels from the Levante to the Ponente twelve million, two hundred and forty four thousand and nine hundred and twenty two leagues, more or less, in one hour.

Of all the infinity of Stars in this eighth Heaven, the Astronomers only pay attention to a thousand and twenty two of them, and fifteen of these, by being greater than all the others, they call Stars of first Magnitude, and each one of these is greater than the earth one hundred times. To forty five others they call second Magnitude, by not being as great as the first fifteen and each of them is eighty nine times greater than the earth.

The Stars of third Magnitude are two hundred and eight, and each of these is greater than the earth seventy times.

The Stars of fourth Magnitude, or most of them, are four hundred and seventy four, and each of them is greater than the earth fifty three times.

The Stars of fifth grandeur or Magnitude are two hundred and seventeen, and each of them is thirty five times greater than the earth. Those that they say are the fewest of them all are those of sixth Magnitude, and these are sixty three, and each of them is greater than the earth seventeen times. Finally, any Star which our sight can see in the Starry Sky, no matter how small, is greater than the globe of earth and water, and given that each Star is of a different nature we will not name their qualities and effects, for this would be an endless job.

Chapter IX

Of the ninth, tenth and eleventh Heaven

The ninth Heaven is call Aqueous or Crystalline. It is called thus due to Psalm 148; *Praise him, you highest heavens; and you waters above the skies*. Saint Augustine says of these waters that they are in the form of a most thin mist. Others have said that these are frozen as a very splendorous crystal. In this ninth sphere or Crystalline Heaven the Astronomer consider the location of the Zodiac with the twelve Signs represented in the eighth Heaven.

This ninth Heaven is separated from the concave side of the earth by sixty one million, eight hundred and one thousand, three hundred and thirty seven leagues. The size of the body of this orb is not known, given the fact that it does not have any Star by which one may measure its magnitude.

Of the tenth Heaven, the first mobile

The tenth Heaven is what the Astronomers call the first mobile, which is under the Empyrium Heaven; one cannot know how distant this is from the earth by the same reason as mentioned above, nor can one know how many leagues does its circumference have, nor the size of its body. It is called first mobile for it is the first Heaven that moves and makes all the other inferior Heavens move, making a full circle from the Levante to the Ponente in twenty four uniform and regular hours, without it never being any faster.

Of the Empyrium Heaven

Who will ever be able to say the distance, magnitude and grandeur of the eleventh Heaven, which the Theologians call Empyrium, the place of quietness and rest? Saint Basil says of this in the *Hexameron*, Book 2, that God our Lord created it on the first day, and that this was immediately filled with Angels, being in such great number that Saint Dionysius says that there is no comparison to even the greatest things on earth. It is a spherical and round body like all the other inferior orbs which it embraces and contains within itself. It is most subtle and so clear and splendorous and this is the reason why it is called Empyrium Heaven. And may the Divine Majesty permit all of us to enjoy it. Amen.

DIALOGUE

OF DOUBTS REFERRING

TO THAT WHICH WAS SAID IN THE LAST TREATISE OF THE ELEMENTAL

AND CELESTIAL REGION

THE INTERLOCUTORS ARE

The reader of this work and its Author

Reader: Many doubts did arise in me regarding the treatise of the elemental and celestial region, dear Author; however, so as not to bother you or extend your work, I will only wish to ask you those which caused me difficulty.

Author: I am very relieved that you, discreet reader, doubting or not doubting, should ask them, for I know that I did not write or declare many things; some due to not being that notorious, others due to not being too relevant to the subject, and others so as you may ask them. And now is the occasion presented, so propose and ask with brevity, for I, with the favor of God, do intend to answer.

Reader: I am most content, and the first doubt is about the four principal winds, on which you have said that the Levante wind is cold and humid, and the Ponente hot and dry; and I do say that you are right, for this is what happens in your motherland and Kingdom of Valencia; however, not in Castile, where experience shows otherwise, for the Levante wind that in your Motherland is humid and cold, is hot and dry in Castile; and the Ponente, which is so dry and hot in Valencia, is felt as dry and humid in Castile; and even the Angelic Doctor Saint Thomas has said this while writing about Meteors, as you refer in your perpetual Lunario, and so explain to me the cause of these changes, if you offer to do as such.

Author: I say that I am content, and know that the cause why the Levant wind is felt fresh and humid in the Kingdom of Valencia is due to this being close to the sea; and as this wind passes through it, it gathers humidity and freshness from the many vapors which continuously rise from the immensity of the waters by virtue and strength of the Sun's Rays. And passing this wind on to Castile, it loses this cold and humid quality, which it had gathered by accident, receiving its proper and natural condition, which is being hot and dry, this by finding a multitude of hot and dry exhalations which perpetually rise from the earth, which was already explained, aiding in this not just the heat carried by the Sun's rays, but also the reverberation arising from the earth due to them, and by this reason is this wind made hot and dry in Castile; and for this same reason is the Ponente felt cold and humid in Castile and hot in Valencia; and for this reason do I see what Saint Thomas says regarding the Ponente being cold and humid when speaking of Castile.

Reader: I am satisfied with the answer and I now understand the cause of why in Castile it is common to rain with the Ponente and in Valencia with the Levante. And beyond what was said, I gather that the Northeastern wind, which is felt as so dry and cold, upon passing to the Midday is made humid and hot and it shall turn cold and dry if it passes to the Septentrion. And so I am resolved regarding this doubt, and I would very much appreciate if you could resolve another which causes me greater difficulty; and this is that I cannot understand that the Heavens are as many as you claim in the fifth treatise of the Ethereal Region, when in truth our sight does not discern more than one; as also many ancient and learned Philosophers claimed that there wasn't any more than a single Heaven; and even the Holy Scripture claims this in Chapter 1 of Genesis; *In principio creavit Deus Cælum & terram*. Where it is clearly stated that God our Lord in the beginning created one Heaven and one earth rather than many Heavens as you claim.

Author: Regarding that which you claim of Genesis, you should know that all the Doctors and Theologians declare that in this passage by Heaven one should understand all the Celestial orbs and by earth all of the four simple and composed elements, and further more in the same Scripture there are many places which confirm this interpretation of the Theologians and of that which I write. Firstly you should read Psalm 18 of David, which says: *Cæli enarrant gloriam, Dei*. Which means that the Heavens manifest the glory of the Lord and his power. And Saint Paul claims that he was taken in rapture to the third Heaven. And the same David in Psalm 95 says: *Lætantur Cæli & exulted terra*. And this means, may the Heavens rejoice and the earth celebrate. And Daniel, in the Song of the Three Holy Children, confirms this by saying: *Benedicite Cæli Domino*. And finally Christ our Redeemer confirms this in the Dominical Prayer of the Our Father, and in infinite other places are there mentions of the Heaven being many. Regarding what you say of great and learned Philosophers I respond, with Aristotle, that they made a mistake due to an even greater error, which was that they thought that the Stars moved through the Heaven as fish do in the water and birds in the air, and it is proven by Aristotle that this is the exact contrary, as he demonstrates that all the Stars are fixed in their orbs just as wood knots on a board are stuck to that same board.

Reader: Thou has proven it well with the Holy Scripture that there are many Heavens, and in this do I believe, and further still do I give credit to what Aristotle said, as he is the first among Philosophers; however, it would greatly relieved me if you could prove this with reason, so as I may believe and see it with my own eyes, if this is possible, or at least to the furthest reach of my understanding.

Author: I say that not only will you understand it but you will also see it. And note that should there be a single Heaven the Stars would have to be fixed in it, as well as the Sun, the Moon and all the other Planets; and from this one gathers that all of these Planets would always have the same distance between themselves, as would the Stars in the eighth Heaven, and thus there would never be different aspects between them nor could they cause these with the other Stars, and consequently there wouldn't be so much variability in the changes in weather as there is. And as the wise and careful Astrologers have seen that these Planets do not keep the same distance with each other, as do all the Stars in the eighth Heaven, but that these rather separate from one another as time goes by and also come closer together, as these many times eclipse each other, making them fall out of sign and luminosity. Then they came to understand that each Planet or Star of these seven should be fixed in its own orb or heaven, and that one orb would necessarily need to be beneath the others in their own order, like the peels of an onion, with some placed within the others, for in any other way they wouldn't prevent each other's sight. And you can see this with your own eyes every time that there is an Eclipse of the Sun due to the Moon, as this places itself under the body of the Sun, an evident and manifest sign that the orb and Heaven of the Moon is lower than that of the Sun; and we can further see this every month in the conjunction of the Moon, that as the Moon is under the body of the Sun we cannot see it nor can it communicate the clarity it receives from the Sun to us until it parts from its corporeal presence.

Also the Moon many times covers the Planets Mercury and Venus, which they call the Morning Star, for the orbs of both are above that of the Moon, and the Morning Star, due to being above the orb of the Planet Mercury, is many times eclipsed and covered. For the Sun every day, shedding its light on us, prevents our sight of the Planet Mars, Jupiter and Saturn and of all the Stars in the firmament, as these are higher than the same Sun, which would not happen, and neither would the Sun be able to cover them, if they were all in the Heaven or orb of the Moon, as these are, as we have said, greater than the Moon more than fifty times.

Reader: Now do I say that I not only understand that you are right, but I have also understood this by having seen a notable eclipse which happened in the year of ninety, last July, and with a mirror placed in a vase of water I was seeing the Moon placing itself under the Sun and eclipsing it; and now do I certify myself that all the Stars are not fixed in a single Heaven, but rather in different ones, and of this I have no doubts. However, do know that I have difficulties with two words you have said above. One is that the Planets are occasionally placed together and other times separated; and the other is that you have said that the Moon received its light from the Sun; for in truth I thought that the Moon had its own and natural light, and that it did not receive it from the Sun.

Author: Regarding the first you should know that when we say that the Moon is in conjunction with the Sun, this is saying that the Moon is under and in front of the body of the Sun; and being that the Sun is separated from the Moon by more than two million leagues, when the Moon eclipses the Sun it seems to us that both these circles are joined together, which is not the case since the Sun is in the fourth Heaven and the Moon in the first, and because of this do we say that they are joined and separated. Regarding your doubt if the Moon receives its light from the Sun or not, know that not only does the Moon receive its light and clarity from the Sun, but also all the other inferior and superior Stars; for should the Moon have its own light and clarity, never would it by any means lose it; but as the Sun communicates this light, at the same time that the Moon places itself under the body of the Sun, we lose that light which is communicated to its upper part; and as the Moon travels away from this same Sun, so does it communicate to us the light it receives from it. That this is true can be clearly seen when one has a lunar eclipse; for we see that it is the shadow of the earth (caused by the Sun), placed between the Sun and the Moon, that makes it eclipse and lose its light; for as the earth is a solid body, and the Sun is diametrically opposed to the body of the Moon, its rays cannot pass and hit the body of the said Moon and thus it is completely obscured, or at least in part, according to the degree that these are more or less diametrically opposed.

Reader: I am satisfied of these last doubts, and of all I have proposed so far; however, a new one does beckon which I have carried in my memory for a long time and I have never had the opportunity to ask it; and this is that I have read in some Lunarios or Repertoires, and even in yours, that the conjunctions or turnings of the Moon happen in some lands before they happen in others, and I cannot understand how this can be; for it seems to me that the time of the conjunction in Valencia should be the same for the whole world.

Author: You are not the first who feels this difficulty and you will surely not be the last. However you should be warned of two things and you shall be clarified; the orb or Heaven in which the Moon sits, beyond its movement from the Levante to the Ponente, which it has in twenty four hours, has another contrary and natural movement, as do all the other Heavens, which is from the Ponente to the Levante. The other cause you should notice is that when the conjunction of the Moon happens, or a solar Eclipse, these always begin from the side of the Ponente, which means that the Moon with its own movement, even if it seems to us to be faster than that of the Sun, starts to place itself under the same Sun by the side of the Ponente; and so it first covers the Sun's rays to those that inhabit the Ponente rather than those who live in the Levante, and by this cause it happens that the Occidentals will notice the conjunction and the Eclipses before the Orientals, some more some less.

Reader: I say that you are right, for in that eclipse of the year of ninety I have mentioned before, I do remember it starting from the side of the Ponente, for before it began I saw the Sun on the side of the Levante and the Moon on the side of the Ponente; however I do not know if it was the Sun which placed itself firstly above the Moon or the Moon which placed itself under the Sun; for do know that this case of the nine Heavens having two contrary movements at the same time has caused me great confusion. And if this is thus (which I do not believe until you prove it to me) it may very well be that the Moon is the first to enter under the body of the Sun.

Author: You were greatly scandalized because I said that the Heavens have two contrary movements. Well do know that the Astronomers consider other movements in the Heavens which they call access and recess or trepidation, different from those we have pointed out above; but as this is not our intent, we will not deal with them now.

Reader: Those two movements which are at the same time contrary I do wish that you declare them to me, for I cannot understand how can one go forward and at the same time go backward.

Author: Do know that one does not require great Metaphysics to make you believe so, and further more to see it; for, should you notice a ship sailing through the sea, you can see those who are inside it, and these can walk in the opposite direction of the movement of the ship and they nonetheless go forward to where the ship is taking them, and thus at the same time they have two contrary movements. The same can be observed in a great river, as I have myself seen, that a paddle boat, wanting to go upstream will instead be taken downstream by the fury of the waters, without nonetheless moving up, be it little or not. The same happens with fish in similar rivers, as they naturally travel up the stream, the rivers takes them down. Above all do notice a visible example and very appropriate for the contrary movements of the nine Heavens; and for this consider that you are moving and turning a wheel towards the Ponente, and that on that wheel there are nine ants which represent the nine Heavens, and that these ants are moving towards the Levante, which is the contrary part to which you are moving the wheel; it is clear that the ants would have two contrary movements at the same time, and this without any repugnance. One movement would be that which you would give them by turning the wheel to the Ponente and the other the one which they themselves would have by traveling to the contrary part, some more and some less, according to what would be natural for them. For do know that the same happens in the Heavens, as an Angel or intelligence, as Aristotle claims (which I do not admit, but in truth do I understand that it is proper and natural for the tenth Heaven to move towards the Levante), moves the tenth sphere, carrying with it all the nine Heavens from the Levante to the Ponente, however, these with their own natural and proper movement are traveling from the Ponente to the Levante, some more and some less, and thus do they continuously have movements some forward and some backward, without there being any contradiction or repugnance.

Reader: I say that you have left me content and satisfied, and this I do not have to deny, for each night I saw the Moon setting to my great discomfort, occasionally later and occasionally earlier, for some nights, the sunset, is found more to the Ponente and some other times in the mid sky, and others in the Levante, and this is an evident sign that the orb and Heaven in which it sits has another different movement from that which is given by the first mobile from the Levante to the Ponente in a time of twenty four hours. And I have no more doubts in this, however, I would be greatly relieved if you should tell me in how much time does each Heaven or Planet finish its own revolution and full turn, traveling from the Ponente to the Levante.

Author: So as to satisfy that which I have promised, and so as to give you enjoyment, I shall say this with brevity; and do know that the ninth Heaven moves so slowly that in two hundred years it does not move more than one degree and a half of the three hundred and sixty in which the Astronomers divide the Zodiac.

This ninth Heaven finished its course and full turn, traveling to the Orient in the time of forty nine thousand years, at the end of which Plato has said that all things would return to their first state; however, the holy Doctor Saint Augustine, Book 12 of *De Civitate Dei*, proves the contrary.

The eighth and starry Heaven has its full turn by its natural movement, which is what the Astronomers call access and recess, in the time of seven thousand years; and these even give it a third movement to the Orient, which perfects the forty nine thousand years as a year, for in this way it will have its measure and natural movement.

The Planet Saturn, which is in the seventh Heaven, gives a complete turn by its own movement in the time of twenty nine years, two months and two days and a half.

The Planet Jupiter, which is in the sixth Heaven, finishes its course and natural movement in the time of eleven years, ten months, thirteen days and a half.

The Planet Mars, which is in the fifth Heaven, finishes its own revolution in a year, ten months and almost twenty one days.

The Planet Sun, which is in the fourth Heaven, as lord of the Planets, with its own movement gives a full round around the universe in the time of one year; traveling in the said time fourteen million and twenty eight thousand leagues, which is the circumference of its orb; and it travels in each day, from the Levante to the Ponente, almost a degree.

The Planet Venus, which is called the Morning Star and is in the third Heaven, and the Planet Mercury, which has its seat in the second Heaven, finish their revolution and full turn in one year, as the Sun; but one should be warned that even if these two Stars finish their trajectory at the same time as the Sun, they do not travel as many leagues as this; for the width of the circumference of their orbs is much smaller than that of the Sun as was said above. The curious man who wishes to know the leagues that each Planet or Heaven travels in a year, month or hour, should divide the leagues of the circumference of each orb by the years or year that the Heaven takes in finishing its full turn, and once these are known for a year, one may also know the ones for a month, day and hour.

The Moon is in the First Heaven, and closest to us; and this finishes its full turn by its own movement in the time of twenty seven days and almost eight hours; this is in such a way as each day it falls back thirteen degrees and ten minutes and a half towards the Orient, nonetheless, moving forward to the Ponente in that same day the three hundred and sixty degrees of its orb or Heaven, which are seven hundred and fifty six thousand, seven hundred and sixty eight leagues.

Reader: I am very content for having received the knowledge of the time that each Planet takes in its natural revolution; but from what was said it seems like the Moon travels in its movement more than the Sun and more than any other Planet if I am not mistaken, for the Moon takes less than twenty eight days to perform its revolution and the Sun takes a whole year.

Author: The reason why the Moon seems to be faster than the Sun and the remaining Planets is not because it travels more, but rather because of the reason I have said earlier, which is that its orb is much smaller than that of the Sun and the other Planets, and in this way if one divides the leagues that are in the circumference of the Sun by three hundred and sixty degrees you would find that each degree contains over thirty nine thousand, six hundred and sixty six leagues; and the thirteen degrees that the Moon moves in its orb during one day barely have twenty eight thousand leagues.

Reader: This must be the reason why it seems that the Moon is faster than all the other Planets; and I have no difficulty in this, however, and this comes in this same vein, I would be very much relieved if you could tell me what's that obscurity which covers the body of the Moon, for some times those seem to me to be eyes, and other times some kind of spots.

Author: They are neither, nor could they ever be any of this, for up there there are no spots. So as you may know what those are, you should note and be adverted that the cause for the Moon and all other Stars to have their light is because their bodies are more condensed and thick than the Heaven and orbs where they rest; and as the Sun's rays hit the said dense and opaque bodies, they receive two things: light and clarity, which they then communicate to us, becoming Stars; and that darkness which sometimes is seen on the body of the Moon is nothing else than that particular part of its body not being thick and condensed, and by this cause the Sun's rays do not touch it, passing through it, and so that part is left without light and clarity, and this is what in the Moon seems dark. And of this truth we have an example and root manifested in crystalline glass, which, when placed under the Sun, should it have any steel on its other side, it stops the Sun's rays in that same glass and they reverberate, casting light and splendor; and should it not have any steel on its back, the rays will pass right on through, penetrating the same glass without any of these rays being stopped, and thus it is darker when compared with before. And the same happens with the body of the Moon.

Reader: I must say that I am greatly relieved for having been corrected, for I always thought that the Moon had eyes, noses and mouth, given what I could see on it; and as I have no more doubts regarding this, I would very much be grateful that you could tell me what is that band or white strap which covers the whole Universe and which is commonly called the Path of Saint James.

Author: This strap, or milky way, which is what the Astronomers call it, isn't anything else but the multitude of the Stars, which are very close and almost put together around the eighth sphere; and I say put together because this is what it seems to our sight, due to them being so small and being very high up, in such a way as we do not see the light they receive from the Sun as clearly and distinctly as all the others except in their whiteness, and even if I say that the Stars are small do not think that any of them is smaller than the earth, but these are rather bigger, for, should it be any other way, one would not be able to see them given the great distance that they have from us.

Reader: By solving one doubt you have created in me another, since you have reminded me of something; my doubt, should ten thousand people hear it (and should these not be Astronomers) maybe two would believe it, and this is that you say that the body of the Sun has a circle of one million leagues, plus seventy five thousand, six hundred and eighty, and being this true our sight does not see it any bigger that a small coin.

Author: You do not know much of Perspective; and this might surprise you, but should the whole earth, as dilated as it is, be covered with living flames, and in such a way as you would be looking upon it from the fourth Heaven where the Sun is, this would seem to you so small and minimal as the light of an insignificant candle. And if this causes you any difficulty to believe, then you should make the experiment with a bonfire the size of a mill stone, and have this at the top of a high mount and be at a distance of ten leagues, and you shall see that that great fire will look to you as being smaller than a *vintem*, and this only after ten leagues. So now, raise your point of consideration and make another discourse and intellectual comparison, or Arithmetic, and should the fire that you sees be the size of a *vintem*, by being ten leagues away, let us conjecture the great body which is the Sun and it will appear as a coin by being at a distance of two million leagues, and you shall find that this is a good discourse and calculation, then you shall not doubt what I say regarding the size of the body of the Sun, and you should know that every million leagues contains a hundred thousand leagues.

Reader: Surely, thinking about it, you do seem to be right, and one may piously believe in such, and even make the experiment you mentioned. However, I remember that you said that the ancient Astronomers made a great deal of the planetary hour so as to understand certain things and not take care of others, and as such I should very much like to have some rule so as to know which Planet reigns in each hour, for once this is understood I would know it for every man and as such not make a mistake in considering their conditions and tendencies.

Author: This I do gladly; even if you do need to take note that in this deal of births this rule isn't as certain as that which the Astronomers can give you by means of an Astronomical figure; however, for the ancients that invented it, this was meant for manual things, but I, with your pardon, do say that it is neither good for one thing nor the other. To understand this rule one should write down the Planets as I give them here: Sun, Venus, Mercury, Moon, Saturn, Jupiter and Mars. Be warned that the Sun rules over Sunday, and it also has the first hour of the Sunrise. Venus dominates on Friday and its hour is the first of the Sunrise. Mercury dominates Wednesday, whose hour is the first in the morning during the Sunrise. And thus Moon is on Monday, Saturn on Saturday, Jupiter on Thursday and Mars on Tuesday. Knowing this very well, one should know the hour at which the Sun rose in any day of the year (which can be found in our Repertoire and Lunario). Now, in order to know which Planet dominates in each hour of that day, checking if it is a Monday, Tuesday or Sunday, etc, for the Planet will be according to this day, and the first hour will be the hour of that Planet, in each hour change the Planet in the order which I have given above until you arrive at the hour which you want, and the Planet in which it falls is the one reigning and dominating in that hour.

Reader: As far as my intentions go, I have understood it, even if not completely; as such, I would be greatly relieved if you could repeat an example, for in my understanding examples are the best way to interpret what is said and written.

Author: You are right, by examples does one reach the true meaning and declaration of any doctrine, mainly in matters such as rules, which always require a certain artifice; and so as we do not lose any more time, let us say that I wish to know, on a day of birth which is on a Thursday of this present year, which Planet will rule right at the Sunrise and at what hour in the afternoon; I find that the Sun comes out at seven in the morning, and that will be the dominion of Jupiter, by being a Thursday, and at four in the afternoon Mars will dominate, for attributing to each hour its Planet, as was said, it so happens that Mars falls at three in the afternoon, and there its dominion starts, and since it lasts for a whole hour, it follows that at four Mars will dominate, and this is a terrible hour for anything, according to the ancient Astronomers; and let no one make the mistake of saying that Sunday begins on Saturday, even if it is true that for Astronomers it does have its beginning there, in the midday of Saturday, for regarding the Planetary hour, this is not counted, but rather the hour at which the Sun rises on each day in each hemisphere.

Reader: I have received this rule with great joy, more than any other thing I have heard so far, even if this has all given me great pleasure and contentment; however, I have heard that should the artificial day have more or less than twelve hours, one should regulate it through those same more or less than twelve hours; and if this is so, there should be more to understand.

Author: You do not need to know much, nor is there any necessity to make the hours longer or shorter than the ones given by the clock, for the Planets rule a single sixty minute hour, and no more.

Reader: I am aware of everything; however, what use is there in knowing the hours of the Planets if I do not know to what this is used for.

Author: You are also right and as such do note the things that the ancient Astronomers left written to us about what things to begin and not begin on certain hours according to the Planet which is dominant; even if these for me are of no consideration or efficiency, as I have said; but I have nonetheless repeated what they have said.

Reader: But to completely conclude my questions I further ask you to tell me if that eclipse which occurred at the death of our Redeemer Jesus Christ was miraculous or natural, for I understand that there are several opinions regarding this.

Author: I very well know that not everyone has the same opinion, however, the most certain and true is that it was miraculous and not natural, as I will prove through the Holy Scripture; and do note that should that Eclipse be natural, necessarily would the Moon have to be in conjunction with the Sun, and this was however not the case, nor could it ever be, for that is against the Holy Scripture; then it was not natural but miraculous, and not only on that day was the Moon not in conjunction and under the Sun, but these were greatly separated and opposed, as is written in Leviticus, Chapter 23, and in Exodus, Chapter 12, where God expressly tells the Hebrews to celebrate Passover at the fourteenth day of the Moon, and it was in this time that the Redeemer of Life celebrated the day before he died, and thus one may gather that the Moon on that day was opposed to the Sun, and as such could not have Eclipsed the Sun, and thus it is proven that that Eclipse was not natural, but rather miraculous. But do note that a natural Eclipse cannot be total nor universal to the whole world; and on the day that Christ died, Saint Luke says, Chapter 22, and Saint Mark, Chapter 14, that the Sun was obscured in such a way as the whole Universe was in darkness, and even Dionysius the Aeropagite, a great Astronomer, being in Egypt, saw such great obscurity in the Sun that it would make it contrary to nature, and he came to say that either the whole world was ending or that the God of Nature was dying, and thus I do not doubt that that Eclipse was supernatural; there is no shortage of learned men who repudiate this truth (as Francis of Asculi[234]) by saying that in those days a Comet called Miles was formed, which placed itself over the Sun on that day in which Christ our Redeemer died on the Cross, and that the Sun was darkened for those three hours which the sacred Evangelists mention for this reason. Also, this opinion is against all reason and natural Philosophy due to the fact that an Eclipse cannot pause nor take the time in darkness as that one took; as also that supposed comet could not have Eclipsed the Sun, for it is commonly considered that Comets are a made of some very pure, subtle and resplendent exhalations; and thus, even if these could place themselves below the Sun, not only would these not Eclipse it, but on the contrary they would cause even more light and splendor. Others have said that Venus and Mercury were the cause of that Eclipse, for they are below the sphere of the Sun, and on that day it so happened that both of them were in conjunction with the Sun, and that this was the cause of that Eclipse.

This opinion does not deserve credit, for none of those Planets, neither alone neither together are enough to Eclipse the Sun, this for two reasons; one is that the Planet Mercury is so small that its body does not have more than an Italian mile, which is the third part of a Portuguese league; and the other is that even if the Planet Venus, which is larger than the Moon, by being so close to the Sun it is impossible for it to Eclipse it; and if the Moon can Eclipse the Sun it is because it is quite distant from it and close to us, and also, since Christ our Lord has died until this day never have we seen or read that these Planets have Eclipsed the Sun, and thus it is concluded that the Eclipse which happened on the death of Christ our Redeemer are miraculous and not natural.

Reader: I assure you that I am most satisfied with all your responses, and thus I thank you for the work that you undertook; and I ask God to grant you graces so as you may further commit to more and greater works. Amen.

---

234. Translator's note: Also referred to as Francis of Marchia, a XIVth century Franciscan Theologian.

TREATISE

BRIEF AND VERY CURIOUS

of the significances and causes of the white and black signs which appear on one's fingernails. With a further notable correction of priceless value and advantage regarding the way of curing wounds that today some people claim to do with wine, olive oil and orisons

On certain occasions it is customary to appear on one's fingernails some white and black signs, and both of these proceed from the four humors that dominate, in different proportions, the human bodies; and these humors are blood, phlegm, cholera and melancholy, which, by being subjected to the influence of the heavenly bodies are altered, augmented and diminished from time to time, causing various and diverse effects, some which are in all bad, and others which aren't at all good. This can be seen in the variety and changes of the four times of the year, for in each of these one of the four humors is dominant; and given that this is the cause, the Holy Mother Church (according to the Saint John of Damascus) has ordered for fasting on the Ember days of the year, institutionalizing the first of these in Spring, so as this fasting may repress the sanguine humor, which in that time is dominant and usually incites mortals to lust and vainglory. The second Ember days are ordered in the beginning of Summer, in order to repress and diminish the choleric humor, which in the second part of the year usually dominates and provokes in men wrath, hate and deceit. The third Ember days are ordered in September, so as to repress in us the melancholic humor, which in this time usually dominates and causes boredom, sadness, illness, greed and even suspicions, desperation and many other things which are of a melancholic nature. Finally in the entry of Winter we fast the last Ember Days so as the phlegmatic humor may be diminished, which is the one that in this time dominates more than the others, causing great laziness and weakness, both spiritual as bodily. In this way, as the said four humors are subjected to the variety and changes in the weather, caused by the diversity of the celestial aspects, and should these be well or badly disposed in our bodies thus will they cause good or bad effects, and among many, they cause the white and black signs which usually appear in one's fingernails, and be warned that the black signs precede and are generated from bad and hot humors, denoting their great malignant and terrible effects which they cause to those who have them, also, aiding in the influence of any bad Planet. The white signs also denote an excess of some humor; however, as these are generated from cold humors they are not as malignant as the black signs, and even if they are under the influence of a bad Planet they do not denote such terrible things. And if any curious may wish to know in which part of the body and finger of one's hand each Planet dominates, I shall say this shortly.

The Planet Venus has natural dominion over the kidneys and in the thumb of a man's hand. The Planet Jupiter dominates the liver and the index finger. The Planet Saturn naturally dominates the arms and the middle finger. The Planet Sun has its dominion in the heart and stomach of man, and in the ring finger. The Planet Mercury directly dominates the spleen and the little finger.

The Planet Moon dominates the head, mainly the brain, and the mount which is between the little finger and the wrist. The Planet Mars has its strength and dominion in the bile and from there corresponds in influences to the middle of the palm, inside the triangle of palm lines. These last two Planets help in the influence of the other Planets on the said signs, some more some less, according to the disposition and aspect which they may have with them, and all of which we have said we subject to the obedience and correction of the Holy Roman Catholic Church.

Following is a notable correction of the method of healing with wine, olive oil and orisons

Natural reason and experience has finally taken note of a marvelous method of curing all and any fresh wounds with wine and olive oil, without the application of words, orisons or by the placing of certain cloths in this or that way, which are all great mistakes and manifest superstitions, for the virtue of closing and healing a wound is not in words or orisons, which are uttered by those who thus cure, neither by placing cloths in a cross as they do, but rather, only wine and olive oil have virtue and natural strength to heal and preserve from all corruption and sores, conserving them always fresh and without any matter until they are sane, as experience shall demonstrate and show to those who wish to experiment. This method of curing new and fresh wounds was taken from the sacrosanct Gospel of Saint Luke, in Chapter 10, in which it is said that a man, coming down from Jerusalem to Jericho, came across some thieves, who not only robbed him but also dealt so many wounds on his body that they left him for dead. And there, the Redeemer of Life says that a Samaritan passed, and seeing that poor man was moved, and he tightened his wound with wine and olive oil; and from this example did some take the cue to cure wounds with wine and olive oil. And as human malice witnessed the cures and rare effects that wine and olive oil could perform, it covered them with holy words and blessed and devout orisons; so as only a few could enjoy such a great and important benefit. And so as this may be made clear and manifest, the virtue and strength to heal new and fresh wounds is only in the wine and olive oil, and not in the words or orisons which are said by those who heal, and note and be warned that never could these heal old and ancient wounds, and these people themselves confess this. And I now say (and I think many will say with me) that if the virtue of healing was in word and orisons, these would heal both new and old wounds; but what we see is the contrary. Then it is most logical that the virtue of healing new and fresh wounds, and of always conserving them fresh and without matter, proceed from the wine and olive oil; and those who make the experiment will be set clear. And some may ask the why of wine and olive oil not being able to heal old wounds, and the answer is very easy; and this is because the virtue of wine and olive oil is not enough to remove any malignity which has deeply rooted itself and combined with fistulas and old wounds; yet, they still have plenty of virtue and efficiency to heal any fresh and new wound, even if it is large and terrible, but also to conserve it fresh and not consenting that any matter be generated in it; as it happens with unguents, which as soon as they are applied to any wound they immediately generate matter and more matter; also by this cause can a wound dilate and not close, and even sometimes it grows old and becomes a fistula; which will never happen with wine and olive oil. I then ask all and every one in particular, that new and fresh wounds be healed with wine and olive oil, for it is most certain that with those two preservative and conservative medicines all new and fresh wounds will be healed much better than they would with the said unguents and with much less harm to the patient. And as we are all mandated to use the quickest, best and easiest remedy for our necessities, as well as for those of our fellow man, I ask and petition once again that the experiment be made, using this method of healing fresh and new wounds with wine and olive oil, for with all brevity and softness will the desired end be reached, which is that of health.

The method which should be used to heal new and fresh wounds with wine and olive oil

Firstly, gather five or six very clean small cloths, of a similar size as the wound, and place some white wine in a vase and put a small amount of water into this, so as the wine is made softer for the wound, which you should wash with a linen cloth with this white wine. After the wound has been cleaned, anoint the surrounding area with a little bit of common olive oil, the one used for food; but before you do this it is a very holy and Christian thing to bless the wound in the name of the Father, the Son and the Holy spirit. Once this is done place the said cloths, made wet with the wine, on the wound in the form of a Cross, or in any other way you may see fit, for it is really not important that you place them in any way, and neither is the number of cloths important (and there is also some superstition in this). And do note that the reason why one uses so many cloths is just because they can soak up more wine and in this way the wound is conserved fresh for a longer time and it won't be able to create any matter.

Greatly necessary secret to repress the blood flow from wounds

Sometimes there is so much blood coming from a wound that many, not having any remedies are immediately finished; and this is not only in wounds, but also from nose bleeds or on the occasion of some bloodletting and also from the natural blood flow of a woman. For to avoid similar dangers, Master Constantino[235] writes, and this is confirmed by Master Pedro Logrero[236] that one should apply powder from roasted frogs on this area, and the blood flow will immediately stop. One of these Masters says that if a woman or man carries these powders with them, in contact with their bodies, they should not fear any blood flow, even if they have one.

Method of preparing the frog powder

Cast any amount of these animals into a new pan, and this should be covered in such a way as no breath may escape from it; place this pan over some living embers until the frogs are completely roasted, an after this grind them and sieve them thinly; and one may use this powder on the above mentioned occasions; and do note that these also have the virtue to close open veins.

Precious unguent to heal any fistula or old wound and other evils

Since we, with the favor of God, have declared all that one needs to know in order to cure new and fresh wounds, it will be good to also say and declare a strange secret of an admirable unguent to heal any fistula or old wound, whose recipe and method of production is as follows:

In a pound of rose oil cast four ounces of rosemary flowers, this in a well covered bowl, which should be placed under the Sun for a month. Once this is done cast some of this oil in a new bowl and place this to heat, and put a generous quantity of good wax into this bowl, so as it be made into a neither very thick nor very liquid unguent. And once the wax is melted and well incorporated, take the bowl from the heat and place it to cool, and should you see that it has become too thick and hard, cast some more oil into it; and should it be too soft, add some more wax to it; and in this way you will have an unguent with which you can cure fistulas and old wounds; but this effect is even better experienced in new and fresh wounds. And note that if one places the above mentioned bowl of oil and flowers into a quantity of horse manure (that should be still warm), and conserves it buried like this for a month, and then makes the unguent from this, it will result in something so perfect and of such virtue that with this you may cure cancer, ringworm and pustules that may grow on the heads of young boys and also mange and any burn. But be warned that in order to heal all of these harms, which are of a lesser nature, one should apply the unguent more dilute and soft, which is what is usually done so as it will stick to the wounds; and in this way, with the virtue of this unguent, and mainly with the aid and favor of God, the mentioned evils will be cured and many more.

---

235. Translator's note: uncertain reference.
236. Translator's note: uncertain reference.

SECRETS WHICH ARE ADDED

TO THIS PRINTING

Secret to remove moths from barley

When barley is attacked by moths one should spray it with some vinegar, or one should close the room where this is kept so as no light comes in, and no matter which one of these secrets you use, they will all die and your barley will be free of that plague.

Secret to make glue

So as no flies will be attracted to the glue one may make, or come to the things where this is applied, one should grind and mix into it some alum, when one is mixing the water and the flour.

Secret in order to free a house from flies and mosquitoes

Take feathers from a Hoopoe and burn them in the house or room where these are, and they will be gone and never return.

Another secret

Take some cumin powder, white wine and a new branch of a vine or any other plant which has green leaves, and having this wet with the said wine and cleaning the walls, doors and windows with it, no mosquitoes will enter.

Another secret

Take some elderberry leaves and cumin, boil these in water, and spray the walls with this mixture and flies will be driven away.

Another curious secret

A curious man asked in a conversation with many other people what thing could a man place in a vase which is already filled with water. All the present made several experiments and could not discover it until the man who asked the question took a portion of ash and filled it. This is a curious thing and very easy to be tested.

Secret to clean, whiten and strengthen one's teeth

Burn goat horns, and by rubbing the teeth with this powder they will be made white and the gums tightened.

Another secret

Cleaning your teeth with pine wood is good, and these will not become weak, but rather tightened.

Another secret

If one rubs his teeth with the root of a walnut tree it will make them clean, white and tightened.

Very curious secret to make virginal milk

Virginal milk is very useful for women who have hot faces and who have a fiery liver and it has the virtue of cleaning wrinkles from the face. And this is the method of making it: take some strong vinegar, in a bowl melt some salt in water, and this should be well melted; mix in a glass or in the palm of your hand some of that salt water and two drops of the vinegar and you will instantaneously see how this is converted into milk.

Secret so as to have a candle that lasts three months

Take four quarts of saltpeter, six quarts of incense, three of sulfur, seven of common olive oil, seven ounces of virgin wax and incorporate all of this and make it into a candle. Place this in a bowl of water and light it.

Secret to make colorful ink

Melt half an ounce of gum Arabic in three ounces of rose water, and in this place some vermilion or some other color.

Secret to make green ink

Take rue juice, verdigris and saffron, everything mixed and ground, and place this in the gum water.

Secret to make blue ink

Take some Prussian blue, also called Berlin, gum water and a little rock sugar, and this needs to be in an infusion in a glass vase.

Secret to make yellow ink

Take saffron and place it in an infusion of gum water and it is done.

Secret to make gold ink without gold

Take orpiment and crystal stone, one ounce of each; grind and mix these as finely as possible over some slab; then mix into these powders five or six egg whites, very well beaten until they look like water; mix everything very well and you can paint and write with this.

Secret to make ink the color of silver without silver

Take one ounce of the finest tin and two of quicksilver; mix these two metals until they become as an unguent, then mix in the gum water; and this can be used to paint.

Secret that the powder masters use in order to make flames of different colors

Camphor, mixed with the composition used in fireworks makes a white and uncolored flame.
Ivory filings make flames with the color of silver, tending to lead.
Greek tar makes a flame the color of bronze.
Black tar makes a dark flame, with a shadow, similar to a thick smoke that obscures all the surroundings.
Sulfur, mixed in moderation makes a blue flame.
Ammonia and verdigris make a green flame.

Powdered amber makes a straw colored flame.

Raw antimony makes a red color, and iron filings and sieved glass make a clear fire with a long tail.

Secret to write on a scroll on which one may erase the letters whenever one wishes

Melt cannon gunpowder in clean water and write with this; when you wish to erase these letters rub them with a cloth and they will immediately disappear.

Secret to make a scroll, or calf, golden

Take some garlic juice and powdered saffron, and this you should pass over the scroll two or three times, and you should let this dry for a while; and when this is dry you should make it hot with your breath and in an instant you should place the gold on this with some cotton and when it is dry it will be burnished.

Secret so as cordovan becomes as new

Take dyer's ink, mixed with lemon juice and rub your cordovan with this bath and it will regain the same luster it used to have.

Secret to make marble golden

Take some Armenian bole, the finest you can find, and mix this with flaxseed or walnut oil, and when you wish to make the operation make sure this is not too strong or too weak.

Secret to make a master's water so as to dye with all colors

Take some roman vitriol, alum, a small mirror, salt ammoniac, two pounds of each, and one pound of vermillion; place all of these in a retort and distill it, carefully saving the water which arises from this operation; when you wish put this dye on anything, drop in some of this water the colored powder, and after this is well mixed you will have what you want; the same can be done with all the other colors, and these will always be kept beautiful and pleasant.

Very curious secret to make a vase which, if drunk from, becomes stuck to the lips; this is a humorous trick

Take two *adarmes*[237] of fish glue, two *adarmes* of gum Arabic and place this in a bowl half filled with glue water and let it boil until it is reduced to half the volume and with this composition you should anoint the vase or glass belonging to the one you wish to trick; in order to unglue this anoint with vinegar or lemon juice.

Secret to cure dog bites

Cucumber leaves, macerated and placed on top of the bite of a rabid dog is of great help. Pliny says that you should mix this with a little wine; and this same mixture is good against the bite of centipedes.

Secret to remove spots from the face and roundworm

Cucumber leaves will clean spots from the face, and macerated and mixed with good honey will heal roundworm.

---

237. Translator's note: and old unit of measure equivalent to 1,79g.

Secret for those who cannot urinate and for those who are broken

Those who cannot urinate should boil some cress seeds in wine or olive oil, and place this on their lower hairs, it greatly purges cholera and makes it come out from below; it also has the virtue of consolidating breakings, mainly in young creatures, and for this one should leave these seeds in milk and give this to drink; and the mothers or wet nurses who are raising them should also eat cress, for this is greatly advantageous to cure whatever breaking they may have.

Secret to write letters that can only be read during the night

Take gall from frogs, rotten willow wood and fish scales, in equal parts, and you should make these into a very subtle powders and make it into a liquid unguent with some egg whites, and with this mixture you may write on a wall or door and this will not be able to be read except at night. And this is due to a kind of natural phosphorous, for any of these things has by itself the ability to shine in the night; surely there will be no shortage of people who know of this public secret, but I was solicited to put it in this recompilation.

OTHER NEW SECRETS

NOW ADDED

Sweet and sour capers

Depending on the base portion, one should follow this recipe until these are covered: one *azumbre*[238] of strong vinegar where you should have mixed half a pound of honey; this should be boiled in a casserole in which one should put three or four cloves or nutmegs, one of these, with a piece of cinnamon and all of this should be macerated and added when the vinegar and honey are boiling; as soon as this is done remove it to a glazed casserole, as it cools one should remove the capers from this broth, and once this is done these should be very well covered, and one may taste them. Should they be too sour then one may add some honey, and if they are too sweet one may add more vinegar.

Secret to remove stains from cloth or silk

Take a small feather, or your own finger if you don't have this, and wet it in some wine spirit and pass this over the stains until these are made wet, but not too much, and after a while you may rub this that these stains will disappear.

Secret to clean spots from mirrors

Take some very well ground and sieved ocher, and after this take a cloth and wet it in some water and in this ocher, and by washing the glass with this and drying it with another cloth it will be made clear and very bright.

Secret to kill Mice

Prepare one plate with flour and another with the same amount of lime, and this needs to be very active, very well ground and sieved, and mix these two together. As the Mice eat this, with

---

238. Translator's note: an old unit of measure equivalent to 2,016 l.

the humidity of their bodies, the lime will be activated and burn their entrails; and if one also places there a bowl of water they will immediately die. This secret is safe and without any danger. There are many other secrets to do this, but these are risky and for this reason I will not write them here, and one should take care that this should be in a place where no Cat or Dog may reach it, for they will die.

Secret so as to write letters on paper that no one will be able to read except he who they are intended for

Firstly write in onion juice, fig tree milk, lemon juice or alum water, and when one wishes to read it, this should be placed over the heat of a fire, and one will see the characters.

Another

White lead untempered with gum placed under the light, and distilled. Any writings done with this liqueur will be occult.

To remove ink stains

Fig tree milk and white lead, by making this into a thin mass and softly passing it over the paper will make it white again.

Curious secret of your own urine

Write on your hand or any other part of your body, after this is dry burn some paper and pass the ashes over what was written that the letters will turn black; this is proven.

Secret

In order to loosen a lock do the following: first dip it in olive oil and have it like this for six or eight days; once this is done take it out and try it, after this place it in very hot water and it will be loose.

Various secrets to have gray hair

Gray hair is like a putrefaction on the head or hair; sometimes this occurs to the young, due to some illness; sometimes from too much sea travel, and once this ceases they once again gain black hair. This happens much more to the lustful, or parents who have children late in life, or to those who have been fed by an old wet nurse.

Secret to dye gray hair

Take some powder of fish gills fried in olive oil and after these are dried mix them with green walnut peels and boil this in rain water. Also good is a Crow's egg beaten in a copper vase, and by anointing your head or eyebrows with this mixture. *Carpaso*[239] juice will also make them black and thick. Also ant eggs mixed with flies and used as an anointment on the eyebrows *nisi levigatum cum aceto illitum*, which means that Crow oil will make the eyebrows black.

Secret in order to warm up various things which may be in a glass vase, be them ointments, oils or other things that might be at hand

---

239. Translator's note: This name can refer to a number of plants, but it is likely the *Cistus psilosepalus*.

Take a bucket of copper or brass and fill it with cold water, and over this place some brown paper and over this paper place the glass vase, and all of this should be put over a fire and without any risk this will heat up, and it may even boil.

Another curious and different method for the same end

Take a clay pot from Alcorcon, not glazed, big or small according to the size of the glass vase; in this clay pot place some very fine sand so as this will be half a finger high, and over this sand place the vase, adding more sand to it so as around the vase one will have three or four fingers of sand; place all of this over a fire and you may heat it as much as you want, be it a lot or a little; and this is a curious and true thing and it costs very little.

Another secret

Take a vase, be it crystal or ordinary, and fill it with water, after this take the peel of an orange and rub the outside of the vase with it; after this you may smell the water and see how it will smell like orange, and sometimes it will even taste like orange.

A game for laughter

Take a hat that should have a soft top, and you should also have a cape on your lap and a mortar hidden in this, and you may say to him that you want to embarrass: I challenge you to break this egg I have here. And this challenge should be accepted as is natural. Place over a table part of the cape and on top of this the egg, and you should take your hat before you put the egg down and show it to all the present, and with great skill of hand place the mortar inside the hat with its mouth down and place this over the egg; and at this point the challenged one will try to break it and fail and severely hurt his hand, and the one who makes this game should once again lift the hat with the mortar, hiding this in his cape and once again show the hat to all.

Another game

Take an egg and place it on a table and say that no one with be able to break that egg with his fist. There should be plenty of people who will take up this challenge. You should then place yourself behind the table and grab it with both hands, and as the man is about to throw his punch, pull the table and he will miss, causing great laughter in all those present.

Another game for laughter

Take a cloth and say to the one you wish to trick: take the tip of this cloth that I will hold the other end. You should be separated by three palms and you should then say: being this close to me, do you think you will be able to punch me when I say so? And the other will surely say yes, and at this point you should walk with this other person to an open door and step outside, closing the door afterwards while still holding on to the cloth, and then you may say: throw that punch now. And he will thus be fooled for he will not be able to do so; and this is a thing of great laughter.

Another game for laughter

Take a common mortar and placing it upside down sit on top of it, now extend your legs and place one foot on top of the other in the following way: one foot will have its heel in contact with the ground and its tip pointing up, and the other placed on top of it in the same conformity. In this position try to put a thread through a needle and it will be a thing of great laughter, for you will fall to one side or the other.

Three birds were in a tree, a man took a rifle and killed one, how many were left? Should anyone respond none because the other two flew away, since one may know of this question, say that two were left.

Very effective remedy to heal wounds in the breasts of women who are breastfeeding and also to cure the pustules and scabs that usually appear to boys and adults on their mouth, lips and nose

Take some old bacon that should not be rancid and macerate it in a mortar mixed with some white lead powder and melt this in some rose water, in such a way as this is made into a mass. Apply it to the breast and conserve it there for twenty four hours and do not feed the creature during this time and you will effectively heal. The same will happen if you apply this unguent to the scabs on the lips, nose or any other part of the body, for it refreshes them and dries them softly and the patient will be readily cured; both remedies are experimented and one may use them without fear of reprisals.

Secret to bend hot iron with your own hands

Take some purslane juice and Bull's gall; once this is done you may anoint your hands and grab any hot iron and bend it without burning yourself; and this has been tried by this Author many times.

LAUS DEO

TREATISE OF THE ANIMALS

OF THE LAND AND SKY

AND THEIR STORIES AND PROPERTIES; SPEAKING
OF EACH OF THE LAND AND THE VIRTUE WHICH IS
MOST AUGMENTED AND MARKED IN THEM WITH THE
AUTHORITY OF THE DOCTORS AND SAINTS

COMPOSED BY
JERÓNIMO CORTEZ, VALENCIANO

The Doctor Domingo Ximeno de Llobera, general inspector of this Archbishopric of Valencia and by the most illustrious sir Friar Don Isidore Aliaga

I, Antonio de Olmedo, Scribe of the chamber of the King our lord and of those who reside in this Council, give testimony that I was shown by these same lords a book entitled History of the Land and Sky Animals with their Properties, that with their license and privilege was printed and charged at three maravedis[240] per folio, containing thirty of these which amount to ninety marevedis; and it is ordered that for this price it may be sold but no more; and this charge should be placed on the cover of each volume of the said book so as one may understand what is asked and charged for it, without this price being allowed to exceed this value in any way. And this should contain the order given by the said lords of the Council of the request made by Angela Rull y de Cortez, widow, wife that she was of Jeronimo Cortez born in the city of Valencia. In this City of Madrid, at the fourteenth of the month of November of sixteen twelve.

Antonio de Olmedo

---

240. Translator's note: an old Spanish coin in circulation between the XIIth and XIXth century.

FROM THE KING

By the part of Angela Rull y de Cortez, widow of Jeronimo Cortez born in the city of Valencia, a request was made that your mentioned husband completed among other works a Treatise of the Land and Sky Animals and their Stories and Properties, which was printed in the same city of Valencia by virtue of a license that had been conceded to him, whose authenticated copy you have presented together with this same book. And given that you have become a widow and poor and with many children to feed you have decided to try to extract the greatest possible benefit from this work so as to remedy your necessity, and you have asked and begged that we give you license to print this book in the kingdoms of Castile for this time; with the prohibition that no others may be served with it.

Regarding this book, our pragmatic diligences over it arrived at the following: it was agreed that we should order that this license be passed by the mentioned reason which we have as just. And as such we give license and right, for the time of four years, which should be fully counted from the day of this our license, that you, or anyone empowered by you and no one else, may print and sell this book which was mentioned above. And by the present license the printers in these Kingdoms you have named may not print this book that our Council has seen, and this should be signed and confirmed by Antonio de Olmedo, our Chamber Scribe, and by one who resides in our Council, so as before it goes on sale you should bring it to them together with the original so as they may determine if this new printing is according to it, or you may bring this in public form to a Corrector nominated by us so as he may analyze and correct this new printing according to the original. And we order the Printer who may print the said book that he does not print its beginning and its first run, nor should he deliver more than one book with the original to the author and person who ordered the printing, nor to any other person for correction before the first book is corrected and taxed by our Council, and in no other way may the first run be printed, and this should immediately be given license, approval, tax and errata, and it may not be sold by you or any other person until this book is in the form we have mentioned, this under penalty of falling under the laws of our Kingdoms that deal with such matters. And we order that during this time no person without your license may print or sell this book, under the penalty that his earnings be lost and also any books, molds and devices related to it that he may have, and he will incur a penalty of fifty thousand maravedis for each time he does otherwise, and one third of this penalty shall revert to our Chamber and the other third to he who denounced him. And we order those of our Council, President and Attendees of our Audiences, Alcaldes,[241] Alguaziles[242] of our house and all Cities and Towns and places of our Kingdoms and lordships, and each of these in their jurisdiction, both those in service as well as those in service in the future, that you keep and follow our grant and favor and do not move against it, nor pass nor contend it under penalty of ten thousand maravedis to revert to our Chamber. This is closed in San Lorenço el Real, at the twenty second of the months of September of sixteen twelve.

I THE KING

By order of the King our Lord
Jorge de Touar

---

241. Translator's note: A traditional Spanish title for a municipal magistrate.
242. Translator's note: A traditional Spanish title used for a number of judicial positions.

ROYAL PRIVILEGE

OF THE CROWN OF ARAGON

Don Philip by the grace of God, King of Castile, Aragon, Leon, of the two Sicilies, Jerusalem, Portugal, Hungary, Dalmatia, Croatia, Navarra, Granada, Toledo, Valencia, Galicia, Mallorca, Seville, Sardinia, Cordoba, Corsica, Murcia, Leon, the Algarves, Algeciras, Gibraltar, of the Canary Islands, of the Western and Eastern Indies, Islands and solid earth of the Ocean, Archduke of Austria, Duke of Burgundy, Brabant, Milan, Athens and Neopatria, Count of Hapsburg, Flanders, Tirol, Barcelona, Roussillon and Cerdanya, Marquis of Oristano and Count of Goceano. By reason of the supplication of Angela Rull y de Cortez, widow of Jeronimo Cortez, which called to our attention the expiration of the ten year license given to the mentioned Jeronimo Cortez, her husband, to print in the Kingdoms of the Crown of Aragon the following books: Practical Arithmetic for all trades; Animals of the Land and Sky; Lunario and perpetual prognosis general and particular for each Kingdom and Province; Physiognomy and various secrets of nature; which were composed with great labor and cunning, and are greatly useful and necessary to the Republic and very well received in it, and that given her poverty she could not have them printed nor extract the benefit from them her husband did, and who also has five children to raise and does not have any other thing in the world but these books and works, we give mercy to prolong the said license for another ten years, and we have this as a just thing, and these ten years should be counted from the day the first license expires. By means of our sure science we deliberately prorogate, extend and amplify to the mentioned Angela Rull y de Cortez our mentioned license of printing the above mentioned books in the Kingdoms of our Crown of Aragon for another ten years which should be counted from the day the first ten are expired, as was said. We prohibit and explicitly ban, according to the same means, that during the time of the present prorogation no other person may print, sell, nor carry prints to other regions of the mentioned Kingdoms except the mentioned Angela Rull y de Cortez, and this may come to a penalty of five hundred gold florins of Aragon[243] and the loss of all molds and books; and this should be divided into three parts, one for our Royal Coffers, another for the mentioned Angela Rull y de Cortez and another for the denouncer; and this with the condition that the books that are printed with this our prerogative be fully in accordance with those that were printed with the first license and approvals recognized by our supreme Council of Aragon. And we order by the same present means of our most certain science and Royal authority that this be followed by all the General Chancellors, Vice-chancellors, Chancellery Regents, trade Regents and General Governors, Alcaldes, Alguaziles, *Vergueros*,[244] Retainers and any other officers and superior Ministers in the mentioned Kingdoms and lordships of the Crown of Aragon, constituted and constituents, and their Lieutenants and Regents of the mentioned trades, and not doing so will incur our wrath and indignation and a penalty of a thousand gold florins of Aragon to be given to our Royal Coffers. The present prorogation, license and prohibition, and all in it contained should be kept, obeyed, guarded and observed by the mentioned Angela Rull y de Cortez without contradiction and this should not be given any room for contentions should our grace be valuable to them, that or our wrath, indignation and the above mentioned penalty. In the City of Madrid, on the eighth of the month of January, year of the birth of our Lord Jesus Christ, sixteen twelve.

I THE KING

V. D. Didacus Clavero Vicechacelor V. D. Montes de Guard. Reg.
V. Ferro Reg. Thesau. Genel. V. Roig. Fis.& Patr. Advoc.
V D. Pji. Tallada Reg. V. Ortiz pro Confer.Gñel.

---

243. Translator's note: An old Aragon coin first minted in the XIVth century.
244. Translator's note: uncertain translation.

PRIVILEGE OF PORTUGAL

I the King announce to those who read this license that I find it good and pleasurable to give Angela Rull y de Cortes, widow of Jeronimo Cortes from the City of Valencia, license to print, by herself or by any person she may empower, for the time of ten years which should be counted from the date of this document, in any of the Kingdoms and lordships in the Crown of Portugal, the book that her mentioned husband composed entitled: on the Properties of the Land and Sky animals, and during the mentioned time of ten years no other person of any state or condition, be it by himself or by empowering of any other one, may print the mentioned book, nor have it printed outside of the mentioned Kingdom, and those who do not follow as such will incur the penalty of paying ten thousand reis[245] for each offense, half of which reverts to he who accused him and the other half to our Vaults, and beyond this they will lose all volumes, molds and whatever other instruments used in the printing of this book that may be found. As such I order all officers of justice and people knowledgeable of this element that what is written here be followed and kept without any doubt or embargo, and this should be printed in the beginning of the mentioned book and it shall act as a license, for its effect lasts more than one year without any embargo to the ordination which determines otherwise. Made by Luis Prego de Avelar, in Madrid, on the thirty first of the month of May of sixteen eleven, written by me, Francisco Nogueira de Betancor.

KING

Francisco Nogueira
By order of the Council

---

245. Translator's note: an old Portuguese coin in circulation between the XVth and XXth century.

TO THE DOCTOR

Domingo Ximeno de Llobera general Visitor of the Archbishopric of Valencia by the most illustrious lord Friar Don Isidoro Aliaga

Carefully thinking in these past days to whom to dedicate this book on the nature of the Land and Sky animals that was composed with great labor by Jeronimo Cortez, my father, after a long study on authors who deal with this topic, being the last that was brought to light after his Practical Arithmetic, his Natural Physiognomy and his Lunario and perpetual prognosis were so well received; I was fortunate to have particular knowledge of the valor, Christendom and letters of your Excellency and the weight and spiritual rule you have over this Archbishopric and the total trust that his Illustrious has in you, which is such a grave and important thing which will surely cause admiration to those who do not know of your Excellency's experience in business, and the satisfaction that you have in treating these, be it those ordered by His Majesty, the offices you have served as also in the government of the City of Saragossa, the times you were a judge in Zalmedina and an ordinary procedure judge, and when it came to the position of Governor of that Kingdom, all placed their eyes on you with general acclamation, and you very much deserved to be proposed to his Majesty for this position with great certainty of reaching a great success, rising even higher than the good memory of the most excellent lord Don Iayme Ximeno de Llobera, your Excellency's uncle, Bishop of Teruel that he was and Viceroy and general Captain of that Kingdom; all these things were deserved by your Excellency as these are well known and proper of a Prelate who the whole world knows is meant to do great things since he took the main positions of his most illustrious Religion as Bishop of Albarracin and Tortosa, as those churches publicize, ignoring you and making you a much lesser service than deserved, for these have a holy envy of Valencia for having taken you from them. With these premises, without mentioning other such things from my part, solely based on the fact that your grace knows much better than all others the will and spirit I have in serving you, I have determined to dedicate this small work to you (even if for me this is a great work and of great esteem by the respect I owe to my father, and by having had weighed on him so much). I beg that you receive it under your protection and may you favor it in an explicit way, that may the hope of your grace accepting it be certain, for never before did I have the daring of having offered it to you, and in this way I see it better to fulfill my desires. My God keep you your Excellency, in Valencia, 20th of December of 1612

Bartholome Cortez

APPROVAL OF THE DOCTOR

Juan Bautista Ballester, Archdeacon of Murviedro, Evaluator and Ordinary Judge of the Holy Office of the Inquisition, Professor and Examiner of Theology and Synod member, etc.

By order of the greatly revered Sir Don Thomàs Martinez Rubio, Dean of Teruel, Officer and General Vicar and Governor of this Archbishopric, is this Book on the History of land and sky Animals and their properties reviewed; and being this a matter which usually demands great volumes to be filled with such hard matters, in this book are the most selected things compiled, so as they may be a field for the curiosity, learning and a document of vitality; and due to this do I judge that one may offer license that this book may be printed a third time, seeing as it has nothing which is against our Holy Faith and good customs. Thus are my feelings now and continuously, etc. Valencia, 18th of December of 1669.
    Doct. Juan Bautista Ballester.

Imprimatur   Imprimatur
Martinez   *Gilirt.F.A.*
Off.V.G.

FIRST PART

OF THE LAND ANIMALS

Chapter I

Of the Lion and its Excellences

Among the Learned and Natural Philosophers there is the question of which among the crude land Animals is the greatest and most principal; for some say that one should give the advantage to the Elephant, and that this deserves to be king and master of the Animals, for it among all of them is capable of discipline, and it is the most calm and discreet, and also the largest and most respected among the brute Animals (even if the Lion is more feared); and this Animal is of such a natural gravity and sense that any offense, be it in deeds or words, given to it, it receives it with such notable harm and feeling that it may even become sick over it; and equally, it also knows and recognizes all courtesy and respect which is given to it and it reciprocates with notable appreciation to those who respect it. And regarding strength, power, valor and effort, none of the brute Animals is greater than it, nor can these even come close regarding the weight, load and work it can take on; and these are things which belong and are the business of a King and Captain, so as he may govern his subjects. Regarding discretion, prudence, spirit and strength, it is said (as will be shown below) that no one has the advantage over it, and thus it is given the lordship and rule over all Animals.

Others say (and these to me seem to be on the side of reason) that above all land Animals, the one that should take the prime place and advantage among them is the Lion, this by the royal, magnificent and natural conditions that it has, as well as for that reason that nature, and its Creator, seem to have wanted to mark the Lion as the supreme King of all land Animals for it was endowed with royal temper, strength, generosity and great respect, and it was further given a crown of its own hair so as to be made the king that it is, and this is the proper and natural insignia of the King. Furthermore it was armed with strong teeth and ferocity of face, so as all other Animals may be remitted and respectful; with sharp and powerful claws so as it may beat and prostrate its enemies and rivals; with a will and bravery in its heart so as not to fear anything nor have difficulty in imposing upon those that might rebel and disrespect it; it has such valor and strength in its arms (where it is said that it has all its strength) so as to be able to fight and beat all and any Animals, even if greater in their size than it; lightness and dexterity in all its body so as to be diligent in any work. Finally it was imbued with nobility and generosity in its condition so as all could surrender and subject themselves, for it is a most certain and verified thing that any Animal is made to subject itself only by the Lion's benign and merciful stare, without causing it any harm in any way. And thus do I, without any damage to any other Animal, give to the Lion the prime position and advantage over all the land Animals, having the solemn charge and lordship over them; and for this reason does it seem to be right to begin this present history by the mentioned strong Lion.

Natural conditions of the Lion

The Lion has a most hot nature, by which it normally has a great desire for coitus, and this is even truer of its female. It is an Animal of a bold, frank, strong and noble condition; it is generous and haughty of heart, with recognized will and intensity; it does not fear adverse confrontation with any, for it feels itself superior to all Animals. It sleeps with its eyes open, and the Natural Philosophers say that if it by accident it sleeps on a ship then it will be in danger of drowning. When it urinates it raises its leg like a dog, it has five fingers on its hands and four on its feet, as a wolf and a dog. It has curved claws, very solid bones, in such a way as these are entirely like inner cores. Arnaldus says of this Animal, Chapter 7, that should you break a Lion's bone with steel you will be able to produce fire from it. And when it is walking, it erases its footsteps with its tail, and in this way hunters cannot follow or chase its steps. And Isidore says that the Lion has great virtue and strength in its chest, firmness in its head, and its will can be found on its forehead and tail; and its esteem is such that even if it is being chased by hunters it will not flee, but rather it will always turn to face those who follow it. And if it happens that it needs to go down some slope or up a hill, in such a way as it cannot see those who chase it, it will do this very quickly, so as not to lose its honor and reputation of not fleeing, this because it will not be seen during this period. It is most generous with those that subject themselves to it (as was mentioned) and the Natural Philosophers say that it will show its nobility to a greater extent to children and women than with men and other Animals; and this is in such a way that should it run into any child, not only will it not harm him, but even caress him with its tail.

Solinus, Pliny and Aristotle write that the first time a Lioness gives birth it will have a litter of five; the second time it will have four; the third three; the fourth two on the fifth it will only give birth to one, and in this way is it concluded and no more will it conceive. Isidore, the great Philosopher, writes that its pups are born as if dead, being in this state for three days, and this they say is due to their natural extreme hotness, and their parents will not cease giving out great roars and shouts in their ears, and after the three days they awake and are revived, as if awakening from a heavy and deep dream. And it is also true that the Lion is wild and fierce, and all land Animals respect, fear and recognize its superiority and advantage, but even with all of this, the Natural Philosophers say that it will flee in a great hurry in the presence and sight of a Rooster, and even more if this is white or painted white; and not only does it fear its mere sight but it will be made to tremble by its singing alone. This is surely a thing worthy of admiration and wonder, to see such a fierce Animal, so presumptuous, brave and strong that trembles and runs from the presence of a Rooster and its singing, which is such a small Animal, with such meager strength and pleasant to the sight; surely there must be some natural virtue and hidden property in the Rooster by which it can cause this dread in the bravest and strongest of Animals. Some Learned men, and among them Pero Lucrecio[246] Poet, have said that the Rooster's feathers have a certain property that causes great pain and disturbance to the sight of the Lion, and that it, not being able to bear such feathers, runs from their presence, but I however would say (*illorum pace*) that if it not only runs from this presence but also from its singing, then the virtue and strength of this effect must not be in the feathers alone, nor in some exterior quality of the Rooster, but rather from a superior cause and celestial influence. And one should note that the ruling Planet of these Animals, the Lion and the Rooster, is the Sun, infusing in them its royal and magnificent nature; and even if the Rooster is small and of little strength, it participates much more than the Lion in the influence and nature of the Sun; and from this does it arise that the one with the greatest quantity of strength respects and fears that with the smallest strength and body, by reason of this greater virtue of celestial participation, which for us seems as something hidden but for the Lion is most natural and manifest. From what was said one can gather that, should any one find himself confronted with a Lion, it is a most convenient and right thing to use a Rooster, carrying one with them, for this fearsome Animal will sooner run than be in the presence of Rooster; but below we will give an even better and easier remedy. The Lion is of such haughtiness that it will not eat any game left over from the previous day. And one should note that when a Lion wishes to hunt it will give out two or three terrible roars, by which it will cast fear into all Animals, leaving them surrendered, fearful and half dead, and thus he may hunt them without fatigue, and this also allows those others which may have more spirit about them to run and it will chase and catch them to cure its hunger. This Animal does mind a great deal if the Lioness which is close to it mates with some other Lion; and, should this happen it will recognize this by its sense of smell and punish her most cruelly. In this way it also has a very wide, sharp and penetrating sight.

Aelianus[247] writes that when a Lion is old and can no longer run or catch its prey, the younger and more robust ones will kill for it and either guide it to the dead Animal or bring it its meal; it has such great memory that should anyone ever harm it, even if many years may have passed, it will recognize this person and it will seek revenge, and in the same way is it greatly appreciative and thankful to those who did it some good and have pleased it, as may be seen in the discourse of its stories. One should note that the Lion, according to Avicenna, will first move its right hand and foot, and only then the left, as the Camel.

Stories of the Lion and of its gratitude

Being the Lion so fierce, cruel and brave against those who resist and oppose it, it is still extremely generous and thankful, in such a way as it will never forget anyone from whom it might have ever received a particular benefit; and to him who has done so it will always serve, pay and thank on any occasion that might come up; as one may see in the examples given below taken from trustworthy Authors.

The Lion is so furious when it is chasing some Animal, hare or rabbit to eat, that it does not take notice of any bush or wood, and as such it will run into such bushes and trees when it is chasing its prey; and it is common that some splinter or thorn will get stuck in one of its feet or hands, as these are so meaty, soft and large; and God Our Lord has given it such a natural instinct

---

246. Translator's note: uncertain reference.
247. Translator's note: Claudius Aelianus, a roman author of the second and third century, writer of *De Natura Animalium*.

that it knows and understands that only man can extract this thorn and end its pain; and thus they call to him with moaning and friendly and sad complaints.

Pliny writes in his *Natural History*, Book 8, that a man named Elpis, disembarking in Africa and going on his way to a village, saw a fearful growling Lion come in his direction; filled with dread he climbed a tree, and the Lion, approaching this tree, lifted its hand to him many times, in which it had a stick pierced across it, and it gave away many saddening and painful grunts, as if wanting to say: "Have mercy on me." Elpis, losing his fear and moved by pity, came down and took out the thorn from the Lion's paw, and, curing the wound with some wine he carried, made a band aid with a cloth; and this Lion was so thankful that every day it would bring a piece of game to the ship so as to offer it to Elpis and his companions.

In the story and life of the Doctor of the Church Saint Gerome, one may read that this same thing happened to this saint, that, while in the desert, a Lion came to him with a thorn in its paw, and the Saint removed this and healed the wound; and this Lion, in recognition of this good deed, was never parted from the Religious House in which the Blessed Saint lived, and it always accompanied a certain Jenny in gathering wood for the said House. One day it happened that the Lion was somewhat unvigilant, and separated from the said Jenny, and some travelers passed by and seeing the Jenny alone took it; and the Lion, not being able to find its Jenny, did not want to return to the House of the saint without her, and thus it went away and returned to the desert. After a few days and a few months, those who took the Jenny returned to those lands once again, and this time they took a different road, which, for their inconvenience lead them straight into the hands of the Lion, the custodian and guardian of the Jenny; and as the Lion recognized the Jenny, it immediately rushed against the travelers, making them run; and taking the Jenny by its halter with its teeth, guided it back to the House and Monastery of the Glorious Father Saint Gerome, persevering its usually fidelity and guardianship, without ever going one step away from its dear Jenny.

Of another Lion we may read in the Conquest of the Holy Land, in the time of Godefroy de Bouillon; a knight called Golfredo de Torres, roaming the Province of Judea, saw by chance a fight between a Lion and a fierce and amazing Serpent, which had gripped the said Lion and had it so tightly squished that the knight thought that it was defeated and would surely die; as such he felt pity for the Lion, taking on the Serpent himself and killing it. The King of the Land Animals, upon finding itself free, was so thankful to the knight for his benefit and help that it never again parted from his side, and in this way he saved him from many dangers and combats he had in that campaign of the Conquest of the Holy Land, keeping danger at bay and always keeping an eye out for him; and its affection was such that when this knight was dining it would always lay at his feet, and it slept at the side of his bed, and it would not allow him to leave his home alone. It came to happen that Golfredo, needing to travel and not wanting, and also not being allowed to take the Lion on the ship, left it on the shore; and the sad Lion, seeing Golfredo leaving him and not being allowed inside the ship, jumped into the water so as to follow him; and not being able to fight against the waves of the sea was drowned, without anyone being able to save it.

Aelianus writes in the Book of *Animalium*, this rare case of a Lion, which Aulus Gellius[248] relates of Apion[249] the Greek. The case was that, as in Rome some solemn festivities were taking place, in order to celebrate this more completely it was custom to fill a very well walled avenue called the Coliseum with many beasts, such as Lions, Tigers, Bears and Bulls, and in this place there were also men who had been condemned to death and rebellious slaves; and if these, fighting these beasts would beat them, they would be allowed to walk away with their lives, having given proof that they were free and frank. It so happened that one time one of these men was the slave of an African Consul, called Androclus, and among the beasts there was a great and fierce Lion which was brought from Africa, and for being so great and of such terrible aspect, all had their eye on it, watching and waiting for the moment when it would charge the slave and tear him

---

248. Translator's note: a second century author famous for his *Attic Nights*.
249. Translator's note: a first century Greek author who first documented the common folktale of "Androclus and the Lion". All his works have been lost, but the folktale in question was preserved by the above mentioned Aulus Gellius.

apart. The Lion looked at the slave for a long time, and after having looked well upon him started walking towards the said man who was awaiting death, and as all watched the Lion came closer without bursting out into fury, as all others had done before, they were in a great suspense; and the Lion approached the man as if very tame and very gentle, licking the hands and feet of the slave Androclus, to the great surprise of all attending, but even more to this slave. Seeing himself the target of the Lion's affections, he recovered his spirit and strength and also started to pet the Lion dearly; and being both so embraced he recognized it from a particular case which had happened in Africa (that we will explain); the Roman Emperor, seeing such a remarkable case, called for the slave and asked him to explain the cause for that Lion to have such great respect and courtesy. The slave Androclus then declared and said that in Africa, while serving his master on a certain occasion, he wandered from his usual path, and entering into the desert saw a Lion coming towards him, and for fear of death took refuge in a cave nearby, with the Lion following him with a limp and also bleeding from its foot where it had a thorn; and it approached the slave very gently, showing its foot and moaning with great sentiment and pain. Androclus, losing his fear and moved by compassion, took its foot and took out the thorn, healing and tending to the wound as best as he could; and the Lion, feeling relived from its suffering, took shelter with the slave for a long time; and as Androclus was in that place for a few days, the Lion would greet him with fresh game every day, which he was forced to eat over his great hunger, and this life lasted for him for three months; and not being able to stay he returned to his master the Consul, who, when coming to Rome gave him up to that circus of Beasts where he found the same Lion to which he had given that service and good deed in Africa, and recognizing him it did not want to do him any harm, as was clearly seen. The Emperor upon hearing the case ordered that Androclus be set free and that the Lion be given as a slave of the slave, now a free man; and no matter where Androclus went, the Lion would follow with remarkable obedience and respect, as if it had reason and senses like a man. And how much is piety worth for the brute Animals, when towards men it is worth so little, that it is so rare to see any man show any gratefulness for any good deed which is done upon him.

Of Alexander's wars there are two stories and notable cases of Lions, and this is mentioned by Plutarch in the story of his life. The first was that Alexander, over some disappointment that was given to him by a knight called Lysimachus, ordered that he be given to a wild and fierce Lion, so as it would tear him to pieces; and Lysimachus, arming his right arm in secret with an iron plate with steel thorns, upon seeing the Lion charging awaited for it with great spirit, and as it rushed to him with his mouth open he pushed his arm into it and the Lion could not make prey of him over the armor, and as such Lysimachus grabbed it by the throat; and even if the Lion with its claws greatly injured Lysimachus, bringing him close to the point of death, the brave soldier never released it, and the Lion found itself defeated and suffocated, and Lysimachus free from all danger. Alexander seeing the spirit and effort of Lysimachus, not only ordered the wounds he received to be healed, but also, from that day on, he kept him as a close friend. And after this case we find an even more remarkable one, and this was that a Philosopher called Callisthenes, visiting Lysimachus while he was recovering, said to him these words: Lysimachus should you have studied you would surely have reached this rare secret that I know of so as to be free from the fury of any Lion, this with much less work and danger than the one you went through! And even if Lysimachus constantly asked for this secret with great insistence, the Philosopher did not give it to him. It so happened that after Lysimachus was healed from his wounds, and having a close friendship with Alexander, he told him of what the Philosopher had said about this notable secret to be free from Lions without any weapon or danger, and that even if he greatly asked to be taught this, it was not at all possible. Alexander upon hearing this gained a great desire to also know this secret, and he asked Lysimachus to procure it from the Philosopher in such a way as he would know that it was Alexander who asked him this. Lysimachus, through every means possible tried to learn this secret from the Philosopher and still this was to no avail; and so he returned to Alexander and told him of what had happened; Alexander, enraged, ordered the Philosopher to be thrown into a cage of Dogs, which are naturally envious, so as they would treat him as such over his envy of this secret; Lysimachus however, wanting to know this secret, asked the King that the Philosopher be put in a cage of Lions instead, so as in that way he could use of this secret and the King might see it; and this was with the added condition that should the Philosopher live, then he should be forgiven, and otherwise the claws of the Lions would be his payment. This seemed well to the King and he immediately ordered him locked in the Lions' cage without any weapon and that the Lions not be fed for three days. The Philosopher went into the cage with bread and water for three days and also with three very large wax torches, and he walked into that cage where there were five Lions, and placing himself in a corner of this cage with one of the torches lit in front of him, the Lions were so frightened by the light emanating from it that they never dared come close to the Philosopher, nor move from their spot, even if they were enraged by hunger; and over this was the Philosopher set free and Alexander satisfied with the experimented secret under Lysimachus' advice; making this very useful secret public. In such a way are Lions so fearful and terrified of fire which is lit near to their eyes that, should they have room to escape, they will run endlessly without ever stopping, and should they not be able to do so they will cower in a corner trembling, without daring to come close to the person carrying this flame; and this is due to not only them having a very sharp and delicate sight, but also because they naturally fear fire. And this should be more than enough for me to move on to the other Animals that are still to come, and those wanting to read more stories of Lions should read, Aulus Gellius, Aristotle, Pliny, Solinus and Plutarch in his book of Animals, where there are many cases such as these about Lions.

Natural properties of the Lion

Lion skin, according to Aesculapius, applied to hemorrhoids, or even if one just sits over this in such a way as this skin is in contact with these wounds, will reduce and dry them.

He further writes that should one anoint the loins, or the area around these, with Lion fat, he does not need to fear Wolves or any other wild beast; for this smell causes in them a great fright, and they can sense this from a great distance and they will be made to run without stopping.

Avicenna writes that the fat of a Lion will very quickly heal the hardness of any aposteme.

Pliny says that the fat of a Lion, mixed with rose oil, can make a woman's face very beautiful, and this will not acquire any spots; but these will rather be made clear and this will also blemish any sunburns.

Dioscorides writes that the said fat, or this fat mixed with wine, once drunk, will counteract any venom and remove the strength from any poison, from whose scent and strength, it is said, all venomous Animals flee, but particularly serpents.

The bile of a Lion, so says Pliny, mixed with rose water and placed over the eyes will make the sight clearer and sharper.

Pliny writes that a dried and powdered Lion's heart, drunk with wine, cures the quartan and tertian fevers, and this should be taken during the fever's decrease or increase.

Hali brags of Lion's fat in that it reduces and resolves any hardness and swelling.

Isaac writes that Lion meat, which is most hot, heavy, thick and hard to digest, causing pain and stomach torsions to those who it eat, is nonetheless marvelous for those who suffer from imaginations, ghosts and illusions; and it heals any ear pain, this by dropping two of three drops of juice from this meat into them.

The Lion, by natural instinct, knows from one year to the next if there will be an abundance or lack of supplies; and should it realize that there will be a lack, it will move from one region to another, and when this is not the case it will not move.

Of strength and its excellences, by occasion of the Lion

We have mentioned the Lion, and noted the many virtues and natural excellences which to me seem to be championed by this Animal, and of these, those of greater splendor are its strength and thankfulness; and in this way we will say something of these two virtues with the authority of Saintly and grave Authors.

Strength, says Aristotle, is located in the bones and nerves.

Strength is lacking where reason is also lacking, and this is justified by Plutarch.

Strength is a virtue whose purpose is to always fight for that which is just. Cicero.

Strength does not have necessity for rage. Plutarch.

Strength does not face danger without an honest and just cause, for in this way it would be more madness than spirit and effort. Lactantius.[250]

Saint Ambrose says that death is always close to the spirited and effortful, and of this truth we have many and great examples in the divine and human letters; and these I will not mention more than two, so as not to delay this work.

This first is the effort of Samson, by whose strength, spirit and bravery suffered all the labors we know of, that he was forced to work a millstone as a Donkey, blind; and in the end he died by his great strength, ending his own life and that of thousands of Philistines in one swoop by embracing the column of the Temple and casting them to the ground; even if there was a great mystery to all this, etc.

The other example is reported by Valerius Maximus[251] of an Italian which was so given to effort that he did not hesitate in applying himself to anything which required strength; and it so happened that seeing on a mount an oak tree, which had two extremely strong branches, by whose weight the tree had almost broken apart, this Italian took the opportunity to prove his strength once again, deciding to finish the job and break the tree; he took his hands and with his great strength opened the tree a little more, but once again the tree returned to its original state and his hands were thus stuck and he could no longer escape and he died in that place, without anyone being able to rescue him.

Strength without direction is always dangerous; and if accompanied by prudence one will always achieve victory over that which he may undertake. Stobaeus.[252]

Saint Gregory says that strength is preserved and augmented with prudence.

A man who kills his enemies by treachery cannot be called strong. Euripides.

The strength of necessity is greater than the strength of men. Titus Livy.

Strength is always lacking where there is a lack of reason and justice. Plutarch.

Saint Chrysostom says that there is no greater strength than being a man of the earth and earning Heaven.

Of thankfulness and its benefits

Thankfulness is to not underestimate a good deed which is received, nor to forget it.

Saint Bernard says that he who does not give thanks to God over everything he has, more than being unappreciative, is nothing but a thief.

The thanking of a good deed is never too late, should there have not been negligence nor occasion to do the thanking. Cicero.

A good deed deserves double the thanking if it is done without any thought of payment. Common saying.

The ungrateful deserve to be counted with the unjust and the thankful with the just. Stobaeus.

He who does not thank does not receive satisfaction. Seneca.

A belated thanking is ungrateful; but that which is given readily, or when the occasion presents itself, is a great recognition. Ausonius.[253]

The earth does not generate a worse thing than an ingrate, and it does not produce anything better that a thankful person. Common saying.

---

250. Translator's note: Lucius Caecilius Firmianus Lactantius, an early Christian author, adviser to Emperor Constantine I.

251. Translator's note: A Latin writer of the first century, author of the *Facta et dicta memorabilia*.

252. Translator's note: Joannes Stobaeus, a fifth century writer of a compilation of Greek authors.

253. Translator's note: Decimus Magnus Ausonius, a Latin poet and master of rhetoric from the IVth century.

A thankful person is the cause for a do-gooder to be spirited and do more good; and the opposite kills the joy of acting thus and it changes his character. Seneca.

Saint Bernard says that being thankful is the cause and source of piety to increase towards a man, and an unthankful man not only causes the source of piety to dry towards him, but also that of mercy and the stream of grace.

Any thankful man is shameful; and an unthankful man is not only shameless but he also keeps an open door to all vice. Stobaeus.

Saint Augustine says that to God one must always give grace, even if he never answers our pleas. Regarding this I know of a Hermit who was doing penitence for many years, and he was constantly giving many graces to his Creator for all he had received from his hands; and it happened that one day a dark Angel disguised as an Angel of light appeared to him and said: Why do you torment yourself so, giving so many graces, if you are marked and condemned for Hell. And this Hermit was disturbed, thinking this to truly be an Angel of light, and responded to him: Angel of God, even if I am to end in Hell, that is not a reason for me to stop giving graces to my Creator for all that I have received from him. And as soon as he said these words this evil Angel left, and he became so worthy that God sent a good Angel to console and strengthen him, for thanking God is a powerful thing. And this truth can be seen in the beginning of the world, with those first men who were born from our mother Eve, who were Cain and Abel, brothers; and as the Divine Majesty gave so many graces to the just Abel, for he was so thankful that he offered as sacrifice to the Lord the best of the fields and his cattle, He took him by the hand and he died a Saint. And contrarily, Cain had God drop his hand and condemn him, for he was greatly unthankful to his Creator, to whom he gave the worst of the fields as sacrifice.

So plead to the Divine Majesty that we may be always thankful to God, above all, and afterwards to those who do us good. Amen.

Chapter II

Of the Donkey and its great Excellences

Nature and complexion of the Donkey

The Nature of this Animal is in everything contrary to that of the Lion, which is hot and dry, and the Donkey is cold and humid; the Lion is brave, fierce and wild, and this one is simple, benign and humble; the Lion is impulsive, ready and vengeful and this one is calm, late and long-suffering; the Lion is light, voracious and impatient, and this one is heavy, temperate and very patient; finally the Lion is strong and daring; and the Donkey is weak and contrite.

Aristotle, in *de Animalibus*, writes that any Animal with a heart which is smaller than its natural body requires will be very spirited; and those who have it larger than their bodies require will be very fearful. And because the Lion has it smaller relative to its body, and also because of its great heat, it is daring and furious. On the contrary, the Donkey is very fearful, for it has a heart larger than the proportion that its body requires, and also because it is of a cold complexion. And in this way the Lion fears heat and the Donkey fears the cold.

Verses and privilege of the Donkey

When to the Chaos of this world
The sacred Omnipotence
Gave to it being with its being,
By which things are made
It ordered the easy Air
To create Birds and that among them

Some would be marked
In virtue and preeminence
Such as the Eagle
The Phoenix, Saker and Stork
And other birds whose graces
I do not say for they are immense.
It also ordered that Fire,
Which it enclosed in the fourth sphere
Give to the Sun its rays,
So as to heat us with its strength.
To Water that it produced
The innumerable amount
Of fish which in its interior
Inhabit and feed;
And that this reveal
Such strange greatness,
As the *Caimanvaste*,[254]
And the voracious Whale,
The treacherous Crocodile,
That cries with caution,
With that sweet singing
Of the tricky mermaid.
And as the most beautiful
Made it so Mother Earth,
After producing the plants
It also sustains the beasts,
Giving bravery to the Lion,
Cowardice to the Panther,
Lightness of the Dromedary
Strength to the Elephant;
And among those
Wise Nature chose one
That in the service of men
Is greater than all
Giving it virtues,
Graces and excellences,
Of Strength and skill,
Availability and patience.
It is most friendly to man,
And peaceful to all beasts,
Helpful in the Cities,
And esteemed in the Villages.
This Prince is the Donkey,
And may the Reader forgive me,
For Christ did praise it,
As well as his true mother;
And this do I mean to praise
If you give me some time.
And after having created
The divine providence
Man in its likeness
And Heaven as his inheritance.

---

254. Translator's note: uncertain translation.

And as soon as from Paradise
It casted out his disobedience
Our first Father
And our first Mother.
From this Animal they took the help,
As Heliodorus[255] tell it,
So as to pass through the labor
Of exile and penitence.
The greatest powers
Which featured in the old Law,
On Donkeys traveled
With rich mantels.
From the second of Kings
We know that Abraham was a famous Patriarch
Rich in honor and possessions;
And he when of his son
Was to make a bloody oblation,
He took a Donkey, and he was witness
Of its great faith and obedience,
This Text also mentions
That when beautiful Abigail
Went to marry David,
On a donkey she was riding.
And the rich Shulamite,
Who for some time hosted the Prophet
Known due to his cloth
As Steven over the rocks,
On a Donkey went seeking
A Man for his dear daughter
From the Kingdom of death
To life he returned.
King Saul of Israel,
Before the Populace anointed him
The Donkeys of the King his father
He gathered from the field.
And his children being Kings
Always to the greatest feasts
On Donkeys did they ride,
As Misibosete tells us,
Of this same Misibosete,
Son of the King of Judea,
In that Royal History,
The Sacred Letters says,
That when with King David
Went to calm a certain war,
On two Donkeys did the two go,
And not on Horses or Mares
And the People of God
Needed these so many times,
It was without a doubt
For greater honor and greatness.
The same with the Gentiles,

---

255. Translator's note: uncertain reference due to excessive options.

As Nason[256] tells us.
That on Donkeys did the Gods ride
To give punishment and penalties
To the furious Giants,
That putting strength against strength
Wanted to climb up to Heaven,
And run over the Planets,
And one only needs to know
That it is more than perfect
This Beast, for triumphant
Was Jesus Christ seen on it,
And this was the day he made
To his Eternal Majesty
The entry into Jerusalem,
With such joy and festivity.
And when that Lady
Gave birth, remaining Damsel
In Egypt it was with a Donkey,
Being the Queen of the centuries.
The Donkey on which Balaam roamed
God wanted that to him an Angel appear
Before the blind Prophet,
And this even he could see.
Saint Augustine claims,
That of our Mother Church,
Its new figure was a Donkey,
As it was the Donkey that of the old.
The first to plow the fields
Was Noah, and this is an old thing,
That it was with a Donkey and an Ox,
That he opened the earth.
Aristotle and Pliny,
And Varro do advise us,
Of the virtues of this Animal,
Its properties and preeminence.
The Philosopher Apuleius
Is not affronted nor unappreciated
Of being a Donkey he wrote
Of being transformed into its Efficiency;
And being worthy of a heroic book,
That in all of Libya and Media
The Golden Ass was called
Over its sharp sentences.
Job was greatly wealthy,
And his greatest possessions were
To have Donkeys, and it is known
That they were more than five hundred.
And the Famous Romans,
As merchandise and stock,
They had the dealing of Donkeys,
As Marcus Varro tell us.
It is also said that one made

---

256. Translator's note: uncertain reference.

In these times a sale
Of a Donkey which was worth
More than three thousand coins.
Besides this the Donkey also has
So many secret virtues
In its body that this is reason
That it be held in high esteem.
Dioscorides warns us,
That if a sick man has for lunch
Its liver he will heal
Of *gota coral* and leprosy
And in the same chapter
Says that powder from broken
Nails, to those that drink this
Will reach a certain health
It is also said, that powder
From the front legs
Will heal scrofula
If you mix these with vinegar.
Pliny writes that the milk
Of a Jenny, drunk is good
For poison and venom,
And to free one from pestilence;
And mixed with honey
Cures dysentery;
And placed with nail powder
It heals blindness.
Another greater property,
Is that among all beasts
Only the Donkey and the Dove
Do not have any gall.
Some other examples
Of its praise do I have,
But so as not to bore
With my Donkey I'll speak.
It seems as it is said
That some with a serene face,
Have in the Donkey their kin,
For there are those who have disgust of it
To those I say and respond,
That there isn't a thing that moves me
More than speaking of the virtues
That in this Animal are kept.
Of all we have raised
We see that the Donkey is used
Better than all other Animals,
And not counting its price
The Donkey alone can make
The trade of all other beasts,
For it can sow like an Ox,
Carry loads like a beast of burden
Run like a horse,
No trade does it discard

For it serves in Atahona,
For the uses of war;
To stop one only says "xo"
And it is worth more than thirty reins;
To make it walk one "arre"
And it is worth more than twenty spurs
No Animal is more valiant
Than a Donkey that is sure,
Place a Donkey and a Lion
And the Lion will be killed.
And even Plutarch claims
That he saw Tigers killed
By Donkeys and even more can be seen
In the Canary Islands.
And not only alive
Has the Donkey its strength
For Samson with its jaw
Killed the Philistine people;
About ten times one hundred,
Did he throw to the earth,
With the jaw bone of an Ass,
In a single battle.
This Animal is the one that gave
The five vocal letters
For every time it heehaws
A, è, ì, ò, ù it gives us.
The Roman Monarchy
Drew in its Flags
In order to denote silence
The Donkey's ears;
The Persians a white skin
Of a Sheep;
Assyrians the skin of a Wolf;
Of the Minotaur the Greeks.
But the Arabs and Egyptians, as Ptolemy tells us,
Placed the skin of a Donkey,
For they wanted silence.
This I ask of the Reader,
That he read with patience
These things of the Donkey
Printed in Valencia,

Curious question

Of a great marvel
For being so proven.
I ask to the discreet man,
If he can reach it;
Say, from where and from which part,
In which Climate or at what distance
In which season and in which weather,
Or in which celebration
Did a Donkey sing with its voice

With certainty and such strength
That all in the world heard it
All without exception?

Answer

In Noah's Ark
Do I feel the answer,
To this question
And new tale.

Of the advantages of the Donkey, of the great favor and privileges that from its Creator and Our Lord it has received

Among the Animals of little respect and those that are held in less consideration by men, is, in my opinion, the Donkey, given its bad disposition, as it seems, and by the simplicity that it professes; for it seems to me that no one in the World offers respect to those who are not respected, nor care for those who are not cared for, nor makes an effort for those that one doesn't need; rather it seems that simplicity and humility are most boring things, and that pride and severity are enthroned, respected and loved, and for this cause is this Animal held in little regard by many, and by most as an extreme bore. And I don't know what other Animal, which serves man has received more privileges and favors from its Creator, nor which is more useful and helpful, nor which one is more subjected to the obedience of man than the Donkey, for to all which is done unto it does it subject itself, for should one want it to sow it sows; should one want it to carry a load it will carry it; and should one want it to walk it will walk without any need of spurs to do so, nor does it need a spur to make it serve, nor a bridle so as it will stop; for it is most obedient. And this Animal is so patient and accommodating that it makes no difference in the works or chores which might be given to it like it is with other Animals; for some are good for one job and others for another job; some need bridles and other don't; some admit to a saddle and other don't and some can use an *albarda* and other can't even bear to see it; only the Donkey does subject itself to everything, without carrying about bridles, halters or saddles. Besides obedient this Donkey is also very contrite and silent, for it does not moo like the Ox, nor like the Mule, nor does it raise itself like the Horse; and regarding its normal spending and adornments, with little does it content itself, and with even less does it maintain itself and with almost nothing is it decorated and it works more than all others.

Finally, it is good for the rich and useful for the poor, serving all to whatever extent these may want it; and referring to riding it, with more commodity, simplicity and security in one's life and those of its riders can this Donkey carry them, and why is this most beautiful Donkey underappreciated? And even if it is true that in our time this Animal is held in such low regard, in times past it was greatly esteemed, and its service was appreciated by the greatest, most grave and honorable people that the World has ever known and ever will know; and it was held as the most honorable and safe of all cavalries, that no other Animal was known and written about as this; and thus we will tell of the esteem and mention cases of some most grave people before the coming of Christ Our Redeemer, such as Abraham, Job, Saul, Kings and others as these. Of Abraham one can read that he addressed his Donkey when he went to sacrifice his son, and by this did he represent the act of humility and obedience that he was about to perform. Of the most patient Job (Chapter 1) it is told in the Divine Scripture, that he had fifty Donkeys, which were one of the greatest temporal riches he possessed. Of Saul it is written that when he was anointed as a King, by order of God, he went to collect the Donkeys of his father. More does the Text say of the beautiful Abigail, that when she was on the way to marry King David, she was riding a Jenny, and from this may we believe that all damsels carried themselves as thus. Another principal lady was the daughter of Caleb, called Achsah, so the Scriptures says, which was riding one of these Animals. And the good Shulamite, the one who hosted the Prophet Elijah, a rich and principal woman, and the Scripture says that she rode a Donkey and she met the Prophet so as he could resuscitate her son. And even beyond these people of such quality and authority, of this same thing we can read of many Prophets and Saints, who always rode on similar Animals, and didn't think of them as any lesser, as these days it seems common. To all of this the Reader could reply and say that the mentioned people, even if grave, were very humble, and that they did this out of humility. And to this do I respond that you should read what is said of Absalom, son of King David, and Achitophel (Kings 3) that both used these humble and simple donkeys as rides. And the sons of King Saul also rode Donkeys. Also of Misibosete (who was one of the said brothers) the Scripture mentions (Kings 3) that he ordered a servant to decorate a Donkey to accompany King David, who would certainly be riding another one. And the Scripture says (Judith 10) that those thirty brother, sons of Prince Galadites (Judge of the Hebrew people), rode thirty young Donkeys, being Princes and Lords of thirty Cities. In this way one cannot argue that only through humility were these people riding such Animals, for not only do the small and humble use them, but also the great and enthroned, and even Kings very much loved this cavalry and had them as the most honored, safe and simplest of all, and it truly is. And we also know that Apuleius the Philosopher did not hesitate in saying that he saw himself transformed into a Donkey in that Book he wrote called the Golden Ass, where many beauties and excellences of this Animal are mentioned.

Story of the Donkey

The Sacred Doctors, and Saint Augustine among them, say that the Donkey on which Christ Our God rode on Palm Sunday was the figure of the New Church and the Christian People. And that the Donkey which Christ our Redeemer also rode on that same day and voyage, was the figure of the old Synagogue and the law of the Jews. And what greatest favor and privilege could the Donkey reach than carry its own Creator made man? This is not found of any other Animal, except this one, this due to it being so humble and so patient. And further still do I ask, what other Animal did God say that he had need of, except the Donkey? As the Sacred Evangelists wrote that Christ our Redeemer, on Palm Sunday, sent two of his Disciples to untie the mentioned Donkey and bring it to him; and he warned them that should anyone ask why they were untying it that they should answer that the Lord had need of it. Oh benignity and meekness of the Savior that being absolute Lord of all things would say that he had need of this Animal for what it represented as was said! Oh favor and particular worth of this Donkey, for in the day of greatest worth and human honor, when the King of Glory wanted to triumph over his enemies, he rode in this Donkey to enter triumphantly in Jerusalem! And one should be warned that by honoring the Donkey, he also honored and gave a great favor to all Christians. This truth I have just said was already prophesized many years before God was made man by the Prophet Isaiah, Chapter 62, who, while speaking to the Jews in Prophetic spirit, told them: *Filia Syon ecce Rex tuus venit ad te manfuetu super Asinam, & pullum.* Which means: Daughters of Zion, rejoice, for to you I am sending a meek, benign and humble King. And so you may see and believe, that he is coming as I am saying, he will be riding a Donkey, which are the most humble, simple, peaceful and meek Animals on the whole of the earth for the said ministry. What more can I say or write in honor and favor of this Donkey besides that which was said by the Prophet and that Christ our Redeemer worked on it, and all of this for our documentation and example?

What can we say of that story and colloquium which happened between the Prophet Balaam and his Donkey (Chapter 22) when they were on the way to talk badly of the People of Israel, that riding on it, with this determination, a angel appeared to him with its sword unsheathed, warning the Prophet not to pass beyond? And as the Donkey saw the Angel with such rage and its sword risen and unsheathed it changed its path, and the good Prophet (or should I say bad and blind), not being able to see the Angel in his path, started to beat the poor Donkey terribly, making it return to the path, and upon seeing once again the Angel so enraged against the Prophet once again it turned away; not being able to see the wrath of the Angel, as the Prophet was blind (from his eyes), he once again started to beat the Donkey until it returned to the path. And as it was seeing the Angel, it did not move to one part or the other and fell at the feet of the Prophet, who, losing his patience, once again started to beat the sad Donkey so badly that God Our Lord its Creator, feeling sorry for it, gave it the faculty of speech so as it could talk and complain to the Prophet; and so it told him: Why have you injured me and mistreated me three times? (Oh rare event! Oh story never before heard! Oh miracle never seen and worthy of being noted!) To this complaint that surprised the Prophet he responded: For you did not want to obey me, nor walk forward and for this did I hurt and mistreat you; and should I have a knife I would have ended you. To which the Donkey responded: Have I ever not been obedient to you, without ever contradicting your will and service? And the Prophet responded: This is true; you have never been disobedient. And as Balaam said these words God opened his eyes, and he saw the Angel with its sword placed against him, and he gave a humble reverential greeting. Then the Angel sternly reprehended the Prophet, saying: Were it not for the obedience and respect of your Donkey, I would have put you to death, leaving the Donkey with its life. Oh rare privilege of this Donkey, and a never before seen case, that not only God all Mighty had compassion and pity for a Donkey, giving it the faculty of speech, so as it could complain, but also that an Angel would defend it, threatening with death the Prophet over his mistreatment of it! For who today has such care for these beautiful Donkeys, treating them well and supporting them without such anxiety and mistreatments? And I believe that if men did not underestimate and abandon the Donkey as a ride, and if they did not bring up so many harnessed Horses and garnished Mules, it would be much better than these, both in body and spirit, for there wouldn't be so much haughtiness and there wouldn't be so much expense in food and dressings as there is; nor would so many offenses to the Creator be made, as we see today, for humility is content with little things, and the superfluous would not be an expense. Some might say to me that the Donkey has an ill temper and disposition for it to be a good ride and cavalry. And to this I respond that it has this to better serve the purpose which God created it for; and more, should it be treated and handled as it should, it would have a different spirit, which would be much better than the one it has; for if it was garnished and presented as a Mule or Horse, I assure you that it would have a better disposition than the one it presents. And if it is as such, it is because it is ill treated, and men don't make much case of it.

Regarding its big ears, not growing a tail or hair or any other things which may be counted as missing by those who don't like Donkeys, I say that those are just whims and vanities of those said men, and shallow tastes applied to their gravities and appetites; for these are not essential or necessary; for the truth is that to the Horse one wants it to have hair and a tail, and in the Mule these are cut; and on some they want ears and on others not; draping them in some and cutting them in others; in such a way that having this or not having it is not a necessity, but rather customs and opinions of human whim.

I also want to respond with a story to some that may tell me and claim that even if these Donkeys are good for work and more safe to ride, they are nonetheless not good for war; to this I say that it was a privilege, particular grace and a singular mercy of God that he made them so bad for the exercise of men killing each other; the Divine Majesty did not wish for it to be apt nor disposed to be in a war, but rather out of it; and men should take this cue to also not damn themselves. Even if we have a story from Plutarch, in the life of Alexander, who saw a Donkey kill a strong and brave Lion by kicking it. The ancient Poets also spoke, even if in a lie, that these were apt for battle, for the Gods of the Gentiles rode on Donkeys when they were doing war with the Giants; and in this way did they beat them.

Also note another story of the strength of these Donkeys in the dealings of war, for not only do they make war and damage to their enemies during their life, but also after death, for they submit all rebels, as can be read in Samson, who with the jaw of a Donkey killed a thousand Philistines. And from this jaw did the Divine Majesty operate another rare marvel, that when Samson was dying of thirst, God offered him water through means of that same jawbone, making an abundance of water come forth from it, curing his thirst. In this way was the said jaw used as a defense and weapon against his enemies, and also as a fountain and pleasure for his person.

There is no shortage of people who will say that even if all that was said is true, Donkey meat has no taste or advantage as food, and to this do I respond that it is only because it is not in use, and because men do not have it as a custom, that this meat does not seem good; for we do know from stories that the Flemish in their banquets and invitations, so as to offer a grand feast and greater enjoyment to their guests, they fed them Donkeys, and it is told that these are extremely tasty. And the same is surely still the case; however I do understand that it was respect, discretion and prudence that caused one to not eat the meat of an Animal which offers such advantage to the service of man as the Donkey, for this would be to win one over the loss of one hundred.

In Book 4 of the Kings, Chapter 6, one can read that as Samaria was besieged by the King of Syria, they arrived at such an extreme of hunger that a single Donkey, meant for food, was worth eight hundred *reales*. And Plutarch writes that in a certain war of King Artaxerxes, one saw another Donkey going for seventy *reales*. In this way one may see that in the necessities of both war and peace, always was the Donkey an asset. Finally, the necessity and advantage given by these Donkeys is of such importance that, if the Majesty of God Our Lord had not given them to us, we would be deprived of many and great delights and rest, and we would suffer from great labors, more than we already do; and with them do we live somewhat more rested; for they serve us and offer us rest in all they can and this is quite enough; apart from this they also provide us with a certain different kind of Donkey, even if sterile, which are stronger and more robust, which work even more than their parents, which are the infinity of Mules and Hinnies that are conceived from Donkeys and Jennies, even if through adultery, if such a thing can be said.

How one makes Mules and Hinnies, and the cause of why they are sterile

As it is appropriate, one should say how and why one generates the said Animals and the cause of these not conceiving or generating offspring. Regarding the first I say that the mating of a Jenny and a Horse generates a Mule; and the mating of a Donkey with a Mare generates a Hinny, and to this do I call adultery for this is the mating of Animals of different species which cause such great mixture. From the mating of a Donkey with its own species one always obtains a Donkey or a Jenny, as is confirmed by the great Philosopher Aristotle with that famous Philosophical saying: *Omne simile generat sibi simile*. This mean that all similar generates another similar; and this is what experience has shown. The cause of why the Mule and Hinny cannot conceive, some say, even if falsely, is because God cursed the Mule in Bethlehem when the Virgin Mary placed her new born Son Jesus in the manger, near which was an Ox and a Mule. And they claim to say that the Ox covered and heated the baby God with its breath, and the Mule uncovered him, and for this reason God cursed it. But this is a great falsity and fable; for no such thing is said in the divine Letters, nor is this read in any grave Author worthy of faith. What can be truthfully said regarding the Mule and its praise is that as soon as God was born as Man, the Redeemer of life choose as rest and residence the stable and home of this Donkey, and as bed its poor manger, this rather than the heavy and adorned houses of men, and this is no small praise to this animal.

But returning to our purpose, I say that these mixed Donkeys are not sterile over what the vulgar say, but rather because nature, feeling offended by the mating of different Animal species, does not allow for them to conceive, so as these may not generate any more of their kind.

And the curious should note and the Farmers be adverted, that this we have just said of sterility is not only true of the land Animals, but also it happens in grafted trees; even if it is true that these produce very good fruits; but should these be grafted with trees of a different kind they will produce fruit which is neither good nor bad; and this is surely worthy of being noted and experimented. As such, by what was said, these Donkeys cannot conceive, and also because God Our Lord did make them in this way so as with the greater commodity they could serve us, and with less embarrassment they could aid us; for conceiving diminishes and reduces strength; and giving birth, raising a young one and being pregnant is a great impediment for service and work; and because of this do I faithfully believe that God Our Lord made these Donkeys, that are so necessary to human life, sterile, so as with greater effort and liberty they could serve and obey us.

Properties and Virtues of the Donkey

One of the excellences which should be noted, and which is also experimented in the Dove, is that these do not have gall; and this we say with Aristotle regarding the Donkey.

A drum made with Donkey skin, so says the Natural Philosophers, played in war raises the spirits of the Soldiers much more than if it is made from any other Animal.

Dioscorides writes (Book 2, Chapter 42) that a Donkey's liver and nails, burned, made into a powder and drunk with a stew is good against decrepitude and *gota coral*.

Pliny (Book 28) and other grave Authors write that Donkey's milk, drunk, is good against all kinds of venoms; and mixed with honey cures dysentery and alleviates the pain from gout.

The above mentioned Author writes that Donkey's milk, mixed with powder from its nails, makes the sight clearer and removes pain from the eyes.

Donkey's milk, so say it every great Medic, is an important remedy to heal the phthisical, as experience has shown.

Pliny and Suetonius[257] write that the wife of Emperor Nero, who was called Poppaea, washed her face and her whole body with Donkey's milk, and that she lived with great health and had a greatly beautiful face; and wherever she went she took with her five hundred milking Jennies just for this reason.

Donkey urine has a great virtue and efficiency in curing kidney pain, if this is applied still hot on wet cloths over the afflicted area.

Galen says that wild Donkey urine, or of those raised in a field, is good to break the stones which are generated in the bladder.

Donkey manure, placed over a blood flow will retain it and completely halt it.

Donkey blood will retain this same flow, should it be applied to the ailing part.

Field Donkey manure made into a powder, and drunk with good wine, cures a Scorpion bite.

Aesculapius says that drinking four or five drops of Donkey blood, with good wine, will heal normal fever.

Donkey spleen, melted in water and applied to the breasts of a woman will attract milk to them.

Jenny milk, if drunk, mitigates and softens the womb; and used to wash the mouth makes the teeth firmer, according to Dioscorides; and some say that it stops a runny nose. And it is further said that Donkey urine, if drunk, will heal the frenetic.

Hali says that powder from Donkey lungs, drunk with some meat broth or white wine, cures cough.

Pliny writes that if one carries a ring made from the leg bone of a Donkey he will be kept from decrepitude.

If a Donkey is seen walking around a field, hitting his hooves on the ground many times, this is a sign of rain.

It is further said that should one fumigate a house with powder made from Donkey lungs, that neither poisonous Animals nor serpents will live in it.

Camillo[258] writes in the history of the Donkey that if one of these Animals lays on the ground and does not want to get up, no matter how much one hits it, should a woman approach it and say (as if playing a trick): "get up sir Donkey", it will immediately rise, heehawing and jumping with pleasure.

Of obedience and its rare excellences, by occasion of the Donkey

Because we have noted that the Donkey has such obedience and natural subjection, it seems good for me to say something of this virtue, with the authority of Saints and most learned men, so as one may see the valor of this and of he that with virile spirit professes it.

---

257. Translator's note: Gaius Suetonius Tranquillus, a first century Latin author, famous for his biography of Julius Caesar.

258. Translator's note: uncertain reference.

Saint John Climacus says that obedience in man is a perfect abnegation of the body, declared with fervor and will of the soul; the contrary is the abnegation of the Soul, declared by exercise and works of the body.

Seneca said that obedience to God is a frank liberty of the soul and body.

Saint Gregory says that perfect obedience cannot be found in respect and servile fear, nor in fear of penalty, but solely in the love of justice and affection for charity.

Saint Gregory says that obedience is not only a virtue, but rather the mother of all virtues.

Saint Augustine further says that more than being the mother of all virtues, it is a guardian and custodian of all of them; and he also says that obedience is a greater good than continence.

This is of such exigency and acceptance to God, who loves it, that he desires it more that any sacrifice. And Saint Gregory says, in Morals 13, that with reason is obedience greater than sacrifice, for with sacrifice one offers the flesh of others, and with obedience one offers his very will.

Seneca, a Gentile Philosopher, says that obeying God is liberty. And he says furthermore that Kingdoms are quieted and made peaceful by obedience, and that this is to have true peace, quietness and freedom.

Saint Paul (Romans 13) praises obedience in such way that he says that a Superior man, even if bad, should obey a Christian, not only to avoid punishment but also to obey his consciousness.

Solomon says that an obedient Man will sing victory.

Aristotle says that the more one obeys the more graces he will gain from him to whom he obeys.

Stobaeus says that there isn't any greater evil in the world, or outside of it, than disobedience.

Saint Gregory says that with obedience does one defeat Demons; and with the remaining virtues does one fight them.

Saint Bernard says that faith leads to obedience; for it is a mirror of Christ, and thus only obedience professes the merit of faith.

Saint Paul (Philippians 2) says that Christ was made obedient, until the death on the Cross.

By the obedience that Abraham had to the Commandments of God, in wanting to sacrifice his Son, did the same God promised him that his children would be as many as the Stars in Heaven and the sands of the Sea.

Chapter III

Of the Camel and its natural conditions

    The Camel is a misshapen, gibbous and disgusting Animal, and it is most effortful, so much so that it can carry the load of six regular Animals; and when one wishes to load it, it is only necessary to hit its front legs with a stick and it lowers itself to be loaded, for it is so tall of legs and high of body that men cannot reach it to place any baggage on it, and it overcomes this problem by lowering itself. When this Animal drinks, the Natural Philosophers say, and also experiences shows it, it cannot drink any clear water, but it will rather make it murky with its muzzle and it will even put its feet into it to move the dirt under it, and this, it is said, so as not be able to see its ugly face and figure. Others say that this is not the reason why it does such a thing, but that it is like a child watching himself in a mirror, trying to grab its own face with its hands; thus the Camel seeing itself in the water wants to do the same as the child; and this seems to me to be best reason of why it does this. And more do they say about this behavior, that if it cannot make the water murky it becomes irate and furious, grinding its teeth; and because of this those who deal with these Animals only offer them water to drink during the night and in the dark, and in this way they will not have the chance of seeing their face in the water and becoming angry.

    The pace of a Camel is as fast as that of any other Donkey, for they give very long and fast strides, and for this reason are these Camels used to travel those long stretches of land of two of three leagues in length; and this for three reasons. The first is because these can walk on sand as easily as on solid ground. The other is so as to not be covered by those mounts of sand; for these, with the regular wind, move very fast during the afternoons and they change from one part to the other, and should men not be on Camels, which are very fast, they would find themselves in great perils and binds. The last aspect is that they have such great sense that they never forget their path once they have passed by it; and as those paths are destroyed and covered by the sands, which commonly shift and move due to the winds, given their great sense they will not lose sight of their journey, and they guide themselves safely.

The real Camel has a hump in the middle of its spine, and it does not have distinct gall like other Animals, but rather it has some very fine veins where it stores its gall. If it eats grain it will swallow it whole and during the night ruminate it. They are fit for war, the females more than the males. There is another kind of Camel which they call the Dromedary, of whose species were those which carried the three Kings from the Orient to see the new born God and King of the Jews; and these are so fast that if they run, they can cover more ground than any race horse, for they can cover fifty or sixty leagues in a day without tiring too much; and these Dromedaries are the ones which have the two humps, one in front of the other, and one of these can be used as a saddle in the middle of its spine. When the Camel is incited by Nature to the venereal act it becomes strangely furious. And should its female approach any other Animal, it will charge it with bravery and fury, for it is very zealous and lustful.

The Female is pregnant for a year, and during this whole time it will not be joined with a male, which, even being so given to that vice, will not join itself with pregnant females; and after these give birth they go another year without mating. And like these there are other Animals that do not mate with pregnant females or those which are raising their young, and in this they are better than many men.

The Camel has a strange excellence, and this is that it can go three or four days without drinking, which is not a good regiment for sane, light and temperate living, fitted for travel and other ministries.

Story of the Camel

Even if it is true that the camel, due to its Nature, is very given to the venereal act, it is also true that the Natural Philosophers and Aristotle (Book 9, Chapter 47) say that they have never seen it mate with its own mother, and regarding this they tell a story which is worthy of being known; and this is that in order to really know if the Camel has filial respect for its mother, they awaited for the appropriate time when Nature incites and moves these Animal to the said act, and they locked together a Camel with its mother, and never in any way did the Camel mate with her. After these were taken out, a trick was used to see if the Camel would mate with its mother, and this was that they covered and disguised it very well, in such a way as it could not see its face; in this way did the son Camel take its mother and being in this position they uncovered its mother's head; and the Camel seeing that this was its mother immediately came down from her with great grief and it charged furiously at him who uncovered her head, understanding that this was the one responsible for that betrayal, and there it kicked him, breaking him into pieces! Oh filial respect never before seen among the brutes! Oh strange countenance with the mother of such a libidinous Animal! Oh rare example, and confusion to so many children with little respect for their parent! Oh admirable example of suffering shown to all, for on that occasion one could doubt the restrain of the Camel and the respect it has for its mother; and of this do the Natural Philosophers say, and experience shows it, that they live more than one hundred years, and to this age only the Elephant can reach; and it seems that the Camel has reached this blessing of long life which God gives and promises to those men who respect their fathers and mothers.

Properties and natural virtues of the Camel

The juice taken from the hump of the Camel, taken from below, has the virtue of healing hemorrhoids. Avicenna.

The blood and brain of the Camel, dried, made into a powder and drunk with vinegar, cures epilepsy. Avicenna.

Camel meat, eaten, provokes urine. Avicenna.

Camel blood, fried with olive oil, and taken through the mouth, retains blood flows. Avicenna.

This same fried blood, if taken by a woman, prepares her to conceive and it also has the virtue of stopping venom. Avicenna.

Camel milk is better and it does less harm than any other milk. Avicenna.

Camel urine has the virtue to heal the hydrophobic, if taken through the mouth, and it stops the stink of the nose and it breaks blockages. Avicenna.

Camel's white manure, dried and mixed with honey, applied as a dressing, prevents tumors, and it comforts the humors. Diaf.[259]

Fresh Camel manure breaks away warts, and applied to the nose represses blood flows. Pliny.

Of Praise and other things by occasion of the Camel

Many and great praises do the Donkey and Lion deserve, of which we have spoken here, over the great virtues and excellences we have noted; however, many more do seem to me to be deserved by the Camel, simply over the great restrain and natural respect it has for its Mother, and over this we will say what is praise and we will say of what this consists of.

Praise, so says Aristotle, is not anything else than a practice that further beatifies virtue, as we have just said of the Camel.

True praise, Sallustius[260] says, is a proven thing.

Glory and praise, says Cicero, are similar to honesty.

Praise, says Seneca, has a shadow of virtue.

Fame itself, says Marcus Aurelius, should depend of the praise of others, and not of one's own self, for this is a vile thing.

Saint Luke says that no one should be praised while he lives; for this may be the cause for him to slip and fall, and about this did Christ say: to none shall you commend along the path, which is the same as saying: To none shall you praise while he lives.

A friend who praises in public, Solon[261] says, reprehends in private.

To praise in one's presence, Aristotle says, is a thing of flatterers; and in one's absence it is a thing of honorable men.

There isn't a softer practice than the praise of one's kin in their absence. Xenophon.[262]

There isn't anything so low and so small that there isn't something about it that can be praised. Pliny.

To praise oneself is a thing of a vain man; to vilify oneself is thing of a mad man. Maxentius.[263]

Make such works, Periander[264] says, so as to be praised in life and blessed in death.

---

259. Translator's note: in the 1672 edition this name is given as Liaf.
260. Translator's note: Gaius Sallustius Crispus, a fist century BC Roman historian.
261. Translator's note: An Athenian lawmaker and poet from the VIth century BC.
262. Translator's note: Xenophon of Athens, a Geek philosopher, student of Socrates.
263. Translator's note: Marcus Aurelius Valerius Maxentius Augustus, Roman Emperor of the third and fourth century
264. Translator's note: Corinthian tyrant of the seventh century BC.

Chapter IV

Of the Wolf, and its perfidious conditions

The wolf is a fraudulent and deceitful Animal and the ancients called it the wild Dog, due to the similarity it has with this in its form as in its howl, even if this does not bark. It is daring and voracious, and it does not eat anything else but meat, and in such a way as it is said to swallow it whole in great pieces.

The Natural Philosophers say that the Wolf does not feel so much hunger during the day as during the night, and it can go for three days without eating; but when these are up, it breaks its three day abstinence; its brain, they say, increases and decreases *ad motum Lunæ*, as that of the Dogs and Genets.

Pythagoras writes a notable thing of the nature of the Wolf, which is that should one take out one if its eyes before killing it, dogs will run from this eye at its mere sight.

Porta says that not only do they run at its sight but also by its mere scent, and they will be unable to bark.

Saint Ambrose mentions a strange and natural thing about the Wolf, and this is that if a Wolf sees a man before he sees it, this man will become hoarse in such a way as he will not be able to shout at the Wolf nor raise his voice; and in this way the wolf will make little case of the man and his hoarse voice (should he be able to speak at all), and it will continue to look upon him, eye to eye, as if mocking him without any fear. But should the contrary happen, if a man sees a Wolf before it see him, and he shouts, the Wolf will become so frightened that it will immediately run.

And in this does the mentioned author say that there is a great difference between seeing and being seen. And in this same way is that saying true: A cautious man is worth four; or as others say, has won half the fight. From the Wolf discovering a man was born the saying: *Lupus est in fabulæ*; which is said when whispering about someone and this person appears, upon which one then says: Hush, for of whom we speak is present. This Animal has an amazing and fearful howl; and Pythagoras says that if a Dog or any other Animal passes over the urine of a Wolf it will never again conceive or become pregnant. Isidore says that the Wolf does not mate in more than twelve days with its female throughout the whole year. And more, that it mates like the Dog and its penis is made of bone.

Story of the Wolf

In the Kingdom of Valencia, in a Town called Penaguila, it happened that a certain Fenollar, going into a mountain to hunt, found a pack of Wolf pups, still suckling, and as one of them seemed good for him, he killed all others and took this one to be raised and domesticated; and this pup become so house broken and so protective of its home that it guarded it better than any Dog, and he gained such affection for its master that it would never allow him to go alone anywhere he went. But as it is said, those who have a bad genius late or never do they lose it, and it happened that once, upon leaving the house he left the Wolf on guard, as he had done many other times, and this Wolf approached the stable and in friendship took to the Animals in there, and among the Donkeys there was one that it was so fond of that it beheaded it, and after having its fill of its blood and flesh left and never returned. Oh what a warning this to man, so as not to invite into his home that which will give him grief.

In the Kingdom of Catalonia there is a case of certain Wolves which deserves a story, and this was that a blind man, traveling from one Town to the next, and carrying his flute and drum so as to make his living, was traveling along a very deserted path when night fell; he then started to hear the great howls of Wolves (for there are many and very large in that land) and fearing encountering them, decided to turn back from where he had came from. As he was going back the young man who was guiding him said: Over here I see a corral and a pen; "let us go there then", said the blind man. Arriving at the door, as this was not locked, they entered, and the boy guided his master to a room with a wooden stair; and once they had climbed in they removed the stair, and shortly after a dozen wolves entered into the pen, and, as the blind man had opened the door, they entered the house.

Even if these had an easy way in they did not have an easy way out, for the door closed after them; and as all of them were inside the house, thinking game was about, they started to hunt. As the blind man was being told by his guide what was happening, that twelve Wolves had entered, he said: take the drum and I'll take the flute, and let us give them some music for we are safe and secure. And as they started to play the Wolves were so terrified, scared and amazed that the poor things realized that they could not stop the sound nor escape, as the door was closed, and so they killed and ripped each other apart, without any of them surviving; and at day break the Musicians left, very happy with their feat, that they achieved victory solely with a flute and a drum.

Another very grave story of the Wolf, which happened in Italy

Among the many and grave stories that Aristides[265] writes regarding things from Italy, one of them, and not one of the lesser, is of a she Wolf that due to a certain case became the wet nurse of some boys, giving them her tits and milk for some time. These boys were Remus and Romulus, who, from Sheepherders became great soldiers and valorous captains and were founders of the great city of Rome, head of the Universe.

This story is told by this prestigious author and Lucius Florus,[266] in Book 1 of his *Epitome,* and Livy, in Book 1 of the *Ab Urbe Condita*; also the glorious Doctor Saint Augustine mentions this

---

265. Translator's note: uncertain reference.
266. Translator's note: Lucius Annaeus Florus, a Roman historian from the first and second century.

story in the book *De Civitate Dei*; and Pliny in the eighth book of his Natural History. And the case was thus: Ambitious Amulius brother of King Numitor, having the desire to reign, killed in secret the said King Numitor, who left a son and a daughter of little age to whom the kingdom rightfully belonged. Amulius, so as to rule alone, killed his nephew during a hunting trip and had his niece locked away with the vestal virgins; and she became very much infatuated by a very brave, even if mean and adulterous, boy named Mars (whom, after his death, was titled by those Gentiles as the God Mars, God of Battle, for being so valiant). This young man had contact and friendship with this vestal virgin, impregnating her, and at its time, she gave birth to two extremely beautiful and robust boys. This birth wasn't so secretive that the news didn't reach the tyrant King Amulius, who had the boys brought before him; and once he saw them he delivered them to a very trusting servant of his so as he would take them to the Tiber River and throw them in. The servant, moved by compassion, did not dare to accomplish the order and cruelty of his master, and so he went around a mount near the river and left the boys in a cave; and just by chance (or by disposition of the Heavens), it happened that a she Wolf had just given birth in that cave, and as this Wolf was returning from the field, and seeing those two boys, gave them her tits and reared them for a few days. It so happened that a sheepherder called Faustulus was passing with his cattle near that cave and heard voices in it; and upon approaching the cave saw the Wolf feeding the boys; and retreating he waited for the opportunity when the Wolf would be away so as to take the boys to safety; and so he did, giving them to his wife so she would raise them, and she was called Acca Larentia. These, after certain respects and considerations, imposed on the boys the mentioned names of Romulus and Remus. These, as time went by, came to understand the cause of their banishment and life with the sheepherder, from whose house they left at the appropriate age and made themselves into soldiers, and given their good fortune they rose to the rank of Captains and they avenged the death of their grandfather Numitor and their mother's banishment; and this story is remembered by Virgil in the first book of his Aeneid, by saying the following:

> Ilia the fair, a priestess and a queen,
> Who, full of Mars, in time, with kindly throes,
> Shall at a birth two goodly boys disclose.
> The royal babes a tawny wolf shall drain:
> Then Romulus his grandsire's throne shall gain,
> Of martial tow'rs the founder shall become,

Medicinal properties of the Wolf

Wolf's heart, Aristotle says, well dried becomes very aromatic, and burned in an oven, made into powder and drunk with good wine will heal epilepsy.

Wolf's liver, dried and made into a powder, so say it the Physiologists, drunk with good wine, is good against the intemperance of the belly, mainly for diarrhea.

Boiled Wolf meat will cure those suffering from fantasies, with fantastical imaginations and imaginary illusions. Aesculapius.

White Wolf's manure is good against colic. Hali.

Wolf meat, according to Avicenna, is of very bad digestion, and the stomach cannot take it; unless one has hemorrhoids, for these will be cured.

Eating Wolf's blood cures colic. Avicenna.

Wolf's intestine, Albertus says, placed across any path and covered with dirt will not allow that any four legged Animal pass over it, especially Sheep, and this experience was done by Saint Thomas of Aquinas.

Wolf skin, if place together with skin from a Lamb or Sheep, will consume it, according to Hali.

Of Gluttony and its great evils, by occasion of the voracious Wolf

Given that we have not noted or found any virtue or good natural condition of the Wolf to speak of, but solely vices and complaints, such as it being voracious and gluttonous, it seems right to me to say something of Gluttony, and with the authority of learned, grave and saintly men.

Gluttony, according to Medina,[267] isn't any other thing than a deformed appetite to eat and drink, and this, he says, is mother of laziness and the principle of all vice, for it causes the blindness of the senses, blockage of temper, hardness of heart, vice in words, and inattention in work; and furthermore, it is the cause of infirmity and miseries. And those who are given to this vice, only through a miracle will have health and they will never be constant.

Gluttony, Saint Climacus says, is the inventor of whims, shallow dressings and trinkets and also of new vices.

The said Saint says that he who waves a soft hand at a Lion is in a position to tame him; but he who waves his body with trinkets, makes it wild against him.

Plutarch says that a meal should be taken as remedy and medicine for hunger, not for the pleasure of the body.

The gluttonous, so says Plutarch, lives to eat; the temperate eat to live.

Saint Gregory writes that the feasts of the Soul are the words of God; and Saint Gregory says that bread and water satisfy nature.

In eating, so says Hugo,[268] one should keep such equality that this does not become a dishonesty nor something outside necessity.

Diogenes, a great Philosopher, was asked which the best hour to eat was. He responded that for the rich it was when he felt like it, and for the poor when he had anything to do so.

Over Gluttony did Esau lose his firstborn right, which he sold for a plate of lentils.

The man who is given to Gluttony welcomes in every vice

Too much eating and drinking causes decrepitude and numbing of the body.

---

267. Translator's note: uncertain reference.
268. Translator's note: uncertain reference.

Chapter V

Of the Lamb, Ram and Sheep

The Lamb is the simplest and most benign Animal of all Animals, and it is so gentle and innocent that even when sheared it stays silent, and it does not complain if mistreated; and if taken to the slaughter it does not quarrel, nor shout nor scream, as all other Animals; it is not malicious like the Ox, nor cunning like the Fox, nor voracious like the Wolf, nor envious like the Dog, nor brave like the Bull, nor furious like the Lion; and you may see that it does not have teeth to bite, nor claws to scratch, not horns to charge, nor anything with which to defend itself; but rather it is from head to toe bland, soft, useful and necessary to human life without there being anything in it that might be lacking. And even if it is true that the conditions and properties of this little Animal are known to most, given that it is so common, it is much more common to stay silent about them; but even with all of this, so as not to break with my intention, I will say something of the great deal which is known of it.

Of the great and wide advantages of the Sheep

Firstly Ram's meat is the best and most common of all, with which almost the whole universe is sustained; and it is a marvelous thing, and even miraculous and worthy of praise, seeing as a Sheep does not give birth to more than one Lamb per year, and at the most two, which is a rare event, and that thousands upon thousands of these are killed everyday throughout the World; and this being true there is still such an abundance of these in each City, Town and every corner of the earth that one must admire at how these are so multiplied and spread, without there being a way to know how this is done. Of Sows we know that they give birth in litters of seven or eight in a year, and sometimes more, and of Wolves we see that they give birth to this same amount of pups per year, and natural reason would expect that Sheep would be in a much larger number, but yet these are not, not even one third or one fifth; for should we kill the amount of those indomitable Pigs and fierce Wolves as we do Sheep, these would not last for the whole year, and I even doubt that they would last one month. And in this way there is a great deal to take into consideration regarding the multiplication of this cattle, which is so necessary to human life, and the diminishing of all other Animals that aren't as necessary or useful; this particularly regarding the enemy Wolf, which giving birth to the litters they do, through the bushes and woods of a Province one only finds a hundredth or thousandth part of the number of Lambs. And it is the supreme providence of the universal Creator who ordered that we had less of these enemies; and of those which we require we had more. And by this, and by all other benefices we receive from his Blessed Hand, may his Holiest Name be praised and glorified. Amen.

What can we say of wool, that it so frankly gives us, and with such abundance for the dressing and human pleasure, for men cover themselves with it, and in it do they sleep restfully, and by it do many states of men live and make their livelihood, as those who own and sell it. Those who sell it and with it make an infinite amount of cloth of different textures; the Dyers, which make them of various colors; the Store owners who sell them; those who polish and fix it; the Taylors and knitters that with their cutting and sewing make an honorable living; and from those to the Weavers who make it into sheets and blankets; the mattress makers makings mattresses, and the hat makers making hats. Finally the lords and Kings, who have these as great and beautiful treasures.

Of the leather and skin of these Animals, who can say the service these make and the advantage they give to so many varieties of trades and people? For if we look at Herders, with these skins do they cure the Winter's cold and are they protected and kept cool in Summer. The Tanners earn their keep with their tanning and in strengthening and giving them color. The Shoe makers, making it into a thousand different boots, shoes and slippers. And the Violin Makers, Scroll Makers, Glove Makers, Printers, Booksellers, Pouch Makers and Notaries live and have honorable incomes with these skins; the Scribes and Copiers of Church books, honor with these the Chapels, Churches and Parishes in their Choirs and Archives. Finally, who is the man who does not have necessity of one of the above mentioned works and products? Such as money pouches, shoelaces, jackets, straps, boots; shoes to wear; and Princes and Great Lords who adorn their houses and quarters with the skins of these humble Animals, of several textures and cuts, with that variety of colors and dressings which are made unto them.

What can we say of the service, pleasure and enjoyment that we make of Sheep's milk, for it seems to me to be one of the necessary supplies and pleasures that human life requires; for with it does one make a thousand different stews and dishes, so many cheeses, with such diversity of tastes and flavors. Finally do I say that these Animals are as necessary for human life as all others which are raised for its sustenance; and it seems to me that would they be missing in the World, it would be missing its best and most necessary part for the life of man, regarding all that which is for his sustenance, not counting bread. There is so much to say and write of these Animals that this would mean not speaking of any other; and one can say that in living they give us life and after death they conserve it, for with their wools we dress and adorn ourselves, with their meats do we maintain and sustain ourselves, for it is the best addition to the bread that God Our Lord has created for the conservation of human life.

And it is a notable thing that, when killed, there isn't a single thing in the Lamb that does not have a use and utility for the service of man; beyond the benefit that its meat, milk, wool and skin gives us. But of this Animal we take and use all giblets, without there being a thing that goes to waste, as their intestines, from which are a variety of musical instruments made, which is a thing of the greatest entertainment, softness and contentment that man has in this life. From the fat of this Animal are the most beautiful candles made, that are not only used in the setting of a table, but also in the houses of great Lords, Princes and Kings and also in Temples and Altars of our Christian Religion.

What can one say of the great service given through the glue which is made from discarded parchment or skin of this Animal; without which so many Officers would not be able to fulfill their duties, mainly Book sellers, Carpenters, and Instrument Makers, of Guitars and Harps and others; And even their feces are good for the fertilization of the fields &c…

Story, privileges and excellences of this Animal the Sheep

Given what we have said, more relevant than count the privileges and excellences of these Animals would be to narrate stories of them. Granullachs tells in his Chronography that this Animal sleeps one half of the year on one side and in the other half it sleeps on the other, and as such we know that from the time the Sun enter the Sign of Aries, which means Ram and which is on the twenty first of March, it sleeps on its right side until the twenty third of September; and from this date until the Sun once again enters the Sign of Aries, it sleeps on its left side. And from this we learn that the right side signifies fertility, good weather and Spring, which begins in the mentioned twenty first of March, which is when the Sun enters the image and figure of the Sign called Aries or Ram. And on the left side is harshness and unfavorable weather manifested, which is when the Sun is as detached from the Sign of Aries as much as it can possibly be. And in this way when the Sun enters the image of the Ram, are all plants increased, tree blossoms and herbs grow; the land rejoices, the fields smile, the flowers bloom and the fruits begin to grow. Finally in this time do the ships begin to sail, commerce starts, birds sing and an infinity of other delights, which all of them are received because the Sun has entered the Sign of Aries of which we speak. For when the Divine Majesty of God Our Lord created the Sun on the fourth day of the world, all Astronomers say that he established it in the image and first degree of Aries, so as our first Fathers could enjoy that happy and smooth weather, which from the four parts of the year is the best and most enjoyable; and in which all created and living things of this life prepare themselves for the generation and increasing of their individuals, without which their species would not be able to preserve themselves. And when the supreme Creator wanted to create Man for love of Man, he waited for the luminaries of the Sun and Moon to be found in this sign of Aries, which was on the twenty fifth of March, with the Moon being in conjunction with the Sun; and this is not without a great mystery, for the true God and Sun of Justice, the purest Lamb was joined with the beautiful and always Virgin Mary, Holy Sheep *per carnis Assumptionem*. And when Christ the Redeemer Our God and true Man, was ordered to be given unto death, it was with the Sun in the said Sign of the Ram, in which time the days are equal to the nights.

Being the Sun in this Sign of Aries or Ram, did God make that wonderful rescue of the Hebrews from the Egyptians on the Red Sea, where these all drowned, and this rescue is an expression of the other even greater rescue that the Majesty of Christ God and Man would eventually make in dying for all men on the Cross in the appropriate time, which was with the Sun in the Sign of Aries, drowning all the sins of the World in the Red Sea of his Passion and Blood. For this mercy and favor that God gave unto the Hebrews, freeing them from captivity and servitude of Pharaoh, do they celebrate that solemn Feast and Passover of the Lamb, this by commandment of the same God on the fourteenth of the Moon of the same month in which they were freed from slavery, which was when the Sun was in the Sign of Aries of which this chapter speaks of, for in this same time and occasion would the immaculate Lamb Christ Our Good die as he did at the age of 32 years, three months and ten days, in the Moon of March, which was on the third of April, and so can we say that as the Sun was in Aries the God Lamb and True Man died. And the Passover Lamb, which we have mentioned, which God ordered (Exodus, Chapter 12 and I Leviticus, Chapter 23) that the Jews eat, and that five days before it should be killed and brought from the field, which should be white and immaculate, and that they bring it in with green branches, as the type and figure of Jesus Christ the white and immaculate Lamb, who entered into Jerusalem with branches of Palm and Olive trees five days before he was killed, which was on Palm Sunday. And when Abraham was to sacrifice his son by order of God, already with the knife risen to cut his throat, an Angel stopped him, revealing a Lamb hiding between the bushes, and told him that that Lamb was the one to be sacrificed and not his son, the figure of the True Messiah Lamb and Redeemer of Life, which would be sacrificed to the Eternal Father on the Holiest Cross for our sins. Finally, when the Redeemer of the World wanted to be revealed to the World, he ordered his precursor, Saint John the Baptist that he manifest him as a Lamb by saying: *Ecce Agnus Dei, ecce quitolis pecata mundi*. And this means: behold the Lamb of God, Behold he who takes away the sins from the World. And in this way did Jesus Christ Our God want to be compared to the Sheep, as did the Prophet Isaiah write in Chapter 53 by saying: *Tanquam Ovis auctus est ad occisionem*. Which means that Christ was taken to the slaughter with that same patience of a Sheep upon death; and in this way is he compared to the Lamb due to its meekness and to the Sheep over this great patience and suffering. The dignity and excellence of these blessed Animals is such that they were determined to be the custody and property of grave men of Royal blood, as can be read of the Prophet Daniel, who was a herder of this cattle when God called him to be a King. And of just Abel do we know that he died being a herder of Sheep. And the Patriarch Jacob, who doesn't know that he was the custodian of this cattle for fourteen years, as the Divine Scripture says, where it is told of the great labors he went through by being a herder of these Animals, and the good he acquired from them? And when the Majesty of God appeared to the Shepherd Moses in the green bush which was on fire without consuming itself, this cattle was he keeping. Of Remus and Romulus who were famous Captains and almost rulers of the whole world and founders of the great City of Rome, head and queen of the Universe, Titus Livy and other grave writers mention that they were first Shepherds of this cattle; and from Shepherds they would become great soldiers and Captains. Leaving these great Men, who so much loved the keeping of this cattle, which says something great of these excellent Animals, and what shall we say of the supreme maker and Creator of all things Jesus Christ Our God, who more than all of these is said to be a Herder of Sheep, even if figuratively; for one does not call him Herder of Goats, or Billies, nor of any other cattle, but that which we currently deal with, for this is the most naturally peaceful, tame and patient of all the others. Great favors did God Our Lord make unto the Herders of the cattle, as we have said and may do so, as it was to these that God and man was first manifested and not to the magnates and Kings of the World, as is told in the Divine Letters.

Natural properties of the Lamb

Lamb, according to Isidore, knows the voice of its mother, this more than any other Animal, and it is also the one which most suffers should it lose sight of it in the middle of other cattle; but at the slightest sound from its mother it recognizes and joins it.

Galen says that Lamb meat isn't good for the stomach; Isaac says that it is indigestible and it generates viscosities.

Avicenna writes that Lamb's blood, drunk with wine, cures epilepsy, and clotted blood is good against any poisonous bite, if placed on top of it.

Lamb brain, according to Albert, distilled over a fire with walnut oil and sugar and drunk, is a remedy to break bladder stones and expel sands; and it greatly reduces kidney and urinary tract pain; and in this same way does he say that it is good for all those who urinate blood. And you should know that this is proven.

Lamb gall is good against cancer, this by anointing that region with it.

Properties of the Ram and Sheep

Ram, which in Latin is called Aries, mentions Isidore that *quia fuit in aris à gentibus immolasum vade dicitur: Ideó Aries quiæ mantatur ad aras*. Which means that to the Ram they called Aries, for the Gentiles offered it on their altars as sacrifice to their Gods; and even the Jewish people offered it to God as sacrifice for their sins.

Avicenna writes that Ram's meat, burnt and made into powder is good against morphea, if placed over the region.

He further says that the powders of burnt Ram's meat, together with those of its mother, drunk with wine, are good against Serpent, Scorpion and also against rabid Dog bites.

He further says that the said powders are good against clouded eyes.

He also says that hot Ram's lungs, placed over a skinned foot or an infected scraping, will heal it marvelously without need of any other medicine.

Aesculapius says that the juice of a lung distilled over fire and drunk is good against the tertian fever and it heals kidney pain.

Pliny writes that Ram's broth is good against Crab bites.

Hali says that Ram's gall cures ear pain arising from coldness.

The powders of burned bones, from Lamb, Ram of Sheep, can remove oil stains from paper and silk, by placing them on top of this and making pressure with a good amount of weight for seven days.

The manure of these Animals, is most useful for the land, for it makes it very fertile.

The nails and horns of these Animals are good for a great deal of medicines; and even Silversmiths use the ashes of these in their trade.

Every time the Rams mate with their females, if the Aquilon wind is blowing, they will give birth to males. And if the Austro wind is blowing, they will give birth to females. Pliny.

Note this proven secret which is that if you tie the left testicle of a Ram, it will always produce females. Pliny.

Of the virtue of humility and its advantages

Over these Animals, the most humble and gentle of all that exist on the earth, it seems to be appropriate to say something of this such heroic and principal virtue, without which no one may enter Heaven, as is clearly said by Christ Our Redeemer in Saint Mark, Chapter 18, by saying that to he who doesn't humbles himself as a child will not enter into Heaven. And Saint Bernard says of Our Lady that with her virginity she pleased God and with her humility did she conceive.

When Hyssop asked Chilon[269] how he understood God, he answered that he elevated the humble and lowered the proud.

True humility, so says Saint Chrysostom, consists of four things. In disregarding oneself. Not disregarding others. In disregarding all that makes the World. And in disregarding offense and not paying attention to insult.

Humility is the root of peace, and is born from self knowledge, Saint Gregory.

Humility is the keeper and receptacle of grace, Saint Bernard.

Humility is what disposes the heart to receive other graces and virtues. Diego de Estella.[270]

Humility, according to Saint Gregory, is the door and foundation of all virtues; and whoever wants to have virtues without it is like carrying ashes in the wind.

Humility, so says Saint Bernard, is more important in being awarded Heaven than virginity, it is the keeper of peace and Ecclesiastic accordance.

Saint Chrysostom says that humility is the principle of Blessedness, that the more one lowers and humbles himself Christianly, the more he rises.

The humble, so says Estella, lowers himself not because he is of smaller worth, but because he is of greater weight, as good wheat.

Job, speaking of the praise of humility, says that the humble can be secure and persevere in this virtue for he will reach glory in the end.

Solomon says that the road to glory was, is, and will be humility.

Christ says in Saint Mathew 11: Learn from me that I am gentle and humble in heart. Idem, Chapter 3, says that in order to find the narrow path into Heaven one need to enter through the door of humility.

The humble, so says Estella, with his humility edifies his fellow man, confounds the devil and compensates God for all offenses.

Saint Gregory says that an evident sign of the chosen is humility.

Only humility escapes all snares of the Devil.

---

269. Translator's note: probably Chilon of Sparta, one of the seven Sages of Greece.

270. Translator's note: probably Diego Ballestero de San Cristóbal y Cruzat, a XVIth century Spanish Franciscan theologian and ascetic.

Estella says that Heaven does not receive any one else besides the humble; furthermore, he who gathers virtues without humility is throwing straws at the wind and dust in the air, with which he is blinded.

Saint Augustine says that should anyone ask him what is the path to Heaven, he will always say humility; and many times was he asked and he always responded that there is no other path to Heaven but through humility.

Also says that our works grow before God in merit, the more they decrease in our eyes through humility. And he further says that one of the reasons why God wanted us to overcome in this life our praises is because to be a friend of God one needs to be humble.

Saint Augustine says that humility is not just having old clothes and walking with a lowered head, but mostly to reveal ourselves in an insult received.

The same Bernard says that true humility is offered immediately to repair a fault.

Saint Gregory says that the more the humble are put down, the more do they become like God; and that only the humble can behold God, and these will come to occupy the place of the prideful. Regarding this it is told in the books of Esther, Chapter I, that Queen Vashti, wife of King Ahasuerus, lord of one hundred and twenty seven Provinces, was repudiated and deprived of being a Queen over her arrogance and disobedience; and the beautiful Esther, due to her humility and simplicity was seen as graceful in the eyes of King Ahasuerus, and thus he took her as Wife and Queen, and she did not seek to acquire jewels and adorations as all other damsels who did so to look pleasant in the eyes of the King, but rather she adorned herself with humility and self-consciousness, and this made her beautiful, graceful and even a Queen. The most expressed figure was the Blessed Virgin and Mother of God, being the most humble and graceful of all who were and will be, due to the great humility of conceiving the Son of the Eternal Father. And regarding this Saint Bernard said of the Virgin: *Virginatate placuit, & humilitate concept*, as was said.

Chapter VI

Of the Goat and Buck

Among the Animals of great interest and advantage to man are the Goat and the Billy, for the whole of them, from leather, meat and hair is useful to man, even if not as much as the Sheep and Ram. Regarding things as fighting, the Goat is much better for the making of shoes than the Ram. Meat should be taken from the Ram and leather from the Billy. This is a light, temperate and risky Animal; its natural living is walking and roaming the Mountains and cliffs, walking without care, without rest, eating solely the tallest leaves and herbs; and should it be able to reach a tree it will gnaw at its bark and destroy it, and for this reason is it important that a Herder be light, fast and temperate in order to jump after them and be able to grab them. The Goat is an Animal that is maintained with any plant, and of any herb it makes use, and even if this is poisonous it does not harm it; and if by any chance it tastes any honey it will die from it. Constantino[271] writes that if these Animals eat a plant which is called tamarind, or drink from a vase made from its wood, their spleen will melt. Serapion[272] writes that he saw some of these Goats that ate of these plants and no harm came to them. Of the Turkish it is said that they give powders of this plant to the Janissaries when they are young, for it reduces their spleen and in this way they are made more temperate and light; and this works in such a way as they can catch a deer in a single breath.

And when a Turk leaves his house or is on the road, he takes with him these temperate and light Janissaries, which are sons of Christians, given to the Great Turk as pariahs from Greece, and now these can be found in many regions of Turkey. Returning to our purpose, I say that the Goat is naturally insane; and in this way may one understand why an incipient and insane man is customary to be said to have Goat eyes; and this Animal sees further in the night than during

---

271. Translator's note: uncertain reference.
272. Translator's note: there are a few authors and physicians which this can refer to, Serapion of Alexandria, Serapion the Elder or Serapion the Younger, but it is most likely the first, from the third century.

the day and it has teeth in both gums, a thing that the Sheep and Ram do not have, for these have solely four teeth; the Billies have more teeth than the Goats and they normally live between eight to nine years. The best pasture for a Goat that has just given birth is, according to the experts, salt, for this generates in them a lot of milk and it also makes them fat and bright. But they say that this should be given in dry weather, after they have gone out to eat and giving them something to drink afterwards, and they will become very fat and produce an abundance of milk.

The Herders should be warned that occasionally an Animal will approach the Goats in the afternoons, which is called Caprimulgo and in regular tongue Nightjar, even if it is sometimes called Mamacabras.[273] This one approaches the Goats carefully when these are resting and it sucks their milk, and they think that this is their Kid and they consent to this; and when this happens their milk dries up and some of them lose their sight.

Story of the Goat and Billy

In the descendants of the Marcuses, a noble lineage of Catalonia, one may read of a certain Goat and Kid, that even if this was but a dream it did have its effect; and this was that a nobleman called Marcus, who over the disgrace and vanity of his ancestors came into great misery, and by being a nobleman and very poor he lived in great distress, always trying to discover a way in which he could be free from that poverty; and with these thoughts it happened that he dreamt that if he were to leave his land and travel to France, under a Bridge near the City of Narbonne, he would find a great treasure.

When he woke up, and was thinking about this dream, illusion or this desire to abandon his miseries, or maybe imagining it while awake, he decided not to pay attention to it, but as he once again had this dream, he determined to go test this venture. Arriving at the said Bridge one day or another, it happed that another Nobleman of that City every morning and afternoon passed by it, and he noticed this foreigner sitting in the middle of the Bridge for many days, and no matter how early he got up or how late he got back, this foreigner was already there, and so he decided to ask him the cause of this. The Catalonian Nobleman, after his insistence, responded: You should know that a dream brought me here, which said that, should I come to this Bridge, I would find a great treasure. The other man started to cross himself and jested saying: What a good idea it would be for me to leave my house over a dream I had the other day in which I went to Catalonia to the house of a man called Marcus and under a ladder I found a famous treasure. The Catalonian Nobleman hearing this other dream and the Frenchman's reprehension said his goodbyes, keeping his name a secret. Once he returned home he started to dig in secret the place that other man had mentioned; and after a few days he found a large iron chest, inside which there was a very large Golden Goat and Kid, made of solid gold. And with these two pieces he paid all his dues and all that he owed and he abandoned his misery, and the first thing he did was to build five chapels, which, as I know, are still standing today in the city of Barcelona.

Lodovico Celio[274] and Bolaterano[275] write that in Calabria a rare case occurred with a Billy; and this was that a herder called Cratis, while keeping some Goats near the River Cratis (from where he took his name) was so affectionate to one of his Goats that he had unlawful contact with it, and treated her with great delights and did not allow her to walk together with all the others. A Billy, which had dealings with this Goat was prevented from seeing or even getting close to it, and it took such malignancy to the Herder that one day, while he was sleeping, the Billy approached him and head butted him to death.

It then happened that within a few days the Goat manifested the contact the Herder had with her, for she gave birth to a monstrous half baby half Goat. Who will not admire at this strange case? That an Animal so incapable of reason would avenge an offense made onto the Goat with which it had contact! And who will not cross himself in knowing that there are men in the world

---

273. Translator's note: goat suckler.
274. Translator's note: A sixteenth century professor of Latin and Greek, most often known through the name Caelius Rhodiginus.
275. Translator's note: uncertain reference.

so without reason and sense, and of such vile and low thought that they cannot resist a brute Animal and not have interest in his legitimate wife!

From this case do I understand that it is custom to call those who do such things in Spain *Cabrones*, and in Italy *Cornuti*, speaking ironically with them, calling them in these terms, so as to awaken them from this deed done with this Animal.

Medicinal properties of the Goats and Billies

Goat milk is the best of all for children, after that of women; and should it be boiled it is very good for old men, but it is best if this is from black Goats rather than from white ones, and it is very healthy in the morning.

Goat milk retains diarrhea if drunk, or given with some *guijarros luzientes*.[276]

The milk from these Animals makes the skin of the face softer and it removes spots from it.

This milk, if drunk temperately, causes a good sleep, and in excess causes nightmares.

If drunk, this is good against all poison.

From Goat are many beautiful cheeses made; but one should be advised that these generate sands and stones, and those who have difficulty urinating should not eat of this cheese, nor from any other Animals, and this is advised by Grecio,[277] Bartolo,[278] Avicenna and Pliny. And the same is advised for women who are having their rules, for this is dangerous and harmful.

Milk serum, with fumus terrae[279] juice, drunk every morning makes a purge through urine and from behind, and it diminishes one's heat.

Goat and Billy horns, burned and made into powder are good to clean the teeth, for it cleans them, makes them white, strengthens and tightens the gums and removes pain.

The rennet of a Kid that has never grazed is good to soften the harnesses which are generated inside the breasts of women. And if drunk it cures decrepitude and it prepares the *madre* for conception.

The manure of these Animals is of great use for the fields, and if boiled in vinegar it heals the pain of any scorpion bite or that of any other poisonous Animal.

Columella[280] writes that whoever has the custom of eating Goat meat will always have a good and wide sight, and he will be temperate and light.

Kid blood, the Natural Philosophers say, makes diamonds softer, being true that one cannot do this with a hammer, and with a touch of this blood they becomes soft.

Goat urine, placed still warm into ears which are hard of hearing will remove the impediment; the same is done with gall.

Billy urine, drunk, breaks bladder and kidney stones, and it expels sands. And this we have said and shall say is mentioned by the above authors and Dioscorides among them.

Goat and Billy fat is very good for many illnesses, it softens any hardness and it is also good for shrunken tendons and nerves.

Cows will run from the smell of roasting Goat meat.

Ashes from Goat horns prevent the smell from the feet and armpits, if this ash is applied there.

Goat grease, mixed and melted with roses, removes the grains which are generated on one's face and also pustules; and distilled and placed in the ears will cure deafness, if this is not too old.

Smoke from burnt Goat hair applied to the nostrils prevents blood flows.

---

276. Translator's note: uncertain translation.
277. Translator's note: uncertain reference.
278. Translator's note: uncertain reference.
279. Translator's note: *Fumitory Fumaria officinalis*.
280. Translator's note: Lucius Junius Moderatus Columella, an extremely relevant agricultural writer from the first century.

Of necessity and danger, by occasion of the Goat

For having noted in these Animals two great flaws, especially in the females, as these are naturally indiscreet, placing themselves in danger by climbing up ravines and cliffs, in such a way as they many times fall, it seems to me to be appropriate to speak of necessity and danger.

Necessity, says Saint Augustine, isn't anything else but poorness of spirit, and that under the name of necessity are all vices hidden.

Necessity and madness are always together. Bion.[281]

Constantly walking in a rush or moving one's hands too much without a reason is a sign of necessity and madness. Demetrius.[282]

Seneca says that it is better to be poor than a fool, for the poor has necessity of money and the fool has necessity of reason.

When the Philosopher Apollonius was asked who was the poorest, he responded the greatest fool. Philostratus.[283]

Marcus Aurelius says that the Wise compensates what he lacks from nature with the Letters, and the fool compensates with malice what he is lacking in direction, and because of this do the greatest fools sin for malice.

Aristotle says that from ignorance and necessity do events occur.

Cicero says that necessity is the greatest evil of all evils of fortune and of the body; and that it is a characteristic of the fools to notice the flaws of others and not take care of their own, and that it is natural for a man to fail and only persevere in front of a fool.

One cannot dispute the Letters with the ignorant, nor insist with a fool.

A fool cannot and does not know how to be quiet. Solomon.

There is nothing more bold nor daring, so says Menander,[284] than necessity and madness.

The fools are always whining and ready to give their opinion. Idem.

Saint Gerome says that to serve a Wiseman is freedom, and to order a fool is captivity.

Saint Gregory says that one is as much a fool as he wishes to seem Wise, while being ignorant.

Saint Augustine says that under this name of necessity are contained all vices.

Cicero says that necessity is the mother of all evils.

Of Danger

Saint Ambrose said that offering oneself to danger without good cause is insanity.

Seneca said that it is a great madness to offer oneself to danger in the hope of a remedy.

The Wise says that whoever loves danger will die from it.

In great trust, so says Peisistratos,[285] there is always great danger.

Seneca says that danger should not be taken, but rather received. And that never is a danger defeated if not by another danger. And he further says that he who wins without danger wins without honor.

To escape danger is a great sanity, and to seek it is necessity and madness.

---

281. Translator's note: uncertain reference.
282. Translator's note: uncertain reference, but probably Demetrius the Cynic.
283. Translator's note: author of *Life of Apollonius of Tyana*.
284. Translator's note: A Greek dramatist from the third century BC.
285. Translator's note: An Athenian tyrant of the sixth century BC.

Chapter VII

Of the Dog and its great loyalty

The Dog, according to Isidore, is the most intelligent of all Animals and the one of greater sense; and according to the Physiologus it exceeds all other Animals in three things: in discernment and knowledge, in love and loyalty and in diligently serving its master. It is amiable, festive and caring; even if envious in everything and it is docile and accommodated to anything. It has five finger on its hands and four on its feet, as the Wolf and the Lion (the Bitch has many tits, like a Sow) and it is hairy like all other Animals except the Sheep. The Dog, to its master, is ready in obedience, diligent in service, thankful in his treats, recognized in its sustenance, loyal in its handling, faithful friend on any occasion, perseverant in danger, confident in work and finally, in life and in death, it loves and recognizes he who is good to it with an admirable enthusiasm. The ancients, in order to denote the great fidelity and obedience of the Dog, painted it with its head always turned to its masters during the hunt, and with this they meant that the obedience of the Dog is stronger than its natural inclination; for in the chase of a hare, it will call its master and ask for his instructions. Only the Dog among all other Animals has hate, spite and envy of another Dog, and only it and man will once again eat what they have vomited; The Dog its food, the Man his sin; this Animal is light in its running, good for hunting, and good as a guard. Among these Animals there is a great difference in kinds, and each one has its own trade, for ones are called helping Dogs, and these are used in dangerous meetings, for they are risky, wrathful and spirited, and they can take on one, two or three men without these knowing how. Others are called mastiffs, and these are natural for the keeping of cattle, for they are most zealous in this work, keeping an eye on it day and night, circling it as sentinels and giving out some barks and howls to keep the enemy Wolves away. To other Dogs they call bloodhounds, and these have an immense sense of smell, for they can track beasts that hunters and mountain men can then kill with their arms and arrows, and this without seeing them, and the mere sound of a rifle will make them jump on the prey in order to return the dead or wounded Animal. To others they call water Dogs, which are attentive to the sight of a hunter and are in charge of returning game should it fall in a body of water, and they do not leave the water until they have found this piece of game to bring it back to the hunter; and these are in such a way friends of the aquatic hunt that they will jump in the water should they see any fish, in order to try to catch it. To others they call greyhounds, and these are light, natural and convenient for Hare hunting. Some of these are so loyal that they will hunt by themselves and bring back to their homes, to the hands of their master, a piece of game without having eaten any of it. To others they call Podengos,[286] and these are natural for hunting rabbits. Others they call Pointer Dogs, which have such a sense of smell that in the middle of the woods they can discover Partridge, and if these stop they will not move a muscle, staring eye to eye the Partridge until the hunter kills it.

And one should note the respect and fear the Partridges have towards these Dogs, for should they be discovered by it, they will not move unless the Dog abandons its purpose. Finally, to other Dogs they call guard Dogs, which are only good for this trade, which is to guard a house, and these are as important for this job as all the others for the other jobs we have mentioned; and from this difference of Dogs there are some who are so cunning and of such great sense, that they can recognize thieves solely by their smell; and if they feel these during the night, they will circle the house barking and they will not shut up until the smell of those 'honorable' people is gone. And there are also some little Dogs which are used for the entertainment of ladies, or in other words, to waste time.

Signs in order to recognize a good Dog

In all created things there are those who are more or less proper, and since we are talking of Dogs, it will not be inconvenient to provide the signs by which these may be good for any job and trade in which one may use a Dog. The Natural Philosophers say that when a Bitch gives birth, one should see which of the pups opens its eyes the first, for it is said that this is the best one, be it for guarding a house, guarding cattle or hunting, this one is always the best for this work. Pliny writes that in order to know which of the pups is the best and finest one should take the pups from where their mother gave birth, in such a way as she will not see them, and that pup which its mother brings back first to the place where she gave birth and was raising them is the best. Others give different signs to measure their quality, and this is that when they are little one should take them by the ear and raise them in the air by it, and the one which can take the most pain without yelping or complaining is the best and finest. For the guardship and custody of a house a black or brown dog is best; to guard cattle it should be white, or tending to the white, with a big head, a wide and open mouth, large lips, droopy ears, black and bright eyes, rightful bark, short and thick neck, husky and hairy chest, back, hips and arms and a fierce and amazing face, so as to frighten its enemies.

Signs in order to know when a Dog has rabies

It seems to me that it isn't of any less importance to teach how to know when a Dog has rabies, for all we have said and will say, and life will not be reduced by knowing this.

Rabies in a Dog is always, or most often, arising from the great thirst and heat these Animals suffer, both natural and accidental, for they are very hot and also the dry and hot weather makes them dryer and it heats up their blood, and even more in the Canicular Days, and so in this time they suffer from rabies more than in any other, and may the Divine Majesty of God free us from this, Amen. And even if Aristotle says in the *Natura Animalium*, that if a rabid Dog bites a man he will not suffer from rabies as it happens with other bitten Animals, this is false, as experience has shown; for we see that men bitten by rabid Dogs not only become rabid but they also die from this illness.

---

286. Translator's note: Portuguese dog breed specialized in rabbit hunting.

When a Dog runs from its own shadow, as if afraid of it, it is evident that it has rabies.

When a Dog is staring at its shadow and is barking at it, this is a sign of rabies.

When a Dog runs from its own master without cause, this is a sign of rabies.

When a Dog doesn't recognize its master it is a sign that rabies is starting to dominate him.

When a Dog doesn't recognize the house of its master, nor does it seem to know how to enter it, this is a sign that it is about to go rabid, and in this case one should immediately apply that which will heal it or put it down.

When a Dog is depressed, with its ears low and hanging, while previously it had them straight and raised, this is a sign that it has rabies.

When its eyes are brighter than normal, and it is foaming from the mouth, this is a sign of rabies.

When its bark is coarser, and other Dogs run from it, this is a sign of rabies.

When it doesn't want to eat and if it gets wet it runs ways, this is a sign of rabies.

When it runs without end, and it has its tail between its legs, this is a sign of rabies.

When the Dog has rabies, confirmed if water is cast on it, it will bang with its feet on the ground and die.

The Natural Philosophers say that a Dog that crosses its hands when lying down on the floor will never be taken by rabies.

The Dog that has above its eyebrows a white, brown or black sign, over each of them, will never be taken by rabies.

Natural remedies so as a Dog will never have rabies, unless it is bitten by another

Columella writes that one should take a pup that is forty days old, and one should twist the tip of its tail, in such a way as the first joints of this become loose and dislocated from the others, then cut a bit of the skin and you will find a small nerve, which, should it be cut, will cause that a Dog will never become rabid, unless it is bitten by another rabid Dog. Others say that in order for a Dog not to become rabid one only needs to cut the tip of its tail when it is forty days old, or a little more; but never younger, for the Dog will die.

Remedy against Dog fleas, worms and mange

Against the fleas which are generated in a Dog it is good to wash them with water in which henbane was boiled, or with the green part of the said henbane, and if the Dog is washed two of three times with this water it will not have a single flea; and should it have ticks in its ears, by washing them with this water they will die.

Against worms and Dog mange, it is important to take a Ram's head and boil it very well in water, and then mix this broth with a some aloe, and then give it to drink, and it will be healed of both these things. Washing them a few times with Sea water will also cure them of mange.

Story of the Dog

Friar Luis of Granada tells of a Hare which was roaming by the sea shore and ran across a tiny Dog, which started to bark and chase this Hare with great noise, which did not apparently care about this barking and continued on its way; and this little Dog felt so offended with its tiny bark that it lost its patience with the Hare and started to fight with it, and so as not to stains its teeth with its blood, it dragged it to the Sea, and placing its hands on it, drowned the Hare.

Friar Luis of Granada tells of another Dog that was accompanying its master to the market, who had to momentarily abandon the path so as to take care of his necessities, and in doing so forgot his money pouch and belt; as during this the Dog was having its fun through the fields, it did not see through which path its master went, and going back to the path it could not find him, and so it stood there guarding the pouch and belt; and when its master returned through the same path three days later, he found the Dog guarding the pouch and belt, dying of hunger, and as soon as it saw its master it died, keeping with its customary fidelity.

Pliny tells of a Dog that had such love for its master that when he died it no longer wanted to live; and as such it stopped eating and died of hunger.

Of another Dog I can speak for having witnessed it, and this was a Notary from this City, called Chaves, who had a Dog that when its master was ill would never leave his bedside; and when this Chaves died the Dog no longer wanted to live, as it stopped eating, and it died three days after the burial of its master; and of this case there are many witnesses in Valencia.

Of a half Ram half Dog

In our days, in the City of Valencia, a monstrosity happened which is worthy of memory, and this is about a blanket maker called Juan Lior, who had a Bitch for the guarding of his house, and in this same manner he raised a Lamb for the entertainment of his children, which soon enough become a Ram. And this Animal had such familiarity with the Bitch that they always walked and slept together, and from this friendship and company it so happened that the Bitch became pregnant from the Ram, and when its time came it gave birth to six pups, with their skin similar to their father the Ram. And not knowing of this gathering of the Bitch with the Ram, they got rid of five of them, leaving only one, so as the Bitch could raise it well and with little fatigue. In a few days they noticed that the pup was covered from head to toe with wool, and that it had its muzzle, front and head as a Ram, even if not with horns; the teeth were flat, its hands and feet were those of a Dog and the tail that of a Ram; it had the bark and growl of a Dog and it urinated like a Ram, for one never saw it raise its leg to do this. And it had a very contrary nature to the other Dogs, as these are very much enemies of the poor and all those with old clothes, but this was so much a friend of them that when it saw a Cleric or a Religious man it become so joyful that he would follow them for a great deal of time.

In Valdechrist, the Monastery of the Carthusian Friars, which is about nine leagues from Valencia, there was a Bitch which usually made the trip from the Monastery to the City with the Procurator of this house, and it so happened that one of these times it was pregnant, and mere days away from giving birth; on this occasion the Procurator needed to go to Valencia and the Bitch, seeing him leave, went along with him. Arriving in Valencia at night the Bitch went in labor and gave birth to five little pups, of which the Procurator took away two and left behind three, so as the Bitch would be able to raise them better. After tending to the new mother the Procurator retired to his chambers; and returning in one hour he did not find neither the Bitch nor the pups, and thinking that these would have been hiding in some corner of his house he searched through all of it and still he could not find them. The next morning the Procurator wrote to the Convent, and among many things, related what had happened with the Bitch. The Monastery wrote back saying that they had found the Bitch early in the morning at the door of the Monastery; and that all were amazed that a newly mother Bitch could have made a journey of fifty four leagues in a single night, for she would have forcibly had to make the trip three times in order to take the three pups, for she wouldn't be able to take more than one at a time, which would be impossible.

And what is surely the most amazing thing is that it managed to take the three pups before the gates of the City were closed for the night.

Plutarch tell of another story and notable case of a Dog; as King Pyrrhus was marching with his army he came across a Dog that was keeping watch over the dead body of its master, howling terribly; the King ordered the body to be buried and that the Dog be given a daily ration; and furthermore, he order that research be done on the cause of death of the master of that Dog; it so happened that the killer was not found, and so all the men were ordered to pass in front of the King, at whose feet the Dog was sitting, watching all the Soldiers; and upon seeing those who had killed its master it charged at them with great fury and threw them on the ground. The King, seeing the fury and daring of the Dog, immediately suspected those soldiers, and had them arrested and tortured, and they then confessed to having killed the master of that Dog; and for this they were condemned to death.

In the year of 1447 a strange and miraculous case happened in Valencia regarding a certain Dog; and this is a story I wish to tell here. The case was that a Judge of this great City of Valencia was a man called Genis Ferrer, married to the daughter of a rich farmer from Payporta, a place neighboring Valencia. And a man was complaining to this lady that her servants had mistreated him and destroyed a farm he owned near hers; and she, not making much of a case of the complaints of this poor man, did not bother to reprehend her servants, nor did she order that they not bother this man again; and it happened that the man once again complained to her, saying that if she did not compensate him for this damage he would have to resort to the local Justice. The good lady, feeling the seriousness of this man, ordered a Black Slave of hers to kill this farmer, and she told him not to worry, that should he be caught, she would save him from any harm. This Black man decided to fulfill the desire of his mistress (and by this reason do many servants and some friends surely end up in hell), and he went on to find a place to hide in the farmer's house, and in the dead of night he stabbed the poor man, his wife and two sons he had, and not being able to see one other little girl of six of seven years old that was still alive in another bed, he escaped through a window, just as a Dog that was guarding the house was rushing towards him, and not being able to follow him through the window it could not catch him and the Slave was able to reach safety. When the day broke the girl called for help and all neighbors rushed there, but they could not know who had done this nor the cause for it. And this case was made silent, for in those days surely things of Justice were not as refined as they are now, nor was human malice so great. And it happened that after a few months the Dog that was unable to avenge the death of his master when he was murdered arrived in Valencia, and it went up to the Hall of Judges, having all of them inside, and it started barking and giving great howls at the door, and these were so remarkable that all inside came out to see what was happening and they chased the Dog away. The following day the same Dog returned to the Hall of Judges at the same time, and it gave out greater barks than last time, and once again it was chased at the end of a stick; and one of the Judges warned the others that the coming of that Dog twice with such barking always at the same hour should not remain a mystery; and so he ordered that this Dog be followed after coming to the Hall of Judges, and so was done. As the Dog returned at the same time it was followed to the mentioned place of Payporta, where he stopped; and upon asking the locals to whom that Dog belonged to they responded that it belonged to that good man who had been killed with his wife and two children during the night in his own house, and that with that Dog, also a girl of six or seven had escaped this fate. With this information they returned to the Hall of Judges, and as this was appropriate, they called the girl there and they had her between two guards of this City; for the girl said that she would be able to recognize the Black man who had killed her father should she see him, and so it happened that one day she found him, and said that that was the Black man who had killed her father, mother and brothers. The Black man was arrested and taken to a dungeon, and as he was trusting of the word of his mistress, he immediately confessed, saying that this lady had ordered him to do this, and she was immediately arrested and sentenced to death, along with the Black man, and Divine Justice took this Dog, that for so many years had eaten the bread given by its dead master, as an instrument of such a just sentence.

In our own days another case of a Dog happened in the remarkable City of Toledo, and this was that a certain Knight of this City had died, and his Dog was so saddened by this that as the body of his master was taken to be buried, it was so hurt that in order to close the Church doors they had to chase him away with a stick, and as the door was closed it remained there, moaning and barking to be let in so it could keep company with the body of its master, and it stayed there for many days and months; and if not for a good man who passed everyday by the Church with some food it would have surely died of hunger and thirst, all this because it did not want to be parted from its master, nor seem ungrateful to he who had fed it.

Another Dog I can mention for having witnessed with my own sight this example of discretion and natural foresight; and that was that every time it was given a piece of bread it would eat it; but should the piece be too big it would carry it to a stable and dig a hole in the manure gathered there, placing the bread inside and covering it; and should the day come when somebody forgot to feed it, it would dig up this hidden bread and eat the amount necessary for the day, once again burying the remaining bread.

In the time of Emperor Charles V, in the city of Palencia, there lived a Clergy member who was a Precentor and Teacher of the local See, and he had a Dog with such great sense and knowledge that everything that the Precentor taught it, it would learn so well that all were admiring and some were even suspicious that it had received a devil in its body, and it was necessary to perform exams to prove that this was solely the natural instinct of this Dog and the great industry of the Teacher. And among the many skills this Dog had, one of them was that it was charged with fetching the students, whose names the Dog had memorized. And when the said Teacher needed to address any of them, he would call the Dog and tell it, either by signs or words: go get me Juanillo, and it would immediately fetch him even if he was hiding among the other youngsters, finding him with no problem and taking him back to its master. And should the Teacher ask it to fetch Perico, it would not make any mistakes, and it would fetch Perico and bring him with great haste. And in such a way could it distinguish the students that it was as if it had reason. Even to fetch meat there was no better servant than this Dog, for leaving it a basket with the money wrapped in some cloth or paper it would carry it in its teeth, take it to the Butcher and place it in front of him who then gave it the meat in the same basket and the Dog would return home, without touching any of the meat. If by any chance the Teacher was at Church and it started to rain, he would just stand at the door and wait for his Dog and, taking off his cap, he would place this in its mouth and say: Find my sister and ask for an umbrella; what a rare thing! That as the Teacher had a mother and sister living in the same house the Dog would find the right one and, giving her the cap, she would immediately understand what the Dog wanted and she would give it to it by tying the cape to its back and it would safely carry this to its master in its mouth. And if the Teacher was at church and found a dirty cloth, he would walk out, give it to the Dog and say to it: Take this cloth and give it to my mother and bring a clean one; and the good Dog would go straight to his master's mother, give her the cloth and wait for a clean one, and should it be delayed or if someone was slow in giving it the cloth, he would bark throughout the whole house, and when it got it, it would march back; and it had one other excellence which was that it never entered the Church, but it would rather wait outside of it until its master would come out to get whatever it was that he was carrying. If the said Teacher wanted to get up extremely early on any day, he would call the Dog to his sleeping quarters and by tapping on the door he would transmit to the Dog what he wanted; and thus the Dog, before the Sun was up, would rush to his quarters and would not stop scratching at the door until its master opened it. Finally, should he ask for the Breviary it would also understand this; if he asked for his slippers it would get them; the gloves, it would bring them, and also many other things which he had thought this Dog and of which I will not write for being too many; I will however tell one other thing of great consideration that happened with this Dog. And this case was that a great friend of this Teacher had a journey to make, and fearing that some harm would come upon him he was ready to abandon this obligation; the Teacher, perceiving this, said: Do not abandon your obligation, for I will lend you my Dog so as it may accompany you (for this Dog was great of body, strong, brave and robust). And to this his friend responded: I would gladly go with the Dog should it want to come with me, but I doubt that it will follow me. Hearing this, the Teacher called the Dog and pointed at his friend with his finger and said: go with this man and do not leave his side until you return, and watch over him as you would me. Marvelous thing! That as soon as this was said the Dog left the side of its master and went with his friend. And as these were on their way, stopping in a certain inn the man wanted to hear Mass, and by not wanting to lose the Dog when he went into the Church he left it in the quarters where they were living. The Dog, seeing itself locked in and without his company, jumped out of a window and following its scent went through the path its companion had followed, and found him at Mass, and he was greatly astonished and no longer did he try to separate himself from it; and when they had returned to their City and home, the Dog did not want to leave him until he went to see the Teacher, to whom he then told all that had happened with the Dog during the trip.

Over these and other things did some people try to buy this Dog for fifteen hundred ducats, and the Teacher never wanted to sell it; and upon taking it one time to the presence of Emperor

Charles, this Dog died on the way, and as one was lost so was the other, for it wasn't without great sentiment that this man found himself deprived of his faithful servant, and he could not present it to whom he wanted.

I have known a Dog of such great sense and scent that anything that its master left on the field or inside his house, even if hidden, as he would ask for it the Dog would go get it. And this Dog's master wanting to show this to one of his friends, took him to a farm he owned and hid among the woods a cloth in the presence of his friend and in the absence of the Dog, and upon returning home he called the Dog and showed it the pouch, indicating to it that his cloth was missing and said: Find this; and the Dog no sooner went than it returned with the cloth in its mouth, which wasn't of little admiration to all the present, me included. The things that this Dog did and understood were of the same fame as some Italians which roam the World, that no one is admired by these, for they are such and so many that we see them and do not believe them.

Medicinal properties of the Dog

The great Aesculapius writes that Dog's blood, drunk, will cure tremors in those that suffer from this ill.

The same is said of the powder of Dog meat, or powder of burnt Dog head, that should these be drunk they will cure tremors. And powder from Dog teeth will heal the bite of the same Dog, and it is also said that these cure tooth and gum ache.

Dog gall, mixed with honey, cures eye mists and cataracts; and its milk will make hair and beard grow; and it is further said that Dog fat heals gout or the evil of the feet, and also ear pain.

Avicenna says that Dog's blood does not allow for hair to grow, or at least hair which was pulled out previously, should that area be anointed with this blood; and the same is written by Galen.

Dog's urine, placed over a wart will make it disappear and dry. Avicenna.

Dioscorides writes that the milk from a Bitch's first litter prevents the growth of hair after these have been cut with a razor, by anointing that region with this milk.

Furthermore it is said that Dog urine, mixed with saltpeter, cures leprosy.

He further writes that the white manure of a Dog, produced and boiled during the Canicular Days, and dried also in this time, is of great use to retain belly fluxes, if drunk.

Pliny writes that to reduce the strength of any poison, so as it does not harm he who has drunk it, there is not better remedy than Dog's blood.

The same Pliny writes that milk from a Bitch's first litter, placed in the eyes melts away mists and clears up the sight; and if placed in the ear, still warm as if right off the tits, removes pain and heaviness.

He also says that anointing one's head with Dog fat or bone marrow will kill lice.

He further says, in Book 30, that the skin of a Dog, wrapped around any finger of the hand, prevents all distillations of the head.

He also says that by anointing one's feet with Dog's gall will remove pain from these which might originate from gout.

Furthermore he says that fresh Dog urine will cure any kind of wart.

Also, by licking any wound with its tongue, a Dog will heal it; for it is a property and virtue of the said tongue to clean, dry and re-flesh.

The Dog is born blind, and it is an Animal that over a bone will lose its food and even the friendship of its parents.

Of friendship and loyalty, by occasion of the Dog

Among all the Animals, that which professes the greatest friendship and loyalty towards man is the Dog, as can be seen by the examples we have mentioned, and in each day do we see this and touch this with our own hands; and its fidelity is such that it is much greater in many pounds to that of many men, even if these are true friends, and as such it has seemed appropriate to me to say something of true friendship.

Friendship, so says Saint Chrysostom, is a conformity sealed with love.

Saint Augustine says that true friendship is the bond of all things.

Aristotle says that friendship isn't anything else than a soul guiding two hearts and one heart that lives in two bodies.

Saint Augustine says that true friendship is perpetual.

Pope Pius the second says that true friendship doesn't have a price.

Saint Gregory says that a good friend is a keeper and helper of his friend's soul.

A friend, so says common wisdom, is a rock castle from where one defends the honor of a friend.

In all things, Seneca says, one should consult with a friend.

Seneca says to reprehend your friend in private and praise him in public.

Cicero says that in adversities does one know his friends.

Aeschylus says that among friends there should be no need for more than one yes and one no.

Hermogenes says that friendship is always certain in abundance and prosperity, and that one will know its truth as soon as these pass.

Chilon says that half of me is my friend, and half of my friend is me, and in this way he may seek me and I him, for he is me and I am him.

When Saint Gerome talked with Rufinus[287] he told him: When you find a good friend, you should treat him better than Gerome, for this isn't just found on any corner, and it is very hard to find, and one finds it very few times; it is conserved with difficulty, it is lost easily, it is appreciated very late and is missed very soon.

Cassiodorus[288] says that one should have the same esteem for an enemy who does you no harm as to a friend that does you no good.

Plutarch says that prosperous things gather friends, and adversities put them to the test.

Those who separate good friendships deserve that the Sun separates from them. Cicero.

In both fortunes, Plutarch says, true friendship is a sweet thing.

Seneca says that it is a more pleasant thing to make friends than to have them; and that a good friendship has less strength than a good kinship.

Jerónimo de Arbolanche[289] tells of two such friends that one of them confessed to being the other so as to free him from death, by offering himself up instead him, and he would rather die than see his friend die. Orestés was one of them, and Pilades the one who wished to die for his friend.

This same Author writes in his Book 7, that one friend loved the other so much that as one died the other was buried alive with him, by seeing himself deprived of such a good friend.

Oh Faithful friendship to what thing you force, as King Alexander, so as to free his friend King Luis from leprosy and help him claim once again his Kingdom, he killed his only two sons and with their blood healed him of that leprosy and restored him to his first condition and prosperity, preferring to see himself deprived of his sons than of his friend.

Of vomit invented by the Dog and its great advantages

The Dog, according to Pliny, Avicenna and other grave authors, was the inventor of the vomit (an extremely important remedy for a thousand different ills) for as it feels pain in its guts, it will immediately rush to the grasslands and from eating of these its stomach is moved and it provokes a vomit, and so it is set free from that weight. The ancient Medics, solely with this remedy, cured all infirmities that arose from three distempered humors, except those of the sanguine one. And not only did vomit free man from many and great labors but it also conserved his health and

---

287. Translator's note: Tyrannius Rufinus, a fourth century monk, translator of Greek patristic writings into Latin.
288. Translator's note: Flavius Magnus Aurelius Cassiodorus Senator, a fifth and sixth century Roman statesman.
289. Translator's note: A sixteenth century Spanish writer.

increased his life, this by cleaning the stomach area of over fluidities, crudeness and viscosities and terrible humors which are gathered there, causing an infinity of infirmities, and this sets man free from all of them. Particular of vomit, so says the Medical doctors, is that it cures all head ache and migraine; it prevents hand tremors, clears the sight, cures any boredom and heaviness of the stomach, unties and unclogs the veins, liver and spleen; retains diarrhea, belly fluxes, even if these are of blood; it does not allow for stones or sands to be generated, cures jaw pain; prevents water retention and blockages; and should these two infirmities be confirmed, vomiting will break them, and should this be done twice a month, one must never fear colic nor urination pain, nor gout, nor sciatic.

Finally, this great medicine and singular remedy will cure quartan fevers arising from the melancholic humor; it heals the tertian fevers which arise from the choleric humor and also regular fevers which are generated from the phlegmatic humor and other such acute and terrible illnesses that for not being of my specialty I will not mention. Everything which is affirmed and confirmed by the great Medic Hippocrates in that sentence and aphorism which says: *Vomitus, vomitum curat*; which means that vomit will cure another vomit, which is the greatest symptom and accident which may happen in the stomach; we may then see that vomit can cure the greatest accidents and most terrible of all ills, which is vomiting and not being able to retain food in the stomach, and it will also cure all the above mentioned infirmities and many more.

This can be further confirmed by the authority of many and great Authors and famed Medics; but as it seems to me that the authority of Hippocrates is sufficient I will make all others silent and I will solely write what our Patron Saint Ferrer says in the book of his life and miracles; who, wanting to persuade men and make them enthusiastic about vomiting their sins, for this is a much necessary medicine to cure spiritual infirmities and conserve grace and the friendship of the Creator, he says in the following manner: that as to conserve heath and corporeal life doctors advise men to vomit twice a month; so too is every Christian advised to perform a vomit of his sins, by confessing them twice a month so as to be cured of the infirmities of the soul and conserve the grace and friendship of God Our Lord.

Very important prescription for vomit

The most effective and helpful vomit, according to the learned in this faculty is the following: Take half an ounce of *Gera de Gale*,[290] or a full ounce, depending on each one's temper, in a powder or as a confection, even if it is better as a powder; melt this in a small amount of white wine and drink it, keeping it in the stomach for a quarter of an hour, and after this drink a big bowl of water in which you have boiled radish greens, spinach or Urgel chamomile, with a little bit of vinegar; and having drunk this try to vomit by putting your finger into your mouth or a feather with some olive oil, and in cleaning your stomach in this way many times you will be healed of many infirmities from the head to the toes.

Of what are the Gera powders made

So as one may see how important the *Gera de Gale* is, both for children as for adults, especially those that have worms, I will say the things which go into this. The first and principal thing which is in the Gera, or Gerapiega, is aloe, after this it's cinnamon, saffron, *almecegas*, spikenard, *assaro*,[291] xylo, balm and lastly citron sandal, and all of these are aromatic spices and comforting powders, and so they comfort the stomach and liver; fortifying and strengthening all close and principal parts of the belly. One should note what was written of the Gera in a notebook of a great and famed Medic, which said as follows: Oh Gera, Gera, what would be of the Medic, if the World knew of you? And further down it says: and if every fifteen day you are taken no one will be ill. Which is the same as saying: If man knew and used Gera, the Medics would die of hunger.

---

290. Translator's note: uncertain translation.
291. Translator's note: uncertain translation.

Chapter VIII

Of the Fox and its great treasons

The Fox is a cunning and treacherous Animal. It has the same condition as a bird of prey, and according to Saint Ambrose, it is bothersome to man and also to all Animals, except to one, which is called *Tiro*,[292] with which it has friendship and company, for these have the same condition.

Saint Isidore says that the Fox never makes a den or a home of its own, and yet it is never without a roof; and this is because it steals it from another Animal which is called Genet, and this with a strange cunning and deceit, for awaiting for the Genet to leave its den, the Fox will enter and leave there its manure; and when the Genet returns and smells the terrible odor it turns away running and never returns to its home; and with this treachery the Fox has a habitation without any work. Of the Fox also Constantino writes that it has a notable cunning and treachery; and this is that when it's hungry it barks like a Dog, so as with this bark the Rabbits will awaken and move; and with this trick it discovers their homes and catches them, curing its hunger. Another diabolical invention of the Fox, the same Constantino writes, is that when it is suffering from great hunger, and it cannot solve this with the treachery of the bark, it will lie down on some brambles with its feet up and its tongue out, so as to play dead, and as birds start to come near it, with its known cunnings, it catches them and is made satisfied.

Another cunning of the Fox regarding the Hedgehog is mentioned by Aelianus, for as this Animal feels a Fox about it, it makes itself into a ball; and as the Fox does not have a way to make its kill due to the sharp and penetrating weapons nature has given the Hedgehog, the Fox starts to roll it around and urinates on it until the urine reaches the nose and muzzle of the Hedgehog, and this, not being able to suffer this stench, opens up, and in doing so the Fox kills it and cures its hunger.

---

292. Translator's note: uncertain translation.

Stories of the Fox

Regarding this there is a story of the treachery of the Fox, and this was that during a certain night a shopkeeper was carrying some chickens and roosters, and as a Fox heard this noise it decided to eat them, and arriving on the path, place itself as if dead on the road through which the shopkeeper would pass; arriving near it, and thinking it was dead, he touched it with the tip of his foot, and seeing that it had no movement thought it was dead, and so as to take advantage of its fur, picked it up and placed it on his donkey, near the chicken cages. The cunning Fox saw on this occasion the perfect opportunity to kill some of the Chickens, and it was gone before they reached Villadiego, where the shopkeeper saw the damage and trickery of that cunning Animal.

It once happened (as many other times before) that an Eagle came upon the ground to catch a Hare, and as soon as it had it in its claws a Fox came out and took it from the Eagle; offended by this robbery, the Eagle went back to its perch and fell over the Fox, which, seeing itself caught between its claws was helpless; and as a shepherd was watching this fight he went closer in silence and taking his staff he struck all of them down; and thus he took with him all three pieces of game at very little cost.

In a certain village a Farmer had raised a Fox since it was little, and this was so domesticated that it would never leave his house; but, as the saying goes, many times man brings home his own sorrows; and as habits are never lost, the Fox was once left alone with the Chickens, and these were more than fifty and yet none were left alive; and fearing the punishment that would fall upon it, the Fox left the house and never returned.

Another Fox is mentioned in this tale of cunning; and this was that as it entered into a Chicken coop, which had very low walls from the outside and very high from the inside, and in this way, as it had its fill of chickens, killing them all, the Fox could not escape. Soon after, the owner of that house arrived, and seeing the dead Chickens and the Fox trying its best to jump out of the coop, he got down in order to grab a stick so as to give it what it deserved; and as this happened, the cunning Fox took the opportunity to jump on his back and from there jump over the wall and run away, using the man as a bench or ladder; and over this, or over other similar situations, should one say the old refrain, which goes: *Audaces fortuna invat, timidos quæ repellit*. And this means that fortune favors the daring, and the cowards it abandons.

And because these stories and treacheries of the Fox are infinite, and one would never end them and there wouldn't be any more room for the things yet to come, it will be better to leave these then in the inkstand, and I will only say that Samson, in order to destroy the fields and vines of his enemies, over a treachery that these had made unto him, used the most treacherous Foxes. And to these he tied their tails together with some hay and he set them on fire, letting them lose in the fields and vines of the Philistines, and as it is written, they burned and charred all of them; and as Samson took these treacherous Animals as instruments of his vengeance they are compared to hypocrites and double faced people; and do note a very important thing, that the Fox always walks with a limp, for its right leg is always a little shorter than the left, and so it is said that a man should guard himself from a limping Animal as if it was the Devil.

Medicinal properties of the Fox

Cold olive oil with Fox meat, according to Hali, is good to break any hardness from any part of the body.

Fox fat, fried in olive oil, is good to cure tooth and ear pain. Hali.

Water in which the meat of a Fox was cooked is good to cure joint pain, by washing these parts with that water. Avicenna.

Fox fat, Avicenna says, distilled and placed in the ears, removes their pain.

Powder from Fox lungs, drunk with good wine, cures those with asthma. Avicenna.

Fox fur is the hottest of all Animal fur. Avicenna.

Fox testicles, dried, made into a powder and drunk, are good against absent mindedness, but they move the appetites of Venus. Avicenna.

Of treason

The natural condition of the Fox is of extreme treachery; and it is dedicated to weaving treacheries, deceits and tricks, and so we will say something of treason and treachery.

Treason, says Livy, is treachery made against carelessness, and may we be free from it.

There is no safe place, says Saint Ambrose, wherever a traitor lives.

There is no punishment, so says Cicero, which can compare to treason or an unjust treachery.

One cannot trust, so says Livy, anyone who has ever been caught in treachery.

Traitors, so says Marcus Aurelius, always enter with kind words and leave with evil deeds, for they greet to fool, they promise to not give, and they secure to kill.

Vegetius[293] says that a single treachery can cause more damage than the weapons of an enemy.

Plutarch says that one should not have loyalty to him who betrayed his Country.

Maxentius says that traitors, and those who make pleasure of sowing evil among their kin and relatives, rarely end well; and thinking that there will be a reward for their treasons, they receive their just deserts, which is pain and terrible punishments.

---

293. Translator's note: Publius Flavius Vegetius Renatus, a Roman writer. Very little is known of him, except his two remaining works, a book on veterinary medicine and a military guide.

Chapter IX

Of the Pig and its advantages

The Pig is a fierce, imprudent and wrathful Animal, its nature is very lazy, dirty, impatient and grunting, from where one has the expression: If one wants noise he should raise Pigs; of it Aristotle says that it is incapable of acquiring a good habit, as it happens with the Elephants and other Animals, and it is always wild, indomitable and fierce; roaming the hills it is much more fearsome, terrible and wild than when it is raised in a corral; it has immensely strong teeth, and they are always destined for death, for they have no other use. The Natural Philosophers say that when one is to hunt a Pig, and this happens after it urinates, it becomes impossible to reach it, for as they relieve their bladders they become terrible and light, seeking the highest cliffs and slopes; but if a Hunter seeks it in the morning, before it has urinated, he can catch it easily. However, a Hunter should take care not to fail in his raid, for its fury is terrible and its fangs aren't anything short of spear heads. If this is found running up a slope, its chase will be difficult; but should it be found coming down a slope easily will it be put to ground, for as its hands are shorter than its legs, it will soon fall and become vulnerable. And should it have to pass any river, it will sooner kill itself[294] than do this, due to their hands being so short.

These Animals are good for Farmers, both for provisions and supplies of a house, as well as for pleasure, for there isn't any meat, neither fresh nor salted, that is as tasty as ham; and also because they can make rich a man who raises them; this because of the great amount of litters they have if they are well treated; and these give birth twice a year, and each time these give birth to seven,

---

294. Translator's note: uncertain translation.

eight, nine or more Piglets. And one should always take care when raising them to not let them loose, especially Farmers who have new born children, this because they will eat a baby with the same ease as if it was a stock of bran, and of this there have been a few examples and experiences; and not only do they eat the children of others, but if their hunger is great they will also eat their own; and if one does not keep them under control, or put a ring in their snouts, they will tear a house down, for they will dig all the ground around the foundations of a house with their noses. In this way it is best to keep them well supplied with food, for these are naturally voracious; and these will either eat, sleep or grunt, and they are so indomitable and incapable of correction, as Aristotle says, that even if one beats them to death with a stick, they will never be corrected of anything; and these are so dirty that their enjoyment is but mud, and these are so lazy that if they can eat while laying down they will not get up; and this is to such an extent that being hungry they will fill a house with their shouting so as to eat, and as they will not get up nor move they will shout until food is brought to their mouths.

Stories of the Pig

The Sacrosanct Gospel of Saint Matthew, Chapter five, tells of a strange case which happened with these fitly and fearsome Animals (even if their meat is very tasty), and this was that a Gentile Saracen man was possessed by demons, and he was living in some dead man's caves, and from there he would raid the paths with great fury and rage, scaring and mistreating all who passed there, and it happened that Christ our Redeemer passed by that place, and this possessed man seeing him ran in his direction and worshiped him and in high voices and shouts saying: Jesus, Son of the God of the most high, by God do I ask you, do not torment me. Then that Lord ordered the demon to leave that afflicted man; and he who knows all, Jesus Christ our Lord, asked the demon its name. And Satan responded: Legion is my name (and this means multitude) for there were many devils, and they pleaded to the Lord not to cast them out of that Region; and more did they plead to him to let them enter into the bodies of a group of Pigs nearby. And as the Redeemer of Life gave them license, they left that human body and entered into the Pigs, which, in a strange fury, cast themselves into the sea and never came back, and it seemed like more than two thousand of these were drowned. And the Saracens saw that, as Jesus Christ passed through that land these Pigs had drowned, they asked him to leave.

See the reason why those cursed Saracens casted Jesus Christ out of that land. Let us keep the divine goodness and not cast the God of our souls out for this same reason, over that or some other viler and vainer reasons than Pigs; what good is here to be felt and wept over, and what more would there be to be written; but as this is not our purpose, we will move on.

Story and tale which happened in Barcelona

In the City of Barcelona there is a certain lineage of people called the Porcelles, which in the Catalonian language means Piglets, and this last name is taken from these grunting Animals because of a certain tale which happened in this City to a married couple. And the case was that a lady of an average social status had convinced herself of something which is outside of common reason, and this was that someone had told her that a woman who gives birth to more than one child at a time indicates the sign of infidelity and that she had had commerce with more than one man; and as she saw herself pregnant and with a very large belly, she feared giving birth to more than one son, and she had imagined that she would be seen as indiscreet, thinking that it was true that giving birth to two, three or more sons, meant that while being married she had betrayed her husband. Upon giving birth it happened that she gave birth to nine male children, and as her *Comadre* was giving her the news of what was going on, she was thinking about what to do about her imagined affront (even if this was not true) and thus she persuaded her *Comadre* to hide the case and say that she had only given birth to one son, as she would find a way to remove the others from the world. With this intention she called a maid and ordered her to take those eight children and carry them to a field outside of the city and bury them there; and as she was taking them in a basket out of the City the maid ran into her master, and he asked her where she was going and what was inside that basket, and she responded in the Catalonian language; My Lord, these are some Piglets, and from this did they acquire the name of Porcells. Her master wanted to see them and opened the basket, finding eight beautiful babies, even if small and weak; and seeing this treachery and evil he immediately understood what this was, and asked the maid if his wife had given birth to these; she responded yes, giving him the full account of what was happening and the cause of why she wanted to bury them. Her master then, as a father and discreet man, he gave them to be raised without anyone's knowledge, except for the maid's; who he threatened so as this was not divulged, which she fulfilled. And after three years this father had a great feast organized, without his wife knowing to whom this was dedicated; and as all was prepared he had the eight boys come in with their nurses; and as all sat at the table the father started to declare the purpose of that invitation, and the story of those eight children who had come in with their eight nurses, and their mother not only received a small affront and scare, but she also received a great contentment as a mother, for seeing and understanding that those were her children, who by her own imagination had been sentenced to death after having just been born. And the father then ordered that all eight children from that day on be called the Porcells; and to this day are their descendants called thus, and this for the maid having said, when she was on her way to bury them, that the basket was carrying Porcells.

Medicinal properties of the Pig

Among all the meats with sharp hair, the best and the one with the best taste is bacon. Columella, Crescentiis, Lactantius, Herrera and Pliny are the authors of these properties.

Bacon fat, melted in vinegar and diluted in two or three times the water, is good to cure pain of any burn.

Pig's fat is good to ripen and stop any swelling and abscess.

This same fat kills lice on one's head or any other region.

Pig's lard can be used in an infinite amount of medicines and stews, and from it can one make unguent for any ill.

The marrow from the jaw of a Pig removes pain from teeth and gums.

Fat, eaten raw, is good against any poison which was drunk, and against mercury it is the best remedy, should be eaten immediately after.

Boar skin is the best for making shoes for dry weather, for as soon as it rains they are useless.

Pig's urine, mixed with rose oil, removes urination impediments, any ear pain and it break bladder stones.

Boar manure, dried, made into powder and drunk with wine, cures diarrhea, even if this has blood.

Pig's lungs, if eaten, will cure and prevent drunkenness.

Pig's fat is good to close and heal old wounds.

Fresh Pig's manure, placed still warm over a region with blood flow, retains and strops it in no time.

Pig's brain heals carbuncle.

Many other healings and advantageous properties has the grunting Animal; which one may read in the mentioned authors; but I will only say one more thing, for these mention this one with great exaltation, and this is that should plague be confirmed with buboes, the said Authors say that these should be very well anointed with Pig's fat and scrubbed with a cloth of warm wool, and this will kill the disease and prevent it from spreading, and there will be no danger to the patient.

Of laziness, by occasion of the Pig

For having noted that these grunting Animals are so lazy, it seems to be a good idea to say something of this, so as to show the damage this can cause.

Laziness, says Medina, isn't anything else but weakness and a decay of the heart, from which all vices originate; and it is so dangerous and poisonous this vice that it destroys all good and saintly works, and it causes pusillanimity and desperation.

Laziness and negligence, according to Saint Gregory, make a virtue into a sin.

The principal effects of laziness are talking too much, working too little and babbling.

Laziness will always bring those with it to poverty and an unfortunate end.

Laziness, so says Saint Basil, is always accompanied by malice.

Saint Augustine says that laziness and greed are always together.

Saint Bernard says that the weak and lazy are bad for any good works, and these are never found in prayer.

God Almighty and Our Lord, said through Jeremiah: Cursed be the man who makes my work with laziness, weakness and deceit.

Bias[295] says that laziness is a terrible mother for virtues, and that it is a well where they all drown.

---

295. Translator's note: Bias of Priene, one of the Seven Greek Sages.

Chapter X

Of the Deer and its properties

According to Aristotle the Deer is forewarned and prudent, and more than any other Animals it is discreet, light and extremely fearful, and this is due, according to the same Aristotle, to it having a very big heart; and of this he says that every Animal which has a heart bigger than the necessity of its body will be fearful, and should it be smaller it will be more daring, even if inconsiderate and wild.

This Animal has branch like horns and these begin to grow when it is two years old and until it is six, and every year a new branch is born, and from this age on no more branches are born even if they do grow in thickness; and among all the Animals the Deer is the only one whose horns fall and grow once again, with which it displays great contentment and joy. All Animals, and man with them, have a nerve under the tongue, like a worm, and this same nerve the Deer has in the middle of its forehead, and over this nerve the female is greatly troubled. Even if the Deer and Doe are greatly frightened by the voice of a Fox, they rejoice in the voice of man, especially if they hear soft singing, and they will follow this voice in such a way as they are easily hunted. The Natural Philosophers tell of a strange thing about the Deer, and this is that when two Deer fight, the loser will afterwards follow the winner throughout the rest of its life as a slave, showing submission and obedience, recognizing the winner and his superiority.

Stories of the Deer

One can read in the story of the life of Saint Giles, Abbot, that as he parted from the esteem of men and their troublesome company, he went into exile on the other side of the Rhône River in France, where he lived in a cave, and near this there was a fountain of very clear water, and a Doe that was near the fountain become very happy about seeing this new guest and humbled itself in front of Saint Gile, who then decide to live there with that Doe. And the Abbot Saint stayed there, eating roots and herbs in the company of the Doe that many times gave him its milk, and in this way he spent some time there in Prayer and Contemplation. It so happened that the King who ruled

France one day went out with his Dogs on a hunt, and these found the Doe that was the companion of Saint Giles, and seeing itself pursued by Dogs it took refuge in the cave where the Saint was doing his prayers and it threw itself at his feet as if asking for help regarding that danger. The Saint seeing it in such distress made a Prayer for it, asking God to free it from that harm, and so it was that the Dogs did not dare come into the cave, and as such the Doe was set free; but even if they did not enter they still barked at the interior of the cave, and the King arriving there with his hunters, not being able to enter the cave over the impediment of a great bush, had one of them shoot an arrow into the cave so as to see what was inside that made the Dogs bark such, and in this way he injured Saint Giles Abbot. The hunters approached, cutting their way through the bushes, until they arrived at the cave, and they saw the injured Saint inside, with the Doe lying at his feet, and from this story a great advantage came to that King, and to all those living in that land, and much glory to God Our Lord, may he be always Blessed and worshiped by his Servants. Amen.

The Deer have this instinct and natural love among themselves, that should they have to pass thought a great River, they help each other in this way: as they enter the river one after the other, the second will place its head in the middle of the buttock of the first, the third will do this to the second, the fourth to the third and so forth. And when the one that is leading is tired, it will switch to the end, changing its post, and they help each other in this with love and discretion. Sometimes it happens that as they pass, the strength of the river is too much and one of them may be taken by the waters, and should this happen, and the others realize that they cannot help it, they all throw themselves into the water, preferring death than surviving without one of their own.

The Natural Philosophers write that the Deer have a strange dislike and animosity toward snakes, and this in such a way as they will go to the caves and water holes where they take refuge, and they start digging and making noises until these come out and they tear them to pieces with their feet and mouth. And once they are finished with this they leave with great lightness seeking fresh water for fearing the poison, and they drink from this and vomit it once again, and in this way they get rid of all the venom which the snake might have had. Regarding this an Author writes of a certain Deer that while it was killing a snake, having it between its feet, it rolled up and bit it on the snout; and in this way the deer and the snake were rolling around in a fight without end, and as a man was watching them from the distance, he approached carefully and with a knife he cut off the head of the snake, freeing the Deer; and its contentment and gratitude was such that it never again wanted to leave the side of that man, and in this way it went with him; and one should actually not be amazed by this, for this Animal is the one (not counting the Dog) who has more friendship and familiarity with man, and even more if he sings or plays an instrument, for it is a great friend of hearing music.

Medicinal properties of the Deer

On the left side of the heart of the Deer there is a bone (which is a thing never seen in any other Animal) that if made into a powder and drunk with some regular water will heal every ill of the heart and diminish the melancholic humor. And this same powder is used against blood flows and hemorrhoids. Plateario.[296]

He who carries with him a Deer horn, according to Aesculapius, does not need to fear snakes, for these will run from its mere smell. The same Author says that the marrow of a Deer can remove any pain, this by anointing the ailing region with it.

Deer rennet, according to Hali, if eaten is good against bad mushrooms, and he says that Deer urine removes kidney pain, viscosities from the stomach and intestines, and it also heals wounds in the ears.

The tip of the tail of a Deer, according to Avicenna, is poisonous, and should anyone eat it, it will cause great harm and agonies of the heart, and little by little death.

Dried Deer lung, made into a powder, according to Pliny, mixed with honey and eaten, will heal coughing and asthma, no matter how old.

---

296. Translator's note: uncertain reference, but most likely Matteo Plateario or Giovanni Plateario, Italian Medics.

Deer rennet, according to Pliny, is a good remedy for *mal de madre*.

Deer horn powder, burnt, according to Pliny, if drunk, will heal decrepitude, and mixed with rosy vinegar they heal headaches, if a cloth made wet with this vinegar is placed over them. He further says that these powders are good to whiten and clean the teeth, and even remove pain from them; and this is even good to make them stronger for it tightens the gums; these are also good for blood flows. Finally, he says, if these are drunk with white wine, they dry and cure head rashes; and mixing these powders with white wine, they heal any pustule, by making them wet with this wine.

Pliny says that the right horn of a Deer is an antidote and remedy for many ills.

Aristotle writes that a Deer will hide his right horn from hunters as much as it can, for due to natural instinct it knows that this is the reason why it is being hunted.

Of dread and its advantages and harms, by occasion of the Deer

Dread is a fear conceived in the understanding of some present or future evil. Iuris.[297]

He who fears God, so says Solomon, will accept serving him.

The path to God, so says Saint Gregory, begins with fear, and through this it reaches perfection.

He who is without fear, so says Tertullian, is without shame or correction.

Divine fear, according to Saint Gregory, is the foundation of faith.

Fear without hope, according to Saint Augustine, is the cause of desperation.

A holy thing is, according to Saint Bernard, to live with fear and divine dread, so as to reach the grace of God.

Shame, according to Terence,[298] is something of a free man, and fear something of a slave.

Fear, according to Titus Livy, is always stronger than shame.

A fearful Dog, according to Cicero, has a worse bark than bite.

Aristotle says that any Animal with a naturally large heart is fearful, and those that have it smaller than their bodies require are daring, shameless and reckless, as we have mentioned.

Saint Augustine says that he who always lives in fear is always tormented.

Little or no things, according to Quintilianus,[299] have any effect on he who is fearful.

He who can ask without fear gives rise to denial. Seneca.

He who fears God keeps his precepts, is secure, lives quietly, sleeps a good sleep, asks without suspicion and reaches all that he desires.

He who fears God loves humility, lives peacefully, follows humbleness, learns what he wants and lives restfully.

He who is feared by many will forcibly be afraid. Periander.

It is not good, according to Publius,[300] to fear that which cannot be avoided, but one should rather receive it with manly spirit.

He who lives without fear is in great danger, according to Mexía.[301]

Cicero says that even if there are many things that we love, we will always fear even more; for love is easily changed, but fear is difficult to resolve.

He who always walks among enemies, according to Euripides, is always filled with dread, and so this man says (and with reason) that if for no other reason, we should seek to not have enemies, and that there are innumerable respects in this life, and we at least should seek to have friendship with all men, and this is the principal commandment of God our Lord, which is convenient to all.

He who fears God has great patience, is given to prayer, makes penitence, has devotion, follows obedience and controls his passions with prudence.

Good is, according to Saint Bernard, that even if a man is troubled he should not be disturbed.

---

297. Translator's note: uncertain reference.
298. Translator's note: Publius Terentius Afer, a Roman play writer from the second century BC.
299. Translator's note: Marcus Fabius Quintilianus, a Roman rhetorician from the first century.
300. Translator's note: Publius Cornelius Tacitus, a Roman senator and historian of the first century.
301. Translator's note: Pero Mexía, a Sevillan writer and humanist of the XVIth century

Chapter XI

Of the Cat and its cunnings

There are three different types of Cats in Spain; one is the Domestic, the others are called Genets and the others are called Civets.

The Domestic Cat is a cunning Animal and it is a natural enemy of the Mouse, or should I say a friend, for it will spend three or four days waiting at the door of a barn so as to catch one. It is a cowardly and daring Animal; it is a coward if it has a place to run, and it is daring and valiant if it is cornered, and on this occasion it will show its claws and demonstrate such spirit and courage that it will make even the bravest tremble. And this should be noted by anyone trying to catch one, even more if this is trapped and without any place to run, and for this reason it is called in Italy the House Lion; and this is with good reason, for seeing itself in a bind it will scare away even the most valiant. So much joy does the Cat have when it catches a Mouse, that unless someone stops it, it will play with it for two or three hours and once it understands that it is dead, it buries it in its gut by eating the body with such contentment as if it was a fish. It has such crystalline eyes that they shine in the dark just as coals; and it has such a sharp and penetrating sight, that it sees as easily in pitch dark as it does in midday, and it has another property in its eyes, and this is that as the Moon is increasing, so do its eyes, as experience has shown.

This Animal is very tractable and amiable, if it is treated with kindness and cuddles; but it is terribly indomitable and intractable if it is treated with force and harshness. It cannot stand to be tied or locked or tightened, and he will rather kill and rip itself apart than allow to have its body or neck tied. The claws of a Cat, besides being sharp and penetrating, are also poisonous; and even if their wounds do not kill these cause so much pain and become inflamed in such a way that if these aren't treated with some salt or wine, they will be enough to lose a finger and cripple a hand, as I have seen. It has a very harsh tongue, more so than tufa stones. It is extremely gluttonous, and the one which isn't is not fit for hunting Mice. And even if these are terrible and valiant on the occasions we have mentioned, should one of the long hairs they have near their nose be cut, they lose all their spirit, pride, strength and they become very limp and cowardly, in such a way as they are not longer fit to hunt Mice. They are great enemies of touching water with their feet, and unless they are extremely thirsty they will refuse to drink so as not to enter into water; and among all Animals no other can withstand hunger more than a Cat, and it is common that a miserable man, filled with illness and who never dies, is said to have seven lives as a Cat, which is the same as saying that he has great strength, spirit and endurance, as does this little Animal. It is so clean that in order to defecate it will seek a hidden place with loose earth, so as it may cover it and prevent the smell. Oh admirable cleanliness, for it not only covers it but it also smells it once and again, and should it still find any scent, it will cover it up once again, no matter how faint the smell! For who will not admire that natural virtue and property which is that no matter from how high it falls, it will always fall on its feet. Oh admirable symbol of the just man, that no matter how high he rises, this will never get to his head, and he shall always land on his feet and is always standing. Oh heroic virtue of the just, that even if from such heights one falls, he does not let himself go down or become depressed; and be this a rich or poor contentment, *sempre idem ipse est*.

Stories of the Cat

A certain Knight had in his house such a well instructed and ordered Cat, that every time he was dining, the Cat would be holding with its little paws a lit candle on the corner of the table, taking the place of a lamp; and due to this he would say that the art, industry and cunning of man was such that it could impose on the works and forces of nature. This Knight had in his house, as a Teacher for his sons, a Student, very fluent in Philosophy, and he tried in many ways to persuade the Knight of exactly the opposite; and seeing that arguments and good reasoning were not enough, he decided to have him touch and see this with his own hands, that nature was more powerful than all industry, cunning and art of man. And to do this the Student got a live Mouse, and he waited for the evening, when the Cat was holding the candle with its hands, providing light for its master at the table; and the Teacher started to tease the Cat with the Mouse, which he had tied up over a board, and when he saw that the Cat was staring at the Mouse, following it with its eyes, he let it loose over the table, and the Cat, forgetting all obedience and art which had been taught to it, dropped the candle on the floor and went with his natural inclination, chasing the little Mouse and catching it between its claws, and it had such a greater joy in catching this Mouse with its claws than holding the candle for its master. And in this way the Knight at last confessed that natural inclination is more powerful in the brutes then the cunning and art of man.

Riddle of the Cat

A Master of Grammar, who was reading to some Students in his home, on a certain occasion we will mention, said this riddle to his Disciples with great rush and high voices: *Videntes Asper currit. Gaudium portat; si non securritis super abundantiam, tota requies destruetur*. And seeing as none of them responded due to not having understood it, he declared this enigma in even higher voices over the danger he was in, saying: Students, a burning cat is running, but should you not save it with water the whole house will burn down.

And the case was that as a Cat was sitting by the fire, its hair became ablaze, and feeling the burning it ran into an empty room that contained some straw, and in a quick improvisation the Teacher mixed up the names of all things by something similar to them, calling the Students *Videntes*; for it is certain that those who study know, and those who know are the ones who can see; and thus with reason did he call them *Videntes*. To the Cat he called *Asper*, for it being as it is in its tongue, as we have said, as well as in its claws, fangs and voice. To fire he called *Gaudium*, which means delight, contentment and joy, and with reason did he call it thus, for it is a pleasure to the sight and joy to the entrails in keeping us from the cold which is so contrary to our nature and without which man could not live nor be joyful. To water he called *Super abundancia*, for there isn't anything which is more abundant in the earth that this. Finally to the house he called *Requies*, which means rest, and with reason, for our enjoyment, relief, pastime and good living is in one's house.

Rare treason of the Cat

In the City of Gandia, in the House of the Society of Jesus, a certain case happened with a Cat, most notable and always incredible, and this was that after the fields there had been watered, a Cat went into the wet soil; and being it true that all Animals of this species are extremely unfriendly to water and to getting their feet wet; this one on the other hand not only got them wet, but it even searched for mud so as to better get them dirty, and it did this over a certain cunning and treason that this Cat had thought up. After doing this the Cat went up to a certain room filled with wheat; and it started taking up this wheat with its little hands and feet, and, keeping it tightly grabbed, it got close to the wall (next to the said House of the Priests) and lying down with its paws up, filled with wheat, which with all the mud stuck to them, and being in this position for two hours, playing dead and displaying this wheat; sooner or later a Bird came down, thinking that this was solely wheat, and it started picking at it, and in this way it became a prey of this cunning Cat, to great admiration of all observers; and this happened many times and it attracted more and more attention and it was always for the same goal.

Of the Civet Cat

The Civet Cat is a wild Animal, impossible to handle like the Domestic one, which is tractable with goodness, and with evil it becomes impossible to handle; but with the Civet there is no good or evil way into friendship. Its hair is all striped and spotted, and it has some similarities with the Wolf, even if its face, teeth, eyes and nose are all of a Cat; it can see much better than the Domestic one, to the point of being able to see past solid things; its tongue is similar to that of a snake and its neck is like that of a Wolf.

One should warn that the eyes of a Civet have tricked many Hunters and Shepherds, who think that this is some Animal carrying some hot coals in its head, and as it has so sense, as soon as it hears a noise it turns its eyes and back and disappears, and in this way these men are fooled and tricked.

Of the Genet Cat and of how one makes its liqueur and from what

The Cat which they call Genet is the one from which an important liqueur is made of very smooth scent called Algalia, the most admired of all scents, for it is so strong and penetrating that it transcends all other scents.

This Animal is of the shape and color of a domestic Cat, even if it has a much more spotted skin, similar to the Civet Cats, and they are also somewhat bigger than the regular ones, and if these are well kept and treated they provide you with plenty of Algalia, so much that for each month one can gather one ounce of this liqueur. It creates this liqueur in some pockets it has near its testicles. And so as this is better produced and with more abundance, these are made to run and jump for a while every three or four days, and with this movement those pockets are greatly filled, and this is then removed with some little silver spoons, and in this way it is made stronger and with a more penetrating scent than otherwise. And when these pockets are full they cause them so much pain that if they are not emptied every three or four days, they would burst with pain; and should one forget to remove this they will roll around on the ground so as it may fall out, and so is this humor and scent taken out, which is worth many ducats. And regarding this, one can mention that in the City of Lisbon a certain man left to his son twenty four Genets with a clause and pact in his will saying that he wished for those Cats, now given to his inheritor and his descendants, to be increased and not decrease, in such a way as if a single one of those Cats were to disappear they would have to pay to the Hospital of Mercy, which is in Lisbon, three thousand ducats. And so as not to lose that amount, in that house thirty Cats were raised, which produced the equivalent of three thousand ducats and some change, not counting the costs of their maintenance of very good meat, for the better the food one gives them the better the Algalia they produce. And that liqueur is very important to remove pain and to quiet ear buzzing and to treat gloves and dresses. And one should note that any clothes with this scent will not attract moths.

Medicinal properties of the Cat

Only two medicinal properties of Cats are mentioned by the great authors, and these are the following.

Aesculapius writes that Cat manure made into powder and mixed with vinegar and well ground mustard, cures ringworm, an almost incurable ill.

Hali writes that Cat meat or skin, still fresh and warm, applied over hemorrhoids will decrease them and remove all their pain; and in this same way he says that this will remove any pain.

The rich and greedy have discovered another property in the Cat, and this is that its skin is very good to store money inside it.

Of earthly and mundane love, by occasion of the Cat

It is most remarkable the love that the Cat has for its children, for it is certain that it will eat them so as to prevent them from being hurt, and over this we will say something of earthly and sensual love, with the authority of the Learned and Saints.

Mundane love is a forgetfulness of reason, very close to madness. Plutarch.

Earthly love is a friend of novelty, and a breaker of promises; it is an enemy of restfulness and enemy of peace; it is the fall of the happy, and the waste of the fortunate, it is the cage of the mad and a chest of troubles. Finally, Marcus Aurelius says that it is the principle of many miseries and the extreme of misfortune.

Love, guided by low and sensual appetites brings man to an unfortunate and miserable end. Ovid.

This love misleads like a child, weakens like an old man, and it guides like a blind man. Marcus Aurelius.

Love is an I don't know what, sent by I don't know who, from I don't know where, it is generated I don't know how, it is felt I don't know when, it is maintained by I don't know what, finally it kills and I don't know why. Ovid.

This love is a hidden flame, a delicious venom and a very sweet herb; it is a joyful torment, a tasteful infamy; finally it is a penetrating wound and death that soon ends.

The point where one starts to love the earthly things is the one where one starts to fear.

Mundane love does not have reason, order or firmness.

True love roots out all fear. Saint Gerome.

The effects of earthly love, according to Saint Climacus, are the dispersion of possessions, debilitation of strength, obscurity of mind, and deprivation of freedom and feeling.

Only he who loves without self interest can be said to truly love. Erasmus.

Chapter XII

Of the Ox and its advantages

    The Ox is a very heavy Animal, but very necessary to the life and rest of man; for not only is it useful in life on any occasion one needs to work or carry a cargo, but also after death it sustains us, ending our hunger with its flesh, with its skin being used for a thousand different things and services for human life. And this is in such a way as we could call the Ox our companion, for with all of its species, it is a continuous aid in work, as can be seen in Italy, France, throughout all of Castile and in many other Provinces, where barely any other beast of burden is used besides Oxen; and even if these are good with carrying cargo, they are further valiant in pulling carts, and this is of great rest for man. And I think to myself that it was the Devil, as the enemy of our good, who invented the games with Bulls, so as these may eviscerate many men, and so as men would kill and eat so many of them as they do throughout the world; and this arises from us having less consideration for them than did the ancients; for there used to be a law mandating that anyone who killed an Ox maliciously would be charged with nothing else than his own life; and today we have it as a great feat and bravery to kill them in such a dangerous way, as it happens in what they call the game of Bulls.
    And even if these Animals seem so brave and malicious as they appear in the arena, this is because they are provoked and forced with those spikes and sticks that are driven into them; and this is not because they are thus inclined, but they are rather forced; and it is a thing worthy of consideration to see the friendship and conformity they have among themselves. For when any beast or Wolf approaches any of them, it is remarkable to see how they come together, buttock to buttock, with their head outward ready for battle, showing their horns to their opponents, and

in this way no Wolf can get past them, and there is no way to break this circle, and any predator will give up its intent quickly.

The fighting of Bulls among themselves, so say those who have seen it, is the best of all Animal fights, for, not counting the tricks, cunnings and treacheries that they use in order to defeat each other, they have a great consideration, never before seen in any Beast, and few times seen among men; and this is that, should the fighting be tight, and one of them finds itself tired, they will break off the fighting for a moment until it is rested, returning to their battle when they are both ready. And they say another thing of these fighters which is of no smaller consideration than the previous point; and this is that the one who wins a fight will return to a herd of cows, lying with them and manifesting the pleasure and contentment of its victory; and the defeated Bull not only will not join his other companions, but it will seek a more distant place where it may find good grasses so as to grow bigger and recover its strength, so as to return, with more spirit and courage, and seek the victor and have another bout with him, which it will surely win; after this, the newly defeated, burning with fury will seek out a man on which to have its revenge, and upon doing this to one it immediately becomes calmer.

Rare case of nature

Of these Animals a rare thing is told and written by most grave men. Abencenif[302] and Palladius write that should one lose a Bee hive, that one may extract these from an Ox with abundance.

I will recite the method of extracting Bees as they mention; for even if Marcos Barròn says that Bees are created from a dead Calf, he does not say how or when. But Crescentiis refers to this in the following way: Garnish a small square dry and hot chamber or room, and the Sun should hit it when it rises and sets, and may it have some waxed windows, in such a way as light may come in but not air, and if this chamber can be sealed with Ox manure it will be very good. Now they say that one should take a Calf, which should be completely red, two years old and very fat; cover its nose and beat it to death with sticks, making sure its bones are well broken[303] but that its entrails are not pierced. With it still warm, make several openings in its body, wherever you want, and fill these with plenty of Rosemary, Thyme, Mint, Oregano, Winter savory, Parsley[304] and other such herbs of good scent, and once again close these openings and any other it may have, such as the nose, ears and mouth and place inside this chamber many of the mentioned herbs on the ground, walls and under the calf. Once this is done close this chamber very well, closing any crevice with Ox manure, so as no air can come in nor any breath or heat come out, and from this arrangement some imperfect maggots will grow, without legs or wings, and little by little nature will form them, giving them legs and wings and these will become perfect Bees.

Further on Abencenif writes the same in a different way; and this is that one should take the blood of a Calf, by making a hole in its throat, and then you should sew this hole up, and put this blood once again inside its body through the mouth, and then close all the holes in the Calf's body by sewing them very well, in such a way as no heat or breath may escape; and even better will be to seal every hole with Ox manure. Then place this Calf on the ground and soften it up with sticks, in such a way as not to damage its gall bladder and intestines; and by placing it in a chamber as described above for three whole weeks, after this time open this chamber, so as that breath may escape and new fresh air may enter, and once again close this very well, just as before; after another three weeks you will have that whole room covered with Bees, which will be trying to get out, and from that Calf only its hair, horns and bones will be left, and everything else will have converted into Bees. And Abencenif further says that it is from its brain and spine marrow that the Queens are generated; and he says that to gather these Bees up you should have their hives ready and these should be fumigated with almond flowers, or sprayed with honey water, and these should be placed in front of the windows and the Bees will enter by themselves,

---

302. Translator's note: I haven't been able to find much on this author, except through secondary sources, such as Alonso Herrera's book.
303. Translator's note: Jesus!
304. Translator's note: uncertain translation.

following the good scent, for these are great friends of good smelling things; and in this way, with no work, you will be able to recover your Bees.

This certainly seems to me to be a thing worthy of being noted by those who have the possibility, time and place to perform it. And do note that this is not a difficult thing to believe in; for one should note what happens with a dead Donkey, from which are born and generated certain Beetles which grow wings over time, and these fly with such fury that should they hit a man's face they will leave it greatly damaged, as many travelers and workers of the fields have noted.

The same happens with dead Horses, which generate Hornets with such hard stings that if they bite an Ox they can pierce its horns; and one should not be amazed, for, as says the Philosopher: *Que corruptio unius est generatio alterius*. Which mean that the corruption of one thing is the cause for the generation of another; and this we see and touch every Summer with Flies in apples, and from every other corrupted thing are so many others generated that we can see with our eyes; and in this way it is common today that a good year for fruit is also a good year for Flies. And isn't that what this is? As there is no Summer in which we do not see so many Birds being born and generate in threes, for our bother and fatigue. And these Birds are called Mosquitoes, which are generated in some small pouches in white poplars, that, should it be possible, I would have all of these cut down, so as such bothersome Birds may not be generated. And even if these critters cannot be perfectly called Birds, we will however say that from other trees are many other perfect Birds generated, whose meat can be very well cooked and eaten. All of this was said so as we may not marvel ourselves, nor place any doubts on the fact that a dead Ox generates Bees, especially if this is mentioned by such Authors which are owed a great deal of credit, and any wise man one can make this experiment, for this is the mother clearness.

Another modern Author writes of an easier way of producing Bees than the previous ones; and this is that one should take the belly of a Cow or Calf, and as this is still warm and filled with manure, put this in the middle of some muck and cover this with warm manure, and have this in this way for fifteen days, after which the whole belly will have converted itself into round worms; and if you leave them there uncovered, these will grow and develop wings and they will become perfect Bees, but this Author says that this method does not generate any Queens.

Story of the Ox

Even if of these animals there are many well known stories, coming from the games with Bull, as these show their bravery and make prey of men, killing and breaking them apart here and there with many cunnings and treacheries, I will nonetheless simply mention two or three of these cases, for having happened in my own days.

In the year of 1561 a notable case happened with an Ox; and this was that there was a Bull run in a Village of the Kingdom of Valencia called Pego, and they got an Ox to run in the Plaza of the said Village, where there was a very wide stairway heading to the House of the Judges, and in this stairway many of those who handle the Bulls usually take refuge. Having thus enraged the mentioned Ox, one of these went up the stairway, and as the Ox followed him up all men there ended up taking refuge in the Judges Hall, thinking that the Ox would not follow them, as it indeed did, finding them in the Council room where it did a great deal of damage. A boy who was in this room, in order to escape from the Ox, stepped into a window, strongly grabbing the top rail, and as he was in this position, half of his body inside and the other half outside, the Ox, seeing this, charged at him, and as the boy finally got his body up, the Ox fell out of the window, breaking its legs upon hitting the ground; but not even this made it lose its bravery or courage, for even if it was thus fallen, it would raise its head to the window, giving out great shouts as if complaining for having missed the shot.

In Valencia, among other memorable cases happening with Oxen we can name one which happened when they were running a single Ox in the street which they call Barcelona, and a man was inciting and pricking it from the top of some stairs; and the Ox turned to him and followed him up until it came to a dining hall where there was loom, under which a boy was hiding, thinking himself very well hidden and safe; but as he was showing his feet, the Ox did not stop until it destroyed the whole loom, discovering the boy and picking him up by his jacket and dragging him down the stars, leaving him safe but severely broken; after this the Ox needed to be taken down with ropes; and in this same tone one could tell and write infinite stories, or better put, of these disastrous successes of Oxen and men, caused by our tastes and vain pleasures.

I cannot let the opportunity pass without telling of a rare thing which happened with a Bull in the Kingdom of Valencia, and this was that as two Bulls were gathered to fight, and one of them was beaten, it had such courage and spirit that it ran through all paths as a raider, seeking out men so as to avenge the offense it had received from the other Bull. And as a traveler saw the shouting beast come in his direction, he climbed up a tree, and the Bull charged the tree with such fury that its right horn went into the trunk half a palm, in such a way as the Bull was stuck to the trunk without any way to free himself. And the man, seeing the Bull stuck to the tree, decided to go down; and when the Bull saw the one he was pursuing, it grew in courage in such a way that it broke off its horn and continued to charge that man who thought he was safe and who did not even take a breath to look back, but he simply ran, finding in time another tree; and as the Bull saw him go up, it had acquired such malignity towards him, that it did not leave the tree that whole afternoon, nor did it leave that place during the whole night, only leaving in morning as some other people passed by that site and the Bull decided to chase them; and the man who was in the tree started to shout out at those traveler, warning them of their near future, and they immediately ran in all directions; and in this way all reached safety and the Bull was tricked and left without a horn.

And this should be enough about the Stories of these Animals; for if I had to mention the disasters and rare cases that have happened with these, there wouldn't be enough paper in the present work, and it would become a very boring and dull thing for my Readers, who probably know of these matters more than I do, as they are so frequent and noted throughout the whole world.

Medicinal and deadly properties of the Ox

Avicenna writes that Ox gall, mixed with saltpeter is good to cure any kind of pustules which grow on the head; but one should first anoint them with some olive oil so as to remove the crusts, and after that apply the unguent of gall and saltpeter.

Note also this remarkable and easy unguent that cures and heals any pustules; and this has been known to also cure some forms of ringworm.

Take two or four *dineros*[305] of *Diaquilones*[306] and mix and melt these in a pot with some rose oil, and this should become somewhat clear, and you may place this on any pustule or on any other ill which may grow on one's head, and it will heal, and this is most proven.

The same Avicenna says that Ox gall removes pain and cures hemorrhoids.

Pliny writes that the marrow from the leg bone of an Ox, mixed with the blood of the same Ox, can be applied for hair loss, and this will cause hair to become stronger and stop falling.

The same Pliny writes that the gall of an Ox, mixed with Goat urine, cures deafness and heaviness from the ears.

Hali writes that the gall of an Ox, placed in the ears in some cotton, removes pain and noise from them, even more if these are caused by coldness. And he further says that anointing hemorrhoids with this gall will remove pain from them.

Pliny writes that Bull's blood, boiled with some cabbage and applied over a blocked belly will unblock it, and it will do the same for the spleen.

Hali says that Ox manure will resolve any swelling and aposteme hardness; and furthermore, the powder of this manure, burnt and applied to the nose will retain blood flows.

He further says that this manure mixed with cow butter, and made into a dressing, applied to a belly swollen with water, will heal this retention and completely solve it.

---

305. Translator's note: uncertain translation, but probably a Spanish unit of measure I'm not familiar with.
306. Translator's note: an unguent composed by various herbs, lead oxide and olive oil.

He further says that an Ox's liver, made into powder, burnt and drunk with some wine, retains diarrhea and blood flows.

Bull's penis, burnt and made into powder, is good to heal hemorrhoids, by first washing these with hot white wine, and immediately after applying this powder; and these will be cured after three times.

More: the whole world knows that to seal a Bee hive Bull's manure is the best, as it is also good for the reeds where one raises silk worms; and if this is dried and set on fire, it is useful to keep away Mosquitoes and many other things, and this is very much discussed by Dioscorides and in *De Natura Animalium*.

Fresh Bull's blood, if drunk, is deadly, as was experimented by King Midas, according to Plutarch, as he says that this King, seeing as he could not cure certain spasms and tremors that he had, nor free himself from certain terrible visions which tormented him, decided to kill himself by drinking Bull's blood.

Plutarch writes that a captain, called Themistocles, seeing himself banished and without any hope of once again seeing his homeland, sacrificed a Bull and drank its blood, dying immediately after.

Finally, Cow's butter is of a great advantage for infinite medicine, and a pleasure for human life, as all know, and because of this I will say no more.

Of malice and its damages, by occasion of the Ox

As we have noticed the strength of the Lion, the obedience of the Donkey, the danger of the Goat and the zeal of the Billy; in the Ox one should note its considerable malice, as is experienced by those who run with them; for we see that even if they manage to throw a man to the ground, this is not enough for them to forgive him, as the Lions do, which are so generous and without malice that should any one fall completely surrendered at their feet, it is forgiven and set free; the Ox is the opposite, for the more a man surrenders to it the more its malice grows and it does all it can to finish him off, and as soon as it sees that one no longer moves, thinking him to be dead, he will release him, for it has no more enjoyment. In this way the Ox is particularly vengeful and malicious, and because of this it seemed right to say something of this vice, so as one may see how evil and harmful it is to our nature, so as we may keep ourselves from allowing its entrance in our heart.

Saint John Climacus says that malice is a vice which resides in nature; but it is not in this naturally, for God is not the Creator of vices, but rather of our good natural virtues.

Saint Bernard says that a malicious man is always inconstant and uncertain in his actions.

Saint Gregory says that the malicious man always lives with labor, for he constantly plots and is thinking malice against his kin in such a way that he constantly fears them.

Cicero says that malice has a better chance to create friendships than virtue; even if these are not secure, but rather very dangerous.

Saint Chrysostom says that a malicious man does not admit to advice.

Lactantius says that malice infects many and it forgives few.

Saint Augustine says that evil and malice cannot flourish for long.

The same Saint says that no one is malicious by nature, but only through vice; and that the malicious desire that all become like them.

Aristotle says that virtue and malice discover the spirit of each man, in the sense of him being a villain, a free man or a slave.

Plutarch says that the greatest instrument on the occasion of poverty is malice.

Saint Augustine says that malice and misery always walk together.

Aristotle, a Gentile and a Philosopher, says that it is worse to do harm and damage out of malice than out of weakness.

Chapter XIII

Of the Ant and its great foresight and natural instincts

Even if the Ant appears to be a useless Animal for human life, we will however find in it great examples, not only of discretion and foresight for our good government and regiment, but also of singular and perfect friendship for the preservation of our lives and possessions; and without these virtues there can be no peace nor agreement between men, the law of the Republics, the maintenance of states, nor the security of our lives. For it is certain that where one does not have any foresight, there will be no prudence, which is the mother of good government; and where one lacks union there is no peace, without which everything else is also lacking, for division is certain, and as the Sacrosanct Gospel says: *Omne Regnum in se devisum dissolavitur*.

Who will not mention and exalt the virtues and excellences of the Ant, even if this is disregarded by man, we see that the wise brag and exalt it in the Proverbs, using it to reprehend men over their relaxations and uncaring, saying that they should learn their duties with the Ant, that they should save in the time of plenty for the time of shortage. And more do they warn men that Ants know without having a Master, and they obey without a King, and they govern without a Captain. They know for they are prudent and diligent in seeking out all which is necessary and they do not allow the present to pass them by without taking their opportunity.

And they obey and never have any quarrels among themselves, but they rather conserve such peace that they have this as an advantage over all other brutes and an advantage regarding many men. Finally, they manage and govern themselves with such discretion that, as Cicero said, there is no City, Kingdom or Republic in the World that is as well governed and concerted as an Anthill. Considering Saint Ambrose in his *Hexaemeron* the discretion and prudence of the Ant, he says great things of them. For Pliny and Aristotle and Aelianus mention it and do not cease to sing of its excellences and these are such that they almost seem as like rational men rather than brute Animals, and these may serve us, not only as an example but also as punishment as we shall see. Pero Mexía in his *Silva*[307] shows the makeup of the various parts of the Ant, saying a great deal about its waist and posture of its body, of the fierceness and composition of its face, the disposition and make up of its feet and hands, that there isn't anything like it in the Griffon or Lion, in such a way that should the smallness of its body be equal to that of the Lion, Bull or Elephant, none would dare step on it as they do now. Nor would anyone even dare to look at the horrible and amazing face it has. For this is what happens regarding some great and fierce Ants in Septentrional India, of which we will speak of in the end of this Chapter.

Returning to our purpose, it is remarkable to see the spirit and strength that nature has given it, for even if it is small it can carry cargo seven times greater than its own weight; and should it find any grain in its path it will break it apart, no matter how hard it is, simply with its teeth; and it is amazing to see the will it has when with its two pincers it finds something which it determines to be sustenance, that it will completely break it apart.

There are so many and great foresights and natural discretions of the Ant that they seem to be more virtues and reasonable foresight than natural instincts; for if we observe the order, concernment, dealings and friendship they have with each other, we will see that all of them live in a single whole, without any boredom or harm, with so much peace as if each of them would have its own room; and this does not happen with all the other brutes, as also with men, who having the use of reason and the obligation of peace and friendship, are almost never able to conserve it for long; and I'm not saying this about many, for even just two of us are unable to maintain peace for long. Oh our misery and the happiness of the Ant, oh most lament worthy case of all mortals, and most worthy praise for the Ants, oh human misfortune and misery, that the natural instinct of the Ant is greater that the free will of the human understanding and heart. What can we say of the agreement, foresight and discretion they have when they come to pick food, that thousands of them, coming and going, never bother each other, and it is such a marvel that they see each other and never stand in each other's way, but rather they organize themselves with such discretion in the most narrow places that they amaze the human judgment. And note that if they stop in their path, contacting with each other, it is a most certain sign that it will rain, and in most haste and care they carry their provisions back before any rain falls, and with greater hurry they stop their journey. And should any of them be carrying something which is too heavy, it is a remarkable thing to see that they will help each other and they will offer aid to all those that are in trouble. And should any pass by a dangerous place, or need to go uphill, some will pull it from high up and others push it from below with such admirable arrangement until it is completely safe, and after this they will let its carrier go on with its job.

All other Animals keep their food for themselves, and they will even quarrel about who carries it; but Ants do no such thing, for each one of them seeks to work for all the others, and all of them are in charge and taking care of a single one, depositing all grains in a single granary, and from this do all of them eat, at their own time and order, having always in consideration if Winter will be long or short, so as nothing may be in shortage. Oh rare prudence, concerted abstinence, oh admirable discreetness, if one can say these things.

And it is certain that one may say that these eat to live, and not live to eat, as it happens with many mortals.

Of the cave and home of the Ants

The ancient Philosophers, investigators of hidden causes, wishful to know the properties of the brute Animals, and mainly those of the Ants, found that in any cave or Ant tunnel there are always these three chambers, organized with such order and arrangement for their own purpose that they exceed the art of any stonemason. And according to Aelianus among the Ants there are those that are male and female, and that in one chamber are those Ants which have eggs, where these are hatched and raised and, in their time, small Ants come from these; in the second chamber there are those Ants that don't have eggs, as also the males, so as with the communication of males and females their numbers may increase; and the third is exclusively a

---

307. Translator's note: *Silva de varia lección*, a miscellany of several humanistic topics.

granary, where they take and keep the grains and the supplies they find in the Summer in order to sustain themselves in Winter. And when these make their cave it is an impressive thing to see the hurry they have in carrying out this dirt, sometimes ten and twenty at the same time, and this without any bother to each other, as we can see when they come out in April and go back in June. And to see the arrangement with which they mount the earth around this so as to make a defense and protection from the celestial injuries. Who is not admired in seeing the turns and twists they make at the entrance of the cave, which seems more like Troy or the labyrinth of Crete than a hole or straight path; and of this the mentioned Authors say that it is not done without purpose, for should any critter want to enter to harm them, it will be lost right at the entrance, and it will not be able to find its way out, but it will die and they will be kept safe.

Other discretions have been noted by other Natural Philosophers, and this can still be seen in these days in many parts; and this is that, should it rain in such a way as water may enter into their cave, being more than their walls can handle, and get their supplies wet, these will wait until the weather improves and once this is so they will take out all the supplies which got wet and place them outside so as these may dry; and after this is done they will carry them back inside with a strange diligence. And this case, should it be well considered, seems more like industry and rational foresight than natural instinct.

We can read of another greater prudence of the Ants; and this is that, so as the grains they keep do not rot due to the humidity of the earth, they break them in half, and they constantly eat the part which seems to be the worst, and in this way they keep their supplies from being consumed.

Even if it is true that they are close to nine months entombed, none should think that they are resting; for they actually continue with their work, constantly moving their grains and supplies so as these don't go bad. Oh rare example, oh marvelous doctrine for all those given to laziness, for as soon as working for one's duty is done there is an infinity of games with which to waste time, working one's body and offending the Divine Majesty with one's soul.

These Animals have another natural instinct; and this is that, when the time to gather supplies comes, the biggest and most robust of them come out of their cave so as to examine the fields around it, and they return with news and proofs of what they found; to the point that we see them in a great hurry, many of them at the entrance of their cave, waiting for those that come carrying their findings, and they drop these in the front of the cave so as the others may recognize them. And the Natural Philosophers say that the Ants that are at the door of the cave are the oldest. And should any bring a grain which is bigger than the door of the cave, they will gather and break it in as many parts as necessary to make it enter.

Many other properties and excellencies have the Ants, but so as we do not greatly extend ourselves we will merely say what Pliny and Aelianus write in Book 11, Chapter 30, and in Book 3, Chapter 27, and this is that the master Ants, during the time when they come out in search for food, do not leave their caves on certain days, and these are the 9th of the Moon, and this is attributed to religion and to the thanking of their Creator, and so they do not want to work on these days; I on the other hand would say that (*illorum pace*), should the above said be true, that on these days they do not come out to work, the cause of this must be because the 9th day of the Moon must be prejudicial to their nature, as we know and see with our experience; that there are certain days of the Moon which are good for some things and bad for others, and thus this 9th day of the Moon must be inconvenient to Ants, and all other days must be beneficial and helpful for them; for it is a very possible thing that they would know which day of the Moon would be good or harmful by natural instinct, as other Animals do.

Finally, the same prestigious Authors says that the Ants always seek twice as much supplies as they will require for Winter or for the time when they are enclosed, and they always know when good weather is coming.

Stories of the Ant

Aelianus writes in his Natural History of a notable discretion and great mercy of the Ant, and this is mentioned regarding the Philosopher Thleante;[308] and this says that this man was roaming the fields day and night, contemplating and speculating on the natural things, and among many things, those of the Ants, as they came and went with their supplies to their caves, and he saw certain Ants which were very different from the others around them and also in their size, and these were carrying a dead Ant, similar to the local ones, and arriving at the door of the cave with their dead Ant, they left it there; and as they did this he saw how many Ants came out of the cave and joined together with the foreign ones which had brought the dead one; and this Author understood that these were thanking them for having brought their dead companion; and this lasted for a long time, as some came in and others went out, showing great recognition and thanking the new arrivals. After a while he saw that from inside the cave they brought a small worm, which they gave to the foreign Ants, which took it and left, leaving the dead Ant there, which they had brought so as it could be buried; and of this case, this great man says that they traveled for about ten paces from their cave, placed it on the ground and covered it with dirt, returning to their cave afterwards, leaving us with a rare examples of piety and mercy, so as we mortals may do as such with our next of kin.

And a Knight of this City of Valencia called Don Luiz, lord of Sanz, heard that I was writing this book on the Stories of Animals, and among the many things he told me of the Ants, one of them was that he had certain caged birds as his entertainment, and placing these in some very high wall, greatly separated from the ground, it happened that a few days after he had given food to his birds, the grains would be completely gone; and the cause of this was that Ants would go up to the roof and down to the cages with such diligence that in a single quarter of an hour they would have taken all of the grain, and the birds would grow continuously weak because they didn't have time to eat any of the grain. The Knight, not knowing of any of this, would cast the blame on his servants, thinking that they were doing this, for these were hemp seed, which are big and tasty grains. And finally his servant, feeling themselves free from any guilt in that case, placed themselves as sentinels and discovered the Ants coming down from the ceiling and stealing all the grain, going back up and down the wall with great loads and joy. Informing Don Luiz of this case, and as he saw what was happening, he sought to find where these Ants were coming from; and once the cave was discovered he had a great deal of water poured inside and also he covered their entrance, thinking that with this he would finish them off; however, a few days later, even if the Ants knew themselves found, they once again got back to their task of stealing the grains from the cages; but this was with cunning and rare understanding, as these would not do this during the day, but solely during the night, and safe in this way they would steal all the grains from the birds. And as the Knight kept seeing that no matter how much grain he would give his birds in the morning not a single one would be left, he once again believed that this was his servants, even if these denied it. Then this Knight, not thinking that this was a treachery of the Ants, determined to lock all of his servants in their sleeping quarter, so as to clear his suspicions; and putting a great deal of grain in the cages he came to find not a single one in the morning. Amazed, he could not believe that the Ants were doing this, for the cages were placed inside his house during the night; but these were actually coming in through a crack in the windows, and without being seen or felt, they took their needs; however, after a great deal of vigilance they were caught red handed, and they were condemned to eternal banishment by flooding their cave with boiling water, and they never returned.

Lorenzo Palmireno,[309] admired in seeing and understanding the foresight and good government of the Ants, decided to prove from where this foresight and natural instinct came from.

With this designation he went in the early morning to a field seeking an Anthill, and having found one placed around it a great deal of white honey (which he was carrying for this purpose)

---

308. Translator's note: uncertain reference.
309. Translator's note: Juan Lorenzo Palmireno, a sixteenth century Spanish play writer and humanist.

so as to see what method they would use to cross this to be able to seek their usual sustenance. Having done so he placed himself watching, and after a while he saw the first one coming out the door of the cave and come across the deadly path. And after a few of them came out to see this, they thought of a method to solve the problem; and this was that all of them started to take dirt from the inside of their cave and place this over the honey, one after the other with such diligence and arrangement that soon they made a broad bridge and all of them could pass thought it without any danger. Palmireno seeing this unthinkable sagacity and sudden solution, by which all of them were saved, prepared for them a different impediment and trick, no less dangerous than the previous one, for when they came back; and this was that he dug a moat around the Anthill and filled this with water. As the Ants returned, seeing a new obstacle, they all dropped their provisions of wheat (for this was the time of drying this grain) around the moat, and they rushed back to bring some straws and they placed these over the water, one next to the other with admirable arrangement and diligence. Making in this way a bridge, as if this was made by barges, and they passed with their provisions into their cave very content and free from danger. Admiring these solutions, this Author, not at all tired of experimenting and testing the Ants, took some Juniper oil and dripped this down the entrance of the Anthill; and returning the following day he saw that they had opened a new entrance and the previous one had been closed with dirt from the outside.

Of Ants as big as Dogs

Pero Mexía writes (Chapter 5), and as is also mentioned by other grave Authors, that in a certain part of Septentrional India there are some Ants which are as large as Dogs, and these are feared as Lions, or maybe even more; and these inhabit caves under the earth as those we have over here; and they say that these make their extremely deep homes in regions rich in gold and silver, and as these dig the earth they will take out great chunks of these metals; and a few have lost their lives in seeking this ore, for as these Ants feel that someone is touching the earth they place around their cave as protection, be it by their scent or hearing, they come out with such fury that all they come across they break into pieces. But it is said that the greedy who want to take this earth should wait until the time when the Ants are hatching their eggs, for in this way they are greatly entertained and they do not dare to leave their cave; but should these come out, even if one has a very light Camel so as to escape, this will not be enough to outrun them; and the only way is to throw some pieces of meat at them, so as these will become entertained with these, for they are most fond of meat; and with this trick, as well as others which were invented by the locals of that land, can a man make himself rich, should he escape the lightness and bravery of the Ants.

Medicinal properties of the Ants

Pliny writes in his Natural History that from Ant eggs, macerated with some dog's milk, one can make a compound which cures ear pain.

He further says that from Ants ground with salt one can make an unguent to remove marks and spots from the face.

He further writes that Ants are the principal medicine for Bears to free themselves from their infirmities; and as these feel themselves ill, they seek to find some Ants and in eating these they make themselves better.

In Catalonia, Ants with wings are used to catch birds, and one can catch a great deal of them like this.

Ant eggs, taken with a sip of red wine, will cure and coldness in one's belly.

Remedy against Ants

It hurts me to talk and write against the Ants, for their excellences and properties are so many and so great, and even if it seems like cruelty to do harm to those that give us such admirable examples, I am however even more obliged by the common good of man than to that of these critters. And in this way I will put aside the examples they give us and focus on the damage they make, and I will say a few remedies so as to get rid of Ants.

Pliny writes in his Natural History, Chapter 10, that in order to get rid of Ants one should place ground sulfur into their cave, or oregano powder, and this will make them die.

He further says that if one places some quicklime in their caves, that this will consume them.

Aristotle says that oregano or sulfur powder will kill or drive them away.

Pliny says that if one covers the top of their caves with mud or water from the sea, that they will never again come out from there.

He further says that if one places the herb called Sunflower in the mouth of their caves, they will never again come out.

A grave Author says that if one burns some Ants in front of their cave, that these will go to another place.

He further says that should one place some Juniper oil inside the cave, they will all die; and these remedies seem like enough to get rid of the mentioned Ants.

Of peace and good government, by occasion of the Ant

Should the reader consider this chapter on the Ant well, he shall see that there are two virtues which are splendorous and principal, and these are peace and good government; and with these they marvelously teach us how we should have treatment with our fellow man, and in what way we should govern ourselves in our homes and outside of them. And these Animals are so advanced in peace, quietness and knowing how to govern themselves without any guides or captains, that it would be good for us to say something of these so important and necessary virtues for the conservation of our corporeal and spiritual lives, without which there cannot be any quietness, peace and anything good in general or particular.

Of peace and its great advantages

Of the gifts of the Spirit that we know (at least we Christians), the third of these is peace, with which man calms storms and conserves a meek and quite spirit. Medina.

Peace isn't anything else than a quiet and calm liberty. Cicero.

War is a cause for peace, and one should not intend on war for any other purpose than peace and quiet. Sallust.[310]

True peace is to fight vice so as to be in agreement with good customs. Casianus.[311]

The root of peace is humility. Saint Gregory.

Peace is the daughter of humility. Saint Augustine.

The peace of Christ is acquired with simplicity of heart, with humility of spirit and with the forgiveness of offenses.

One of the greatest gifts left by Christ to his disciples when he left this world was peace, by saying: Peace I leave with you; my peace I give you. John Chapter 4.

Better than assured peace, so says Titus Livy, is an expected victory.

By peace and agreement are the Cities conserved, and with discord are they destroyed and finished. Saint Augustine.

---

310   Translator's note: A contraction of the Latin Sallustius, which likely refers to either the Ist century Roman historian Gaius Sallustius Crispus or the IVth century Greek philosopher Sallustius

311.   Translator's note: uncertain reference, but probably Saint John Cassian, an early Christian writer and monk.

Peace is accompanied by the glory of our God and Lord, and as God was born into the world as a man the Angels sang: Glory to God in the highest, and peace on earth, good will toward men, Luke, Chapter 2.

He who wants peace should be ready for war. Vegetius.

I would rather have, so says Erasmus, peace in some bad manner, than a very just war.

God gives peace upon peace to his chosen. Saint Isidore.

Those who love peace love the Author of it, which is God; and in return for this they are called Sons of God. Saint Isidore.

Of good government

He who governs, so says Cicero, should not just observe and order what happens in the present; but also in what is to come, as do the Ants.

He further says that a government isn't anything else besides a law which speaks.

He who governs should keep the laws and rights. Cicero.

A City, he further says, without law and good government is like a man without reason.

The office of government, so says Saint Gregory, should be denied to those who desire it, and given to those who run from it.

One should first see if a man who rules others can rule himself. Solomon.

A Republic, according to Aristotle, is better to be ruled by a good man than by a good law.

A position of government reveals how a man truly is. Aristotle.

A position of charge always carries animosities, hates and spites. Simonides.[312]

The laws of government should be harsh and strict, but their enforcement somewhat merciful. Stobaeus.

He who rules over all should have been elected by all. Pliny.

Those who rule not only should be prudent, vigilant and diligent, but also benign and patient. Pythagoras.

Two things, according to Democritus, rule and sustain the world, and these are reward and punishment.

There is as much necessity in a Republic, so says Seneca, of letters and good council, so as it may be ruled, as there is of weapons and valiant man to defend it.

He who governs, according to Saint Augustine, should seek to be more loved than feared.

If those who rule and govern do not have peace among themselves, as do the Ants, then all men and Republics will be ill.

---

312. Translator's note: probably Simonides of Ceos, a fifth and sixth century Greek poet.

Chapter XIV

Of the Dragon

The Dragon, according to the Physiologus and Isidore, is larger than any land Animal, and of it Aristotle says that it is generated in Ethiopia, and according to other Authors it is also found in the Oriental India. Saint Augustine says that this Animal is extremely fierce and very cunning; and as it is always warm, it always lives in and inhabits caverns and under the earth; and as soon as it feels cool and humid air it will immediately go out into the field, and with the wings it has on its sides, it immediately refreshes itself. This Dragon of which we speak has a crest on its head, even if grotesque it has a large body and a blunt and short snout, and it almost does not have a tongue, for it being so short, and its feet are like those of the small Dragons which are created here in our walls of Spain, and these have very large and sharp claws, even more than the Lion; and this Animal grows so much that some of them are larger than twenty five cubits. These Dragons are of such nature and they have such a complexion that if they eat any poisonous Animal this does not harm them, according to Aristotle, and as such they always seek Vipers, Scorpions and other similar Animals so as to eat them. Pliny says that these Dragons have a normal animosity with the Elephants; and Saint Augustine says that they fight them and wrap them with their great tails and squeeze them, and in this way they achieve their victory. Saint Isidore says that these Dragons do not have strength in their teeth, but only in their tails; and in this way, when they fight, they do not use their teeth and claws as much as they do their tails, for after having caught the enemy with their tails they squeeze them with such strength that the said Animal is quick to be torn apart. This is a meat eating Animal, and they never get tired of it, and should it have the occasion it will eat enough for three days, and it comes out of its den every day; it also has a stone on its head called Draconitides, which is of the color of Venetian glass, and it has such virtue and excellence that no Author has ever been able to say all of its properties, of which we will say a few. But one should note and be warned that the mentioned stone cannot be taken if the Dragon is dead, but rather before it dies, for according to Albertus and other such grave Authors, once the Dragon is dead the stone loses its virtue, strength and value, and in this way they say that it needs to be taken *ad huc vivendo*. And they further say that once the Dragon is dead not only does this stone lose all of its virtue but it also loses its color and being, and in such a way as it is no longer distinguishable.

Virtues and excellences of the Dragon stone, called Draconitides

Albertus says that this Dragonitides stone, taken from a Dragon before it is killed, gives a great spirit and strength against the enemies of him who carries it.

He further says that he who carries this stone cannot be poisoned.

He also says that should he drink venom this will not harm him.

He also says that he who carries it cannot be poisoned by any venomous animal.

Also that whoever brings that stone with them, in contact with the skin, and falls ill of a deadly disease, the mentioned stone will change color, and from a clear glass it becomes black or gray: *mirabile dictu si ita se habeat*.

Also, should any venom be placed on this stone, or this stone be placed on any venom, this will lose all its strength.

Stories of the Dragon

Pero Damiano[313] writes that in Armenia there was a Dragon which had a terrible and admirable grandeur; and as one day the Dragon was lying down, with its head concealed in some bushes, a group of travelers passed by it, and one of them, who was probably tired, thought that this was a great tree trunk, and sat on it. And the Dragon, feeling some weight on it, quickly turned with its teeth and swallowed him; his companion, who also wanted to sit down, seeing his friend disappear so suddenly, ordered himself to God and even if his feet were tired, ran off.

In the book *Hortus Sanitatis*,[314] there is a story of a Dragon that lived in the time of King Philip II. And in the first years of his reign it so happened that on a certain narrow path near a mount in Armenia there lived two Dragons which were so fierce that all who passed by there would die suddenly, without these Dragons being the cause of it, for these did not manifest themselves nor did these men die at their hands.

As this news reached his Majesty, he asked the cause of this and none could discover it; however, after a few days of inquiring on the cause of death of those men, a Courtly Knight responded in this way: Oh Catholic King, if Your majesty gives me permission, I will tell you the cause of that terrible damage, for I have seen it with my own eyes. And being given license, this Knight brought in a mirror, and placing it in the hands of the King, he saw in it the two great Dragons of which we speak, and these were with their mouths and noses very much opened, and these produced so much smoke, and this was so thick and poisonous, that it corrupted the air in such a way that all who passed by this path had their entrails corrupted and would suddenly fall dead. Having seen this in the mirror, his Majesty ordered that people well equipped with corporeal and spiritual weapons be gathered so as to destroy and finish these fierce Animals, and this was done and from that day on that path became safe and without any danger.

In the first book we have mentioned there is another case worthy of admiration, and this Author says that once he was retired in a certain country house, which was almost in a desert, and that at a certain point nine great and terrible serpents passed by that place; and the owner of that house and his servants came out, armed with swords. The master took to the front and charged the serpents, and these in turn charged them with such hisses and venom that his servants immediately surrendered and passed out, but the master gained such spirit and strength that in a little while he had sliced them into a thousand pieces.

---

313. Translator's note: uncertain reference. The only relevant Pedro Damiano I know was XVth century cheese master and pharmacist, but I doubt it's the same one mentioned here.

314. Translator's note: The first encyclopedia of Natural History, published in 1485 by Jacob Meydenbach.

As I saw this, writes the Author, I asked what was the cause of such effort and bravery, and the valiant soldier responded; do not be amazed by what you saw, for I have a Draconitides stone with me, which is the stone of the Dragon that this chapter mentions, and as I asked to see it and he opened his left hand and showed it to me; and similar to that instance he told me of many others which had happened, and he attributed his victories to the virtue of the said stone.

And as another case happened before my eyes (that said Author mentions) I would like to share it, and this was that a few days after that incident with the nine Serpents, a great and deformed Serpent, hissing terribly, passed by that desert, and the mentioned house keeper went out to seek it, taking a sling, and in finding it he threw one single stone and with it shattered the serpent in a thousand pieces. And I, seeing this case (the Author says), wanted to see if he was carrying the Draconitides stone, and he was carrying it in his hand. Rare cases and events are these which have happened as I so believe, and any one may give them credit for two reason; one, because the said stone has great virtues and excellences, this according to all Natural Philosophers; and the second, because in a book of such authority one cannot believe that such grave things could be written by an Author unless they were true.

Medicinal properties of the Dragon

The Physiologus says that Dragon's gall, boiled with wine and drunk, is good against numbness of the members; and if those regions are anointed with the mentioned wine it will immediately cure this numbness.

Dragon fat, the same Author mentions, is good against all venom.

He further says that the head of a Dragon will bring fortune to any who owns it; and this is because of the stone it carries, which is called Draconitides.

He further says that Dragon meat, eaten, will greatly refresh the sensual and unruly appetite of he who eats it.

He also says that in Ethiopia the meat of this Animal is frequently eaten, and it is considered to be very good, and it also cures thirst and the will to drink.

Dragon's blood, which is sold in the Botanical shops, is the resin of a certain bush, for it has in itself the natural color of the blood of a Dragon, and for this reason do they say that this is Dragon's blood.

Of venom, with some stories by occasion of the Dragon

I take this occasion to discuss venom, as I have noted that the Dragon has such virtue and natural strength in its complexion that all poisonous and venomous Animals it may eat it can convert into good and smooth nourishment, without it doing it any damage, and in this way let us say something of venom.

Venom is something contrary to the nature and blood of man, and as soon as he touches this, or this touches his heart, it kills.

Pliny says that there are many sources of venom, and these are the following: the black poppy, henbane, wolfsbane, cantharidin, the *tapsa de cosco*,[315] dungwort, ruby sulfur, arsenic, the *solimão* and other confections of mixed pestilences that are composed and invented by the mortals to consume and finish each other.

There are a species of Serpents which are called Ancocias that when it seeks to kill, it coils itself up and when the time is right it stretches itself with so much fury that wherever it touches it leaves its poison, and should this be a living thing it will die and change color. Andromachus.[316]

There is another species of Asps which are so poisonous and evil that they spit their venomous saliva with such precision that they never miss their mark, and they always kill that which they hit, and of these Asps there are three species and all are deadly. Another species is called Chersea,

---

315. Translator's note: uncertain translation.
316. Translator's note: There are two Greek physicians with this name, father and son, one was the inventor of the theriac and the second was the author of an extended written work on pharmacy.

with which Cleopatra killed herself. Another one is called Cerastes and this one has seven horns, and it is a most cunning Animal and it kills with great cunning and treachery. Andromachus.

This acclaimed Author further says that there are other small land Animals and these are so venomous that they kill by stinging or biting, such as the Hydra,[317] the Land Crab, the Scorpion, the Spiders, the Horned Frog, the Rana Rubeta and the Amphisbaena snake with two heads and many others that nature produces throughout the whole world.

Note that if one takes the body of a Viper and, cutting out the head and tail, for this is where it has its poison, and washes the insides very well, this may be used as a theriac, which they say is the best and it works against all poisons, either eaten, drunk or even if one was bitten by one of these Animals. Galen.

Andromachus in his *De Theriaca, ad Pisonem*,[318] says that the Drino is a Serpent of such evilness and bad nature that just passing over one will make the skin from one's feet and legs peel off, and this generates such apostemes that even the hands of those who may treat this will suffer.

Galen speaks of the Basilisk, which is a Serpent between red and yellow, and that just by staring or being stared at by it can kill, be it Animals or men. And he says that many Animals will die just from hearing its hiss. And he further says that if any Animal approaches another one which has been killed by a Basilisk it will also die. Finally this Animal has such poison that all other poisonous Animals are afraid of it, and it fears none of them.

Claudius and Galen say that there is a beast, which is called Hemorro, and he who is bitten by this will immediately have a blood flow from his nose, mouth and any other opening in his body, and he will be left dry and without any remedy.

He further says that the Dipsa is another poisonous beast, and those it bites acquire such continuous heat and thirst that these can never be satiated and they will soon die.

Avicenna writes that in his time there were men of such bad nature that poisonous Animals wouldn't come near them; and he saw these being bitten by these Animals and the Animal died, not the man.

Galen writes of a girl who was used since very young to eating a poisonous herb called cicuta, and in this way she became accustomed to this poison, and could convert it into nourishment, and not only did this poison not harm her but it actually killed all those who slept with her.

Alberto Magnus writes of a girl from Germany who since she was very young would take spiders from the walls and eat them, and this lasted her whole life, and not only did these not kill her, but they would even make her fat.

Pliny writes that in Africa there was a certain lineage of men that just by looking at a field would dry it, and not a single green thing would survive; and should these cast their eyes with this same intention on a young boy, he would die.

Plautus[319] writes of King Mithridates[320] who, having been beaten by Pompey, so as not to die by his hands took some poison, and this did him no harm due to the robust and strong nature and complexion he had; and seeing that this poison could not kill him, he then used a dagger.

King Alexander, after having conquered so many parts of the World, died from poison given by his soldiers.

Emperor Otto,[321] after the many battles he had with Crescentius died poisoned by a pair of gloves the wife of his enemy sent him.

Emperor Claudius died at the hands of his wife who used poison. Pliny.

It is also written how Pope Victor III died from poison which had been put in his chalice while he was saying Mass.

---

317. Translator's note: uncertain translation.
318. Translator's note: this book was actually written by Galen.
319. Translator's note: uncertain reference, even though there is a Titus Maccius Plautus, a Roman play writer, but he was born well before King Mithridates.
320. Translator's note: Mithridates VI of Pontus, a very successful Roman enemy.
321. Translator's note: Otto III, Holy Roman Emperor.

Chapter XV

Of the Elephant and its rare knowledge

Even if it may seem like we have offended the Elephant by not having said anything of it until this point, we hope that it will not seem like we do not appreciate it, for it is rather the contrary; for we now place it in the middle of the land Animals in the same way as the Sun is in the middle of the Seven Planets, giving light and clarity to them all.

Aristotle, Aelianus and Celio write in the *de Animalibus* great things regarding the Elephant, worthy of being known and imitated by man. These Authors say that the Elephant, is among all Animals the one which is capable of the greatest discipline and it is the most fitting for learning and understanding all which is taught to it; it is a self-conscious, benign and affable Animal, and it is most obedient to man, mainly if this is a grave man, for it will recognize this gravity and lordship, and have towards him a great respect.

This Animal lives for two hundred years and he walks very calmly and more than any other Animal, for it gives the widest strides. When it is in captivity it will mourn and cry with many painful complaints for seeing itself without freedom, and these it makes during the night, in a low voice, so as no one will hear it, this over his self-consciousness and the esteem it has of itself; and if while it is doing this complaining anybody walks in on it, it will immediately become quiet and cease its cries, dissimulating its complaints with a joyful and serene face.

Should anyone say offensive words at it, it feels them so badly that it may even become ill with anger and hurt feelings, and this should only be understood when it is in captivity, for, should it be free no one would dare to say anything to it, for it is a very vengeful Animal, a great friend of honor and praise. It is a most zealous Animal, not only in its honor and esteem, but also in the companies it has contact and friendship with; it is most chaste and an enemy of adultery, and each one of these will be content with one single mate once it has found and taken to it; and should this one ever disappear, it will never again find another one. What admirable example is this for our day! What rare and straight reprehension does this Animal give to all disconcerted widows, men or women. The shame the Elephant feels when approaching its female is such that it will not do this in public or in any place where it can be seen, but it will rather hide and seek a place far away and secluded. And should it understand that it is being seen in this act, it becomes so enraged that it will rush to him who saw it with such rare fury that it breaks him into pieces.

Aelianus writes, in Book 6, that the Elephant is greatly bothered by the libidinous and adulterers; and it has such knowledge of this that by simply seeing one it will recognize him, and should two men approach it, being that one is chaste and the other not, it will not only avoid the face of the dishonest, but he will refuse to even look at him. And this same property the Bees also have, which will be discussed in their proper time.

The Elephant is so much a friend of its honor, that when the female with which it has contact has any conversation and contact with any other, it will beat and kill her without any mercy. Should it be hit by any arrow or dart, it will take it out with great ease, and be set free and without any damage; and its strength is such that with its strong and large fangs it can take down trees, break walls and great buildings.

Avicenna writes that frequently the ancients used Elephants in war, placing on their backs great towers and wooden buildings so as to fight from up there and climb the walls of their enemies. And they also used the strength of these Animals to bring great ships to land.

The Elephants are well supplied and great of body, and according to Aelianus they are taller than seven cubits, and some even nine and they have five of width; their ears are three palms in height and half a palm in width; it has a very thick and soft body, with some hair, and when it shrinks itself it makes so many wrinkles and folds that during the Summer, when these are molested by Flies, one of these folds can fit five hundred of these Flies, and it can tighten these folds in such a way that none of these will survive, and in this way they defend themselves from bothersome Flies.

In the front of their snouts they have a trunk of more than an ell[322] in width, and this is used as their nose and also to pick up food and place it in their mouth. Some Authors claim that these Animals do not have any joints; and others say that they do, which I do believe, and even if this is so, should they fall to the ground they will not be able to get up, but this is no reason to believe that they don't have joints; the truth is that they cannot use the joints they have in the middle of their legs except when they are young, for as soon as their hide becomes thick and hard they can no longer bend their legs, except by the joints they have close to their bodies, and they use these to walk; and their legs are so thick, strong and massive that they barely get tired, and they give great strides with a very calm walk (as was said) in such a way as they can walk more than any other four legged Animal; and these large strides are caused by having their joints so high, and in this way they can walk a great deal, but they cannot get up without help should they fall.

The teeth and fangs of these Animals are made of ivory, which is greatly esteemed by all, and over this are hunters always hungry for them, hunting and inventing a thousand different tricks and traps; and the Elephants have such foresight that when these see any hunters they know and understand by natural instinct that the cause that they are being hunted is so as they can take their fangs, and in this way they hit them against some tree or cliff with such fury that they break them, so as the hunters will be entertained with these and they can find safety; and these teeth are so large, which come from the sides of their mouth, that grave Authors, and Aelianus among them, say that these are greater than five palms in many of these Animals. But there are other hunters who do not hunt these out in the open, but rather with great cunnings, and this is that they keep watch over the trees where the Elephants usually retire to rest, and they saw these in half right thought the middle of the trunk, but not all the way through, and as some Elephants lean over on these they fall to the ground, and thus the hunters come out, disguised, and greatly beat them, leaving them very tired. After this they are substituted by different men who start to demonstrate

---

322. Translator's note: a unit of measure related to the cubit, currently 18 inches.

great sorrow over the mistreatment of the Elephant, and they show great demonstrations of pity, humility and reverence, and they help it back on its feet, and in this way the Elephant is made tame rather than enraged, for these men are not disguised as the previous ones, and this is the best and safest way to catch these. Cassiodorus writes that the Elephant desires by nature to be honored and respected, for it recognizes in itself, due to the greatness of its body and subtlety of its temper, a superiority and advantage regarding all other four legged Animals

Philostratus registers three different Elephants, and he says that one of these is called the aquatic, for these are found and hunted in some lakes in India, and these have no knowledge or discourse. Others are raised in thick woods very much separated from contact with any other Animal, and these are uncorrectable and treacherous. The third type is that which is raised on the plains, and of these do our stories deal with, for they are the greatest and best of their species. They have great respect for those who treat and maintain them, and they not only respect them but they also fear and obey them; and should any of these give them some humility and reverence they will be greatly enjoyed, blowing their great trunk; but should the opposite happen, and they are treated with harsh words, they become greatly saddened, making their nose or trunk diminish by three palms; which it also uses to murky up water when it drinks, and some say that they do this so as not to drink it clear, but I say that this is not the reason, but it should rather be similar to what we have said in the Chapter of the Camel, that it also does this same muddling of the water. And because in this mortal life there isn't a single thing, be it great or small, that doesn't have an opposite, thus the Elephant has a great enemy in the Dragon, which constantly stalks pregnant Elephant females so as to kill their newborns; however, this female, by understanding and natural instinct, knowing the animosity the Dragons have against it, in order to give birth it steps into some water until this is up to its tits, and there it safely gives birth to a single baby (and I say single because it doesn't give birth to more than one in all of its life, as Isidore confirms), accompanied by the male, and as soon as it is born they dry it and never do they let it out of their sight until it is of a certain age. Isidore and Aristotle say that the female is pregnant for two years, and that during this whole time the male doesn't have contact with her, and after it gives birth it takes another three years until they have contact once again, and this time comes during the Summer, and they seek very hidden, secret and obscure places, as was said, and this is over the great shame and embarrassment they feel in this act. And after they have done this they walk around to see if anyone has seen them, and should they discover any Animal they punish it with death; oh rare temperance and rare chastity of the Elephant, and what example of virtue and continence for man!

Rare Stories of the Elephant

The Elephant is strangely bothered by the treason of adultery, for it is not only unable to dissimulate it, nor can it suffer this in its companion nor any other who may have done this. Regarding this, Aelianus tell of an Elephant that a certain Lord had on a farm and garden, for his enjoyment and contentment, which he greatly loved; and his wife was somewhat frivolous, or better put, was very frivolous, and she greatly betrayed this Lord and her husband, and she did this betraying in the same garden where the Elephant was kept, and this once approached them in this act and pierced them from side to side with its horns or teeth, and left them dead. Over this example and rare event do grave Authors, and among them the very learned Francisco Velez de Arciniega,[323] Apothecary of the City of Madrid, say that men who suffer similar bedrails from their wives are called *cornudos*, by which name one may try to awaken these to not suffer the provocation that the Elephants also do not, for with its horns (that in Latin are called *cornua*) an Elephant killed two adulterers as a faithful servant of its Lord. Or as Francisco Velez intends, that this actually means "naked of heart", for these surely do not have one in order to suffer such villainy and treason, by which they live without it and without honor and the grace of their Creator, which is the worst of all, for the Divine Majesty does not wish that men suffer such.

---

323. Translator's note: a very well respected seventeenth century Apothecary and pharmacist. There are a number of books written by him on pharmacological topics.

The Learned Bishop Miedes of Albarracin tell in the book he wrote in Salé of a notable case with an Elephant, and this was that in the city of Rome they had ordered certain Elephants to a very skilled master of dancing and other such games and inventions, so as he may teach and tame them in some form of dancing for when any sort of festivity was made in this mentioned city of Rome. It so happened that when this master showed these Elephants to the public, so as they might exercise the games or dance he had taught them, one of them made a mistake in a turn of the dance, and the master, greatly bothered by this, went at him with a stick, and the Elephant, very ashamed about its mistake and the beating it was taking went back to its pen; and when night fell it sought a place removed from all the others and exercised the dance under the light of the Moon, so as to not make this same mistake again and not be beaten by a stick. Returning the next day, the said master with his Elephant students went to the square where the festivities were taking place, he placed his Elephants to dance, already holding a stick so as to take it down on any one that failed; and it seemed to one of the citizens there that if the Elephant that had received the punishment last time were to see the master with his stick in his hand, it would certainly become nervous and it would not be able to follow the game as it should, and as such he asked the master to let go of the sick; and in this way the punished Elephant made his game with such grace and dexterity that it was the best of the whole lot. Once the game was ended, instead of going with its fellows and master, it went with this Citizen, not wanting to part from him, for it had noticed and seen that he had been spared some hitting and it wanted to thank that good work by following him.

In this same city of Rome, an Author tells us, there was an Elephant that was so cunning and dissimulated that it would take all the water it could carry in its trunk, and going out into a square where there are always many people, and placing itself in the middle of everyone, it would go around blowing the water out of its trunk and it would make everyone there wet, and this it enjoyed greatly, and all would admire the treachery and skill with which it did this.

Father Acosta tells us in the history of the Indies of an Elephant that once was not fed by him who was responsible to feed it, and so this Elephant went to him as if asking for its food; and this man told it with signs and words: If I do not feed you it is because the pot on which I carry your food has a hole, take it to the potter so as he may fix it. And the Elephant took the pot to the Master, and it returned shortly after for it, for its hunger was great, and the mender gave it back without fixing it. And as the man in charge of feeding the Elephant saw that the pot was not fixed he told it to once again take it to the Master, and he once again did not fix it. And reaching the pot, the Elephant, before heading home, took it to a river and filled it with water, seeing that it was leaking, a proof that it was not fixed; seeing this it returned to the house of the Master, shouting greatly at his ears, which greatly terrified him and he begged forgiveness, explaining to all passersby what had happened; and as such he fixed the pot in front of this same Elephant, and taking it with its trunk it went to the river to fill it with water, to where it was followed by many people, and seeing that it was not leaking, it took the pot home and they could once again feed it.

The same Author tells us of another case with this Animal, and this was that this Animal, wanting to return to its pen to rest, was told by a ship's Captain: Do not go yet, for you did not put this ship in the water; and even if reluctantly it started to move it, at a certain point it stopped and did not want to go any further; the Captain then started to tell him very loving words, saying that the King of Portugal had need of an Elephant such as it; and the Elephant, seeing as he was being treated with such courtesy, turned back to the ship and with a muffled voiced said: *hoo, hoo,* that in the native land of this Elephant, which is Malabar in India, means, I want I want, and with great spirit and effort, and greater contentment than before, it placed the ship at sea.

The same Father Acosta in this same place, tells that in the city of Kochi, in a certain square, some soldier were having some fun and they threw a coconut at an Elephant, hitting it on the head; and as this Animal saw who had done this it took the coconut with it trunk, and carefully followed the soldier until it found him distracted, and it threw the coconut back at his face, and thus it was avenged.

Elephants often become enraged over a certain illness which hits them once a year; and being in this disposition, one of them was roaming with such fury that a slave walking with a baby was so frightened that she dropped the child and ran away; as the Elephant approached the child, recognizing it, picked him up with its trunk and very carefully placed him on a roof nearby, for this was the child of a woman who sold food at the market, and every time this Elephant passed by, she gave it some of her wares, and because of this benefit it received, it did not wish to do any harm to the boy. And one should not be amazed at this, for the Animal with the greatest discretion and reason, after man, is the Elephant.

In the mentioned city of Kochi it happened that a certain Indian who had an Elephant suffered a treachery by another Indian, and the Elephant, seeing the offense given to its Master, wanted to charge at this other Indian, and avenge this injury; but as it was prevented from doing this and its intent was bared, it kept its memory for a few days; and finding himself near a river with this man, it picked him up and threw him into the water, and as he did not drown, it once again picked him up and carried him in the air for a long time, and as it saw that all the people around it were begging it not to do any harm to that man, it let him down in the same place it had picked him up.

Julius Frontinus[324] says, Book 1, that when certain Elephants, carrying with them the great Captain Hannibal on his way to war, refused to pass a certain river, he ordered a soldier to hurt the Elephant closest to the water, and that then he should pass the river himself. The soldier obeyed his Captain, and so he injured the Elephant, entered the river and walked to the other shore; and the Elephant, so as to get revenge on this injury, entered the river after the soldier; and as all the other Elephants saw that that one could pass it, they all did the same, and with this cunning was Hannibal able to make all these Elephants and his soldiers pass the river.

Anteon[325] writes, Book 13, Chapter 30, that an Elephant had become so close to a newly born boy that it would not eat or drink unless it was in the company of this child; and it loved this boy so much that with its trunk it would rock its crib until he fell asleep, after which it would stop, and its greatest joy was to watch him, keeping away the flies away with its trunk.

These Animals, Pliny and Aelianus say, are raised and inhabit hot lands, for they are naturally hot, and they feel cold terribly, and because of this reason they cannot live in cold regions. In the History of Natural Things it is written of a natural instinct of the Elephants: and this is that when they wish to get pregnant, they seek, both the male and the female, a herb with is called mandrake, and they both eat from this, and afterwards they have contact, and from this single time does the female conceive, and according to Aelianus, this single time is the only one in all their life, and their chastity and cleanliness is such that if it weren't for them to continue their lineage and species, they would never mate, even less the males, which are much more continent than the females.

Medicinal properties of the Elephant

Pliny[326] writes that all poisonous Animals run from the smoke of burnt hair and nails of this Animal, and this smoke prevents generation, according to Avicenna.

He further says that male Elephant blood is greatly useful to prevent the flux of rheum from the eyes; one should burn this blood and melt the resulting powder in some white wine and if applied to the eyes this will heal and clear them of clouds and cataracts.

Avicenna writes that if anyone anoints himself with grease or fat of an Elephant, poisonous Animals will flee from him.

Plateario writes that Elephant's teeth can be used as a calamite, and he says that the best calamite invented, either by the ancients or the modern, is the one from Elephant. This calamite is very well known by Medics and Pharmacists, and it is a simple medicine which is mixed with other simple ones so as to produce marvelous effects in many cases and illnesses; and those who

---

324. Translator's note: Sextus Julius Frontinus, a roman senator and writer of the Ist century.
325. Translator's note: uncertain reference.
326. Translator's note: In some editions instead of Pliny this line is attributed to Isidore.

wish to know how to produce and burn the Elephant's tooth, so as to make this calamite, should read the history of four legged Animals by Francisco Velez de Arciniega.[327]

Plateario says that the powder from an Elephant's tooth, burnt and mixed with boiling plantain water cures dysentery and colic.

Of adulation and flattery, by occasion of the Elephant

Among the land Animals, none wishes to be taken into such account and respect as the Elephant, and this is such a friend of flattery that even if it is greatly offended, with a single reverence or humble word that might be said to it, immediately will it be cured, and it will follow he who said this word with great contentment and joy. And because of this it seems to me to be a good occasion to say something of this disregarded virtue, or better said, this abominable vice, which is used by many, for there seem to be many men of the condition of the Elephant, that desire and die to be honored, and in order to be so, allow themselves to be sold and tricked by all adulators.

Flattery, Solomon says in his wisdom, is like the echo in the mountains, which without any speech speaks; without laughter, laughs; without crying, cries; and this same job and property have all flatterers.

He who flatters a friend may be a friend, but is treating him like an enemy. Plutarch.

When asking Diogenes what Animal bite was the most poisonous and dangerous, he responded that among the wild Animals it was that of the bad mouthers and of the gentle ones that of the flatterer.

To speak well of he who is absent is a thing of honorable men, and in front of him is something of a flatterer. Aristotle.

More lands and treasures are spent by Kings by flattering than by war, Curtius,[328] Book 8.

Never did the Alchemists find such a great treasure and sure merchandise than flatterers and adulators, but beware of them. Terentius.[329]

Always are adulation and flattery more accepted and more pleasing than correction and good advice. Demosthenes.[330]

Among the cruel Animals, the greatest is the tyrant, and among the domestic, the flatterer. Bias.

The Gypsies have as a common and natural thing to flatter, and so as not to inherit this cursed habit, Moses, while he was a child, never wished to suckle on the breast of the Gypsies of Egypt.

The flattery and adulation of the Devil was the reason that the earthly Paradise of our Mother Eve and Father Adam was lost and were destroyed and cast into the mud. And the same still happens today to many who are lost to sweet flattery and adulation.

Flattery and self interest are as beloved brothers, and in this way there isn't any flatterer who does not have some interest, and these always frequent the houses of Princes and Kings.

Saint Chrysostom says that there isn't any who know more of flatterers than the greedy. And he further says that flattery is the job of cheaters.

Saint Gerome has as a blessed man he who does not know how to flatter, nor give credit to flatterers, for in this regard he does no harm nor does he consent to it.

The adulators have a place anywhere, and they please all men, for to the extravagant they call liberal; to the greedy they call wise and prudent; to the talkative discreet; to the vengeful honored; to the nosy diligent; to the daring valiant; to the lazy grave; to the overly diligent they call lords of their homes. Finally, to the stubborn they call constant. Oh what sweet deadly poison. Oh smooth

---

327. Translator's note: The book mentioned is the *Libro de los Quadrpedos, y Serpientes Terrestres, Recebidos en el Uso de Medicina, y de la Manera de se Preparacion*, the *Book of Four legged Animals and Land Serpents Used in Medicine and the Method of Their Preparation*.

328. Translator's note: probably Quintus Curtius Rufus a Roman historian of the Ist century.

329. Translator's note: uncertain reference, probably either Marcus Terentius Varro, a Roman scholar and writer, or Publius Terentius Afer, a poet and play writer; alternatively Publius Terentius Varro Atacinus, a poet.

330. Translator's note: A Greek statesman and orator from the IVth century BC.

Siren song. Oh soft words of flattery, said unto the blind who hear them and do not see them. Oh false, cruel and tyrant adulation, how many do you kill, rob, destroy and finish without any knives, for your mother is none other than covet and your father Satan.

The Majesty of God our Lord does not permit that in the sacrifices be given honey, for he is bored by sweet and adulating words. Leviticus 3.

Chapter XVI

Of the Horse and its arrogance

The Horse is a generous, lively, haughty, belligerent and arrogant Animal; it is daring, valiant, spirited, and even more if it is vain, for when it is adorned with beautiful dressings, it raises itself to such honor and it will ride with such fury that if it was not for the harness it would be impossible to live with, for it would gladly run over all, for it seems to not be able to handle such joy, and it will spring and jump, knowing himself to be adorned, and over this it has a great deal more spirit and freshness than before.

Among all Animals, the Horse is the most faithful and loyal to its lord, after the Dog, and thus writes Pliny and Solinus, of many Horses that were greatly loyal to their lords, as we shall say. And its strength is such that God our Lord, while speaking with Job, mentioning his condition and his efforts said: Are you by any chance, Job, powerful enough to give the Horse the strength I have given it?

It does not fear encountering its enemies and it does not make a case of the sound of weapons, but rather it will rush at them; it has no esteem whatsoever for its own life, nor does it make a case of any danger; with its feet it hits the earth, with its ears it shows its spirit; if it sees itself in battle it will foam at the mouth, boiling with rage it runs over all so as its master may walk away with honor. In a war, feeling the drums, it will gain even more spirit, with the noise of trumpets and horns it becomes joyful and it is not content nor peaceful until it sees itself in the middle of a battle, and feeling the spirit and effort that the Captains transmit to their soldiers, it will be besides itself with joy. It can feel a war from a great distance, only by seeing the movements and mobilizations of men, and in this way it will not be kept in the stables, feeling itself arriving late to the rush and clamor it can hear.

In the book *De Rerum Natura* the nature and condition of a good Horse is greatly described; and it is said, and true, that in almost every part of the world are Horses born and raised, however, the best for things of war are those from Scythia and Cappadocia; and among their colors, the black and the white have a greater advantage above all others.

It is further said that the haughty Horse will never forget the Mare which birthed and raised it; and in this way, when it is grown, it will never approach its mother so as to take her, but rather it will keep its respect and courtesy, as does the Camel towards its own mother. And being this true, among all Animals, the one with the greatest desire for coitus, apart from man, is the Horse; and still, no matter how much it feels the tightening of the lustful appetite, it will never dare to take the mother which gave it birth.

It is an Animal of great memory and sense, this because it will never forget something which is taught to it (according to Aelianus), be it in matters of war, riding or pleasure. Also, because it senses from a great distance any loud noise and it recognizes and understands with ease that which it is taught to it. Aristotle also lets us know that when these Animals reach their old age, their teeth become whiter than they were when they were young.

This knowledge is vast, for Marcus Varro gives us this news with greater punctuality than Aristotle, and he says that any Horse, when it reaches two and a half years, changes its four front teeth, that is, two from the upper and two from the lower jaw; and when it reaches four years it will change four more teeth, which are the ones on the sides; and from this moment on other teeth will grow, which in the Animals are called the fangs. In their fifth year this same Author says that they change their fangs, and after these are done they will be six years old, and when they are seven they will have the full set in equality. And finally, when they pass fourteen or fifteen year of age this is demonstrated by their eyebrows turning white, and these will have some great concavities under them. This Animal has a great desire for coitus all its life. It lives until it is thirty or thirty five years old, and the female until it is forty. They have various eye colors, like man; and according to the opinion of many, the Horse does not have gall, as does the Donkey. The Horse is so furious that when it is pressed by libido, if this is not castrated no one will be able to handle it.

Stories of the Horse

Pliny and Solinus tell of a Horse owned by the king of the Scythians that, this king having died in a battle, as an enemy soldier approached the body so as to steal his royal dressings, the Horse saw this and charged the soldier with such fury and courage that it broke him into pieces with its hooves, and afterwards it stayed there as guard to the body of its lord until his friends arrived to take the body, and it then followed them showing great evidences of sorrow over the death of its lord.

The mentioned Authors also write of another Horse owned by King Nicomedes, that when it realized that its lord was dead it no longer wanted to eat and as such it died of hunger and pure sorrow for never seeing its master alive again.

Aelianus tells of a Horse owned by Alexander called Bucephalus, that whenever it was adorned, it became so haughty that it did not allow for anyone else besides King Alexander to ride it; however, should it be without any dressings, and in a battle, anyone would be able to ride it. It is further said of this Horse that as it was injured in a battle, King Alexander got off from it and got up on another fresher Horse, so as to continue with his battle; and in seeing this, the Horse Bucephalus charged this other Horse and beat it down with its hooves, for it did not allow its master and lord to ride any other Horses, and humbling at the feet of Alexander (as was his custom) the King rode it, and the prodigies and valorous deeds it did were such, and so great the valor and bravery it had, that it freed Alexander from many dangers and battles. And after his enemies where defeated, this Horse died from its wounds, and given this fidelity and other such things Bucephalus had done, Alexander had it buried with great festivities and he wrote its name on its grave so as to perpetuate its memory.

The mentioned Authors writes, and Eulogelio[331] with them, that Alexander founded a city in the place where Bucephalus was buried, and he gave it the name of that Horse, and in this way today we have the city of Bucefala, for this Horse aided in the conquering of this place with his great spirit.

---

331. Translator's note: uncertain reference.

The Horse has such sense and good memory, even more if it is pure, that a trustworthy Knight of this City tell us of a strange thing which happed to him, and this was that in the time when duels were more frequent than today, two noblemen challenged each other, and as each of them wanted to do good, they did not wish to have any company or any third party present, and so they went out by themselves to a deserted place away from any path by one thousand and five hundred passes. As this Knight was passing by a path close to the place where the two men were fighting, his Horse did not want to move forward, but it rather wished to abandon that path and follow the sound of the blows he was hearing, or the shine of the swords it could see due to the bright Sun, and as the one riding the Horse was unaware of what was going on, nor did he understand why the Horse wanted to leave the path, he was greatly mistreating it, injuring it with his whip and spurs. But the will of the Horse was greater and it indeed left the path, going forward with its ears upright (an evident and manifest sign that what is happening has a great interest in its entrails), the Knight released it and allowed it to go at his will, also for wanting to see what had caught its attention and what was the reason for such defiance. And it was a rare thing that as soon as he gave it license and dropped its reins, the Horse went with a strange lightness throughout the fields and shortly after discovered those two who could barely lift their swords in order to hurt and kill each other, for they had been fighting for a long time, and they always aimed at each other's heads. The Knight then discovered these two duelers after his Horse, and in finding them stepped in their way, and much wasn't needed for them to give up on this fight, and thus they were all set free and in friendship; and the Knight understood the stubbornness of his Horse in wanting to leave the path and come to this faraway place.

To support the sense of the Horse it happens that if it is taught to dance it will learn this very well and with great ease, as can be noted by a Horse of King Phillip II, which danced with such grace as if it was capable of reason.

Aelianus tells of a strange event and of a great loss and pity for those of Sybarita, a region in Arcadia, who, for having taught all of their Horses to dance were defeated and killed in a war. And the case was that the Sybaritas, as soon as they received a Horse, the first thing they did was to teach it how to dance, and they were so used to this that if they heard music or anything of the sort, no matter if these were tied in their stables or being ridden, they would start to dance. It so happened that the Crotonits, enemies of the Sybaritas, arriving at the field of battle, instead of carrying many weapons (even if they still had a few) came with drums and a great abundance of musical instruments; for they knew what was happening and how the Sybaritas had taught their Horses to dance; and as they were standing front to front, they started to play their instruments and the Horses of the Sybaritas instead of charging started to dance, with such leaps and jumps that they broke the whole army; and in this way they were killed at the hands of their enemies, or better said, at the hands of their Horses, for they were to blame, given that they were taught this damned trade, whose inventor is Satan. Many deeds and accomplishments are said of this most strong Animal; and I can tell of a certain Horse for having seen it, for this happened in the Duchy of Gandia, where I lived at the time; and this was that as a certain man, wanted by the law, was staying in this town, and he was warned that the *Alguaciles*[332] of Valencia were coming for him, he, with no further delay, jumped on his Horse, in which he had a great trust, but as soon as he left the town he ran into the *Alguaciles*. By pressing his Horse, they eventually ran into a steep slope of twenty eight cubits of height, which ended in a river which passed by the town, and without any fear, his Horse jumped off, falling in the middle of the river, disappearing for a long time, after which the Horse appeared at the surface and walked out with great spirit, saving its master, even if shortly after the Horse died in the service of its master.

Medicinal properties of the Horse

Horse manure, burnt, made into a powder and placed over bleeding wounds will retain and marvelously staunch the blood; by placing these powders on bleeding noses will also stop this flux. Dioscorides.

---

332. Translator's note: an old Spanish judicial title.

This same Author says that Horse's blood is most effective to incorporate and mix corrosive medicines.

Hali writes that Horse rennet is wonderful to slow and solve any hardness or swelling.

He further says that the breath and smoke from Horse manure is good to purge dead creatures from their mother's womb, by receiving this smoke from below, for it greatly attracts the *fetum mortuum*.

Aesculapius writes that Mare's milk, drunk, mitigates the pain and burning of the *madre* of women; and the rennet of the male, melted in some wine and drunk, removes all pain from the belly and stomach.

Pliny says that the nails or feet of a Horse, ground and placed on the gums, mitigates tooth pain.

Avicenna writes that powder from Horse feet, drunk with wine, stops the poison of any Animal bite.

Dioscorides writes that the mentioned powders, drunk with vinegar, heal the *gota coral*.

If a pregnant woman wants to speed up her labor, Adamo,[333] a grave Author, says that they should drink the blood from a Horse's shinbone.

Dioscorides further says that Horse manure, burnt and drunk with wine, makes any dead creature immediately leave the pregnant one.

Finally Adamo says that Horse fat is good for women's menstruation and internal wounds.

Of boastfulness by occasion of the Horse

Of the Horse we have truthfully said that it is arrogant and boastful, for it gloats and becomes haughty over seeing itself well dressed and beautiful, and for this reason it seems to me that it would not be inappropriate to say something of boastfulness, so as one may see the harm that this, and arrogance, can cause.

Boastfulness isn't anything else than an esteem and demonstration of the self and related things.

Saint Cyprian says that boastfulness and ostentation, in themselves, are hateful.

Saint Gregory says that boastfulness moves and excites the greatest daring that one's forces permit.

Aristotle says that it is ostentatious and boastfulness to attribute to oneself things of others, counting them as belonging to you.

The arrogant and boastful, Diogenes says, to none are good, not even to themselves.

Juvenal[334] says that virtue is not in the nobility of the lineages, but rather in good customs and spirit.

Erasmus says that true honor is not given by lands, but rather by the river of virtue.

In the Roman decrees one may find this sentence: that a man with honor should offer his life to assure his fame.

Seneca says that the greatest thing on earth is honor.

This same Author says that a man with a generous heart would much rather die with honor than live without it.

Cicero says that it is much more honorable he who deserves honor but does not get it, than that he who has it without deserving it.

A great penalty is given to him who in evil is lost; but he who in evil is glorified much worse does he deserve.

Saint Augustine says that if in the end of the world boastfulness and ostentations disappeared, we would all be equal.

Better is a humble confession in evil than vainglory and presumption in virtue. Jurisprudence.

---

333. Translator's note: uncertain reference.
334. Translator's note: probably Decimus Iunius Iuvenalis, a Roman poet of the Ist and IInd century.

Chapter XVII

Of the Tiger or Panther

  The Tiger or Panther is the cruelest and most vengeful of all the brutes of the land, and it is most swift, as is mentioned in the commentary on Hosea with: *Nil Leone fortius, nihil Panthera velocius*. In the way the Lion is greater than all Animals in terms of strength, the Tiger is in speed, and for this reason it is painted with flames coming out of its mouth, denoting through these the speed with which it runs. It is an Animal which gets along with all other Animals and according to Isidore it only has animosity with the Dragon, and this is not without reason, for among all only this one stalks the Tiger's young so as to kill them. The Panther or Tiger is very beautiful, even if cruel to man, and it has over its body as if half Moons, or some spots very pleasing to the sight, which (according to the Book *Hortus Sanitatis*) grow or decrease according to the movements of the Moon. Many and grave Authors call the Tiger or Panther, *Pardal*,[335] and even if these are different in their condition and beauty, they are nonetheless of the some species, like Dogs, which some have a certain form and posture and others one very different from this; some are strong and valiant, and others gentle, weak and cowardly. This same difference exists between the Panther and the *Pardal*: but one should note that what the *Pardal* lacks in beauty and bravery, Nature compensated this by giving to its skin, even if rustic, a scent and fragrance so great that many birds and land Animals will follow this Animal so as to enjoy it, and when

---

335. Translator's note: this is a somewhat old fashioned term to designate a big cat, such as a lynx or ocelot. I don't know to which one it is referring to in this context.

these least expect it, they become food for the *Pardal*. I seem to be able to hear a curious reader saying that I have just contradicted what I have said, and that he cannot believe nor understand that the Panther and *Pardal* are of the same species; and that the similarity with the case of the Dog does not convince him. To this I respond that should they remember or read the Chapter on the Donkey, they will find their response, for there we say that experience shows that the Mule and the Donkey are brothers, conceived in the same womb, and they are also extremely different among themselves, as all know, be it in condition, disposition and beauty, and one is apt for breeding and the other not. And the cause of this is written and narrated in length in the mentioned Chapter of the Donkey, and as such I do not wish to tire my quill here, but I will merely refer that one should consult in this place on how two Animals, sons of a mother and father, can be so different as we have said; however, one should know and understand that from the joining of the Lions with the Panthers or Tigers the Bear[336] is born, and from the Lioness and Tiger is the Brown Lion generated, and so these are brothers, even if not by father and mother, &c. Finally, the Tiger is an Animal with claws like those of a Lion, the body and tail like a fox, and the ears of a Donkey, and these are often raised on the shores of the Tigris River, and these run with such fury that it almost seems like a Horse, and from this it took the name of Tigris, given the similarity this Animals and this river have regarding their speed, for this same thing is what the word Tigris means in Greek. Many paint Tigers with wings, claiming that in fact these have them; but this is not true, and they do not have them, and if they are painted with wings this is to denote the great speed it has while running.

Stories of the Tiger

Pliny writes in his *Natural History* of the great love and affection the female Tiger has for its children, while it is cruel to all others. Of this Pliny says, Book 8, Chapter 18, how some hunters were once out on the shore of the Tigris River, which is around Babylon, and they saw, by chance, four Tiger pups in a certain hole, and not seeing any impediments, for their mother was absent, they picked them up and took them with them on their path across the river. After some time the Tiger went to its cave, and not finding its children immediately went out to search for them, and due to their scent it found the path those who took them were on; and as the hunters were alert and well warned, seeing the speed in which it was coming to seek its children, they dropped one of them; the good Tiger recognized its pup and took it to its cave, coming out with even more fury and following the same path as before; and as the hunters saw it coming back, they dropped another of the pups and picking it up it once again it took it to the cave, once aging coming out in a fury for its other children. As soon as the hunters arrived at the River they released the third pup, and no sooner had they let it go than it was taken as if by a lighting. And not forgetting the fourth child the Tiger came back out eager to get it back, and arriving at the edge of the River it saw that the hunters had already boarded a ship, and it was so struck by sadness and pain that it made the very hunters feel sorrowful, and as they kept on their path they lost sight of it and did not know if these feelings and cruel sentiments ended.

Another Tiger story tells us that as some hunter had taken its pups while the mother was out in search for food, when this Tiger returned and did not find them the rage and courage it gained was such that it no longer wanted to return to its den nor eat any more food, but it preferred to rather stop eating and die of hunger and sadness over having lost its children. In this way there are Animals that due to loving their children such, will die of sorrow if these are taken, and there are others who want them so badly that if these are not taken from them they will eat them, making them into their own blood and flesh, thinking that in this way they will be better kept safe; and these are the Cats, that over the fear of losing their children will swallow and hide them in their stomachs.

This Animal is so bothered by the sound of drumming that, according to Plutarch, it will become altered in such a way that it will rise to such a fury that it may kill itself.

---

336. Translator's note: uncertain translation.

The same Pliny, in the above mentioned place, tells of how hunters who are seeking these Animals (surely in Hyrcania, for in this region there are plenty of them) will take some large mirrors and when they catch the pups and begin to flee, smartly do they leave some of these mirrors behind, so as the Tiger will see some of these and detain itself looking at it, seeing there its figure, thinking this to be one of its children, and it will be entertained there licking and cuddling it, as if this image was really one of its children, and in this way may one perform this theft which represents so much danger in catching and hunting such fierce and cruel Animals as the Tigers, and in this way are they raised in cages or other such places prepared for them.

On many occasions can we see how cruel and fierce the Tiger always is towards man, especially in festivities and public feasts that the Gentile Romans used to make when they achieved some victory over their enemies, celebrating their false Gods; and this was that they had a proper place for some men, which they had condemned to death or sold as slaves, to fight such beasts, and he who could free himself from this danger he would be set free. In those places there were all sorts of wild Animals such as Lions, Tigers, Bears, Bulls and other similar ones; and when a Lion fought with a man, and the man surrendered, this Animal would be satisfied, this unless it was hungry, and should a man fight a Bull, if he were to lie down without moving the Bull would be satisfied, even if to some it is not enough to play dead, and should a Bear come out, and should this be victorious, maybe it would kill the man, and then return to its den; but should a Tiger come out to fight a man, and should it indeed be victorious, it would not be satisfied with seeing him beaten or dead, but rather torn to pieces for such is its fierceness and cruelty.

Medicinal properties of the Tiger

The skin of the *Pardal*, according to Pliny and Aristotle, has a great odor and fragrance, and it has the virtue of keeping away poisonous Snakes. A very grave Author called Hildegard,[337] writes that anyone with leprosy, should they apply to this the heart of a Tiger, this will heal and health will return; for according to the learned Francisco Velez de Arciniega, speaking with the authority of the above mentioned Author, any leprosy that touches the mentioned heart will become attached to it, and so the one with this disease will be healed.

Avicenna writes that this Animal and the Leopard, should they by any chance eat any poison, they will hurry to find some human manure.

Of cruelty by occasion of the Tiger

Being that the Panther or Tiger is so cruel, it seems to me that this is an occasion to say something of cruelty, for this vice is greatly bothersome to all, even if very much used.

Cruelty, according to Aristotle, is an inhumanity, a detestable fierceness and a vice of wild beasts.

Cruelty, according to Mexía, is an enemy of all reason and justice, and it is worse than the sin of Wrath and Pride.

Cruelty, says Seneca, is not a feature of man, but rather of beasts, for it is used by he who likes blood and evil cunnings.

Supreme cruelty is to increase a penalty. Seneca.

Cruelty is exercised by he who reprehends his friend in need. Seneca.

To the cruel and proud, the more the punishment is belated, the more grave and harsh it becomes. Titus Livy.

Of Nero, Marcus Aurelius writes that he was so cruel that in his life he did not concede to anything, not even to his own mother, for out of pleasure he had her killed and the whole of Rome burnt, looking over it for seven day while it was burning.

To the cruel, says Curtius,[338] the more you plead the more he becomes cruel.

---

337. Translator's note: Hildegard of Bingen, an XIth century Benedictine abbess and polymath, writer of the book *Physica* on the medical properties of plants, stones, and animals.

338. Translator's note: Quintus Curtius Rufus, a Roman senator and historian of the I[st] century

Atreus, King, was so cruel that he killed the children of a woman called Tiestes in front of her, and more, he cooked and prepared them as food. Arbolanche, Book 7.

This mentioned Author writes that the Etruscans were so cruel that they had men tied together with the dead, and in this way they died miserably.

Herod, King of the Jews, was so cruel that so as to kill the Baby Jesus, had one hundred and forty four thousand babies killed, and his own children with them, and after he died, still wanting to be cruel, had all the lords of Jerusalem gathered and enclosed in a room, and had his daughter kill them all after he had died.

Chapter XVIII

Of the Beaver

The Beaver is half land Animal and half water Animal, for it enjoys and lives in both of these elements, and it cannot live solely in one of these, and as such, at times it is in the fields and at times it is in the water, and its greatest resting place is in this last one, where it will have a house, built with wood cut with its own sharp teeth, near the shore, where it spends the nights and some parts of the day. And this den is made with such skill so as the Beaver may be in and out of the water, and this should be known, for the bottom half of this den is underwater and the upper half above, for the Beaver breathes through lungs. The upper half of its body is similar to that of the Otter, especially its head; and the lower half is similar to that of a fish, at least its tail, and those who have seen and tasted it say that this tail not only has the shape of that of a fish, but also the scent and the taste of fish. The hind feet are flat, so as with them it may swim and sustain itself in the water, and in this may one see the foresight of nature, for seeing the necessity that this Animal has in using the water to live its life, due to the inclination given by its tail, it provided it with flat and wide feet so as to be sustained in it, for if it were any other way it would drown under water, and if it couldn't enter the said water it would not be able to survive. The skin of this Animal is delicate and very soft, in such a way that many hunters are solely interested in it when hunting this Animal; even if it is true that this Animal is also greatly pursued for its testicles, given the great virtues and excellences that it has for many unguents and necessary medicines for human life. The Physiologus, treating the composure and admirable dwellings the Beavers make in rivers and fountains, mentions that the sticks and wood which are used to fabricate these are from plants with a bitter bark, and that these firstly peel this part away and eat it, for they are most amicable of sour and bitter things, and after this do they use these sticks to make their dwelling. This same Author, and others like him, write that the Beaver, upon seeing hunters, naturally knows that these are seeking its testicles, and that as these draw closer, with a strange feeling and rage, it cuts its own testicles and drops them, becoming very relieved that these will no longer pursue it, for they were given that which they sought. This is mentioned by several grave Authors, but I for one say that they cut their own testicles not due to the fact that they understand the thoughts of those pursuing them, but rather because as these see themselves pursued by Dogs and hunters, they cut themselves for their testicles are a great a obstacle for them to run, for these are very large, and by cutting them with their razor sharp teeth they not only run but they almost fly, for they become very light, and in this way they will not be caught. Oh rare consideration of a brute Animal without reason, that it would rather lose that which it greatly esteems over that which is worth the most, which is its life and liberty; and of this the Wise say: *Non bene pro toto libertas venditur auro!* Which means that liberty should not be traded for all the possessions in the world. Oh strength of living, what things you achieve and force on an Animal that with reason is called Beaver (Castoreo), for from this effort of life it becomes chaste! Oh how many do not have their rest, life and freedom in this sad and short life, and even in the next, joyful and long, for not doing as the Beaver does with its will, seeing death with their corporeal and spiritual eye, &c.

The Beaver, according to the Natural Philosophers, has friendship with all Animals, except with the Dog, which it holds as its capital enemy; and it has such a nature that in the water it is always alone, and in the fields it is always accompanied, and it itself will seek out other Animals so as to entertain itself with them.

Stories of the Beaver

The Natural Philosophers, writing of the Beaver, greatly admire its spirit and bravery, as well as what we have already mentioned of it cutting its own testicles, and as well over the story which is told, which greatly shows the spirit and heart it has.

This case was that when certain hunters were seeking a Beaver, and finding its water dwelling, they understood that the Beaver had taken refuge in it, and they set their Dogs on it, but none dared enter; but the racket and noise these made outside was such that the Beaver did come out and started running, with the Dogs after it, and as one of the Dogs was faster than all the others, being close to the Beaver, this turned on it and with two bites ended it, continuing its run immediately after. As this was happening, another Dog was beginning to approach it, leaving all the other Dogs behind and almost reaching the Beaver, and it once again turned on the Dog and with one bite it was put down; continuing with its run, this same thing happened with the third, fourth and last Dog, as the Beaver always waited for its opportunity to take revenge on its enemy one at a time and in this way escape them all. And the hunters seeing that it was about to escape from their grasp could not believe that it was still carrying its testicles, judging by its speed, and as such they began to search along the path it had taken to see if they could find them; not being able to they returned to its den and while looking at its composure and art, they discovered the testicles that the poor Beaver had cut so as it could escape without any bother and run faster. There is no shortage of Authors who say this Animal does not cut its testicles so as to run faster, but rather to incite within itself greater fury and rage, so as it may fight with greater audacity and with wrath defend itself from its enemies, and also be inflamed by rage so as to run and fight with more fury, as the Lion does, that in order to become enraged, beats its own body with its tail, hitting itself with great blows, and with these blows it becomes more furious. But be it for this reason or the other it is a most difficult thing to cut its testicles with its own teeth, and this shows a great spirit and a great heart, as no other Animal has, and over this I intend to say something of heart a little further down.

Medicinal properties of the Beaver

The testicles of the Beaver are also called Castoreos, and these have great virtues and excellences. These are dried in shaded and well ventilated places and can be preserved for many years, even if the younger they are the better.

Plateario says that the said testicles have an admirable virtue and efficiency in resolving and marvelously comforting nervous parts and regions.

By giving Beaver (testicle) powder to drink with rue juice, or as a decoction with red wine, it will cure any headache arising from coldness. Plateario.

These powders have the virtue of curing inflammations of the tongue caused by a blockage in the phlegm, this by placing these powders under the tongue, one or several times. The same virtue and efficiency has a decoction of wine with these powders, drunk, this to cure paralysis of the body and shrinkage of the nerves; it comforts the brain, promotes sneezing, provokes menstruation, banishes dead creatures from the womb, speeds up births and promptly expels the placenta. Idem.

Dioscorides writes of great virtues of such powders, and above all he says that these are good against the bites of poisonous Serpents.

Beaver oil, according to Arnaldus de Villa Nova, has many properties, and the three first among these are the same we have mentioned of Plateario, that they are quick to resolve, attract and fortify all tendons, nerves or any weak and debilitated member.

It is said that these testicles can be falsified by those coming from the island of Ponto, and in order to know which ones are fake or real, Dioscorides says that the true Beaver testicles are united, and these have nerves uniting one to the other, and this can be no other way.

These powders, drunk, are worth against absent mindedness, and nervous shakes. Dioscorides.

These powders, drunk with wine, cure flatulence and any superfluous windiness, it reduces belly pain and they do not permit that any poisonous drink may cause harm. Dioscorides.

Avicenna says that these powders, drunk in the morning, are good to increase memory; and mixed with litharge, vinegar and rose oil will marvelously cure coldness from the ears and deafness.

Beaver gall, drunk, prevents decrepitude. Avicenna.

Of heart by occasion of the Beaver

Speaking of the spirit with which the Beaver cuts its own testicles (even if some do contradict this, there are more who affirm it) we promised to say something about heart, and for this being the root from which spirit or cowardice of all Animals arises, we shall say something according to the Learned.

The heart is placed, as a King, in the middle of the chest, surrounded by all the principal members which govern the regiment of the body, and according to Aristotle and other learned medics, only man has his heart on the left side, and all other Animals have it in the middle of the chest.

It is a most hot member, which infuses the heat of life in all other members, and according to Aristotle, it is the first thing which is formed in man, for it is the most principal of all members and it is the source of natural heat, and it is the last member to die in man, and it is so sensitive and delicate that it cannot be injured, or this will end a man's life.

The heart has within itself two vacancies, one on the right and one on the left, between which there is a thin wall of very tense and hard flesh, so as to keep inside it a certain hot blood. From one of these vacancies is the blood passed so as to be refined through some very thin pores into the other vacancy, and as this passes these pores are immediately closed so as this may not return back. Should these vacancies be small one will have a great spirit, should they be large then one will have little spirit and little bravery; the cause of this, according to Aristotle, is that all Animals who have a large heart are cowards, and all which have a small heart are brave; for by having a large heart so will the vacancies be large, and having a small heart so will the vacancies be small;

and being small these receive less blood and as such this is conserved hotter and boiling, which would not happen if there was a great deal of it; and from this one may gather that the hotter and livelier this blood gathered in this vacancies is, the greater spirit does one demonstrate, and on the contrary &c.

Those who have a soft heart have a great spirit and great thoughts, and all of this arises from this fact.

Those who were killed by poison, according to Suetonius, can be discovered by placing their heart over a fire, for it will not be consumed.

In the heart are the thoughts and words conceived, and there is happiness and sadness born, and from there arise the effects of fear and love, according to Aristotle and Saint Bernard.

The heart by itself is most hot, and from it do all other parts and members of the body receive their heat, for even with excess heat it is not consumed, for nature (guided by God) provided it with a lung that always keeps it cool, receiving fresh air and casting away the hot one, and thus it is sustained.

Seneca said that among all human things, there isn't anything greater than the heart who knows to underappreciate the very great things.

It is a natural thing for a merciful heart to be affected and feel sadness over seeing things and labors in which it cannot help. Cornelia.[339]

There isn't a more loyal or certain thing to a man than his own heart.

Never does a hurting heart have good news as certain nor bad new as doubtful.

The distressed heart finds greater rest in narrating its pains than in hearing the joys of others. Marcus Aurelius.

Saint Bernard says that the hearts of men are judged by their words, and the words of God Our Lord are judged by the heart.

So as to know the type of heart a man has, so says Cassiodorus, one should pay attention to the words he says and the actions he does.

Saint Gregory says that the soul and heart of God are his Holy Scripture.

The heart of a lover is more in that which he loves than where it lives. And so says Saint Gregory that even if we don't have a more certain neighbor than our heart, this is many times, or almost always, separated from us, for it always has its own wants, loves and thoughts.

The same Saint Gregory says that the heart of the Priest isn't any other thing that a Reliquary of God. And he further says that the number of times one gravely sins, the number of times one is without a heart.

---

339. Translator's note: Probably Cornelia Scipionis Africana, daughter of Scipio Africanus, famed over her great virtues.

Chapter XIX

Of the Unicorn

The Unicorn is not a very big Animal (even if it has an equine body) but it is extremely strong and it has a terrible spirit, inexpugnable and harsh; and according to Pliny and Aelianus, it is such a wild and brave Animal that it would rather be killed than caught, and its body, according to Solinus, is that of a Horse, the head of is that of a Deer, the feet of an Elephant and the tail of a Pig. It has in the middle of its front a straight and pointy horn, even if twisted like the shell of a snail, and around two palms in length; it is so strong that anything which is not iron will not bother, break or pierce it. Some Authors call Unicorn to the Indian Horse, given the similarity in posture and bravery, such as Pliny and Aelianus. Other, such as Solinus and Saint Isidore claim that the Unicorn is the Monoceros, or Rhinoceros, as can be read in Greek, for that which is found written about this Animal attributes to it all the qualities, properties and posture of the Unicorn, and so they believe that these are one and the same; those wishing to read arguments in favor and against this issue should read the History of land Animals written by Francisco Velez de Arciniega, Apothecary of the City of Madrid, for he discourses there in a gallant and subtle way on these topics; for my intent with this small work is not to deal with questions, but solely to speak of the nature, properties and stories that to each Animal belong in an open and accessible way. The horn of the Unicorn has great properties and excellences, and for this it is required that we say something of its form so as one may not be taken as the other. The above mentioned Authors, mainly Solinus, say that the horn of the Unicorn is twisted as a flint stone (as was said) even if it is straight and thick, and it is surrounded by thick and brown hairs at its base in the Animal's nose.

And this becomes gradually thinner and twisted towards the tip, and it is as solid and strong as a tooth and fang of an Elephant, but the clearest indications that this is effectively the horn of a Unicorn, according to Aelianus, is its radiance and the way it is twisted towards its tip, and these two natural excellences are not found in any other horn of any other Animal except the Unicorn.

Even if the Unicorn is so indomitable, fierce and brave, many weaker Animals come close to it, so as it may aid and protect them against other cruel beasts, and the Unicorn does defend them and keep them under its custody, fighting on their behalf until victory or death, without ever manifesting or showing a hint of cowardice, and it is even in the moment before its death (according to these Authors) that it finds the greatest spirit and bravery. Saint Isidore, speaking of the Unicorn says: its natural habitation is in the deserts and the furthest possible place from the contact of man, and this is so valiant that it exceeds all Animals in spirit and strength, and it would rather lose its life than its effort, and its legs are shorter (even if robust) than its natural size would require. And it is true that of the horns of these Animals very little or almost nothing is said, and according to Aelianus this is due to them being so indomitable, fierce and cruel; but should we read the History of Animals by Francisco Velez de Arciniega, one will find a lot being said in that place about these twisted horns, and the Author himself has seen a few, as he so writes in his natural history, for human industry can overcome all, and pave a path over any difficulty; and thus, in order to hunt this indomitable Animal they have found a certain invention of man which is most incredible (even if I find no difficulty in believing this, for the same is written by Saint Isidore). And the case is that in order to hunt these indomitable and intractable Animals one should take a beautiful damsel, very well disposed and humble, and place her in a place where the Unicorn may see her (in such a way as she may be safe), and the affection that this Animal gains towards this beautiful damsel and her beautiful dress is such that it will sit at her feet and rest on her lap, where it will sleep, and with this industry is this Animal hunted and taken in certain wooden cages specially made for this purpose. And even if they do not kill it, it, seeing itself imprisoned, kills itself, for it has the same condition and nature as the Cat, which does not permit it to be caged and much less tied. To many this method of hunting the Unicorn mentioned by Saint Isidore is hard to believe, which is the risking of the life of a young damsel for the prison of a brute; and to this difficulty I answer (even if it is true that this is written by Saint Isidore, as I do believe) that one may take on to the mounts and harsh lands where these Animals are raised a well adorned damsel with beautiful dresses and scents so as the Unicorn may be caught off guard and be hunted, but one does not need to put their lives in danger; for even without this invention I have just mentioned, the human judgment would discover another, and another thousand inventions so as to hunt this Animal, and it seems to Saint Isidore that the invention and method of hunting the Unicorn, with its terrible strength, seems to symbolize our God and Lord, who, before being made man (according to the Holy scripture) was very terrible and strong, *& Deus ultionis*. For in order to treat and tame such a wild Lord, and make him change (if this can be said) his condition of Unicorn into something soft and tame as a Lamb, it was necessary to place before Him a beautiful and humble Damsel, adorned with all virtues, which was the always Virgin Mary, His Mother and our Lady. And as this same Lord wished to change His condition, and treat man with familiarity and softness, His Majesty brought on the creation of the mentioned Damsel, with such beauty, humility and grace that she exceeded (as she does) all pure creatures. And seeing her the divine Unicorn (as he always sees) so perfect and complete, filled with all graces, He became affectionate of her (as He always was) and was so pleased that He surrendered and laid on her purest lap, taking from her human flesh and making Himself man for the love of men; and so it could happen that from this contact He could be arrested and become a remedy for this world. For as the horn of the Unicorn, when placed in poisonous water removes all poison, allowing other Animals to drink from this without danger (as is written by grave authors, such as Archdeacon Gomez, Bishop of Abarracin in the book he wrote in Salé, as also Pomponius Mela, in his history of the Animals) in this same way was also the strong horn of the death and passion of Christ our Redeemer placed at the front of the Holy Roman Catholic Church, cure for all poison of deadly, venial and original sin, as he has ordered of our Mother Church.

Medicinal properties of the Unicorn's horn

Lusitano,[340] writing on Dioscorides, mentions that which we have referred from other Authors about the Unicorn's horn, that if placed in poisoned water it removes all poison. This Author then says that, as well as with others of great authority, in the lands where the Unicorns are raised there are an abundance of poisonous Serpents, which at night take refuge in fountains, where they vomit a great deal of venom, and they make these waters poisonous. And it is a rare thing that as all other four legged Animals come to drink from this water, none dare to come near until a Unicorn places its horn in it, and after this they all can drink secure and without any fear of being poisoned, for the touch of this horn makes those waters pure and free from venoms. The discreet Arciniega gives us the order by which to prepare the Unicorn horn in the book he composed on the land Animals, and whose powders are used to treat many ills; and as such I remit the Reader to the mentioned Book, Chapter 4, on the Unicorn.

Powder of a Unicorn's horn, drunk with wine, kills any poison. Lusitano.

These powders are worthy against burning hotness and smallpox. Idem.

They are also good against worms and they can be used to speed up childbirth. Idem.

Hildegard writes in Book 4, Chapter 7, that anyone who carries a lock of Unicorn hair placed in contact with the skin will not suffer from hotness.

He who carries the skin of the feet of a Unicorn will not suffer from swellings nor pain on his feet and legs, and he will always have these dry, given that this is in contact with the skin and flesh. Idem.

Should one place under the bowl in which one eats stew the nail of a Unicorn, and should this be hot, it will not boil if there is any venom in it; and if this is cold, smoke will arise, should there be poison. Idem.

Of custom and its effects by occasion of the Unicorn

A custom, should it be bad is pernicious, but should it be good, is greatly advantageous and agreeable to the eyes of God and of the peoples; and custom can do a lot both for the brutes as for man, that those never abandon it and these with great difficulty can separate it from themselves; and custom is such a powerful and sticky thing that it becomes co-natural, and part of he who has it; in such a way that the Philosopher came to say that *consuetudo est altera natura*; and this means that a well kept custom is converted to nature; and declaring this, it further means that that which is natural cannot be separated or repressed, at least not without great difficulty; in this same way custom has such strength, and even more than that which is natural. And this we can see very well in the Unicorn, that since it is accustomed to living in such remote areas and so separated from man, it is made indomitable, intractable and fierce, without ever allowing itself to be approached or dominated by its lord man, and it is in the way we mentioned that it may be caught and either killed or broken into pieces. Which does not happen to others which are more fierce, wild and cruel Animals, which, given time and patience, allow themselves to be handled, ruled and governed by man; and only the Unicorn remains free in its liberty, and it only respects a damsel and to her yields its harshness and terribleness. And one cannot know if this obedience is given over subjection or surrender (or if this sentiment does not exist in it) or if it is solely due to the knowledge and intrinsic association that the Damsel's virginity has, which it recognizes in the same way as was said of the Elephant (and will be said *Deo savente* regarding the Bees), that agrees with it haughtiness and customary presumptuous, and this custom has moved my spirit to say something of it with the authority of grave Philosophers and Saints.

Custom, according to Saint Isidore, Book 2, is a certain right constituted by this same custom which by law is received and is maintained while it is needed.

Seneca says that custom demonstrates that a man is suffering through labors which he does not require.

---

340. Translator's note: probably Amato Lusitano, a XVIth century (Jewish) Portuguese medic and writer.

Master Medina says that custom not only can abolish a law, but also interpret it and constitute a new one.

Cicero says that customs in labor makes them easier.

The custom of sinning makes one doubt its evilness. Cicero.

Custom has the authority and power of a Prince to make and break laws.

Saint Ambrose says that customs and the use of things are the cause of the invention of art.

Saint Bernard says, Psalm 37, that from customs are virtues made, and not in nature, for it is normal for man to use evil to make vices and use good to make virtues.

Saint Chrysostom says that custom changes and corrupts the rights and actions of nature.

Greatness is more related to the use of a thing than its possession. Idem.

Greater force and more victorious are good customs than strength. Quintilianus.

Seneca says that fortune does not have power over customs.

Saint Ambrose says that bad customs wage greater wars on us than our enemies.

Aristotle says that all which is a custom is a delight, from which one may gather that even things which aren't pleasant are made so by custom.

Saint Augustine says that it is a hard thing to fight against habit and custom.

This same saint says that one should not change anything in a custom while this does not contradict reason.

He further says that there is nothing as firm as a custom, even more if it is favored by truth and reason.

Chapter XX

Of the Mouse, and by its occasion we will say something of the Thief

The Mouse is the household enemy of man, and it is very prejudicial to all his things; and it is so insistent in seeking its common sustenance that it gnaws and cuts everything, without forgiving a single thing which is for the food or use of man; and natural inclination is so powerful in the brute Animals that, should they be set free, they will not miss one mark of that in which nature has inclined them. And as to these Animals nature has given such caring affection of always seeking all things of their sustenance with such insistence, they do not care of the danger they place themselves in at each step; and their natural conditions are so similar to those of the Thieves that, in being fearless and covetous of that which is not theirs, they differ in nothing; and so one as the other exercise their malice by always waiting for the careful hours, so as no one may see them, for the fear of being caught with their theft in their hands is great. For if these feel, even if a slight noise, that they are discovered, it is a thing worth seeing, how disturbed, fearful and scared and disoriented they become: one losing sight of their hole and hiding place and the others the sight of the door; and in this way one falls into the hands of the cunning Cats and the others into the hands of the heavy executioner. And both of these (the Mouse and the Thief) are so voracious, one for eating and gnawing and the other for stealing, that they do not care for any danger, but they are rather always neck deep in it, and in this way they will always be killed or imprisoned, as is claimed by the Wiseman of the Proverbs by saying: He who loves danger will die by it.

Pliny talks of three types of Mice in the Cyrenaica region, and about the same amount I say that there are of Thieves in the terrestrial region, ones that have a sharp forehead, and these are cunning and bent on gnawing and to wasting things. Others have sharp hair, so that it stings as that of a Hedgehog, and these are cruel and tyrants. Finally there are other Mice that to the sight seem almost like rabbits, but they are not, but another very fine kind of Mice, and these are traitorous. In this same tone do I say that there are three kinds of Thieves: the first are those who by nature are inclined to such a vile trade as stealing, and these exercise this trade so cunningly and insistently that they cannot abstain from it, and sooner or later they are caught in theft and they end up paying for it; the second are those that because they maintain a certain vice or pleasure in gambling or women, are given to steal farms and lives, and these are frequently roadside bandits and can be usually found on the gallows. The last ones are those who do not look like Thieves, and these are very prejudicial to the Republic, for under the title of doing good they suck the blood of the poor; and in this last category one finds many different kinds of people, &c. Returning to the Mice, I say that in everything and over everything they are similar to the Thieves in their stealing and fear, and even in their increase and growth in numbers are these similar, that I do not understand what kind of Animal or lineage of man can grow so much and be so abundant as are Thieves and Mice, for according to Aristotle, in the *Animalibus*, it is said that none of the brutes are as fertile and ready for generation as the little shy Mouse. This truth is confirmed by Aelianus, by saying that in a certain region of Italy there grew and abounded so much of this species of Animal that they did not allow for a single herb or root to grow in the field, for they would gnaw and eat it; and for this reason, filled with hunger, the inhabitants of that region had to leave until those Mice left over the lack of food.

The same happened in the Islands of the Cyclades, that the great multiplication of Mice was the reason why those populations had to leave for a number of years. And this is the same tone, it seems to me, that the lineages of the Thieves is following; and there are so many of these that if the Majesty of God Our Lord did not provide us with so many Cats and Ministers of Justice to handle the Thieves, one could no longer live in this world, for the Mice would pursue our food and the Thieves our houses and lives. And there is another inclination and condition which is similar, and this is as the Mice are always lurking in the house, climbing the walls and watching over all; so too Thieves are continuously looking for a place in which they may enter in order to enact their evil intent, not caring neither one nor the other of the danger they are in.

The greatest enemy of the house Mouse is the Cat; and of the Thief it is the Dog; and in the same way as in a house with a Cat there are no Mice, so as in a house with a Dog Thieves do not enter.

Aelianus says that Mice run from the hiss of the Viper, in such a way as they will leave and seek another place to live far away from that sound. This same thing happens with Thieves, who run away from the lands where one can hear the hiss of justice which is most strict against them. Finally these great Mice are most bothersome for all men, even if not of all, for there are those who take pleasure in having these for the fun they can have with them; for according to what Plutarch writes in his *Moralia* and Pliny in his *Natural History*, these Animals are most amicable towards metals, and even more of gold. And thus in the houses of those who work with gold there are always some crumbs of this that fall to the ground; and as the neighboring Mice catch all of these, for hearing their noise they gather these pieces, which they cannot in any way digest nor consume, by being an incorruptible metal, and these are kept in their stomach for a long time; and in their time, all neighbors hunt these with their Mouse traps, and opening them up they take this gold and are made rich. In the same way are Thieves bothersome, even if not of all, for there are those who receive them in their homes for the advantages they can get from these, from their backs and evil minds (this until the executioner takes his share by opening them up with a beating). And I believe that there wouldn't be as many Thieves in the world if there weren't those who consented, covered and took them into their homes.

Stories of the Mouse

Aristotle, in the *de Animalibus*, Book 6, Chapter 37, speaking of the second generation and abundance of Mice, and of how it is certain that the females can get pregnant without contact with males, says: In a certain part of Persia there is mention of a female Mouse which was so large and had such a grown belly that people, over the curiosity of wanting to see how many little Mice it had inside, opened it up and among the many they found there was another one that was also pregnant, with still many little Mice inside this one, in this way it was pregnant before even being born; and this mother not only had inside it many children, but also grandchildren.

Strange case and story of the Mice

Aelianus writes, in Book 6 and 11 of his History, that the Mice know and understand when anything is about to fall; and when something is about to fall they move away from it very quickly, with great fear and surprise, running around without knowing where to hide in their disturbance. Regarding this, it so happened in Valencia, in the street of Saint Vicente, a most prodigious and notable case; and this was that at ten o'clock on that day some very large Mice came out of a house with some others very small, and these were running from one place to the other along that street, very fearful and dazed; and in this way the neighbors, and all those passing by this place, seeing the Mice started shouting. And over all this noise all those who were inside the house from where the Mice had come out came also into the street in order to see what was happening; as all grown men and children were out of this house, looking at the disturbed Mice, the house fell to the ground behind them, without causing any damage to any person; and this caused a great amazement in all neighbors and indeed the whole of Valencia.

Story and harmful case of a little Thief

Having spoken of Thieves by occasion of the Mice, I thought of telling this case of a little Thief (more over the fact that he succeeded and over whom). And the case was that while two honorable old men were in a lookout place, they saw a famed Thief enter into the *Tirador*, which is a very large square where the Wool Carders spread their cloths so as these may dry and harden. And in this *Tirador* there is a sentence, the lightest being life, to all who touch even a single palm of cloth from there. And being these two old men watching this Thief and speaking of his famous prowess and cunning, a young boy of ten or twelve years old came up to them, saying the following: Most honorable Fathers, what will you give me if I steal from this Thief you so brag of everything he carries on him, including his shirt, this without him even noticing it until I am done? The old men, not believing the treachery of the boy, said to him: Listen boy, are you cheating us or making fun of our faces? And the boy responded: I am not cheating, for to all this do I dare, and I further say that if you give me two *reales*, I will fulfill what I promise; and if I don't then you can take your hand to spank me. The good old men offered him the two *reales*, maybe just over the daring the boy had in tying to trick them, for they did not believe he could do as he said.

The boy went down to that patio of the *Tirador* where the Thief was walking, awaiting his turn. In this the boy came close to a well that exists in this place and started to cry, shouting out in a great and loud voice, and the Thief came closer, asking the boy what was wrong with him and why he was crying; and he responded, crying even louder: Oh poor me that I will be killed if I do not bring back the plate of gold and silver which just fell into the well when I wanted to drink some water. The good Thief, moved much more by greed than by compassion, told him: Be quiet and do not cry, I will fetch this; and he took off his clothes and as he was about to enter the well he thought of some treachery (even if this was to no avail) so as to keep this imaginary plate, and he told the boy: Go and bring me some olive oil so I can have this in my mouth when I go under water. And as soon as the boy turned his back, doing as he was asked, the Thief jumped in the well, and in this same instant the cunning boy picked up everything the greedy Thief had as clothes and kept his word; and thus he charged the two old men his two *reales*, and the one who had come to steal wool was left without it and was betrayed; And over this, or over some other similar case, the following verse was composed:

He who cheats is cheated,
He who affronts is affronted
If his habits he does not change,
He will be cheated by another.

Medicinal properties of the Mouse

Rhazes, writes in his history of the Animals that Mouse blood, placed on a wart will make it dry and fall off.

The same Author says that roasted Mouse, eaten or drunk as a powder with white wine, will stop the flow of saliva that some have in excess, and this will make it dry and stop.

The same author says that powder from Mouse manure, mixed with honey and drunk, will break bladder stones and expel sands.

Galen writes that the mentioned Mouse powders, mixed with vinegar, will cure alopecia; and if this is drunk it breaks stones which are formed in the bladder.

The same Author says that these powders, drunk with honeyed water, make boys have a big belly.

Rhazes writes that the mentioned powders, mixed with incense and some honeyed water and drunk will break bladder stones.

A dead Mouse, opened in half and placed over a wart will made it fall off.

The same Authors mentions that Mouse manure boiled in water, and with this still warm one washes around the bladder, it will make a man urinate, and should this water be drunk a man will urinate better.

He who carries with him the tooth of a mole, which is a type of Mouse (as is said in Valencia), will not suffer from gizzard ills, according to Pliny, in Chapter 3 of the thirtieth book of his history of the Animals.

Remedy against Mice

Pliny writes that with the juice of a herb called *Camalconte*,[341] mixed with water and olive oil, will very well kill any Mouse that tastes it.

From the juice of a tree called Yew, Pliny says Mice ran away from.

Should one want to get rid of these immediately, with little effort and less work, he should open some four or six grapes or figs, and place inside this some arsenic, and close them back up again, placing these near the places the Mice usually wander, and without any effort they will all die.

If you can find a Mouse of medium size, with this one you will be able to get rid of all the other in the following way; take some of the skin from its head and place in this place some salt and let it go in peace, for it will wage war on all the others.

Another great remedy is to take some powdered cheese and arsenic, placing this inside a cloth very well tied together, making as if some little dolls, and then place these along places where the Mice walk around at night, and these, feeling the smell of cheese, will immediately go to the dolls, and they will take these to their homes, and all others will get a hold of these and they will all be finished; and this trick I once used to get rid of them all, as I was unable to defend myself from them, seeing as I did not have a Cat.

Many and great tricks have men invented in order to be able to fight and be free of the harm and damage done by its household enemies, and as these are so many, and so as not to extend this work further, I will, from the great number of them, give you one more, by being curious, subtle and ingenious.

Take a clay vase, not very big and not very small, with an average size mouth, and you should cover this with a wet scroll, very well tied around the mouth; and when this scroll gets dry and becomes hard, make a cut as a cross on it; and we should further warn that in this vase you should have some water, about half of the vase; and you should further place something good to eat that smells good, such as a piece of cheese or some bacon or any other thing, inside the vase, in such a way as it does not touch the water. Once this is done, as the Mice approach the scroll, they will fall inside the vase without being able to leave, for the cut will open, making the Mouse fall

---

341. Translator's note: uncertain translation.

into the water, and it will once again close. And do note this clever artifice, for it is curious and advantageous, for many Mice will fall inside without being able to warn each other.

Of Nature, by occasion of the Mouse

For having mentioned that Nature can do a lot in Mice, and in each one of the brute Animals; we shall say something of it with the authority of the Learned and Saints.

Livinio[342] Philosopher says that this word of nature does not mean anything else but the will of God, by which all that was created moves and changes at its determined times; and due to this do many learned say that nature is nothing else besides the Divine will.

Saint Augustine, Book 21 of the *Civitate Dei*, says that there is a *Natura Naturans*, which is God; and another *Natura Naturara*, which is the natural effect that by Divine will operates on creatures.

Cicero says that Nature is a force given to creatures so as they may form and produce their similar and attend to their natural inclinations.

Aristotle, in *de Caelo*, says that nature does not do anything which is not founded on reason and proportion; and that it is the principal of movement and quietness of that same thing which is principal by itself and not by some other accident.

The same Aristotle says that in nature there is never shortage of necessary things, nor is there excess of those which seem superfluous.

A difficult thing, according to Plutarch, is to resist the strength of our natural affections; and that the works of Nature do not have necessity of Fortune.

Seneca says that he who in everything follows nature has no need to imitate the artifices.

Cicero says that a man who obeys nature will never offend nor harm another.

Saint Augustine says that our nature never consented to being beaten or subjected.

The first Master of mercy was nature, in the history of Saxony.

Cato called nature a secure and straight Captain, with which we cannot go wrong.

Finally, nature, according to Livinio Lenio, isn't anything else but the will and Divine reason, causer of all created things and its conserver after they are created, according to the quality of each one of them.

---

342. Translator's note: uncertain reference.

Chapter XXI

Of the Frog

The Frogs, according to Saint Isidore, are called *Agarruliate*, for they are constantly croaking and singing without ever ceasing; and they are so insistent with their nefarious singing that many have abandoned the towns and houses that are close to any lake or water tank where these may live. Even if it is true that the Frog is a fish, as the Catholic Church has received it, for it allows for the faithful to eat them on fasting days; seeming appropriate to eat it not as a land Animal but as a water Animal, for it is raised in the waters and is considered a fish; however, this has four feet, like all the other brutes, and some Frogs are raised in the fields, without ever seeing water; and over these and other reasons it has seemed appropriate to discuss them here. From this species of Frog, according to Isidore, there are three kinds: ones that are raised in water, whose croaking and singing is so continuous and heavy that it is impossible to bear its harm. Other frogs are raised in thick forests and fields where there is an abundance of trees and thick woods, and these will never be heard singing or croaking; and of these Isidore says that they have such a property that should they be put in the mouth of a barking Dog, it will forever lose its bark, and it is no longer any good to guard any houses, for it can no longer give out its warning. The third kind of frogs are called Rubetas, or Toads, and these are raised in dry areas and they are very poisonous; and these rarely open their mouths to sing, only at night do they put out some noise, and only this species of Frog does not leap when it runs, as the others do.

The water Frogs, after they are born, are like some little black fish, and they are practically just a head with a very thin tail; and as these begin to grow, this head will grow larger and begin to form its body and legs, with its tail converting itself into their back legs, according to Isidore.

Pliny, in Book 9, Chapter 51, says regarding the Frogs that these give birth to tadpoles, and that from these are water Frogs raised and generated.

Aristotle says that all land, air and water Animals, have a particular care in raising their children, except the Frogs, that, as soon as they breed (according to Pliny) their little Frogs, or those tiny pieces of black flesh, they no more care for them, and as such they leave them in the water, and they go on their way, shaking their tails through the water, and they thus increase and grow, taking the form of Frogs, and as Aristotle says: *Omne simile generar sibi simile*; And this means that all similar generates its similar, even if in their beginning some Animals do not appear to have the form of their parents such as these newborn tadpoles, and such as the children of Crows, which have white feathers, and only after eight or nine days do these fall off and the black feathers of their parents and peers grow. The Frogs, when they wish to produce loud voices (according to Aristotle) put one lip under the water and another above it, and like this they shout and call out terribly. *Et multo magis clamat tempore totius*, according to Isidore, Book 2.

Secret so as the stop the voices and shouting of Frogs

Take some of the Fireflies that are usually found by the fields and place the amount of these you wish in a bright glass dome, with some herbs so as they may have something to eat and not move so much; and with this dome very well covered, so as no water may come inside it, place it in the water in a place where Frogs usually give out their voices; and while those Fireflies produce any light the Frogs will not sing. And this is proven.

Medicinal properties of the Frog

Powder made from Frogs roasted in an oven, or over a fire in a well covered pan, when these are put inside it still alive is, according to Constantino, extremely helpful for the retraction or stopping of blood flow from a wound, this by applying the said powders.

Pedro Logrero further says that anyone who brings these powders with them, in such a way as these may touch their skin, should not fear bleeding, nor suffering from blood flows.

Avicenna, according to the Canon, says that should one cast Frog powders on any blood flow this will repress it and it will no longer bleed.

Boiling a Frog in olive oil and salt will result in an oil which can be used to heal leprosy by anointing the afflicted region with this oil. *De Natura rerum.*

Five or six drops of this oil, drunk, will kill any roundworm or maggot which might be raised in the stomach and belly. *De Natura rerum.*

Frog broth, drunk without having any other thing to eat before or after, for a good period of time, will heal coughing marvelously. In the book of *Hortus Sanitatis.*

If a frog is burnt alive in a new pot, the powders of this frog, mixed with liquid tar or white honey, will cure baldness. Idem.

Brunt Frog gall powder, if drunk, will cure hotness. *Eodem loco.*

The decoction of Frogs, or their powder, is good to mitigate teeth pain. *Eodem loco.*

Fat of Frogs is good to pull out teeth. Ibidem. And it is further said that should one put one of these Animals between one's teeth, this will make them fall out.

Fabulous Story of the Frog, in which it competes with the Mouse

Not being able to find a true story, we will offer a fabulous one, for these always contain in themselves something to be learned, as the present one, for under it comes a discreet and important warning to all those who with their wanting, cares, and even with litigations and quarrels seek positions or lordship, which are many times the cause for total ruin and perdition, as the present fabulous story of the Frog declares and manifests.

A fierce and dangerous battle
At odds (even if with no blood) and stubborn
Without harness, nor saddle nor any other thing,
That could stop such fierce sword.
A bravery and monstrous fury
Which was never seen in armed men;
I sing of a naval challenge,
That even if solely in writing it will cause amazement.
Let the naming of such warriors
Not cause the slightest laughter,
That seeing them so robust and fierce,
Will cause fear and reveal their badge.
See the strength and cunning of lightness
The stir of one or the guise of the other,
The impetus, the courage and the boldness,
Which remains while the chest lasts.
The Frog and the Mouse the armed chest,
With the harness given by nature,
Are two fierce Soldiers,
That my quill here seeks to write.
They come into battle in dressings,
Each one with a strange vestment,
One brings his cover in green,
The other with color and uncertain hair.
Thus these contenders with their spears
Run along the creek to the hard hit,
Braver and more spirited than Lions,
Lighter than the Deer or Lynx.
In their hands the hardest spears
That there is no power that can reach them;
Made from a fine reed,
Which one of them will be hurt, killed or maimed?
It was then the occasion of this fight
The desire to rule in vice
Among the people of the granary, and the desire
To be in the Republic admired.
Among them there isn't one that does not believe
That this lordship is his by right
Of a great lake where they lived
And solely for this little honor did they fight.
How much is committed over this vain honor
(even if to them it seemed like a great thing)
Committing lowly and obscure things
Of swollen pride and ambition;
So as to rule they unrule themselves, insanity
For they leave consciousness to danger,
And they lose their virtue, fame and rest
So as one may rule without pleasure.
Thus placed both in this bale
So hard as dangerous and uncertain,
The cunning Mouse hides his harm
Covered among the flowers.
The Frog on which greater fame is found

With a leap it charges and finds him
Over the green herbs with its spear
Holding it in seeking revenge.
From one side to the other it tries and pushes,
Leaping, turning, running and fleeing
The spear of its enemy
Among the green herbs finding it.
The Mouse, with trickery charges,
Aims, wounds, looks and does not fail
The Frog, that is more nimble and light,
Does not fall to distractions and kills all tricks,
In this way that these two in their fighting
So immersed and equally matched
That the Kite passing in the sky
Looking from up above is not seen.
These two in their own favor are so invested,
That no other thing did they see.
And thus the cunning Kite both of them hunts,
With its beak and nails tears them up.

Declaration of the fabulous story

And this does happen
Among revolted peoples,
That in order to rule and have valor
Are put to lose
Their possessions and honorable life.
Very little does man see and consider.
That it all ends with death;
What is it worth to rule
If this is taken by the brave and fierce Parca?
If we must go through this line,
Those who seek to rule and those who find it,
The rule and honors of this lot
Are sweet in life and bitter in death.

Of silence and secrecy, by occasion of the Frog, with a Story

The very nature of the water Frog, as was written before, is to constantly croak and never shut up, by which reason it has seemed to me appropriate to say something of silence and secrecy, and its great advantages; and I do not wish to speak of the great damage of speaking too much, for of this we have ample experience at every step of our lives. And I also do this from, for the great benefits arising from silence, one can collect the damages that speaking too much may cause.

Silence, according to Euripides, is the safe and custody of security. And over this it is said that the mute lives safer than the mouthy.

The Egyptians painted their God with a finger over its mouth, denoting the secret and silence each one should keep.

Secret is that which is not noted. Medina.

Madness is, according to Seneca, not wanting for a secret to be known from a person you have broken it to. Which is the same as saying that if you could not keep a secret you should not expect someone else to keep it. Do not believe such things.

Saint Bernard says that the discreet man should keep this rule unto himself. My secret is my own.

What you wish to do, says Pittacus,[343] you should not disclose, for if you end up not doing it you shall be mocked.

The same Pittacus says that he who does not know how to be quiet does not know how to speak.

Pliny says that it was no less wise for the speaker to be quiet than to know how to speak.

He who discloses his secret sells his liberty. Peisistratos.[344]

The rise of silence is the security from danger. Stobaeus.

If you wish to not be disregarded, hear a lot, speak little. Stobaeus.

He who wishes vengeance on his enemies should be quiet. Chrysostom.

Seneca says that there are things which are worth more to be quiet about that to say them unashamed.

The silence of Christ our Redeemer, so says Saint John Climacus, achieved the admiration and reverence of Pilates who judged him.

No matter how discreetly a woman speaks, she will always do better in being quiet. Plautus.

Cato said that nothing causes as much regret as the discovery of a secret, especially if this is done by a woman.

Hyssop once asked to the wise Chilon what was the most difficult thing to do; and he responded that it was to keep a secret. This for where there is no silence there can be no freedom.

For those who speak little (so says Plutarch) little laws are required.

The ignorant never stops speaking, as one who cannot be quiet can ever be wise. Plutarch.

Saint Ambrose says that he saw many err over speaking to much, and only one over being quiet.

Aulus Gellius[345] and Macrobius[346] tell of a story of a Roman boy who knew how to be quiet and keep a secret. The case was that the Senators of Rome, when they entered into counsel, took with them their sons since these were young, so as to teach them to keep quiet and keep secrets. It so happened that one day these came out of the Council very late; and they were addressing a serious business they could not finish on that day, and as such they had decided to do so the following day. And as one of the Senators was returning home very late with his son, the mother asked her son in secret for him to tell her why they were so late and what this thing they were discussing was. The boy remained quiet and discreetly dissimulated with his mother, who, the more the boy was quiet the more she was curious about what the Senator had discussed; and so she treated the boy with punishment, he then, feeling pressured by his mother told what was happening (this by lying, as we will see shortly), so as not to reveal the secret which was discussed in the Senate; and he said: my Mother, what the Senators are dealing with in secret was which would be better to increase the Republic: to give each man two wives or to each woman two husbands, and seeing as this was such a serious matter they could not finish it this day. The mother, as the woman that she was, believed what the boy had said, and went without any more consideration to go and tell all the other Roman matrons of what was happening, asking them to ask all Senators to not concede to such an unjust law as that of a man having two wives, but that they should rather consider the contrary, that a woman should have two husbands. With this determination all of them went to the Senate the following day, and placed their request in front of all; who, amazed by this novelty, were gazing upon each other asking what was the cause of such a shameful petition. The discreet boy then said that they should be lead out that he had discovered the reason for that alteration, and as such he told of the case as it had happened; and from that day on no more was any boy admitted in the counsels, except that well warned boy, for he knew how to be quiet and keep a secret; and thus they dressed him in a Toga and the clothes of a Senator, and as such he would enter council and give his opinion, as all the other Roman Senators and elders.

---

343. Translator's note: Pittacus of Mytilene, one of the seven sages of Greece.
344. Translator's note: an Athenian tyrant of the VIth century BC.
345. Translator's note: A Latin author and grammarian of the IInd century.
346. Translator's note: Macrobius Ambrosius Theodosius, a roman writer of the Vth century.

Chapter XXII

Of the Monkey or Simian

This Animal can be counted among the monsters, for in many exterior parts of its body it is similar to man, and in many others similar to the other brutes, for it has a face like a man, even if this is ugly and monstrous. Its head is round and not elongated as that of the remaining brute land Animals. It has hands and feet very similar to those of a man; and having the remaining brutes their tits on their belly, this one has them like humans. And in this one may see how wise and prudent is nature, for seeing as the Monkey had hands to grab its children, and so as these could have access to all they needed, it placed its tits on its chest, and in all other Animals it placed them below this. It is a temperate cunning and vengeful Animal, in such a way that if anyone angers it, even if years have passed, it will remember this offense and always seek revenge; it is a great friend of playing games with children and playing tricks on them, even if these sometimes are dangerous. It is a great imitator of things, and of copying all that it sees, which is the cause for their capture; for those who seek and hunt them use this trick which consists in bringing some bags and trousers, and placing these under the trees where they live, in a place where the Monkeys can see them, they put their trousers on and take them off many times and then place these tied together in a bag. As the hunters walk away into a place where the Monkeys cannot see them, these immediately come and go into the bags to imitate those men and put on the trousers, and in this way they become tied to each other. And seeing them thus trapped, the hunters rush to them with a great riot, in such a way that with the fright they cannot get themselves lose nor can the other Monkeys try to free them, and thus they are caught and some good coins made off of them.

These Animals have a great taste for nuts and fruits, and the physiognomy of their face is very restless, as such they can never be still, always rising and lowering, running or jumping, making a thousand ugly faces, tricks and fooleries, and this is due to having a very light blood. And in this way when a boy grows up very boisterous, lively and restless, it is customary to say that he has Monkey's blood, which, if not for sleeping, would never stop and be still, and when it is sleeping it dreams like a man, even if in this it is joined by other Animals, such as the Dog, the Cat, the Lion and many others.

This Monkey is very obedient and given to its Master, and it is gentle and docile in any game, even if it is wrathful and fierce when it is offended, not having any forgiveness in it (as was said), unless this is received from its owner, in which case it will suffer it with great submission and patience.

Story of the Monkey

In a Village that is called Sueca, in the kingdom of Valencia, there lived a Master of the Order of Montesa, lord of that Village, and he had nominated for his position a Governor to take care of that whole place. And this governor had in his home a terrible Monkey, and everything it saw it would imitate. And this Governor had a servant who was married, and his wife had a still suckling baby, and as the Monkey had seen how the mother tended to its diapers, it learned this is such a way that every time this child was put on its bed, the Monkey would rush to it, take him in its arms, untie its diaper and retie it, with such precision as could only be done by his mother. It happened that one day, this Monkey took the child, for which it had acquired a great affection, and carried the baby up to a Tower which was in the house of this same Governor. And climbing onto a wall, it stayed there in sight of all the people standing in the market, dancing and playing with the crying boy, and the more this cried the more the Monkey would jump along that tower so as to calm him. As the people were seeing the danger the boy was in, they started to shout at the Monkey and throw rocks and sticks at it, and the Monkey always stood firm on the wall, making faces and jumping from wall to wall, not wanting to come down; and seeing as shouting was of no use, they decided to go up there with a mattress, and catch the boy with it; and in this way the Monkey came down from the wall, and the boy was made safe and free, and his father later took revenge on the daring of the Monkey.

In the City of Madrid, living there Vice-chancellor Frigola,[347] he had in his home a Monkey which was a great imitator of things; and as this one saw that some maids had placed some chestnuts on a flaming brazier, and had then removed themselves from the room, this Devilish Monkey decided to eat them, and it approached the brazier and, not having anything with which to take them out, it grabbed a Cat that was resting by the fire, and holding it firmly by the back, placed it over the embers; and as the Cat felt himself burning, it started to paw away desperately at the embers, and in a short period all the chestnuts were cast out of the fire; and having this done, the Monkey threw the Cat away, which was already with no hands or feet. And having done this it took its time to eat the chestnuts, giving rise to great admiration in all surrounding people over its devilish daring.

Of deceit, by occasion of the Monkey

Speaking of these restless and half monstrous Animals, we made mention of the trickery used to catch them; and because of this we will say something of this detestable vice, with the authority of the doctors and Saints.

Deceit, so says Saint Chrysostom, always shows itself in the appearance of good. And thus deceit is nothing else but a hidden treachery with a title of kindness.

Saint Augustine says that it is worse to fool someone by lying than to be fooled by believing.

This same Saint says that deceitful and fake kindness is a doubled evil.

Terence says that it is a normal thing for a deceitful to call another deceitful.

---

347. Translator's note: probably Simon Frigola a XVIth century member of the Council of Aragon.

There is no greater treason and destruction in this life that a dissimulated deceit. Cicero.

Saint Chrysostom say that nothing unearths good as a deceitful trickery.

Mimo Publius[348] said that it is a deceit, and a great one, to receive from a man something which one can clearly see that he will not be able to return.

Deceit, says Cicero, drives away good and loyal friendship.

It is worse, so says Saint Gerome, to fake with deceit Sainthood than for a man to sin manifestly against another.

This same Saint says that he who asks with deceit, does not deserve to hear a truth.

---

348. Translator's note: uncertain reference.

Chapter XXIII

Of the Lynx

The Lynx, according to Isidore, Book 12, is similar to the Wolf, even if different in its eyes, in the hair it has around its lips and in its fur, which is spotted; and regarding these, as we have said, it is similar to the Civet Cat, and in all other parts of its body it is similar to the Wolf. These Animals are generated in several parts of the world; but they are more abundant in the regions of Africa, from where a few were taken into Italy and Spain. Among all the brutes the one that sees better during the day and farthest during the night is the Lynx, even if it is true that the Owls, Cats, Lions Wolves and Mice see well during the night, their sight cannot penetrate solid bodies, as can that of the Lynx's.

To hunt these Animals with ease, the experts write, one should take some small pieces of glass or crystal, for they say that seeing bright or translucent things troubles their sign, and many learned even say that these may even go blind if they stop to look at these things for too long. And they say that it is for this reason that these Animals do not drink from the fountains and rivers during the day; for they fear blindness or the disturbance of their sight, and in this way they will suffer thirst until night falls. Learned men say that the Lyncurius stone is made from the urine of the Lynx, and this is confirmed by Pliny, Dioscorides, Isidore and Christoval de Encelio,[349] in the *Remetalica*,[350] where he says that by freezing the urine of the Lynx, this will become hard in such a way that it becomes no different from a stone, and of its virtues we will say something here and further down in this work. Dioscorides says of this stone, Book 2, Chapter 74, that: *Lotium Lincis quem multi ligarium vocant mox ubi minxerins lapis fir*, where he does not deny that which the modern do deny, that the urine of the Lynx can be converted into a stone. There is no shortage of opinions contrary to what we have just said, that it cannot be reasoned that the urine of a Lynx can be converted into a stone; I am sure that there is no impossibility in this matter, for we see by experience that in the ulcerations of men sometimes are generated stones which are so strong and hard that one needs a hammer to break them; for if just as in the ulcerations of men, stones are generated from the heat and thick humors, the nature of the Lynx has it that once its urine falls to the ground it should be made into a stone with the cold and frost, for if instead of cold there is heat, this will not become hard, and it will be like the urine of any other Animal.

And this I write in order to defend the opinion of much learned men who confirm it, and whose intellects would not be moved to say this without great reason and fundament, for if this does not contradict reason, nor is it impossible to nature, it shouldn't be denied nor should the ones who so profess be reprehended. This stone does not have a certain form, as some have thought, for if the said urine falls into a mold with a round figure, this will generate a round stone; and if the figure and dispositions of the earth in which the urine falls is square, this stone will not become round or triangular, but rather square; and thus, according to the dispositions of the mold will the stone be formed, which, should it be made warm by rubbing it with a cloth, it will attract to itself straws and small things that may be around it, as the magnet stone does to iron.

The Natural Philosophers write that the Lynx is an envious Animal, for having urinated it will spread or hide its urine, so as man will not be able to use this; and should this be so, it is indeed a thing of consideration and even admiration, that an Animal would have this natural instinct, that it would understand that its urine is of use to man; and so as this may not be used for his benefit, it hides it, and this it does out of evil. This same instinct also has the Elephant, as we have said, that it knows and understands that its fangs are esteemed by man, and that it is pursued over these, and it will itself break them and give them freely as long as it is left alone.

And the thing that happens with the Lynx in it being envious, is the same that happens with the Dog, which is always envious of other Dogs should they come close to its Master and should he have any attentions with anyone else besides it; and in this way one should not be surprised if the Lynx is envious of man and does not want for its things to be enjoyed by him, and this truth is further confirmed by Solinus in the book *de Animalibus*, Chapter 8. And Ovid in Book 15 *Metamor*, and the great Philosopher Aristotle in book *de Admirandis nature*, Chapter 1, and another infinite amount of other trustworthy Authors.

The tongue of this Animal is serpent like. Its nails are very long and like those of a bird of prey. It has a ferocious aspect even if by nature it is shy and a coward. The females only give birth to one cub each time they become pregnant, and no more than this, and these Animals have their union as the Hares and Lions, which is from behind, and the cause and reason for this is given by the Philosophers in their stories, by saying that all Animals that urinate to the back have their union in the opposite way as those who urinate to the front, as are the mentioned Lions, Lynxes and Hares.

No story is known of this Animal, and should there be any, I have never heard it, even if I have searched in all Authors which have written of such things. And as we do not know any stories, we shall say something of the stone which is created by the freezing of this Animal's urine.

---

349. Translator's note: uncertain reference.
350. Translator's note: a XVIth century book by Bernardo Pérez de Vargas (to the best of my knowledge) dealing with minerals and metals.

Medicinal virtues of the Lyncurius Stone, made from the urine of the Lynx

Iorath and Rabanus[351] say that the Lyncurius stone is made from the urine of the Lynx which is frozen within seven days; and it has the virtue of attracting straws and small things, should it be rubbed with some wool cloth.

Helinandus,[352] Book 10, Dioscorides and Theophrastus say that by taking powders of this Lyncurius stone this will remove stomach pain, restore color to the face, and retain belly flux.

The Philosopher says that this stone is of a cold and dry nature, and that applied to sores it will heal them and attract to itself any iron which is in any wound.

This stone, according to Pliny, has the color of fire; and according to others it is somewhat darker.

Arnaldus says that any fierce Animal will become strangely calm when finding this Lyncurius stone, staring at it and taking pleasure in its sight.

The book of the Nature of Things, when mentioning this stone in Chapter 75, says that in the deserts of Libya there is one such stone with admirable greatness and virtue; and when any wild Animal is oppressed by a hunter, they take refuge in this stone; and being in the presence of this stone they think themselves greatly secure; and they are *mirabile dicta, aruqe factu si ita se haber*. Isidore seems to want to say and feel the same, for he says; *Liparia, ò Lyncurius suffita gentiles omnes bestias avocare traduntutur*. Which mean that this stone, made into an incense, will attract to itself every wild Animal of the land.

Of envy and its harm, by occasion of the Lynx

Speaking of the Lynx we have said with the authority of Aristotle, Ovid and Solinus, how envious this Animal is, for, with great diligence does it scatter and hide its urine, or the stone that is produced from it, so as man cannot take advantage of it, and for this reason we will say something of envy, a sin with no excuse nor gain, with the authority of the learned and Saints.

Envy, according to Aristotle, second topic, is an Animal passion, and a deadly sadness in seeing someone else with honor, imagining that this is in determent of his own.

The ancient painted envy with the tongue and eyes of a venomous serpent, in this way declaring the poison this carries with it.

Master Medina says that envy is daughter of greed, and its companions are detraction, whispering, hate and spite; and those with it are joyful with the ill and sadness of others, and to the contrary they are made sad with their good and pleasure.

Envy is a sad sin, without any pleasure or taste, rather, it torments the heart of he who carries it, and thus it wastes and consumes him as a worm in wood. Medina.

The end of envy is boredom, Pliny the younger.

Envy, so says Ovid, is always in battle with the most high.

There isn't any envy as dangerous, according to Seneca, Book *de Ira*, than that which is born from prosperity; for it will outlast one's good fortune, and it will outlast the envy of others.

Saint Paul says that through envy did sin enter the world, which was the total perdition of humanity.

Origen says that from loving oneself too much envy will grow to such a degree that it will cause a man to have spite of all those who are his inferior, for they are not his equals; of all his equals, for they are not his inferiors; and to those greater than him, for they do not subject themselves.

Cicero says the following: I would rather my enemies have envy of me, than have my friends tainted with such.

Envy, so says Licenciado Aranda, can never settle in an honorable and generous breast, but rather in those of vile and low spirits.

---

351. Translator's note: uncertain references.
352. Translator's note: Hélinand of Froidmont, a XIIth century medieval poet and chronicler.

What ill and damage has envy caused and still causes in the world, for it levels everything, Courts, Palaces and Chapels, it will run through all. Medina.

Envy is the proper sin of the Devil, who, not having all advantages, had envy of the divine benefits reached by men. Medina.

Over envy did the sons of Jacob mistreat and pursue their brother Joseph. Genesis 30.

Over envy and covet of swelling his kingdom, King Herod, who was the king of the Tatars, killed his brother Mithridates, who was the King of Babylon, in the public square.

Other infinite cases there are of envy which are told in the divine and human letters, in such a way as these would make this work never end, should we want to tell them all; however, those which were said are enough for one to see the harm and damage that envy, daughter of greed and ambition can cause; and may God keep us from it. Amen.

Chapter XXIV

Of the Hare

    The Hare is a feeble Animal and weak of heart; it is very fearful and elusive and it is very suspicious and always thinks that one is out to get it; it is light, a great runner, its back feet are much larger than its front feet, and in this way it runs better uphill than downhill. Among the four legged Animals the one which can make the greatest leaps is the Hare, and it is constantly changing places, and it will never be found in the place where it was born and raised; and over food and hunger it can run three leagues in one night, and where it does find food it will indeed stop, never caring about the place from where it came, this over the fear it has of being caught by hunters. And should there be snow in the places it passes, it will not walk by stepping, but rather by leaping, so as its tracks cannot be followed by hunters or Dogs; should it hear any human sound it will leap and where it falls it will stay motionless, and even if hunters are walking around it, it will not move, not even if it is stepped on, this unless someone tries to grab it, in which case it will leap and start running.

    The Hare gives birth to two or three little ones already covered in fur and with their eyes open, and it does not give birth to them in a burrow, but rather in the woods, and there it lets them be the whole day, being always somewhat separated from them until the time when it wants to give them sustenance, for it is afraid of being caught with them. Every time it approaches one of its young it does so by hopping; and this, it is said by those who know of these things, so as not to leave a track for hunters which these may be able to follow, for such is the fear that it has and suspicion of being caught. It sleeps with great care and with its eyes open, and this is said by those who know and also by the learned and the Natural Philosophers, that it does so out of the great fear of being caught off guard. Some Hares are hermaphrodites, which means that they are male and female; in this way they can use both masculine and feminine sexes, and this means that the males can make each other pregnant and give birth like the females; but these male Hares do not give birth to more than one little one at a time. This is confirmed by Terence with these words: *Turem qui es Lepus, & pulpamentum quaris?* Which means: See here, six Hares that are using the trade of a female so as to solicit men? Of this truth there are today many testimonies of hunters who have seen and experienced this; and this was confirmed to me by a Knight of this City of Valencia, a great man given to this type of hunt and of other more noble and large, called Don Luis Sanz, who has written with his own hand a very curious book on hunting, very wisely written, and in which he says many great things of this shy Animal, and among them those that which we will narrate, just as they were witnessed.

This shy and murmuring Animal has a lot of lip shaking fear, for not only is it pursued by men who are interested and affectionate of this game, but also by Dogs who are hungry for it, as these are mortal enemies of the Hares, and also many other land and air Animals; among the brutes these are the Foxes, the Genets, Lions and others such as these; and among the birds the Eagles, the Falcons, Gyrfalcon and other brides of prey, and these seek them so as to catch them.

Saint Ambrose says that the hair of these Animals changes to white in the Winter. In the Summer this returns to its natural color, according to Pliny.

Medicinal properties of the Hare

Avicenna writes that Hare's brain, eaten roasted, stops and prevents hand, feet and head tremors, should these be due to some accident and not due to old age.

The same Avicenna writes that rubbing the gums of children with the same Hare's brain, will make them softer and thinner, and it has the virtue of allowing for the teeth to be born quickly and without pain.

Hare meat, according to Rhazes, even if it is heavy for digestion, will perfectly stop diarrhea.

Hare's liver, roasted and melted with white wine, drunk, is good for those who have their hands burned due to excess heat from their liver. Rhazes.

Those who have bad urination, or stones, should take Hare powders, made from it whole and still with hair, roasted for an hour in a dry and very well covered furnace; these powders should be taken with white wine or chicken broth, and it will make urination easy again, breaking bladder stones should you have them. Idem.

Hare manure, dried and mixed with vinegar, used as an unguent on face wrinkles, will remove them marvelously. Idem.

Hare's blood, very fresh and placed over face spots and Sun burns, will remove them completely. Dioscorides.

Hare rennet is good against *gota coral*, and against all kinds of venoms and bites from any poisonous Animal, this by melting the rennet in vinegar and drinking it. Dioscorides.

Powder of Hare head, drunk, will heal apoplexy.

If these powders are mixed with Bear fat, and one anoints the region from where one has lost hair, this will make them grow back. Dioscorides.

Since we could not write and narrate any story of the Hare worthy of consideration, we will bring forth a fable of the great terror it has of being caught by the hands of its enemies, as we have mentioned before; and of the effort and spirit one should have in any difficulty, for this is the right guide and it insures hope in any labor.

A fabulous story of the Hare

A great blast in the mountain was heard
The fearful Hares hear,
They run with lightness and arrive
At a great lake and with a ruckus.
The Frogs, as they do, jump,
Into the water and disappear;

The fearful Hare noticed,
And of the present case consulted.
One who among all is the wisest
And it said with effort and boldness:
What is our impertinent terror?
From what do we so much cower?
For our lightness is evident,
Let us show with effort and haughtiness
And our fear let us refuse it,
And this new clamor disregard.

Declaration

Virtue is a great and praiseworthy thing
A strong man will never lose it
Be it in a firm case or in a changeable one
That his hard fortune may offer him.
The generous and favorable fate
In his praise and glory is converted,
That fortune it so seems
To the fortunate shines.
He who has his spirit down
Over a single sad and not thought of case.
Very fearful, weak and small
Shows his debilitated heart.
Does not deserve the honor that the daring
Much more pursues with boldness
Felicity is enjoying it,
And valor and security not to fear it.
All we have seen in this life
Of little effort and heart are noted.
That in a turn and prosperous avenue
Make acts of fame known.
That the same occasion offers late
Makes them greatly valiant and spirited,
And these are often the occasions.
The feeblest coward and the most fearful
With the desire for honor is inflamed.
And making clear the doubtful,
Heroic thing of fame does he perform.
There is nothing difficult for him.
His own blood at the price of honor he sells.
That to cowards the occasion makes this effort,
And from shame makes strength.

Of murmuring, and its little use and great damage.

As the Hare seems to be constantly murmuring, for it is always moving its lips; there are also men who never let their tongues cease, that they are always gossiping of others, and it seems that no food tastes good to them if it is not salted by gossip; and for this reason we will say something of this so widespread vice, and deeply fixed in the entrails of many, which has no use.

Gossiping, so says Hugo, isn't anything other than a talk born from envy or from wishing evil, and it seeks to taint and darken the life, fame and virtue of another.

Gossiping, according to Saint Augustine is a deadly poison for friendship.

Seneca says, Epistle 122, that the gossiping of someone is that person bad mouthing himself.

The gossips, so says Saint Gregory, are like those who bow into the dirt and become blind because of the dust that rises from it.

Euripides says that gossiping is the occupation of women, not men.

Saint Bernard says that the tongue of a gossip and bad mouth person is the brush of the Devil with the ink of hell and venom of a viper.

It is a heavy and hard thing to be the judge of someone else's life if you cannot even govern your own. Friar Louis of Granada.[353]

Saint Gerome says that one should keep himself from gossiping, and from hearing any such thing; and a Christian chest is obliged to always hear both sides.

Those who gossip (in my own mind) intend to do two things, and these are to discredit those they bad mouth (for in truth, gossiping and to say bad are the same thing) and to speak highly of themselves.

Cicero says, Book 3, *De Officiis*, that a man should lose his wellbeing before gossiping or saying anything bad of anyone else.

Homer wrote in the Iliad, Book 10, that all which is bad in men, one should not say in their faces, nor gossip in their absence, for there is no one free from guilt.

---

353. Translator's note: A sixteen century Dominican theologian and writer.

Chapter XXV

Of the Rabbit

The Rabbit is an Animal very similar to the Hare in its fur and fearful condition. Even if Pliny says that these are of the same species and nature, the Hares are larger than the Rabbits, and regarding their breeding, these are more fertile than the Hares. It is above all an extremely fertile Animal, for it gives birth every month of the year, and it gives birth to five or six at a time, more or less. And it is a thing worthy of admiration that as soon as the Rabbit gives birth to its young, it is already pregnant with some more. The cause for this is that after it gives birth to its litter, it will immediately come out of its burrow to look for its male, that is waiting for it right at its door, and there they have their union and after this it goes back in to give birth to a new batch, and as soon as this is born, it will get back out to meet with the male again, and in this way it is raising and generating at the same time. As such these Animals are never empty, except during the strongest months of the year, which are July and August; but in all others it is conceiving and giving birth as we have been told by trust worthy men given to this kind of game, and they have many and great experiences of this truth, even if the authority of Pliny, Book 8, Chapter 55, also confirms it. It is an ingenious and cautious Animal, for it makes its cave and den with great skill, as this den has many turns and curves, and it always has two entrances, given that one is always covered by dirt so that it may use it to escape due to the Ferrets that the Hunters use to chase them. In this way, should the Ferret enter through one hole, the Rabbit will escape through the other, and should no one be waiting for them on the other end with a Dog or stick, they use this trick to escape their enemies; and when the male, female and their children are inside the burrow, they will have both entrances covered, so as they may avoid their enemies, which are many, for these are the same as we have mentioned of the Hares and even more. And should it be that they didn't have so many enemies, than it would be impossible to live with them, for they would be so abundant that there wouldn't be enough fields for them, and they would enter through our farms and destroy everything, as has happened in a certain Village of Spain (according to the writings of Marcus Varro in his History) that so many Rabbits abounded there that it was necessary for the inhabitants of those lands to leave them. These Animals gather, male and female, in a contrary way to all other Animals, and this is rear to rear, for the male has the virile member placed below its tail. Pliny writes in the above mentioned place that the Rabbits are also hermaphrodites, as the Hares, meaning that the males can get pregnant, and even if he is of this opinion this could not be proven by sight or experience, but rather, all the modern Authors say that only in Hares can one find this monstrosity, and not in the Rabbits. And this, it seems to me, that the authority of Aristotle comes into play here: *Stulum est abducere raioem ubi experiential demonstrate in contrarium*. Which mean that there is no point in calling to reason arguments or the authority of the learned if experience shows otherwise.

Medicinal properties of the Rabbit

Rabbit meat, according to Isaac, provokes urine, comforts the stomach and is better digested than Hare meat.

This same meat cures swellings of the belly by causing the expulsion of gases and thick humors.

Rabbit fat is good to cure ear pain, and against the sores created in the fingers when there is cold.

This same fat is good to cure swellings of the neck, behind the ears, and these are very harmful and are called parotids, which usually swell after some grave illness; and when this happens it is actually a sign of health, for all the illness is accumulating in that place.

This fat is the principal remedy for paronychia which is generated in the tips of the fingers.

Fabulous story of the Rabbit

For not having found a true story of the Rabbit, it has seemed to me to be appropriate to bring a fabulous and exemplary one, so as from it one may understand that he who does not hear bad of himself will not say anything bad of someone else, and nor will he underappreciate anything if he does not want to be under appreciated.

> In the great brawl of lineages
> (custom among the vile)
> With the proper disuses, with outrage
> Disgusting the good fortune and life.
> New fierce, spites and courage
> Of esteem misunderstood
> This non foolish fable tells us.
> Of the wise Rabbit and the Fly.
> On its side the Fly contented
> In its favor a thousand things, claiming
> To be noble, to fly and to live
> In royal palaces in delight;
> Of the precious meals given there,
> Of sweet smelling wines enjoying.
> Of herbs and stews very costly
> It always had tasty tastes.
> The Rabbit was said that he lived
> In a dark place,
> And that with weak herbs it was raised
> Drinking from the lakes and Rivers
> In burrows and hidden places he lived,

Exposed to the cold and the heat.
The Fly was always revolted by the comparison,
Neither did she recognize him as a neighbor.
The prudent Rabbit responded,
That he had no shortage of nobility;
But that his luck had always given him the placidity
Of living without soreness nor vileness.
To all he was agreeable and grateful,
Having peace securely held,
An example to all of prudence,
Of concernment, reason and diligence,
The Fly, would point out a thousand flaws,
That in her were correct and fit
Vagabond and sickening it was always called,
Of what it wants it was always
Unwelcome, and bothersome of all,
That in Winter dies and decays,
To all it is bothersome with reason,
Prevention of quietness and joy of life.

Declaration

He who says what he wants,
Hears what he doesn't want;
And he that as a madman is stubborn
Will reap what he doesn't want.

Of blessing by occasion of the Rabbit

Blessings, says Saint Augustine, are valid for fertility and generation, and seeing as the Rabbits have this particularity of being very great in abundance, more than any other land Animals, it seems proper to me to say something about blessings with the authority of the holy scripture and the Saints.

Saint Augustine says that blessings are many and diverse, and that all come from God, for all contain his Holy name.

Blessings are of such merit and esteem that Ecclesiasticus says that almost all of them are presided by the holiest Trinity, Father, Son and Holy Spirit.

Saint Augustine says that the blessing of a priest should be greatly esteemed, given the great power it has by coming from God.

David, in Psalm 113, says that the Lord gives his blessing to all those who fear him, from the greatest to the smallest.

Regarding blessings, there a story which is worthy of every good son; and this was that a lord of many servants, not being married, had a son from a certain black slave he had in his home; and this became such a good son (even if a bastard) that the father was greatly attached to him, this due to him being greatly obedient, but also because he was loved and respected by all of his father's servants. And because of this, and also over other convenient respects a father must have, when he was sick and nearing his death, he married that mentioned black slave, and in this way he made his son legitimate, who then had rights over his father's estate. Once the father was dead, the slave became a free woman and a lady, and her son the heir of that place and farm. And because in this life there is no shortage of people who care about the affairs of others, there was no shortage of envy (a sin with no use) and it so happened that the son and slave were put in a bad position with the King, being accused of the crime *Lege Majestatos*, and they were arrested and chained because of this. But before he was taken, he begged the Judges to be allowed to say goodbye to his mother, and being given this favor, he went on to kiss the hands of his beloved mother, who, not being able to speak correctly gave him her blessing with these words: *Come good time my son, me from the father, me from the Son, me from the Holy Spirit, chains of iron now, chains of gold will become.* Most admirable, for it happened as the mother had predicted, for as the King ordered that the crime be investigated, he was found without any guilt and was considered a good Knight and loyal vassal; and as pay for his loyalty, the King gave him a chain of gold from his own neck and placed it on this faithful and loyal subject with his own hands, and thus he returned to his mother with the luck she had prophesized by giving him her blessing. Let all disobedient sons hear this example of obedience and respect of this Knight for his mother; and it was not an accident that every time that this Knight was riding, should he pass by his mother, he would get down from his horse and take off his hat until his mother had passed and gave him her blessing, after which he would get back on his horse and ride off.

The blessings of a father and mother always bring with it the hope of success to their son in any work he may enter into.

Chapter XXVI

Of the Crocodile

The Crocodile, according to Pliny, among all Animals is the only one that does not use its tongue except to taste its food, as it does not speak, as all other brutes; and according to Isidore, it is a great and terrible Animal, of about twenty cubits in length; it has a saffron color, four legs as the brutes, and in the day it inhabits the fields but in the night it enjoys the waters. Aristotle and Pliny, Book 8, Chapter 25, are admired by the greatness of this Animal; and they say that there is no other that from such a small beginning grows to such extreme; and they are amazed that from an egg like that of an Anser it can get to be twenty cubits is length. It has claws like a bird, and teeth like an Animal, and its tongue is short like that of a fish, and stuck to the lower jaw; and according to Pliny and Solinus, while this Animal is alive, it will always grow, and this same thing is said by other Authors, that it never stops growing. It will flee with great fury and fear from anyone chasing and challenging it; but it will also pursue with great spirit anyone who fears and runs from it; and should it catch any man, it will kill him, and after he is dead, according to Pliny, it will begin to moan and cry with great sentiment over that human body it sees in front of it.

Stories of the Crocodile

The Crocodile lives and inhabits the streams of the River Nile, and when its female lays its eggs, it does so near this River, and once they are laid, their mother will not part from this place more than two or three leagues; and when this Animal lays its eggs near this River, one can be sure that in that year the mother will not leave that place, nor will it roam the fields, as was said, and it will always remain near its eggs. And Pliny and Solinus say in the above mentioned place, that the nest, or the place where the Crocodile eggs are laid, is an omen and indication that the River Nile will not rise nor grow in that year beyond the place where these eggs are laid, for this Animal knows by instinct, grace and gift of nature, to what point the Nile will grow in that year that it laid its eggs. This story and knowledge of the Crocodile seems to be confirmed by the bird Halcyon; for according to Saint Ambrose, and other learned men and Saints confirm this, this bird lays its eggs in the sand and sea shore, and during its hatching (which lasts for fourteen days) the Sea will never alter itself, nor will the waves reach these eggs, but rather, all the waves near these eggs are repressed and broken onto themselves, so as not to reach these eggs. Marvelous thing this, and most worthy of note, that as these birds raise their eggs every year near the Sea and Rivers, and, in the middle of Winter, never are the winds altered, nor are there storms at sea for that amount of time. And of this truth are Sailors very certain, and certified by their great experience of many years in these affairs, and so they call these fourteen days the halcyonic days. But there is one difference between these two Animals, regarding the fact that both of them lay their eggs near the shores of water; and this is that the Crocodile, by its natural instinct, of knowing that the water will not rise nor grow on that year, lays its eggs near the shore; but to this Halcyon bird and to its young, the winds, the Sea and the storms obey and respect, this against all customs of nature during the Winter time. The cause for the Crocodile to lay its eggs near the streams of the said River, so say it the Natural Philosophers, is due to the fact that this Animal during the night very much enjoys to be in water, and for this reason it raises its young near this, even though it is said that it will not enter water during the time it is raising them. Pliny and other Authors says that this Animal does not manifest nor is seen during Winter, but only in Summer; and that during this whole time when it is not seen, it does not seem to eat, or it will only eat once in many days. When the Crocodile is indisposed and bothered by worms (for having a great deal of them) it will place itself with its mouth open in the Sun; and Pliny and Solinus says that there are certain birds on the shores of the Nile that seeing the Crocodile with its mouth open, will enter there and go down to its stomach and belly and in this way they clean it of all worms by eating them, and in this way it is made healthy and free from these. These same Authors say, and also the Physiologus, that there is a kind of Serpent, which is called Ennydros, that hides in the grass and often eats Crocodiles, this when they find themselves in their mouths or stomachs; Isidore says that often the Crocodile will be walking among the grass, and the Ennydors will enter its mouth through the openings among its teeth, only stopping inside their belly, and there they will start to eat their entrails and pierce their stomach; and in this way they can leave this place safe and sound, and the Crocodile will be killed. Even if it is true, according to these Authors, that the back skin of these Animals is so strong and thick that blows from stones and even iron will not damage it, and the leather from its belly is so soft and weak that with ease do these Serpents pierce it, and in this way they beat and kill that which they pursue; and for this reason does Pliny say that naturally the Crocodile fears and flees from Serpents.

Properties of the Crocodile

Pliny writes, Book 8, that from the manure of the Crocodile the old women of those regions make an anointment that once applied makes them look young and beautiful.

The same Author says that this anointment, mixed with oil of sour almonds, will make wrinkles disappear.

Of the tongue and its advantages and damages

For having mentioned the tongue of the Crocodile, which, according to Pliny, it does not use for anything else besides to taste food, as we have said, we shall say something of the great good and evil it causes mortals.

The tongue, so says Mimo Publius, is a shouter for the heart, in such a way that if this is in love then it will sing of love; if it is in pain, of pains it will speak.

Isidore says that life and death is in the hands of the tongue.

When words do not come from a good heart or thought, then regret will follow.

In talking too much there is never a shortage of sin. Sapiential Books.

It is not less prudent to know how to be quiet than how to speak.

Aristotle says that general conversation does not move as much as particular.

Seneca says that the large majority of all labors which befall man are not so much because of what is done but of what is said.

Words are the shadows of Work. Lucius Florus.

The kindness or malice of the soul is easily known through the tongue.

Faith is located in understanding, charity in wanting; knowledge in the eyes, hearing in the ears; mercy in the hands; abstinence in the throat; chastity in the body; love in the heart; but life is solely located in the tongue.

If one thinks himself good but does not hold his tongue, then his goodness is in vain. Saint Jacob.

A great sin did Cain make in killing his brother Abel; but a greater one was saying that his guilt was greater than the mercy of God.

The greedy wealthy man does not ask for healing to any part of his body except his tongue, for it feels the greatest torment and pain of all others, for with it he denied to the poor the crumbs from his table, and maybe because he operated more sins by talking that by working.

He who speaks no ill of any person is perfect. Saint Jacob.

Nature placed all the strength of the Eagle in its beak, in the Unicorn in its horn, in the Serpent in its tail, in the Bull in its head, in the Bear in its arms, in the Horse in its chest, in the Dog in its teeth, in the Pig in its fangs, in the Dove in its wings, and finally in woman in her tongue.

Speaking well is part of living well. Quintilianus.

He who knows his sins restrains his tongue; but he who does not restrain it, will never know himself. Saint Climacus.

By his speech is a man known and also by the sound of metal. Quintilianus.

One cannot talk too much without sinning, and he who holds his tongue, saves his soul. Proverbs.

He who speaks all he wants, hears what he doesn't want. Chilon.

The mirror of the soul shines on words. Saint Ambrose.

He who does not know how to shut up cannot know how to talk. Plato.

Saint Augustine says that there is no better sign to know a liar than to see someone who talks too much.

Of the discreet Hysop, a great Philosopher (even if a Slave), one may read that as his master asked him to arrange delicacies, he came up with a great deal of tongues, indicating in this way that there was nothing better in the world than a good tongue. And as his master asked him on another day for the worst food possible, this same slave brought him the same dish of tongues, without any salt, indicating in this way that when these are not tempered, they are most awful.

Chapter XXVII

Of the Chameleon

The Chameleon, according to Isidore, is a four legged Animal, with a small body and a long tail, that according to the Natural Philosophers, lives off the air, and which can appear in many colors, whose cause, so says Aristotle, is due to it being very fearful, and when it feels anything about itself, it will all tremble and change into a hundred colors, as it happens to some mortals, that when they receive some offense, fright or disgrace, their face will turn to several colors. Aristotle says, Book 2, Chapter 11, that the cause for this Animal to be so fearful and frightful is because it has so little blood, and from this it so arises that it can change into so many colors; and Avicenna says this Animal can change into every color of its imagination, and so it can change with ease into so many colors as its sight can see. Solinus writes that the skin of this Animal is apt to recreate any color which is placed in front of it. According to Avicenna and Aristotle, the Chameleon has a face like a lizard, sharp nails like those of a bird, a rough body, a very hard skin like the Crocodile, two very deep eyes, which are always open, without ever closing; and these are very movable, for they are continuously rolling from one side to the other, and its meat is very weak and soft; and finally, it does not have a spleen. Aristotle says that this Animal has its face partially similar to a Pig, and partially similar to a Monkey, and every time it is oppressed or exalted, it changes its color. Pliny writes, Book 28, that the Chameleon has such a virtue that it attracts to itself several birds of prey, which are called Falcons, and having them in their power it gives them to other Animals so as they may tear them apart; and according to Solinus, many of these Animals are raised throughout all of Asia.

Medicinal properties and incredible things of the Chameleon

Pliny, speaking of the Chameleon, says great things of the properties of this Land Animal which seem useless and without advantage. He then says that the right eye of a Chameleon, taken out while it is still alive, cures marvelously the mists of the eyes and clears the sight; but he says that one should mix and grind the eye of this Animal in Goat's milk, and in this way, applied to the eyes, it has a great virtue.

Democritus writes a rare and amazing things about this Animal (of which Pliny laughs about), and this is that if one takes the head and throat of the Chameleon and burns them with Oak wood, this will emit so many vapors and thick fumes that great clouds will form around this and these will be so thick that they will cause thunder and rain; marvelous thing this one: *Si ita se habet*. And I do not wish to prove it nor disprove it, even if Pliny condemns it, for we known *In rerum natura*, of many prodigious and almost miraculous things, as the ones which can be read of the Heliotrope stone, which, should they be true, say that should this be put in a large metal vase filled with water and placed under the Sun's rays, it will produce so many thick vapors that these can make a whole hemisphere dark, and make it seem more like night than day.

Those who have thought (even if falsely) that the eclipse which happened on the death of Christ our Redeemer was not miraculous but natural, in order to prove this mention this Heliotrope stone, and the vapors that it naturally emits if placed in water, and that these can darken a large portion of the earth, from where one may extract this experiment. Those who might wish to read more on this should read the Dialogue of Doubts which we have in our book on Natural Physiognomy, and one may find this there copiously written. And those who wish to see and understand the great marvels and prodigies, naturally made by the artfulness of nature, should read all the Chapters of the fourteenth book of Pedro Berchorio,[354] *Morales*, and one may find marvelous things in there and much more about the Chameleon, with the authority of Democritus.

If one carries the heart of a Chameleon, this is good against quartan fever. Pliny.

---

354. Translator's note: uncertain reference, although this name appear associated with many religious texts.

Carrying the right front foot of a Chameleon on the left side, is good to fortify the heart and one does not need to be frightened of visions, nor nightly terrors. Idem.

The right tit of this animal, carried by a person is good against fear and frights. Idem.

The left foot of the Chameleon, burnt in an oven with the herb also called Chameleon,[355] and these powders being very well mixed with scent pellets, have a the virtue of, if burnt, creating such a thick and condensed smoke that, should it be placed at the feet of a man, it will make him invisible, for he will be covered in such a way as the eyes of other men will not be able to reach him, and in this way are men made invisible, and these do not disappear, as some erroneously think. Idem.

This same virtue and nature has the liver of this Animal, burnt in an oven. Idem.

He who anoints his face with the gall of a Chameleon, will cover any sadness of the face.

And this means that no matter how sad one may be, by anointing the face this will not show.

Of blood, by occasion of the little that the Chameleon has

Blood is one of the most important parts of the human body for the conservation of life.

Blood is like the water from the sea, that is never still nor peaceful, and at times it will be restless and altered to such a degree that it will overthrow the week boat of our body and throw us in the deep abyss of death.

Aristotle says that the body is the seat of blood, and blood is the seat of the soul; and in this way the body is no more alive than when its blood is preserved.

The sanguine, according to Galen, are very lustful, and very little times will they keep to their faith, especially with women, that the more they see the more they want.

The death of least torment and labor is that of the one who dies from blood loss.

The blood is like a clock, that if the four weights of the humors are not unbalanced, always has its movements concerted.

The blood of the red man, should it be taken when he is angered, can turn to poison.

Regarding blood, we described the following verses with a noted Artifice[356]

Quo	An	di	tris	Mulce	pa
S	guis	rus	ti	dine	vit
Ho	San	mi	Chris	dulce	La

---

355. Translator's note: *Houttuynia cordata*.
356. Translator's note: this is probably a humorous riddle and a play on words, which, as is obvious, is pointless to translate (should it even be possible).

Chapter XXVIII

Of the Salamander

It is the opinion of learned men, according to the book *de Natura rerum*, Chapter 129, that the Salamander lives rather than dies if placed in fire, and it will extinguish it and make it calm; even if they say that once the fire is extinguished the Animal will also disappear; *Ut fertur ibidem*. And according to Pliny, Book 10, Chapter 68, it is not known how this Animal is born, nor how it is generated; and that these Salamanders only appear in very humid and rainy weather and that they never appear in dry or serene times; and because of this, in those regions of Asia, when it rains or there is very humid weather, these are discovered frequently in the fires of ovens used to make glass. But Pliny says, in Book 29, Chapter 4, that from the leather of Salamanders are the belts of kings made, which, after these are worn out, by placing them in a fire they are renovated and once again become beautiful and new, without being consumed.

It is said as a very certain thing that Pope Alexander had a garb made from the leather of these Animals, and when he needed to have it cleaned he would order that it be put over a fire; and not only was it not burnt, but it would rather emerge beautiful and repaired.

Often, the Roman Emperors one may read about regarding the gentile times, so as their memory would be kept, as also that of the men marked in war, virtue, letters and good government, had their bodies burned and turned to ashes; and the vase in which these were burnt was a sack of the leather of these Salamanders, inside which the body of the deceased was placed and put in the fire, turning to ash but leaving the sack untouched and even newer than it was before, where these ashes would be kept and saved and then placed atop the tall pyramids as today we can still see in Rome. Also Pliny, Book 19, Chapter 1, mentioned a certain linen which is made in the Indies which is used to make sheets and tunics, that in order to be cleaned one needs to put it over a fire; and a friend of a certain man close to the King our Lord Phillip II (may he be in Heaven), in a conversation was told as a most sure thing that his Majesty had some cloths that in order to be cleaned and made white needed to be placed over a fire, and that in this way they were made very pure and clean, but we do not know if this was the same linen as mentioned by Pliny or if this was from the leather of a Salamander. For if such a thing does happen, as we may piously believe, that these sheets do not burn nor are consumed in the fire, and that the Salamander is conserved in it, than it must have a most cold and resilient nature.

The whole of the Salamander is poisonous, and there isn't a single good thing about it, rather it is written that should its saliva touch any herbs, plants or trees, it will dry them and destroy all health around it. Should it happen to drink from any water source, then this will infect all which may also drink from it. And all the Natural Philosophers say that the malice of this poison and saliva is such that should it touch a man it corrupts and completely poisons him; and this must be the extrinsic (not intrinsic) cause of why fire does not burn it; for not only is it not burnt, but with its poisonous saliva it will diminish and reduce the strength of the fire until it is extinguished.

The modern, however, are of a different opinion, and Dioscorides agrees with them, and he cannot believe nor be persuaded that such an Animal can live in fire and not burn itself. I say that he is not right, for other Authors just as grave as Dioscorides believe the contrary, such as Aristotle, Pliny and Aelianus, in their histories of the Animal; and this is even confirmed by Saint Isidore as he refers to it in the book *de Natura rerum*; And these not only claim that this lives in fire, but they even say that it is generated there, and as it grows, with its poison, it is able to incite the flames, should they be weak; and, should they be strong, that it will remain alive, and without any injury; regarding any other intrinsic virtue it might have so as to be conserved in fire, like that of gold and no other metal, or like that of fish which are created and sustained in water, to which the eternal wisdom made it so as they did not need to breathe, so as they wouldn't drown, this is unknown to us. For as fish are conserved in water, and men, and the brutes of the land in the earth, and the birds in the air, so too are the Salamanders able to conserve themselves and live in fire, as also are Animals raised and conserved in the ice and snows, as Aristotle confirms and writes, Chapter 19, Book 5, that a certain worm is generated and conserved in the snow, and that it lives there with great contentment; and should it be separated from this it will die; and not considering this, there are juices from herbs and other simple and composed elements that, should a man anoint himself with them, he will be able to enter into a fire and not be burnt, some of which we mention in our book on Natural Physiognomy and various secrets of nature. And although in this book I deny this marvelous marvel, by taking into consideration the works of nature, and how grand and prodigious they are, I have come to accept that this may be so and also accept how such learned and grave men have written and with great efficiency confirmed this. And finally do I say that *sapientis est matute concilium in melius*. And I have as a certainty that if we did not have as much experience of this same thing as we have with gold, which placed over fire does not consume itself, there would also be those who would deny it; and if anything is diminished and consumed in gold when it is placed over a fire, that this not the gold, but rather some impurity or the mix of some other metal, for it will come out even more beautiful and lustrous, and it seems that its proper and natural place and contentment is the crucible, as the water is to the fish, the air to birds, the earth to the brutes, the Heaven to man and to the Salamander the fire. And this same fire cannot be still nor cease to burn, and it will not suffer a hard or strong thing without softening it; nor a soft thing that it will not melt; nor a melted thing which it will not consume, this except for four things, which are gold, ashes, clay and the Salamander.

Of fire and its kinds, by occasion of the Salamander

For having noted in the Salamander that virtue and strength of resisting fire, it has seemed to me appropriate to say something of this voracious element.

Fire, according to Aristotle, is the noblest, rarest and principal of all the elements, and as such it is in the heights and most honorable place of them all.

Saint Augustine says that there isn't anything as pleasant and delectable to the sight, nor clearer and more beautiful than fire; for beyond being fiery and bright, in its heat it has a great virtue of balancing and vivifying our cold nature; for it not only consumes but also cures, alters, refines, cleans, hardens and softens.

We know that there are three kinds of fire, one which is called elemental fire, which inhabits the conclave of the Moon; and for being so rare does not prevent our view of the Heavens.

The other kind of fire is called material, and that is the one we see and enjoy while it has matter to burn or any other thing to sustain itself; and once this matter is consumed it disappears.

The third kind is called infernal fire, which is the one that torments the condemned; and this is so terrible and strong that many Saints say that our fire is but a pale image of that one. And being this true, we know as certainty and Faith that it does not end nor consume the bodies and souls of those who pay their debts there, and it never leaves them nor does it ever cease burning.

END OF THE FIRST PART

SECOND PART

OF THE VIRTUES AND PROPERTIES OF THE

Air Animals

Chapter I

Of the Eagle

    The Eagle stands above all birds, and it is Queen and ruler over all of them, whose sight is so sharp and strong that it can gaze at the body and rays of the Sun face to face, with such firmness and confidence that it can be for two or three hours in such a position that it will not blink or tire its eyes; and regarding this one can find the proof and experience in its chicks, for it makes them face the Sun; and those that do not divert their gaze, these it raises as its own; and the others who by chance or weakness look away, those it casts away from its nest and company, and the others it will sustain, comfort and raise with care. This bird raises its young in very high and safe places, and this is always in the same place, where it is said there is a stone called Eagle Stone which is famed to have many and adorable virtues; and so as one may know if these are true, this should have another stone inside it which is lose and movable; and the learned say that the Eagles carry these to their nests; and this they do so as their eggs will not be boiled due to the great heat that these Eagles have; for they say that this stone or stones can temper the excessive heat of the Eagle. However, other Philosophers say that they bring this stone to their nest so as they may release their eggs from their body, and without this stone they would not be able to lay their eggs, for they are extremely narrow in their rears and this stone makes them swollen and in this way they can lay them easily, and for this cause do women who are about to give birth use and take advantage of this stone, for the virtue that it has in opening and dilating.

Pliny says that in the Septentrional region there are certain Eagles with a great body and these do not lay more than two eggs, and they wrap these in hare or fox fur, and in this way they leave them under the heat of the Sun without roosting, waiting until their shells break by themselves; and as soon as the chicks emerge from these then the parent will take care and raise them until they can fend for themselves. The Eagle has a strange natural instinct, and this is when it feels itself getting too old and tired, it will rise up through the sky above the clouds in the direction of the great heat of the Sun, until its sight is almost consumed, and from this heat it dives into cold water, and from there it flies to its nest where it should have its chicks already grown and ready to hunt, and there do all its feather fall, due to those two extremes of heat and cold that it receives from the Sun and the water; and shortly after, due to the heat of their young, its feathers grow back, and its sight is restored and all its strength returns, and it once again becomes robust and strong.

Story of the Eagle

In the city of Sexten, Pliny mentions in Book 10, Chapter 15, that a certain damsel raised from young an Eagle, and the love and affection this damsel had for this Eagle, and the Eagle for this damsel, was such that they could not stand to be separated. And when this Eagle was of appropriate age, the damsel took it to a high tower and set it free; and this Eagle, understanding that it was being released, thankful for the love with which it had been raised, and the freedom that was now given, would frequently return to visit the damsel, bringing her every day a fresh piece of game. After some years, the Eagle bringing its customary gift and not being able to find the damsel, for she had died the previous night; it looked through all the windows of that house and not being able to find her, it cast itself into a living fire that it found in the room it usually visited her in, and so it ended its days, paying in this way the love that the damsel had given it.

King Pyrrhus[357] had in his Palace a certain Eagle that at the mention of this king would give great shows of pleasure and contentment, for it loved him dearly and this to the point that when Pyrrhus died the Eagle no longer wanted to eat, and thus it finished its days because the king had died, of whose name it so much enjoyed.

Souidas[358] writes in Book 4 of his history, a marvel of the Eagle, and this is that a boy being lost and alone in a field, without its mother (for a certain reason that we will not mention for being too long) an Eagle would come to him during the night so as to keep him from the cold and during the day it would make a shade with its wings and with quail blood it raised him; and with these diligences was this boy kept for many days, and he was called Ptolemy Soter,[359] son of Arsinoe, until he grew, and this because this Eagle had such great care in keeping this boy from the Sun and cold and did not allow him to die of hunger.

Plutarch writes of another case, not any less prodigious than the previous one, and this was that among the Lacedaemonians a great plague struck, and as such these went to consult the Oracle on what they should do in order to be free from that disease, and it was responded that they should sacrifice a young damsel, and that this would cause the plague to vanish. The Lacedaemonians drew lots on which damsel should be sacrificed, and this ended up being one who was called Helena, who had raised, for her own pleasure and entertainment, a beautiful and great Eagle; and as the said Helena was being taken to the place where she was to be killed, the Eagle constantly circled her beloved and dear Helena; and as the executioner took the knife to cut her throat and approached her, the Eagle came down with a great fury and it took away the knife

---

357. Translator's note: A 3rd century Greek General, king of the Molossians.
358. Translator's note: A Xth century Greek lexigrapher, creator of a relevant glossary.
359. Translator's note: One of the generals of Alexander the Great, later King of Egypt.

from the executioner's hand; and given this strange case they forgave the damsel, and in this way she was freed from that sentence due to her dear and beloved Eagle.

Phylarchus,[360] a Philosopher from Athens, Chapter on the Eagle, writes of a no less serious case and no less worthy of note than the previous ones, and this was that a certain boy, being very much a friend of raising birds, raised among them an Eagle, and he was so affectionate of this one that he would continuously tend to it. And as this Eagle one day fell ill this boy was continuously tending to it with great care so as it would recover, and in this way it was freed from that illness. And it happened that a few days later the boy fell himself ill, and as the Eagle would see all those from that house so sad and troubled over the indisposition of the boy, it also become as such, constantly visiting its beloved patient. The boy ended up dying from that disease, and as he was being carried to be buried, the good Eagle followed the funeral, and it did not want to be parted from the dead boy, and so it ended its days, preferring to die than to live without that dear boy.

Aelianus writes, Book 12 of *de Animalium*, Chapter 21, of the case of an Eagle as rare as the ones mentioned, and this was that to the King of Babylon called Saccor[361] was prophesized by the Chaldeans that, due to the daughter of his niece, that they would find themselves free from his heavy rule, which was afflicting the country at that time. Fearing that prognostication, the king ordered the girl to be locked in a Tower, and she had been made pregnant from a black slave (even if one with a handsome face and good looks). And in that place that lady gave birth to her child, calling this black man there and placing the child in a basket so as to be lowered to his father and be raised, and as in this tower there lived certain Eagles, one of them seeing the basket, took it through the air, ending up in the land of the Chaldeans (who were the ones who prognosticated their freedom from the rule of the king of Babylon), leaving the basket at the door of a certain rich and powerful Chaldean, and by good disposition of Heaven, the owner of that place saw the Eagle come down and leave the basket; and very eager to see what was inside he found a beautiful baby, even if of a mixed color. As the Chaldean become very effectuate of this boy, he had him raised and instructed in all good customs and military arts; and so as to make the story short, he was raised with such disposition and affection to the arms, and also so valiant, that the Chaldeans elected him their captain. And he, after some time, overthrew his great uncle and freed the Chaldeans, who were those who had raised him, and this happened by intervention of an Eagle.

Laurencio Surio[362] writes miraculous things of the Eagle, which happened to a saint called Medardus, and this was that when he was a boy, and as his parents had sent him on a errand, it so happed that it started to rain a great deal, and it also happened that an Eagle came down from the sky and, opening its wing over the boy, kept him from getting wet, and the admiration of all of those who say this was not small, for it was a prognostication of the goodness of the saintly boy Medardus.

The same Surio writes of the rare case of the body of Saint Benedict, in the way that an Eagle discovered it after it had stayed for a great deal of time in a river, where those that had destroyed the Monastery of Montecassino in Italy had left him, and where this holy body was buried with that of his sister Saint Scholastica. And as the body of Saint Benedict was in the river, an Eagle would spend the great part of the day circling around that place; and this went on for so long that eventually someone was suspicious and went there to investigate, finding that precious relic of Saint Benedict.

Medicinal virtues of the Eagle

The gall of an Eagle, mixed with honey and applied to the eyes of those with a weak sight will heal them and sharpen their sight, and according to Pliny it make sight very clear and penetrating.

This same product of gall and honey, so says Pliny, is good to clear mists and cataracts from the eyes.

Eagle feet, tied to the lower back, are good to remove pain from this area.

---

360. Translator's note: a Greek historian from the IIIrd century whose actual works have not survived to present days.
361. Translator's note: uncertain reference.
362. Translator's note: a XVIth century German hagiographer

Eagle brain is good against gout. Pliny.

The Eagle Stone has great virtues, which it has in its nest, less in India than in the region where the Chinese live, Albertus says that these stones can be found in Persia.

Eagle feathers, placed in the middle of other feathers, will consume them.

Serapion says that this stone is carried by the Eagle so as it may lay its eggs with ease; and that it causes this same effect in women who are in labor, and it dilates and opens the door from where the creature is to come out; and it is even said that it will forcibly attract this, by tying it to the left thigh of the woman, should she be pregnant with a girl; but should it be understood that she is pregnant with a boy one should tie this to the right side. And he says more, that once a woman has given birth, one should remove this stone, for it will attract more blood than is convenient.

Rhazes says that tying the stone under the knee of a woman who wants to give birth will speed up the birth and make it easier. And this same Author says that he has experimented this many times and it always resulted in a quick and safe birth.

Evax[363] writes in his *Lapidario* that this stone, tied to the right arm of a pregnant woman, will cause her great relief and keep her from abortion and a bad birth; but more useful than this is the *Agnus Dei*.

This stone, if carried with a person, will free her from decrepitude, and even from being poisoned, according to Albertus.

Albertus further says, and this is also said by the Chaldeans, that should anyone be suspicious that there is any poison in one's food or drink, that they should place this stone in it, and one will learn if there is any poison; and this is because it will immediately change color; and should there not be any poison, it will retain its own and natural figure.

Of good and bad company, by occasion of the Eagle

For having noted in the Queen of the birds the good company it has always had with the men and women who have raised it with the bread from their tables, it has seemed to me to be appropriate to say something of good and bad company, with the authority of the learned and Saints; so as, seeing the good and advantage one can gain from good company, we may embrace, love and conserve them; and, seeing the contrary, and noting the damages bad company can cause, we may be parted and flee from them, as we do from pestilence.

Good and saintly company, so says Saint Isidore, confounds one's enemies and edifies our next of kin, and it even glorifies the Supreme Creator.

In the good and saintly company, so says Saint Chrysostom, is where God will always be found, and He says as such: Where ever two or three may be gathered in my name, I will be among them.

A confederate company is obliged to defend all others, unless it is in an unjust war. Jurisconsult.

Those who are companions during work will also be during rest. Saint Bernard.

There is no firmer thing to defend and support a Republic that a good, unanimous and appropriate company. Saint Chrysostom.

Of bad company

Bad company is like a fine lime, for until the damage is evident, no one feels it.

Each one can be judged by the company he keeps; and from here one has the proverb: Tell me who your friends are, and I'll tell you who you are.

The company of the bad is uncorrectable, and one should always keep away from these, for they will always end badly. Saint Bernard.

Bad companies and practices corrupt the customs. Saint Jerome.

Bad company is a moth to fame, and once wealth is lost it is a danger to life. Saint Augustine.

Of bad conversation, and likewise company, is under appreciation created. Jurisprudence.

---

363. Translator's note: Damigerón Evax "king of the Arabs", probably a fictional author to whom is attributed a book of the properties and effects of precious stones.

Chapter II

Of the Dove and its virtues

The Dove is a most simple Animal, without bile or malice. Even if Aristotle says that it has bile, but that this is simply not located in the same region as in the other Animals, but close to the intestines, it is actually most certain that it does not have it, for experience thus shows. The Dove is among the Animals which are very strong in flight and in generation, and most simple in its condition; and by natural instinct it can recognize if a bird of prey will be able to sense it in the air or land, and seeing that it will be caught in the air, it will fall to the earth; and if it sees that its enemy will prevail on land, it will rise through the air with such fury as no other bird can match it. If the Dove is left in its freedom it will not raise its young in low places, but rather in the highest and safest; it pays extreme attention to its own feathers, and when it is to do any high flight, firstly it will prepare and compose its feathers, so as to better fly. It takes great pleasure in water, for being extremely hot, and when it is having its pleasure in some water basin, the Natural Philosophers say that it is looking at the water so as to see if any bird of prey is flying above it, and that by the mere silhouette, it will know if any bird is a friend or foe, and thus it will know if it should seek refuge or keep still. The manure it generates and leaves in its nest is so hot that it harms the eyes of its young, and every once in a while it will have to throw this out; and by making this diligence it incites its young to do the same with their beaks. And these are of such a benign and merciful nature that if they see another mistreated Dove, they will take care of it and support it. They drink water differently from other birds, for they do not raise their heads, nor do they take their beak from the water until they've had as much as they need. The Dove has a great labor in laying its eggs, and should the male see that this is being detained and delayed, it will pursue the female and peck her until she has laid them; and should these have a good supply of water and grain, they will lay egg all year round, generating new Doves every month; and Aristotle further says that the Doves of Autumn and Summer are better than the ones born in Winter and Spring, and as these are just one year old, or even less, the males and females will begin to join together. And should there be no male available, the females will come together and court and kiss, and from this they generate eggs, but these do not bring forth young Doves, for they lack the generative virtue of the male.

Story of the Dove

Mandeville,[364] in the book he wrote on the marvels of the world, tells of a wonderful story of the Doves; and this is that in the Orient there is a certain kind of Dove that works as a messenger, taking letters from one part to the other, especially when the distances are long and filled with enemies; and he says that this is done in the following way: after two, three or more Doves are raised in a certain land, they are then taken to another where they are kept locked and not well taken care of; when occasion presents itself, they tie a letter or note to the body of the Dove, and this one is cast free and the door of its cage closed, and it will by itself return to its own motherland and place where it was born and raised and where it was well treated; and once this Dove is collected, the letter or note is taken and in this way one may know what is happening in the land where the letter was written.

And who doesn't know of the great comfort and joy that the Holy Patriarch Noah received in the Ark of the Deluge by a certain white Dove that brought him a twig of olive back to the Ark on its beak, announcing that the Deluge was over, &c.

In the Kingdom of Valencia, our motherland, a case happened regarding Doves which is worth being known, and this was that in the Island of Mallorca, certain people were raising a great deal of Doves, and it also happened that those lands were struck by a great shortage of supplies and grain; and as those Doves saw themselves oppressed by hunger, they left not only the coop where they were raised, but also those Islands entirely, ending up in the Kingdom of Valencia, in the place and village today called Muferos; arriving there, they found a great field of peas, which is their proper and natural food, and they ended their hunger there. The owner of that field, seeing the damage that those hungry Doves had caused, armed that field with a great deal of nets, and he caught them all and kept them with him for a few days; and as he could not discover who they belonged to, he wrote a piece of paper and tied this to one of the Doves which he set loose, which, seeing itself free returned to Mallorca from where it had come; and as its sad owner saw it he was greatly pleased and made it so as it would return to its previous coop, and during the night, approaching it, maybe in order to kill it, so as it would no longer escape, he saw the letter; and it read as follows: In the Kingdom of Valencia, in Muro, a great deal more were seized; and if after seeing this they are not claimed, all will be finished. The owner of the Doves was happy in part and sad by seeing that the deadline of this letter was very short, and he decided to go shortly to that place and he paid for the expense and damage they had made and he returned with more joy and contentment that can be put in words. And from this case we have an interesting question: Which of the two men liked the Doves the most, their owner who crossed the ocean and risked his life to get them back; or the other man by not killing them after catching them in their theft.

And as I understand that there are many people who are affectionate of Doves, both high and low born, I wish to say something of the differences which exist between the different kinds of Doves. I will then say that the differences in pleasure Doves, regarding their colors and postures, are fifteen, although some speak of many more; however the most frequently used are the following: Gavinos veros, Vayos, Filacotones, Saffron, Blue, White, Mouse or Rat hair, Black, Tenados, Red, Dog hair, Overos, Botafogos, Argentados, Xalandrinos and Monginos, and recently there was a breed brought from Argel called Bolteadores, which, while flying, gave a thousand loops in the air, which is very enjoyable.

The Gavinos are in two ways, the veros and the tostados. The Gavino vero will have three colors, blue, white and black, and this mix is what makes it a Gavino vero, and each feather will have its own color, and these will be very small. On its head it will have more white feathers than

---

364. Translator's note: John Mandeville, a fictional character described in the XIVth century travel memoires *The Travels of Sir John Mandeville*.

of the other colors, with very black streaks on its wings; and these, as also the tostados, will have a great body, and have feathers down to their fingers, even if these will be very short. The Gavinos tostados have these same colors, except that their backs will be much blacker than the rest of their bodies.

The Vayo Doves are streaked with bright crimson on the tips of their wings. On their neck, body and head they will have these same streaks; and those that have their head completely brown are not as fine, and these will have a white back, yellow eyes and a black beak. The Filacotones are not very white, with bright saffron streaks; the neck, back and head are very white, and if these areas are very bright, then these are the best.

The Saffron Doves will have the back, neck, chest and head with the same saffron color, the brighter the better, and these should have some saffron colored spots above their neck which make a graceful circle like the Moon when they fly, and on the tips of their wings these should also have saffron spots which are a great adornment and pleasing to the sight; their eyes should be hazel or yellow, and the beak should be white, like that of the Filacoton.

The Blue Doves should be gray with brown and wide black streaks; the back will be very white, the beak black and the eyes yellow. And their blue should be very light, the lighter the better.

The Rat hair Doves have the same color as the Vayo, only lighter and with a brownish chest with black streaks and a white back, and their body will all have the same color; their eyes are bright yellow or hazel.

The Black Doves are extremely black, as a raven, with a black beak and bright and yellow eyes.

The Tenado Doves arise from the mating of a Black with a Blue, and so they no longer become black, and they make the blue darker; and in this way, the lighter the Tenado the better; but these should have yellow eyes without any streaks and their whole body should have the same color.

The Red Doves should be completely red, however, this color should be brighter on their backs, neck, head, under their wings, and on their tips they should have some dirty white, and on each of these feathers they should have a red streak, and on their necks some red spots, which open up as the Moon when they fly, which is very graceful; of these there are also colored, but these are not so good.

The Dog hair Doves are like dark Blue ones, with black streaks and white beak, and these are produced by the mating of two Doves of which one should be Tenado and the other Blue, and these should have feathers on their fingers, or at least short feathers.

The Overo Doves are the ones which have an imperfect color tending to the rosy, and these are born from the Rat hair and the Filacoton.

The Botafogo Doves are those with patches of imperfect colors, with plenty of white on their neck and head, and with some marks on the rest of their body.

The Argentado Doves are those that have streaks all over their body, with a very bright spot on their chest with streaks; and under this spot, and all over their neck they have feathers that shine like silver, and they have a black beak; and these can be black or blue.

The Xalandrino Doves have a high crown, cropped at the sides with some twirls that grace them greatly; and of these there are many colors.

The Mongino Doves are the ones with a crown and a cloak, tunic or veil; and the tunic is white without a single spot; and the cloak is of their own color, and some are like the Tenados, others black, others brown and of other colors, and this cloak covers their whole back, chest, head, crown and neck down to the chest; and the wider and rounder the veil the better. In the cloak and hood there should be no white, and the tunic should cover the wings and neck and all under the wings and legs, in such a way as they resemble a venerable monk.

Medicinal virtues of the Dove

Aesculapius says that a Dove, killed and opened, and placed in this way still hot over any bite, will remove the pain and any poison, and even rabies, should this be the bite of a rabid dog.

The hot blood of a Dove is the principal remedy for illnesses and pain in the eyes; and this will be better if taken from under the wings of the Dove. Aesculapius.

Dove manure will dry any humor, break any swelling and remove pain.

Dove blood retains the blood flow from the nose. Dioscorides.

New Dove meat is good (as was said) against serpent bites. Pliny.

Young Dove blood, taken from under the wings, warm and fresh, placed over the eyes is good for those with excessive blood. Pliny.

Dove manure, melted in vinegar as an unguent, and placed over any scar from healed wounds, will smooth them and remove any stitch marks and signs. Pliny.

Dove manure, mixed with linen seeds, melted in vinegar and applied to carbuncle will heal and cure this part entirely. Pliny.

Dove blood is good against gout in the feet, by anointing them with the said blood. Avicenna.

Young Dove blood is good to heal mange, even if very old; and it is the principal medicine to remove joint pain. Avicenna.

Of self knowledge, by occasion of what we have noted of the Dove

Self knowledge is a very high philosophy and reached by very few.

To our father Adam it was very easy to name all things, for he had knowledge of the nature of all of them, and himself he did not name.

Having presumptuousness or arrogance, according to Saint Augustine, is the cause for us not to know ourselves; for from knowing and understanding ourselves we will realize that before we were man we were earth, and before we were earth we were nothing; and thus man is a son of the earth, and a grandson of nothing.

From one knowing himself does he become humble, simple, affable and communicable, and from not knowing himself does one become terrible as a Lion, cruel as a Tiger and fierce as a Dragon.

From man knowing himself, according to Saint Bernard, does a man become forewarned; and from knowing God he may become learned; and from fearing Him, even more learned and forewarned.

Men complain, says Petrarch, that the sea is stormy, the air is corrupt, that friends are treacherous, that the weather is changeable, fortune is uncertain, but none, he says, complains about himself, and this is born from not knowing himself. These, says Petrarch, are like the bad player, who if he loses, does not place the blame on himself, but rather on the game.

Macrobius says that, while consulting an Oracle of Apollo, he asked by which way he would become venturous, and this was responded with: by knowing yourself.

Asking the Philosopher Thales[365] which was the most difficult and the easiest things, he responded that the most difficult was to know oneself, and the easiest to know of others.

The great perfection of a man comes from him knowing his imperfections.

The principal of finishing and closing a deal, is knowing it well.

---

365. Translator's note: Thales of Miletus a pre-Socratic Greek philosopher of the VIth century B.C.

Chapter III

Of the bird called Halcyon

This bird is called Halcyon because of a man which was thus called, who gave news of a great marvel and natural property of this bird; and this is that it lays its eggs and raises its young in the strongest weather of the whole year, which is Autumn, contrarily to all other Animals; and what more needs to be noted of this bird is that it lays its eggs on the shores of the Ocean (where it lives) close to the actual sea, and in seven days are these hatched and in another seven days does it raise them. And it is a marvelous thing, that with the normal rainy, windy and inconstant weather, the sea does not alter itself in any way, nor are there any rains during those fourteen days in which this bird Halcyon is nesting and raising its young.

And these fourteen days are so notorious and well known by all sailors, and these have such confidence that the sea will not alter nor move in those days, that they sail without the slightest fear; and for this are these called the Halcyonic days, and this is the same as saying, days of calmness and peace in the Ocean.

Chapter IV

Of the Mallards

Mallards live with greater pleasure in water than on land; and the male is different from the female in which it has its head and neck green, and their face is wide and its wings between them white, green and black; and the fury that these males have over the act of coitus is such that they may kill the female, and when these emerge from the shells of their eggs, they are so agile and lively that they can raise themselves, as it happens, that sometimes they are raised without a mother.

Curative virtues of the Mallards

Avicenna says that the Mallards are hotter than any other domestic bird and that eating their meat increases and clears up one's voice, and their grease *valet ad coitum & multiplicat esperma*. And it is also good to cure any pain.

Mallard meat causes many over fluidities and it is most bothersome, and the best part of this is the breasts.

Chapter V

Of the Geese or Goslings

The Geese have the same issue as the Pigs, as they are always grunting, and in this way they are never quiet; and the ones which are wild and live their freedom are always flying from one place to the other making noise.

In the Alps there are a kind of Geese which are so heavy that they are easily caught with one's hands; and among the Animals, the one with a better sense of smell to detect man is the Goose.

Curative virtues of the Goose

Avicenna and Dioscorides say that Goose fat is most useful to cure burns and harshness of the face and lips caused by cold.

This is also good to remove ear pain; and it is also good and advantageous for the womb.

Aesculapius says that the said fat of the Goose is good to resolve any hardness.

The same fat, melted in onion juice and poured in the ears, will make any water which might have entered there come out, or it will make any aposteme that might be there come out.

Dioscorides mentions that the said fat of a Goose will marvelously reduce any pain.

Chapter VI

Of the bird called Bernace[366] and of another called Carbates

This bird called Bernace, Isidore says, is born from the bark of a certain tree which grows in Germania.

And Aristotle says that that tree is also found in Flanders. Others say that this bird is generated by the putrefaction of the mentioned tree. Iacobo Attonense, Bishop, says that this tree from which these birds are born is created near the sea shore in the Oriental regions, and he says that these are born from its branches as a kind of nodes, and inside each of these nodes a little chick is generated, and little by little these grow with the humidity of the tree, and once these are grown they grow wings and after this they are released from the node which is their beak, and once free they fall and immediately return to the tree, being fed by the leaves and fruits of this same tree.

The second kind of Animal, called Carbates, is generated in certain trees which are grown on cliffs by the Sea, and in this way, as the fruits from these trees fall to the Sea, they rot and this putrefaction generates these birds; and after this they generate more birds by themselves by the coming together as males and females, generating eggs which they then raise. This says the Author of the book called *Hortus Sanitatis*. And he further says that he and many others have seen this with their own eyes.

From all of this one cannot but be marveled and this cannot be doubted, for we have in our own Europe and in Spain the birth of birds from trees, which are called Mosquitoes; and the only difference from those birds and these is that those are created large and these are very small and are a source of harm to human life; but these are nonetheless birds and they fly like all others.

---

366. Translator's note: Barnacle Goose.

Chapter VII

Of all kinds of Birds which are placed in cages for the recreation of the ears and sight of man

The birds which are commonly caged for pleasure and entertainment of man are the following: Goldfinch, or Seven Colors, as they are called in Castile, Canary, Linnet, Siskin, Serin, Yellowhammer, Thrush, Blackbird, Plush-crested Jay and Parrot, &c.

The Goldfinch in Castile are called Seven Colors, for this means that for this bird to be a fine one it is necessary that it has seven colors, even if these commonly do not have more than five in their feathers, which are white, black, brown, yellow and red, and some will have six. It is also true that some of these have under the wings or under their chest a few green feathers, and if we consider the color of their skin, which is red, we can say that they have more than the mentioned five. So as a Goldfinch is as fine as possible, and does not have any problems with singing, it should have the above mentioned five colors; furthermore it should have a big body, and it should be well kept and joyful in its cage, it should have a wide tail and be well extended in its extremes, the legs should be well separated from each other, a tall and straight neck, a round head, a wide beak, very black at the top, a high, clear and sound full singing; the best food for it is hemp and sometimes millet and linen seeds, and as a treat sometimes some greens, and should it have lice, spray it with your mouth with some white wine under the Sun.

The Canaries are very well esteemed and appreciated birds, and these are brought from the Canary Islands, and for this reason are they given this name; these should have a good size, not too big nor small, nicely polished, a high and risen neck. And one should be warned, when choosing one, not to confuse the female with the male, for the female is not good for singing, and the male has a greener and brighter color than the female, and it has a fatter and rounder head, and the female has a slicker one.

The Buntings or Royseñores have a large body, the size of the Thrush, and they have brown feathers; the males can be distinguished from the females by the fact that these have a thick and round head with a ring of black color around the neck. These are very esteemed birds for having a high, solid and wide singing; the best are very eager to sing, so much so that they never stop singing throughout the whole day.

The Royseñores have a good and delicate singing, softer than the other caged birds, and they exceed them all in their senses, in singing loudly and chirping. They start singing at the end of April or the beginning of May; and these have an odd particularity, and this is that when the female lays its eggs, the male will entertain her with its singing around the nest, and these are raised very close to the ground and close to myrtle; and they are great friends of farms, gardens or bushes; they sing in small trees near running waters. Finally, the birds Royseñores are great friends of music and soft and delicate singing and they will approach anyone who might be playing or singing and they join in with their twitting; these eat meat, and they are so delicate that occasionally they may be found dead; and for being such early risers, in some regions these are called *Lucinas*; and they have such affection for singing and twitting that even if they may fight and quarrel, and one of them is beat and mistreated by the others, it will not stop singing, as it happens with all other birds, and they will sooner lose their life than their will to sing. They have such knowledge of singing and music that they can learn any different tone they may hear, being able to make twenty different ones in one singing; and what is more remarkable is to see in such a small bird so much power and duration of singing; however, when this comes together with the female it loses much of its voice's softness. These are usually called Royseñores due to the noise they produce being so soft to the ears of tasteful lords of good sense.

The Lennets also have a very pleasant singing, these are traveling birds that are always coming and going and changing place; the disposition of these bids is the same as the Seven Colors, and their food is also the same as the Goldfinch.

The Siskins are some little birds, smaller and more subtle than the Linnets; they are most benign and gentle, so much so they are easily caught with one's own hands by giving them some pine nuts. They have a low singing but this is soft and appeasable; they have a green color and they are never still in their place; these should be treated like the Seven Colors or Goldfinch.

The Serins are the smallest of all singing birds; they have green feathers, the males much more than the females, with a round and fat head, and their singing is a great confusion with which they entice, move and bother all others to sing; and these should be treated like any other.

The Greenfinch is a little bird larger than the Goldfinch, and they have green feathers. And even if these are also raised here, they are also traveling birds, and they roam the whole world; they have a reasonable singing and they should be treated like the Linnets.

The Thrush are birds of great sense and in this way they can learn to talk; and the one that manages to have a clear talk is worth a great deal, for it is of great entertainment; they learn much more during the night than during the day, for during this time they are much more attentive, listening to everything they hear, and all they learn they reproduce, such as the barking of a dog, the cackling of a chicken, the coughing of a person, even calling servants by their names. These birds will eat anything, such as meat, bread, figs, worms, flies, cooked rice and another thousand things.

The Blackbirds, even if they do not learn how to speak, have a full and comely singing, and this lasts for two months, which are April and May.

The Plush-crested Jays, if caged from a young age, may acquire a great speech, and sometimes they will speak so clearly that if these are heard but not seen, one will think that this is indeed a person and not a bird, and their cages should be made of wicker, three or four palms in height and round; and these will eat anything which might be given to them, like the Thrush, whose nature is to hide anything it may find; and if these can they will tear up papers and make other kinds of evils. The Plush-crested Jays are raised in very high pines with thick branches, and they hide their nests as much they can, this because of the cuckoos, which break their eggs and place their own in their nests, as they do to other birds, for these are so inept that they do not know how to hatch and raise their own, even causing their death, and for this reason they seek out with caution and treachery those who, not knowing or feeling it, will raise them.

Parrots are birds that are not raised in this region, but these are rather brought from the Indies; and among these there are a few differences, for some differ from others in terms of size and plumage; they have their feathers painted blue, green, yellow and other colors. These birds require iron cages, and not of wood, for these have such a sharp beak that in this way they can cut anything. They are most gentle if they are cared for and well treated, otherwise they become so wild that they cannot be tamed nor managed. If one of these Parrots learns to speak it is worth fifty ducats, and maybe even more. They learn what they hear better at night than during the day, and should a mirror be placed in front of them they will marvelously repeat what they hear and see, and this naturally and very clearly. Many of these birds are raised in Peru and in the Gelboe mounts; they don't make much noise and they don't fly too much; and in this way they are very easy to catch.

It is written of the Parrot that if it gets wet with rain water it will get sick and die, and from any other water does it receive this damage; it is such a friend of the virginal aspect, that by placing a well disposed and dressed damsel with her face in front of it, it will tweet, talk and make a thousand different dances, having so much pleasure in seeing her; should it be given wine it will become drunk like a man, and in this way it will speak better than before.

Chapter VIII

Of the birds of prey that are kept by many lords as entertainment and enjoyment in the hunt, such as the Goshawk, Hawk, Peregrine, Kestrel, Lanner Falcon, Bornis, Saker Falcon, Gyrfalcon, Merlin, Sparrowhawk, Hobby and Aplomado Falcon

There are two types of Goshawks, ones are called the *Niegos*, and these are raised and trained for low hunting; and the others are named *Zahareños*, and these are raised to go up in the air, and in this they are much better, for they can rise to the tops of any wood when any partridge is hiding in it, and by seeing it, it will fall upon it and kill it. However the *Niego* Goshawk will go into the woods, chancing, searching and falling on its prey, and the partridge has a thousand opportunities to hide and not be seen nor felt, and the Goshawk may end up fooled; and these have another fault, and this is that if its prey escapes it, it will not chase it again, as does the *Zahareños* Goshawk, which will turn and return to its prey. This bird is the best and most pleasant for hunting, and it is more useful than all others and of a greater entertainment than all of them, due to the many more pitches and flights one can make with it in a day; and it has a great contentment in seeing game running and the hounds running with it. Of the Goshawks which are raised in Spain, the best are from Liena, and in the Asturias the ones from Oviedo; and the Catalonian ones are the ones from the high peaks of the Pyrenees; and if these are the ones that have a spot between their eyes and their beak, then they are the best. These Goshawks are also raised in Sardinia, Ireland, Navarra and in other regions, but as these are not good hunters I will not name the lands from where they come from.

Of the Hawk

Of this species of the Hawk there are four kinds. The first are the ones with a large body, very domestic and with a very joyful and affable face, bright eyes, thick feet and very long nails. These will chase any bird, without any fear and with a strange fury. The second ones are those with a smaller body than these first, they have shorter and thicker wings than their bodies would require, bigger and darker eyes; and these are brave and almost indomitable. The third are even smaller, and these are the fastest and hardest to tame; however, they are most delicate and very given to those who raise and tame them. The fourth and last are the smallest and lightest of the four, and they are most given to hunt, even if they are extremely delicate in their rearing. The first thing that a Hawk will do when it hunts, according to Aristotle, is to eat the heart, and these are sustained solely from this meat and according to Augustine they die with bread.

According to the *Physiologus,* should this bird come across any other during the night, it will catch it and keep it all night in its claws, without killing it; and when dawn comes, even if it has hunger, it will let it go free. And still it is said that should by any chance it run across this bird it released, be it alone or in the company of any others, it will never pursue it, nor touch the others which might be with this one, this out of respect for that one which it set free.

The Hawks always raise their young in cliffs or tall mountains, and they have the property of changing the color of their eyes and face.

Curative properties of the Hawk

Pliny writes that, Hawk boiled in rose oil, is good to heal any ill and damage of the eyes. And he also says that ash or manure of a Hawk, mixed with honey and applied to the eyes, will remove mists from these and clarify them.

Aesculapius and Hippocrates write that Hawk fat, melted with olive oil, by anointing misty eyes with this, will they be marvelously healed, and it will generate a much purer and clearer sight.

Of the Peregrine

There are three kinds of Peregrines with which the lords of Castile and even those of the kingdom of Aragon hunt: ones are brought from Flanders with the Saker and Gyrfalcons, and these are very well conditioned and appeasable. Others are those that are taken from the Kingdom of Castile and Aragon, and these are very wild and terrible to tame and train for hunting, even if they are the best and the most proud and given to the greatest gentleness; and in this way they are more esteemed and appreciated than the others, and these cost and are worth more. The third are brought from the Indies; and these are birds that give good tests and fly a lot and these can hunt Herons and Kites, and these are easy to handle and train; and of these from the Indies, much like all others, it is not known where they are raised; even if there are opinions that these might be from cold regions to the North and to the Tramontane; and once these are raised they will travel to diverse regions of the world. The Peregrines hunt with great spirit and diligence a great deal of birds, such as Partridges, Stone Curlews, Owls, Kites, Storks, Flycatcher, Cranes, Seagulls and Herons.

Of the Kestrel

The Kestrels are birds of a beautiful plumage and great spirit, and they are general for any game, and they are such great fliers that they can almost compete with the Peregrines in many areas; these are birds which are raised in many parts. Of these there are *Niegos* and *Zahareños* and one is as good as the others. I have said that the *Niegos* are those that enter into the woods, and the *Zahareños* are those that hunt in the air; and this is because the Kestrel *Niegos* can be let loose for fifteen or twenty days, and because of this I say that one is as good as the others. In the Island of Suisa many of these are raised, and from here one has very good ones, even if the ones from Mallorca and Minorca are very beautiful; and the ones from Mallorca can be better than the ones from Suisa, but above all these are the ones raised in the Pyrenees for these are greatly chosen due to their qualities. These are raised in Aragon, in the mountains of Xaca, in Castile, in the Kingdom of Valencia and in an infinite of other regions. These however are only born in the month of March, and their young are born by the time of Saint Jorge, and after six days these can be taken for rearing.

I only wish to warn hunters about one thing of the Kestrels; and this is that after they have been taken to hunt, and if these do not catch anything, do not tire it, nor abstain from feeding it when you take it back; but rather one should give them a treat and feed them as if they had killed a Heron, and in this way will they become affectionate and one may accomplish from them all that one may wish; and if one does not do as such, then they will be lost; and, as I have said, the Kestrels are good to hunt any bird, and even Rabbits and Hares, and these are so valiant that they risk hunting Cranes and Herons; and those that fly and hunt the best are the *Cernicalos* and the *Picazas*, which are of great enjoyment.

Of the Barbary Falcon

The Barbary Falcons are very noble, tasteful, appeasable and spirited birds, and these are such good fliers that they can compete with the Peregrine; and this can be seen especially with the *gallinitas ciegas*,[367] that only the Peregrine can catch and also the Barbary Falcon. These birds are taken from Oran and Algiers, and the Arabs bring these on Camels from Zara, a land of black people, where they go for dates and other merchandise which is brought every year by traversing those so long, wide, deserted and dangerous sand fields, and should any wind lift up in these one cannot escape without being buried in the mentioned field, and thus they bring their Camels in order to pass these quickly and lightly; and before they enter into these sand deserts, they do great calculations for the wind, so as to avoid danger; and yet some do not escape, and to these men which the sand buries is their meat turned to powder and they are called mummies, which

---

367. Translator's note: Uncertain translation, but probably a type of beetle.

are used for many remedies, as is mentioned in its proper place. Returning to these Barbary Falcons, these (the ones which are the true ones) have a red and bright color, and around their necks, near the nape, they have a redder collar, and these are as big as the Kestrel; and when their hoods are removed, these will make two thousand little games and movements with their heads. And finally, they are great companions and they can hunt almost anything.

Of the Lanner Falcon

The Lanner Falcons have a woolly like plumage, and these are raised in Africa and from there they are taken to Oran where they come to Spain via Algiers; they have a whitish color, but some are grayish; all these Falcons which are brought from Oran are good, because the Arabs know them well and they do not bring the bad ones, but only the best and well proven ones. They are villainous birds and in this way they do not have the necessity for so much care and treats, nor do they give as much to the hunter as the Peregrine or the Kestrel; these Lanner Falcons are very good at hunting Partridges. The *Torzuelos* are good for Rabbits, Hares, Stone Curlews and Owls; the *Picazas* are good for Rabbits and Hares.

Of the Bornis

The Bornis are also Falcons with a woolly plumage; these are raised in Navarra, and in the Asturias in Oviedo and in the mountains of Levana, and their plumage is somewhat blacker than the Lanners; these are moved to the Partridge, Rabbit, Hare, Stone Curlews and Owls, with greater spirits than the Lanners. These are brought from Flanders, together with the Peregrines, Gyrfalcons and Saker Falcons, and these are very well picked to hunt Owls and all other birds.

Of the Saker Falcon

The Sakers are birds with a woolly plumage, and these are brought from Lepanto to the Court once a year, and these are birds with a great body and long tail. One should notice that these are villainous and harsh to handle, and this in such a way as if you have already bought, taken care of them and have them in your home for many days, they might still decide to leave; and should a hunter intend to claim its prey, it may even fall on him and not allow him to do so, and as such one should not have pity or mercy in their handling, and constantly quench them and spray them with cold water so as these may gain their reason. For the hunting of Cranes and Kites the Saker are very good, for they are limber and light, and they fight with great rigor, and for Hare and Rabbits rarely does one find better help, for in one single swoop they will put a Hare or Rabbit down.

Of the Gyrfalcons

The Gyrfalcons are brought to the Court as the Sakers. These are highly appreciated birds and they are worth a lot of money. They are very strict and have a great body and strength, so much that with a single swoop they can kill a Crane, and can drag off a Kite. These are very hot birds and as such they require very cool lands, this because in a hot one they will not last long, and as soon as one has these birds on his hand, one can feel the great heat coming from inside them, and for this end it is good to give them butter mixed with sugar and one almond. These are raised in cold lands to the North, in which the day isn't longer than four hours; and thus they are better and fly more in Winter than in Summer, and this is one of the three birds that are best to beat the Kites. From this it is said that the Kite does not yield or submit to any, except for the Saker, the Peregrine and the Gyrfalcon, and above all, the Gyrfalcon will beat and run it over.

Of the Merlins

The Merlins are the most appreciated of all birds, and the ones which are most useful for the hunt, and this is because these are caught with a net, and on the first day one may tie their feet that these will be still on one's hand without fighting, and here they will eat what is given to them; on the second day they will fly back to the hand; on the third or fourth day they will fly from the hand to the ground; and on the eight or tenth day one may put them to fly and hunt. These are birds of little care or demands and of great entertainment; the equipment to hunt with these is very little, for one only needs a horse and a dog in order to move the Partridges from the woods where they may be hiding; and once these are raised, the Merlins will just take off with them; and it is most pleasant to see them lift, rend and go back down until all Partridges are done.

Of the Sparrowhawks

Of all I have said about hunting birds, I place the Sparrowhawk as first among these as the most noble of them all; and the Sparrowhawks have such a privilege that if in the same load one has Hawks, Goshawks and in the middle of these any Sparrowhawk, even if dead, these will not have to pay any taxes in any port nor Kingdom, as long as they have proof written by the hand of a Notary that that dead Sparrowhawk was picked up alive from the place where those other birds of prey were brought. Of these two things which have been read and written here we will never know the cause, for this is how those who deal with the hunt have written; one is that the Sparrowhawk is nobler than all other hunting birds and it is thus placed first among these; and the other is the privilege that neither it nor any other bird that may be brought in its company may pay any taxes where they may arrive; and these two difficulties I will leave for the curious.

Another notable thing is written of the Sparrowhawk, and this is that when there is a great cold and frost, it is said that (should it be in its own freedom) it sleeps with another bird between its feet; and some say that this it does so as to sleep with its feet warm, and in the morning, even if it is dying of hunger, given the benefit it has received from that bird, it will release it, and if this one goes to the left, then the Sparrowhawk will go to the right so as to not come across it and kill it, should it not recognize it, and for this nobility it is said that this is a noble bird; and from this it is understood the two things that the author confesses that he does not know.

Of the Hobbies

The Hobbies are small birds, almost the size of the Merlins; and these have a white ring around their necks near their head; these are bird that while flying can catch Partridges, Larks, Martins, Swallows and Swifts; these can go for many hours in the air, without flapping their wings, and they can fly more than any other hunting bird, and their wings are larger than their bodies require; these are raised in cliffs like the Kestrels. With the Hobbies one can put them to fly and hunt in the Summer, but not in Winter, for they feel the cold in extreme, and they make efforts to always go to more temperate lands and thus during the night they may try to escape their perch and end up hanged; and should these be tied to the ground, they will give many leaps to try to escape; and many times it has happened that these are better set loose than being allowed to kill themselves.

Of the Aplomado Falcons

The Aplomados are birds which are brought from Peru to Spain; and these are similar to the Hobbies; they are good for Partridges and Magpies. These are elusive and very wary of Dogs and Horses, so much so that they flee from them, and thus they are not very well considered, nor do I wish to say more about them. I will solely say the conditions, posture and sizes that all these birds of prey should have; first and foremost, these should have a round chest and busty with flesh; the back should be well composed and round like the chest; a small beak and very large and sunken eyes, so as these may see more and farther; and birds with these characteristics will be very spirited and daring; and the ones with large and bold eyes will not be able to see far and they are useful for little, and they are also cowards. They should have big hips, large hands with long and thin fingers; they should have their legs well separated, so as not to be as fussy as the ones that have them narrow; the tail should be prominent, and when these are on one's hand or on a perch, this should point to the front, not the back, and the wings should slightly cross like those of the Swallow. And the wings and the tail should be wide and the feathers grainy, the color should be black, red or gray; although the Goshawks and Hawks are very good if whitish; and I finally say that these should not have many signs on their backs resembling stones, which are referred to as *apedreados*; and the less of these signs they may have on their backs, the better they will be.

Chapter IX

Of the Rooster

Among all the domesticated and campestral birds, the Rooster, as it seems, is the most vigilant and early riser; and this is so much so that in order to shake away its sleepiness and raise itself from the night well and awake, it flaps its wings, hitting its own body in doing so. This vigilance and natural care proceeds and is born from the great zeal and care it has with its entrusted chickens, so much that it will not allow anyone to touch them; and as nature has given it spirit, bravery and strength, this will not cause anyone to doubt its will to take any one of its darlings.

The vigilant Rooster, according to Dioscorides, and this is shown by experience, is very noble and liberal, for everything it has as a meal it will divide among its allies, calling them with haste and insistence, preferring not to eat so as they may take their fill. It is so restrained and courteous that in order to note that a man is well raised, it is said that he is as courteous as a Rooster; and the mentioned Author says, in the Chapter of the Rooster, that from what he gathers, it is arrogant, haughty and daring, for he has seen it have contentions with an Eagle, the Queen of the Birds, and this Eagle would rather give up this fight than contend with the haughty Rooster.

Saint Gregory in his Morals says that the Rooster is the messenger of the day and knower of the nights, and it is further the distinguisher of the hours and exhorter of the peoples.

Saint Ambrose writes that the nightly singing of the Rooster is very soft and advantageous, for it makes for a good company in one's home; and this warns, represses fear and awakens with diligence. And these three properties and excellences are found and verified in the Apostle Peter, vicar of Jesus Christ, when on the night of the arrest of his Master and our Lord, a Rooster woke him from that deep sleep of sin which he was in, and not only did this awake him with great diligence, but it also reprehended him with admirable dexterity, for through its singing and sight of Christ, *flevir amare*.

The repeated singing of the Rooster, some say, is due to its weak memory, for they say that as soon as it finishes singing it already does not remember that it has sung; and it is for this opinion (even if false) that in order to make fun of those who easily forget the things which are said to them one may say: come now that you have the memory of a Rooster. I would however say (*illorum pace*) that it does not repeat its singing so many times due to lack of memory, but this should rather be due to the great zeal it has with its darlings, so as that they may understand that it so much cares for them, it repeats its singing so many times. It can be proven that the Rooster does not have a lack of memory over the fact that should any one mistreat it with a stick or in any other way, it will never forget the person who did this, and it will flee at his sight, and should this be one of the fighting ones, it will even charge this person *& expertocrede Roberto*.

It is a very well known thing, and something which is experienced by all, that the Rooster has great knowledge of the night and even more so of the hours, for we see that every night it will sing its rough voice at midnight and at the break of day, and this with great punctuality and concernment; knowing by natural instinct these moments and times. And it is certain that there isn't a more accurate clock, nor more punctual candle, nor as vigilante Crane as the Rooster, neither are there any as good so as to at midnight sharply awake the Ecclesiastics and Men of Religion so as to make these rise and perform the Divine remembrances. And in this same way, at the break of dawn, it sings, warns and wakes all officers and workers of the fields so as these may give themselves to work and all walkers may go on their different ways.

Why the Rooster sings at midnight and at the break of day

Many books have I read and no few stories I have searched, this only to inquire of the reason why the Rooster sings, should he be a good one, so punctually at midnight and neither before nor after the dawn of day, and I have never found anyone who has any memory of this, being such a notable thing (such as the turning to the North of the Lodestone, whose precise and certain cause is not known). I then say that in order to understand and know the cause of such knowledge by the Rooster one should be warned that the Planet Sun influxes directly into the Rooster, as it also influxes into the Lion, the Bull and the Ram, and in other similar Animals; but the one which has a greater part with the Sun is the Rooster; and by this cause does the Lion, King and lord of all Animals, not having any fear nor respect for any of them, fears and trembles with the mere presence and sight of the Rooster (as was noted in the first Chapter). Being this thus, that the Rooster has so much part and friendship with the Sun, much like the Lodestone, that without any reason, placed free, will turn and face North, as if turning its eyes even if this does not have any; so does the Rooster always know, and with more reason, for this one has eyes, of the Sun, from which it receives influence and natural instinct as a second cause. And as such, when the Sun is below the Earth, when it passes beneath the feet of the Roster going to the Levante, which is the point of midnight for those living in the same place as that Rooster. And at this point, as the Sun is passing beneath the feet of the Rooster, it will know of this marvelously, this by the great participation and knowledge of its Planet as we have mentioned; and for this reason it sings and shows signs of contentment and joy, giving the news of midnight to all around it with its voice and singing. And as day approaches, a little before dawn and the first break of the Sun, it will once again sing, showing signs of even greater contentment, having a greater tone in its voice by understanding that its good Planet of the Sun is dawning, a sight that it finds strangely joyful and comforting. And one should note that as the day approaches, more and more does the voice of the Rooster become clear.

Great things could one say and write of the spirited and vigilant Rooster, as about the great care it has with its darlings, as of other infinite properties and excellences that nature gifted it with, more than any other flying Animal. Regarding this first virtue, what husband was there ever seen that had as much zeal for his wife as the Rooster has for its darlings? What Prelate or shepherd is there that takes care of his sheep as much as the Rooster takes care of those that are in its charge? What father or mother are there that oversee as much the well being of their children as the Rooster watches over the well being of those in his guard? From this care we have ample experiences, for we see that at the time the chickens go up into their coop, should any of these fall down, it is most worthy to see the care with which it calls for it, and seeing that it does not come up, it will go down with great calm and walk around it until it has come up the coop; and once this is done it shows its great pleasure and contentment. Oh what tacit reprehension and rare example for all of us who have children and families, let us imitate this vigilant and caring Rooster and take watch over those we have in our care.

Finally, what soldier or Captain, placed in a fight, uses as many tricks, inventions and skills to beat their enemies as the Rooster weaves and performs when placed in such a fight?

What Caesar, Hannibal or Tucapel[368] has ever been seen in a hand to hand combat with such zest, bravery and spirit as has been seen and noted of the Roosters in the City of London during the time of Henry VIII, as we shall say.

Story of the notable challenge of the Roosters

Dioscorides Laguna[369] writes in the chapter of the Rooster, a great story of a rare challenge of two Roosters; the story is grave due to the grave people which will be mentioned in it; and this challenge was rare given a certain case that in it happened. This Author then says that in the Kingdom of England and in the City of London, King Henry VIII had in a place which was called the Coliseum, two famous and brave Roosters fight, and in this fight there were many ducats won and lost. And given this interest in betting, as well as in honor, even if vain, many were dedicated to raising brave and spirited fighting Roosters, saving them for the days of the greatest festivities of the year.

As the day of festivities arrived, in order to add to the enjoyment, they placed in the Coliseum two valiant and famous Roosters; and what all did see was that, as soon as both of these were placed in their positions they readily approached each other, as if understanding the reason why they were put there. Placed thus one against the other, it was a thing very much worth noting and marveling, to see how these two Roosters stood still staring at each other for a long time, with (as it is called) beards trembling. Having thus stared and penetrated with their sights, they began their mortal combat, moving one towards the other with measured and careful steps, lowering and raising their crested heads, with such compass and concernment that one could not tell which was the first and which was following with this lowering and raising of the head. And as they jumped, putting body against body, they fell together, and once again raised with such lightness that one could not say which one of them was the first without losing some pretention to honor.

> It was certainly an amazing spectacle,
> Seeing two Roosters so harshly in battle
> Filled with blood and copious sweat
> Their faces and eyes in flame.
> The breath is heavy and fast
> And the neck thick with strength,
> Without giving one step back from the fight,
> Without there being an advantage or upper hand.
> All the present were surprised
> With that hard firmness and bravery,
> Seeing them in a thousand parts wounded,
> And the blood that made the soil moist.
> The faces, and crests torn,
> And as no match or fight there is
> Without one falling dead
> But both of them dying was the most certain thing.

---

368. Translator's note: A famous Chilean leader who held great resistance against the Spanish.
369. Translator's note: Andrés Laguna de Segovia, a Spanish physician, botanist and pharmacist particularly famous for his commented translation of Dioscorides' *Materia Medica*.

Finally, with the fight having lasted for nearly two hours, one of them, having avenged its blood well, fell to the ground dead; and the other, seeing his enemy beaten and dead, gained a new strength and spirit (they say), and as a sign of victory climbed over the defeated dead and began to sing with its harsh voice, and before it could finish, it lost its lively drive and fell also dead, over the one which had caused his death. Oh deadly rage, oh cruel envy! Oh case of lamentation and worthy of tears, for we see two homely and domestic birds, of the same species and gender, and who desire such ill to each other, that I doubt that there is any other so badly matched, and over this the following sayings are offered:

Sayings of the Rooster

Observe the nature
Of the Rooster and its strangeness
With notable sharpness
It was said that
Its strength could not be tamed.
For so much is its scorn,
Haughtiness and fierce pride
That I so consider,
That two Roosters do not sing well
In the same coop.
The fighting is continuous
Between these two so fought
The joyful victory shall be
Sung by the victor.
With grave pity and pain,
Caused by this rigor,
The defeated is silent,
And in his own coop sings
Each one much better.
For nobility and valor,
And for not consenting
In his own home anyone superior,
Over the doing and the saying
With such effort and vigor,
Over the rare vigilance
That I speak of in this Animal,
And for its strange constancy,
We may very well say without boasting
The King is my Rooster.

Story and notable and miraculous case of the Rooster

In Santo Domingo de la Calzada, a city in Castila la Vieja, a case and marvelous wonder happened regarding a Rooster, worthy of being perpetuated in memory, as is done in this City with great care and vigilance. And this case was that two people were coming from Flanders, a husband and wife, having with them their son of perfect age and going on rote to visit the Holy House and Temple of Santiago in Galicia, which is located in the City of Compostela. The three Pilgrims, arriving at the mentioned city of Santo Domingo, went to an inn for the night, where there was a not so honest servant girl, who made propositions to the young Flemish Pilgrim, and as he did not consent to these dishonest requests, this woman gained such a rage against that man that she did not stop until she managed to slur his name. And so, on the day the mentioned Pilgrims wished to leave the inn, this impatient and ill intended maid placed a valuable silver cup in the baggage of the young man; and shortly after the Pilgrims had left, this treacherous woman began to shout, saying that a silver cup was missing, and this was a cup which the Pilgrims had drunk from, and that they must have taken it. Immediately were these Pilgrims chased, and they found the cup on the young man's Donkey; and as this was seen by the Judges and Regents of the City, he was sentenced to death, set to be hung soon. Let each one consider what the parents of this unfortunate boy would do; for they did not let this discourage them, and they continued their Pilgrimage until arriving in the City of Compostela, where the house and body of Saint James rests in Galicia. And this story further says that the two honorable old parents of this man, who they had left in Santo Domingo de la Calzada, would each day give all the food they could part with to the poor, both on the way to and from that place. Arriving in Santiago, they fulfilled their duties and came back around through the same path, being guided by the passion they had for their beloved and only son, who they would perhaps already find on the gallows, for Santiago de Compostela is separated from Santo Domingo de la Calzada by about eighty leagues, and they took about thirty days to go and return. Arriving at the place of the execution, and seeing their son hanged, they began once again to cry with feeling. Their son, who was alive and hanging, seeing how his parents were crying bitterly, began consoling them by saying: parents of mine, do not cry for I am alive, even if hanging, for the blessed and devout Saint James has sustained me and conserved my life. The parents, hearing their son and the reason for him to be alive, if they were crying with sadness, in that instant began crying with joy and contentment, giving graces to their Creator and to the Apostle James of such a great mercy and benefit; and amazed at such marvel, they sought to discuss what was happening with one of the Lawmen of that City, who at that moment was preparing for his meal and had two birds on a plate, and these were a Chicken and a Rooster, and he had not yet touched any of these, and upon hearing that the young pilgrim they had hung a little over a month ago was still alive at the gallows, thought that this was surely a lie. The honorable parents of the hanging boy began to insist on this with great felling; and as the Judge did not believe them, they asked that he send there some well reputed people so as they could testify to the truth of these Pilgrims. And to this the Lawman responded: That hanged boy is as living as these two birds I have roasted here; marvelous thing that both these bird rose up alive; and the Rooster began to sing. Amazed by this case, without waiting any further, all believed them, and they went to see the hanging boy, and finding him alive they took him down and delivered him unto his parents; and these went on their way in peace; and that false woman was arrested, and confessing the truth was killed by it.

The truth of this miraculous case was well investigated and testified by the Greater Church of Santo Domingo de Calzada, where one can find the breed of Roosters and Chickens which were resuscitated in testimony of the mercy that God gave to those Pilgrims by intercession of Saint James. Another marvel and miracle should be noticed in this Rooster and Chicken; and this is that before these were killed to be roasted, they had black feathers, and when the Omnipotent God and Our Lord brought them back to life, he dressed them with the most white feathers, the same white that these today can be seen with coming out of their eggs.

Signs of a strong and good Rooster

The great Farmer Alonso de Herrera writes, in the chapter of the Rooster, that in order for a Rooster to be a fine one it should be small and very lively, with a high and full voice, and it should be constantly challenging and fighting with other Roosters of its age, and mounting all larger chickens. Further, it should have a very ridged head comb and not like a saw; the head should be thick, the beak sharp and wide; the ears should be white and full; its beard should be long and a mix between white and red; the neck should be risen and well adorned with wide golden feathers. It should have its feet and chest very hard; big wings, a high and wide tail, black eyes and very visible, and it should be daring and have the courage to challenge a man; its color should be black or red, and it should be joyful in its nature. And should you see, when they are still little, that any of them have a small yellow mark over the tail, these will not be good for Roosters, but rather for eating while they are still young.

Medicinal properties of the Rooster

Avicenna says that Rooster broth is good to cure stomach pain arising from a sharp wind. He further says that the broth of an old Rooster, boiled with Polypodium and Dill, two well known herbs, very well cooked, is marvelous against cholera.

Galen says that a marvelous thing about the Rooster is that one should take an old and fat Rooster and it should be made to run until it falls tired, after this one should cut its head, remove the entrails and intestines and place inside it a great deal of salt until the body is full, and then close it and place it to boil, in twenty bowls[370] of water, this until these have been reduced to three, and these three, if drunk, are very good to cure chest asthma, tremors from the hands, feet, head and anywhere in the body, and it marvelously cures joint pain.

Aesculapius says that Rooster's brain, drunk with wine, is good against any poisonous bite, and he also says that this brain has marvelous virtues, but he seems to have left them in his ink stand.

Aristotle says that a Chicken is raised from the white of the egg, and it is maintained by the yolk while it does not come out of its shell. When a Rooster is old and is over seven years of age, and can no longer have contact with the Chickens, its semen will corrupt it, given that it can no longer expel it, and this is then converted into a small egg, and it then casts this out; and should this fall on any manure which is still warm it will generate a Basilisk.

Inside the gizzards of a very old Rooster, one will find a somewhat brownish stone, the size of a small fava, which, if carried inside one's mouth will keep it constantly fresh, and it will cure any thirst; this is the principal remedy for the hydropic and those with any urinary blockage, and for those with diarrhea, for all these infirmities, and any others, cause a great thirst; and this stone will stop and fully cure these.

Young chickens, before they begin to sing, are good for the whole month of July, this more than in any other time.

Of zeal/jealousy[371]

For having noted that the Rooster has an extreme jealousy towards those in its care, it has seemed to me that it wouldn't be without purpose to say something of this, and of how prejudicial this can be.

Jealousy isn't anything else besides a damned suspicion and fantasy, and an infernal thought about a loved one.

Jealousies are a secret fire that consume the entrails, a worm that is constantly gnawing at the heart, and they are a perpetual restlessness, and an eternal unrest that is not ended until the one with it is ended.

Jealousies are born of thought, and are raised in fantasy, and as such they are nothing more than a suspicion of something which was not confirmed.

Jealousy and suspicion are very different things, for jealousies are the cause of great bother, and suspicions provide the occasion for a man to increase his wanting; and thus, suspicions aren't any other thing than a fear of losing that which is loved; and where there is no suspicion there cannot be true love. The ill of jealousy is so bad that it does not give room for the proper use of reason and freedom.

Jealousy by a different name is called vengeance, for this will cause vengeance to fall on those who keep it.

The more one loves the more jealousy will grow; and he who is generous and a lord of his own mind will never have bad suspicions of the thing he loves, for he will be certain that he who loves becomes the loved one; and being one and the same thing, he will not imagine of it what he cannot think of himself.

---

370. Translator's note: this should refer to a unit of measure I'm not familiar with.
371. Translator's note: in the original this reads 'celoso', a complicated translation which can be taken as both zealous and jealous

Lodovico Celio says that a Billy Goat killed the Shepherd Cratis (as we have seen above) out of the jealousy it had for another Goat over the contact which he had with it, and he fed it with his own hand.

The zeal for charity is sent by God, according to Saint Bernard, and this is a sign that the same God has come to a man's soul.

The zeal of mercy burns softly, and it fills the soul with virtue and efficiency.

Chapter X

Of the Chicken

This name of Chicken (*Gallina*) is derived from Rooster (*Gallo*), just like from Lion one makes Lioness. The Chicken is the most fearful and cowardly bird of them all; so much so that of a man who is a great coward one may say: You are as a Chicken; but even if this Animal is a coward and fearful, when it is raising its little chicks, it is so spirited, valiant, and daring that no land or flying Animal is its equal; and it is so protective of its little chicks that it does not fear the Kite, the Eagle or the Fox, but, in a mad frenzy, it charges against all of these so as these may not take her little ones; and it is not without a cause that Christ our Redeemer took example from the Chicken, by saying to those of Jerusalem in the following way: Oh Jerusalem, how many times did you keep your children near, just like the Chicken keeps its young under its wings.

And the Chicken is of such profit and advantage that neither the Goat nor the Sheep provide as much as it, should it be well kept, treated and maintained. And because regarding this point there are infinite things to be said, I will remit them all to the Book of Agriculture of Alonso de Herrera, where it is explained how a man can make himself rich and have an easy life in a short time without much expense, especially if he lives in a City with a great deal of people; for these very much need all the things that the Chicken provides, such as fresh eggs, young chicks, Roosters, Capons and their mothers, even if old, for Chicken meat is the best one of all the birds.

Medicinal virtues of the Chicken

Chicken meat is the best and the one of the greatest nutrition and substance of all other birds, and it is the tastiest and less dull of them all.

The greatest white feast one may have is that of chicken breasts.

Columella and Abencenif say that there is greater advantage in one hundred well treated Chickens than in one hundred sheep, even if pregnant.

Chicken fat is good for an infinity of medicinal things, for it is good to soften any hardness, opening swellings, repress and alleviate pain, &c.

Aesculapius says that Chicken fat is useful to resolve pustules and swellings in the eyes.

He further says that the legs and feet of Chicken, boiled in olive oil, salt and vinegar, are good to cure neck pain.

He further says that fresh Chicken manure is good to reduce the phlegm that is generated in the nose.

Chicken eggs should be eaten above any other type of eggs.

The white of the eggs is very good to cure eye burning, and it clears the sight and gives luster to the face, it reduces spots and burns made by the Sun, artificial fire from Saint Anthony's fire.[372]

Fresh eggs, drunk while soft, are good to cure kidney pain and bladder sores; and should these be drunk raw and warm, just as they come out of the Chicken, they will be much better to clear one's voice.

Fresh eggs, boiled with vinegar, repress diarrhea, be them soft or hard.

Egg white, as is well known, is very important for fresh wounds, even if olive oil and wine in a wet cloth is better, as is largely discussed in our book on *Physiognomy and various secrets of Nature*, in its third printing.

Beaten egg whites with salt or clean sand, placed inside a bowl of thick and clouded wine, will clear it up marvelously, whose experience has been often shown.

Egg whites, mixed with lime, make a good concrete to put together any broken thing, even more so if this is glass; and finally there are many other things mentioned of eggs in the above mentioned book of Physiognomy.

---

372. Translator's note: a medieval name for a form of Erysipelas.

Young Chickens are good until the end of September, and Chickens and Capons are good for all Winter.

In its gizzards, Chickens have a membrane that if taken out, made into a powder and drunk with white wine, will break bladder stones, and it will cast out any sands.

Chapter XI

Of the Capon

The Rooster is the only bird we know and see that can be castrated, and to these we call Capon; the cause of this, we all know, is so that it will get fat and become tender for eating. This should be castrated in an old Moon, which should not be in one of the Signs dominating the genitals, and it should be without food or drink for a whole day before, for in this way the process will be safer; and it can be castrated in one of four ways. The first is to cut their little testicles with great care; and once this is done the wound should be covered with ash so as to repress the blood, and it should be given a wine soup, and it should eat it either by its own accord or forced, and it should be kept isolated in a sheltered place.

The second way of castrating is to burn its two nudges with a very hot iron until these open up and reveal the little balls, and as soon as you cut these you should cover that place with a bit of clay or some clean brick powder, this instead of using an unguent.

The third way is to burn the lumps right off, and immediately cover this with clay or brick powder.

The fourth way is to use a very hot iron to burn a little wart it has on its tail, without damaging the tail itself; and in this way it will lose its Rooster haughtiness and it will no longer be able to generate or sing, nor have contact with Chicken; and thus it will become fat and become good and tender.

Chapter XII

Of the bird called Griffon or Grippes

    This bird has two natures, for it is both a land and a sky Animal, for it has four legs like a beast, and wings like a bird; and its body, tail and feet are those of a Lion, and its wings and beak are those of an Eagle; many of these Animals are raised in Scythia and in Asia, a land which is abundant in gold and precious stones, such as emeralds and many crystals; and those who live in Scythia arm themselves very well and ride horses in order to hunt this Animal and take these stones and crystals, for these birds will go out to meet them and fight with such force that they kill and rend them without any difficulty.

    This bird is raised in not very high places, and it brings to its nest the stone called Agate, where some of these may always be found, and the cause of this is not known, but it is thought that it brings these stones for many reasons, and these are that there are a great variety of these Agate stones, with various colors, and some are colored like the skin of a Lion, and these cause spirit and strength in he who carries them; others have a black color with some white streaks, and these cause agility and lightness in the one who carries them with him.

    Finally there are other stones which have a color like that of coral, and these have the virtue of giving effort and spirit to the heart of he who carries them with him. And Evax further says that this is good in aiding one to beat any danger should it be carried by the heart; and for one of these properties, or for all of them, are these taken by the Griffons to their nests.

Chapter XIII

Of the Crane

The Cranes are birds that have very long legs, and nature is so wise and prudent that to every Animal with long legs it also gives a long neck so as in this way they may be able to reach their food, and this name (*Grulla*) was given to it due to the voice of its squawking.

These birds have a King to whom they obey and have a great deal of respect for, as the Bees; and when they sleep they place their head under their wings and stand on one foot for the whole night; and one of them is always standing as guard, with its head raised high and holding a stone in its risen foot, so as in case it falls asleep, the stone will fall and it will once again awake. And this guard duty is shared among them, with each one serving it for one night; and in this way each one will have their turn. The Cranes have the habit of making bands and factions among themselves and fighting each other; and the beaten ones become quiet and the victors will always give out great voices of pleasure and contentment for the victory they achieved. I have mentioned that the Cranes have a mortal enemy in the Pigmies, a people which are no taller than a cubit, with whom they have field wars, and according to Aristotle these peoples live near Egypt and they fight the Cranes with such commitment, and they are so immersed in their fighting, that one can just catch them with bare hands. When these feel that it is about to rain, they give out terrible voices, and they all gather around their King to cover it; and when these come down to the land to eat, all will do so except the King, which stands with its head high and watches over the whole lot, after this they all stand as guards and the King may eat; and when these fly they do so in a row. It is said that once Winter comes these travel to the Oriental regions, and that before they leave they swallow a certain sand which is all made of gold, and that in their stomachs these will group together into one stone; and once they pass the ocean they vomit them; and these stones, if placed in a fire, become very fine gold, and regarding these, those with experience in such matters say: Crane stones, gold found.

Chapter XIV

Of the Swallows

The Swallow is a greatly benign, affable and good bird to the eyes of man; with its three extreme colors which represent chastity, penitence and charity, which are the white of its chest, the black of its wings, and the red of its neck. This little bird is the announcer of good weather and Spring, in which it awakes and invites men in the morning to go to the Tabernacle of their Creator, as it also does. In some of these birds one may find the Celadine stone, in its liver, and those of experience say that the Swallows that are in their nest can be recognized as having this stone, for these give great peace to all others, and those that don't have it, if they are resting in their nest, they do not go near any others. The Swallows show that they are prudent in the construction of their nests, and they further show themselves to be extremely honorable, for they do not resort to tricks in the making of their nests, but rather they do these in open sight of the owner of the house they are building on, and they show themselves to be well warned for they announce what is to follow, for by making their nests they assure us of the stability and firmness of that house, and this will have no danger of collapsing; and a house where they build can be sure that it will not fall. These little birds have the property and nature of the fig tree; and this is that it gives fruit two times per year, and also the Swallows lay eggs twice; the first time, according to the Physiologus, due to excessive cold, their eggs are frozen and lost, and this happens in the Apricos Mountains, where these bird take refuge in these warmer lands. The second time they lay eggs is over here, in our homes, and these reach their perfect age. In the making of their nests they are so well forewarned that they make their base the strongest, understanding that the foundation should be stronger than all the rest; and then afterwards they start to cover the rest with mud in the form of a dome. In the belly of these birds there are two stones, in the liver, and one has a red color and the other white, and of their properties we have made memory in our treatise of the stones. The Swallows have a strange order and concern in feeding their children, always starting with the biggest, with no concern for the rest of them. The Swallows all know how to raise their young in the roofs of our houses, and it sometimes happens that, due to excessive fire and smoke that may be made, their young can sometimes become blind, and as this happens their parents immediately seek out the Celidonia herb, which restores their sight, making it clearer and stronger than before, and from this have men gathered that this herb is good to clear one's sight.

Curative properties of the Swallow

Dioscorides says the following of those two stones which are found in the Swallow's stomach: one is of great advantage and utility, and the other of great damage; and the mentioned Author adverts that when one opens the stomach of the Swallow in order to extract the mentioned stone, one should take care that these do not fall or touch the ground; and he further says that one of these Stones, which is called Celidonia and has a red color, tied to a piece of Deer leather, and carried by the neck, is good against the illness known as Epilepsy.

Old Swallows, burnt and made into a powder and mixed with honey are good to cure eye mists and marvelously clear one's sight. This is also valid for those suffering from angina and this also placates throat tumors by gargling with it.

Aesculapius and Avicenna say that the ashes of burnt Swallows are very good for one's sight, for it cleans, clears and purifies it; but this should be melted in white wine, and this wine should then be placed on the eyes; and should these be too strong then it should be mixed with rose water.

Aesculapius says that powder of burnt Swallow's heart, drunk with white wine, will prevent the generation of any illness in the eyes.

Pliny says that Swallow manure boiled and drunk, is good against the bite of a rabid dog.

Avicenna says that Swallow manure, melted in fennel juice and mixed with white wine, is a marvelous water to cure eye mists and *experto crede Roberto.*

Chapter XV

Of the Crow

The Crow is a filthy bird and very different from all others that eat meat; for these others seek to eat it fresh, like the Eagle, the Falcon and the other birds of prey; but the Crow seems to always seek dead and horrible meat; and it is a common saying about the Crow that if it circles a certain house while squawking, it denotes plague, for it can feel the infectious, corrupt and spent air in the regions where they live.

Fulgencio[373] says that the Crow, even if it does not know how to sing any other song besides its crowing, it is capable of making sixty four different tones; and he says that when it is shouting at other birds, it immediately rushes to peck their eyes; and that the Crow is a natural friend of theft; and regarding this it is told that a certain Crow was once raised in a certain house where there was a habit of counting gold coins over a certain table, and it was so cunning that without anyone noticing, it would several times take away a coin, and it would hide it in a patch of land in that house near a tree; and one day by mere chance it was discovered with the loot in its hands.

The Crow knows its own color, so much so that as the little Crows come out of their eggs, it will not feed nor raise them for eight days, for these are born with a white plumage, and thinking that these are not its children it neglects them; however, after eight days, this white plumage falls and the natural black one grows, and then its parents can recognize them as their children and they then maintain and seek out food for them with much diligence and care; and this the Divine Letters mentions, in one verse of David: *Qui datiumentis esca, & pullis Corvorum invocantibus eum.* And in this way, the Lord and Creator and universal provider, has the particular care of maintaining the little Crows during that time of eight or nine days in which their parents leave them, thinking that they are not Crows nor the children of Crows, &c.

---

373. Translator's note: uncertain reference.

Chapter XVI

Of the bird called Woodpecker

The Woodpecker is a bird of great properties, of which the Natural Philosophers tell great excellences. Isidore says that this bird took its name from one of the Suns of Saturn, which was called thus (*Pito*) and it was used it in his divinations. This bird is raised in trees, and in small holes in mountains or castles, away from human contact. It has a red back, saffron chest; near its neck it has some green feathers; the wings have the color of wax, and the tail feathers are shiny and bright; it has curved claws and a beak so sharp that it can pierce through the bark of any tree, no matter how hard. The Natural Philosophers say that this bird is raised in any hole or concavity in a tree, and should any iron or nail be in this tree, it will fall off, for they say that it is a natural property of this bird to keep away from it anything made of iron. Others say that this property is not with this bird, but rather with a herb that it takes to its nest. Regarding this it is said that in order to discover what herb this is, the curious try to find a place where this bird is being raised, and upon finding it they nail an iron plate in front of its hole, in such a way as it cannot enter to raise its young; and seeing this impediment, it seeks out this herb which has the virtue of casting away any iron, and they say that once this herb is brought and placed in the front of the hole, the nails will fall off and the plate will fall with the herb, and in this way one may find out what herb this is; whose properties I will not mention for not being decent nor appropriate for Christian chests.

Chapter XVII

Of the Pelican

The Pelican is a very benign bird and strangely pious with its young, which it raises in Egypt near the Nile; and as its young are growing, they are constantly pecking at their mother's face; and as she feels this pain, she eventually turns on them, and by pecking them they are killed; and seeing that they no longer move, she begins to moan and to make a great sentiment, to the point of pecking her own chest, drawing out blood and sprinkling her young with it, which then revive, and in this way the mother becomes very content and peaceful.

Others say that this bird wounds its own chest so as with this blood it sustains its young when it does not have anything else to feed them; but be it as it may, this is a great act of love, spirit and effort.

Chapter XVIII

Of the Partridge

The Partridge is one of the most pursued country birds, this by its meat being of so good a quality and taste; and these are not only pursued by men, who hunt them with a thousand cunnings and inventions; but these are also coveted and hunted by many birds of prey.

These birds have in the past been protected by public and general edicts; but these are so much coveted by man that there is no use in making threats, penalties or royal prohibitions, in such a way that in our time there is no memory of such pasts edicts; and certainly it seems that these past edicts were right, and that it is fair that these birds not be hunted at least between the month of February and Saint John, for this is the time when the Partridges hatch their eggs and raise their young, and in this way there would be an abundance of hunt during the rest of the year, both for the sick as well as for the sane. The Natural Philosophers say that the Partridge is very cunning, even if it does have a great weakness, and this is that, in feeling itself pursued, it will solely hide its head, thinking that its pursuer in this way will not see it, and as such they are caught; the greatest killing of these is in the months of April and March, done with the singing of a caged Partridge; for in this way the males will be blinded with heat more than in other times of the year; and as in the mentioned months the females are sitting over their eggs, the males feel the calling of the caged female Partridge and run to it, not caring about the trap set for them.

There are three kinds of Partridge; ones have a red beak, and these have little feathers and plenty of meat, and they are very easy to catch, for they are most heavy and they have more strength than lightness. The other kind of Partridge is different from these in that they are smaller and lighter, with brown feathers; and of these there are plenty in Castila la Vieja. The third kind are the Partridges called Guinea, for they are black with a wide and round chest.

It is told, as a very certain thing, and this was written in the Physiologus, and by Ambrosio[374] and Michele Savonarola,[375] Medic, that the Partridges steal each other's eggs, and when these think that they are stealing and cheating, they are themselves cheated, for after the stolen eggs are hatched and the little Partridges are born, by hearing the voice of their natural mother, the one which laid and generated them, they will run to it, leaving behind the one that had all the work of hatching and stealing them, and in this way they are left cheated and without children; and this is also mentioned by the Prophet Jeremiah in a certain parable when he says: *Perdix fovet que non perit fecit divitias, & non in iudicio, indimidio dierum fuorum derelinquet eas, & in novissimo erit incipiens.* Which means that the Partridge sustains and raises that to which it did not give birth, and applying this to man, it says that he acquires wealth with deceit and without reason or justice, and in his best day these will leave him, and in sweetness he will be cheated.

The Partridge raises its eggs like a Chicken, and it raises its young around it, calling them and giving them shelter under its wings; and it has such a nature that as soon as these come out of their shell they already know how to walk and run. And when their mother sees or feels a hunter it will start to sing, making the little ones run and take themselves to safety, after which it will do the same; and after the danger is over it will start to sing with great joy, so as its children will hear this and come out, hiding once again under its wings.

Healing properties of the Partridge

Isidore says that Partridge meat is the best of all wild meat, both in taste and for health, and regarding the breasts, the upper one is better than the lower one.

---

374. Translator's note: uncertain reference.
375. Translator's note: Giovanni Michele Savonarola, a XIVth and XVth century Italian medic and humanist, writer of the *Speculum Physionomie* and grandfather to the Dominican Girolamo Savonarola.

Partridge gall, mixed with an equal amount of honey, is the best mixture to clear one's sight, Dioscorides.

Hali says that the liver, cut out, made into a powder and drunk, is good against epilepsy.

Pliny says that Partridge broth, beyond comforting the stomach, gives vigor and strength, prevents decrepitude; and should anyone have such an illness, he will be healed.

Chapter XIX

Of the Turtledove

The Turtledove is a bird of a very solitary nature, a friend of the desert, avoiding any contact and human conversation, contrarily to the Dove, which loves and seeks the company of men, living and becoming soft and loving among them.

The Turtledove, when it is raising its own, brings to its nest a herb called Scilla, this for fearing the Wolf, for it knows by natural instinct that the Wolf is an enemy of this herb and it is a friend of eating its babies; and with the said herb placed in its nest, the Turtledove is secure that its enemy will not come close.

The Turtledove has such love for its male companion that if by any chance this is to die, be it hunted or imprisoned, it will never again seek nor take any other companion, but it will rather spend the rest of its life moaning and crying, being in pain and mourning over the absence of its direct companion; and this feeling is such that from that day on it will never be seen in the company of other Turtledoves, but it will always live in solitude, thinking it would do some offense to its absent companion if it was to join any other Turtledoves. Oh widows of our times, should any of you hear of this advice or have news of it, consider it with attention for charity's sake, and do note this feeling and pain that this little bird has over its lost companion, and similarly suffer with discretion and prudence your absent husband, crying your sad longing.

One other thing is mentioned by the Natural Philosophers about the Turtledove which is worthy of being noted; and this is that after they have lost their companion, they always seeks out the dry branches of a tree, and among these they entertain themselves without caring about the fresh and green ones; being it true that before becoming widows they did not care about the dry branches, nor did they even stop in these, but they would rather only seek out the green branches and the ones with the most flowers in the most enjoyable, delectable and fresh places. For what shall the honorable woman who has lost her company do? Should this be a reason for her to seek out the fresh gardens and human conversation, and the fresh places or the madness of the galas of this life? Surely that the discreet and well warned widow will say no, for all her daily enjoyments have ended on the day that her beloved husband was lost, this by imitating the Turtledove (an Animal incapable of reason and discipline).

This little bird usually lays three eggs, and it doesn't raise more than two, like the Dove, and it always builds its nest in the holes of tree or in their roots; it is kept with grain and it can live up to fifteen years like the Doves; and its blood, according to Avicenna, is good to remove ear pain and to clean the eyes and sharpen the sight.

Chapter XX

Of the Hoopoe

The Hoopoe has a crest like a crown, and its plumage is very beautiful and it is most pleasant to the sight; however, its condition and nature is terrible, for its living and its well being is in dead places, and it is extremely fond of the manure of man, and its blood has the property of making one see ghosts and illusions in their dreams, if this is rubbed on one's wrists, it causes melancholia and sadness, as is declared in Leviticus: *U pupa lugubris estluctam amans*; which means that the Hoopoe is a sad and melancholic bird, a lover of crying and sadness.

The children of this bird recognize the debts they have with their parents, for the Physiologus says that when their parents are old and cannot see nor fly because of their old feathers, their children will feed them and heat their eyes with their mouth, sustain them in their nest and cover them under their wings until new feathers can grow and their sight restored; and by seeking food for them they in this way give some payment for the great deal they owe their parents. Iorath[376] in the book *de Animalibus* says the following about this bird: *U pupa pulli paentes suas foventes anhelat super oculos ipsorum, ut vistam recuperent*.

Healing properties of the Hoopoe

Pythagoras, in the book *Romanorum*, says that the blood of the Hoopoe causes devilish dreams to him who anoints himself with it.

The feathers of this bird, carried on the head, will remove pain from this place.

The tongue of this bird, burnt and its powders carried on one's head, are very good for memory.

The heart of the Hoopoe makes ants flee with most haste.

The smoke from Hoopoe feathers will kill mosquitoes.

---

376. Translator's note: uncertain reference.

Chapter XXI

Of the Peacock

    The Peacock is a most beautiful bird, and it knows of this extremely, for if one see it and does not say some compliment it will become sad; and if it understands that it is being bragged about or that someone is enjoying looking at it, then, with great joy, it extends its wings and tail, making a most beautiful and perfect circle with it and it will show itself very haughty and proud; and if by any chance anyone looks at its feet, seeing as these are very ugly, it will immediately close its wings and close its tail with sadness over the ugliness of its feet. And if during the night it should wake up and not be able to see the beauty of its tail, it will start to lament and voice regret and mourn; and as is natural, every year its feathers will fall and new ones will grow, and during the time when they haven't grown out yet, it will remain hidden, for it cannot stand to be seen without its beauty.

    Varro writes that among all the birds, Nature gave this one the palm of beauty and the pride of well dressing, and it did not give it anything else, for Aelianus says that the Peacock may be adorned with feathers, but it is weak of flesh; it has a head like that of a serpent, with a crown of wide and purple feathers, it has a collar the color of sapphire, a bright neck, red wings and a silky back tending to the red. It has a strange beauty in its tail, for in the extremities of this one may see some circles of green and blue, which look like sapphire and gold. When it wishes to have contact with the female it will give out voices and shouts, with which it frightens away all serpents and all poisonous Animals, and in this way one will never see any of these Animals nor any Serpents near any Peacock, which can live up to twenty five years. And when it is still young, should it be made wet and muddy, it will die of sorrow for seeing itself without any beauty.

Atheneus[377] says, Book 13, that in Lefcada a Peacock become so affectionate of a young damsel that once she died it no longer wished to eat, and it died of sadness, and its body was said to not rot or give out any foul smell, but it rather conserved itself, as if it was embalmed with sweet smelling things; and this seems to me to be due to them having such weak flesh.

Medicinal properties of the Peacock

Peacock manure, drunk, cures the *gota coral*, or decrepitude, marvelously.
Peacock broth cures back pain.
Peacock giblets, melted in rue juice and honey, cures colic.
Burnt Peacock eggs, ground and mixed with vinegar, will cure leprosy.

Of human beauty, due to that which we have noted in the Peacock

Beauty, says Heliodorus, Book 4, is a gift of nature that attracts hearts to it as the magnet stone attracts iron.
Beauty, according to Aristotle, is the measure of perfect equality of all bodily members.
Beauty, according to Euripides, is an unhappy thing, for it often is spoiled.
The ancient Philosophers called beauty a brief gift, for this is temporary.
Marcus Aurelius said that rarely does one find beauty that is not accompanied by madness.
Aristotle said that beauty moves more than pleads and letters.
The true and real beauty, so says Saint Bernard, is the most high God, and to he who becomes affectionate of this all the rest will seem like trash.
Juvenal[378] says that rarely does one find beauty and chastity together.
If you are beautiful, so says Democritus, do not ugly your beauty with ill deeds; and should you be ugly, good deeds will make you beautiful in the eyes of God and men.
Beauty, according to Theophrastus, is a silent deceit, for by being quiet it attracts and fools.
Beauty, so says Ovid, has a great closeness to pride, and also with vanity and madness.

---

377. Translator's note: uncertain reference.
378. Translator's note: likely to be Decimus Iunius Iuvenalis, a Roman poet of the first and second century.

Chapter XXII

Of the Vulture

The Vulture is a very large and heavy bird, which is always hungry and seeking to eat, never being filled or content; and the Natural Philosophers says that it can live up to one hundred years; and in eating and swallowing, no bird is its equal, given the amount of heat it has in its stomach, that they say can even digest iron. Regarding these voracious birds it is told here in Valencia that a good man wished to see if it was true that this bird could eat iron, and as such decided to give one a key he carried tied to his money pouch by a string; and as soon as this key was in its beak it ended up in its stomach together with the money pouch and the string, and the man was left without key, pouch and money.

Saint Ambrose says that these birds are born without any contact from a male, and they are raised in high mountains or very high trees. The Natural Philosophers further say that the last eggs a Vulture lays cannot be hatched nor raised, for these come out with a much thicker shell than those before, and as the Vultures do not have enough heat for these, they do not generate. The Commentator,[379] and other such grave Authors say that these Animals usually follow soldiers, for they naturally know and understand that in their wake there will be many dead bodies; and in this way they shall have plenty to eat, and this incites and moves them to follow any war and to have joy in it; and this same thing is mentioned in a comment of Leviticus which says the following: *Lex vulture comedi prohibit, qui bellis, & ortuis gaudet.* Which means: the Law of the Scripture forbids Jews from eating the flesh of the Vulture, for this bird takes pleasure in war and in the death that this causes. It is further said that this bird feels the scent of dead bodies from over five hundred miles away; and this also happens if there is a plague, for as the airs are corrupted and infectious, they recognize this and they can feel the future illness, and thus they

---

379. Translator's note: a common way of referring to Averroes.

rush to the villages, and they stop in the places where these airs are detained; and this is a sign and evident prognosis of plague, when there are many of these birds or Crows above any village; and according to Saint Isidore, they can feel the scent of dead bodies from one shore of the sea to the other.

Medicinal properties of the Vulture

Aesculapius says that the feathers of this bird, burnt, drive away serpents, for these cannot stand this smell.

He further says that Vulture liver, melted in its blood and taken for ten days relieves decrepitude.

Further still, its blood, mixed with horehound juice, is good to cure obscurity from the eyes.

The feathers of this bird are the best for writing, and for this reason these are desired by many.

The juice from Vulture manure, taken through the nose, will immediately cause a woman to give birth.

Chapter XXIII

Of the Caladrius

The Caladrius is a little white bird which is usually found in the courtyards and great homes of Kings, usually making its nest on the walls there. This little bird, so says Aristotle, the Physiologus and many other grave Authors, is a true prognosis of the health or death of a sick person, and in the following way: should this bird be placed in front of a sick man, if the illness is deadly it will turn its face from it, not wanting to see the sick person; but, if it is not deadly the little bird will remain calm and gaze upon the sick, taking all which is illness into itself, which sometimes causes it to die and the sick to be healed; but, should it be allowed to go free, it will disperse all the ill it took into itself through the air and in this way it will not die.

Medicinal properties of the Caladrius

The Caladrius has a somewhat thick bone in its leg whose marrow is good to clear the sight, by anointing any darkened eyes with it.

Aristotle, *Calandrius, infirmum si mori debent, non respicit; sed se ipsum videre velit, abillo omne infirmitatem ad se trahit.*

The legs of this bird, made into ashes, are god to cure blindness due to weak eyes.

It is said that this bird was brought from Persia to these regions by Alexander.

Chapter XXIV

Of the Phoenix

The Arabs call this bird Phoenix for being the only one in the world which lives for five hundred years, and more it is said in Arabia that when it knows that it has reached the end of its life (according to Isidore), it will gather a pile of branches and aromatic tree barks, such as incense and myrrh and other like these which are extremely hot. And having made this pile as a kind of dome, is crawls inside it and lays there under the fire of the Sun, as it is dying it is set on fire in a most hot and deadly flame and as this happens it flaps its wings so much that those branches and barks are set ablaze, and thus it dies burning and it turns to ash; and from this ash, with the humor of the dew of the night, a small worm is generated, which grows with the heat of the Sun and from the ashes around it, and little by little it lives and grows and in a few days some small wings will grow from it, and this bird then returns to its first and optimal state, fresh to live another set of years as it has before, and in this way the Phoenix bird never dies. This is said by Isidore, but Ambrose goes through a different path, which seems more natural and according to reason. He says that after the said bird makes its bed and residence with the mentioned tree barks and crawls inside, with the great heat of the Sun and the aromatic wood it is set on fire and it dies; and he doesn't say that the wood itself burns, but only the bird dies from the heat; and from the humor of its flesh a worm is generated, which, little by little acquires wings and grows to its past size. Who does not admire such a rare and prodigious work of nature, and example and marvel from which one may extract a most powerful conclusion and confirmation of the Resurrection (which is *à minore ad malus*); that if in nature there is so much wisdom and power, that once a living thing is dead it may once again live the life it had, what will the supreme Creator of all things be able to do so as to work so many marvels such as the ones we know? Isn't it obvious that he will have much greater power and knowledge to make much greater things, so much so that they may exceed the capacity of human and angelical reason? Returning to the topic, Solinus says that this Phoenix bird has the size of an Eagle, with its head greatly adorned with feathers resembling hair, it has a crested throat, near the neck it has feathers like bright gold and above this some of purple color; in its tail it has feathers with the color of the sky, and others will have the color red on their tips.

Chapter XXV

Of the Stork

This bird has very tall legs, long neck and a large beak; they are great enemies of the serpents, or rather, great friends, for they not only eat those they might come across, but they even seek them out with the intention of eating them, and these they take up through the air and drop them so as to kill them.

Storks only raise their young in towers and tall buildings, and it is said as a very certain thing that these do not raise a litter without having one of their young fall off the nest; and the Natural Philosophers say that this they do so as to thank the owner of the tower or building where they are living in, giving him a little Stork as payment for the place where they inhabit and raise their own. Others say that these pay God their tithe, recognizing the benefit that they received from the hand of their Creator, like the Ant, which for each Moon keeps for one day from seeking its food so as to give thanks and pay God some of the great debts it owes; and this day, as was said, is the ninth of the Moon. Be it as it may, either one or the other are nothing short of a great mysteries. And to prove this the Natural Philosophers give an example which has been proven and tried, and this is that in Thuringia, a land where there is no tithe, Storks do not live nor raise their young; and by this may one understand that in a land were one does not pay back one tenth of the fruits which God provides they do not wish to live. It is written of the Storks that when their father or mother are old, these will themselves fall into their nest, where they raised their children, and there these maintain and entertain them until their lives have ended, for these are very grateful birds and of great understanding.

Story of the Stork

A strange case is told of the Stork that, should it be true, deserves to be known, remembered and discussed; and this was that when a male is joined with a female for the first time, these remain as if married for their whole lives, without ever the male parting from the female or the female from the male, this unless the male understands that the female has betrayed it. And regarding this, a case is written in which two males and one female Stork were living in a certain castle in Castile; and the owner and lord of that castle was greatly entertained and had great enjoyment in seeing and contemplating how they raised their young; and he saw many times that when the male left the nest to seek out something to eat, the other male would approach and have contact with the female, leaving afterwards, and after this the female would go down from the tower and into a water ditch and would return to the nest. Once the male arrived it would not know of anything, for he did not see this betrayal that the female was doing. The lord of the castle, having seen what was going on, ordered that no water be kept in the ditch, so as the Stork could no longer go down from the tower to refresh itself after the betrayal; and as this could no longer wash itself, it returned to the nest. As its companion arrived, with its scent it knew of the betrayal that the female had done; and the lord saw how it mistreated its companion, leaving afterwards, and the following day it returned with a great deal of female Storks and they pecked the adulterer to death.

Medicinal properties of the Stork

Pliny writes that the ventricle of a Stork is good against any poison, should it be carried.

This same ventricle, boiled with wine, according to Pliny, removes pain and swelling from any meaty area.

Dioscorides says that Stork manure, drunk with water, is good against *gota coral*.

Chapter XXVI

Of the Sparrow

The Sparrows are cunning and treacherous, they are friends of the villages and they raise their own in holes in roofs, for they are always fearful of their enemies, and they are never out in the open. These birds cause great damages to the crops of wheat and barley, and because of this there was an Edict in Valencia in which a man who caught five hundred Sparrows, and showed these alive or dead, would be paid five *escudos*, and these birds could stay with he who hunted them.

The Sparrow is a most warm bird, and very given to coitus; and because of this Aristotle says that these birds do not even live for three years, for they age prematurely over this use they have with the female. And Aristotle further says that the man who performs this act too much will become gray, and consequently will become old too early, and this not to mention the great incurable damages that this may cause. Aristotle writes that these birds suffer from decrepitude and his cause for this is that these usually eat hyoscyamus or henbane, which may cause in men great laughter and sadness, and sometimes these will make them mad, even if they will recover within twenty four hours.

Finally the Sparrows are most cunning, so much that the Comment of Psalm 24 goes as follows: *Passer aliquot strepitum magnum faciente volat; ne laqueo venantium copiatur*. And this means that these birds are heard to make great noise and chatter for no hunter can catch them in a noose.

Chapter XXVII

Of the Owl

The Owl is a nightly and religious bird; it is nightly because it is during the night that it flies and hunts, and it does not come out during the day over the fact that it has such bright and large eyes that it cannot see. And it is said to be religious for it constantly visits churches and checks the lamps so as to drink the olive oil. It maintains itself mainly on Mouse meat. It also visits pigeon houses so as to take their eggs, and should it be discovered it will fall to the ground with its claws up so as to defend itself. This bird hunts a thousand other tiny birds, and these are always found around some small twigs anointed with some glue, and these are there caught and trapped, for as they see this never before seen bird, they rush to it wanting to peck its eyes, and in this way they fall into its trap and are hunted.

The Owl and the Crow are mortal enemies because of their eggs; this because the Crow seeks the nest of the Owl during the day in order to eat its eggs; and the Owl does not rest during the night until it can find the Crow's eggs, and from this is that animosity born.

The *Mochuelo* is somewhat smaller than the Owl, and it is also a bird that cannot stand the light of day, and thus it roams and hunts during the night those birds that are careless and sleeping in trees, it pursues Mice and it is hated by most other birds. It is also used in the hunt with Goshawks and Hawks, for by taking it with its head covered to the hunting field, as they uncover it, because it cannot see in the Sun, it will immediately fly to the ground, and all other birds, by seeing this will think that this one has found something, and as such all approach, and at this point the Goshawk or whatever bird of prey is taken is let loose and these other ones are caught with ease.

Chapter XXVIII

Of the Cuckoo or Cubet[380]

The Cuckoo has a name according to its singing, and this bird does not know more than one song, and this one it constantly repeats and some take it as a bad omen when it is heard; and it is never in the place where it is thought or be, for if one thinks that it is to the left it is in fact to the right. This is a treacherous bird, for it constantly seeks those birds that have eggs which are similar to its own, and it waits for these to leave their nest so as to lay its own in it and have others raise them. And it uses different treasons, and this is that it steals eggs from the nests of these birds so as they may not realize that new ones have been laid there. And the children of the Cuckoo are naturally so cunning and treacherous that they steal the food from the mouths of those other ones which are not of their species, and in this way they eat and grow fat while the others become weak. And the mother by seeing these so healthy and bright will love them more and be greatly bored by its own natural ones, for seeing them so weak and consumed, and it will not perceive this betrayal.

The *Cubet* is a very luxurious bird, so much that even if the female is on top of her eggs the male will still take her and break her eggs; but the female, by being experienced in this, in seeing the male coming will jump up from the eggs so as these may not be broken; other females of these species, better adverted and warned, hide their eggs somewhere where the male cannot find them, for, according to the Natural Philosophers and also Aristotle, if the male finds them it will break them so as the female will not lose time with them and it may have all the contact it may desire.

---

380. Translator's note: uncertain translation.

Chapter XXIX

Of the Hooded Crow

The Hooded Crow is a bird able to prognosticate the weather, for when it is about to rain a great deal it will give out great voices, and of this it is said: *Tunc Cornix plena pluviam vocat improba voces.*

The ancient augurs of gentility made a great deal regarding the voices of the Hooded Crow, saying that it not only prognosticated future rain, but also coming events. This bird is naturally libidinous, and it is constantly seeking the eggs of the Doves.

Chapter XXX

Of the bird called Swan

This bird is white and very beautiful in its feathers, but it is black and ugly in its flesh; it lives in lakes of water, and it maintains itself with fish. This is a bird with an impatient, wrathful and choleric complexion.

Emilio[381] says of this bird that sailors take it as a prognosticator of good weather, when it is found at sea, and thus they came to say these verses:

Cignus in auspicis simper litissimus ales.
Hunc optant Naute, quia non semorgit in vadis.

The Natural Philosophers say that this bird will never feel good in singing, at least while it is alive, for when it approaches the hour of its death it will sing, contradicting its customs, and with such softness and melody that all other birds stop so as to hear, astonished and amazed by its funerary song.

The feathers of the Swan are good for writing, even if in some the ink does not flow well, and for this it is good to anoint the tip of the feather with a bit of garlic, and after that the ink will flow well, and of this secret I have plenty of experience.

---

381. Translator's note: uncertain reference.

Chapter XXXI

Of the Bees

There are so many (dear reader) properties and excellences in the most remarkable Bees that there is no quill that can write them or language that can declare them, no Lynx that can penetrate it, nor human understanding that can reach them; for even if these little birds are small in their bodies, they are great in the good they do us, and even more for the warnings they give us. For if we observe the order and foresight with which they compose their homes, organize their boxes, decorate their homes and build their combs, we will see that their industry and concernment is greater than all human fabrications. For to see the prudence with which they organize and govern themselves, the order with which they govern themselves, the love for their labor, the friendship with each other, the prudence with which they regulate themselves, the patience they can suffer, the rigor with which they can punish, the care with their work, the diligence they have in carrying out their duties, their eagerness in always being busy without there ever being any laziness, giving in this way a tacit reprehension to all vagabond men.

Among all the Flying, Swimming and Land Animals, the Bees are the ones which are the proudest and most careful in electing a King or leader, who they respect, serve and obey, without missing one single point in the custody and guard of their Captain or King.

This King or leader of the Bees has a larger body than all others that are subjected to it, and it is more royal and generous than all of these.

The King of the Bees, according to the Natural Philosophers, does not have a sting; however, an experienced man says that they do, but they never use it, and in this do these little birds show themselves to be prudent, discreet and warned, for they elect the Bee which is more clement and without malice, that it may have a sting but never use it.

So much is the obedience that the Bees give to their King and leader that, even if these have been guarding him for ten years, they will never leave his side; and if ten Bees need to go to work, they make sure that there are ten carrying supplies to tend to the King and be sure that he will never be left alone and without any supplies. A most excellent warning so as all vassals learn how to tend to their King.

And should their King wish to move to another place, it is a thing worth seeing and noting, how they surround him and follow him wherever he goes; and they take him so well covered among them that it is impossible to see or discover this King, this due to the number that is constantly accompanying him.

He who wishes to take or see a swarm of Bees in which the King travels, should be warned, for these will furiously charge against anyone who approaches in order to defend their King, this out of fear of losing it and being left without a leader.

Should they by any chance feel that their King is in any way tired, they will all gather and place themselves under him, carrying him so as he may rest, and each one of them will seek to be the first in doing this service.

And should their beloved King fall ill and indisposed, it is a most admirable thing to see the feeling they all have, surrounding him by all sides (even if separated), buzzing with sorrow, without ever leaving, and one may see that this will make all their evil impulses cease. And if by any bad luck the disease prevails and their leader dies, they all fall in pain and in an odd feeling, giving out such painful buzzing, that one may clearly see that they loved him; and their sorrow is so great that they no longer want to eat nor leave for the fields for a few days, and even the Sunlight seems to bother them. And on this occasion the Drones (which are a kind of large Bees which work as slaves) take the dead King and remove him from the presence of the mourning Bees, and they bury and hide him with the same solemnity and ceremony which their natural instinct has taught them from their early age to have regarding consideration and foresight, according to the Natural Philosophers. Having the body removed from the presence of the sad Bees, and curing their sadness over a few days, they elect a new King with the same conditions as we have said. And one should say that there are always a few Bees which are apt for the position and ministry of being Kings. And should by any chance some Bees rise up wanting to take this position of being Kings and leaders of all others with tyranny, all of these will join together and conspire against them, banishing them from the hive and ending their intentions by ending their lives.

Let us see the method and industry which they use in the fabrication of their cells and quarters, which is most worthy of being noted. The first thing they do is to make a paste of very bitter and sour herbs which they place around their homes so as to make a good foundation and keep away any Animal which might want to steal their honey; so as these, upon running into such sour taste will give up in their intention and not do them any damage; and for this reason is honey not made in the first three layers of the hive. Secondly they fabricate and prepare the cells or six sided holes; and they do not build these straight, but rather oblique, so as to be more protected from the wind and from any harmful Animal, for these will not be as easy to assault as it would be if they were built straight.

It is of no less consideration to see how they distribute their work and positions of labor and ministry; for some are charged with guarding the King, being as soldiers, never leaving its side with the order and concernment mentioned above. Others are busy in the garrison, and are on watch as valorous soldiers at the doors of the Beehive so as to resist all enemies who might assault them to eat their honey and also to take their lives. Others go out into the fields seeking the liqueur with which they make their honey and the flowers which they use to make wax. And one should note that each Bee carries four loads, two in their hands and two in their feet. And should by any chance wind come up when they are in the fields, they immediately fall to the ground and grab a small rock, so as with this weight they may prevail against the wind.

If by any chance some Bees are left out in the field when night falls, they fly to the soil and lie down with their backs to the ground, and they then sleep with their feet up so as not to get their wings wet by the night dew and become unable to fly. Others are waiting at the door of the hive for those that come back carrying flowers so as to unload them and take the said flowers which they use to make the honeycombs. Others are kept polishing the cells already made. Others, finally, bring water for the Bees which live inside; and these are the Drones, which are used for lowly jobs such as putting cement on the hive walls, bringing water, cleaning the quarters and burying the Bees that might die; and these Drones are so vile in their nature that they are forced to suffer a thousand abuses and offenses from the other Bees.

Of these Drones it is said as a very certain thing that they don't have a sting, and as these are very hot, they are used to heat up and vivify the eggs of the other Bees so as these may be born faster; but, should the Bees find these Drones to be lazy or eating the honey that they are making, not only do they sting them and cast them out of the hive, but they also finish them; for more than being great enemies of gluttony and Thieves, laziness, and those who partake in this, bother them to the greatest extreme.

The charity they have among themselves is so great that should any one of them be sick, they take it to the sunlight so as it may be made joyful, and there it will be visited by the others, all showing their grief and lament over the labor and sickness of their companion, and they bring it food and make a thousand demonstrations of charity and affection, not allowing that it do any work until it is fully recovered. And one may also see the care which they have in taking this one back inside before nightfall so as not to be exposed to the cold of the night. And should this Bee die, they bury it in the honey combs, and are filled with sadness and pain.

And seeing the silence they keep during the night, and this with the many thousands of them that live in a hive, they are so still and peaceful as if there were in fact none; and these keep their sentinel work, keeping guard over all of them; and above all of these they have a crier and morning caller, so as soon as the day breaks, waking before all others, with two or three strong buzzings it may awake all others; and with this warning each one of them will get busy with their own labor and ministry. And should this one with the responsibility of waking all others, for its back luck, forget its job, it will pay sevenfold, and the least with its life.

Regarding honey, there are different opinions regarding how it is made, for some say it is made from the dew that the Bees collect and take on their wings before the rise of the Sun; and that this honey is as a manna, which when brought into the combs is coagulated, thickened and is converted into a smooth and sweet honey liqueur. And it is further said that if the comb was made with Rosemary flowers, that that dew which is placed there will take on that taste of Rosemary. And if the comb is made from the flowers of Lavender, this honey or liqueur will take on that taste; and from this it is said that the honey takes the name of that same Lavender or Rosemary. This opinion is not grounded in a good foundation; for it is most certain that should the wings of the Bees be made wet with dew they would not be able to fly, as I have proven above.

Others say, and with reason, such as Pliny and Dioscorides, Book 2, Chapter 74, that honey is not anything else than a dew that falls from the sky during the night over the flowers and herbs of the fields; and this dew, by falling on these flowers, becomes soft and sweet by natural virtue of the said flowers which themselves have a certain sweetness (as experience shows) and the Bees then gather and collect this dew and liqueur with great contentment. And after having this somewhat altered in their stomachs, feeling themselves full, they take care to empty this in the combs which they fabricate especially for this, with the purpose of having this as provision and sustainment for the time when there are no flowers in the fields; and also for those times when they cannot go out due to the excessive rain and bad weather that is common in Winter. And one should note that even if this dew falls on flowers which are bitter and sour, the Bees, by having this in their stomach, make it soft and sweet, for this is a property of the stomach of the Bees, to turn the sour into sweet and the harsh into soft; and on the contrary, Spiders turn all the sweet they eat into poison.

The wax, as we have said, is made from flowers with which they make their combs and cells where they deposit the dew and liqueur converted into honey.

Properties of the Bees

The Bees are great friends of cleanliness and diligence; and thus it is convenient for one who keeps them to be clean and a hard worker, as they are.

He who goes near a hive should take care of not having eaten garlic, onion or any other food which may smell bad, nor should he have any bad smell, for they will pursue him with the greatest fierceness.

Beyond being extremely clean, the Bees are also extremely chaste; and in the same way should he who tends to them also be, for, according to Aelianus and other such great Authors, they know by natural instinct the man who is not chaste and is libidinous; and they even say that by their sense of smell they can discover a man who has had recent carnal contact with a woman; and by being so chaste the Gentiles gave the custody of the Bees to the Goddess of chastity.

If a Bee is a great deal of time without working or going out into the field, it will become ill; and for this reason they are never lazy, nor does time permit this.

When Bees have among themselves a discord inside the hive, letting out a great buzzing, this is a sign that they want to leave that place and home. And when this is evident to the Beekeeper he should immediately go there with some sweet wine with a soft aroma, and sprinkle them with it, so as they may not leave. And one should know that three days before they intend on leaving they give signs by letting out some very clamorous and strange buzzing, as they are preparing to leave.

The Bees can predict future bad weather in such a way that if the day is to become rainy they will not leave the hive; and if there is to be a good weather there isn't a single one that doesn't go out into the fields.

At night, after all have entered and gone into their cells and quarters, they entertain themselves with some murmuring and singing, until one of them comes out and with a harsh sounding buzz and silences them all until the break of Dawn, and the same Bee which marks them for silence also wakes them for work. Pliny.

The Bees, according to Pliny, cannot be without a King or leader; and should they lose one they become sad and full of mourning (as we have said) this until they elect a new one.

In the year where Spring is humid, according to Pliny, there will be little honey and the Bees will grow a lot; when the weather is dry there will abundance of honey and the Bees will be diminished.

As a Bee drives its sting into any flesh, it will lose this sting and its entrails; for as it only has one intestine, and one is connected to the other, in losing one it will also lose the other; and this one will no longer make any honey, for it dies. The cause for it to lose its sting and entrails upon stinging is because, as its sting enters any soft thing, like living and feeling flesh, this will alter itself, and being altered it will tighten and the sting will be stuck, and thus it will not be able to be pulled out. If on the contrary it stings a hard thing in which the sting will not be able to pierce, it does not lose it, as the same will happen should it sting a soft thing which will not alter itself or tighten.

Bees, according to Avicenna and Palladius, make honey twice a year, and this is in the Autumn and Summer, and they say that the honey of Summer is much better than that of Autumn, and the reason for this is because the flowers are much newer and stronger.

Bees, according to Pliny, love soft sounds and concert music, so much so that if one is outside of the hive and hears some sound near it, it will immediately return.

Bees are great enemies of olive oil, and in this way it is a good idea to go among them while having one's face and hands anointed with olive oil.

One should note that should a Bees sting, if you immediately anoint that region with olive oil, it will not become swollen nor will this make any damage.

Powder made from dried Bees mixed with Mouse manure and laurel oil will make hair that might have fallen out due to some disease grow again.

These are great friends of clear and clean water, so much so that these will prefer to die of thirst than to drink muddy water.

What can we say of the use and service that we have from these and the honor and advantage that we take from the wax and the honey they make and offer us, for not only do Kings and great lords use wax in order to illuminate their tables and quarters, but also is the Church honored to light the altars with this wax. With it are processions organized and funerals made grand. Finally, with it are the Saints celebrated and the Brotherhoods made magnificent.

And from honey are composed the virginal washes, of which so much excellences and advantages are gained, this without counting the innumerable medicines, remedies, boilings and beverages that every day do men invent, for these are so many that I will have to direct you to the Apothecaries and Monasteries so as they may be able to tell you of how much there is to know, for I do not dare to do this here, for I have yet to speak of other things.

In the chapter of the Ox I have written of three methods by which to obtain and create Bees when one has completely lost them and so I remit the Reader to this section. Here I will speak of a way and artifice, not for generating Bees as I have before, but rather to attract them from the mountains and hollow trees where many swarms usually live and where they produce a lot of honey.

A man who wishes to have Bees from those places I have said (and not the ones from his fellow man, that this is not permitted among men of reason, much less Christians) he should seek a creek or a fountain like those which are common outside of any village, where plenty of Bees have the custom to drink, and he should take with him a hollow tube, the wider the better, in which he should have some water with honey, and this should be somewhat thick, and by placing this near the water where these Bees go to drink, you will immediately see how they will rush to the smell of honeyed water and many of them will go into this tube; and as soon as you think that there are enough inside the tube, close it. Once this diligence is made one should make another, and this is that one should open the tube just enough for one Bee to come out, and no more than this, and he should follow it as best as possible; and should this go out of his sight he should let another one go; and should this one once again disappear he should let another one go and so forth until he can follow them to where they have their garrison, and in this way these Bees will reveal where they live.

Warning about the Bees

Should you wish to do a no less curious diligence instead of the previous one in order to know if the Bees are far away or not, one should take with him some ink, and when the Bees arrive to drink some water one should mark them with the ink placed at the tip of a small feather, and he should then wait until it leaves and once again returns, and one will be able to see the marked Bee, and if the hive is far away it will take a long time to return.

Returning to our purpose, I say that, after having found a swarm or swarms of Bees, one should have a hive or hives prepared in the way we have mentioned in the chapter of the Ox. Now place the hive in front of the place from where they are exiting, and cast some smoke under the opposing part, that all of them will immediately come out due to the sweet smell and enter the hive (as is described in the above mentioned place) with no difficulty; and with this industry and diligence one will be able to acquire and own Bees in abundance.

Of Diligence

If the Reader had curiosity and attention in the reading of the chapter of the Bees, then he should have noted that the two particular virtues and excellences of these little Animals are Diligence and Chastity, of which we will say some excellences and praises with the authority of the learned and the Saints.

Diligence is a physical act proportionate to a work of virtue.

Diligence is the mother of good fortune, which, should it be just, according to Estobeus, is immune to reprehension.

Diligence, according to Saint Bernard, is the proper trade of a Prelate and of the one who rules, Book I.

Diligence and solicitude, according to Curtius,[382] have their seat on peace and rest, Book 4.

Terentius says that Diligence is a companion of industry and that to these two are events obedient.

In the dealings of war, so says Vegetius, readiness and Diligence are of better service than virtue and strength, Book 4.

Saint Augustine says that that which is done with Diligence is done right; and from this does the saying come: That which is already made, is well made.

Saint Gerome says that too much Diligence is also the cause of suspicion.

Estobeus says that Diligence with industry is worth more than good cunning.

Dreams and wine are the things which are more contrary to Diligence. Columella, Book 10.

There is nothing that is not beaten or reached by strong Diligence. Seneca.

A thing will be easiest to reach and make the more it is done with Diligence. Erasmus.

Saint Gregory says that too much use and Diligence in earthly things disturbs the effects of prayer.

Saint Bernard says that God our Lord is very diligent and ready with all those who are also thus in serving Him.

Of Chastity

By Bees being so chaste and virginal, I wish to write something of Chastity with the authority of the learned and Saints.

Chastity is one of the twelve fruits of the Holy Spirit, which conserves the soul chaste and the body clean. Medina.

Without fasting and moderation, Chastity will not be properly conserved. Friar Estella.

Chastity arranges a soul and makes it ready to receive a clear understanding of God, and it prepares it for the secrets of Heaven. Idem.

Among all the Apostles Saint John and Saint Paul were virgins, and one of these was taken to see the third Heaven, where he saw that which he had the courage to say, Corinth, Chapter 12. And to the other was revealed great secrets of Heaven in the bosom of the Lord.

By being Chaste was Joseph able to declare the dreams of the Servant and Baker which were in prison, and also those of Pharaoh the King, by which he would come to reign over the entire kingdom of Pharaoh, lord of Egypt, Genesis 40 and 41.

The daughter of Phanuel lived until 84 years with the cleanness of Chastity, and in this way she was worthy of having a prophetic spirit, to see and know Christ incarnate. Luke, Chapter 2.

Saint Thomas of Aquinas lived as a Chaste virgin, and for this he was so splendorous (as we all know) in the Church of God with great wisdom. Friar Estella.

The humble and chaste is victorious over demons, who are dirty and proud spirits. Idem.

Moses had all women killed except the virgins, letting them free solely for being as such.

Noah was spared the Deluge because he was such a chaste man, and he was five hundred years old when he got married and had those three children: Shem, Ham and Japheth. Idem.

God loves Chastity so much that he ordered Noah to place all filthy Animals in the Ark two by two, and the clean ones seven by seven. Genesis, Chapter 7.

Plutarch said that in order to conserve Chastity one should sometimes even abstain from one's own wife, so as this may not be an occasion to be incited towards others.

Erasmus says that Chastity is not to lack concupiscence, but rather to overcome it.

Plutarch says that the good and chaste woman should cover and keep her body, even inside the walls of her own quarters.

---

382. Translator's note: probably Quintus Curtius Rufus, a Roman historian of the I[st] century AD.

Story and miraculous case of the most chaste Bees

The holy and sacred Doctor Antonino, Archbishop of Florence, writes, in part 3 of *Theologica*, title 12, c.7.§.2, of a rare and prodigious miracle, and he says the following: a rustic man who had a great desire and lust to be wealthy was thus constantly seeking inventions and tricks so as to become rich; and a Magus advised him that, should he want to be wealthy, he should keep and conserve the Holy Sacrament in his mouth when he went to commune during Easter, and that he should not swallow this; and he should take this to his hives and place it inside one of them, and once this had been done all the Bees from all his neighbors would rush to that one and would start to make honey in that hive. This simple and greedy man took the advice of the cursed Magus; and it was a rare case that indeed the Bees of this rustic and those of his neighbors started working with an admirable concernment and industry to build a tiny chapel made of wax with an extremely beautiful Altar inside the hive. Having come the time to take out the honey, this man went to his hive and found it empty of honey and Bees. And amazed at what he saw (or rather, what he didn't) he went to the hive where he had put the Holy Sacrament and he saw that a multitude of Bees were flying around this, buzzing with an admirably soft hum, and singing with a strange and arranged melody. Wanting to get near to this hive where the flesh of God and Man rested, all these Bees rushed at him with great fury, as if wanting to avenge the injustice made to their Lord and creator. The rustic, seeing this great force and fury of the Bees, understood the virtue of God and went away, going immediately to his Priest to confess his betrayal and evilness, relating also this same miraculous case which he had noticed in the hive. The Priest, understanding the case, had the whole village congregate and many other people came from around this region; and in this way they all went in a procession to the Beehive. Oh grave case and great respect of the Bees, for as soon as the Priest arrived at the hive where the bread of life, the Holy Sacrament rested, all the Bees came out of the hive, flying out with joyful buzzing, singing with great softness and melody. And as the hive was opened, all could see the Church and Chapel of wax that the Bees had built and made with its Altar, on top of which was the Holy Sacrament. Finally, with great reverence, the Priest took out the Holy Sacrament with the Church and Altar, and took it in the procession with tears of joy and great rejoicing in all the village where these relics are kept.

What Christian will not be beside himself with pure contentment and joy by seeing that the most High God and our Lord, permits and desires such works and such marvels for confirmation of our holy and immaculate faith? What Heretic or Moor is not confounded in seeing and understanding such prodigious miracles, and does not surrender himself to the rightful obedience to the holy Church and our Catholic faith?

End of the first and second part of the

Animals of the Land and Sky

Appendix I

Below are several sections, tables and calculation present in the 1836 Barcelona edition of the *Lunario*. These have not been added to the main body of the current compilation of this same book due to the fact that these rely on concepts and elements which are incompatible with the original text and layout of the *Lunario*, most notably the use of the Epact. These are shown here as an example of the various alterations and permutations this book has undergone throughout the centuries, as its original content has lost its scientific accuracy but its name, and that of its author, has not at all lost any of its appeal.

***

Prologue

To the Reader

Reader, if for the most curious Lunario written by Cortez you have cultivated, before this new printing, a special affection, I trust that, in your piety and prudent knowledge, the reformations and additions I have made unto it shall not be the motive for you to lose your affection; but rather that you take it to an even greater regard; for the additions made were made under advice of some great enthusiast of the Lunario; in short, all that which it was missing so it would be able to correspond to the title of Perpetual. Should you be a Mathematician you will not require this; and given that, to him who knows, too much practice becomes dull, I ask you, due to your knowledge, to give it to some friend of yours who is less knowing. If you are not, and you extract from it some leisure, or use it to some benefit, then give graces to God our Lord, and do not honor this book or this new reformation of it; for it is my obligation to express these most curious things that the Mathematical sciences deal with for the common good; and if you neither have such diversion, nor find anything you like in it, for not being of such curiosity, nor have any kind of affection over things of this sort, I ask you to not cast it out, but rather give it to a Priest or to man of the cloth, and he will take it to great esteem; for in this book are expressed many things which are good for one to know (even if not obligatory), at least by the fact that it contains news of that which may be taken from the Calendar which is in the beginning of the Missals, Breviaries and all other Prayer Books about the days on which one shall celebrate all movable feasts.

Explanation and practice of the perpetual Table of the Dominical Letters from the year of 1600 forward

We have removed the wheels of the Dominical Letters and Golden Number, which were found in this Lunario, for having been found lacking and disturbing in the finding of perpetualness of these same Letters and Golden Numbers.

The Dominical Letter is used to find the Sundays and all other days of the week; for once we know which day of the month is Sunday we can also find out when it is Saturday, Monday, Tuesday, Wednesday, Thursday, etc. So as one may know all of this by this Letter, it was inserted into the Roman Ecclesiastic Calendar; and this is referred as such because these may be found in all the Missals, Breviaries and other prayer books, as also in all Repertoires and Lunarios; and from this we may find great facility: that once the Dominical Letter is known one may search for it on the edges of the Calendar and one will find the day of the month which is a Sunday.

The Dominical Letter may be taken in many ways, because these are cyclical, having 28 letters, passing one letter per year, except the leap years, which have two letters; by which one may understand that in the 28 letters, two are repeated seven times, which means that in those 28 years there are seven leap years, for four times seven is 28, which is the length of a complete cycle or period; and once this is finished it once again returns to the beginning. This method will then last forever, without there being a necessity of corrections over the anticipation of the Equinoxes, of which we have mentioned above; from this arises the use and utility of the wheels and ancient tables used to find the Dominical Letters. And even if many methods have been invented to find these letters, I don't find it preposterous to offer another, since among so many, one more will surely fit.

In the Table of the Dominical Letters, below, there are four rows, going from margin to margin, and each one of these rows has 28 divisions, and in each of these there is one Dominical Letter and in every four divisions there are two Letters, which indicate the seven leap years of the 28 years. These four rows have the title: *First Table used for the centennial leap years*. This means that this Table, with its 28 divisions is to be used for all centennial years of which are leap years; for in every 400 years you have centennial leap years, and for these is this row reserved.

The title of the second row is: *Second Table for the first centennial which is not a leap year*; this means that this Table or Row with its 28 letters, is used for the first centennial in which we drop the leap year of those 400.

The title of the third is: *Third Table of the second centennial, which is not a leap year*; meaning that in the 400 years this is the second in which we do not have a leap year.

The title of the fourth row is: *Fourth Table for the third centennial which is not a leap year*; meaning that this table is for the third centennial from the 400 years which is not a leap year, and of these non leap centennials the first will be in 1700, the second 1800 and the third 1900, which, as we have said, are the 300 years in which we remove three days, and the removal of these days causes a change in the order of the Dominical Letters; and for this are these four rows used.

This Fourth row has beneath it the sign *, and following this, there will be the number one beneath the letter F and two beneath E, and three beneath D, etc. Under the sign * there is the number 28 and under this the number 56 and 84 and the number 99 shall be beneath the letter C. These numbers are the years following from one centennial to the next, which indicate the Dominical Letter without any sort of work.

These years until 99 both serve for the 28 letters of which they are beneath, but also for the other three rows above, with the exception that the Second, Third and Fourth rows do not use the two letters above the *, for they are not leap years, but they solely use the bottom letter, and the one above this one will be used in 28 years, which will be a leap year; and having said this there isn't much room for doubts.

We take the first row, which is for the leap year, from 1600 until 1699, which, dropping the 1600 gives us the letter D for the 99, which means that the Dominical Letter of any year after 1600 (and before 1700) shall be found in that row in this same way. Let us suppose that we wish to know the Dominical Letter of the year of 1674: dropping the 1600 we seek out the 74 in the common years and I find that to 74 corresponds the letter G and so I may say that the Dominical Letter of the year of 1674 was G, and I may see that in this same column is also used for 1618 and 1646, for these numbers are in the same division, and the same should be done for any other year in such an easy way that I do not need to offer further examples.

The second row is used for the year of 1700 until 1799 in the following way. The year of 1700 is the first centennial that is not a leap year, and the order of the 28 letters is not changed from the first row; but, since we have one less day our calculation needs to be different. We should know that the Dominical Letter of the year of 1700 is C, which is under the D for the years of 1728, 1756 and 1758, which are the number in this division, 28, 56 and 84, and so can I say that the years of 1728, 1756 and 1784 are leap years, for their Dominical Letters are C and D. By understanding this, one example is enough so as one may find the letter of any year between 1700 and 1799, and lets see for the year of 1716.

Operation: from this year of 1716 I drop the 1700 having 16 left, which, seeking in the row of the common years and which is correspondent in the Row of the Dominical Letters for the first non leap year I find E and D and so I say that in this year of 1716 the Dominical Letter is C and D, for this is a leap year; and the same is also true for the years of 1744 and 1772, for they are in the same division as 16. *Anytime a year has two Dominical Letters, this is a leap year.*

The third row is used for the years between 1800 and 1899, for this is the second centennial which is not a leap year; in this year of 1800 the Dominical Letter will be E, but the years of 1828, 1856 and 1884 will be leap years and shall have the letters E and F. Following the same as before we shall see of the Dominical Letters of the remaining years up to 99, and we shall have the example of the year of 1809.

Operation: I drop the 1800 and I am left with 9; I seek this in the common years and see its correspondence in the row of the second centennial, which gives A, as thus I see that A is used in the years of 1837, 1865, 1893 for this is the common division for 9, 37, 65 and 93.

The fourth row is used for years between 1900 and 1999, for it is the third centennial which is not a leap year; thus, the Dominical Letter of the year of 1900 is G, but that of the year of 1928, 1956 and 1984, which are leap years, will be A and G, in the same way the Dominical Letter of all common years which are below one hundred can be easily found; let us take the year of 1910.

Operation: from this year of 1910 I drop the 1900 and I am left with 10, which, by seeking in the common years will correspond to the Dominical Letter B, which will be the same for 1938, 1966 and 1994, for 10, 38, 66 and 94 are in the same division.

The year 2000 is a leap centennial, and as such we return to the first row, and thus the letter B and A, just as was used for the year of 1600 are once again used for 2000, and due to the arrangement of the common years, these letters of B and A, which were used for 1600, 1628, 1656 and 1684 are once again used for 2000, 2028, 2056 and 2084, for these are all common years in the same division.

All that is left is to give the rule by which to perpetuate the four rows, and this is so easy that with what has already been said one could discover it; but I do not wish to let this pass, so as these matters may not offer any work or challenge and so as the Table may be indeed perpetuated; and this is as follows:

Perpetual table for the four Rows of the Dominical Letters

1	1600	2000	2400	2800	3200	3600
2	1700	2100	2500	2900	3300	3700
3	1800	2200	2600	3000	3400	3800
4	1900	2300	2700	3100	3500	3900

This Table perpetuates the four rows of Dominical Letters in the following way: the numbers of 1, 2, 3 and 4 are the ones corresponding to the years of 1600, 1700, 1800 and 1900, as well as to the years of 2000, 2100, 2200, and 2300, and so forth; this means that the fourth row of Dominical Letters will be used for the years of 1900, 2300, 2700, 3100, 3500 and 3900 and so forth until infinity for every 400 years, and the same being valid for all centennials, such as 1600, 2000, 2400, 2800, 3200 and 3600, which are all in the first row which is the one of the leap centennials; and from this one may see that there is no effort in increasing any centennial in this small table.

One should further note something, should the curious reader not be able to extract it from this explanation: that in every non leap centennial only one letter of the two that are presented in the beginning of each row is used, in this way the years of 2100, 2500, 2900, 3300 and 3700 will have the Dominical Letter C, just as the year of 1700.

The years of 2200, 2600, 3000, 3400 and 3800 have the letter E, which is the one from the year of 1800.

The years of 2300, 2700, 3100, 3500 and 3800 have the letter G, which is the one of the year of 1900, and one should not make a case of the letters above these until another 28 years have passed.

APPENDIX I

First Table used for the centennial leap years

*	1	2	3	4	5	6	7	8	9	10	11	12	13	14	15	16	17	18	19	20	21	22	23	24	25	26	27
B	G	F	E	D	C	B	A	G	F	E	D	C	B	A	G	F	E	D	C	B	A	G	F	E	D	C	B
A				C				E				G				B				D				F			

28	29	30	31	32	33	34	35	36	37	38	39	40	41	42	43	44	45	46	47	48	49	50	51	52	53	54	55
A	G	F	E	D	C	B	A	G	F	E	D	C	B	A	G	F	E	D	C	B	A	G	F	E	D	C	B

Second Table for the first centennial which is not a leap year

56	57	58	59	60	61	62	63	64	65	66	67	68	69	70	71	72	73	74	75	76	77	78	79	80	81	82	83
D	B	A	G	F	E	D	C	B	A	G	F	E	D	C	B	A	G	F	E	D	C	B	A	G	F	E	D
C				E				G				B				D				F				A			

Third Table of the second centennial, which is not a leap year

84	85	86	87	88	89	90	91	92	93	94	95	96	97	98	99
F	D	C	B	A	G	F	E	D	C	B	A	G	F	E	D
E			G				B				D				F

Fourth Table for the third centennial which is not a leap year

A	F	E	D	C	A	G	F	E	C	B	A	G	F	E	D	C	B	A	G	F	E	D	C	B	A	G	F
G		B				D				F				A				C				E					

Of the Golden number, explanation of its tables and the method of extracting it perpetually

After the Romans had invented a great deal of tables and wheels, and they made them functional with the conjunctions of the Sun and Moon, and made them work perpetually to be fitted to the Calendar given to them by Romulus, everything was found to be defected; for in a few hundred years the errors of these tables became obvious. Numa Pompilius, who followed Romulus, emended the Calendar and declared that every calculation made from it up to that point had been faulty. To correct for this he ordered that a new calculation be made, which lasted until Julius Caesar, which was in the year of 45 before the coming of Christ to the world. And among all the calculations made since the time of Numa Pompilius to work the conjunctions of the Sun and the Moon, ones were those of the Golden Number, which was made in the year of 432 before the coming of Christ to the world. Historians say that it was Meton who invented it, and that this inventor was from Athens, the son of Pausianas; and they further speak of its use by the same Meton and that the Romans received it with great enthusiasm, for they found it to be stable, and as such they placed it in the margins of all Calendars in golden characters, from which the name Golden Number arises.

Still, this Golden Number, over time, has been seen to also be defective, not by its own fault, but by that of the solar year; for many observations have put its errors to light. And so, in the reformation of the Calendar , made by Gregory XIII, it was substituted by the Epact.

This Golden number forms a circle whose full period consists of 19 years, and after these 19 one once again counts the number 1.

It will also be good to understand the following two tables. The first contains the following title: *Table one, used for the Golden numbers of the centennial years*; after this one there is another with the following title: *Golden numbers used for the roots of the common years*.

The second table has the title: *Second Perpetual Table of the Golden Number, which is used for the common years*; and next to this there is the title: *Years after the centennials*.

Once these tables are known with ease will the Golden Number be found on any centennial as well as common year. We call centennials all those years that are made up of hundreds, as they are displayed in the first table with their corresponding Golden Number. We call common years those that are less than one hundred, and these are found in the second table after the title *Common years etc*; for one may see that these are from 1 until 99, for if these were to reach one hundred they would belong to the first table, whose title is: *Table one of the centennial years*: from which we may comprehend that once the Golden Number of the centennial year is known, you can transport it, or, by looking in the heading of the second table, and from the side of the common years, this will make a straight angle and find the Golden number. And this may be better understood by some examples, and by this one will save on the whole explanation of the second table which would be necessary for those who are not used to these subjects, this unless we provide examples.

The first of these will be the year of 1500. This, being a centennial, I say that its Golden number is 19, and so shall it be for the years of 3400, 5300, 7200 and 9100. This for the reason that these centennial years have 19 at their edge on the first table, which is the Golden number that will serve for these years.

The second is of the year of 1700. I seek this in the first table and I see that on the edge this year has the number 10, and so can I say that the year of 1700, as well as those of 3600, 5500, 7400 and 9300, have 10 as their Golden number; and in this same way can know this for every centennial.

Third example: The year of 1600, by looking at the table do I see that it corresponds to the number 5; but, should I wish to know the Golden number of the year of 1649, I drop this number of 1600 and take the number of 49; I go to the second table and in its heading I seek the Golden number 5, which is the number of 1600, and making a straight angle with the common year of 49 I find the Golden number of 16.

Another example: the year 1716, I drop the 1700 and take the 16. See that the year of 1700 has the Golden number of 10, which, seeking in the heading of second table and making a straight angle from the 16 in the common years I find the number 7; and so we may say that the Golden number of the year of 1716 is 7.

Another example; the year of 1724, of which 10 is the Golden number of 1700, as before, I seek this number in the heading of the second table and coming from the 24 in the common years I find the Golden number of 15 for the year of 1724, and so forth for every other years, for we can spare any further examples.

First Table used for the Golden number for the centennial years

1	0	1900	3800	5700	7600
6	100	2000	3900	5800	7700
11	200	2100	4000	5900	7800
16	300	2200	4100	6000	7900
2	400	2300	4200	6100	8000
7	500	2400	4300	6200	8100
12	600	2500	4400	6300	8200
17	700	2600	4500	6400	8300
3	800	2700	4600	6500	8400
8	900	2800	4700	6600	8500
13	1000	2900	4800	6700	8600
18	1100	3000	4900	6800	8700
4	1200	3100	5000	6900	8800
9	1300	3200	5100	7000	8900
14	1400	3300	5200	7100	9000
19	1500	3400	5300	7200	9100
5	1600	3500	5400	7300	9200
10	1700	3600	5500	7400	9300
15	1800	3700	5600	7500	9400

(Golden number of the centennial years)

This table can be easily perpetuated by adding another column to it, and another further still, and in these write in the new years in intervals of 100 in the natural order, as can be seen.

Perpetual Table of the Golden Number

Root of the centennials					Years after the centennial																			
1	20	39	58	77	96	1	6	11	16	2	7	12	17	3	8	13	18	4	9	14	19	5	10	15
2	21	40	59	78	97	2	7	12	17	3	8	13	18	4	9	14	19	5	10	15	1	6	11	16
3	22	41	60	79	98	3	8	13	18	4	9	14	19	5	10	15	1	6	11	16	2	7	12	17
4	23	42	61	80	99	4	9	14	19	5	10	15	1	6	11	16	2	7	12	17	3	8	13	18
5	24	43	62	81		5	10	15	1	6	11	16	2	7	12	17	3	8	13	18	4	9	14	19
6	25	44	63	82		6	11	16	2	7	12	17	3	8	13	18	4	9	14	19	5	10	15	1
7	26	45	64	83		7	12	17	3	8	13	18	4	9	14	19	5	10	15	1	6	11	16	2
8	27	46	65	84		8	13	18	4	9	14	19	5	10	15	1	6	11	16	2	7	12	17	3
9	28	47	66	85		9	14	19	5	10	15	1	6	11	16	2	7	12	17	3	8	13	18	4
10	29	48	67	86		10	15	1	6	11	16	2	7	12	17	3	8	13	18	4	9	14	19	5
11	30	49	68	87		11	16	2	7	12	17	3	8	13	18	4	9	14	19	5	10	15	1	6
12	31	50	69	88		12	17	3	8	13	18	4	9	14	19	5	10	15	1	6	11	16	2	7
13	32	51	70	89		13	18	4	9	14	19	5	10	15	1	6	11	16	2	7	12	17	3	8
14	33	52	71	90		14	19	5	10	15	1	6	11	16	2	7	12	17	3	8	13	18	4	9
15	34	53	72	91		15	1	6	11	16	2	7	12	17	3	8	13	18	4	9	14	19	5	10
16	35	54	73	92		16	2	7	12	17	3	8	13	18	4	9	14	19	5	10	15	1	6	11
171	36	55	74	93		17	3	8	13	18	4	9	14	19	5	10	15	1	6	11	16	2	7	12
18	37	56	75	94		18	4	9	14	19	5	10	15	1	6	11	16	2	7	12	17	3	8	13
19	38	57	76	95		19	5	10	15	1	6	11	16	2	7	12	17	3	8	13	18	4	9	14

APPENDIX I

Explanation of the Epact and of the methods of its tables, so as one may use them perpetually

Although many times before the Lunario has been printed with the title of having been reformed, in none of these was the Epact added, and as such all of these are defected, and do not fulfill that which they propose themselves to be. The current aspiration of achieving this may be able to overcome this wrongness which has been expressed in its practice; to make everyone understand this is to have achieved the intention of having all understand all things of the calculation of the Calendar, so worthy of all Ecclesiastic men and all curious people whose occupation is not related to the mathematical sciences but who rejoice in knowing briefly of such practices.

This Epact is the most real invention of all things which can be invented so as to understand the conjunction of the Sun and Moon; and this was ordered into the margins of all Calendars in the year of 1582, replacing the Golden number. Even thought this Lunario, due to its brevity, does not allow for us to explain fully why the Epact was changed, or why 29 of these are usable for 100, 200 and 300 years, causing great varieties due to the three days which are dropped in these years and the one day that the conjunctions of the Sun and Moon move up in 312 years and a half, in determent of the Epact or the Golden number.

With all of this we shall give the rules so as to make the equation of the Epact perpetually, without paying attention to the 312 years and a half and the day that moves up in the conjunctions, and we shall neither count the three days that are dropped in every 400 years. With this I will be able to dispel the doubt of those who do not have an understanding of such things and have read Galucio,[383] who is the man who in Spanish has written more about this than any other, but that has never offered any rule so as one may increase the centennials in his wheel. From this defect have some doubts arisen, as I have said, such as has happened to Don José Valdés y Vega, priest of the parish of S. Ramon of Salamanca, chaplain of his Majesty (may God keep him) and the royal chapel of Saint Marcus, *mayordomo* of the most Excellent Señor Calderon, bishop of the said Salamanca, and his general treasurer of Pias Memorias; for by seeing this difficulty I find it good to enter upon it, for he does not make it possible to resolve this with what he has given, even if he communicated with many mathematicians, which were unable to help with his doubt, and so I shall remove it for him. And so as this may not happen to any other, these perpetual tables are given and with these will you be able to add the centennials of Galucio and perpetuate his wheels of the Epact.

To find the Epact it is better to first explain the tables of the Epacts. The first of these begins in Epact * and ends in Epact I, and it contains all 30 Epacts. Each Epact here has its corresponding centennials, as can be seen by the years of 1700 and 1800, which are in Epact *. The years of 1900, 2000, 2100 are in Epact XXIX. The years of 2200 and 2300 are in Epact XXVIII and the years of 2400 and 2500 in XXVII, and so forth with all centennials. With this Table of Epact Equations one may perpetuate the wheels of Galucio, the title of this table is: *First Table of Equations of the Epact*.

The second table is used for the years after the centennials, and its title is: *Second Table of the Epacts for the common yea*rs. This table has 30 Epacts and it starts at the empty epact or the star *, and it ends in Epact XXIX. The Epacts in this table, from one to the next, mark the difference between the solar and lunar year; and so from one to the other there is a difference of eleven, which is the same as eleven days.

To find the Epact in any given year, one does not need to do anything else than to search in the first table for the past centennial year closest to the year in question; upon finding this in the table I will search in the second table of the common years; and this may be found by counting the Golden number of the Epacts; and the end result will be the Epact of that year.

---

383. Translator's note: uncertain translation.

Example

The year of 1710, of this the centennial is 1700, which gives me the equated Epact of * from the first table; I seek this Epact on the second table, and I find it at the top of the table; I count from this Epact the Golden number of the same year of 1710, which is one, and it falls on the same star Epact; and so I say that the Epact is *.

Another example

In 1715 the Golden number is 6, which, counted for Epact *, which is the one for the year of 1700, gives us Epact XXV for the year of 1715.

Another example

In the year if 1700 the Golden number is 10, I count 10 from Epact * and I have Epact IX

Another example

The year if 1719 has the Golden number 10, and by this reason the Epact is IX as before. This same rule is then valid of the year of 1890; for 1700 and 1890 are in the same Epact of *.

Another example

In the year of 1954 the Golden number will be 17, and the year of 1900, in the table of equated Epacts corresponds to XXIX; I seek this Epact in the second table and I count the 17 of the Golden number and I find the Epact XX, and so I can say that in 1954 the Epact will be XXV.

Another example

In the year of 1942 the Golden number will be 13, and from the first table I have Epact XXIX (which is the Epact of 1900), and by counting on the second table I find Epact XXII, and this Epact is the one for 1942.

And this calculation is valid for 300 years, for in the division of Epact XXIX one has the years of 1900, 2000 and 2100, which, by knowing the Golden number of the desired year, and counting from Epact XXIX will result in the corresponding Epact of that year.

One should note that anytime one reaches the end of the second table, when counting the Golden number, as it happens with the two examples mentioned before, that one should return to the top of the table and keep counting from Epact *.

It seems to me that in this first table there are enough centennials to last until the end of the world, for we have them from 1700 to 29600. But should the world last more than this I wish to offer the rule by which one may increase these 30 centennial Epacts so as this may earn the title of perpetual.

From the mentioned reasons of dropping 3 days in every 400 years and the coming early of the conjunctions in one day every 312 years and a half, it results that every 10000 years the equations of the Epact repeat themselves but merely change the position while running the various periods of 200, 300 or 100 years.

This can be done in the fowling way: let us suppose that the year of 11700 was the one where the cycle of 10000 ended, and this was not in the table, as this would end in Epact XVIII, where we have the letter D, and as such in order to begin another 10000 year cycle we needed to use the first centennial of 11700; I cheek where 1700 is, which was 10000 before, and I see it was on Epact *, where it sits with 1800, and I then write in Epact XVII 11700 and 11800, and in Epact XVI I place 11900, 12000 and 12100 and in Epact XV I place 12200 and 12400, for in Epact XXVIII we

APPENDIX I

now have 2200 and 2400, 10000 years before. And in this way we may increase the centennials by 10000 years, with exactly the same equations but different Epacts; and this calculation goes on in 20000 years in Epact V, where the letter C is, which is in the year of 21700 and after another 10000 we will have Epact I. And this must be examined in the table with care, for it is not easy to perpetuate it, and given the small size of the Lunario we have extended this in three hundred thousand years, for after this time the equations of the Epacts return once again to their beginning and we have once again the same Epacts. And this is taken to be very clear by Clavius,[384] but such is not so for those who are not familiar with these themes.

Father Clavius, as wise in the mathematical sciences as he was, made through certain methods, or quarter minutes, other few equations over these and came to the following conclusion: that of the year of 8200 one should drop one day, in 21900 another day and in 35700 another, and not a single more thing needs to be done, but that the year of 8200 falls on Epact II, and by removing one day it will fall on Epact I, and the year of 1900 is in Epact III and it shall change to Epact II and the year of 35700, which is in Epact V will become Epact IV, and with these equations are the Epacts corrected.

First Table of Equations

*	XXIX	XXVIII	XXVII	XXVI	XXV	XXIV	XXIII	XXII	XXI
1700	1900	2200	2300	2600	2900	3100	3400	3800	3500
1800	2000	2400	2500	2700	3000	3200	3600	3900	3700
		2100		2800		3300		4000	
8700	9000	9100	9400	9600	9800	10100	10300	10600	10800
8800		9200	9500	9700	9900	10200	10400	10700	10900
8900		9300					10500		
15600	15900	16200	16500	16400	16700	17000	17300	17500	17800
15800	16000	16300	16600	16500	16800	17100	17400	17600	17900
		16100				17200		17700	
22600	22900	23100	23400	23600	23800	24100	24200	24500	24700
22700	23000	23200	23500	23700	23900		24300	24500	24800
22800		23300			24000		24400		24900

---

384. Translator's note: Christopher Clavius (1538-1612), a German Jesuit graduated in the University of Coimbra. One of the great reformers of the Gregorian Calendar.

Continuation of the Table of Equations

XX	XIX	XVIII	XVII	XVI	XV	XIV	XIII	XII	XI
4100	4200	4500	4700	5000	5100	5400	5700	5900	6300
	4300	4600	4800	5200	5300	5500	5800	6000	6400
	4400		4900			5600		6100	
11000	11300	11500	11700	11900	12200	12300	12600	12900	13100
11100	11400	11600	11800	12000	12400	12500	12700	13000	13200
11200		D		12100			12800		1300
17900	18200	18500	18700	19000	19100	19400	19500	19800	20100
18100	18300	18600	1800		19200	19600	19700	19900	20200
	18400		18900		19300			20000	
25000	25100	25400	25700	25900	26200	26300	26600	26700	27000
25200	25300	25500	25800	26000	26400	26500	26800	26900	27100
		25600		26100					27200

Continuation of the Table of Equations

X	IX	VIII	VII	VI	V	IV	III	II	I
6300	6600	6700	7000	7300	7500	7800	7900	8200	8500
6500	6800	6900	7100	7400	7600	8000	8100	8300	8600
			7200		7700			8400	
13400	13500	13800	14100	14200	14500	14700	15000	15200	15400
13600	13700	13900		14300	14600	14800	15100	15300	15500
		14000		14400		14900			15600
20300	20600	20700	2100	21300	21500	21700	21900	22200	22400
20400	20800	20900	21100	21400	21600	21800	2000	22300	22500
20500			21200		C		22100		
27300	27500	27800	27900	28200	28500	28700	29000	29100	29400
27400	27600	28000	28100	28300	28600	28800		29200	29500
	27700			28400		28900		29300	

Second Table of the Epacts for the common years

*
XI
XXII
III
XIV
XXV
VI
XVII
XXVIII
IX
XX
I
XII
XXIII
IV
XV
XXVI
VII
XVIII
XXIX
X
XXI
II
XIII
XXIV
V
XVI
XXVII
VIII
XIX

By what was explained about the Epacts we may not know what were the Epacts before the year of 1700, for the table of equations started in this year and not before. To find the Epacts before 1700, one should know that the Epact of 1500 and 1600 was Epact I, and this is the Epact one should take for the calculation with the Golden Number.

Example

In the year of 1699 the Golden number was 9, which, counted from Epact I on the second table gives us Epact XXIX, and this is the epact for 1699 and so on for all others.

Explanation of the perpetual Table of movable feasts

Having explained the Epact and the Dominical Letters, it will be also good to explain the method of finding the dates of the Movable Feasts, a thing that the Lunario never did by giving the necessary rules for this calculation; for it relied on the Golden Number, and this needs to be corrected every 100 years, for it is a defective method.

In order to find the Movable Feasts perpetually first one should know the Epact and the Dominical Letter, and this Dominical Letter should be found among the seven of this table; and the Epact should be found in the division corresponding to that Letter; once this has been found one only needs to follow that row and find the days of the Movable Feasts.

If the year has two Dominical Letters then it is a leap year, and every time this is found one should go with the second Letter, and to those Feasts which are before March should be added one extra day; this is the Septuagesima and Ash Wednesday that usually fall before March, and should Ash Wednesday fall on March one does not need to change it, only the Septuagesima which is always in January or February.

Example

In the year of 1712 the Dominical Letter is C and B, which makes it a leap year, and so we used the letter B. Its Epact is XXII. I find in the table the letter B, and in this division I find the Epact 22 and I see that the Septuagesima falls on the 23rd of January and Ash Wednesday on the 9th of February; seeing as this is a leap year the Septuagesima turns to the 24th of January and Ash Wednesday to the 10th of February; Easter is on the 27th of March; the Litanies on the 2nd of May; Ascension on the 5th of May; Pentecost on the 15th of May; Corpus Christi on the 27th of November.

Another example

In the year of 1717 the Dominical Letter is C, and the Epact is XVII, by finding this in the row of the Letter C I find the Septuagesima on the 24th of January; Ash Wednesday on the 10th of February; Easter in the 28th of March; Litanies on the 3rd of May; Ascension on the 6th of May; Pentecost on the 16th of May; Corpus Christi on the 28th of May; Advent on the 28th of November.

This Table may also be found in the Breviaries and Missals, and these repeat Epact 25 two times in different colors or different characters. If these are in color, and if they are in black, then the 25 is in red, or, if they are using Castilian numbers, they place the 25 in common numbers,[385] as is done in this Lunario.

In order to understand this Epact, and which one should be used, one only need to understand Epact 25 when the Dominical Letter of the year is C, and in every other year that it is not a C one does not need to make an issue of this. In order to know which one of these should serve, one should look upon the Golden Number of the year whose Letter is C and the Epact 25, and once this is known you must see if the number is eleven or smaller than eleven; if it is so then one should take the Epact of the common color or common character, that which in this table is next to the 24; and if the Golden number exceeds eleven then one should take the one with a distinct color or character, that which in the current table is next to the number 26.

From the non observation of this rule such a remarkable mistake has risen that in some Missals and Breviaries we see in the Movable Feasts that in the year of 1737 Easter falls on the 18th of April, when it should be on the 25th, and these are the years when the feast of Saint John and the Corpus Christi fall on the same day.

With this calculation does Father Clavius respond to the heretic Mitilineo,[386] who wrote against the Gregorian correction.

---

385. Translator's note: the reference to Castilian numbers seems a little strange, but what is meant by this is Roman vs Arabic numerals.
386. Translator's note: Cristoforo Mitilineo.

By this table one is able to calculate the Movable Feasts from the year of 1712 to the year of 1741. And because one does not take care to observe these calculation of Epact 25 over the letter C, in those years in which the Corpus Christi coincides with the feast of Saint John (which are the years in which this error happens) I place these here until the year of 4900, as every time we have Epact 25 (taking those conditions given for the Golden Number) with the letter C, the Corpus Christi will coincide with the feats of Saint John.

Years:	1732	1886	1943	2038	2190
2258	2329	4214	2673	2630	2782
2877	2945	3002	3097	3154	3249
3306	3469	3537	3621	3784	3841
3993	4088	4156	4224	4376	4528
4680	4748	7900			

Of the Day on which one my save a soul by the Bull of the Holy Crusade

Many are those that are unaware of the day on which one may save a soul from Purgatory, for not paying attention to the days mentioned in the Bull of the Holy Crusade, or because this is not usually given in the calculations of the Movable Feasts. For removing a soul from Purgatory follows these rules, and you can do this ten times in a year. The first is on the same Sunday of the Septuagesima; the second is on the first Tuesday of Ashes; the third and fourth on the third Saturday and Sunday of Lent; the fifth on the fourth Sunday of Lent; the sixth and seventh on the Friday and Saturday of Palm Sunday, this is, on the Friday and Saturday before the week of Lent; the eighth is on the Wednesday of the Easter week; the ninth on the Thursday of the week of Pentecost; and the tenth on the Saturday of this same week. And this repeats itself every year.

Perpetual Table of the Movable Feasts

Letter	Epact	Septuagesima	Ash	Easter
D	23	18th January	4th February	22nd March
	22, 31, 20, 19, 18, 17, 16	25th January	11th February	29th March
	15, 14, 13, 12, 11, 10, 9	1st February	18th February	5th April
	8, 7, 6, 5, 4, 3, 2	8th February	25th February	12th April
	1, *, 29, 28, 27, 26, XXV, 25, 24	15th February	4th March	19th April
E	23, 22	19th January	5th February	23rd March
	21, 20, 19, 18, 17, 16, 15	26th January	12th February	30th March
	14, 13, 12, 11, 10, 9, 8	2nd February	19th February	6th April
	7, 6, 5, 4, 3, 2, 1	9th February	26th February	13th April
	*, 29, 28, 27, 26, XXV, 25, 24	16th January	5th March	20th April
F	23, 22, 21	20th January	6th February	24th March
	20, 19, 18, 17, 16, 15, 14	27th January	13th February	31st March
	13, 12, 11, 10, 9, 8, 7	3rd February	20th February	7th April
	6, 5, 4, 3, 2, 1, *	10th February	27th February	14th April
	29, 28, 27, 26, XXV, 25, 24	17th February	6th March	21st April
G	23, 22, 21, 20	21st January	7th February	25th March
	19, 18, 17, 16, 15, 14, 13	28th January	14th February	1st April
	12, 11, 10, 9, 8, 7, 6	4th February	21st February	8th April
	5, 4, 3, 2, 1, *, 29	11th February	28th February	15th April
	28, 27, 26, XXV, 25, 24	18th February	7th March	22nd April
A	23, 22, 21, 20, 19	22nd January	8th February	26th March
	18, 17, 16, 15, 14, 13, 12	29th January	15th February	2nd April
	11, 10, 9, 8, 7, 6, 5	5th February	22nd February	9th April
	4, 3, 2, 1, *, 29, 28	12th February	1st March	16th April
	27, 26, XXV, 25, 24	19th February	8th March	23rd April
B	23, 22, 21, 20, 19, 18	23rd January	9th February	27th March
	17, 16, 15, 14, 13, 12, 11	30th January	16th February	3rd April
	10, 9, 8, 7, 6, 5, 4	6th February	23rd February	10th April
	3, 2, 1, *, 29, 28, 27	13th February	2nd March	17th April
	26, XXV, 25, 24	20th February	9th March	24th April
C	23, 22, 21, 20, 19, 18, 17	24th January	10th February	28th March
	16, 15, 14, 13, 12, 11, 10	31st January	17th February	4th April
	9, 8, 7, 6, 5, 4, 3	7th February	24th February	11th April
	2, 1, *, 29, 28, 27, 26, XXV	14th February	3rd March	18th April
	25, 24	21st February	10th March	25th April

Continuation of the Perpetual Table of the Movable Feasts

Ascension	Pentecost	Corpus Christi	Sunday between Pent. and Adv.	Advent
30th April	10th May	21st May	28	29th November
7th May	17th May	28th May	27	29th November
14th May	24th May	4th June	26	29th November
21st May	31st May	11th June	25	29th November
28th May	7th June	18th June	24	29th November
1st May	11th May	22nd May	28	30th November
8th May	18th May	29th May	27	30th November
15th May	25th May	5th June	26	30th November
22nd May	1st June	12th June	25	30th November
29th May	8th June	19th June	24	30th November
2nd May	12th May	23rd May	28	1st December
9th May	19th May	30th May	27	1st December
16th May	26th May	6th June	26	1st December
23rd May	2nd June	13th June	25	1st December
30th May	9th June	20th June	24	1st December
3rd May	13th May	24th May	28	2nd December
10th May	20th May	31st May	27	2nd December
17th May	27th May	7th June	26	2nd December
24th May	3rd June	14th June	25	2nd December
31st May	10th June	21st June	24	2nd December
4th May	14th May	25th May	28	3rd December
11th May	21st May	1st June	27	3rd December
18th May	28th May	8th June	26	3rd December
25th May	4th June	15th June	25	3rd December
1st June	11th June	22nd June	24	3rd December
5th May	15th May	26th May	27	27th November
12th May	22nd May	2nd June	26	27th November
19th May	29th May	9th June	25	27th November
26th May	5th June	16th June	24	27th November
2nd June	12th June	23rd June	23	27th November
6th May	16th May	27th May	27	28th November
13th May	23rd May	3rd June	26	28th November
20th May	20th May	10th June	25	28th November
27th May	6th June	17th June	24	28th November
3rd June	13th June	24th June	23	28th November

Table of the Times

Years	Letter	G. Number	Epact	Septuagesima	Ash
1836	C D	13	XII	31st January	17th February
1837	A	14	XXIII	22nd January	8th February
1838	G	15	IV	11th February	28th February
1839	F	16	XV	27th January	13th February
1840	E D	17	XXVI	16th February	5th March
1841	C	18	VII	7th February	24th February
1842	B	19	XVIII	23rd January	9th February
1843	A	1	*	12th February	1st March
1844	G F	2	XI	4th February	21st February
1845	E	3	XXII	19th January	4th February
1846	D	4	III	8th February	25th February
1847	C	5	XIV	31st January	17th February
1848	B A	6	XXV	20th February	8th March
1849	G	7	VI	4th February	21st February
1850	F	8	XVII	27th January	13th February
1851	E	9	XXVIII	16th February	5th March
1852	D C	10	IX	8th February	25th February
1853	B	11	XX	23rd February	9th February
1854	A	12	I	12th February	1st March
1855	G	13	XII	4th February	21st February
1856	F E	14	XXIII	20th January	6th February
1857	D	15	IV	8th February	25th February
1858	C	16	XV	31st January	17th February
1859	B	17	XXVI	20th February	9th March
1860	A G	18	VII	5th February	22nd February

APPENDIX I

Table of the Movable Feasts

Easter	Ascension	Pentecost	Corus Christi	Advent
3rd April	12th May	22nd May	2nd June	27th November
26th March	4th May	14th May	25th May	3rd December
15th April	24th May	3rd June	14th June	2nd December
31st March	9th May	19th May	30th May	1st December
19th April	28th May	7th June	18th June	29th November
11th April	20th May	30th May	10th June	28 November
27th March	5th May	15th May	26th May	27th November
16th April	25th May	4th June	15th June	3rd December
7th April	16th May	26th May	6th June	1st December
23rd March	1st May	11th May	22nd May	30th November
12th April	21st May	31st May	11th June	29th November
4th April	13th May	23rd May	3rd June	28th November
23rd April	1st June	11th June	22nd June	3rd December
8th April	17th May	27th May	7th June	2nd December
31st March	9th May	19th May	30th May	1st December
20th April	29th May	8th June	19th June	30th November
11th April	20th May	30th May	10th June	28th November
27th March	5th May	15th May	26th May	27th November
16th April	25th May	4th June	15th June	3rd December
8th April	17th May	27th May	7th June	2nd December
23rd March	1st May	11th May	22nd May	30th November
12th April	21st May	31st May	11th June	29th November
4th April	13th May	23rd May	3rd June	28th November
24th April	2nd May	12th June	23rd June	27th November
8th April	17th May	27th May	7th June	2nd December

Of the Movable Feasts and of the difference these have with the fixed one

The Movable feast are different from the fixed by many reasons; the main among these is that the fixed only mark the festivities of a Saint whose celebration is on that day, and on such a day is his life and death celebrated, without any further mystery than that of his virtues, and there is no change in this day on which he was born or died; the movable ones have in themselves a greater and much more innumerable mystery than the fixed ones; for these were institutionalized by our Redeemer Jesus Christ, in memory of that mystery of the redemption of the human kind, as may be seen by each of the movable feasts according to their own order.

Of the Letter of the Roman Martyrology

Before we explain the following Calendar of the days of the Saints, it will be good, since we explained the Movable feasts, to provide the rule to find the Letter of the Roman Martyrology, which is used for prayers; but these are only needed by Ecclesiastics, and since it is their business to know the why that A, B, C, etc, are upper or lower case I will not provide this information, but

I will provide the letters for the years. In order to learn this one only needs the Epact of the year; and once this is found in the tables below, the Martyrology letter may be found in such a simple way that it does not require an example.

P	N	M	H	G	F	E	D	C	B
*	XXIX	XXVIII	XXVII	XXVI	XXV	XXIV	XXIII	XXII	XXI
A	u	t	s	r	q	p	n	m	L
XX	XIX	XVIII	XVII	XVI	XV	XIV	XIII	XII	XI
k	i	h	g	f	e	d	c	b	a
X	IX	VIII	VII	VI	V	IV	III	II	I

Explanation of the Calendar of the days and non movable feasts

Following there is a calendar with the days of the Saints and the non movable feasts. Those that have the sign of ✠ are the ones that should be kept; those that, have the sign †, mean that one may work before or after Mass; and those with ✷ are for the Court; but as this Lunario is to be used by many provinces, both in Spain as outside of it, each one should insert their own special feast of their Patron, and those that in their province are kept for Court. This one was made according to Madrid, with its precept and Court feasts. The letters coming from the 1st of January and following the order A, B, C, D, E, F and G are the Dominical Letters, that once these are known they can be sought in the edges of the month and they will indicate the days of that year which will be Sundays. The Epacts give the days of the conjunctions, by being sought in the same way as the Dominical. Before this point Cortez usually places an explanation of the General Prognostication of each Kingdom and Province; and this is merely summed up by paying attention to the first thunder of the year, and this prognosis he then places at the end of each month, when speaking of the works of Agriculture and as such we do not include this section here. And one should note that the vigils are only changed on Sunday, this mean that if these fall into any Sunday it is an indication that the Saint in question will be celebrated on Monday. The Abstinences are decided by vote in the City, as that of Saint Michel; and others are made by devotion, being it a day for the Virgin our Lady; and as such, on those that are decided within the City is it allowed to eat meat outside of Madrid, but not in those belonging to any special day of the Virgin. In this Edition we have made some more variations, making the Calendar in accordance with the custom of Barcelona.

JANUARY, 31 days, and 30 lunar

Epact			
*	A	1	✠ Circumcision of the Lord
XXIX	B	2	St. Macarius Abbott
XXVIII	C	3	St. Daniel Martyr
XXVII	D	4	St. Titus Bishop and Confessor
XXVI	E	5	St. Telesphorus Pope and Martyr. Beginning of the Nuptial Blessings
25 XXV	F	6	✠ Day of Kings
XXIV	G	7	St. Raymond of Pennafort Confessor
XXIII	A	8	St. Lucian Martyr
XXII	B	9	St. Marcellinus
XXI	C	10	St. William Archbishop and Gozalo Confessor
XX	D	11	St. Hyginus Pope and Martyr
XIX	E	12	St. Victorian Abbott
XVIII	F	13	St. Hilary Bishop and Confessor
XVII	G	14	St. Felix Presbyter
XVI	A	15	St. Paul 1st hermit and St. Maurus
XV	B	16	St. Marcellus Pope and Martyr and St. Fulgentius
XIV	C	17	✶ The Sweet name of Jesus and St. Anthony the Abbot
XIII	D	18	Cathedra Petri
XII	E	19	St. Canute King and Martyr
XI	F	20	St. Fabian and St. Sebastian Martyrs. *Sun in Aquarius*
X	G	21	St. Fructuosus Bishop and Martyr and St. Agnes Virgin
IX	A	22	St. Vincent and St. Anastasius Martyrs
VIII	B	23	St. Ildephonsus and St. Emerentiana
VII	C	24	Our Lady of Peace and St. Timothy Bishop
VI	D	25	St. Paul's Conversion, Apostle
V	E	26	St. Paula and St. Polycarp Bishop
IV	F	27	St. John Chrysostom, doctor
III	G	28	St. Julian and St. Cyril, bishop
II	A	29	St. Francis de Sales and St. Valerius Bishop
I	B	30	St. Martina Martyr and St. Adelelmus Abbott
*	C	31	St. Peter Nolasco founder

FEBRUARY, 28 days, 29 lunar

Epact			
XXIX	D	1	St. Caecilius and St. Ignatius
XXVIII	E	2	✠ Purification of Our Lady
XXVII	F	3	St. Blaise Bishop and Martyr and the Blessed Nicolas of Longbardis
25 XXVI	G	4	St. Andrew Corsini and St. José of Leonisa
XXV XXIV	A	5	St. Agatha Virgin and Martyr and the blessed Martyr of Japan
XXIII	B	6	St. Dorothea Virgin
XXII	C	7	St. Romuald Abbot
XXI	D	8	✱ St. John of Matta founder
XX	E	9	St. Apollonia Virgin and Martyr
XIX	F	10	St. Scholastica Virgin and St. William
XVIII	G	11	The 7 Blessed servants of Mary
XVII	A	12	St. Eulalia Virgin
XVI	B	13	St. Catherine de Ricci
XV	C	14	St. Valentine Presbyter
XIV	D	15	St. Faustinus and Jovita Martyrs
XIII	E	16	St. Juliana and the five thousand Martyrs
XII	F	17	St. Peter Thomas Bishop
XI	G	18	St. Simon Bishop and Martyr
X	A	19	St. Conrad Confessor
IX	B	20	St. Leo Bishop
VIII	C	21	St. Felix Bishop and Confessor
VII	D	22	Cathedra Petri in Antioch
VI	E	23	St. Margaret of Cortona Widow
V	F	24	† St. Matthias Apostle
IV	G	25	St. Aventanus Confessor
III	A	26	Our Lady of Guadalupe Mexican
II	B	27	St. Baldomerus Confessor and St. Maurice Martyr
I	C	28	St. Romanus Abbot

In a leap year this month has 29 days, and the feast of St. Matthias goes into the 25th

MARCH, 31 day, 30 lunar

Epact			
*	D	1	St. Rudesind and St. Albinus
XXIX	E	2	St. Jovinus and Basileus Martyrs
XXVIII	F	3	St. Hemiterius and Cheledonius
XXVII	G	4	St. Casimir Confessor
XXVI	A	5	St. Eusebius and Blessed and Nicolás Factor
25 XXV	B	6	St. Ollegarius Bishop and Confessor
XXIV	C	7	St. Thomas Aquinas Doctor
XXIII	D	8	St. John of God Founder
XXII	E	9	St. Frances Widow and St. Pacian Bishop
XXI	F	10	The forty Saintly Martyrs
XX	G	11	St. Eulogius Presbyter and Martyr
XIX	A	12	St. Gregory Pope and Doctor
XVIII	B	13	St. Leander Archbishop
XVII	C	14	St. Florentina Virgin and St. Matilda
XVI	D	15	St. Matrona Virgin and St. Raymond of Fitero
XV	E	16	St. Heribert Bishop and Confessor
XIV	F	17	St. Patrick Bishop
XIII	G	18	St. Gabriel Archangel and St. Braulius Bishop
XII	A	19	† St. Joseph husband of Our Lady
XI	B	20	St. Nicetas
X	C	21	St. Benedict Abbott and Founder
IX	D	22	St. Ambrose of Siena
VIII	E	23	St. Victorian Martyr
VII	F	24	St. Agapetus Bishop
VI	G	25	✠ Annunciation of Our Lady
V	A	26	St. Castulus Martyr
IV	B	27	St. Rupert Bishop
III	C	28	St. Sixtus III Pope and Confessor
II	D	29	St. Eustace Abbott and St. Berthold Confessor
I	E	30	St. John Climacus Abbott
*	F	31	St. Balbina Virgin

APRIL, 30 days, 29 lunar

Epact			
XXIX	G	1	St. Venantius Bishop and Martyr
XXVIII	A	2	St. Francis of Paola Founder
XXVII	B	3	St. Theodosia Virgin and St. Benedict of Palermo
25 XXVI	C	4	St. Isidore Achbishop and Doctor
XXV XXIV	D	5	St. Vincent Ferrer
XXIII	E	6	St. Celestine Pope
XXII	F	7	St. Epiphanius
XXI	G	8	St. Dionysius and St. Alberto Bishop and Confessor
XX	A	9	St. Mary of Clopas
XIX	B	10	St. Ezekiel Prophet
XVIII	C	11	St. Leo I Pope and Doctor
XVII	D	12	St. Zeno Bishop and Martyr
XVI	E	13	St. Hermengild Martyr
XV	F	14	St. Peter Gonzales also called St. Telmo and St. Tiburtius
XIV	G	15	St. Basil and St. Anastasius Martyrs
XIII	A	16	St. Turibius Bishop and St. Encratia
XII	B	17	St. Anicetus and Blessed Mariana de Jesús
XI	C	18	St. Eleutherius Bishop
X	D	19	St. Hermogenes Martyr
IX	E	20	St. Agnes of Montepulciano
VIII	F	21	St. Anselm Bishop and Doctor
VII	G	22	St. Soter ans St. Caius
VI	A	23	St. George Martyr
V	B	24	St. Fidelis
IV	C	25	✶ St. Mark Evangelist and St. Anianus Bishop
III	D	26	St. Cletus and Marcellinus Popes and Martyrs
II	E	27	St. Peter Armengol and St. Anastasius
I	F	28	St. Prudence Bishop and St. Vitalis Martyr
*	G	29	St. Peter Martyr Inquisitor
XXIX	A	30	St. Catherine of Siene and St. Pelegrin

MAY, 31 days, 30 lunar

Epact				
XXVIII		B	1	St. Philip and St. James Apostles
XXVII		C	2	St. Athanasius Bishop and Doctor
XXVI		D	3	† Feast of the Cross
25 XXV		E	4	St. Monica Widow
XXIV		F	5	St. Pius Pope and St. Angelo Martyr
XXIII		G	6	St. Ioannis ante Portam Latinam
XXII		A	7	St. Stanislaus Bishop and Martyr
XXI		B	8	✶ Apparition of St. Michael Archangel
XX		C	9	St. Gregory Nazarene
XIX		D	10	St. Anthony Archbishop
XVIII		E	11	St. Anastasius, St. Eudaldo and St. Pontius
XVII		F	12	St. Pancras Martyr
XVI		G	13	St. Peter Regulatus
XV		A	14	St. Boniface Martyr
XIV		B	15	† St. Isidore, the Farmer
XIII		C	16	St. John Nepomucene
XII		D	17	St. Paschal Baylon
XI		E	18	St. Felix of Cantalice Confessor
X		F	19	St. Celestine Pope and St. Ibo Doctor
IX		G	20	St. Bernardine of Siene and St. Baudilius
VIII		A	21	St. Secundinus Martyr
VII		B	22	St. Quiteria and St. Rita of Cascia
VI		C	23	Apparition of St. James the Apostle
V		D	24	St. John Regis Confessor
IV		E	25	St. Gregory Pope
III		F	26	St. Philip Neri Founder
II		G	27	St. John Pope and Martyr
I		A	28	St. Justus Bishop and Confessor
*		B	29	St. Maximus Bishop and Confessor
XXIX		C	30	St. Ferdinand King of Spain
XXVIII		D	31	St. Petronilla Virgin

JUNE, 30 days, 29 lunar

Epact				
XXVII	E	1		St. Simeon
25 XXVI	F	2		St. Marcellus, Peter and Erasmus Martyrs
XXV XXIV	G	3		St. Isaac
XXIII	A	4		St. Francis Caracciolo
XXII	B	5		St. Boniface Bishop
XXI	C	6		St. Norbert Bishop and Founder
XX	D	7		St. Paul bishop and Martyr
XIX	E	8		St. Medard Bishop and Confessor
XVIII	F	9		St. Primus and Felician Martyrs
XVII	G	10		St. Margaret Queen of Scotland Virgin
XVI	A	11		✶ St. Barnabas Apostle
XV	B	12		St. John of Sahagun and St. Onouphrius
XIV	C	13		† St. Anthony of Padua
XIII	D	14		St. Basil Magnus Doctor and Founder
XII	E	15		St. Vitus, Modestus and Crescentia Martyrs
XI	F	16		St. Quiriacus and Julitta and St. Lutgardis
X	G	17		St. Manuel Martyr
IX	A	18		St. Mark and Marcellian Martyrs
VIII	B	19		St. Gervase and Protase Martyrs
VII	C	20		St. Silverius Pope and Martyr
VI	D	21		St. Aloysius Gonzaga
V	E	22		St. Paulinus
IV	F	23		John of Sahagún Presbyter and Martyr
III	G	24		✠ Birth of St. John the Baptist
II	A	25		St. William Bishop
I	B	26		St. John and Paul Martyrs
*	C	27		St. Zoilus
XXIX	D	28		St. Leo II Pope
XXVIII	E	29		✠ St. Paul and St. Peter Apostles
XXVII	F	30		The Celebration of St. Paul Apostle and St. Martial Bishop

JULY, 31 days, 30 lunar

Epact				
XXVI		G	1	St. Gall Bishop and St. Secundinus Martyr
25 XXV		A	2	✶ Visitation of Our Lady
XXIV		B	3	St. Tryphon Martyr
XXIII		C	4	St. Laurianus and the Blessed Gaspar de Bono
XXII		D	5	Blessed Miguel de los Santos
XXI		E	6	St. Romulus Bishop and Martyr
XX		F	7	St. Fermin Bishop and Blessed Lawrence Humphrey
XIX		G	8	St. Elizabeth Queen of Portugal Widow
XVIII		A	9	St. Cyril Bishop and St. Zenon and companions Martyrs
XVII		B	10	St. Christopher Martyr
XVI		C	11	St. Pius I Pope
XV		D	12	St. John Gaulbert Abbott
XIV		E	13	St. Anacletus Pope and Martyr
XIII		F	14	St. Bonaventure Doctor
XII		G	15	St. Camillus de Lellis Funder
XI		A	16	✶ Our Lady of Mount Carmel
X		B	17	St. Alexis Confessor
IX		C	18	St. Symphorosa Martyr
VIII		D	19	St. Vincent de Paul
VII		E	20	St. Elias, St. Margaret and Wilgefortis
VI		F	21	St. Praxedes Virgin
V		G	22	St. Mary Magdelene. Canicular
IV		A	23	St. Liborius Bishop and Confessor
III		B	24	St. Christina Virgin and Martyr. *Vigil*
II		C	25	✠ St. James Apostle, Apostle of Spain
I		D	26	† St. Anne Mother of Our Lady
*		E	27	St. Pantaleon Martyr
XXIX		F	28	St. Nazarius and Celsus Martyrs
XXVIII		G	29	St. Martha Virgin
XXVII		A	30	St. Abdon and St. Zenen Martyrs
25 XXVI		B	31	St. Ignatius Loyola Founder

AUGUST, 31 days, 20 lunar

Epact			
XXV XXIV	C	1	St. Peter ad Vincula, and St. Felix Martyr
XXIII	D	2	✶ Our Lady of the Angels
XXII	E	3	Invention of St. Stephen Protomartyr
XXI	F	4	✶ St. Dominic Guzman Founder
XX	G	5	✶ Our Lady of the Snows
XIX	A	6	✶ Transfiguration of the Lord
XVIII	B	7	✶ St. Cajetan Founder and St. Albert Confessor
XVII	C	8	St. Cyriac Martyr
XVI	D	9	St. Romanus Martyr. *Vigil*
XV	E	10	† St. Lawrence Martyr
XIV	F	11	St. Tiburtius and St. Susanna Martyrs
XIII	G	12	St. Clare Virgin
XII	A	13	St. Hippolytus and St. Cassian Martyrs
XI	B	14	St. Eusebius Confessor. *Vigil*
X	C	15	✠ Assumption of Our Lady
IX	D	16	✶ St. Roch and St. Hyacinth
VIII	E	17	St. Liberatus Abbott
VII	F	18	St. Helena Empress and Virgin and St. Agapitus
VI	G	19	St. Maginus Ermit and Martyr and St. Luiz Beltran Bishop
V	A	20	St. Bernard Abbott
IV	B	21	St. Jane Frances de Chantal Founder
III	C	22	St. Fabrician and Sigfrid Martyrs
II	D	23	St. Philip Benizi. *Vigil. Sun in Virgo*
I	E	24	† St. Bartholomew Apostle
*	F	25	✶ St. Louis King of France
XXIX	G	26	St. Zephyrinus Pope and Martyr
XXVIII	A	27	St. Joseph Calasanz
XVII	B	28	† St. Augustine Bishop, Doctor and Funder
XVI	C	29	Beheading of St. John the Baptist
25 XXV	D	30	St. Rose of Lima Virgin
XXIV	E	31	St. Raymond Nonnatus Confessor

APPENDIX I

SEPTEMBER, 30 days, 29 lunar

Epact			
XXIII	F	1	St. Giles Abbot and St. Lupus Confessor. *End of the Canicular*
XXII	G	2	St. Antoninus Bishop and St. Stephen King
XXI	A	3	St. Sandila Martyr and St. Nonito Confessor
XX	B	4	St. Rosalia and St. Rose of Viterbo
XIX	C	5	St. Lawrence Giustiniani
XVIII	D	6	St. Eugene Martyr
XVII	E	7	St. Regina Virgin and Martyr
XVI	F	8	✠ Nativity of Our Lady
XV	G	9	St. Gregory Martyr
XIV	A	10	St. Nicholas of Tolentino Confessor
XIII	B	11	St. Protus and Hyacinth Martyrs
XII	C	12	St. Silvanus Bishop
XI	D	13	St. Philip Martyr
X	E	14	Feast of the Cross
IX	F	15	St. Nicomedes Martyr
VIII	G	16	St. Cornelius and Cyprian Pope and Martyr
VII	A	17	St. Peter Arbues, St. Lambert and Stigmata of St. Francis
VI	B	18	St. Thomas of Villanova Bishop
V	C	19	St. Januarius Martyr Bishop and Martyr
IV	D	20	St. Eustachius Martyr
III	E	21	† St. Matthew Apostle and Evangelist
II	F	22	St. Maurice Martyr. *Autumn*
I	G	23	† St. Thecla Virgin and Maryr
*	A	24	✶ Our Lady of Mercy
XXIX	B	25	St. Mary de Cervellione Virgin
XXVIII	C	26	St. Cyprian and St. Justina Martyrs
XXVII	D	27	St. Cosmas and Damian Martyrs
25 XXVI	E	28	St. Wenceslaus and Blessed Simon de Rojas
XXV XXIV	F	29	† Dedication of St. Michael Archangel
XXIII	G	30	St. Jerome Doctor and Founder

OCTOBER, 31 days, 30 lunar

Epact			
XXII	A	1	St. Remigius Bishop and Confessor
XXI	B	2	The Guardian Angel
XX	C	3	St. Claudianus Martyr
XIX	D	4	✶ St. Francis of Assisi Founder
XVIII	E	5	St. Flora Bishop and St. Placid and companions
XVII	F	6	St. Bruno Founder
XVI	G	7	St. Mark Pope and Confessor
XV	A	8	St. Bridge and St. Reparata
XIV	B	9	St. Dionysius Areopagite and his companions Martyrs
XIII	C	10	St. Francis Borgia and St. Louis Bertrand
XII	D	11	St. Nicasio Bishop and Martyr
XI	E	12	Our Lady of the Pillar
X	F	13	St. Edward and St. Gerald
IX	G	14	St. Calixtus Pope and Martyr
VIII	A	15	✶ St. Teresa of Avila Virgin and Franciscan
VII	B	16	Blessed Maria de la Encarnacion
VI	C	17	St. Hedwig Widow
V	D	18	✶ St. Luke Evangelist
IV	E	19	St. Peter of Alvantara Confessor
III	F	20	St. Juan Cancio Confessor and St. Caprasius Martyr
II	G	21	St. Ursula and the eleven thousand Virgins Martyrs
I	A	22	St. Mary Salome Widow
*	B	23	St. John of Capistrano and St. Peter Pascual
XXIX	C	24	St. Raphael Archangel and St. Bernard of Calvo
XXVIII	D	25	St. Gabinus, St. Crispin and Crispinian
XXVII	E	26	St. Evaristus Pope
XXVI	F	27	St. Vincent, Sabina and Christeta Martyrs. *Vigil*
25 XXV	G	28	† St. Jude and St. Simon Apostles
XXIV	A	29	† St. Narcissus Bishop and Martyr
XXIII	B	30	St. Claudius Martyr
XXII	C	31	St. Quentin Martyr

NOVEMBER, 30 days, 29 lunar

Epact				
XXI		D	1	✠ Feast of all Saints
XX		E	2	✴ Celebration of the dead
XIX		F	3	The Countless Martyrs of Zaragoza
XVIII		G	4	St. Charles Borromeo
XVII		A	5	St. Zachary and Elizabeth
XVI		B	6	† St. Severus
XV		C	7	St. Florentius Bishop and Confessor
XIV		D	8	The Crowed Martyrs
XIII		E	9	Dedication of the Church of the Savior of Rome and St. Theodore Martyr
XII		F	10	St. Andrew Avellino Confessor
XI		G	11	St. Martin Bishop
X		A	12	St. Martin Pope and St. Didacus of Alcalá
IX		B	13	St. Stanislaus Kostka
VIII		C	14	St. Rufus and Serapius Martyrs
VII		D	15	St. Eugene Archbishop and Martyr
VI		E	16	St. Rufinus Martyr
V		F	17	St. Gertrude Virgin
IV		G	18	Dedication of the Basilica of the Apostles
III		A	19	St. Elizabeth Queen on Hungary Widow
II		B	20	✴ St. Felix of Valois Founder
I		C	21	✴ Presentation of Our Lady
*		D	22	St. Cecilia Virgin Martyr. *Sun in Sagittarius*
XXIX		E	23	St. Celement Pope and Martyr
XXVIII		F	24	St. John of the Cross Confessor
XXVII		G	25	St. Catherine Virgin and Martyr
25 XXVI		A	26	St. Peter Alexander Martyr
XXV XXIV		B	27	St. Facundus and St. Primitivus Martyrs
XXIII		C	28	St. Gregory III Pope
XXII		D	29	St. Saturninus Martyr. *Vigil*
XXI		E	30	† St. Andrew Apostle

DECEMBER, 31 days, 30 lunar

Epact			
XX	F	1	St. Eligius Bisho and Confessor
XIX	G	2	St. Bibiana Virgin and Martyr
XVIII	A	3	St. Francis Xavier Confessor
XVII	B	4	St. Barbara Virgin and Martyr
XVI	C	5	St. Sabas Abbott
XV	D	6	St. Nicholas of Bari Bishop
XIV	E	7	St. Ambrose Archbishop and Doctor
XIII	F	8	✠ Conception of Our Lady
XII	G	9	St. Leocadia Virgin and Martyr
XI	A	10	Our Lady of Loreto
X	B	11	St. Damasus Pope and Confessor
IX	C	12	St. Sinesius
VIII	D	13	St. Lucia Virgin and Martyr
VII	E	14	St. Spyridon Bishop
VI	F	15	St. Eusebius Bishop
V	G	16	St. Valentine Martyr
IV	A	17	St. Lazarus and St. Francis of Siena Confessor
III	B	18	Our Lady of Expectation
II	C	19	St. Nemesius Martyr
I	D	20	St. Dominic of Silos Abbot. *Vigil*
*	E	21	† St. Thomas Apostle. *Winter*
XXIX	F	22	St. Zeno Martyr
XXVIII	G	23	St. Victoria Virgin and Martyr
XXVII	A	24	St. Delphinus Bishop. *Vigil*
XXVI	B	25	✠ Birth of Christ our Lord
25 XXV	C	26	✠ St. Stephen Protomartyr
XXIV	D	27	† St. John the Evangelist
XXIII	E	28	† Holy Innocents Martyrs
XXII	F	29	St. Thomas Archbishop of Canterbury
XXI	G	30	Transference of St. James the Apostle
19 XX	A	31	St. Sylvester Pope and Martyr

Marvelous effect of the Moon on the fluxes and refluxes of the sea

Among the various and many effects that the Moon usually causes, one of them, and quite strange, is the flux and reflux of the sea, which raises and lowers twice in a period of little over twenty four hours by the movement of the Moon, and usually detains itself six hours and a fifth part in each rise and low. These fluxes and refluxes usually happen on every Ocean coast and on a few of the Mediterranean, and sometimes are these rising and lowering, such as on the coast of Panama, that the beach is extended by a length of two leagues, sometimes more sometimes less.

As it is convenient and necessary for sailors to know the hour of the day when the tides start, so as they may enter with their ships in the harbors and docks without danger, it is no less important for a Medic to know this marvelous secret; for, as Pliny writes, and Pero Aponiense confirms, every animal that dies a natural death never does so on the rising tide, but rather on the lowering tide; this is a most worthy thing of being noted and it has been proven by Medics.

For one to know perpetually at which hour of the day will each high or low tide begin, one should first know which day of the Moon it is on the day we wish to know the tide. To know the days of the Moon one may do so with the following Table, on the first column at the left, and after that to the right, one will find the hour at which every high and low of the sea begins on that day. And one should know that the following Table is made up of five columns; the first column of this Table starts with what is understood as the day of the new Moon, which is not a complete day, for it is assumed to begin at midday and ends at the midday of the following day. The first day of the Moon is understood as beginning at the midday of that day noted at the edge with the number 1, and it ends in the midday of the number 2; for it is supposed that the first day does not begin but after twenty four hours and four fifths. The letter A at the side of the hours indicates afternoon, and the M indicates morning. In the fifth column one will find the small letters m.d., which signifies midday and m.n., midnight.

In order to know the day of the conjunction of the Moon with the Sun, one only needs to know the Epact of the year of that conjunction; once the Epact is known one should add to it as many days as months have passed since March until the month one wishes to know the conjunction, and this sum one should subtract from 30, if this is the amount of days in the month, otherwise subtract from 31 or 29, and the result shall be the day of the conjunction.

Example

I wish to know the conjunction of the month of August of the year of 1713, whose Epact is 3, and there are 6 months between March and August, which adds to 9, which subtracted from 30 gives us 21, and so I may say that on the 21st of August there is a conjunction; and so forth for all others.

The same can be seen if we search for Epact 3 in the Calendar of the month of August. But here we may see that Epact 3 falls on the 22nd and not the 21st, but this means nothing because in 200 years these become equivalent, both the example and the Calendar. And for this calculation, and all that may follow, one only needs to make this calculation in this manner which will give you the average conjunction.

Days of the Moon	1st high tide			1st low tide			2nd high tide			2nd low tide		
	H.	f.		H.	f.		H.	f.		H.	f.	
1	3	4	M	10	0	M	4	1	A	10	2	A
2	4	3	M	10	4	M	5	0	A	11	1	A
3	5	2	M	11	3	M	5	4	A	12	0	m.n.
4	6	1	M	12	2	A	6	3	A	12	4	M
5	7	0	M	1	1	A	7	2	A	1	3	M
6	7	4	M	2	0	A	8	1	A	1	2	M
7	8	3	M	2	4	A	9	0	A	3	1	M
8	9	1	M	3	3	A	9	4	A	4	0	M
9	10	2	M	4	2	A	10	3	A	4	4	M
10	11	0	M	5	1	A	11	2	A	5	3	M
11	11	4	M	6	0	A	12	1	M	6	2	M
12	12	3	A	6	4	A	1	0	M	7	1	M
13	1	2	A	7	3	A	1	4	M	8	0	M
14	2	1	A	8	2	A	2	3	M	8	4	M
15	3	0	A	9	1	A	3	2	M	9	3	M
16	3	4	A	10	0	A	4	1	M	10	2	M
17	4	3	A	10	4	A	5	0	M	11	1	M
18	5	2	A	11	2	A	5	4	M	12	0	m.d.
19	6	1	A	12	2	M	6	3	M	12	4	A
20	7	0	A	1	1	M	7	2	M	1	3	A
21	7	4	A	2	0	M	8	1	M	2	2	A
22	8	3	A	2	4	M	9	0	M	3	1	A
23	9	2	A	3	3	M	9	4	M	4	0	A
24	10	1	A	4	2	M	10	3	M	4	4	A
25	11	0	A	5	1	M	11	2	M	5	3	A
26	11	4	A	6	0	M	12	1	A	6	2	A
27	12	3	M	6	4	M	1	0	A	7	1	A
28	1	2	M	7	3	M	1	4	A	8	0	A
29	3	1	M	8	2	M	2	3	A	8	4	A
30	3	0	M	9	1	M	3	2	A	9	3	A

And so as this may be made clearer, and this table understood, we shall give an example; by it that we wish to know at which time starts the rising and lowering of the tide on the 4th of September of 1713. I check, on this 4th of September, how many days have passed since the conjunction, and as the last conjunction was on the 22nd, 14 days have passed; I then go to the table and find this number on the left side, and I see in front of this, that the first crescent of the said 4th of September will be at 2 and 1 fifth of the afternoon; and the second crescent will be at 2 hours and 3 fifths in the morning of the next day; and its first low is at 8 hours and 2 fifths in the afternoon of the 4th; and by this example may one easily understand all the others.

APPENDIX I

Of the Canicular days, when they begin and end

Of these Canicular days Cortez speaks in this place, and he, just as any other astronomer, relates the cause of this heat to a great Star called Dog, which is found in Leo; but I have never been able to convince myself that the heat which is felt in these days, called the Canicular, emanated from Canis Major and Canis Minor, but rather that this emanates from the Sign of Leo, on which the Sun enters usually on the 22nd of July; as this is also the beginning of the Canicular Days. This opinion is probable, for this is always felt on the 22nd of July. Geminiano,[387] master of Procio,[388] certifies this 80 years before the coming of Christ our Lord into the world. Of this same opinion are the most relevant astronomer mathematicians, such as Patabio,[389] Lebara,[390] Pliny, Barròn,[391] Columella and Manilio.[392] This, and by that which is told of this star of Dog, which by its movements was seen in March, and today is seen in the beginning of August, and in a few centuries will be seen in September. Another reason which further confirms this truth is that those who follow this Star usually take the Cosmic Setting and Heliacal Rising and depending on the height of the Pole, they vary the beginning of the Caniculars in over 15 days; and by taking a look at the histories of different peoples of the world, living in different Pole heights, they all mark the beginning of this heat at the 22nd or 21st of July. Some astrologers, who are not mathematicians, may argue that this heat is caused by the Star, which is of a Martial nature. And to this I respond that there are plenty of other Stars of this same nature that do not cause such effects when the Sun passes by them as it does when the Sun passes by Leo; Furthermore, in our antipodes, like those inhabiting the austral part, such as Chile, experience the Canicular heat in Winter. For these and other reasons I say that the Canicular should be counted by all inhabitants of the Septentrional zone at the 22nd of July. The heat of these days, it seems to my limited knowledge, to be over the greater heights that the Sun takes over the Horizon in the Opposing Signs; for just as Gemini is the opposition of Cancer, and these signs are around the months of June and July, the Sun ends up consuming all the Humidity of Winter and Summer, a thing it cannot achieve in Gemini alone, but entering in Cancer it consumes all of it, and entering in Leo afterwards so does the heat start. And what causes greater or lower heat from one year to the other are the transit of the Planets through Leo; for we have seen that, while Saturn is in Leo, we experience temperate Canicular, as those of 1710, 1711 and 1712, for in these years Saturn was in Leo. We can conclude from this that the Canicular start at the 22nd of July and last 30 days, as says Gottardo of 1815, but I am not opposed that these last 30 days, depending on the disposition of the Planets around this time, may even extend itself to 40 days, or not even reach 30, nor am I opposed that during these days Medics should avoid purging, bloodlettings or applying any form of medicine without great necessity. Wine, according to Pliny, should be kept safe from this heat; and this is achieved by washing the cellars with fresh well water, as well as the vats where the wine is kept. Women should pay attention to something very curious on these days, that if they grind salt very finely during the Canicular it will preserve itself for the whole year without getting humid, unless you have a very rainy Winter; this curiosity is useful so as silver salt shakers do not acquire mold, for by grinding the salt is all the humidity gone and no more may enter it. Around this time one should take care that dogs have plenty of water; for if they do not, they may become rabid; and may God our Lord Jesus Christ keep us from that evil.

---

387. Translator's note: uncertain reference.
388. Translator's note: uncertain reference.
389. Translator's note: uncertain reference.
390. Translator's note: uncertain reference.
391. Translator's note: uncertain reference.
392. Translator's note: likely to be Marco Manílio, a Roman poet and astrologer.

Declaration of the tables of the conjunctions and fulls of the Sun and Moon, from the year of 1712 to 1742, and perpetually afterwards[393]

In order to know the conjunctions and fulls of the Sun and the Moon from the year of 1712 to 1742, one does not need to do more than to search in the current tables and look for the year one wishes to know about in one of them; on the edge one can then search for the month and on this line one will find the days and hours of the conjunctions or fulls. These hours and minutes are hours like the astronomical mathematicians count them, which is from one midday until the next midday; which results that if the hours do not exceed 12, then these will refer to hours of the afternoon or night, and if they exceed the 12 then these will be hours of the next day. They call all the hours between one day and the next the *horas post meridiem*, which are the ones used in these tables; but the civil calculation takes the ones from 12 in the day until 12 at night, and from the 12 at night until the 12 at day. And all of this will be much better understood with the following examples.

I wish to know the conjunction and the fulls of the Sun and Moon on the month of March of 1717; I find this year in Table 6. In the month of March, which is at the edge of the table I see that the conjunction is in 12 days, 15 hours and 59 minutes, marked with the sign L, and we will not pay attention to the ones marked with M as these are used to perpetuate these Tables, and they will be explained in due time. In the full I see 26 days 16 hours and 27 minutes *post meridiem*; this is, according to the astronomical calculation; which in the civil one these become 13 days, 3 hours and 59 minutes, in the morning; and this because to the astronomical 12 days one adds 12 hours, and because of that from the 15 hours we have subtracted 12 we have 3 hours and 59 minutes left. The full will be on day 25, 4 hours and 27 minutes of the afternoon; and in this same way in all hours which are passed 12, from which one always needs to subtract 12, and what is left is set in the morning of the next day, and this rule should be observed in all the conjunctions and fulls of the Sun and the Moon.

These Tables are 31, and they are used for the years of 1712 until 1742, and after these they are once again useful for another 31 years, starting from 1743 until 1773. To these years we will refer as years of the first revolution, the ones which are marked with 1 R, which mean precisely first revolution. Next to these years there is the number 2 and in some 3; and this means that to these years one should add this number to the days of the conjunctions and fulls of the first revolution, further adding that in these years the conjunctions should be read as fulls and the fulls as conjunctions; the minutes of the edge of the Table are minutes one should subtract from the minutes of the hours of the conjunctions. This meaning that in 31 years one shall have the same conjunctions and fulls, switched among themselves minus the minutes at the edge, which are the ones which are subtracted from two days in the non leap years and three in leap years. The understanding of this is made easier with an example.

In the year of 1743 I wish to know the full of the month of March; by what was said about switching the conjunctions I seek the conjunction instead, and I see that it is at day 22, 11 hours and 18 minutes; adding the two more days this will be 24 days, 12 hours and 18 minutes; and from these 18 minutes I subtract the 25 from the edge, and I have 53 left, but as we are subtracting a number by one which is larger than it, we have to subtract one to the hours, which have 60 minutes, and so we have that the full of March comes on the day 24, 11 hours and 53 minutes *post meridiem*, and since this does not pass the 12 hours it means at 22 and 53 minutes in the evening.

The conjunction is at day 6, 22 hours and 45 minutes; this, by adding to the 6 becomes 8 days, 22 hours and 45 minutes; and from these I subtract 21 from the edge and I have 24, and so I can say that the conjunction is at day 8, 22 hours and 24 minutes, *post meridiem*, which according to the civilian calculation becomes 10 and 24 in the morning of the 9th.

---

393. Translator's note: The tables described are probably riddled with errors, as the original examples have absolutely no correspondence to them, making it a challenge to interpret any of these instructions. I tried my best to align the Tables with the examples given, but I cannot be sure about any of the values mentioned in these.

The conjunction of April of this same year of 1743 is at day 5, 13 hours and 2 minutes, and in an equal manner I subtract the 22 minutes from the edge and I get 40 minutes, reducing the hours from 13 to 12, and by adding 2 to the 5 days I can say that the conjunction of this month of April of 1743 is at day 7, 12 hours and 40 minutes. These hours are *post meridiem*, which are 12 hours and 40 minutes in the evening. And this same process may be observed for all years between 1743 and 1773.

From the year of 1774 until 1804 we once again have the same conjunctions and fulls, adding this time 4 days on common years and 5 on those that are leap years. These numbers are next to each year and above the years we have 2 R, which means second revolution. The minutes at the edge are now subtracted two times, the conjunction are once again the conjunctions and the fulls the fulls; this because after another 31 years and two days the Moon is in the opposite position as it was 31 years ago; and in this same way we can say that after 6 days it will be in the same position it was 62 years ago.

And this may be seen with a few operations of the conjunctions of the years between 1774 and 1804. Be it that I want to know the day of the full of the month of March of the year of 1774, I have 6 days, 22 hours and 45 minutes, I subtract to the 45 two times 21 and I have 3 left, and I add 4 to the 6 days and I get 10; and so I can say that the full of the month of March of the year of 1774 is at day 10, 22 hours and 3 minutes *post meridiem*, and according to the civilian calculation this is 10 and 3 minutes of the morning of the 11th.

The conjunction is at day 22, which by adding 4 becomes day 26, 12 hours and 18 minutes; from this we subtract two times 25, and we have 28 left, and we reduce one hour from the 12 hours, and so I say that the conjunction is on the 26th of March, at 11 hours and 28 minutes *post meridiem*, and in the civilian calculation this is the same hour, for it does not exceed 12 hours and we say it is at 11 and 18 minutes in the evening of the 26th. And this should be performed on all other years

When it happens that the days of the conjunctions or fulls exceed 30 or 31 (which are the number of days in the month) given the addition of days for each revolution, the exceeding days are counted in the next month. Example: The conjunction of September of this same year is at the 30th day, 3 hours and 29 minutes, which, by adding the 4 days will end up being 34 days; I subtract the 30 days of September and have the 4th of October; and so I can say that the conjunction is at day 4, 3 hours and 29 minutes, I subtract from the 29 minutes two times 26 and I get 37 minutes with one less hour, and so I may say that the conjunction is at day 4, 2 hours and 37 minutes *post meridiem*, and according to the civilian calculation it's at 2 and 37 minutes in the afternoon of the 4th of October. Taking this into consideration we should not have to offer anymore examples for the year of 1774 until 1804.

There is one warning left, which is that from the year 1800 on one should add to the conjunctions and fulls, apart from the days already indicated, one extra day, and this is because of the day which is to be removed from 1800 according to the scheduled reformation. And this will be better understood with an example: be it the same year of 1800 which is found in Table 27, which is also used for the year of 1738 without any other addition, I see that the full is on the 4th of March; I add 5 days, which are the ones specified and I get 9, and one more from the reformation and I get 10, and so I say that the full of the month of March of 1800 is at day 10, 21 hours and 8 minutes, minus the two times 24 minutes, which is equal to 20 minutes minus one hour; so finally I say that the full of the month of March of 1800 is in day 10, 20 hours and 20 minutes *post meridiem*, and according to the civilian calculation this is at 8 hours and 20 minutes of the 11th. In this way one may make the same for every year above 1800, always adding an extra day.

For those years between 1805 and 1835, which are another 31 years, one does not need to give any further warnings if one pays attention to the days needed to be added and which are at the side of the years. Near these we have a 3 R, which mean third revolution, and by third revolution it means that we have to add to the hours and minutes the minutes on the edge three times, and as this is an uneven revolution we switch the conjunction by the full, also not forgetting the day we must add to the years after 1800. What was said should be enough to extract the conjunctions and fulls of the years between 1805 and 1835, but it will be nonetheless good to perform an operation, and be it that I want to know the day of conjunction of March in the year of 1815. I find this year in Table 11; next to this year we have the number 7, which are the 7 days one should add, and one more for being a year above 1800, and so we have 8 days, and by adding this to the 2 days of the full Moon, which here stands for the conjunction, we can thus say that the conjunction is on day 10, 16 hours and 13 minutes, which, by subtracting three times 15 results in 28, and thus we can say that the conjunction is on day 10, 15 hours and 28 minutes *post meridiem*, which in the civilian calculation becomes day 11, 3 hours and 28 minutes in the morning.

In May of this same year the conjunction is in the 30th, and 5 and 53 minutes *post meridian*, and this without making any calculation. To do this I have to add 8 days to the 30, seven from the year and one extra over the 1800s, making up 38 days, I subtract from the 38 March's 31 and I have 7, which are the 7th of June, and I subtract from the 5 hours and 53 minutes the 36 minutes of the edge three times, which are 1 hour and 48 minutes, which, subtracting from the 5 hours and 53 minutes, results in 4 hours and 5 minutes, and so I can say that the conjunction of the Sun and the Moon is on the 7th of July, at 4 hours and 7 minutes *post meridiem*; and according to the civilian calculation it is in the same day and hour, but in the afternoon; and in this way may one operate on all months belonging to these years between 1805 and 1835.

For the years between 1836 and 1866 to all Moons one need to add 9 days, which are the days on the top of the Table, and one more for the 1800s, making up 10, and the minutes at the edge are subtracted four times, and in this revolution the fulls are fulls and the conjunctions are conjunctions. And all other effects are like those we have already seen.

This calculation is enhanced or made perpetual in the following manner. Below the year of 1743 one should write 1867, in that of 1774 write 1898, and in that of 1805 write 1929 and in that of 1836 write 1960. Having these years thus placed you will have the year of 1867 in the first revolution, and by it the same 2 days as the year 1743, for the year of 1898 4 days and 2 R, for the year of 1929 7 days and 3 R and for the year of 1960 9 days and 4 R. Once this has been understood one can increase the years in groups of 31, but it is most important to remember to place these years in the correct 1 R, 2 R, 3 R or 4 R, for one always needs to know how many days to add to the conjunctions, for in the year of 1867, one add 2 days, which are the ones from the first revolution and further 9, which are the ones coming from the previous four revolutions, resulting in 11 days, plus one from the 1800s results in 12 days; and one also need to subtract the minutes at the edge 5 times, one for the first revolution and 4 for the last four revolutions. And to proceed with the years from 1867 until 1897, one does not need to do anything else but align to the year of 1744 that of 1868 and to 1745 that of 1869, and so forth for the 31 years between 1867 until 1896, and this will go on until Table 31, which is the one for the year of 1773, and because this has 3 days, those that need to be added are 13, 3 for the first revolution, 1 for the 1800s and nine over the previous four revolutions, always noting that in the 1 R and 3 R one switches the conjunctions and fulls.

For the year of 1898 one should add 14 days, 4 for the second revolution, 9 for the previous four and 1 for the 1800s, which added together make 14, and one needs to subtract the minutes at the edge 6 times, for there are 6 revolutions. The 31 years between 1898 and 1902 are worked in the same way as explained before, meaning that where one had 1775 one should now have 1899 and where we had 1776 one should put 1900, which are in Table 3, and so forth until this ends in the year of 1911 in Table 31 where we have 1897.

In Table 3, where we have 1900, for being a new centennial year, adding to the 5 days that were used for the year of 1776, to the 9 from the previous four revolutions one should add two more days, one for the 1800s and one for the 1900s, and all of this together adds up to 16 days; and for being an even number of revolutions one uses the conjunctions and fulls normally.

The year of 1929, which falls in the same place as the year of 1805, has next to it 7 days, together with the 9 from the previous four revolutions add to 16, plus two from the 1800s and 1900s results in 18 days, and these are the amount of days that need to be added to the Moons of 1929. The minutes at the edge should be subtracted seven times and because this is an odd revolution one switches the aspects.

From the year of 1960, which falls in the year of 1836 one should add 20 days, 9 for the four revolutions, 9 for the days of the year of 1836 and 2 for the 1800s and 1900s. Because this is an even revolution is it not necessary to change the conjunctions.

From what was said one may see that to the years after 1960, which is the one fulfilling Table 31, by adding more years from 1962 on, the same should be observed, always adding to the years of the first Table every 31 years; this means that over the years of 1743 and 1867, one may now put the year of 1991, over 1774 and 1898 one adds 2022, and in this way one may perpetuate the tables to the infinite, observing that in the year of 1991 more than the 2 days which should be added in this table, one should add 20, which may be found from the revolutions ending in 1990, which are now 8 which are added to the 2 days, the 1800s and 1900s should also be added to the days; all this meaning that for every 4 revolutions one should add 9 days; if we have 8 revolutions then these are 18 days, 12 revolutions 27 and 16 revolutions 32. Any time any day is taken from the centennials this day should also be added, as was done in 1800 and 1900. The years which are subtracted from the centennials over the leap years are mentioned in the table for the increase of the centennials for the years of the Dominical Letters, and these are those marked with the numbers 1, 2, 3 and 4, while not making a case of 1700 (in the *Perpetual table for the four Rows of the Dominical Letters*), for this is already arranged in these tables; and so in the tables where we have the years of 2100, 2200 and 2300 one should add 5 days, 2 for 1800 and 1900 and 3 for 2100, 2200 and 2300, not making a case of the years of 2000 and 2400 or those which fall in the number 1; for these are the centennials from which we do not subtract a leap year, and we further remind that one should subtract the minutes on the edge of the table the number of times of the number of revolutions. In the following table one has the method by which to increase the days in the years of the following columns, and it has as a base the principle of the first table with its four revolutions, and next to it its days. Having this into considerations for the first table, one may follow with the rules already explained.

Table of the years and days which should be added to the first table of the conjunction and fulls.[394]

1 R	Days	2 R	Days	3 R	Days	4 R	Days
1723	2	1774	4	1805	7	1836	9
1867	11	1898	13	1929	16	1960	18
1991	20	2022	22	2053	25	2084	27
2115	29	2146	31	2177	35	2208	36
2239	38	2270	40	2301	43	2332	45
2363	47	2394	39	2425	52	2456	54

One may see in this table how the year rises from 31 in 31, as the days from 2 in 2, except on those which are leap years in which it is from 3 in 3. These calculations differs very little from those which are made through rigorous calculus of the motions of the Moon, and it would not be an easy task to offer in this Lunario the rule by which to adjust the conjunctions; for it would be necessary that the readers be familiar with the principles of astronomical computation and calculus; and should this be something which may seem pleasing, you may ask your bookseller for the second volume of the Lunario, in which the paths used to find the locations of the Planets and the Signs may be used as a perpetual ephemeris.

---

394. Translator's note: it should be noted that the days in this table do not include the days one must add on account of the centennial.

1 R		2 R		3 R		4 R	
1743	2	1774	4	1805	7	1836	9

Table 1   Of the year of 1712

Months	Aspects	Days	H	L	Min
March	Full	6	22	45	21
March	Conjunction	22	11	18	25
April	Full	5	13	2	22
April	Conjunction	20	22	31	32
May	Full	5	4	5	24
May	Conjunction	20	6	34	37
June	Full	3	19	32	26
June	Conjunction	18	12	27	40
July	Full	3	10	18	28
July	Conjunction	17	21	2	39
August	Full	2	0	50	18
August	Conjunction	16	4	21	36
September	Full	14	14	13	30
September	Conjunction	30	3	29	26
October	Full	14	2	40	23
October	Conjunction	29	15	38	26
November	Full	12	18	27	16
November	Conjunction	28	4	42	26
December	Full	12	12	44	12
December	Conjunction	27	13	25	27
January	Full	11	8	16	10
January	Conjunction	25	23	46	20
February	Full	10	3	20	12
February	Conjunction	14	24	59	20

APPENDIX I

1 R		2 R		3 R		4 R	
1744	2	1775	4	1806	6	1837	9

Table 2   Of the year of 1713

Months	Aspects	Days	H	L	Min
March	Full	11	20	30	18
March	Conjunction	25	21	19	26
April	Full	10	10	31	25
April	Conjunction	24	9	6	28
May	Full	8	21	36	32
May	Conjunction	23	21	49	28
June	Full	8	6	25	37
June	Conjunction	21	11	28	29
July	Full	7	14	12	40
July	Conjunction	22	1	5	27
August	Full	5	20	52	39
August	Conjunction	20	16	41	25
September	Full	4	4	19	36
September	Conjunction	19	9	12	22
October	Full	3	13	29	30
October	Conjunction	19	0	43	21
November	Full	2	0	54	24
November	Conjunction	17	15	14	21
December	Full	1	15	4	28
December	Conjunction	17	4	44	13
January	Full	15	18	3	25
January	Conjunction	30	2	56	12
February	Full	14	2	12	27
February	Conjunction	28	31	44	13

1 R		2 R		3 R		4 R	
1745	3	1776	5	1807	7	1838	9

Table 3   Of the year of 1714

Months	Aspects	Days	H	L	Min
March	Full	15	6	29	9
March	Conjunction	30	15	15	18
April	Full	13	21	14	13
April	Conjunction	29	6	21	25
May	Full	13	6	32	33
May	Conjunction	28	18	54	32
June	Full	11	17	7	33
June	Conjunction	27	5	4	36
July	Full	11	4	41	31
July	Conjunction	26	13	37	38
August	Full	9	18	39	27
August	Conjunction	24	21	31	37
September	Full	8	10	9	22
September	Conjunction	23	5	21	34
October	Full	8	3	5	18
October	Conjunction	22	14	25	30
November	Full	6	20	36	16
November	Conjunction	21	1	1	25
December	Full	6	13	25	17
December	Conjunction	20	13	54	21
January	Full	5	4	43	16
January	Conjunction	19	5	18	16
February	Full	3	19	40	23
February	Conjunction	17	21	2	14

1 R		2 R		3 R		4 R	
1746	2	1777	5	1808	7	1839	9

Table 4   Of the year of 1715

Months	Aspects	Days	H	L	Min
March	Full	5	4	22	27
March	Conjunction	19	15	39	16
April	Full	3	13	27	32
April	Conjunction	18	8	41	20
May	Full	2	21	20	35
May	Conjunction	18	0	26	25
June	Full	1	5	6	37
June	Conjunction	16	14	12	30
July	Full	14	1	53	33
July	Conjunction	29	23	58	33
August	Full	14	13	34	33
August	Conjunction	28	12	25	27
September	Full	12	27	57	33
September	Conjunction	27	7	45	21
October	Full	12	7	2	31
October	Conjunction	26	20	50	15
November	Full	10	16	17	29
November	Conjunction	25	15	25	12
December	Full	10	2	32	26
December	Conjunction	25	10	5	13
January	Full	8	14	9	23
January	Conjunction	24	2	18	16
February	Full	7	3	18	20
February	Conjunction	22	17	31	21

1 R		2 R		3 R		4 R	
1747	2	1778	4	1809	7	1840	9

Table 5 — Of the year of 1716

Months	Aspects	Days	H	L	Min
March	Full	7	18	0	19
March	Conjunction	23	5	22	28
April	Full	6	9	25	20
April	Conjunction	21	4	25	33
May	Full	6	1	11	24
May	Conjunction	20	22	10	38
June	Full	4	17	35	29
June	Conjunction	19	7	20	40
July	Full	4	4	20	29
July	Conjunction	18	12	26	38
August	Full	2	20	53	29
August	Conjunction	16	21	7	34
September	Full	1	9	41	29
September	Conjunction	15	8	11	28
October	Full	14	22	15	21
October	Conjunction	30	8	18	27
November	Full	13	15	12	14
November	Conjunction	28	19	49	27
December	Full	13	9	13	11
December	Conjunction	28	5	0	27
January	Full	12	5	45	11
January	Conjunction	26	11	34	25
February	Full	10	21	58	14
February	Conjunction	25	1	2	24

APPENDIX I

1 R		2 R		3 R		4 R	
1748	2	1779	4	1810	7	1841	9

Table 6   Of the year of 1717

Months	Aspects	Days	H	L	Min
March	Full	26	16	27	21
March	Conjunction	12	15	59	25
April	Full	11	6	29	27
April	Conjunction	15	4	6	26
May	Full	20	14	27	44
May	Conjunction	24	15	42	27
June	Full	8	22	21	29
June	Conjunction	23	8	48	28
July	Full	8	5	15	40
July	Conjunction	22	22	32	27
August	Full	6	22	5	36
August	Conjunction	21	14	41	26
September	Full	4	20	26	34
September	Conjunction	20	5	34	24
October	Full	4	6	18	28
October	Conjunction	19	19	43	23
November	Full	2	19	0	22
November	Conjunction	18	8	53	23
December	Full	2	11	8	16
December	Conjunction	17	20	39	19
January	Full	1	5	3	12
January	Conjunction	17	7	29	26
February	Full	31	0	17	10
February	Conjunction	14	14	46	7

1 R		2 R		3 R		4 R	
1749	3	1780	5	1811	7	1842	9

Table 7   Of the year of 1718

Months	Aspects	Days	H	L	Min
March	Full	1	18	13	13
March	Conjunction	16	3	35	28
April	Full	14	13	38	20
April	Conjunction	30	1	51	27
May	Full	14	0	9	31
May	Conjunction	29	13	30	34
June	Full	12	13	53	31
June	Conjunction	27	21	52	38
July	Full	12	1	0	29
July	Conjunction	27	5	45	39
August	Full	10	15	38	26
August	Conjunction	25	14	34	37
September	Full	9	7	36	22
September	Conjunction	23	20	56	34
October	Full	9	0	10	29
October	Conjunction	23	6	20	20
November	Full	7	10	32	18
November	Conjunction	21	18	3	23
December	Full	7	8	19	19
December	Conjunction	21	8	14	18
January	Full	5	22	8	21
January	Conjunction	20	0	57	14
February	Full	4	9	47	25
February	Conjunction	18	18	51	18

1 R		2 R		3 R		4 R	
1750	2	1781	4	1812	7	1843	9

Table 8   Of the year of 1719

Months	Aspects	Days	H	L	Min
March	Full	5	19	56	28
March	Conjunction	20	13	2	15
April	Full	4	4	44	31
April	Conjunction	19	5	43	21
May	Full	13	14	52	35
May	Conjunction	8	21	9	27
June	Full	1	15	44	36
June	Conjunction	17	9	24	32
July	Full	1	7	30	35
July	Conjunction	16	20	3	35
August	Full	15	5	13	36
August	Conjunction	29	8	44	26
September	Full	13	13	52	34
September	Conjunction	28	0	29	20
October	Full	12	22	28	32
October	Conjunction	27	18	25	15
November	Full	11	7	44	28
November	Conjunction	26	12	41	13
December	Full	10	18	40	25
December	Conjunction	26	6	42	15
January	Full	9	7	21	21
January	Conjunction	24	22	2	18
February	Full	7	21	54	18
February	Conjunction	23	10	57	24

1 R		2 R		3 R		4 R	
1751	2	1782	5	1813	7	1844	9

Table 9 — Of the year of 1720

Months	Aspects	Days	H	L	Min
March	Full	8	13	55	17
March	Conjunction	23	21	28	29
April	Full	7	5	45	19
April	Conjunction	22	5	58	34
May	Full	6	22	57	23
May	Conjunction	21	12	56	38
June	Full	5	13	52	17
June	Conjunction	10	21	29	39
July	Full	5	3	48	37
July	Conjunction	19	4	51	31
August	Full	3	16	26	33
August	Conjunction	17	14	49	32
September	Full	2	3	46	26
September	Conjunction	16	16	13	8
October	Full	1	1	16	19
October	Conjunction	15	15	36	13
November	Full	14	14	22	28
November	Conjunction	29	29	11	11
December	Full	14	14	53	26
December	Conjunction	28	28	36	12
January	Full	13	13	50	24
January	Conjunction	27	27	14	16
February	Full	12	12	1	16
February	Conjunction	25	25	17	22

1 R		2 R		3 R		4 R	
1752	2	1783	4	1814	6	1845	9

Table 10   Of the year of 1721

Months	Aspects	Days	H	L	Min
March	Full	31	20	42	22
March	Conjunction	27	9	52	22
April	Full	11	21	39	29
April	Conjunction	26	21	10	24
May	Full	11	6	24	35
May	Conjunction	25	14	53	26
June	Full	9	0	8	39
June	Conjunction	24	3	46	27
July	Full	6	20	41	40
July	Conjunction	23	21	0	28
August	Full	7	4	4	38
August	Conjunction	22	11	28	27
September	Full	9	13	48	33
September	Conjunction	21	1	16	26
October	Full	5	0	6	26
October	Conjunction	20	14	1	25
November	Full	2	13	1	19
November	Conjunction	19	10	0	25
December	Full	3	7	20	14
December	Conjunction	18	12	45	26
January	Full	2	2	31	10
January	Conjunction	16	22	14	26
February	Full	31	11	27	51
February	Conjunction	15	9	34	27

	1 R		2 R		3 R		4 R	
	1753	2	1784	5	1815	7	1846	9

Table 11   Of the year of 1722

Months	Aspects	Days	H	L	Min
March	Full	2	16	13	15
March	Conjunction	16	20	2	27
April	Full	15	6	54	28
April	Conjunction	30	21	11	29
May	Full	14	19	43	29
May	Conjunction	30	5	53	30
June	Full	13	7	25	29
June	Conjunction	28	13	59	39
July	Full	12	21	56	29
July	Conjunction	27	21	10	39
August	Full	11	13	4	25
August	Conjunction	26	4	13	37
September	Full	10	4	25	23
September	Conjunction	24	12	40	33
October	Full	9	20	47	21
October	Conjunction	24	0	30	27
November	Full	8	12	9	20
November	Conjunction	22	12	545	21
December	Full	8	1	14	22
December	Conjunction	22	2	36	15
January	Full	6	14	45	24
January	Conjunction	20	21	40	12
February	Full	5	2	4	26
February	Conjunction	19	16	26	12

APPENDIX I

1 R		2 R		3 R		4 R	
1754	2	1785	5	1816	7	1847	9

Table 12   Of the year of 1723

Months	Aspects	Days	H	L	Min
March	Full	6	11	20	28
March	Conjunction	21	10	14	16
April	Full	4	20	22	31
April	Conjunction	20	2	44	22
May	Full	4	5	16	33
May	Conjunction	19	16	19	29
June	Full	2	15	6	34
June	Conjunction	18	3	54	34
July	Full	2	1	49	33
July	Conjunction	17	15	48	37
August	Full	15	21	11	37
August	Conjunction	30	5	31	24
September	Full	14	5	14	35
September	Conjunction	28	12	7	19
October	Full	13	13	52	32
October	Conjunction	28	15	35	17
November	Full	12	0	8	28
November	Conjunction	27	9	31	15
December	Full	11	11	25	23
December	Conjunction	27	1	33	17
January	Full	10	1	16	19
January	Conjunction	25	15	39	21
February	Full	8	17	23	15
February	Conjunction	24	3	29	26

1 R		2 R		3 R		4 R	
1755	2	1786	4	1817	7	1848	9

Table 13   Of the year of 1724

Months	Aspects	Days	H	L	Min
March	Full	9	10	33	16
March	Conjunction	24	13	2	30
April	Full	8	3	44	18
April	Conjunction	22	21	11	34
May	Full	7	19	42	28
May	Conjunction	22	2	59	38
June	Full	6	10	39	28
June	Conjunction	20	12	59	38
July	Full	5	13	34	32
July	Conjunction	19	21	4	35
August	Full	4	10	34	33
August	Conjunction	18	9	20	30
September	Full	2	10	34	33
September	Conjunction	17	23	10	24
October	Full	2	6	36	31
October	Conjunction	16	15	25	16
November	Full	15	9	3	13
November	Conjunction	30	1	42	27
December	Full	15	5	4	12
December	Conjunction	29	10	52	25
January	Full	13	13	52	13
January	Conjunction	28	0	10	22
February	Full	12	15	52	19
February	Conjunction	26	14	15	20

APPENDIX I

1 R		2 R		3 R		4 R	
1756	2	1787	4	1818	7	1849	9

Table 14   Of the year of 1725

Months	Aspects	Days	H	L	Min
March	Full	14	3	48	25
March	Conjunction	28	5	11	20
April	Full	12	14	46	31
April	Conjunction	26	20	43	22
May	Full	11	21	37	36
May	Conjunction	26	12	16	25
June	Full	10	5	17	39
June	Conjunction	25	2	45	28
July	Full	9	11	11	46
July	Conjunction	24	17	37	29
August	Full	7	20	14	36
August	Conjunction	3	6	59	28
September	Full	6	5	59	31
September	Conjunction	21	19	42	28
October	Full	5	18	44	24
October	Conjunction	21	7	5	27
November	Full	4	10	17	27
November	Conjunction	19	17	53	17
December	Full	4	4	30	12
December	Conjunction	19	4	16	27
January	Full	2	33	58	10
January	Conjunction	17	14	39	26
February	Full	1	17	29	12
February	Conjunction	16	1	27	25

1 R		2 R		3 R		4 R	
1757	3	1788	5	1819	7	1850	9

Table 15 — Of the year of 1726

Months	Aspects	Days	H	L	Min
March	Full	3	11	56	17
March	Conjunction	17	12	56	25
April	Full	2	1	20	24
April	Conjunction	16	2	15	26
May	Full	1	13	25	32
May	Conjunction	15	14	32	27
June	Full	14	4	28	28
June	Conjunction	29	5	37	40
July	Full	13	9	13	28
July	Conjunction	28	12	30	40
August	Full	12	10	36	26
August	Conjunction	26	19	37	36
September	Full	11	4	49	24
September	Conjunction	25	1	59	31
October	Full	10	26	33	22
October	Conjunction	24	16	20	25
November	Full	9	6	35	22
November	Conjunction	24	6	42	18
December	Full	8	15	43	24
December	Conjunction	22	23	46	13
January	Full	7	5	46	25
January	Conjunction	21	18	26	10
February	Full	5	17	16	27
February	Conjunction	20	13	58	12

APPENDIX I

1 R		2 R		3 R		4 R	
1758	2	1789	4	1820	7	1851	9

Table 16   Of the year of 1727

Months	Aspects	Days	H	L	Min
March	Full	7	2	52	28
March	Conjunction	22	7	43	17
April	Full	6	22	29	30
April	Conjunction	20	22	46	24
May	Full	4	22	29	31
May	Conjunction	20	11	14	32
June	Full	3	9	20	36
June	Conjunction	18	21	12	31
July	Full	2	22	1	31
July	Conjunction	18	6	18	38
August	Full	1	11	24	28
August	Conjunction	16	12	57	38
September	Full	14	20	46	35
September	Conjunction	29	19	27	19
October	Full	14	5	34	32
October	Conjunction	29	11	19	17
November	Full	12	16	4	26
November	Conjunction	28	4	55	17
December	Full	12	5	2	20
December	Conjunction	27	19	44	20
January	Full	10	20	33	19
January	Conjunction	26	8	37	23
February	Full	9	13	40	13
February	Conjunction	24	11	7	27

1 R		2 R		3 R		4 R	
1759	2	1790	4	1821	7	1852	9

Table 17   Of the year of 1728

Months	Aspects	Days	H	L	Min
March	Full	10	8	53	13
March	Conjunction	25	4	39	31
April	Full	9	2	15	18
April	Conjunction	23	1	55	34
May	Full	8	17	10	24
May	Conjunction	22	21	5	36
June	Full	7	2	34	29
June	Conjunction	21	5	57	36
July	Full	6	18	20	34
July	Conjunction	20	16	15	33
August	Full	5	2	39	35
August	Conjunction	19	4	51	28
September	Full	3	13	21	34
September	Conjunction	17	17	43	22
October	Full	2	22	10	32
October	Conjunction	17	13	2	6
November	Full	2	7	13	30
November	Conjunction	16	3	2	13
December	Full	16	1	45	13
December	Conjunction	30	5	2	23
January	Full	14	16	28	10
January	Conjunction	14	18	39	19
February	Full	13	9	6	21
February	Conjunction	27	9	4	18

APPENDIX I

1 R		2 R		3 R		4 R	
1760	2	1791	4	1822	6	1853	9

Table 18   Of the year of 1729

Months	Aspects	Days	H	L	Min
March	Full	14	20	59	17
March	Conjunction	29	1	54	18
April	Full	13	5	53	32
April	Conjunction	27	16	6	21
May	Full	12	14	47	37
May	Conjunction	27	9	46	21
June	Full	10	21	45	39
June	Conjunction	20	0	19	29
July	Full	10	4	17	39
July	Conjunction	5	14	39	31
August	Full	28	13	14	35
August	Conjunction	24	0	55	30
September	Full	7	0	16	29
September	Conjunction	22	12	45	30
October	Full	6	14	18	22
October	Conjunction	21	23	30	29
November	Full	5	15	58	16
November	Conjunction	20	9	30	28
December	Full	5	2	1	11
December	Conjunction	19	19	44	27
January	Full	3	20	29	11
January	Conjunction	18	6	27	25
February	Full	2	15	46	14
February	Conjunction	16	18	11	23

1 R		2 R		3 R		4 R	
1761	2	1792	5	1823	7	1854	9

Table 19   Of the year of 1730

Months	Aspects	Days	H	L	Min
March	Full	3	7	45	14
March	Conjunction	18	15	9	21
April	Full	2	20	2	23
April	Conjunction	16	20	31	24
May	Full	16	10	51	26
May	Conjunction	31	14	10	38
June	Full	15	1	26	27
June	Conjunction	29	21	5	40
July	Full	14	16	35	23
July	Conjunction	29	8	55	39
August	Full	13	7	26	28
August	Conjunction	27	12	1	35
September	Full	11	12	56	25
September	Conjunction	25	22	59	29
October	Full	11	11	2	24
October	Conjunction	25	16	40	22
November	Full	10	1	2	25
November	Conjunction	24	2	22	16
December	Full	9	11	42	25
December	Conjunction	22	10	46	12
January	Full	7	22	26	26
January	Conjunction	22	16	17	10
February	Full	6	8	36	23
February	Conjunction	21	10	11	13

APPENDIX I

1 R		2 R		3 R		4 R	
1762	2	1793	5	1824	7	1855	9

Table 20 — Of the year of 1731

Months	Aspects	Days	H	L	Min
March	Full	7	18	48	28
March	Conjunction	23	6	1	19
April	Full	6	5	18	29
April	Conjunction	21	17	36	26
May	Full	5	16	30	29
May	Conjunction	21	5	0	33
June	Full	4	2	34	30
June	Conjunction	19	9	50	38
July	Full	3	13	49	29
July	Conjunction	18	21	24	39
August	Full	2	8	38	37
August	Conjunction	17	4	19	38
September	Full	15	11	53	34
September	Conjunction	30	16	32	20
October	Full	14	21	33	29
October	Conjunction	20	8	35	19
November	Full	14	9	12	23
November	Conjunction	28	23	33	20
December	Full	12	23	33	18
December	Conjunction	28	12	59	23
January	Full	11	6	30	13
January	Conjunction	27	0	43	25
February	Full	10	10	50	12
February	Conjunction	15	10	52	28

1 R		2 R		3 R		4 R	
1763	2	1794	4	1825	7	1856	9

Table 21 — Of the year of 1732

Months	Aspects	Days	H	L	Min
March	Full	11	5	19	14
March	Conjunction	25	20	2	31
April	Full	9	22	41	19
April	Conjunction	24	4	45	33
May	Full	9	13	36	20
May	Conjunction	23	13	58	34
June	Full	8	1	53	32
June	Conjunction	21	23	48	34
July	Full	7	12	14	36
July	Conjunction	21	12	32	31
August	Full	5	21	8	37
August	Conjunction	20	1	20	26
September	Full	4	5	28	31
September	Conjunction	18	17	5	21
October	Full	3	13	34	33
October	Conjunction	18	10	27	16
November	Full	1	22	48	29
November	Conjunction	17	4	30	14
December	Full	16	21	47	15
December	Conjunction	30	22	22	21
January	Full	15	12	9	19
January	Conjunction	29	12	4	17
February	Full	14	2	7	24
February	Conjunction	22	5	51	15

APPENDIX I

1 R		2 R		3 R		4 R	
1764	2	1795	4	1826	7	1857	9

Table 22   Of the year of 1733

Months	Aspects	Days	H	L	Min
March	Full	15	12	38	28
March	Conjunction	29	22	59	17
April	Full	23	21	23	33
April	Conjunction	28	14	28	21
May	Full	13	14	41	36
May	Conjunction	28	6	52	26
June	Full	11	12	45	38
June	Conjunction	26	21	5	30
July	Full	10	20	51	36
July	Conjunction	26	8	52	32
August	Full	9	7	4	33
August	Conjunction	24	19	48	33
September	Full	7	9	29	37
September	Conjunction	23	5	39	32
October	Full	7	10	47	20
October	Conjunction	22	15	5	30
November	Full	6	3	29	14
November	Conjunction	21	0	59	28
December	Full	5	13	34	11
December	Conjunction	20	11	33	23
January	Full	4	18	24	12
January	Conjunction	18	22	49	26
February	Full	3	11	36	16
February	Conjunction	17	11	39	21

1 R		2 R		3 R		4 R	
1765	2	1796	4	1827	7	1858	9

Table 23   Of the year of 1734

Months	Aspects	Days	H	L	Min
March	Full	4	1	56	22
March	Conjunction	19	1	30	20
April	Full	3	13	22	28
April	Conjunction	17	16	41	22
May	Full	2	22	17	32
May	Conjunction	17	7	57	34
June	Full	15	23	1	27
June	Conjunction	30	12	25	40
July	Full	15	13	50	28
July	Conjunction	29	19	52	38
August	Full	14	3	51	28
August	Conjunction	28	4	33	34
September	Full	12	16	58	28
September	Conjunction	26	15	52	27
October	Full	12	3	26	27
October	Conjunction	26	6	0	20
November	Full	10	16	41	27
November	Conjunction	14	23	7	14
December	Full	9	3	25	27
December	Conjunction	24	18	9	11
January	Full	8	13	50	26
January	Conjunction	23	13	46	11
February	Full	7	0	18	26
February	Conjunction	27	6	1	14

APPENDIX I

1 R		2 R		3 R		4 R	
1766	2	1797	5	1828	7	1859	9

Table 24 — Of the year of 1735

Months	Aspects	Days	H	L	Min
March	Full	8	11	16	25
March	Conjunction	23	23	30	21
April	Full	6	22	46	26
April	Conjunction	22	2	14	28
May	Full	6	11	20	27
May	Conjunction	21	22	0	35
June	Full	5	0	1	28
June	Conjunction	20	5	39	39
July	Full	4	5	1	28
July	Conjunction	19	12	49	40
August	Full	3	6	5	27
August	Conjunction	17	19	24	38
September	Full	1	21	33	24
September	Conjunction	16	4	9	34
October	Full	15	14	19	28
October	Conjunction	31	3	43	21
November	Full	14	3	14	22
November	Conjunction	30	17	22	22
December	Full	13	19	7	15
December	Conjunction	29	5	31	24
January	Full	13	8	53	12
January	Conjunction	27	16	30	26
February	Full	11	7	10	11
February	Conjunction	26	2	19	28

1 R		2 R		3 R		4 R	
1767	2	1798	4	1829	7	1860	9

Table 25   Of the year of 1736

Months	Aspects	Days	H	L	Min
March	Full	12	2	54	15
March	Conjunction	26	11	54	30
April	Full	10	18	12	20
April	Conjunction	24	22	14	51
May	Full	10	8	4	28
May	Conjunction	24	6	23	32
June	Full	8	20	55	3
June	Conjunction	22	18	38	32
July	Full	8	5	14	37
July	Conjunction	22	7	40	30
August	Full	6	13	6	38
August	Conjunction	21	22	20	26
September	Full	4	20	46	36
September	Conjunction	19	15	7	21
October	Full	4	4	59	33
October	Conjunction	19	7	54	17
November	Full	3	14	44	28
November	Conjunction	17	0	46	16
December	Full	2	2	41	22
December	Conjunction	17	16	40	18
January	Full	31	16	50	18
January	Conjunction	16	6	40	21
February	Full	30	8	8	14
February	Conjunction	14	20	12	25

	1 R		2 R		3 R		4 R	
	1768	2	1799	4	1830	7	1961	9

Table 26 — Of the year of 1737

Months	Aspects	Days	H	L	Min
March	Full	1	2	36	14
March	Conjunction	16	4	19	29
April	Full	14	13	48	33
April	Conjunction	29	12	44	22
May	Full	13	22	28	36
May	Conjunction	29	3	31	28
June	Full	12	5	4	37
June	Conjunction	27	16	12	30
July	Full	11	14	24	32
July	Conjunction	27	3	8	35
August	Full	10	1	45	34
August	Conjunction	25	14	38	31
September	Full	8	15	45	34
September	Conjunction	23	21	48	25
October	Full	8	7	54	33
October	Conjunction	23	6	46	19
November	Full	7	1	54	31
November	Conjunction	21	16	28	14
December	Full	6	20	44	28
December	Conjunction	21	3	20	12
January	Full	5	14	44	25
January	Conjunction	19	52	20	19
February	Full	4	6	24	2
February	Conjunction	18	6	54	42

1 R		2 R		3 R		4 R	
1769	2	1800	5	1831	7	1862	9

Table 27   Of the year of 1738

Months	Aspects	Days	H	L	Min
March	Full	4	21	8	24
March	Conjunction	19	21	31	28
April	Full	4	6	7	31
April	Conjunction	18	6	29	21
May	Full	3	13	49	35
May	Conjunction	18	42	16	24
June	Full	1	5	59	39
June	Conjunction	16	20	22	27
July	Full	1	20	8	39
July	Conjunction	16	4	20	29
August	Full	16	10	37	30
August	Conjunction	14	21	58	32
September	Full	28	20	34	29
September	Conjunction	13	8	42	25
October	Full	27	10	18	29
October	Conjunction	12	22	3	18
November	Full	27	2	43	28
November	Conjunction	11	8	23	13
December	Full	25	20	58	27
December	Conjunction	10	18	44	10
January	Full	25	15	22	26
January	Conjunction	9	5	42	12
February	Full	24	10	64	24
February	Conjunction	7	7	66	16

APPENDIX I

1 R		2 R		3 R		4 R	
1770	2	1801	5	1832	7	1863	9

Table 28   Of the year of 1739

Months	Aspects	Days	H	L	Min
March	Full	9	4	39	24
March	Conjunction	24	8	22	23
April	Full	7	6	17	24
April	Conjunction	23	5	28	31
May	Full	7	7	3	25
May	Conjunction	22	15	13	36
June	Full	5	1	40	27
June	Conjunction	20	21	25	40
July	Full	5	12	19	28
July	Conjunction	20	4	10	40
August	Full	4	2	39	28
August	Conjunction	18	8	4	37
September	Full	2	18	15	25
September	Conjunction	16	23	21	32
October	Full	6	7	52	26
October	Conjunction	31	2	14	24
November	Full	14	22	13	19
November	Conjunction	30	10	17	24
December	Full	13	13	20	13
December	Conjunction	29	21	16	26
January	Full	13	10	36	10
January	Conjunction	28	4	29	26
February	Full	12	5	53	11
February	Conjunction	17	17	58	27

1 R		2 R		3 R		4 R	
1771	2	1802	4	1833	7	1864	9

Table 29 — Of the year of 1740

Months	Aspects	Days	H	L	Min
March	Full	12	23	44	16
March	Conjunction	11	4	28	28
April	Full	27	15	7	22
April	Conjunction	25	14	30	20
May	Full	11	3	30	30
May	Conjunction	25	1	50	30
June	Full	9	13	29	36
June	Conjunction	23	14	25	30
July	Full	8	21	22	39
July	Conjunction	23	8	56	28
August	Full	7	4	44	29
August	Conjunction	21	19	3	30
September	Full	5	12	14	36
September	Conjunction	20	11	59	21
October	Full	4	20	46	32
October	Conjunction	20	4	29	19
November	Full	3	7	16	26
November	Conjunction	18	20	32	13
December	Full	2	21	11	21
December	Conjunction	18	10	42	21
January	Full	1	21	15	17
January	Conjunction	16	23	31	23
February	Full	31	5	37	12
February	Conjunction	15	10	16	17

APPENDIX I

	1 R		2 R		3 R		4 R	
	1772	2	1803	4	1834	7	1865	9

Table 30   Of the year of 1741

Months	Aspects	Days	H	L	Min
March	Full	2	0	2	13
March	Conjunction	16	19	50	26
April	Full	15	4	26	32
April	Conjunction	29	22	59	23
May	Full	14	6	18	34
May	Conjunction	29	23	25	29
June	Full	12	22	15	35
June	Conjunction	28	14	40	34
July	Full	12	8	53	33
July	Conjunction	27	21	45	36
August	Full	10	21	33	29
August	Conjunction	26	5	3	36
September	Full	9	12	28	23
September	Conjunction	24	13	27	34
October	Full	9	5	19	18
October	Conjunction	23	22	14	31
November	Full	8	3	1	15
November	Conjunction	22	8	16	27
December	Full	7	15	15	14
December	Conjunction	21	20	23	23
January	Full	6	9	52	17
January	Conjunction	20	9	28	19
February	Full	5	0	17	1
February	Conjunction	10	1	29	29

1 R		2 R		3 R		4 R	
1773	3	1804	5	1835	7	1866	9

Table 31   Of the year of 1742

Months	Aspects	Days	H	L	Min
March	Full	6	12	5	26
March	Conjunction	20	18	5	17
April	Full	4	21	19	31
April	Conjunction	19	12	45	20
May	Full	4	5	5	36
May	Conjunction	19	2	21	24
June	Full	2	12	34	38
June	Conjunction	17	17	17	28
July	Full	17	6	20	31
July	Conjunction	31	5	29	35
August	Full	15	18	13	32
August	Conjunction	29	26	30	29
September	Full	14	4	41	31
September	Conjunction	18	6	31	23
October	Full	13	14	8	30
October	Conjunction	27	23	1	16
November	Full	12	0	21	29
November	Conjunction	26	12	40	12
December	Full	11	10	26	27
December	Conjunction	26	13	11	11
January	Full	9	19	32	25
January	Conjunction	28	7	34	14
February	Full	8	9	56	23
February	Conjunction	13	23	10	19

Of the reduction and conformation of the conjunctions and fulls of the Sun and Moon for the various places in Spain

	H	L		H	L
Madrid	0	0	Málaga	0	6 S
Alcalá	0	1 A	Medina-Sidonia	0	9 S
Ávila	0	5 S	Plasencia	0	21 S
Burgos	0	10 A	Santiago	0	16 S
Barcelona	0	28 A	Toledo	0	2 S
Badajoz	0	11 S	Tarragona	0	24 A
Ciudad-Real	0	3 A	Trujillo	0	12 S
Cádiz	0	15 S	Valencia	0	15 A
Zaragoza	0	14 A	Choc. De Canal	0	3 S
Leon	0	13 S	Granada	0	2 A
Alcañiz	0	15 A	Jerez	0	23 S

The conjunctions and fulls which are stated in the previous tables, and those set for the coming years are adjusted to the Meridian of Madrid, which differs from the place where one takes to be the first meridian by 21 degree and 31 minutes. In order to adjust these to other regions it is necessary to refer to this table, where one will find the hours and minutes which should be added or subtracted to the conjunctions and fulls. The letter A which may be found near these numbers means "add" and the letter S means "subtract". Once the minutes are reduced according to these differences, one will have them for all cities, town and villages, for taking that place which is nearer to you in this table one may have the same number as given in the table, for in each 50 leagues there is solely a difference in a quarter of an hour, and these are in the longitudinal leagues, that those of latitude make no difference.

Method of extracting the Lunar and Solar eclipses perpetually[395]

This is achieved with great ease, for once the conjunction or full of a day is know, one should seek on which Sign and degree is the Head or Tail of the Dragon; and once this is known, if this is not distant more than 12 degrees from the conjunction there will be an Eclipse, and if it is more than 12 degrees ways then here will not be an Eclipse. This rule should be evident, for from the greatest or smaller distance of the Sun or Moon from the Head or Tail one arrives at their Meridional or Septentrional latitude, and the 12 degrees are within the range of the Ecliptic movement, either on one side or the other; from this we can gather that if the Moon does not differ from this point of the Head or Tail at the time of it being full, there will be a full Lunar Eclipse, for at this time she will not have any latitude; and should the full be during the night then one will see the eclipsed Moon. The same can be said of the Sun, if at the time of the conjunction there is no distance between the Sun and one of these two points, should we be looking at it from the center of the earth. But as we are distant from that point over 1000 leagues, it is still necessary to perform some other calculations.

---

395. Translator's note: Much like the table for the calculation of the Head of the Dragon presented previously, to which this text refers directly, this section is only present in the Barcelona 1836 and 1848 editions.

This rule is cited by Moya[396] in folio 76, when discussing the eclipses in Abraham Zacuto's Almanac.[397] And this can be further simplified by two examples.

Example of the Sun

One should first search in the year one wishes to inquire in which Sign is the Head of the Dragon, and when the Sun approaches this Sign, then it is the occasion for an Eclipse. Be it the year of 1715, we see that in the month of March the Head of the Dragon is in the seventh sign, 23 degrees and 58 minutes, which is in Scorpio, and that the Sun arrives at this Sign in October, and in this time can I expect an Eclipse, as also in May, for the Sun is in Taurus, which is the opposed of Scorpio. Outside of this time in no conjunction of the Sun will there be an Eclipse, and one should not tire studying the conjunctions and fulls that are not those of May and October. I see that the conjunction is at the 2nd of May, at 21 hours and 20 minutes *post meridiem*, and according to the civilian hours this is the 3rd at 9 in the morning and 20 minutes. On this day the Sun is in the Sign of Taurus; and the Head of the Dragon is on 18 degrees and 56 minutes, which subtracted for those of the Sun result in 5 degree and 56 minutes in longitude from the Head of the Dragon at the opposite side of the conjunction, where one will find the Tail of the Dragon and the Sun, and as such I can say that there will be an Eclipse, for this number is smaller than twelve degrees.

Example of the Moon

The full Moon is on the 18th, 0 hours and 26 minutes, *post meridiem*, which according to the civilian calculation is at 12 hours and 26 minutes; meaning that one will not see the Eclipse, for it will be during the day and it will happen below the horizon. I see that the Head of the Dragon is at Sign 7, 18 degrees and 8 minutes; and that the Sun is at 28 degrees of Taurus, which are the 28 in which the Moon is found in Scorpio, the opposing Sign. From this one ends up with 18 degrees and 8 minutes, after subtracting the 10 degrees; and so one may say that there will not be a Lunar Eclipse. According to what was said one does not need to search in any other conjunction or full.

Another example by the Sun

I see that the conjunction is at the 26th of October at 10 hours and 50 minutes, and the Sun is at 3 degrees of Scorpio and the Head is at 9 degrees and 56 minutes of Scorpio. The difference between one and the other is of six degrees, by which we can say we will have an Eclipse; and in this same way one may perform this calculation for every year.

Further tables could be added to calculate which areas would be affected by the Eclipse, but the shortness of the Lunario does not permit it.

---

396. Translator's note: uncertain reference.

397. Translator's note: A brilliant Sephardic Jew astronomer and Kabbalist of the XVIth century, his life is an almost anecdotal example of the persecution of the Jewish people in Iberia. The referred book is his *Almanach Perpetuum*.

Appendix II

Similarly to the previous case, below are several sections, tables and calculations present in the 1837 Madrid edition of the *Lunario*. Although this edition does not add the use of the Epact to the overall calculations of the original text, it does contain several incompatible points with it that should nonetheless be offered as, once again, examples on how this book has maintained its vividness and authority among rural workers of Iberia and South America.

***

Prologue to the reader

Although this is the same Lunario written by Cortez, and which is so esteemed by scholars that it was printed so many times in so many places, it may, dear reader, seem like a different one in this new printing, in which we have corrected the illustrations of chronology of the times, the treatise of the winds and the system of the heavens, and in a single word, you will find it fitted with all the observations of the wisest astronomer of our time.

It contains a succinct annual history of all which has happened since the death of Christ our Redeemer until these latest times.

Regarding prognostications we have not touched on a single thing, for Cortez claims the *non plus ultra*; and also because these prophesies centered on astrology are not well founded. In everything else, should there be anything which may displease you, do have patience, for as Marcial says, Book 1,

Sunt bona, sunt quædam mediocra, sunt mala plura.
Quam legis hic, aliter non fit, Avite, liber.[398]

By which Ovid concludes:

Et veniam pro laude peto, laudatus abunde
Non fastiditus si tibi, lector, ero.

Of the Ethereal region

Saint John of Damascus in Book two of *de Fide Ortodoxa*, says that there are three heavens: The Airy, the Sidereal and the Emperium. We have so forth dealt with the Airy, that this saint comprehends to contain everything from the earth until the Moon; and so we now will deal with the Heaven of the Stars, the Sidereal; and so as we may proceed with greater clarity we offer the following figure.

---

398. Some of what you read here is good, some mediocre, but most is bad: a book, Avitus, cannot be made any other way.

System and position of the world according to the most modern and acclaimed authors

So as this system of the Sidereal Heaven be better understood one must take into consideration that many and great theologians have said that the heavens are solid and that the Planets and Stars are in such a way fixed and stuck to them that they could not perform any of their movements except when these heavens also moved, and by this we can understand that by being the movements of the Planets and Stars so different there should be a great number of heavens; and from this could many discourses regarding various systems be made; but in order to explain what is represented by the figure we do not need to mention any other than Ptolemy, which was the most famous among the ancients.

The earthly globe is made by nine spheres, the lowest of which is that of the Moon, and following their order we then have Mercury, Venus, the Sun, Mars, Jupiter and Saturn, followed by the Stars (called the firmament), and above all of them the *primer mobil*, which is thus called because this heaven, by making its movement from the Levante to the Ponente in 24 hours, transmits its movement to the inferior heavens. King Alphonso, regarding this point, said, in the year of 1240, that the Stars rotated from the Ponente to the Levante with an extremely slow movement (which is called trepidation), and by this it was concluded that between the firmament and the *primer mobil* there should be another heaven, which would communicate to the Stars the said movement; and thus is the Ptolemaic system made up of 10 heavens, and all of them have as their center the earth and the sea.

The phenomenon and movements observed in the Stars are so extraordinary, rising and lowering from one heaven to the other, that those who admit to the mentioned system, in which the heavens are solid, must admit that these cross each other's trajectory, by paths which they call Eccentric, Epicycle, Eccentricycle, Equating, Differentials &c, and with all of this we cannot arrive at any truth regarding the paths of the comets which rise and lower and revolve by lines oblique to the Equinoxes; and having given this opinion let us pass on to explain the true system of the world, which is represented in the figure, and which is much more verisimilar and according to the sacred scripture and the holy fathers and is commonly accepted by modernity.

The region or distance between the earth and the Moon is what we may call heaven, for it is thus called by David when he says: *volucres cœlum nubibus*. Heaven is also the name given to the place which God has destined as home and rest of the blessed, as can be seen by these words of the holy gospel: *merces vestra copiosa est in cœlis: thesaurizate vobis thesaurus in cœli*. To this Heaven calls the Apostle Saint Paul the third when he said: *scio::: raptum hujusmodi usque ad tertium cœlum::: quoniam raptus est in paradisum*. And for this do I say that from the Moon, surrounding the earth, as its center, to the Stars, and from here to the surface of the Emperium heaven there isn't in reality more than one heaven (which is the second heaven) continuous and composed of a fluid, ethereal and subtle matter through which the Planets and the Stars move. And I say in reality, for speaking astronomically we can very well call heavens to the orbits or circles seen in the figure; and these are nothing else but paths by which the Planets pass; in such a way as the Moon surrounds the earth by the lowest part of this heaven; followed by the Sun which has a higher circumference and which is surrounded by Venus and Mercury, which have been observed infinite times as being higher than the Sun; and from this may we prove the fluidity of the Heavens, for if they were solid they would surely break by the passing of the planets through them.

The other circles of Mars, Jupiter, Saturn and the Stars surround the earth like in the Ptolemaic system, with the difference that Ptolemy said that it was the Heavens that moved, by themselves or by some occult virtue, we however say that it is the Planets and the Stars that move, as can be extracted by many instances of the sacred gospel; but this hasn't been determined accurately.

The Planets and the Stars, which have a center in themselves and as such can sustain themselves in the air like the earth, and travel from the Levante to the Ponente; even if their circle isn't perfect, being slower or faster in the 24 hour cycle when arriving at their original position; and this is the reason why the Ptolemaics gave them a particular movement from the Ponente to the Levante.

At the highest point of the figure we have the twelve signs, whose names are: Aries, Taurus, Gemini, Cancer, Leo, Virgo, Libra, Scorpio; Sagittarius, Capricorn, Aquarius, Pisces. These are the sections or parts in which the astronomers divide the heaven, and these aren't just preset in the *primer mobil*, but also in all of the other heavens of the Stars and Planets; but, as this is solely based on imagination, and as these Signs are treated in various parts of this work, we will excuse ourselves from dealing with them here.

Below is the declaration of the following perpetual and general Table for the prognostication of the years

The following table is so clear that to understand it one needs only to look at it; and in this way I will only say that once it ends in the year of 1864 one will once again use for the year of 1865 the Dominical letter of A, as it was done with 1837, and the first day of the year will be Sunday, the lord of the year will be the Sun, and by this influence there will be abundance; and in this way it will follow through the 28 years of the solar cycle until the year of 1864, in which the cycle will complete itself and a new one will begin following the same order of the table for the year 1865, which will be concluded 28 years later in the year of 1892.

In the first column of the table one should note the years in which the Dominical letter changes, and for greater intelligence one should know that by disposition of Pope Gregory XIII the centennial years are leap years only every 400 years, as is explained in this Lunario. The centennial years which are not leap years should be noted in the same places in the first column, where those three are already marked, in the following way: the year of 2101 in the place of 1801; the year of 2301 in that of 1901 and that of 2501 in that of 2301; and so forth for all others, and in this way will this table be made perpetual and it may forever be used.

I wish to know in the year of 2960 which will be the Dominical letter, the first day of the year, its lord, and if it will be an abundant or sterile year; as the year of 2901, as given by the above rule, will fall in the place of 2101, and I thus follow this table starting from the year before as such: 2900, 2901, 2902 until I reach the year of 2960, and I shall see that it is a leap year, and it will be in accordance with the year of 1836, and in this same way for all other years.

Year in which the Dominical letter changes	Dominical letter	Year of Christ	First day of the year	Lord of the year	Of supplies
	A	1837	Sunday	Sun	Abundant
	G	1838	Monday	Moon	Fertile
	F	1839	Tuesday	Mars	Sterile
	E D	1840	Wednesday	Mercury	Average
	C	1841	Friday	Venus	Fertile
	B	1842	Saturday	Saturn	Sterile
	A	1843	Sunday	Sun	Abundant
	G F	1844	Monday	Moon	Fertile
	E	1845	Wednesday	Mercury	Average
	D	1846	Thursday	Jupiter	Abundant
2101	C	1847	Friday	Venus	Fertile
	B A	1848	Saturday	Saturn	Sterile
	G	1849	Monday	Moon	Fertile
	F	1850	Tuesday	Mars	Sterile
1801	E	1851	Wednesday	Mercury	Average
	D C	1852	Thursday	Jupiter	Abundant
	B	1853	Saturday	Saturn	Sterile
	A	1854	Sunday	Sun	Abundant
	G	1855	Monday	Moon	Fertile
1901	F E	1856	Tuesday	Mars	Sterile
	D	1857	Thursday	Jupiter	Abundance
	C	1858	Friday	Venus	Fertile
	B	1859	Saturday	Saturn	Sterile
	A G	1860	Sunday	Sun	Abundant
	F	1861	Tuesday	Mars	Sterile
	E	1862	Wednesday	Mercury	Average
	D	1863	Thursday	Jupiter	Abundant
	C B	1864	Friday	Venus	Fertile

Golden number	January		February		March		April		May		June	
		Days		Days		Days		Days		Days		Days
1	Full	15	Full	13	Full	14	Full	12	Full	12	Full	10
	Conj	29	Conj	28	Conj	28	Conj	27	Conj	27	Conj	25
2	Full	03	Full	02	Full	03	Full	02	Full	01	Full	14
	Conj	17	Conj	16	Conj	17	Conj	16	Conj	16	Conj	29
									Full	31		
3	Conj	07	Conj	05	Conj	07	Conj	05	Conj	05	Conj	03
	Full	22	Full	21	Full	22	Full	21	Full	20	Full	19
4	Full	11	Full	10	Full	11	Full	10	Conj	09	Full	08
	Conj	26	Conj	25	Conj	26	Conj	24	Full	24	Conj	25
5	Conj	16	Conj	14	Conj	15	Conj	13	Conj	12	Conj	11
	Full	30	Full	28	Full	29	Full	28	Full	27	Full	26
6	Conj	04	Conj	03	Conj	04	Conj	03	Conj	02	Full	15
	Full	18	Full	17	Full	18	Full	17	Full	17	Conj	30
									Conj	31		
7	Full	08	Full	06	Full	08	Full	06	Full	06	Full	10
	Full	23	Conj	22	Conj	23	Conj	22	Conj	21	Conj	19
8	Conj	12	Conj	11	Conj	12	Conj	11	Conj	11	Conj	09
	Full	27	Full	26	Full	17	Full	25	Full	24	Full	23
9	Conj	01	Full	15	Full	15	Full	14	Full	13	Full	11
	Full	19	Conj	28	Conj	30	Conj	28	Conj	28	Conj	27
10	Conj	05	Full	03	Full	05	Full	05	Full	03	Full	01
	Conj	19	Conj	17	Conj	19	Conj	28	Conj	16	Conj	16
											Full	30
11	Conj	08	Conj	07	Conj	08	Conj	07	Conj	06	Conj	05
	Full	24	Full	22	Full	24	Full	22	Full	22	Full	20
12	Full	13	Full	11	Full	13	Full	12	Full	11	Full	10
	Conj	27	Conj	25	Conj	27	Conj	26	Conj	15	Conj	24
13	Full	02	Conj	15	Full	01	Conj	14	Conj	14	Conj	11
	Conj	17	Full	29	Conj	01	Full	30	Full	29	Full	28
	Full	31			Full	31						
14	Conj	06	Conj	04	Conj	06	Conj	04	Conj	03	Conj	02
	Full	20	Full	18	Full	20	Full	19	Full	18	Full	17
15	Full	06	Full	07	Full	09	Full	08	Full	07	Full	06
	Conj	24	Conj	25	Conj	25	Conj	23	Conj	21	Conj	21
16	Conj	14	Conj	12	Conj	14	Conj	13	Conj	11	Conj	10
	Full	28	Full	27	Full	28	Full	27	Full	26	Full	25
17	Conj	03	Conj	01	Conj	02	Conj	01	Full	14	Full	13
	Full	18	Full	16	Full	17	Full	15	Conj	30	Conj	28
							Conj	30				
18	Full	06	Full	05	Full	06	Full	05	Full	04	Full	02
	Full	21	Conj	19	Conj	21	Conj	20	Conj	20	Conj	18
19	Conj	10	Conj	08	Conj	10	Conj	08	Conj	08	Conj	07
	Conj	25	Full	24	Full	24	Full	24	Full	23	Full	21

Golden number	July	Days	August	Days	September	Days	October	Days	November	Days	December	Days
1	Full	09	Full	08	Full	06	Full	06	Full	05	Full	04
	Conj	25	Conj	23	Conj	22	Conj	21	Conj	19	Conj	19
2	Conj	14	Conj	13	Conj	11	Conj	11	Conj	09	Conj	09
	Full	28	Full	27	Full	25	Full	25	Full	22	Full	23
3	Conj	03	Conj	02	Full	15	Full	14	Full	13	Full	13
	Full	18	Full	16	Conj	30	Conj	30	Conj	28	Conj	28
			Conj	31								
4	Full	08	Full	06	Conj	04	Full	04	Full	02	Full	02
	Conj	22	Conj	20	Full	19	Conj	19	Conj	17	Conj	17
5											Full	11
	Conj	10	Conj	08	Conj	07	Conj	07	Conj	05	Conj	05
	Full	26	Full	24	Full	22	Full	22	Full	20	Full	20
6	Full	15	Full	13	Full	12	Full	11	Full	10	Full	09
	Conj	29	Conj	27	Conj	26	Conj	25	Conj	24	Conj	24
	Full	04	Full	02	Full	01	Full	01	Conj	13	Conj	13
7	Conj	19	Conj	29	Conj	15	Conj	15	Full	29	Full	28
							Full	30				
8	Conj	08	Conj	07	Conj	05	Conj	04	Conj	03	Conj	02
	Full	23	Full	21	Full	20	Full	20	Full	18	Full	18
9	Full	11	Full	09	Full	08	Full	08	Full	06	Full	06
	Conj	26	Conj	25	Conj	23	Conj	22	Conj	11	Conj	20
10	Conj	16	Conj	14	Conj	13	Conj	12	Conj	10	Conj	10
	Full	30	Full	28	Full	27	Full	26	Full	23	Full	25
11	Conj	05	Conj	03	Conj	02	Full	02	Full	14	Full	14
	Full	19	Full	18	Full	16	Conj	15	Conj	30	Conj	29
							Conj	31				
12	Full	09	Full	'7	Full	06	Full	05	Full	03	Full	03
	Conj	23	Conj	22	Conj	21	Conj	20	Conj	19	Conj	19
13	Conj	17	Conj	10	Conj	09	Conj	08	Conj	07	Conj	07
	Full	27	Full	25	Full	24	Full	21	Full	21	Full	21
14	Conj	01	Full	15	Full	13	Full	13	Full	11	Full	11
	Full	16	Conj	29	Conj	28	Conj	27	Conj	26	Conj	26
	Conj	30										
15	Full	06	Full	04	Full	03	Full	02	Full	01	Full	10
	Conj	20	Conj	18	Conj	17	Conj	16	Conj	15	Conj	30
									Full	30		
16	Conj	10	Conj	08	Conj	06	Conj	06	Conj	04	Conj	14
	Full	24	Full	23	Full	22	Full	21	Full	20	Full	19
17	Full	17	Full	11	Full	10	Full	09	Full	08	Full	08
	Conj	28	Conj	26	Conj	24	Conj	24	Conj	22	Conj	22
18	Full	02	Conj	16	Conj	14	Conj	15	Conj	12	Conj	11
	Conj	17	Full	30	Full	28	Full	28	Full	27	Full	27
	Full	11										
19	Conj	07	Conj	04	Conj	04	Conj	03	Conj	01	Conj	01
	Full	21	Full	16	Full	08	Full	17	Full	16	Full	16

Declaration of the previous table of the perpetual fulls and conjunctions of the Moon

In order to perpetually know by the two previous tables the day of the conjunctions and fulls of the Moon in any year, one should check the Golden number of the year one wishes to know the said conjunction or full, which can be known by the perpetual wheal which can be found in this Lunario. Once the Golden number of that year is known one should seek in the said tables and in front of that Golden number one will find the day of the conjunction or full of the Moon in any month of that year.

We should warn that in the first table one will find the fulls and conjunctions of the first six months; and in the second of the other six months. And so this may be made easier and better understood, we shall give two examples: be it that I want to know in the year of 1805 at which day of January is the conjunction and the full Moon; I then seek in the said wheel which is the Golden number, and I see that it is 1, and I shall seek this in the first table (for this is the one meant for the first six months of the year), and in front of the angle meant for the month of January I see that the conjunction will be at the 29th of the said month and the full Moon at the 15th; and if I want to know in the month of August of this same year at which day was the conjunction or full Moon, I go to the next table and in front of the same 1 of the Golden number in an angle corresponding to the month of August I see that the conjunction is on the 23rd and the full Moon is on the 8th.

Appendix III

Below are presented alternative illustrations to the *Treatise of the Animals of the Land and Sky and Their Properties* taken from the 1615 edition of this book. These have been considered particularly relevant due to the role the *Treatise* had in the history of Zoological and Biological enlightenment in 17th century Valencia and, consequently, Iberia. And nonetheless, being a late example of a bestiary, these engravings can be in fact relevant to those interested in the history of Zoological emblems.

***

Of the Lion and its excellences

Of the Donkey and its great excellences

Of the Camel and its natural conditions

Of the Wolf, and its perfidious conditions

Of the Lamb, and Sheep

Of the Goat and Buck

Of the Dog and its great loyalty

Of the Fox and its great treasons

Of the Pig and its advantages

Of the Deer and its properties

Of the Cat, and its cunnings

Of the Ox and its advantages

Of the Ant and its great foresight and natural instincts

Of the Dragon

Of the Elephant and its rare knowledge

Of the Horse and its arrogance

APPENDIX III

Of the Tiger or Panther

Of the Beaver

Of the Unicorn

Of the Mouse, and by its occasion we will say something of the Thief

Of the Frog

Of the Monkey or Simian

Of the Lynx

Of the Hare

Of the Rabbit

Of the Salamander

Of the Eagle

Of the Dove and its virtues

APPENDIX III

Of all kinds of Birds which are placed in cages for the recreation of the ears and sight of man

Of the Rooster

Of the bird called Griffon or Grippes

Of the Crane

Of the Swallows

Of the Peacock

Of the Vulture

Of the Phoenix

Of the Bees

APPENDIX III

Index I

Authors mentioned in the texts

A

Abencenif 372, 470
Adamo 397
Aelianus, Claudius 313, 314, 357, 376, 377, 378, 379, 386, 387, 388, 391, 395, 396, 406, 407, 411, 312, 441, 445, 487, 500
Aeschylus 355
Aesculapius 316, 329, 336, 342, 354, 365, 370, 397, 449, 453, 458, 468, 470, 476, 487
Afer, Publius Terentius 29, 366, 421, 428
Agrippa 252
Albert 341 is this Albertus Magnus?
Alexios 252, 25
Alfonso, El-Rei (king of Spain) 33, 44, 126
Alfraganus 85, 87, 89, 91, 93, 97, 201, 262
Ambrose, Saint 180, 243, 317, 334, 347, 357, 359, 376, 409, 419, 428, 435, 437, 463, 486, 489
Ambrosio 480
Anatolius 251
Andromachus 385, 386
Anglicus, Bartholomeus 248
Anselm, Saint 263
Anteon 391
Antonino, Doctor 503
Apollonius of Tyana 234, 347
Aponiense, Pero 536
Apuleius 318, 322
Aranda, Baptista 243 *See also* Aranda, Licenciado
Aranda, Licenciado 201, 232, 425
Arbolanche. *See* de Arbolanche, Jerónimo
Aristides 335
Aristotle 44, 201, 231, 235, 236, 237, 250, 253, 260, 262, 268, 269, 271, 272, 275, 286, 288, 312, 316, 317, 319, 328, 329, 330, 332, 333, 336, 347, 349, 355, 360, 361, 364, 366, 375, 376, 381, 382, 383, 387, 389, 392, 395, 397, 400, 404, 405, 409, 411, 414, 416, 424, 425, 432, 435, 436, 438, 439, 441, 447, 454, 458, 468, 474, 485, 488, 492, 494
Atheneus 485
Attonense, Iacobo 454
Augustine, Saint 29, 180, 235, 237, 282, 289, 318, 326, 330, 335, 343, 347, 355, 363, 366, 375, 381, 382, 383, 397, 409, 414, 421, 430, 433, 437, 442, 446, 450, 458, 502
Augustus, Marcus Aurelius Valerius Maxentius 333, 347, 359, 370, 400, 405, 485
Aurelius, Marcus. *See* Augustus, Marcus Aurelius Valerius Maxentius
Ausonius, Decimius Magnus 313
Averroes 509
Avicenna 65, 77, 79, 148, 158, 159, 160, 161, 162, 163, 164, 165, 238, 253, 313, 316, 332, 333, 336, 341, 346, 354, 355, 358, 365, 374, 386, 388, 391, 397, 400, 404, 416, 428, 438, 450, 452, 453, 468, 476, 482, 500

B

Barròn, Marcos 372, 538
Bartholomeo, Luis 233
Bartholomew of England. *See* Anglicus, Bartholomeus
Bartolo 346
Basil, Saint 243, 283, 363
Bede, Saint 44
Berchorio, Pedro 438
Bernard, Saint 317, 318, 330, 342, 343, 363, 366, 375, 405, 409, 418, 430, 446, 450, 469, 485, 502
Bias of Priene 363, 392
Bion, Mathias 252, 347
Bolaterano 345

C

Callistus, Nicephorus 176
Camillo 329
Cardano, Gerolamo 201, 275, 277
Casianus 381
Cassiodorus, Flavius Magnus Aurelius 355, 389, 405
Cato 240, 414, 419
Celio, Lodovico 236, 345, 387, 469
Chilon 342, 355, 419, 437
Chrysostom, Saint 317, 342, 355, 375, 392, 409, 419, 421, 422, 446
Cicero 29, 317, 333, 347, 355, 359, 366, 375, 376, 381, 382, 397, 409, 414, 422, 425, 430
Cirurgico, Josefo 225
Clavius, Christopher 514, 517
Climacus, Saint John 330, 337, 370, 375, 419, 436
Columella, Lucius Junius Moderatus 346, 350, 362, 470, 502, 538
Constantino 251, 295, 344, 357, 416
Cornelia 405
Creponte 240
Crescentiis 165, 201, 362, 372
Crispus, Gaius Sallustius 333
Curtius 392, 400, 502
Cyprian, Saint 397

D

Damiano, Pero 384
de Acosta, José 236, 237, 265, 390
de Arbolanche, Jerónimo 355, 401
de Arciniega, Francisco Velez 389, 392, 400, 406, 407, 408
de Asculi, Francisco 292
de Encelio, Christoval 424
de Estella, Friar Diego 342, 343, 502
de Herrera, Gabriel Alonso 201, 221, 222, 224, 247, 362, 467, 470
de Mena, Juan 235

della Porta, Giovanni Battista 201, 243, 248, 250
Demetrius 347
Democritus 382, 438, 485
Demosthenes 161, 331
de Moya, Juan Perez 248
de Ribas, Pedro 201
de Segovia, Andrés Laguna 465
de Villa Nova, Arnaldus 163, 201, 223, 224, 225, 312, 404, 425
Diaf 333
Diafanes 252
Dimidio 251, 253
Diogenes 337, 392, 397
Dionysus 232
Diophanes of Nicaea 127
Dioscorides 164, 201, 223, 238, 316, 329, 346, 354, 375, 396, 397, 404, 408, 424, 425, 428, 441, 450, 453, 463, 476, 481, 491, 499
Durand, Guillaume 175, 179

E

Ecclesiasticus 433
Emilio 496
Empedocles 262
Erasmus 370, 382, 397, 502
Escoto 201
Estobeus 501, 502
Eulogelio 395
Euripides 317, 366, 418, 430, 485
Evax, Damigerón 446, 473

F

Faras, João 238
Florentinus, Nicolas 152, 201, 251, 255
Florus, Lucius Annaeus 335, 436
Frontinus, Sextus Julius 391
Fulgencio 477
Fulgoso, Baptista 235

G

Galen 32, 162, 201, 329, 341, 354, 386, 413, 439, 468
Galucio 512
Gaudencio 256
Gellius, Aulus 314, 316, 419
Geminiano 538
Gerome, Saint 314, 347, 355, 370, 392, 422, 430, 502
Gomez, Bishop of Abarracin 407
Gottardo 538

Granullachs, Bernardo 152, 340
Grecio 346
Gregory, Saint 29, 52, 317, 330, 337, 342, 343, 347, 355, 363, 366, 375, 381, 382, 397, 405, 430, 463, 502
Guido of Arezzo 151

H

Hali 90, 316, 329, 336, 342, 358, 365, 370, 374, 397, 481
Hélinand of Froidmont 425
Heliodorus 485
Hermogenes 355
Herrera, Alonso 201, 221, 222, 224, 247, 362, 467, 470
Hildegard of Bingen 400
Hippocrates 126, 149, 161, 162, 356, 458
Homer 430
Hugo 337, 429

I

Iorath 425, 483
ibn Zakariyā Rāzī, Muhammad 161, 162, 252, 413, 420, 446
ben Solomon, Isaac Israeli 162, 316, 341, 432
Isidore, Saint 42, 235, 236, 237, 312, 335, 341, 348, 357, 382, 383, 389, 398, 406, 407, 408, 415, 416, 423, 424, 425, 435, 436, 438, 441, 446, 454, 478, 480, 487, 489
Iuris 366

J

Jacob of Palermo 96
Jacob, Saint 436
Jerome 446
John of Damascus, Saint 31, 51, 293, 577
Josephus, Titus Flavius 263
Juvenal 397, 485

L

Lactantius, Lucius Caecilius Firmianus 317, 362, 375
Lebara 538
Lenio, Livinio 414
Leonicus. *See* Thomaeus, Nicholas Leonicus
Leopold, of Austria 54, 61, 63, 65, 69, 71, 73, 75, 77, 79, 81, 82
Livy, Titus 29, 317, 335, 341, 359, 366, 381, 400
Logrero, Pedro 295, 416
Lucrecio, Pero 313
Luke, Saint 292, 294, 333
Lusitano 408

M

Macencio 238
Macrobius *See* Theodosius, Macrobius Ambrosius
Magnus, Albertus 201, 232, 233, 234, 237, 250, 251, 252, 254, 255, 336, 384, 446
Mandeville, John 448
Manilio 538
Marcial 577
Maxentius *See* Augustus, Marcus Aurelius Valerius Maxentius
Maximus, Valerius 317
Medina 337, 363, 381, 409, 418, 425, 426, 502
Mela, Pomponius 235, 236, 237, 263, 407
Menander 347
Mexía, Pero 366, 377, 380, 400
Miedes of Albarracin 390
Mizaldus 201, 250, 252, 255
Mitilineo, Cristoforo 517
Moses 265, 267
Moya 575

O

Origen 425
Ovid 370, 424, 425, 485, 577

P

Palladius 61, 63, 67, 69, 71, 73, 75, 81, 96, 164, 372, 500
Pallopio 254
Palmireno, Juan Lorenzo 379, 380
Patabio 538
Paul of Venice 236
Paul, Saint 29, 286, 330, 425
Peisistratos 347, 419
Periander 333, 366
Petrarch 450
Philo 161
Philonius 240
Philostratus 347, 389
Phylarchus 445
Pittacus of Mytilene 419
Plateario 365, 391, 392, 404
Plato 161, 289, 437
Plautus 386, 419
Pliny 43, 59, 96, 98, 126, 161, 164, 201, 235, 237, 240, 251, 263, 272, 273, 298, 312, 314, 316, 329, 333, 336, 342, 346, 349, 351, 354, 355, 362, 365, 366, 374, 376, 378, 380, 381, 382, 383, 385, 386, 391, 394, 395, 397, 399, 400, 406, 410, 411, 413, 416, 419, 424, 425, 428, 431, 432, 435, 436, 438, 440, 441, 444, 445, 446, 450, 458, 476, 481, 491, 499, 500, 536, 538

Pliny the Younger 425
Plutarch 315, 316, 317, 327, 328, 337, 351, 355, 359, 370, 375, 392, 399, 411, 414, 419, 444, 502
Polo, Marco 236
Ptolemy 44, 123, 126, 148, 263, 273, 578, 579
Publius, Mimo 422, 436
Pythagoras 334, 335, 382, 483

Q

Quintilianus, Marcus Fabius 366, 409, 436

R

Rabanus 425
Renatus, Publius Flavius Vegetius 359, 382, 502
Rhazes. *See* ibn Zakariyā Rāzī, Muhammad
Rufinus, Tyrannius 355

S

Sadoleto 160
Sallust 381
Sanz, Don Luis 379, 428
Savonarola, Giovanni Michele 480
Scot, Michael 238
Seneca 29, 269, 317, 318, 330, 333, 347, 355, 366, 382, 397, 400, 405, 408, 409, 414, 418, 419, 425, 430, 436, 502
Serapion 201, 344, 446
Siculo, Lucio 237
Simonete 251
Simonides 382
Solinus [See email] 235 maybe Gaius Julius Solinus | 312 certainly Gaius Julius Solinus | 237, 316, 394, 395, 406, 424, 425, 435, 438, 490
Solomon 330, 342, 347, 366, 382, 392
Solon 333
Souidas 444
Stobaeus, Joannes 317, 318, 330, 382, 419
Suetonius *See* Tranquillus, Gaius Suetonius
Surio, Laurencio 445

T

Tacitus, Publius Cornelius 366
Terence *See* Afer, Publius Terentius
Terentius 392, 502
Tertullian 366
Thales of Miletus 450
Theodosius, Macrobius Ambrosius 419
Theophrastus 201, 235, 425, 485

Thomaeus, Nicholas Leonicus 235, 236
Titelmanus 275
Tranquillus, Gaius Suetonius 329, 405

V

Varro, Marcus 395, 432, 484
Vegetius *See* Renatus, Publius Flavius Vegetius
Vincencio 248
Virgil 336
Vitruvius 237

X

Xenophon 333

Z

Zacuto, Abraham 575
Zamorano, Rodrigo 166, 247
Zapata 201, 225, 229, 230
Zoroastes 251

INDEX II

ANIMALS MENTIONED IN THE TEXTS

A

ant 172, 184, 243, 252, 288, 376-382
asp 385

B

basilisk 184, 263, 386, 468
bat 184
bear 243, 380, 399, 400, 428, 436
beaver 402-405
bee 97, 127, 183, 222, 255, 372-373, 388, 408, 474, 497
bernace *See* barnacle goose
blackbird 455, 456
bull 111, 184, 302, 314, 338, 371, 372, 373, 374, 375, 377, 400, 436, 464
bunting 456

C

caladrius 488
camel 184, 313, 331-333, 380, 389, 395, 459
   dromedary 332
canary 455
carbates 454
cat
   domestic 184, 367-370, 399, 407, 410, 411, 413, 421, 423
   civet 367, 369, 423
   genet 334, 357, 367, 369-370, 428
chameleon 276, 438-439
chicken 96, 184, 186, 238, 243, 253, 456, 463, 456, 467, 468, 470-471, 472, 480
   capon 470, 471, 472
   rooster 313, 463-469, 470, 472
conger 243
cormorant 171
cow 172, 346
crab 113, 342, 386
crane 171, 172, 459, 460, 464, 474
crocodile 184, 435-437, 438
crow 171, 416, 477, 487, 493
   hooded 495
cuckoo 456, 494

D

deer 183, 344, 364-366, 406
  doe 184
dog 126, 164, 184, 229, 238, 243, 298, 300, 312, 335, 338, 341, 348-356, 357, 365, 366, 394, 398, 399, 403, 411, 415, 421, 424, 427, 428, 431, 436, 449, 456, 461, 476, 538
  wild 334
dolphin 171, 172
donkey 183, 251, 319-330, 331, 333, 373, 395, 399
dove 184, 329, 436, 447-450, 482, 495
dragon 184, 263, 383-386, 389, 398, 450

E

eagle 184, 224, 233, 358, 428, 436, 443-446, 463, 470, 473, 477, 490
elephant 184, 234, 263, 311, 332, 360, 377, 383, 387-393, 406, 407, 408, 424

F

falcon 428, 438, 477
  aplomado 474
  Barbary 459-460
  borni 460
  lanner 460
  peregrine 459, 460
  saker 460
firefly 248, 256
fly 171
fox 184, 338, 357-359, 364, 399, 428, 470
frog 171, 252, 295, 415-419
  horned 386

G

goose 453
  barnacle 454
  gosling 172
goat 67, 119, 162, 163, 174, 183, 251, 344-347, 375, 469, 470
goldfinch 455, 456
goshawk 171, 184, 458, 461, 462, 493
greenfinch 456
griffon 473, 377
gyrfalcon 428, 459, 460

H

halcyon 243, 435, 451
hare 162, 350, 358, 424, 427-430, 431, 432
hawk 171, 172, 458, 462

hedgehog 357
hobby 461
hoopoe 184, 250, 483
horse 184, 251, 325, 327, 328, 373, 394-397, 406, 436
hydra 386

K

kestrel 459, 460, 461

L

lennet 184, 456
leopard 184, 400
lion 184, 263, 311-318, 319, 333, 337, 338, 348, 375, 377, 380, 383, 398, 399, 400, 403, 421, 423, 424, 428, 450, 464, 470, 473
lizard 164, 256, 438
lynx 423-426, 497

M

mallard 452
merlin 461
mole 171, 184, 276
monkey 420-422, 438
mosquito 171, 238, 296, 375, 483
mouse 239, 367, 410-414, 416, 493
mule 325, 327, 328, 399

O

ostrich 184
otter 402
owl 171, 184, 423, 459, 493
ox 162, 171, 183, 211, 325, 338, 371-375, 501

P

panther 398-401
parrot 455, 457
partridge 480-481, 349
peacock 184, 484-485
pelican 479
phoenix 489-490
pig 67, 184, 339, 360-363, 406, 436, 438, 453
pigeon 171, 186, 252, 253
plush-crested jay 455, 456

R

rabbit 411, 431-439
ram 110, 184, 251, 338-343, 344, 345, 351, 464
rhinoceros 406

S

salamander 276, 440-442
scorpion 117, 165, 184, 383, 386
seagull 172
serin 455, 456
serpent 184, 193, 263, 314, 316, 329, 341, 384, 385, 386, 408, 425, 435, 436, 484, 487, 491
serval 184
sheep 79, 84, 172, 174, 251, 336, 338-343, 344, 345, 348, 470
   lamb 67, 251, 336, 338, 339, 341, 407
sheldrake 171, 172
silk worm 84, 97, 183, 375
siskin 455, 456
sparrow 492
sparrowhawk 461
spider 165, 184, 223, 386, 499
squid 172
stork 491
swallow 171, 172, 234, 257, 462, 475-476
swan 171, 496

T

thrush 455, 456
tiger 263, 314, 398-401, 450
toad 276, 415
turtledove 482

U

unicorn 406-409, 436

V

viper 233, 386, 411, 430
vulture 184, 486-487

W

wolf 251, 312, 334-337, 338, 339, 348, 369, 423, 482
woodpecker 478
worm 189, 221, 222, 233, 350, 356, 408, 441, 489, 490

INDEX III

INGREDIENTS MENTIONED IN THE TEXTS

A

acolodina 195
agate
  powder 233
agrimony
  juice 196
  leaf 187
  root 187
aguardente 187, 192, 193, 227–230, 244, 245
alambre 187, 191
alfavaca 255
almecega 187, 188, 189, 356
  oil 257
almond 188
  oil 187, 196, 436
aloe 350, 356
althaea 190, 191, 192, 193
  powder 254
alum 254
amber 191
anise 188
annual mercury 191, 250
ant
  egg 245, 300, 380
  ground 380
Arabic Gum 245
arsenic 254
artemisia 185, 191, 192, 244
  water 191
asato 189
ash 188
  leaf 193
asparagus 189, 190, 196
asphodel 190
assaro 356

B

baby
  fat 193
bacon 195, 302
  fat 362
bagasse 239
balm 356

barley 186, 194
  flour 191
  water 188, 192
basil
  seed 189
bat
  blood 245
bear
  fat 243, 428
beaver
  gall 404
  oil 404
  testicles 404
betony 191, 192
  leaf 191, 229
  root 191
bezoar
  powder 233
black grain 197
black nightshade 191
  leaf 192
  seed 186
blessed thistle 188
boar
  manure 362
borage 189
  water 189
brassica maritima 191
brinzo
  root 197
broom grass 190
  flower 190
  seed 189, 190
broom shrub 239
bull
  blood 374, 375
  penis 375
butter 193

C

cabbage 374
  broth 189
  red 193
caladrius
  bone 488
  leg 488
camel
  blood 332, 333
  brain 332

hump
  juice 332
  manure 333
  meat 332
  urine 333
campanula
  leaf 190
  root 189
camphor 256
carnation 189
  dust 196
carob 222
  pods 188
carpaso
  juice 300
cat
  manure 370
  meat 370
  skin 370
catnip 191
cedar
  fruit 238
  juice 238
celery 191
  root 191, 196
celidonia. *See* swallow (stone)
chameleon
  eye 438
  foot 439
  gall 439
  heart 438
  herb (Houttuynia cordata) 439
  liver 439
  tit 439
chamomile 356
chard 185, 253
chayote 190
  juice 185
cheese 239
cherry
  gum 190, 191
chervil 191
chestnut
  leaf 246
  peel 245
chicken 186
  fat 193, 194, 470
  gizzard 471
  manure 470

meat 470
chicken's bread (Diloboderus abderus larva)
  oil 194
chicory
  water 196
chimney rust 185, 191
cicuta 252
cinnamon 191, 192, 356
cinquefoil 250
citron sandal 356
clove 227
clover 185
comfrey 193
conger 247
coral 190
coriander
  powder 196
cow
  butter 374, 375
  fat 190
  foot
    nerve 193
  manure 192
  milk 192
crambe 189
cress
  seed 299
crocodile
  manure 436
crow
  egg 300
cucumber 190
  leaf 298, 299
cumin 238
  powder 296
  seed 192, 253
curcuma (tumeric)
  root 253
cuttlefish
  bone 190
cypress
  root 190, 192

D

date
  pit 192
deer
  antler 189, 190, 191
  bone 365

horn 365, 366
  lung 365
  marrow 365
  rennet 365, 366
  urine 365
deer tongue (Erythronium albidum) 189
diacratano 194
diaquilones 374
dill 195, 468
dog
  blood 354
  eye 243
  fat 354
  gall 354
  head 354
  heart 243
  manure 354
  marrow 354
  meat 354
  milk 354, 380
  skin 354
  tooth 354
  urine 354
donkey
  blood 329
  bone 329
  liver 329
  lung 329
  manure 329
  milk 329
  nail 186, 329
  spleen 329
  urine 329
dove 449
  blood 449, 450
  manure 244, 450
  meat 450
dragon
  fat 385
  gall 385
  meat 385
  stone 384
dragon's blood 385

E

eagle
  brain 446
  feet 445
  gall 445

eagle stone 444, 446
  powder 233
eel 240
egg 186, 196
  shell 190
  white 185, 186, 187, 189, 191, 192, 193, 247, 254, 470
  yolk 188
elderberry
  flower 239, 244
  leaf 245, 250, 296
elderwort 192, 193
elecampane
  root 193
elephant
  blood 391
  fat 391
  tooth 391, 392
euphrasia 186, 243
eyebright
  water 194

F

fava bean 190, 191
  flour 192, 193
fennel 164, 186, 190, 196
  juice 190, 476
fig
  leaf 246
  tree ash 191
  tree bark 229
fish
  gill 300
flies 300
flint 196
flour 238
fox
  fat 358
  lung 358
  meat 358
  testicle 358
frog
  boiled 416
  broth 416
  fat 416
  gall 416
  powder 295, 416
fumitory
  juice 245
fumus terrae (Fumitory Fumaria officinalis)

juice 346

G

garlic 187
  clove 191
Gera de Gale 356
ginger 227
goat
  fat 346
  grease 346
  hair 346
  horn 296, 346
  kid
    blood 346
    rennet 346
  lard 240
  liver 190
  manure 346
  meat 346
  milk 346, 438
  urine 346, 374
gold bar 189
goose
  fat 453
greater celandine 191, 194
  leaf 189, 191
  root 190
Greek tar 239
ground-ivy
  leaves 186
gun powder 194

H

hare
  blood 428
  brain 190, 428
  liver 428
  manure 428
  meat 428
  powder 428
  rennet 428
hawk 458
  fat 458
  manure 458
hawthorn
  bark 188
hazelnut 244, 248
hemp

seed 189
henbane 186, 350
  flower 192
  juice 252
  root 187
holm oak
  acorn 191
  ash 191
  bark 189
honey 187, 192, 193, 194, 195, 222, 223, 238, 329, 333, 354, 365, 413, 416, 445, 458, 476, 481, 485
hoopoe
  blood 483
  feather 296, 483
  heart 252, 483
  tongue 483
horehound
  juice 487
  syrup 257
horse
  blood 397
  fat 397
  foot 397
  manure 295, 396, 397
  mare
    milk 397
  nail 397
  rennet 397
horseradish
  peel
    juice 187
human
  milk 186
  hair 186
hyssop 185

I

ictiocola 254
incense 196, 413
  powder 194
iron
  powder 244
  bar 189

J

jacinth
  powder 231

K

knotgrass 189
  juice 191, 192, 254

L

lamb
  blood 341
  bone 342
  brain 341
  foot 249
  gall 341
  skin 189
laudanum 189
laurel
  berry 256
  leaf 191
  stick 246
lead
  powder 302
leather 238
lemon balm
  water 189
lettuce 185, 186, 187, 188
  juice 185, 256
lichwort 185, 187, 190
  juice 185
lily 191, 192, 193
  blue
    root 188, 189
  juice 187
  oil 193
lime 244
  juice 190
linen
  seed 450
linseed
  flour 192
  oil 194
lion
  bile 316
  fat 316
  heart 316
  meat 316
  skin 316
litharge 404
lizard 256
  powder 256
loquat

  pit 191
  seed 190
losna 185, 190
  oil 196
  water 191
luberno 196
lynx
  urine 425

M

macela (Achyrocline satureioides) 186, 187, 189, 190, 191, 192
  flower 192, 193
  oil 188, 190, 192, 246
  water 189
Mallard
  egg
    yolk 240
  grease 452
  meat 452
mallow 190, 191
  leaf 192, 193
  root 192, 193
malvasia 190
mandrake 189
marjoram 191
marshmallow
  juice 255
mechoação (Convolvulus mechoacana) 195
melilot
  water 192
melon 190
mercury 248
milium solis 227
mineral salt 256
mint 164, 185, 188, 190
  juice 188
mirabolanos 256
mole
  tooth 413
mouse
  blood 413
  manure 413
  powder 413
mulberry
  stick 246
musk 191
must 225
mustard 164, 196, 197, 370
myrrh 191, 256

powder 194

N

naval tar 192
nettle 187, 189
nutmeg 189, 227

O

oat
  straw 186, 240
old man's beard (Clematis vitalba) 193
  juice 187
olive
  oil 194, 196, 197, 238, 239, 256, 294, 295, 299, 300, 332, 356, 358, 374, 416, 458, 470
onion 187
  juice 453
orange 193
  juice 196, 239
  peel 227, 247
oregano
  root 160
ox
  bile 190, 252
  blood 374
  foot
    nerve 193
  gall 374
  liver 375
  manure 374
  marrow 374
  nerve 192
  penis
    ash 188
    powder 250

P

parsley 185, 188, 196, 244
  juice 192
  root 197
partridge
  broth 481
  feather 186, 191
  gall 481
  liver 481
  meat 480
peacock
  broth 485
  egg 485

giblets 485
  manure 485
pear 240
  pit 190
pennyroyal 191
peony
  grain 190
  seed 191
pepper
  grain 245
pig
  bladder 190
  brain 362
  fat 362
  heart 189
  lard 192, 193, 362
  manure 196, 362
  marrow 362
  urine 362
pigeon 186
  blood 244
pine
  wood 296
pink potassium alum 239
plantain 185, 187, 189, 191, 194
  juice 190, 191
  root 185
  seed 185
  water 186, 195
plaster 239
poaceae 190, 191
polypodium 468
pomegranate
  juice 185, 189
  peel 191, 246
  skin 191
popal
  balm 185
potash alum 195
pumpkin 190
  root 256
purslane 188
  juice 185, 190
  water 191

Q

quince 196
  syrup 257
quinquefolium 187

quinque radicibus 195

R

rabbit
  fat 432
  meat 432
radish
  leaf 356
ram
  bone 342
  broth 342
  gall 342
  head 350
  horn 342
  kidney 186
  liver 186
  lung 342
  meat 341
  nail 342
rooster
  boiled 468
  brain 468
  broth 468
  stone 468
rose 164, 186, 188, 192, 193, 256, 257, 346
  oil 187, 188, 250, 295, 316, 362, 374, 404, 458
  seed 191
  syrup 194, 257
  water 185, 186, 187, 192, 193, 195, 228, 229, 230, 302, 316
rosemary 189, 221–226
  flower 227, 295
rue 160, 164, 186, 187, 190, 192, 238
  juice 160, 190, 404, 485

S

saffron 191, 192, 193, 256, 356
sage 164, 185, 186, 190, 244
  leaf 187, 227
  wild 193
sagunta
  juice 238
  leaf 238
sal ammoniac 253
salt 185, 191, 192, 239, 245, 297, 416, 470
saltpeter 354, 374
samphire 239
saxifrage 190
scabious

leaf 193
  root 193
scammony 256
sea squill 185
sea water 195, 350
sheep
  bone 342
  feet 190
  leather 194
  lung 240
  milk 192
shell 190
silverweed
  water 190
sleepy plant (Mimosa pudica). 186
snake
  rattle 239
  skin 192, 234
snake grass 189
solda (Polypodium vacciniifolium) 189
soles (of old shoes) 186, 191, 193
solimão 238
solimão (mercuric chloride) 194
sorrel 185, 188, 189
spiderweb 185
spikenard 187, 356
spinach 356
steel bar 189
storax 193
stork
  manure 491
  ventricle 491
sugar 192, 197, 222, 223, 229, 230, 341
  rock 186, 187
sulfur 192, 195, 245, 256
  flower 195
sumac 252
swallow
  ash 476
  eye 255
  heart 476
  manure 476
  nest 188
  powder 476
  stone 476
swallow stone 234

T

tamarisk 196

tanner ink 239
tar 416
tetterwort 164, 186
thyme 191
tripe
  broth 192
trovisco
  seed 194
turnip
  root 191
turpentine 194
turtledove
  blood 482
tutia 187

U

unicorn
  hair 408
  horn 408
  nail 408
  skin 408

V

valerian 243
Venice turpentine 193
verbena 164, 186, 238
  juice 238, 244
vine 190
  juice 192
  leaf 195, 245
  stick 246
vinegar 185, 187, 188, 190, 192, 196, 223, 224, 239, 254, 297, 332, 346, 356, 366, 370, 397, 404, 413, 428, 450, 470, 485
vine leaves 186
viola 192
  flower 192
  leaf 192
viper
  body 386
vitriol
  powder 245
  white 187
vulture
  blood 487
  feather 487
  liver 487
  manure 487

W

walnut 247
  oil 341
  peel 300
  root 297
  shell 190
water
  honeyed 413
  rain 300
watercress 190
wax 192, 193, 194, 196, 240, 243, 256, 295
wheat
  bran 192, 243
  flour 193
  flower 189
white lotus 186
wine 160, 185, 187, 188, 189, 190, 191, 194, 223, 244, 247, 294, 299, 316, 329, 336, 341, 358, 362, 375, 385, 397, 408, 468, 470, 491
  hippocras 190, 192
  red 189, 192, 223, 225, 227, 229, 245, 380, 404
  white 160, 188, 190, 191, 193, 194, 222, 223, 294, 296, 356, 366, 375, 413, 428, 476
wolf
  blood 336
  dung 189
  heart 336
  intestine 251, 336
  liver 336
  manure 336
  meat 336
  teeth 251
worm 189
  oil 192
wormwood
  oil 193

X

xylo 356

Y

yeast 223

Index IV

Illnesses mentioned in the texts

A

abscess 193, 362
alopecia 413
angina 476
apoplexy 148, 184, 228, 428
aposteme 316, 374, 386, 453
arthritis 156, 222, 224, 358, 450, 468
asthma 358, 365, 468

B

bladder
　sores 470
　stones 164, 190, 223, 226, 233, 244, 329, 341, 346, 362, 413, 428, 471
bleeding 189, 396, 416
blindness 488
blockage 154, 161, 222, 223, 226, 228, 233, 333, 337, 356, 468
burns 362

C

cancer 184, 194, 222, 228, 233, 295, 341
carbuncle 362, 450
cataracts 186-187, 194, 222, 224, 227, 354, 391, 445
catarrh 161, 221, 222, 227, 269
cholera 51, 205, 225, 293, 299, 468
colic 157, 189, 223, 224, 225, 228, 336, 356, 392, 485
cough 229, 329, 365, 416

D

deafness 187, 346, 374, 404
diarrhea 189, 336, 346, 356, 362, 375, 428, 468, 470
dysentery 223, 329, 392

E

epilepsy 183, 273, 332, 336, 341, 481
erysipelas 470

F

fever 84, 148, 161, 164, 167, 183, 184, 185, 186, 225, 228, 230, 231, 233, 234, 316, 329, 342, 356, 438
fistula 157, 184, 195, 294, 295
frenzy 148, 155

G

gas 207, 222, 223, 230, 432, 468
gota coral 181, 183, 228, 244, 329, 397, 428, 485, 491
gout 161, 172, 193, 221, 223, 226, 228, 234, 329, 354, 356, 446, 450

H

halitosis 159, 188, 222
headache 155, 156, 161, 185, 207, 208, 228, 245, 356, 366, 404, 483
hemicranias 155
hemorrhoids 157, 196, 222, 250, 316, 332, 336, 365, 370, 374, 375
hiccups 188, 257
hydropsy 189

I

impetigo 233
inflammation
  of the eyes 195
  of the *Madre* 191
  of the mouth 223, 228, 229, 404
  of the virile member 192
  red 192
  windy 192
insomnia 184

J

jaundice 196

K

kidney
  pain 228, 329, 341, 342, 365, 470
  stones 190, 233, 346
  swelling 155

L

leprosy 155, 158, 160, 161, 184, 233, 234, 354, 400, 416, 485
lethargy 228

M

mal de madre 97, 109, 221, 224, 228, 233, 366, 397
mange 160, 161, 164, 184, 193, 195, 222, 233, 295, 350, 450
measles 233
melancholy 51, 84, 165, 183, 205, 206, 221, 223, 228, 231, 233, 234, 236, 293
migraine 156, 184, 228, 245, 356
morphea 155, 341

N

nausea 158, 218, 221
nosebleed 187, 232, 295, 333, 374

P

pain
   back 186, 188, 445, 485
   chest 155, 157, 164, 244
   ear 155, 187, 316, 354, 358, 362, 374, 380, 432, 453, 482
   eye 155, 186, 194, 329, 449
   foot 223, 408
   general 156, 227, 231, 233, 365, 374, 450, 452, 453, 470, 491
   gum 160, 346, 362, 428
   heart 156
   jaw 160, 245, 256, 356
   kidney 228, 329, 341, 342, 365, 470
   knee 155
   labor 192
   liver 223
   lung 156
   stomach 157, 188, 196, 222, 225, 228, 244, 397, 404, 425
   tooth 160, 358, 362, 366, 416
paralysis 154, 161, 164, 183, 244, 404
paronychia 432
parotids 432
phlegm 252, 156, 157, 160, 161, 164, 222, 225, 228, 229, 293, 404
phthisis 225
plague 167, 181, 221, 222, 273, 362
pustules 295, 302, 346, 366, 374, 470

R

rabies 349, 350, 4497
rash 164, 195, 227, 366
rheum 155, 163, 164, 222, 391
ringworm 164, 295, 370, 374
roundworm 164, 190, 228, 233, 298, 416

S

schizophrenia 184
sciatica 156, 192, 356
scrofula 193, 194, 233
shrinkage of the nerves 152
smallpox 92, 233, 408
sores 195, 196, 294, 425, 432, 470
stupor 184, 228
swelling
   general 155, 195, 316, 362, 397, 450, 470, 491
   of the eyes 408, 470
   of the eyebrows 157
   of the face 155, 157
   of the feet 408
   of the gums 223
   of the jaw 229
   of the kidneys 155
   of the liver 184
   of the neck 432
   of the spleen 230
   of the stomach 432
   of the thighs 157
syphilis 237

T

tinnitus 187, 227, 370
tonsillitis 155, 188
toothache 185, 224, 351, 356, 361, 420
tremors 221, 224, 226, 232, 234, 354, 356, 375, 428, 468
tuberculosis 183
tumor 193, 333, 476

U

urinary tract infection 190, 228, 341, 356

V

vomiting 183, 222, 223, 225, 234, 247, 356

W

warts 333, 354, 413
water retention 356

Index V

Planets & Signs mentioned in the texts

A

Aquarius 102, 105, 107, 108, 127, 157, 165, 183, 282, 579
Aries 31, 35, 105, 107, 108, 110, 121, 122, 127, 148, 149, 154, 156, 165, 183, 234, 237, 340, 341, 579

C

Cancer 35, 105, 107, 108, 113, 121, 125, 127, 149, 154, 156, 165, 166, 183, 246, 538, 579
Capricorn 35, 105, 106, 107, 108, 119, 121, 127, 149, 165, 166, 183, 246, 282, 579

G

Gemini 105, 107, 108, 112, 120, 121, 127, 157, 165, 183, 246, 538, 579

J

Jupiter 82, 86-87, 97, 108, 109, 112, 113, 115, 118, 119, 125, 149, 184, 277, 280-281, 287, 289, 291, 293, 578, 579

L

Leo 68, 70, 105, 106, 107, 108, 114, 120, 126, 127, 149, 154, 156, 165, 182, 183, 538, 579
Libra 35, 105, 106, 107, 108, 116, 120, 127, 154, 157, 165, 166, 182, 183, 237, 246, 579

M

Mars 82, 88-89, 97, 108, 110, 111, 113, 116, 117, 119, 123, 125, 126, 157, 182, 184, 277, 280, 281, 287, 289, 291, 293, 336, 578, 579
Mercury 82, 94-95, 97, 108, 109, 112, 115, 118, 125, 126, 183, 246, 277, 278, 287, 289, 291, 292, 294, 578, 579

P

Pisces 105, 107, 108, 109, 125, 127, 149, 154, 156, 165, 183, 246, 281, 579

S

Sagittarius 105, 106, 107, 108, 118, 127, 154, 156, 165, 183, 281, 579
Saturn 82, 84-85, 108, 110, 113, 114, 116, 119, 125, 182, 184, 277, 281, 287, 289, 291, 293, 478, 538, 578, 579
Scorpio 105, 106, 107, 108, 117, 120, 127, 149, 154, 156, 165, 183, 575, 579

T

Taurus 105, 107, 108, 111, 121, 127, 149, 157, 165, 166, 183, 246, 575, 579

V

Venus 82, 92-93, 108, 109, 110, 111, 115, 116, 117, 125, 163, 184, 277, 279, 287, 289, 291, 292, 293, 358, 578, 579

Virgo 105, 106, 107, 108, 115, 127, 165, 166, 183, 246, 579

Z

Zodiac 107, 121, 182, 282, 289

www.ingramcontent.com/pod-product-compliance
Lightning Source LLC
Chambersburg PA
CBHW080718300426
44114CB00019B/2416